I0888846

The "Suffering Servant" of Isaiah

According to the Jewish Interpreters

Translated by

SAMUEL R. DRIVER

and

ADOLF NEUBAUER

With an Introduction by

EDWARD B. PUSEY

Wipf & Stock
PUBLISHERS
Eugene, Oregon

Wipf and Stock Publishers
199 West 8th Avenue, Suite 3
Eugene, Oregon 97401

The "Suffering Servant" of Isaiah
According to the Jewish Interpreters
By Driver, Samuel R. and Neubauer, Adolf
ISBN: 1-57910-255-7
Publication date 7/7/1999
Previously published by James Parker and Co., 1877.

The "Suffering Servant" of Isaiah

According to the Jewish Interpreters

PREFACE.

It is now more than two years since the Regius Professor of Hebrew in this University invited Mr. Neubauer to undertake the task of editing a complete catena of Jewish commentaries on the remarkable chapter which has for ages formed one of the principal battle-fields between Christians and their Jewish opponents[a]. The request was gladly acceded to; and the collection in the present volume comprises not merely commentaries strictly so called, but also extracts relating to the same subject from works of controversy and other sources, whether composed in Hebrew or in any of the other languages adopted by Jews from time to time in the varied homes of their exile. These are arranged, as nearly as possible, in chronological order. In the pages that follow (which, with the exception of a few additional references, are substantially a translation of the Hebrew preface prefixed to the companion volume) will be found a

[a] With the addition, naturally, of the three verses of the fifty-second chapter, which have been unfortunately severed from it.

list of the authors cited, with Mr. Neubauer's own account of the authorities consulted by him, and of the sources, whether printed or manuscript, from which in each case the text has been derived.

1. The Septuagint, according to Tischendorf's third edition (Leipzig, 1874), together with such fragments as remain of the 'revised' versions of Aquila, Symmachus, and Theodotion, as given in Dr. Field's *Hexapla* (Oxford, 1874)[b].

2. The Targum[c], or (so-called) Chaldee Paraphrase, of Yonathan ben 'Uzziel, according to the printed editions, and MSS. at Paris ('P.') and Oxford ('O.')

3. Notices in the Talmud, whether of Jerusalem or Babylon, in the Midrash Rabbah, Tanḥuma, and the Yalquṭ Shim'oni[d]; also in Siphré (as cited by Raymundus Martini[e] in his celebrated work, the *Pugio Fidei*), and the P'siqthâ (as cited by Hulsius, in his *Theologia Judaica*, 1643, from the אבקת רוכל).

---

[b] Here ought strictly to have been added the extract cited on p. 412, which shews that already in the time of Origen (190–250), the application of the prophecy to Israel dispersed in exile was not unknown among the Jews.

[c] Information respecting Jewish literature in general may be found in Jost, *Geschichte des Judenthumes und seiner Secten* (3 vols., Leipzig, 1857–9); Grätz, *Geschichte der Juden*, second edition, more especially vols. v–ix; Etheridge, *Introd. to Hebrew Literature* (London, 1856); and Steinschneider, *Jewish Literature* (London, 1857). On the Targums in particular, see the article in Smith, *Dict. of the Bible*, iii. p. 1637 ff.; on the Talmud and other Rabbinical works mentioned under No. 3, instructive notices will be found in the preface to Neubauer's *La Géographie du Talmud* (Paris, 1868); in Deutsch's *Literary Remains* (London, 1874); or Schürer's *Lehrbuch der neutestamentlichen Zeitgeschichte* (Leipzig, 1874), p. 35 ff., where the further literature is quoted, among which should be named in particular Zunz, *Gottesdienstliche Vorträge der Juden* (Berlin, 1832). Reference may also be made to the various articles, 'Midrash,' etc., in Kitto's *Cyclopaedia*.

[d] Etheridge, p. 409.

[e] Of this remarkable man, the learned and powerful antagonist of Judaism in Spain, in the second half of the thirteenth century, scarcely any account

4. The Zohar. Although agreeing myself with the most recent Jewish historians, who assign this book to a far later date[f], and believing, in fact, that the writer lived unquestionably after the time of Naḥmanides (see chap. xx), yet in deference to others, and amongst them Dr. Pusey, who are still of opinion that it is of much greater antiquity, and that its author was none other than the 'Tanna,' R. Shim'on ben Yoḥai, I have inserted the extracts from it immediately after those from the Talmud. In a parallel column is annexed a Hebrew version from a MS. in the Bodleian Library, Oxford (Opp. 107), made in the year 1602[g].

5. The Arabic version of the Ga'on[h], R. Sa'adyah, the earliest commentator whose writings are now extant (tenth century), according to the Oxford MS. (Poc. 32). This was published by Paulus (Jena, 1790–1); some various readings from a MS.

---

seems to exist in English. The Pugio Fidei, a monument of erudition and research, was first published, with elaborate notes, by De Voisin in 1651; *quartum jam saeculum in pulvere sordido cum blattis et tineis luctans Raymundus delitescebat*, writes the Bishop of Louvain, who discovered the manuscript. There is another edition by Carpzov (1668). Compare Grätz, vii². 163, who refers for further particulars to Quetif's *Historia ordinis Praedicatorum* (Lut. Par., 1719), i. 397. It should, however, be observed, with reference to the extract from Siphrâ (p. 10), that the words relating to the Messiah are not to be found in the printed editions or in the Bodleian MS. 150; compare Jennings and Lowe, *The Psalms* (*Book v*), p. 239. But on the question of the accuracy of Martini's citations, and on the confirmation which some, at least, seem to derive from another source, see further below, pp. xxxii–xxxvi.

f Jost, ii. 291, iii. 74–79; and especially Grätz, vii². 219 ff., 466 ff.; Franck, *La Cabbale* (Paris, 1843); Etheridge, p. 312.

g See Neubauer, Catal. of Heb. MSS. in the Bodl. Libr., No. 1561. The Zohar was also translated from Chaldee into Hebrew in Spain, as appears from the *Refutation* of Alfonso di Zamora (1520) preserved in the Library of the Escurial: see *Archives des missions scientifiques et littéraires*, 2me série, v. 428 (Paris, 1868).

h The designation given to the chiefs of the Rabbinical school at Sora, in Babylonia: Jost, ii. 252; Etheridge, pp. 213, 218. The name appears to be an equivalent expression to the Latin *excellentia*, used as a title of dignity. On Sa'adyah, see Jost, ii. 275–286; Grätz, v. p. 302 ff.

recently acquired by the Paris Library (No. 1325) will be found in the *Addenda*.

6. The translation and commentary by the Qaraite[i], Yepheth ben 'Ali[j], a contemporary[k] of Sa'adyah's, according to the MS., No. 569, in the Imperial Library at St. Petersburg.

7. The Midrash known as the Mysteries of R. Shim'on ben Yoḥai, and accordingly attributed to this writer, but compiled, as it would appear in fact, during the eleventh century.

8. A notice by R. Mosheh had-Darshan[l] of Narbonne (eleventh century), in his *B'reshith Rabbâ*—now, unfortunately, no longer extant[m]—as cited by Raymundus Martini[n].

9. R. Ṭobiyyah ben 'Eli'ezer (contemporary of R. Mosheh had-Darshan[o]) in his work, the *Leqaḥ ṭob*, according to the printed edition.

10. R. Sh'lomoh Yiẓḥaqi, the celebrated French commentator, born about 1030 at Troyes, more familiarly known as Rashi[p]. Appended is a fragment no longer to be found either in the printed books or in MSS., but attributed to Rashi on the authority of Raymundus Martini (*Pug. Fid.* pp. 311, 429).

11. The Commentary of R. Yoseph Qara, likewise a French scholar, according to MSS. at Paris and in the Laurentian Library at Florence. These, however, were all injured and partly erased; and it was only after the greater part of both

---

[i] On the Qaraites, the name borne by those Jews who reject the traditions of the Talmud, see Jost, ii. 294–381; Grätz, v. 174 ff.

[j] His translation of the Psalms has been edited by the Abbé Bargès (Paris, 1846).

[k] See Pinsker, *Lickuté Qadmoniot* (Wien, 1860), i. p. 169.

[l] I. e. 'the Preacher:' Etheridge, pp. 423, 427; see also Zunz, p. 287.

[m] See R. Sh'lomoh Buber in the *Maggid*, 1872, p. 281.

[n] It is possible that this also may be the *B'reshith Rabbâ* and *Q'ṭannah* cited by Alfonso di Zamora: see *Archives*, etc., loc. cit.

[o] Zunz, loc. cit. The composition of the *Leqaḥ ṭob* was begun, according to a note in the Oxford MS. (Hunt. 397), in the year 1097: see the new Catal. of Heb. MSS. in the Bodleian Library, No. 162.

[p] See Zunz, *Zeitschrift für die Wissenschaft des Judenthums*, Berlin, 1823, p. 277 ff.; Grätz, vi. p. 77 ff.

volumes were in type that I was fortunate enough to find the missing portions in a MS. in the possession of my friend Herr Raphael Kirchheim. These will be found in the *Addenda* (Hebrew, p. 398; English, p. 569).

12. The Commentary of R. Abraham 'Ibn 'Ezra, according to the printed editions and MSS. at Paris, Parma, and Rome. In the *Addenda*, p. 400, are given readings from some more accurate MSS. employed by Lañado, and also from one which I met with myself in the Library at Leeuwarden. It is expected that before long 'Ibn 'Ezra's entire commentary on Isaiah will be published under the editorship of Dr. Friedländer[q].

13. The Commentary of R. David Qamḥi [Kimchi], according to the printed text, and MSS. at Oxford. The *Sepher ha-Galuy* of his father, referred to by him both in his Commentary and also in his 'Book of Roots,' of which all previous enquirers have supposed no copy to be in existence, I discovered recently in the Vatican Library (No. 402). The author composed it at the age of sixty years: it consists of a series of grammatical observations on the works of M'naḥem ben Saruq, of Dunash ben Labrat, and of R. Ya'qob Tham; there are annotations to it by Binyamin (ben Y'hudah?). I hope at a future time to be in a position to publish it. As to the *Book of the Covenant*, by the same author, also referred to by his son, a controversial treatise bearing that title has been published at Constantinople under the name of Yoseph Qamḥi; it does not, however, contain anything relating to the fifty-third chapter of Isaiah.

14. An extract from the fifth chapter of the *Wars of the Lord*, a work attributed in the Oxford MSS., Mich. 269, Bodl. 58, to R. Ya'qob bar Reuben, the Rabbanite[r], and stated to have been composed by him in the year 1170, when he was twenty, or, according to the acrostic at the end of the MS., when he was thirty-six years old. The MSS. Mich. 221, Mich. 113, Opp. 581, have further

---

[q] His translation has already appeared (London, 1874).

[r] The 'Rabbanites' are the opponents of the 'Qaraites,' so called because they acknowledge the authority of the doctors or Rabbis.

been consulted: the last mentioned commences with the words, 'Says R. Sa'adyah Ga'on . . . ,' and styles the book the *Refutation*, which in fact is also the name by which it is denoted at the end of Mich. 269: Mosheh Kohen cites it anonymously, and R. Shem Tob ben Shaprut (cf. p. 97) ascribes it to R. Yoseph Qamḥi. The work is divided into twelve chapters, a portion of the last of which has been printed[s].

15. The Commentary of Mar Ya'qob ben Reuben, the Qaraite (a contemporary of his namesake the Rabbanite), known as the *Book of Riches*. For this a Paris MS. ('P.') has been used, collated through the kindness of Prof. de Goeje with a MS. at Leyden ('L.')

16. A translation with short commentary, composed in Arabic by an unknown author, on Isaiah, Jeremiah, and the Minor Prophets, from an Oxford MS. (Hunt. 206). At the end of Jeremiah, it is stated that the author completed it in the year 1196. It follows closely the Targum of Yonathan[t].

17. A commentary by a French scholar from an Oxford MS. (Opp. 625). From some verses at the end it appears probable that the author may have been R. Eli'ezer of Beaugenci[u], who wrote likewise the commentary on Ezekiel, and possibly also the one on the Minor Prophets contained in the same MS.[v]

18. An extract from the work *Yoseph the Zealot* by Yoseph ben Nathan, l'Official, of Sens, who lived about the middle of the thirteenth century[w]. The work exists in manuscript at Paris ('P.') and Hamburg ('H.')

---

[s] At least, according to the assertion of Steinschneider, *Catalogue of Printed Hebrew Books in the Bodleian Library*, col. 2032; but I have not myself been able to find it, as in the volume referred to by him the leaves that must have contained it have been torn away.

[t] On the commentary upon the Minor Prophets, see Merx, *Archiv für wissenschaftliche Erforschungen des alten Testaments*, i. ii.

[u] Cf. Zunz, *Zur Literatur und Geschichte*, p. 79.

[v] See the new Catal. of Heb. MSS. in the Bodl. Libr., No. 1265.

[w] *Histoire littéraire de la France*, xxi. p. 509.

19. From the Commentary upon Isaiah by Y'sha'yah ben Mali of Trani, the Elder, a contemporary of Yoseph ben Nathan's, according to MSS. at Paris ('P.') and Rome, in the Angelica Convent, C. i. 5 ('R.')

20. The exposition of R. Mosheh ben Naḥman of Gerona[x] (about 1250–1270), according to MSS. at Oxford, Mich. 500 ('M.'), Opp. Add. quo. 111 ('O.'), at Vienna ('V.')[y], and two in the possession of Herr S. J. Halberstam of Bielitz ('H.[1] H.[2]'), who kindly transcribed them for me. This exposition has been already published by Dr. Steinschneider at the end of his edition of the *Wikkuaḥ* or *Refutation* of Naḥmanides (Berlin, 1860), as he states himself, from the manuscript Mich. 289 (now 500), though the text appears to me to be derived from some different source. An extract from the *Wikkuaḥ* is annexed, from the MS. 'O.,' and the text as edited by Steinschneider ('St.')

21. From the Commentary of Mar Aharon ben Yoseph, the Qaraite, the Elder, author of the Mibhḥar on the Pentateuch. The extract is taken from the *Mibhḥar Y'sharim*, edited by the late Abraham Firkowitsch (Eupatoria, 1836). A short addition from MSS. at St. Petersburg will be found on p. 400 (English, p. 571).

22. A section from the elder *Niẓẓaḥon*[z], as printed by Wagenseil in his *Tela Ignea Satanae* (Altorf, 1681), p. 105.

23. Chapter 8, section 19 of the *Touchstone* of R. Shem Tob ben Yizḥaq ben Shaprut, of Toledo, which was finished in the month Iyar, 1385, in Tarazona. This treatise is usually subdivided into twelve chapters, being based upon the *Wars of the Lord* (see No. 14), which the author tells us in his Preface was assigned by some to Yoseph Qamḥi. Three MSS. have been collated for this, viz. Mich. 113, Mich. 137 (from which I have extracted the *Reply* to Alphonso, p. 97), and Opp. Add. quo. 72.

---

[x] See Grätz, vii. 41 ff.

[y] For a collation of which I am indebted to the kindness of Dr. Güdemann, Rabbi in that city.

[z] So called in distinction from the later *Niẓẓaḥon* (='Conquest') of R. Lipmann (No. 28).

I have also found an abridgment of the treatise by Abraham Eliyyah Kohen in the MS., Opp. Add. quo. 111, fol. 68[b], where the writer states that he made an abstract of the work composed by Shem Tob against the heretics, and in particular against certain of the Christians, and known under the name of the *Touchstone*, adding that a treatise bearing the same name had already been written previously upon different subjects. And on fol. 70[b] he informs us that the Cardinal of Aragon [a], who was elected Pope in the year 1313, had a public controversy with the author. It has not been thought necessary to reprint this abridgment.

24 A. The Commentary of R. Mosheh Kohen 'Ibn Crispin of Cordova, afterwards of Toledo, also at one period of his life a resident at Valencia, where he composed an answer to a casuistical question. He also wrote notes upon the *Gate of Heaven* by R. Yizhaq Israeli. It is possible that these were his earliest work.

24 B. The forty-second chapter of the *Aid to Faith* of R. Mosheh ha-Kohen of Otor-Sillas [Torresillas] in the kingdom of Leon, and afterwards of Avila, composed in the year 1375, after a disputation held by him with two of his compatriots who had deserted Judaism, and who by permission of the king assembled the Jews together for purposes of controversy. He cites the *Wars of the Lord*, though without mentioning the author's name, and the *Moreh Ẓedeq* of Abner [b]. His own book he dedicates to the celebrated Don David 'Ibn Ya'ish[c] of Toledo. I at first was of opinion that the two recensions A and B were by the same hand, and classified them accordingly under one head; but I now feel hesitation upon this point, though the question cannot yet be regarded as definitely settled. Three

[a] I.e. Petro de Luna: see the *Wikkuaḥ* in the Paris MS., No. 831. 4.

[b] I.e. Alfonso Burgensis de Valladolid, Grätz, viii. 337.

[c] Of the same family as, if not identical with, the Ya'ish who, in conjunction with R. Mosheh Abodel, pleaded the cause of the Jews before the king (Grätz, *ibid.* p. 341).

MSS. have been collated, viz. Bodl. 599 ('B.'), Mich. 147 ('M.'), and Opp. Add. quo. 74 ('O.')

25. The Commentary of En [d] Sh'lomoh Astruc of Barcelona (perhaps son of Nastruc Sh'lomoh, the son of R. Sh'lomoh ben Addereth, mentioned in the Bodleian MS. Reggio 32, fol. 253), from an Oxford MS., Mich. 500, which contains likewise his commentary on Ps. cxxxix. The same writer composed also a commentary on the Law, called מדרשי התורה (which may be found in the MS., Mich. 302), in which he states (fol. 177[b]) that he had seen the plague of locusts in the year 1359. A commentary of his upon Esther is in the possession of my friend, Herr Halberstam.

26. The Commentary of Maestro Izaq Eli, the Spaniard, from MS. 59 of the Breslau Seminary. The author, as appears from the dedicatory words of some verses addressed to him by the poet R. Sh'lomoh Bonfed, was an old man in the year 1359.

27. The Persian version, dating from about 1400, written in Hebrew characters in the Paris MS. 97. This contains nothing new, being merely a literal translation: his renderings of the crucial expressions of the original will be found in the note below [e].

28. Section 236 of the *Nizzaḥon* of R. Lipmann of Mühlhausen, composed about 1430, according to the Nürnberg edition [f] (1644) and a Michaelis MS.

29. From the Commentary upon Isaiah by Don Yizḥaq Abarbanel, according to the printed editions. So far as I am aware, the only MS. of this commentary extant is in the Library of the Escurial [g]; but the recent war in Spain has prevented my being able to collate it with the printed text, which is the more to be

---

[d] *En*, in the language of Provence and Catalan, an abbreviation for *Mossen* (i. e. 'Monsieur').

[e] עבדי, simply 'my servant;' יזה, 'will make to speak.'

[f] Steinschneider, *Catal. Bodl.* col. 1410. It is contained also in the Oxford MS., Opp. 593. Compare Ginsburg, *Commentary on Ecclesiastes* (London, 1861), p. 64.

[g] *Archives des missions scientifiques* (Paris, 1868), p. 428.

regretted as the latter is in many places corrupt. I may mention that an abridgment of Abarbanel's commentary on this Parashah exists in the work called the *Glory of God*, in the Library of the Talmudical School at Amsterdam: the MS. was finished at Venice on the first day of Shebat, 1637. At the end of the preface there is a statement to the effect that there being no title to the work, R. Abraham, son of R. Mattathyah of Patras, when writing a preface to it, called it the *Glory of God*[h].

30. The Commentary of R. David de Rocca Martino, the author of the זכות אדם, in the Oxford MS., Reggio 21. The learned Senior Sachs, in his preface to this work, remarks that Abarbanel copied Martino without naming him; but I should myself be rather of opinion that Martino abbreviated Abarbanel. Certainly, according to a MS. said to have been inspected by the late Dr. Carmoly at Amsterdam, David was in Provence in the year 1360; and if this be the fact, I must withdraw my opinion; but both M. Roest and myself have sought in vain to discover the manuscript in question[i].

31. The Commentary of R. Sa'adyah 'Ibn Danân of Grenada (c. 1500), according to the Oxford MSS., Bodl. 108 and Mich. 284[j].

32. The *Mikhlol Yophi*[k] of R. Sh'lomoh ben Melekh of Fez (about 1500).

---

[h] For transcripts of the preface and of the abridgment of the commentary upon this chapter (which, however, it would evidently have been superfluous to reproduce here), my best thanks are due to M. Roest, the learned compiler of the Catalogue to Rosenthal's Library, and to R. Yoseph Kohen Ẓedeq. There is another MS. of the same abridgment in the Library at Parma, No. 75 (see De Rossi's Catalogue, No. 75), written likewise at Venice, in 1690. And there is an abridgment of the abridgment in the Oxford MSS., Mich. 10, § 5, and Bodl. 88, § 6.

[i] See Berliner's *Magazin für jüdische Geschichte und Literatur*, 1875, No. 35. With due deference to the opinion of Dr. Steinschneider, as expressed in his preface to the תגמולי נפש of R. Hillel (Lyck, 1875, p. 23), it is impossible to agree with him in believing that Abarbanel lived subsequently to David de Rocca Martino, at least until he brings forward more cogent proofs than he has done hitherto.

[j] On 'Ibn Danân and his writings, see further Steinschn. *Bodl. Catal.* p. 2155.

[k] Ginsburg, loc. cit. p. 66.

33. From the *Refutation* of R. Abraham Farissol ben Mordekhai of Avignon (born 1451), who resided at Ferrara and composed this work in 1503[l]. In his preface he states that at the request of Messer Ercoli, Duke of Ferrara, and of his wife and brothers, he was prevailed upon to dispute in their presence with two of the most celebrated men of that day, Brother Ludovicus of Valencia, of the Order of the Dominicans, and Brother Malpita, of the Minors. The disputation was renewed upon several occasions, and the course which the discussion took is recounted in his book, which at the urgent entreaty of Bartolomeo Gogo and other learned men he was induced to write, in order that they might have an opportunity of weighing more carefully the arguments adduced, and of judging whether it would be possible to frame a reply to them. It was composed first in Hebrew, and afterwards translated by the author into Italian. Finding two different recensions of it, I resolved to publish both. That marked A is from the MS. Mich. 302, § 52, where it is entitled the *Shield of Abraham*, some lacunae in it being supplied from Mich. 549, § 37, entitled the *Controversy of Faith*. The other recension, marked B, is from the MS. Mich. 284, § 36, entitled *Controversy of Faith*, and from Mich. 319, § 44, called the *Shield of Abraham*.

34. From the Vatican MS., No. 509, fol. 64.

35. From the Commentary on Isaiah by R. Meir Aramah (c. 1540), entitled the *Urim and Thummim*, according to the printed text and a MS. at Paris.

36. Chapter 22 of the *Bulwark of Truth* of Mar Yiẓḥaq bar Abraham Troki, the Qaraite (1593), according to the printed editions and MSS.[m]

37. From the מראות צובאות[n], an exposition of the Prophets

---

[l] Grätz, ix. p. 53.

[m] This is translated into Spanish and Italian in a Parma MS.: see De Rossi, *Bibliotheca Judaica Antichristiana*, p. 19.

[n] Exod. xxxviii. 8.

by R. Mosheh ben R. Ḥayyim Al-Sheikh, of Saphed, according to the printed text.

38. From the *Armoury of Solomon*, a Commentary on Isaiah by R. Sh'lomoh ben R. Yiẓḥaq, the Levite, of Salonica (1600), according to the printed text.

39. Chapter 41 of the *Tower of the House of God* [o], a polemical work of R. Abraham, the Proselyte, of Cordova (c. 1600), translated from Spanish into Hebrew by R. Mordekhai Luzzatto [p]. This is taken from an Oxford MS., Mich. 356, the text having been collated by Dr. Marco Mortara with that of a MS. in the Rabbinical School at Mantua: the original will be found among the Spanish texts at the end of the volume.

40. From the *Jewel of Gold*, a Commentary on Isaiah by R. Sh'muel bar Abraham Lañado, of Aleppo [q] (middle of seventeenth century), according to the printed editions. For the sake of brevity, the expositions of Rashi, 'Ibn 'Ezra, David Qamḥi, and Abarbanel, which are cited by the author almost word for word, have been omitted.

41. From the Qaraite Tataric version of the Old Testament, made for the use of Jews resident in a district of the Crimea, and dating probably from about 1640, according to the edition of Eupatoria, 1840. The translation is a literal one, and is merely given here for the sake of completeness [r]. Since the text is difficult to read in Hebrew characters, even with the addition of points, I have, with the assistance of M. Pavet de Courteille, member of the French Institute, and of my friend M. Joseph Halévi, transcribed it into Turkish characters.

42. From the חבורי לקט, a short exposition of the Prophets and Hagiographa by R. Abraham ben R. Y'hudâh, the Ḥazan (about 1600), according to the printed text.

---

[o] Comp. Judg. ix. 46.

[p] De Rossi, *Bibliotheca Judaica Antichristiana*, p. 7.

[q] Steinschneider, *Catal. Bodl.* col. 2433.

[r] עבדי, 'my servant;' יזה, 'will make to speak;' אם תשים וג׳, 'if thou givest thy soul in place of a trespass-offering.'

43. From the *Hind sent forth*, a Commentary on the Prophets and Hagiographa by R. Naphtali (Hirsch) ben R. Asher Altschuler, according to the printed text.

44. From the *Reformation of the World*, a Commentary upon Isaiah by R. Sh'lomoh ben R. Yiẓḥaq de Marini, Rabbi in Padua (end of seventeenth century), according to the printed text.

45. Part iii, chapter 19 of the *Furnace of the Faiths*, a controversial treatise by R. Yiẓḥaq Lopez of Aleppo, according to the printed copy. The author does little more than borrow from the *Wars of the Lord* (No. 14) and the *Touchstone* (No. 23); the extract has, however, been inserted for the sake of completeness.

46. Chapter 12 of the אשם תלוי [s], also a polemical treatise, by R. Yoshua' Segre, composed in the year 1791, when the author was twenty-three years old. This I transcribed from a Parma MS., No. 1271; and the text has been further collated with the original MS. by the Abbate Perreau, sub-librarian at Parma. After the sheets had passed through the press, I found the work mentioned in Senior Sachs' catalogue of MSS. belonging to Baron Günzburg of Paris (No. 267),—a library which contains also several other works by the same author.

47. The *Stronghold of David and of Zion*, a Commentary on the Old Testament by R. Y'ḥiel ben R. David Altschuler, according to the printed editions. Since the author (as he tells us himself in his preface to the First Prophets) professes only to record what he had received from his father, I have prefixed the name of the latter to the extract.

A series of extracts relating to Isaiah liii, from larger works upon different subjects:—

a. From the Arabic Lexicon of Mar David ben Abraham, the Qaraite, a contemporary of Sa'adyah Ga'on [t], according to an Oxford MS., Opp. Add. fol. 25, *s. v.* אלם. *b.* From the *Book of Roots* of R. Yonah Abulwalid: see the Oxford edition, p. 117.

---

[s] I.e. properly, the *Suspended Trespass-offering* (see p. 307); but the author means his title to be understood as signifying the *Trespass of the Crucified one.*

[t] *Lickuté Qadmoniot*, p. 208.

c. From the *Letter to the South* [Yemen] of R. Moses Maimonides, as given in the *Qobeẓ*. *d.* From the מלחמת מצוה, a polemical work composed by a scholar of Narbonne (probably R. Me'ir bar Shim'on) in the year 1240, and dedicated to R. Meshullam bar Mosheh [u]. Two MSS. have been made use of for this, one at Parma ('P.'), and, for the first part, one in the Rabbinical School of Breslau ('B.'), in the *Liqqutim* of R. Mosheh of Salerno, see below (*f*). *e.* Chapter 5 of the מחזק אמונה of R. Mord'khai ben Y'hosaphah, of Provence, written by him in answer to the convert Paulus Christianus in 1274 [v]. This I have taken from the Vatican MS. 271, with which the printed text has also been collated for me by R. Mordekhai Angelo di Capua. *f.* From the *Objections* collected together and added to by R. Mosheh ben Sh'lomoh of Salerno (about 1240 [w]), according to a Breslau MS., No. 59. *g.* From the *'Iqqarim* of Yoseph Albo (1420), part iv, chap. 13. *h.* A poem by R. Israel (perhaps R. Israel Nagara, of Damascus, who lived about 1550), from the Oxford MSS., M. 310 and M. 189. *i.* From the *Beginning of Wisdom*, by R. Eliyyah de Vidas (1575), according to the Venice edition of 1593. *j.* From the *Shield and Spear* of R. Ḥayyim 'Ibn Musa, of Magreb, also from the Breslau MS. 59. For the transcription of the three last-named extracts I am indebted to Dr. Freudenthal, and the transcript has also been again collated with the original MSS. by Dr. David Kaufmann. *k.* A chapter of an anonymous *Wars of the Lord*, from a MS. in the Talmudical School at Amsterdam: in the course of it, mention is made of a commentary on the Old Testament by R. Ya'qob ben R'uben. This was transcribed and collated for me by the same scholars who kindly lent me their assistance for No. 29. *l.* From the Paris MS., No. 17. *m.* From a Parma MS., No. 1090. *n.* From the

[u] Comp. *Archives des missions*, 1872, p. 556, and Gross in Grätz's *Monatschrift*, 1875, p. 190.

[v] Steinschneider in the *Mazkir*, xvi. p. 42. The Vatican MS. is often very difficult to read, and in many places has suffered obliteration.

[w] *Mazkir*, xv. p. 86.

Book of the Pious, Bologna, 1538, No. 56 (in other texts, No. 31). *o.* From the *Midrash Konen,* following the old printed text, and Jellinek's *Beth ham-Midrash,* ii. p. 29. *p.* From the *Ten Discourses* of R. M'naḥem 'Azaryah of Fano (about 1640), II. 7 of the part headed חקור דין. *q.* Chapter 19 of the *Gilgulim* ('transmigrations') of R. Ḥayyim Vital. *r.* From the *Midrash Ne'lam,* according to the *Yalquṭ Rubeni* (Wilhermsdorf, 1681). *s.* From the later *Yalquṭ,* the portion styled *Souls.* *t.* From a controversial work contained in a Hamburg MS., according to Uffenbach's Catalogue, fol. 146. *u.* From the Prayers for the First Day of the Passover, according to the order observed by the German Jews. *v.* From the *Liqquṭim,* written in German, and printed at Amsterdam in 1699, p. 5[1]. *w.* From the Order of Prayer for the Day of Atonement, likewise according to the German Jews (Hebrew text, p. 394). *x.* From the Commentary on the Pentateuch (Deut. xxxiv. 10) by Levi ben Gershom (fourteenth century). *y.* From the נצח ישראל of R. Y'hudah ben B'ẓal'el of Prague (sixteenth century).

At this point it was originally my intention to bring the catena to an end; but after conferring with Dr. Pusey, I determined to add the following:—

48. From the exposition of the entire Old Testament, called the *Korem,* by Herz Homberg (Wien, 1818).

49. A Commentary on Isaiah liii, by R. Ya'qob Yoseph Mord'khai Ḥayyim Passani, chief Rabbi at Rome from 1852 to 1867. A transcript was made from a MS. belonging to the synagogue at Rome, by Signor Angelo di Capua, and sent to me by the kindness of Dr. Berliner.

50. From the Commentary on Isaiah by Samuel David Luzzatto (Padua, 1867).

Before passing to the Spanish texts, I may indicate briefly certain other commentaries which, although composed by Jewish hands, have yet for various reasons been omitted. Some are

---

[1] This extract is not from the *Fuente Claro,* as Steinschneider strangely thinks, *Catal. Bodl.* col. 2798.

so penetrated with ideas of a cabbalistic or haggadic nature as to be scarcely intelligible; as, for example, the תורת חכם (pp. 16–19) of R. Ḥayyim Kohen, the מסכנות יעקב of R. Yoseph Pardo, the של״ה (Y'shayah Hurwiz) and עמק המלך of R. Naphtali Herz Bachrach: others, such as those by the pupils of R. Mosheh of Dessau (Mendelssohn) and R. Yirm'yah Heinemann, are merely glossaries, or not original: a third class, again, such as that by R. Me'ir (Liebusch) Malbim, are wholly of a philosophical character, or resemble the אחרית ישראל of the late Gottlieb Schwartz, which, in my opinion, does violence to the Hebrew idiom. Lastly, commentaries such as those of S. Cahen, Herxheimer, or Philippson, being written in the vulgar tongue, and in the hands of every one interested in the literature of the Old Testament, it was evidently unnecessary to reprint.

51. Chapter 4 of the *Fuente Claro* (place and date of publication unknown), the only known copy of which, now at Parma[y], is exceedingly corrupt, not merely through the confusion of similar letters (such as ב, כ, and ר; ה and ח; ו, ז, and י; ט and ק), but also from the interchange of Spanish and Italian words, and the presence of frequent *lacunae*. These corruptions were so numerous, that it was impossible to indicate all the corrections that were needed in order to make the text readable, except in cases where they consisted merely in the filling up of the lacunae [ ]. It seems probable that the work was written originally in Hebrew. In decyphering this text I must acknowledge the assistance I have derived from my friend M. Joseph Halévy of Paris.

In the Imperial Library at St. Petersburg (which I was recently commissioned by the University of Oxford to visit, for the purpose of reporting upon the second collection of Hebrew-Arabic MSS. acquired from the late M. Firkowitzsch), I was fortunate enough to meet with two commentaries of the greatest value, viz.:—

52. The Commentary of R. Y'hudah ben Bil'am (c. 1080) on

[y] De Rossi, *Bibliotheca Judaica Antichristiana*, p. 33.

the Prophets. It is probable that Ben Bil'am's commentary embraced the whole of the Old Testament; for part of that on Numbers and Deuteronomy exists in the Bodleian Library, and I have found besides a leaf of his commentary on the Psalms in the second Petersburg collection (No. 619), and some from those on Job and Daniel (all written in Arabic) in the Vatican Library, No. 429.

53. The Commentary of R. Tanḥum ben Yoseph, of Jerusalem (thirteenth century). I must here acknowledge specially my obligations to the Vice-Director of the Library, M. A. Th. Bitschkow, who most courteously permitted me the freest access to the MSS., and also to my friend Dr. Harkavy.

54. A. From the *Khozari* of R. Y'hudah hal-Levi (about 1140). B. The Commentary of R. Sh'lomoh ben M'naḥem, also known as Frat Maimon, and contained in his work, the *Testimony to Israel*, and cited at length in their commentaries on the Khozari, by his two pupils R. N'thanel ben N'hemyah Kaspi (MS. Mich. Add. 11, fol. 74) and R. Sh'lomoh ben Y'hudah (called also Salmon Vivas of Lunel), Opp. Add. quo. 114, fol. 55. The composition of the latter commentary was begun in the year [51]84 = 1424, when the author was thirteen years old [z].

55. From the Commentary on the Prophets by R. Gershom ben Nathan, written in 1594: the MS. is in the University Library at Upsala.

Next follow three Spanish texts written in Roman characters, and the Latin of ben 'Amram.

A. Chapter 41, in the original (see No. 39), from the *Fortaleza del Judaismo y Confusion del estraño* of R. Abraham, the Proselyte [a], of Cordova, according to an Oxford MS. [b] This treatise is also to be found in Baron Günzburg's Library, No. 467.

---

[z] See *Archives des missions*, etc., 1873, p. 573.

[a] Otherwise called Lorenzo Escudero, according to Dr. Kayserling, *Sephardim*, p. 255.

[b] Catal. Mortara, No. 167; Catal. Coxe, Canon. Miscell., No. 544, who says that, to judge from the hand, the MS. must belong to the sixteenth century.

B. The 23rd 'Question' on Isaiah from the *Conciliador* of R. M'nasseh ben Israel (about 1640), according to the Amsterdam edition of 1650, but with occasional corrections, the text as there given being disfigured by numerous errata.

C. Chapters 24–28 from the *Prevenciones divinas contra la vana Idolatria de las gentes* of the physician Orobio de Castro, one of the persecuted Spaniards who, in order to be able to profess Judaism openly, migrated about the middle of the seventeenth century[c] to Amsterdam, where he composed this work in support of the Jewish faith. For the text I have followed an Oxford MS., Opp. Add. fol. 29, and another which came into my hands from M. Montezinos in Amsterdam. For making the necessary corrections in the MS., previous to publication, I called in the assistance of Señor Lucena, Teacher of Spanish in this University. There is an abridgment of this treatise in Portuguese[d], which I had acquired from M. Montezinos, and from which the French translation was made by Henriquez[e]; but as Portuguese is less generally known than French, it was deemed sufficient to reprint the last chapter from the French translation, according to the first edition.

D. Sections 613–647, and 840, 841, from the *Gate of Truth*, by R. Ya'qob ben 'Amram, written in the year 1634. The Hebrew original of this is unfortunately lost, and it exists only in a Latin translation, in a MS. belonging to Balliol College, Oxford, No. 251. On the first page are the words: 'Porta veritatis sive compendiaria via ad beatitudinem, autore Jacob ben Amram Judaeo; haec porta Domini, justi intrabunt per

---

[c] See Grätz, x. p. 202.

[d] Its title is, *Explicaçaõ paraphrastica sobre o cap.* 53 *de profeta Isaias . . . . , feito por hum coriozo da nacaõ hebrea em Amsterdam em o mez de Tisry anno* 5435. See the Cardozo Catalogue, Amsterdam, 1870, No. 1376.

[e] It has been printed twice: once in London, 1770, under the title *Israel vengé, ou exposition naturelle des prophéties hébraiques que les chrétiens appliquent à leur prétendu Messie;* and in Paris, 1846.

eam (Ps. 117, v. 20). Anno de orbe condito, 5394[f].' Latin is still so far from being in England a dead or unknown language that it has been deemed unnecessary to have this Commentary translated; the text itself has, however, for convenience, been reprinted in the English volume.

There still remain four other treatises to be alluded to. *a. Tratado hecho por doctor* [*Elie*] *Montealto sobre el capitulo* 53 *de Isahias,* which likewise is in my possession[g]: this has been omitted, because it is merely a discussion on the sin of our first parents, and not an exposition of the entire chapter. *b. Declaraçaõ do Cap.* 53 *de Iesaya,* by Yiẓḥaq Montealto[h]: this I was unable to see, in consequence of the jealousy of its possessor; it may possibly be a Portuguese version of one of the Spanish chapters mentioned above. *c.* The מנחה בלולה[i], a commentary on Isaiah, by R. Hillel ben Ya'qob ha-Kohen (about 1500?); but this, as Dr. Perles has pointed out[j]—and through

---

[f] The following curious note is inscribed on the cover:—

An Advertisement.

This manuscript was found in the library of the very learned Rd. Cudworth, D. D. Thence it came into the hands of my learned friend P. Allix, D.D., of whom I bought it. I have heard Dr. Cudworth say that he bought of M. ben Israel a MS. for £10, and I believe this to be the same. It has been thought that M. ben Israel was the author of it. I cannot affirm that to be so. But I can affirm that I take it to be the greatest effort against Christianity that I ever saw in any language whatsoever. And for that reason I do declare that it is my will that it be not sold to any private person for any price how great soever, lest by that means it should be printed, without an answer, to the prejudice of Christianity. I rather will that it should be burnt, or given to some public library upon sufficient caution that it be never lent out of the said library, nor transcribed, but locked up by itself and consulted upon occasion, in the library, by such only as shall be allowed by the owners of the said library.

May 9, 1700. RICHARD BATH AND WELLS.

[g] Cardozo Catalogue, No. 1398. [h] *Ibid.*, No. 1405.

[i] See Steinschneider's Catal. of the Hebrew MSS. at Munich, Cod. 365.

[j] Grätz, *Monatsschrift*, 1875, p. 368.

the kindness of Rabbi S. Z. Taussig, the editor of the נוה שלום, who transcribed for me the portion relating to this Parashah, I am in a position entirely to confirm his judgment—is nothing more than a cento from the earlier commentators, and in particular from Rashi and David Qamḥi.

It is possible that other passages relating to the same chapter may have escaped my notice; any such which may be indicated by the kindness of critics, I shall gladly supply should an opportunity present itself.

I cannot end this preface without acknowledging the obligations I am under to my two friends, M. Senior Sachs of Paris, and Dr. Schiller-Szinessy of Cambridge, who have been of the greatest assistance to me while the Hebrew sheets were passing through the press.

The above is a complete list of the texts which have been edited in volume i. For the translations occupying the present volume, with the exception of those from the Spanish, the undersigned are jointly responsible; for the revision of the translations of the Spanish commentaries, they are under obligations to Mr. H. J. Mathews, of Exeter College, Oxford, to whom they desire to acknowledge their best thanks for the aid which he has rendered. It has been the aim of the translators to render the various texts as literally as was consistent with English idiom, while at the same time reducing in some measure the diffuseness and tautology of expression not unfrequently characteristic of the original. They have refrained from offering any criticisms or comments of their own, even in cases where defective philology or palpably false exegesis might seem to invite or demand them. And, lastly, they feel that it is only just to record their grateful recognition of the assistance which, through the whole course of the work, they have derived from the diligent and skilful eye of Mr. Pembrey, to whom the high character borne by the Oriental publications of the Clarendon Press has been for many years due.

A. N. S. R. D.

OXFORD, December, 1876.

NOTE.

Some explanation ought perhaps to be offered of the orthography employed in the present volume in the transliteration of Hebrew words. The current forms of many of the more familiar Bible-names are derived, as is well known, through the Vulgate from those adopted by the Septuagint translators, and often deviate noticeably from such as would be in strict accordance with the present vocalization of the Hebrew text. It was felt that in a work in which unfamiliar names constantly occurring would of necessity call for exact transliteration, an attempt might be made to remove the anomaly of conventional and unconventional forms appearing side by side, and at the same time to secure throughout forms more thoroughly in harmony with analogy and the structure of the language. When thus restored, for example, the proper names Simeon, Moses, Solomon, Isaac, Jacob, Samuel, Elijah, Isaiah, Sennacherib, become, respectively, Shimʿon, Mosheh, Sh'lômoh, Yiẓḥaq, Yaʿqob, Sh'mu'el, 'Eliyyah, Y'shaʿyah, Sanhêrib. In the citation of books of the Bible, however, the usual orthography has been adhered to; and in some other instances also uniformity has not been completely attained. It only remains to explain that ' represents, before a vowel, the soft breathing; before a consonant, the slight *e*-sound almost necessarily heard between two consonants occurring together at the beginning of a syllable; that ʿ represents the rough guttural ʿAin; that *ṭ*, *ẓ*, *q* represent respectively Tet, Zade, and Qoph (as distinguished from Tau, Zain, and Kaph): lastly, that *j* has of course disappeared, being replaced by *y*; and that Cheth (*ch* as in '*Loch*'), to avoid mispronunciation, is represented by *ḥ*.

CONTENTS.

INTRODUCTION

TO THE

ENGLISH TRANSLATION.

THE late pious Dr. Macbride, ever a great lover of the Jewish people, endowed (as is well known in Oxford) an annual Sermon on 'the Jewish interpretation of prophecy.' On one occasion when I was entrusted with preaching that Sermon, it occurred to me that we wanted larger materials than can be within the reach of most preachers.

The extracts indeed from the older writers, which we still have, are copious, and more complete than they could be made in these days[a]. Raymond Martini had before him MSS. which, under the mandate of the king of Arragon, had been brought together from the synagogues within his realm. Raymond de Pennaforti had founded seminaries for the instruction of members of his order, in Hebrew and Arabic, to promote the conversion of Jews and Mohammedans[b]. James I, king of Arragon, commissioned Paulus Christianus[c], 'of Jewish birth and instructed among them in Hebrew literature[d],' among others, to collect such MSS. as were to his purpose. Paul had gone about

---

[a] Those passages only are collected here, in which this section of Isaiah is directly quoted. Wünsche, die Leiden des Messias, has collected into one the passages on the sufferings of the Messiah from Martini, Schöttgen, and the rest. Sometimes also the allusion to this section is contained in the characteristic word סבל (liii. 4, 11): as in the Pesikta Rabbathi, 'Our Rabbins have handed down, the fathers of the world will rise in Nisan and say to him, Ephraim Messiah our righteousness, though we are thy fathers, thou art better than we, because thou hast borne our iniquities and the iniquities of our sons (סבלת עונותינו ועונות בנינו), and many and hard judgments have passed over thee, which did not pass over the former or the later,' &c. (Schöttg. p. 133, the Hebrew in Wünsche, p. 67); and in the account of a pious man, who, when asked why he took suffering on himself, said, 'He also must suffer something, since the Messiah bore the iniquities (סובל עונות) of Israel,' Chasidim, p. 60 in Hengst. Christol. ii. 351 ed. 2.

[b] Acta Sanctt. Jan. 27, i. 212[b], 419[a]; Grätz, vii. 27.

[c] Wolf, Bibl. Hebr. t. i. n. 1912.

[d] Clement IV in Carpzov's Praef.; Grätz, vii. 131.

as a missionary, disputing with the Jews, undertaking to 'prove from the Bible and the Talmud, that Jesus was Christ and God [e].' He knew then what to select: a king's command could not then be resisted in Spain, and penalties were annexed to its refusal [f]. So the books which Martini used, represent the texts, such as existed in MSS. of the Jewish synagogues in Spain in the latter part of the thirteenth century [g]. They are spoken of as 'of the more recondite [h].' The latest historian of the Jews attests his capacities. '[i] He was solidly instructed in Biblical and Rabbinical literature, which he had certainly learned from a baptized Jew, perhaps from Paulus Christianus; he read fluently the writings of the Agada, Rashi, Ibn Ezra, Maimuni, and Kimchi, and used therefrom what seemed to him calculated to prove that, not only in the Bible, but also in the Rabbinical writings, Jesus was announced as Messiah and Son of God.' The distinguished Jewish writer Ben Aderet, who wrote against him [j], objected nothing to the accuracy of his quotations. In his preface (in which he speaks modestly of himself [k]) he says [l], 'I was enjoined to compose a work from the books of the Old Testament which the Jews receive, and from the Talmud, and the other writings authentic among them,—a poniard which should be at hand for Christian preachers and worshippers, either in their sermons to cut to the Jews the bread [m] of the Divine word, or to put an end to their faithlessness,' &c. Jews of course must lay hold of any weak points in it; but they own that '[n] it for the first time introduced Christians into the Jewish world of thought.'

I had hoped that the general statement of the character of Martini, and the circumstances under which he compiled his work, would have sufficed. But he has lately been denounced as one 'guilty of impostures,' 'well-*meaning* dishonesty' (as if dishonesty were not aggravated when the subject is the faith), 'audacious alteration of the text,' &c. An early father appealed to the heathen emperor as to the calumnies against Christians, '[o] What you would not do, you should not suspect others of

---

[e] Grätz, l. c. [f] Bosquet Ep. ad Voisin. in Carpzov Theol. Jud. c. xii.

[g] Martini was engaged in writing the tenth chapter of his second part in A. D. 1275 (Pug. Fid. fol. 316), but he must have collected his materials before he began.

[h] 'Codices reconditiores,' Bosquet Ep. ad Voisin. in Carpzov, l. c. p. 92.

[i] Grätz, vii. 163. [j] Id. ibid. p. 165, note.

[k] Prooem. n. iv. p. 2 ed. Carpzov. [l] Ibid. n. iii.

[m] The poniard being used as a knife for cutting bread.

[n] Grätz, p. 164. [o] Tertull. Apol. c. 8.

doing.' Raymond Martini spent near forty years[p] in his labours for the extension of the truth, which he loved. Although we know him as a writer, yet writing was not his exclusive or prominent occupation. He is said to have been President of eight colleges, founded by the king of Arragon to promote the study of the Oriental languages for the conversion of Jews and Mohammedans[q]. He was also for a short time a Missionary in Tunis, where he was very acceptable to its king, and yet this, too, had its perils, for one of his colleagues became a martyr[r]. He declared his belief that our Lord[s] put it into his heart to begin his work, and he prayed Him to enable him to complete it in such wise as should be to the glory of God, the defence of the faith, the true and beneficial conversion of unbelievers, and to the eternal salvation of himself, the least of his order. It is best to speak plainly. Either Martini was what he has hitherto been accounted, an able and laborious and conscientious man with vast resources at his command, which have since been lost, or he was a forger, a liar, and hypocrite. There is no doubt of his ability. There is a saying that 'he spoke Hebrew and Arabic as fluently as Latin[t].' Did he abuse these powers, lying in the name of God?

Augustin Justinian, bishop of Nebio, in his preface to Porchet's 'Victoria,' the materials of which Porchet professed to draw from Martini, says[u], 'What labour, vigils, expense, helps are necessary to those who would penetrate the secrets of the Hebrews, I have myself experienced. But, being in whatever degree provided with all these, I have myself read in the monuments of the Hebrews a good part of what is cited by Porchet and Raymond, so that there is no room left for any doubt as to the truthfulness [fide] of their citations. Of this we can give fullest proof to any one by testimony of the books, from which this precious store was taken: almost all of which I have obtained for myself, and keep carefully, as kings do their jewels.'

The loss of any book or books, in the time before printing was discovered, or the variation of texts, when they were only

---

p He was appointed President A.D. 1250, died after A.D. 1286. His signature appears in a conventus, July 1, 1284, Diago Hist. Praed. Arrag. ii. 28.

q Herzog, Real-Encyclopädie xii. 570, Art. Raymund Martino.

r Diago, l. c.

s Praef. end, n. 18.

t Herzog, ibid.

u Quoted in Carpzov's Praef. c. 12, p. 104.

handed down by individual scribes, can surprise no one. In many subjects we have to regret our losses. In this little volume an exposition of Benjamin of Nehawend [w], another of Saadyah Gaon [x], both of them celebrated writers, are alleged. They must have existed in the eleventh century, but are, as yet, lost. The remarkable saying of Joseph Ben Caspi, I believe, is known at present through the one writer who quotes him [y]. What would have been thought of Martini, had he quoted from a book [z] anterior to the Talmud, of which those who have previously quoted it are said to have alleged only one saying? A Jewish controversialist [a], who himself supposes Israel to be the subject of the section, says, as an admission, that in the Talmud it is expounded of the Messiah: 'It is not to be found in our editions.' Dr. Neubauer, who has recently been employed by the French Government to ascertain what remains there are of Jewish literature in Spain and Portugal, tells us, '[b] There are not more than 100 MSS. in those countries, the seat of Hebrew learning of all branches during five centuries (1040 to 1490).' All probably, which Martini used, must have perished.

It is almost degrading to an author of accredited honesty to defend him on the ground that fraud would have defeated its own purpose. *We* use Martini as a repertorium of extracts from books which have been lost. But Martini wrote it to furnish materials for those of his own order, engaged in the like studies for the conversion of Jews and Mohammedans, but chiefly of the Jews. But the Jews had able controversialists. The books alleged were their study from early youth. To what end to use fraud which would be patent and rebound in the first disputation? Passages quoted by Martini are also quoted, independently of him apparently, by a Jewish convert, Hieronymus à S. Fide, who had his authorities from his own Jewish studies. *He* also quotes from a 'Genesi magno antiquissimo [c];' but his quotations, while agreeing in the main with those of Martini, vary from them, quoting sometimes a text more of Holy Scripture,

---

[w] Quoted by Yepheth b. Ali; see p. 31.

[x] Quoted by Ibn Ezra, p. 42.

[y] Ibn Danân, p. 203.

[z] Tana d' bê Eliyyahu, below, p. 385; see Wolf, B. H. i. p. 147.

[a] Meir b. Shim'on quoting Sotah, § 1, below, p. 377.

[b] Neubauer, Talm. and Rabb. Literat. p. 9, (an extract from the Annual Report of the Philological Society, London, 1876.)

[c] Hieron. à S. Fide contra Jud. i. 2, in Bibl. Max. Patr. t. 26, p. 533.

sometimes a text less, sometimes omitting a portion of his text, sometimes explaining it in his own words.

Under his name before his conversion, Joshua Ibn Vives Allorqui, he is well spoken of by the Jewish historian, who mentions his expostulations under the form of enquiries from a former convert, well known as Paulus Burgensis [d]. His book, according to the account of the same historian, was the basis of the celebrated disputation of Tortosa, which, amid many interruptions, lasted for a year and nine months, from Feb. 1413 to Nov. 12, 1414, in 68 sessions [e]. The subject of the dispute was whether the position of Hieronymus, that the Talmud attested that Jesus was the Messiah, was true or no [f]. The Jewish historian says [g], 'Hieronymus adduced the notorious Agada-passages out of the Talmud and other Jewish writings, to prove that most incredible thing, that the Talmud itself attested in some degree that Jesus was the Messiah.' He speaks of them as 'insipid.' He denounces in no measured terms the weakness of his arguments [h], or (in the second part) the charges against the Talmud: but he speaks of him as 'the apostate well-read in Jewish literature [i],' and brings not the slightest imputation against the accuracy of his citations. Hieronymus himself says [j], 'I intend by the grace of God to verify, that these 24 conditions were to be in the true Messiah promised in the Law, by authorities and glosses made by masters among the Jews and Talmudists whose words no one of the Jews ventured in any way to deny.' And they were not denied. But among these passages were some for which Martini has been denounced as a clever falsificator.

---

[d] Grätz, viii. pp. 82–84.

[e] Ibid. p. 118. The book contained 24 conditions which the Messiah was to fulfil, as in Hieron. pp. 531, 532. Hieronymus' work is also divided into the same two parts: 1. The testimony to the Messiah; 2. The allegations against the Talmud.

[f] Ibid. p. 120. [g] Ibid.

[h] 'Geronimo first elaborated a writing, to establish out of Jewish writings, that Jesus was the Messiah and was God. He brought together therein, all which his predecessors had produced of apparent proofs, sophisms, perversion of Scripture, resting on a confused and senseless interpretation, added thereto new senselessness, elevated naive, harmless, allusive Agada-passages to essential articles of faith.' 'The writing breathed a patristic and Rabbinic spirit,' 'he assailed Rabbinic Judaism with Rabbinic weapons.' Grätz, viii. 116–118.

[i] Ibid. p. 114. [j] L. c.

The quotation from the Siphré[k] and two from R. Mosheh Haddarshan[l] occur in Hieronymus also, but with variations which shew that his authority was independent of Martini.

In the following volume a passage from the Talmud is quoted with an addition of two words. In this Martini's text is so clearly right, that it can hardly fail to be accepted. It is one in which names of the Messiah are enumerated. With one exception, each consists of a single word. 'Shiloh,' 'Yinnon' (Ps. lxxii. 17), 'Chaninah,' 'Menahem.' In the present text of the Talmud the other name has been made 'leprous of the house of Rabbi.' Such a name could only have found acceptance through the absence of good MSS. Martini's MS. restores the sense: 'The Rabbis say, "the leprous one" [with reference doubtless to an explanation of ver. 4[m]]; those of the house of Rabbi say, "the sick one," as it is said, "surely he hath borne our sicknesses."' This clear case gives a favourable impression as to Martini's texts.

Formerly, Christians used to charge the Jews with falsifying their MSS.: the tables are now turned, and the charge has been made against Martini. There is no ground for these mutual criminations. The Jews had a perfect right to enlarge or contract their texts, which were made for private use, so long as that text itself was not authoritative, as the Holy Scriptures.

It is notorious that MSS. did represent their text more or less accurately. Even with printed books before him, Schöttgen complained of the injuries which the text had undergone. Thus, he shews how, in a long passage, the Pesikta Rabbathi and the Yalkut Shimeoni fill up and correct one another[n]. He restores the Pesikta, 'in a place very dislocated,' from the Echa Rabbathi[o]; and again in some degree out of the Yalkut[p] and

---

[k] Below, p. 10, quoted as *Ziphrat* in Hieron. i. 11. The spelling is throughout very bad; but for *it* he is not responsible. The passage in the Siphré varying in the present editions, I would only add that Edzardi quotes two passages, in which mention is made of 'the merit of the Messiah' (notes on the Pug. Fid. p. 866, l. 7, in Wolf, Bibl. Hebr. iv. 632), and that the Talm. המצטער (Hebr. text, p. 9), 'afflicted himself,' is a Jewish, not a Christian conception of the Messiah (comp. לצום ולהתענות Hebr. text, p. 35). Not knowing of the atoning death, they pictured voluntary self-affliction.

[l] That beginning 'Says R. B'rekyah,' and that '*In the beginning*,' below, p. 33.

[m] See Levy, Lex. Chald. p. 245.

[n] Horae Hebraicae de Messia, pp. 127–134.

[o] Ibid. p. 136.

[p] Ibid. p. 172.

the Rabboth [q]. He supplies from the Tanchuma what Martini quotes from his Bereshith Rabba [r]: he restores from one edition of the Pesikta Sotarta [s] what had clearly been omitted in another [t]. He shews how the Tanchuma may be supplied out of the Bereshith Rabba, as quoted by Martini [u], or how the Bereshith Rabba may be supplied in part out of the Yalkut, but more fully out of that of Martini [v], or from the Yalkut alone [w]. He marks omissions in some editions [x]; he complains also of dislocation and corruptions of the Zohar [y] and the Tanchuma [z]. He notices variations of the 'son of David' and 'house of David' in different citations of the same passage [a]; of the substitution of the Messiah ben Joseph for the Messiah ben David [b]; the omission of מלך משיח [c]. He uses the modern critical canon, that the number of various readings imply corruption [d]. Dr. Neubauer informs me that different collections and copies of Midrashim are more or less full, and that some have been lost. Indeed, I could not but think, that Jewish writers who quoted them, generally had a larger range before them, than we have now. However, I would say that I took upon myself the responsibility of requesting Dr. Neubauer to insert the quotations from Martini, and that he inserted them (as he placed the extracts from the Zohar) in consideration of my wishes, leaving it to me to defend them. Amid the various sources of human mistake, we are bound by the duties of our common humanity, not to assume the very worst, dishonesty; but to believe what a person says that he saw with his own eyes. Enough has been said, perhaps, where demonstration on either side is impossible, since the extracts were made nearly six centuries ago, and the MSS. which Martini had before him have long since perished.

To return. Besides this great and (as I believe on a study of near fifty years) accurate repertorium, drawn from MSS. before the invention of printing, and including extracts from works which have since been lost, are the large collectanea of Schöttgen, as also those in Lightfoot, Sommer on the Theology of the Sohar, Gläsener on the twofold Messiah, Edzardi's works, as also the careful monograph of Dr. Mc Caul on Is. liii, and others.

But while these brought within the reach of all, the older

[q] Horae Hebraicae de Messia, p. 197. [r] Pp. 101, 103.
[s] P. 141. [t] P. 97. [u] Pp. 72, 73. [v] Pp. 161, 162. [w] P. 164.
[x] P. 182. [y] Pp. 109, 241. [z] P. 74. [a] P. 227. [b] Pp. 228, 229.
[c] P. 231 and elsewhere. See other variations, ibid. pp. 237, 239, 240.
[d] P. 159.

traditional interpretations, we seemed to me to have a less knowledge of the later Jewish mind, from the eleventh century onwards. It may be that, as, on all subjects in all nations, the original minds are few, and the mass of writings are but reproductions of the few, so it may be here. However, be this as it may, whether or no it shall appear that the more recent writers among the Jews, follow the few leaders, as Rashi, Joseph Kimchi (himself followed by his son David), Ibn Ezra, and Abarbanel, both in their own interpretations and in their objections to Christianity, I thought that we wanted fuller evidence of their mind.

Those to whom most had access were very few in number; and much remained to be added from MSS. Abarbanel, I found, quoted a commentary on this section by a celebrated writer, Moses ben Nachman [e], which had escaped the vast knowledge of Wolf (Bibliotheca Hebraea) and De Rossi. Dr. Neubauer pointed it out to me in the Michael collection of MSS. which he was cataloguing, as also another wholly unknown. Besides the additions from MSS., I expected that some of the printed works might be filled up or corrected by MSS. Pococke pointed out, more than two centuries ago [f], by aid of the first edition of Kimchi [g] on the Prophets, and two Oxford MSS., that, from different causes, passages directed against Christianity had been suppressed in printed editions. But if we wish to know any one's mind, we must know it wholly.

I requested Dr. Neubauer then to collect for me all Jewish interpretations of Is. lii. 13–liii. end, engaging myself to have them printed. This he willingly undertook, as an important literary work, and has executed with a fulness which could only have been attained by one with his extensive Oriental learning and knowledge of Jewish literature. Twenty-eight [h] of the larger extracts, and nine of the shorter, have been collected from MSS. in the Bodleian, and libraries of St. Petersburg, Paris, Rome, Florence, Parma, Leyden, Breslau, Upsala. Of the printed comments, the familiar names of Rashi, Ibn Ezra, Kimchi (and his epitome, the Michlal Yophi), Abarbanel, Moses Elsheikh, with those of R. Samuel Lanyado and R. Meir Aramah, were probably

[e] It was printed by Steinschneider; see Dr. Neubauer's Preface, p. ix.

[f] Not. Miscell. ad Port. Mos. c. 8; Works, t. i. pp. 241–249, published A.D. 1653.

[g] Ed. Pisaur., A.D. 1515.

[h] The Fuente Claro is also taken from the one printed copy, which exists.

alone in reach of most. Of these, Kimchi, Ibn Ezra, and Meir Aramah were collated afresh, and Saadyah Gaon's text was restored from the single known MS. (that now at Paris has been acquired since).

Thus far I should only have deserved the thanks of Hebrew and Arabic scholars for having suggested the work to one so competent to complete it, who has spared no pains in its execution. I incurred personal responsibility by requesting Dr. Neubauer to have his collection translated into English under his own superintendence. On the one side, the translation, which has been done with great and accurate pains, made the collection accessible to those who, although idiomatically acquainted with Hebrew, and so, capable of availing themselves of it, had not had leisure to become Arabic scholars, or to read Rabbinical Hebrew fluently, and so could make little use of the originals. On the other side, the translation placed this amount of Jewish controversy (as it must be for the most part) within the reach of persons, men or women, who have not the knowledge required to estimate aright any one thing in the book. Yet in these days, in which almost everybody reads everything new, some might use it to confirm their unbelief; some might be discomforted by the repetition of denials of the faith in it. I was myself startled at the strength of Bishop Kidder's protest, and his fears of the effect of one[i] rather common-place work. Yet in these days anything is but a drop in a raging sea. While then I hope that this book may enable us to understand the better the difficulties of our Jewish brethren, I would, while (owing to the circumstances of the publication) I remain strictly on the defensive, briefly say, why this volume in no way shakes the evidence from this great prophecy, but rather illustrates it.

It will be observed on examination, that next to nothing turns upon renderings of the Hebrew. The objections raised by Jewish controversialists in the following volume, in only four or, at most, five words[j], turn on the language. Of this hereafter.

---

[i] See Preface, p. xxi.

[j] I do not include יזה (lii. 15); for although the interpretations are different, it is never mentioned in Jewish controversy, nor does anything turn upon it. הזה is, in the Old Testament, uniformly used of 'besprinkling,' most frequently of blood, but also of the oil, or water with the ashes of the heifer, in symbolic purification. All the meanings ascribed to it by Jewish interpreters are derived from the meaning 'sprinkle.' Two of the earliest, Aquila and Theodotion, have the technical word, used in the Greek of the

The characteristics, in which all agree, are, that there would be a prevailing unbelief as to the subject of the prophecy, lowly

---

Old Testament of 'sprinkling to cleanse,' ῥαντίσει. These render 'besprinkle' with the accusative of the person, which is, as Gesenius observed, implied by the proper name יזיה.

2. Others, in view of the temporal Messias whom they expected, supply 'sprinkle the blood of,' Yepheth (p. 21), Jehudah b. Bala'm (p. 550), Ibn Ezra (p. 44), Anonymous, xvi. (p. 64), or 'scatter,' Tanchum (p. 553), Aaron b. Joseph (p. 86), Ibn Crispin (p. 105, but explaining 'scatter' as 'one who sprinkles blood'), Abarbanel (p. 190); 'expel, perhaps with bloodshed,' xxxiv. (p. 231), Moses Elsheikh (p. 262); 'sprinkle, so as to leave very few indeed,' Lanyado (p. 301), David Altschuler (p. 367).

3. Others, in the same view, render 'scatter' (as, in sprinkling, drop parts from drop), Symmachus (p. 1), Jonathan (p. 5), Saadyah (p. 17); 'sprinkle and scatter,' Gershom (p. 564); 'expel and drive away,' Joseph Kara (p. 41), Ibn Mali (p. 75), Jacob b. Reuben, Karaite (p. 61), xvii. (p. 67); 'scatter,' Nizzachon vet. (p. 90), Naphthali Altschuler (p. 320), *m.* (p. 393), Herz Homberg (p. 402); 'scatter and conquer' (but admitting 2 and 6 to be possible), Abarbanel (p. 171); 'conquer,' Joseph b. Nathan (p. 72); 'cast down the horns of,' Rashi (p. 37), Abraham b. Judah (p. 314).

4. Derived from this, is 'rule,' Ibn Shaprut (p. 94), Christian in Mosheh Cohen (p. 115), and Mosheh Cohen (p. 117), Christian in Lopez (p. 341), and Lopez (p. 350); 'by his knowledge hold sway over them and gain admittance to the table of kings,' Meir Aramah (p. 241).

5. A few render 'teaching' (again, drop by drop). Others, 'will teach wholesome doctrine,' Jacob b. Reuben, Karaite (p. 61); 'his speech will drop upon,' Moses b. Nachman (p. 80); 'preach and prophesy,' Shelomo Levi (p. 279).

6. 'Speak of' (sprinkling words), Farissol (p. 223), or 'make to speak,' Ibn Danân (p. 207).

7. 'Make to speak,' J. and D. Kimchi (p. 50), Astruc (p. 130), Isaac Eliyyah (p. 140), Sal. b. Melech (p. 217), Troki (p. 256), Moses of Salerno (p. 381), Manasseh b. Israel (p. 437), Persian version (p. xi), Tataric Karaite version (p. xiv), Orobio (p. 484).

8. Segre is, of course, alone in thinking that 'יזה is for יורה, omitting the ר for euphony' (p. 301).

I think all these renderings unidiomatic. In no language would a person say absolutely that he 'besprinkled nations,' meaning that he 'shed their blood,' or that he 'scattered them,' or that he 'taught them,' or that he 'ruled over them;' or that, he 'made them to sprinkle,' meant that he 'made them to speak of him.' Still, let any take which of them he willed, the general meaning would remain the same, that he, whom they once despised, did these things which were the acts of one, who had power over them, as a whole. They, at the same time, by selecting one or other of these, shew that though some of them were Arabic-speaking Jews, the favourite modern explanation, made them 'spring for joy,' did not occur to them, as indeed Golius's 'exultavit prae hilaritate' (retained by Freytag) is a slip for 'the ass sprung from its night's resting-place.' Luzzatto alone leaves the Hebrew tradition for the German with his 'made to leap,' 'startled,' pp. 414, 415. Though at variance with the uniform Hebrew meaning, it does not affect the sense.

beginnings, among circumstances outwardly unfavourable, but before God, and protected by Him; sorrows, injustice, contempt, death, which were the portion of the sufferer; that he was accounted a transgressor, yet that his sufferings were, in some way, vicarious, the just for the unjust; his meek silence; his willing acceptance of his death; his being with the rich in his death; his soul being (in some way) an offering for sin, and God's acceptance of it; his prolonged life; his making many righteous; his continued intercession for transgressors; the greatness of his exaltation, in proportion to the depth of his humiliation; the submission of kings to him; his abiding reign.

Now these are apparent on the surface in translations which adhere to the letter. Whatever difference there is in details of single words, all these stand out in the translation of Saadyah Gaon (who is himself stated to have interpreted the whole section of Jeremiah [i]), or the Persian or the Tataric translation [j], or that of Manasseh b. Israel [k]. The question is not, 'What is the picture?' in this all are agreed; but, 'Whose image or likeness does it bear?'

But clearly as all this lies in the words, none beforehand would understand how it could be fulfilled in one person. For none could tell beforehand, how death, which closes all on this earth, was to be the vestibule to a God-given kingdom; or how kings should bow down before one who had been the object of contempt. 'We cannot,' says one of the later of these writers [l], 'interpret each individual detail in it of the Messiah, because we do not know all the incidents of his advent, or the precise manner of the redemption which he will accomplish for Israel;' and another [m] says, that 'it was given by God as a description of the Messiah, whereby, when any should claim to be the Messiah, to judge by the resemblance or non-resemblance to it, whether he were the Messiah or no.'

Those of old, to whom the later Jews referred as authorities, dwelt on the one or the other side of the picture; some on the

---

[i] Dr. Neubauer tells me that this interpretation is not in his book on 'the faith,' some of which is controversial against Christians (Poc. 148), and suggests that Saadyah may have subjoined a short commentary to his translation of Isaiah as he did to that of Job (Hunt. 511) and of the Psalms. His translation of the Psalms is found in MSS., both with and without the commentary; with, cod. Poc. 281; without, cod. Hunt. 416.

[j] Of these two last, I was enabled to judge through the kindness of another.

[k] Pp. 436-440 below. It is otherwise in the paraphrase, ibid.

[l] Ibn Danân, p. 116.

[m] Ibn Crispin, p. 114.

vicarious sufferings of the Messiah[n], some on his exaltation[o], without attempting to reconcile the two.

The faith in the vicarious sufferings survived in the mystical school, so that even a writer[p] of the latter part of the sixteenth century, preserves, from a work quoted as an authority in the Talmud[q], as having been revealed to their great mystical writer Simeon ben Yochai, the remarkable saying[r], 'The meaning of the words "bruised for our iniquities" is, that since the Messiah bears our iniquities, which produce the effect of his being bruised, it follows that whoso will not admit that the Messiah thus suffers for our iniquities, must endure and suffer for them himself.' The belief that the Messiah was an object of contempt survives also in the prayers of the German Jews for the first day of the Passover[s]; his vicarious sufferings are pleaded in their prayers on the day of Atonement[t]. It survived also in the belief of a Messiah ben Joseph, to whom were allotted the sufferings foretold of the Messiah. Those who place the mystical books at a later date bring down also the date, during which the belief in a suffering Messiah continued among them.

But a suffering Messiah, and a Messiah who should deliver them from their enemies, were humanly incompatible in the same person. Before the destruction of Jerusalem, the Jews looked for the coming of a Messiah to save it; afterwards, to restore it. As Christians have looked for the coming of antichrist and the Second Coming of Christ, so the Jews looked for their Messiah[u]. Every token of evil made R. Akiba

---

[n] Jonathan, v. 3 (p. 5); Talmud (p. 7); Midrash Rabba (p. 9); Yalkut (p. 10, n. 3); Siphré, in the time of Martini (pp. 10, 11); Tanchuma, also in Martini (p. 21); Pesikta, in Abkath Rochel, i. 2, p. 7 (ibid.); Zohar (p. 14); Bereshith Rabba, in Martini (pp. 33-35); 'our Rabbis' in Rashi, ap. Martini (p. 39); Tana d' bê Eliyyahu, as from Shim'on b. Yochai (pp. 385, 386); Midrash Conen (p. 394); 'Asereth Mêmroth (ibid.); Yalkut Chadash (p. 398); voluntary suffering, Bereshith Rabba (p. 35), Sepher Chasidim (ab. p. xxix); contempt, Mysteries of Simeon b. Yochai (p. 32). Other passages in which sufferings of the Messiah are spoken of, though not in reference to Is. liii, are in Sanhedrin, dist. Chelek (Mart. fol. 228; Wünsche, pp. 56, 57); Pesikta Rabbathi (Schöttgen, loci gen., n. xcv. p. 133; Wünsche, p. 66) a long passage.

[o] In Jonathan chiefly (pp. 5, 6); Yalkut (p. 9, n. 1, 2); Zohar (pp. 12, 13); Bereshith Rabba (Mart. p. 33, n. 1); 'a Midrash Aggada' in Rashi Mart. (pp. 39, 40); Midrash Tillim on Ps. ii. (Mart. p. 423).

[p] Eliyyah de Vidas (1575), p. 385.

[q] Tana d' bê Eliyyahu, quoted Sanhedrin, fol. 97, 1, l. ult. of the duration of the world for 6000 years; 2000 years, void (tohu); 2000, the law; 2000, the days of the Messiah. See Martini ii. 10 init., fol. 315.

[r] Pp. 386, 387. [s] P. 398 *u.* Pref. p. xvii. [t] P. 399 *w.* Pref. ibid.

[u] Grätz apologises for the expectations among the Jews, which were so

expect the more the Messias, whom he found in Bar Cochab. In the rebellion against Antoninus Pius, the celebrated mystic Simeon ben Yochai said, in expectation of a Parthian invasion, '[v]When you see a Persian [Parthian] horse fastened at the gravestones in the land of Israel, then hope for the Messiah.' Yet even in the controversy with Christians, the belief that the Messiah should die was not extinct in the second century. In S. Justin's time, Trypho is still alleged to declare in the name of his people, '[w]That the Scriptures do say that Christ should suffer, is plain, but we wish to learn if you can prove also, that it should be by a kind of suffering which is cursed in the law.' '[x]That he should suffer and be led as a sheep to the slaughter, we know; but if he was to be crucified, and die so shamefully and dishonourably by a death which is cursed in the law, prove to us, for we cannot bring ourselves to conceive this.' The Jews at that time explained Isaiah, chap. ix, of Hezekiah [y]; they offered no solution of this. The Jews, of whom Tertullian reports, also remarkably limit their objections to this. '[z]Concerning the last step of His passion, you raise a doubt, affirming that the passion of the cross was not predicted with reference to Christ; and urging besides that it is not credible, that God should have exposed His own Son to that kind of death; because Himself said, "Cursed is every one who shall have hung on a tree."' But they do not appear to have set up any counter-explanation; only as Tertullian says [a], 'In the glory of the Second Coming, upon which they fixed their eyes, they overlooked the humiliation of the first.' The first counter-explanation which we hear of is that so often quoted from Origen [b]: 'I remember once having used these prophecies in a disquisition with those called wise among the Jews, whereon the Jew said, that these things were prophesied of the whole people as one, which was both dispersed abroad and smitten, that there might be many proselytes, on the ground that Jews were scattered in the many

often deceived, by referring to the like failure of expectations of the near coming of our Lord, among Christians.

[v] Grätz, iv. 206. [w] Dial. 89, pp. 185, 186 Oxf. Tr.

[x] Ibid. n. 90, p. 186. Mosheh b. Nachman says, 'There is no mention made in the Parashah that the Messiah would be delivered into the hands who hated him, or that he would be slain and hang upon a tree' (p. 84).

[y] Ibid. n. 68, p. 160. [z] Adv. Jud. c. x; Works, t. iii. p. 125 Edinb. Tr.

[a] Ibid. c. 14. S. Irenaeus assigns the same ground for the unbelief of the Jews.

[b] C. Cels. i. 55; Opp. i. 370 Ben.

nations.' The stress is laid on the dispersion, not on the suffering, (for the Christians were at this time, with the Jews, the objects of persecution.) The Jew anticipated that his nation, not the Christians, were to be the converters of the world. But this was no fixed opinion as to the meaning of the section. S. Athanasius, archbishop of a city where the Jews, even after the mutual massacres of Jews and Romans under Adrian, were in considerable numbers, says, that the Jews interpreted Is. vii. 14 of one of themselves, and Deut. xviii. 18 of one of the prophets, and '[c] as to the words, "He was led as a sheep to the slaughter," instead of learning from Philip, conjecture them spoken of Esaias or some other of the prophets, which have been.' In the dialogue between S. Gregentius, archbishop of Taphar in Arabia Felix, and Herban, 'a teacher of the law,' about A.D. 542, when S. Gregentius alleged this section[d], Herban is reported to have expressed himself as perplexed between the declaration of God by Moses of His Unity and 'David and Isaiah [in this section] speaking in truth of him who is called Christ.' Benjamin of Nehawend, a philosophic Karaite of much reputation (A.D. 800–820)[e], still believed that the section related to the Messiah[f]. 'Many,' Ibn Ezra says[g], in the middle of the twelfth century, 'explained it of the Messiah,' on the authority of a traditional saying of the Rabbis. These then must have lived posterior to those Rabbis, on whose authority they rested, yet prior to any extant author who quotes them. Saadyah Gaon, at the revival of the study of Holy Scripture, interpreted the whole section of Jeremiah[h]; Judah b. Balaam thinks this possible, and ridicules Moses ben Gecatalia's opinion that it might be Hezekiah[i].

The interpretation which survived the longest was that which explained of the Messiah the first three verses of the section. This also came to be objected to. The great traditional gloss[j] on the words lii. 13, 'The Messiah shall be "higher" than Abraham, "lifted up" above Moses, "loftier" than the ministering angels,' seemed too great to be interpreted of a mere man. The Christians in their disputations with the Jews, alleged them as

---

[c] Against Arians, i. 55, p. 259 Oxf. Tr. [d] Dial. ii. in Gallandi B.P. xi. 614.

[e] Grätz, Geschichte d. Juden, v. 203, 204; and Note 17. iii, Note 18. ii.

[f] According to Yepheth b. Ali (below, pp. 19, 31).

[g] Below, p. 43. [h] Ibid. [i] Below, p. 551.

[j] Abarbanel quotes it from 'the Midrash of R. Tanchuma,' p. 165. In Martini's time it was in the Bereshith Rabba on Gen. xxviii. 10. It is quoted from the Yalkut, p. 9.

only fulfilled in Jesus, since 'they cannot be true,' Abarbanel[k] reports them, 'except of the First Cause, who is loftier than the loftiest.' Apart from those who quote the saying, without explaining its meaning[l], they said,—

1. That the words did not mean 'greater *than*,' but 'great *from*[m],' i.e. that the person spoken of derived his greatness from Abraham, Moses, and the ministering angels, i.e. that these assisted him to his greatness. The chief writer who so explains it, says that 'the rendering "above" gave occasion to error on the part of the heretics [Christians], pointing, as they do certainly, to the Godhead of the Messiah.'
2. One, held in great respect, said that the angels were the Rabbis[n].
3. Abarbanel admits that the Rabbis did mean to explain the verse of the Messiah[o], but only as applying to it the traditions which they had received respecting the Messiah, without supposing it to be its meaning[p]. Another quotes a saying of 'our doctors[q],' 'Men do not reply to a Haggadah,' though why he should call it so I know not. Another says that 'whatever justice there may be in expressions of our wise men, they are allegorical[r].'
4. Others say boldly that 'the just and perfect man is every way superior to the angels[s].'
5. Ibn Kaspi (A.D. 1280–1340), an ardent admirer of Maimonides and 'a gifted fanatic for philosophic thought[t],' parted with it altogether, and said 'that those who

---

[k] Below, p. 156.

[l] Rashi (who had only heard of it), p. 39; Joseph Kara [early in twelfth century] (p. 41), Abraham b. Judah Chazan (p. 314), both referring it to Israel.

[m] Isaac Eliyyah Cohen (pp. 138, 139) is followed by the unknown writer xxxiv. (p. 230). Abarbanel rejected it as not agreeing with the words of the Midrash, as did Isaac Arama, A.D. 1492 (quoted by Lanyado, p. 299), and Lanyado (pp. 297–300).

[n] En Bonet (Yedayah ha Penini, A.D. 1298; Wolf, i. n. 677) in Abarbanel, p. 154, rejected by Abarbanel (ibid.) and Lanyado (p. 299).

[o] Pp. 165–168. [p] P. 163.

[q] Mosheh Cohen, p. 124; so Chaiim b. Musa, p. 386.

[r] Abraham Farissol (p. 223).

[s] Moses de Coucy (in Lipmann, p. 151), 'with whom common sense agrees' (Lipmann, ibid.), as indeed the Talmud says of the righteous or Israel as a whole; Moses b. Nachman (pp. 84, 85, and notes).

[t] Grätz, vii. 340–345.

expounded the section of the Messiah gave occasion to the heretics to interpret it of Jesus[u].' Passani objects '[v]to bringing the Midrash into the text;' and says that 'Scripture never bears any other than the simple and natural meaning; a different supposition would not allow us to reply to Epicurus' [the Christian].

6. A few only[w], on the ground of it, continued to explain the whole section of the Messiah; one, who speaks glowingly of its meaning, thinks that the section 'relates at once to the Messiah and any righteous one[x].'

Those, however, who would explain the section of the Messiah were met by the great paradox of prophecy beforehand, 'How can the same be put to death and prolong his days and reign?' Hence Moses b. Nachman supposed a readiness only to die[y]; Ibn Crispin, of nearness to death[z]; Herz Homberg, of their 'device to slay him[a];' and the Rabbis explained the last verse of Moses[b], although (as Moses Elsheikh hints[c]) they thereby contracted an obligation not easily discharged, of connecting it with what preceded. Moses Elsheikh himself follows the unanimous opinion of our Rabbis[d], in interpreting the section of the Messiah, yet so great was felt to be the difficulty of admitting the death of the Messiah, that he extended the interpretation, as to Moses, to all the verses which spoke of death[e].

From this difficulty they were freed as soon as they could satisfy themselves to interpret the prophecy of any class of men, some of whom had died, or of any one man except Jesus. The exaltation could be relegated to the future. Of the many interpretations suggested, that which explained it of themselves was too flattering to national feeling not to be extensively adopted. It might naturally have become universal, but for its unsatisfactoriness.

The new interpretation began with Rashi. Rashi's authority

---

[u] Ibn Danân, p. 203. [v] P. 406.

[w] Moses b. Nachman (p. 78), Ibn Crispin (pp. 92, 100), Astruc (p. 129). So also Levi b. Gershom and R. Liwa of Prague on lii. 13 (p. 568). Ibn Danân supposed that the section alluded to the Messiah covertly (p. 203) by a secret and hidden interpretation (p. 215).

[x] De Marini, pp. 324, 325. [y] Pp. 82, 83.

[z] Pp. 110, 113, 114. They introduce actual deaths of Israel, pp. 82, 111.

[a] P. 403. He adds, 'Not actually kill him, else how should he see seed, have long days &c.?' Saadyah ibn Danân is obliged to interpret the words of 'nearness, willingness, purpose,' as to Hezekiah, pp. 211, 212, 214.

[b] See pp. 8, 10. [c] P. 270. [d] Pp. 258–274. [e] Pp. 269–279.

is put forward by some who followed him, with Ibn Ezra, J. and D. Kimchi, who were later than he, but no one before him. His great Talmudical studies, which seem to have been his earliest occupation, did not suggest it. On the contrary, in his notes on the Talmud he followed the older tradition. In that graphic story[f], in which Joshua b. Levi is reported to have made divers enquiries of Elias and Simeon b. Yochai as to the coming of the Messiah, and was told to ask himself, and that he would find him sitting at the gates of Rome among the poor who bare (סובלי) sicknesses, Rashi explains the words 'bearers of sicknesses' by reference to this section of Isaiah. 'Bearers of sicknesses, i.e. stricken (מנגעים), and he too is stricken (מנגע), as it is written, "And he was wounded for our iniquities," and it is written, "And our sicknesses he bare."' But if Rashi wrote his commentary after A.D. 1096[g], the hideous massacre of Jews in Spire, Worms, Maintz, Cologne, by the wild profligate swarm which gathered, after the first Crusaders were gone[h], might well have occasioned it. 'Before the time of the first Crusade, the Jews in Germany' (says their learned apologist and historian[i], who counts as oppression any disparity of condition between them and any people among whom they sojourned) 'were neither in a condition of oppression nor contempt, nor were shut out from holding landed property.' In what has been called 'the iron age of Judaism[j],' there was too much occasion for representing them (as far as man was concerned) as guiltless sufferers.

The interpretation was received by most subsequent commentators. It would indeed have been a strange exception to the language of the prophets, and of Isaiah himself, who, in this later part of his book too, upbraids his people with their wickedness[k], their neglect of God[l], their dulness and blindness[m],

---

[f] Sanhedrin, dist. *chelek*, fol. 98, col. 1. In Martini, as printed, fol. 281, the [ ] are not extended so as to include all which is now attributed to Rashi.

[g] Grätz places the birth of Rashi in the year when the last Gaon was put to death by the Sultan, A.D. 1040 (vi. 70 and 9). Rashi died at 75. He lived then nineteen years after these wickednesses.

[h] Albertus, Hist. Hieros. i. 126–129, quoted by Grätz, vi. 393. The bishop of Spire and archbishop of Maintz tried in vain to defend the Jews.

[i] Grätz, vi. 90, where he describes their independent condition at Spire, granted by the bishop and confirmed by the emperor Henry IV.

[j] Milman, Hist. of the Jews, t. iii, b. 24.

[k] xliii. 24, l. 1, lvii. 3–13, lix. 2–15, lxiii. 17, lxiv. 5, 6 [Heb., 6, 7 Eng.]

[l] xliii. 22, 23, lxv. 3, 7, 11, lxvi. 17.

[m] xlii. 19, 20, lvi. 10–12.

hypocrisy [n], idolatries, and disobedience [o], and who tells them, '[p] Your iniquities have separated between you and your God'—it would have been a strange contradiction had he, in the midst of this, described them as God's righteous servant, who should bear the sins of all the world besides; (Christians and Mohammedans, as they say, Edom and Ishmael;) and that we, when converted, upon their prosperity and our own overthrow, at the coming of *their* Messiah, should own that they suffered in our stead, the just for the unjust, and atoned for us. It is strangely contrary to their solution of other prophecies, or of the disappointment of their own expectations, which point to an earlier coming of the Messiah during the time of the Second Temple, viz. that his coming was delayed by their sins, that he would come if they repented [q].

However, this enabled them without scruple to accept all the most characteristic parts of the literal interpretation. They interpreted of Christians the disbelief in their mission; they put in our mouths the confession, that they bore the sufferings which we deserved, while we thought them afflicted by God; that the sufferer described [themselves] grew up in the presence of God, as a root out of the dry ground, invisibly supported by Him; that he was despised and rejected; that his countenance was so marred as scarce to retain the human form; that he [i. e. some Israelites] actually suffered (as martyrs, some said, for the true faith in God); that he [i. e. such of them] actually suffered death, and was [were] buried with the rich; that kings [i.e. such as should live at the coming of the Messiah] should acknowledge him; that he should intercede for the transgressors. About all this there is no question. Indeed, such is the force of the prophet's words, that the right faith is, by God's good providence, often embalmed in their paraphrases, and their language would often express our belief, if we substituted the name of 'Jesus' for 'Israel.'

What is meant by 'vicarious suffering' is matter of comment; and, in this, they vary among themselves, and, of course, differ

---

[n] xlviii. 1, 2, lvii. 3-5, lxi. 8, lxv. 5, lxvi. 3.

[o] xlviii. 18, 19, lxv. 2, lxvi. 4. [p] lix. 2.

[q] 'For our iniquities, which have been many, those of the years have passed, which have passed' (Sanhedrin, Chelek, fol. 97, col. 1, l. ult.) 'For our iniquities the Messiah came not at the end of the 4000 years' (Rashi, ibid.; Martini, ff. 315, 316; Abodah Zara, fol. 9, col. 1 med.) In Edzardi, Abodah Zara, pp. 65, 66, and 244, 246.

from us. They cannot, as Jews, accept the belief, imperfectly held by their own forefathers, that One suffered for us as the propitiation for our sins. But the Death, the Vicariousness of the Sufferings, and the Intercession they do believe. It will set this before the eyes, to concentrate their sayings on these three subjects,—the actual death, the vicariousness, the intercession,—scattered over these 571 pages [r].

Amid this amount of agreement, the objections of Jewish controversialists to its being a prophecy of Jesus, proceed, *for the most part*, upon renderings of the Hebrew, identical with ours. The literal meaning of the words is assumed, and this is alleged to be incompatible with the history of Jesus or with the Christian belief in regard to Him.

If the facts of the Gospel had been untrue, if Jesus had not risen again, nor were living and reigning now, then this prophecy of Isaiah would, as they urge, not have belonged to Him, since the subject of the prophecy was to 'prolong his days [s],' to be 'exalted exceedingly [t],' to 'reign [u],' 'intercede' abidingly 'for transgressors.' Jewish controversialists could not but assume the untruth of the Gospel history (for if they had believed the Resurrection, they must have believed in Jesus). But this is not a question as to the literal meaning of the words of the prophecy; the objections presuppose the same interpretation of the words.

Nor would the prophecy agree with our faith, unless our Lord had been 'perfect Man, of a reasonable soul and human flesh subsisting.' If, according to the Apollinarian heresy, as is often repeated or implied by the Jewish controversialists [v], His

---

[r] See Note at the end of these Remarks, p. lxvi sqq.

[s] 'What will be the meaning of "prolonging of days" which is untrue of him?' Ibn Ezra (below, p. 43), Kimchi (p. 55). So R. Jacob b. Reuben (p. 60), Moses b. Nachman (p. 84), Ibn Shaprut (p. 93), Lipmann (p. 149), Abarbanel (p. 161), Troki (p. 244), Segre (p. 360), Meir b. Shim'on (p. 376), Mordekhai (p. 381), Moses Sal. (p. 383), Ibn Musa (p. 387), Milchamoth Adonai (p. 388), Buch. d. Verz. (p. 399), Orobio (p. 470), Aaron b. Joseph (p. 571).

[t] 'Jesus was not lifted up, except upon the cross,' Kimchi (p. 55), Ibn Crispin (p. 101), Abarbanel (pp. 158, 159), Troki (p. 243), Naphthali Altschuler (p. 318), Lopez (pp. 343, 344), Meir b. Shim'on (pp. 375, 377); 'this Messiah of theirs is nowhere,' Mordekhai (p. 381).

[u] Moses b. Nachman (p. 84), Ibn Ezra (p. 43), Milchamoth Adonai (p. 390).

[v] It is said by Moses Cohen, 'You yourselves maintain that his soul was the Godhead within him' (p. 122): 'how can you say that his soul died at all, when, according to your creed, it was not his soul (i.e. his Divinity) which was afflicted by death, but only his body?' (p. 124.) 'They next have

Godhead had been to Him in the place of a soul, the objections would have been valid, that—

1. 'Whereas he whom the prophecy describes, should understand, "the body cannot understand[x]."'
2. 'If he is God [and not man], to whom could he intercede[y]?'
3. 'How could it be considered as a future fact that he should be exalted? Is not the Godhead always exalted[z]?'
4. 'How can he be first in a state of depression[a]?'
5. 'How can it be said that he *will* understand, since the Godhead always understands[b]?'
6. 'How does his receiving a reward agree with his nature[c]?' 'Need the Almighty be reassured by such promises[d]?'
7. 'If he is God, he could not be a servant[e]?'
8. 'How could it be said of him, that he did no violence, since God could not do it[f]?'
9. 'How can God be termed despised, forlorn of men, and stricken[g]?'

---

to admit that this intelligence of his is what they call the Father' (Lipmann, p. 148). 'How should trespass be attributed to his soul, i. e. to his pure and absolute Godhead?' (Abarbanel, p. 161.) 'It can only apply to his soul; in other words, to the Godhead' (Lopez, p. 343). 'If he was God, both in body and spirit, he could not be termed servant' (Meir b. Shim'on, p. 377). It is implied in, 'It is taught in your religion that only his flesh underwent death' (Ibn Shaprut, p. 94). 'If they say that he is termed a servant in respect to his body; God, in respect to his nature as a spirit' (Troki, p. 243); 'the travail of his soul is an unsuitable expression, for you hold that his Divinity never endured travail or suffering, but only his manhood' (Lopez, p. 349). 'How could it be stated with any propriety of the Almighty, that he was cut off out of the land of life?' (Mordekhai, pp. 380, 381.) 'How can the expression "makes his soul a trespass-offering" be in any way applicable to God?' (Ibn Musa, pp. 387, 388.)

[x] Ibn Ezra (p. 43), Ibn Crispin (p. 101), Lipmann (p. 148), Abarbanel (p. 159), Lopez (p. 343).

[y] Kimchi (p. 56), Troki (p. 244), Lopez (p. 349).

[z] R. Jacob b. Reuben (p. 58), Ibn Shaprut (p. 93), Ibn Crispin (p. 101), Abarbanel (p. 151).

[a] R. Jacob b. Reuben (p. 58).

[b] Ibn Shaprut (p. 94), Abarbanel (p. 158).

[c] Lipmann (p. 149), Lopez (p. 348).

[d] Mordekhai (p. 381).

[e] R. Jacob b. Reuben (p. 60), Joseph B'khor-Shor (p. 71), Ibn Shaprut (p. 93): 'In their theory of the Trinity, this man was of the substance of the Creator; how could he be called his own servant?' Ibn Crispin (pp. 100, 101), Moses Cohen (p. 121), Lipmann (p. 148), Abarbanel (p. 159), Troki (p. 243), Naphthali Altschuler (p. 318), Lopez (p. 343), Segre (p. 358), Meir b. Shim'on (pp. 375, 377), Ibn Musa (p. 388), Buch. d. Verz. (p. 398), Aaron b. Joseph (p. 571).

[f] Joseph b. Nathan (p. 71).

[g] Lipmann (p. 148), Ibn Shaprut (p. 94), Nizzachon vet. (p. 90).

10. 'If he is smitten by God, how can it be said that he himself is God[h]?'
11. 'If the Lord laid upon him the iniquity of us all, then he is inferior to God the agent[i].'
12. 'If God bruised him, he is inferior to God[j].'
13. 'If he were God, it could not be said, The pleasure of the Lord shall prosper in *his* hand, since it would then be God's own hands[k].'
14. 'The Eternal could not undergo change or death[l].'

Or it would not have been true, that God 'laid upon him the iniquities of us all,' were our faith, that He died for original sin only[m];

Or that there was no taking away sin before[n];

Or that those free from iniquity and transgression now too go down to Gehenna[o];

Or if God's promises extend to those who wilfully reject them[p], whereas themselves must own that of the 600,000 to whom it was promised that they should enter the land of promise, all but two forfeited it, and God calls it 'my breach of promise[q];'

Or if God could not be said to do, what fulfils His will, though done by bad men[r];

---

[h] R. Jacob b. Reuben (p. 59), Moses Cohen (p. 121). 'It would imply that God smote himself,' Lopez (p. 346).

[i] R. Jacob b. Reuben (p. 59), Lopez (p. 346).

[j] R. Jacob b. Reuben (p. 59), Ibn Shaprut (p. 93).

[k] Abarbanel (p. 161), Lopez (p. 348). 'If he was the Creator, the prophet would have said that his right arm saved him,' Orobio (p. 462).

[l] Eliyyah Cohen (p. 146), Lopez (p. 343).

[m] 'Did he meet death for any other cause, than to wipe out the sin of our forefathers in having eaten the tree of knowledge, for which all were going down to Gehenna? He ought rather to have written, "For the transgression of Adam and Eve was he stricken,"' Joseph b. Nathan (p. 71), Christian in Ibn Shaprut (p. 92).

[n] Nizzachon vet. (p. 91).

[o] Nizzachon (p. 91), 'Died for the redemption of souls who *were* in Gehenna.' Lopez (p. 341).

[p] 'If he makes an atonement for those who do not receive him as God, how can he carry their sicknesses? How can Israel declare that "the Lord laid on him the iniquity of us all," if those who do not believe in his affliction derive, as the Nazarenes also admit, no advantage from it?' Naphthali Altschuler (p. 319), Orobio (pp. 463, 464, 466). 'Israelites are not saved by him at all,' Anonymous, *t.* (p. 397), Orobio (pp. 463, 464).

[q] Num. xiv. 34.

[r] 'Instead of saying that he was smitten of God, he should rather have said, that he was smitten of *men*, as was the fact,' R. Jacob b. Reuben (p. 59),

Or if the forgiveness of sin involves the removal of all temporal consequences.

Other objections apply equally, whatever be the subject, and to their own explanations also, as, that it is a contradiction that 'the same should be fair and marred[s];'—at different times, of course.

Abstract arguments—as that the Incarnation is impossible[t]; or against the doctrine of the Atonement[u]; or that Jesus, if the Messiah, ought to have removed temporal death; or to have repaired Adam's sin entirely; or that mankind ought to have been sinless afterwards[v]; or that the Atonement is an encouragement to sin[w]—are irrelevant to this prophecy, or presuppose the same meaning of its words. The ignorant criticisms upon our Lord's teaching[x], or flippancy in which they sometimes indulge[y], are still less relevant.

The argument from the context is also obviously not an argument from language. It excludes the Messiah from being the subject of the glories at the close of chap. lii, as much as from the humiliation in the greater part of chap. liii. It involves also a denial that the prophets spoke of any Messiah at all. For plainly a mention of the Deliverer could not otherwise be out of harmony with prophecies of the deliverance. It became rather a popular objection[z].

Ibn Shaprut (p. 93). 'If the Jews only executed the pleasure of God in putting him to death, did not they do what was right and fitting?' Segre (p. 359), Orobio (p. 471). 'It says, The Lord was pleased to bruise him, and yet they throw the guilt of his crucifixion on us; but if God in his wisdom was pleased through him to accomplish the restoration of the world, why should men be punished for fulfilling his purpose?' Anon. (p. 397.) Abarbanel recognises the principle as to Josiah, 'Because God was pleased to bruise him, it was He, rather than the archer, who caused him his sickness' (p. 195); yet as to our Lord, he says, 'Pleasure is only used of what is done without assignable cause, not of what is done with definite purpose' (p. 161), repeated by Lopez (p. 348).

[s] R. Jacob b. Reuben (p. 57), Nizzachon (p. 90), Ibn Shaprut (pp. 92, 97), Moses Cohen (p. 121), Segre (p. 358).

[t] Abarbanel (p. 158).

[u] Abarbanel (p. 157), Segre (p. 359), Orobio (c. xxv).

[v] Orobio (pp. 465, 466).

[w] Older Nizzachon (p. 91).

[x] Chiefly in Orobio.

[y] As, that our Lord was not silent before his persecutors, because he prayed to God, Segre (p. 360), repeated by Mosheh of Sal. (p. 383).

[z] It occurs first in Moses Cohen (p. 116), then in Lipmann (p. 147), Abarbanel (p. 154), Troki (p. 240), Lopez (p. 342), Mordekhai (p. 379), Buch. d. Verz. (p. 399), Orobio (p. 476), Ibn Amram (pp. 534, 536).

These exceptions against our faith do not touch upon the literal meaning of the words. The criticisms which would affect their meaning are but four: 1. That the word rendered 'grief [a]' is only used in Holy Scripture of bodily ailment, and is not used metaphorically. 2. That the word rendered 'on him [b]' is plural, and, being plural, proves that the subject, elsewhere throughout the section spoken of in the singular, must be a virtual plural, i. e. a collective, not an individual. 3. Some make the same inference from the use of the plural, lit. 'deaths [c].' 4. That the word 'seed [d]' is never used metaphorically, but always of the physical descendants of a person.

Obj. 1. 'You will not find in your own New Testament, that your Messiah ever had a pain, even a head-ache, up to the day of his death: the very terms here employed, "pain" and "sickness," were not realised in his person, and so cannot apply to him.' Ans. Isaiah does use the word in this very section of mental ills (not actual sicknesses), and of the sufferings laid upon the person spoken of in it. 'Our sicknesses he bore [e],' whereas *one* cannot bear the actual bodily ailments of another; and, 'It pleased the Lord to bruise him: he hath put him to grief [f],' both of which manifestly refer to the first, 'acquainted with grief.' It is also so used in the opening of Isaiah [g], and elsewhere [h], as are other derived forms; as, contrariwise, 'healing' is used with regard to mind or estate. It is probably a metaphor of all language, as being, from the relation of mind and body, the language of nature. Indeed, the objection would not have been worth noticing, but for the positiveness of those who use it, and that Abarbanel and the author of the מלחמות י״י are among those who make it. Those who interpret the section of the people often repeat that it relates to 'the sufferings of exile [i]:' one notices that mental pains are far more grievous than bodily.

---

[a] חלי liii. 2. [b] למו liii. 8. [c] במתיו liii. 9.

[d] R. Jacob b. Reuben (p. 59). He is followed by Ibn Shaprut (pp. 93, 97), Abarbanel (p. 160), Isaac Lopez (p. 345), Moses of Salerno (p. 382), Milchamoth Adonai (p. 389).

[e] liii. 4. [f] הֶחֱלִי liii. 10. [g] Is. i. 5.

[h] Hos. v. 13, Jer. vi. 7, x. 19, Eccl. v. 16, vi. 2; the verb, Is. lvii. 10, Jer. v. 3; part., Eccl. v. 12, 13; Nif., Am. vi. 6, Is. xvii. 11, Jer. xxx. 12; Hif., Prov. xiii. 12. Abarbanel himself notices that it is used of Josiah's mortal wound, 2 Chron. xxxv. 23 (and so not of continuous sickness or sicknesses), p. 195.

[i] See e. g. Troki (pp. 244, 245, 254), Ibn Ezra (p. 45); quoted by Abarbanel (p. 174).

Obj. 2. 'למו,' they say, 1. is a plural; and, 2. being a plural, it must relate to the subject of the section, and so shews that the subject must be a collective, not an individual. Ans. 1. There is no ground to assume that למו is a plural; nor, 2. if it were assumed to be so, does anything require that it should be understood of the subject of the section.

1. With regard to למו being necessarily a plural, Kimchi, who originated the argument, at another time denied it. In his challenge to the Nazarenes he says[k], 'Moreover the prophet says "to them" (למו); but then [if it related to Jesus] he ought to have said *to him*, לו; for למו is plural, being equivalent to להם.' In his Grammar he says[l], 'מו occurs as the affix of the 3rd person singular, as in Job xx. 23, xxii. 2.' 'For ם and ו [מו] contains in itself the sign of the plural noun, and indicates the masc. sing. also. For ם is the sign of the 3rd person masc. plural, and the ו of the 3rd masc. sing.; and therefore מו is used both of many and of one.' L'Empereur observed, that the Chaldee version and the LXX also render Job xxii. 2 in the sing.; and Levi b. Gershom and Meir b. Aramah so render it in Job xx. In Ps. xi. 7, 'the [LXX and] Chaldee render it in the sing.; in Is. xliv. 15, the Chaldee again [the LXX is missing]; in Job xxvii. 23, Ibn Ezra and Levi b. Gershom so explain it.' Abraham Farissol[m], on this place, prefers the singular: 'למו will then be singular for לו, as Ps. lv. 20 and often.' R. Judah b. Bala'm[n] [eleventh century], 'By למו he means לו, i. e. that his misfortune came to him from the sin of the people, not what he deserved himself.' R. Tanchum[o] gives the choice of its being singular (which he places first) or plural. Naphthali Altschuler has, 'For the transgression of "my people" had this "stroke" come upon the Messiah[p].' In the Milchamoth Adonai, it is admitted as possible: 'We certainly find למו used occasionally as a singular, as Ps. xi. 7, but only as an anomaly[q].' Gershom, though interpreting it of Israel, explains it as a singular, אליו[r].

Of modern critics, one who himself renders, 'For my people's

---

[k] See p. 55.

[l] Pococke quotes this passage from Kimchi's Grammar, f. 266. 1, Ven., 8vo; notes on the Porta Mosis, c. 8, on this section, as alleged by l'Empereur against Abarbanel. Elias on Moses Kimchi, Shebile haddaath (pp. 240, 241), admits the fact as to Job xx. 23, xxii. 2, but would limit the use to these two places.

[m] P. 225. [n] P. 551. [o] P. 556. [p] P. 322.

[q] P. 389; but he still says, 'Had he meant Jesus, he ought to have said "upon *him*."' [r] Hebr. texts, p. 397.

sin, the plague for them[r],' and says, 'לָמוֹ corresponds to עַמִּי,' himself lays down[s], 'It cannot be denied that the very old ָמוֹ־ is sometimes used by some poets in the sense of a singular, in very little words, as לָמוֹ for לוֹ "to him," as if in it the ו of the singular were especially heard through, Ps. xi. 7, Job xxii. 2, Deut. xxxiii. 2, twice; Is. xliv. 15.' But,

2. In fact, nothing turns upon it. The rendering, 'for the transgression of my people a blow came to them' (whereby the *them* refers to people in the same verse), is just as natural as 'came to him.'

If the word is rendered 'to them,' the obvious meaning would be (as Ewald says) that it refers to 'my people' in the same clause. This makes a complete sense in itself, without introducing the anomaly, that, whereas the subject of this section is spoken of in the singular, sixty times in verbs and pronouns (and three times in this very verse), it is to be spoken of once in this one verse in the plural; and that 'the kings,' alleged to be speaking in the plural 'we,' 'our,' fourteen times previously, should in this one verse speak in the singular, 'my people,' i. e. the people of each of them. This double anomaly is to take place in four words, without any indication in the context. Those who were before spoken of in the singular are to be spoken of in the plural, and those spoken of in the plural are to

---

r Ewald ad loc. Proph. iii. 98.

s Ewald, Lehrb. § 247, p. 625 ed. 8. In his earliest Grammar he said, 'Exceedingly probably it is sing. Job xx. 23, xxvii. 23, where the whole context of ten to twenty verses, in which the sing. occurs throughout, speaks for it. But it is certain in Is. liii. 8, in which the sing. alone appears; Is. xliv. 15, where the plural does not at all suit the sense; and the poet himself explains לָמוֹ in the same connection (ver. 17) by לוֹ; Ps. xi. 7, where "his countenance" can only relate to God. Hab. iii. 4 explains לָמוֹ, Deut. xxxiii. 2, by לוֹ.' Krit. Gramm. p. 365. Böttcher acknowledges the use of מוֹ for the sing. (not in Gen. ix. 26, 27, Is. xxx. 5, Ps. lxxiii. 10, 'where,' he says, 'it might refer to the plural meaning of the collectives in the context'), nor in Ps. xxviii. 8, or Job ix. 23, but in Deut. xxxiii. 2, (as explained by Hab. iii. 4), Is. xliv. 15, liii. 8, Ps. xi. 7, Job xxii. 2, xxvii. 23 (Ausf. Lehrb. n. 878, 2. *a*, t. ii. p. 28). While the Aethiopic use of *mo* as a singular seems for the time shaken by Platt's N. T. (London, 1820) and Dillmann (Böttcher, l. c. note 6), Phœnician investigators (Ewald, Movers, Meier, Schlottmann, Schrœder) have recognised the *m* as a form of the 3rd pers. pron. sing. Ewald (ZKM. iv. p. 416) and Schrœder (d. Phœn. Sprache, p. 153, note 1) have recognised the *mo* as a relic of Phœnician in Hebrew, and Schrœder owns the *mo* as existing, beyond question, as a real sing., Gen. ix. 26, 27, Deut. xxxiii. 2, Job xx. 23, xxii. 2, xxvii. 23, Ps. xi. 7, xxviii. 8, Is. xliv. 15, and here. Hitzig also maintains that לָמוֹ here is singular, p. 573.

be spoken of in the singular. Yet though this objection found eleven adherents, among them Abarbanel [t], nearly twice as many take the one or the other of the interpretations, by which the 'to them' would refer to the people, either as a continuous sentence, 'for the transgression of my [God's] people there was a plague to them [u],' or in two halves, whereby 'the stroke to them' should refer to 'my people [v]' in the same verse. It

[t] The argument begins with Kimchi, followed by R. Jacob b. Reuben (p. 59). It is used in proof that 'it cannot be, as some say, in view of the Messiah,' by Jacob b. Reuben, Karaite (p. 82), Ibn Shaprut (p. 93), Mosheh Cohen (pp. 118, 122), Abarbanel (p. 163), Abraham of Cordova (p. 293), Lopez (p. 347), Mordekhai (p. 381), Manasseh b. Israel (p. 446), Orobio (p. 511), (yet referring למו to 'my people' in the same verse (p. 513), and rendering in the sing. for clearness.) It is not used by Lipmann (p. 149), nor by Meir b. Shim'on (p. 375), and Rashi apparently refers the 'to them' to 'the people' in the same verse; 'for the transgression of his people, the stroke of exile had fallen *upon* the just who were among *them*' (p. 58).

[u] Symmachus, '*He* was cut off, and for the injustice of my people there was a plague upon them' (p. 2). Theodotion, '*He* was cut off, on account of the defection of my people he touched them' (ibid.) Jonathan, '*He* will cause &c. and transfer to them the sins which my people have committed' (p. 6). Saadyah Gaon, 'He was cut off, and for the transgression of my people the stroke was upon *them*' (p. 18). So the Persian version verbatim. Ibn Ezra (as the more correct), 'For the transgression of my people the stroke will come upon them [the nations],' (p. 46 and note.) In Ibn Shaprut (p. 98) the Christian's rendering, 'Because the murderous blow, wreaked upon him, is a blow for them,' i. e. 'they will be in perpetual exile' (p. 97), is not excepted against, although the argument is. Abarbanel, 'For the transgression of my people' (which was the cause of his [Josiah's] death) 'the stroke came upon them,' viz. upon Israel themselves, because it was they who were 'stricken' by his death even more than he himself (p. 195). Ibn Danân, 'The prophet says, "a stroke upon them," because the boil from which he suffered would have injured them still more, had he died from it' (p. 212). Farissol gives this as a second alternative, having preferred the singular (p. 225). Mosheh Elsheikh, 'Hitherto the just one had been stricken for the people's transgression, but henceforth the stroke would be upon themselves' (p. 269). Lanyado, 'From that moment, for the transgression of my people the stroke was to fall upon them, i. e. upon my people, and not upon the righteous, as it had before, when they were suffering for it' (p. 309). 'He was cut off—for the sin of many people [tribe], plague [sickness] came upon him,' Tataric version. Marini, 'For the transgression of my people, there is a stroke upon them,' (viz. upon my people, for he adds) 'a saying which is the reverse of Zeph. iii. 6, 7' (p. 335). The Christian in Segre (p. 357) rendered, 'For the transgression of his people, there was a stroke upon them.' Segre does not make it one of his ten objections (pp. 358–360).

[v] Yepheth b. Ali, 'All this trouble came upon him because of the transgression of my people, for whom this stroke was, i.e. who deserved it' (p. 27). Anon. xvi, 'When my people abandons the transgression which has lighted upon them' (p. 65). Anon. xvii, 'He seemed to have been cut

apparently became a traditional objection, used without much thought; for Abarbanel, when interpreting the section of an individual [Josiah], and Mordekhai do not themselves understand the *to them* to refer to the subject of the section.

Obj. 3. The argument that מתים, 'his death,' should be rendered 'deaths,' and so implies that the subject of the section is not one, but many, is used by Lipmann[w]: 'Observe, he does not say "death," but "deaths;" yet a single man cannot die more than once.' Ans. There is no ground to lay any emphasis on the plural in מתים, 'death,' any more than in חיים, 'life.' Many nouns in Hebrew are used in the plural, where we, Westerns, could hardly account for it. The plural is used of a condition, as a period of life, or a condition of body[x]. There is then no reason why מתים (if there is any stress on the plural) should not mean 'the state of death;' as חיים, 'the state of life.' And this agrees better with the usual meaning of ב, 'in' or 'at.' In the only other case in which the plural occurs, Ezek. xxviii. 10, it is used of an individual, the prince of Tyre (ibid. 1); and 'a single man could not' (in Lipmann's words) 'die more than once[y].' The earlier interpreters render in the singular[z]. Those who explain the section

---

off because of the transgression of my people, [because of] the stroke which should have been theirs' (p. 69). Mosheh b. Nachman, 'He has been cut off—for the transgression of my people—an event which will be a severe blow to *them*' (p. 82). Ibn Crispin, 'למו refers to my people: from the transgression of my people, (which was) a blow upon them, since in consequence of it many plagues fell upon them' (p. 111). Lanyado, 'He was cut off, and slain "for the transgression of my people,"' the stroke intended 'for them' being borne by him instead (of Messiah ben Joseph), (p. 302.) Alternative rendering in Lanyado, '*On account of the transgression of my people*, for which the righteous was to be taken away' (p. 360). Passani, 'The attribute of judgment laid upon him the iniquity of them all, as the text says, *for the transgression of my people*, even the stroke which should have fallen upon them' (p. 409). Luzzatto, 'עמי is here for עמים as Ps. cxliv. 2; *for the transgression of the peoples*, who were themselves liable to bear the stroke which was borne by him, נגע למו which was a stroke to them;' rejecting the rendering, 'a stroke came upon *them*,' as what would not be expressed by נגע ל (p. 421). Mordekhai, 'He was cut off, for the transgressions of my people, a stroke to them' (p. 379).

[w] Lipmann (p. 149).

[x] As זְקֻנִים, age; נְעוּרִים, עֲלֻמִים, youth; בְּתוּלִים, maidenhood; כְּלוּלֹת, bridehood, Jer. ii. 2; חֲנֻטִים, embalming, Gen. l. 3, (Ewald, Lehrb. § 153 *a*); סַנְוֵרִים, blindness.

[y] Luzzatto, I see, uses this expression against its meaning 'death,' in Ezek. xxviii. 10, but does not say what other meaning it can have (p. 422).

[z] במתיו is rendered by the singular, 'his death,' by the Septuagint (and

of a collective, Israel, of course understand 'deaths' of the individuals, who come under that collective[a]. But no one, except Lipmann, uses it as a controversial argument. Those who interpret the section of an individual, whether the Messiah, or Jeremiah, or Hezekiah, or Josiah, must either regard it as virtually singular, or find some other emphasis for the plural, or assign some other meaning for the whole word. If regarded as a plural, the explanation of Herz Homberg (since the affix is singular) is more natural[b], 'the plural "deaths" is used, because piercing him as cruel men do, through and through[b], they would, so to speak, be putting him to death again and again;' much as we might say, 'a thousand deaths in one.' The Christian martyrs underwent tortures, each of which might have ended life. The more popular explanation among moderns[c] has been that suggested by some before Ibn Ezra[d]; 'building over a grave,' בָּמֹחָיו for בְּמוֹתָיו, which, however, is a meaning for which there is no proof. Those who adopted any of these interpretations, manifestly had not Lipmann's objection.

---

there is no variation in the other Greek versions); 'the death of utter destruction,' Jonathan (p. 6); 'his death,' Saadyah (p. 18); 'in his dying,' Pers. and Tataric vers.; 'how the Messiah will resign himself to die,' Yepheth b. Ali (p. 27); 'in his death,' Joseph b. Nathan (p. 73); Abarbanel (of Josiah, p. 195); Marini (p. 335); Lopez (p. 352); Mosheh of Salerno (p. 383); Passani (p. 410); Tanchum (p. 555).

[a] A meaning is given to the plural by Rashi, 'any form of death' (p. 38); 'some,' in Ibn Ezra, 'of those who died in exile' (p. 47); 'the plural is employed, because they used to be put to death in many ways,' Kimchi (p. 57); 'he will expect them to slay him by stoning, &c. This is why מותיו is plural,' Moses b. Nachman (p. 82); 'various kinds of death,' Ibn Crispin (p. 121); 'the prophet uses death in the plural because they condemned them to different forms of punishment,' Astruc (p. 131); Sh'lomo b. Melech (p. 219); 'various kinds of death,' xxxiv. (p. 237), Troki (p. 254); 'in all his deaths,' Lanyado (p. 310); 'any form of death,' Naphthali Altschuler (p. 322), Segre (p. 365), David Altschuler (p. 371); 'death in two forms' [of his person and substance], Mordekhai (p. 380); 'their various deaths,' Manasseh b. Israel (p. 446), Gershom (p. 566).

[b] Herz Homberg (p. 404). In like way the anonymous *l.* (p. 392), 'that they were often put to death, after being pierced through and through,' 'after having suffered cruel tortures' (quoting another Rabbi by his initials, Z A B), and Lanyado, 'he was not to be put to death speedily, but tortured by every conceivable method of producing a severe and painful end; and hence the prophet says not "in his death," but "in his deaths"' (p. 303).

[c] Gesenius, Thesaurus, p. 188; Ewald (Proph. iii. 95); Böttcher.

[d] P. 47. This was adopted by Jacob b. Reuben, Karaite (p. 62), xvi. (p. 75), Abarbanel apparently (p. 181); of 'high places,' Saadyah Ibn Danân (p. 213).

Obj. 4. 'If the disciples of Jesus had been meant, it should have been written "sons;" for the word "seed" only signifies those born by a carnal generation.' Ans. The objection [e] is founded altogether upon a mistake; for the text has not 'his seed,' but '*a* seed.' This exactly corresponds with '*a* seed shall serve him' of Ps. xxii, following upon a prophecy like this, of the conversion of the world: 'All the ends of the world shall remember and turn unto the Lord, and all the kindreds of the nations shall worship before him [f].' '*A* seed shall serve him; it shall be accounted of the Lord a generation; they shall come and shall declare his righteousness unto a people which shall be born' [yet another generation], 'that the Lord has done' very mighty things [g]. This is the characteristic of the kingdom, that it should not pass away, like earthly kingdoms.

The context shews who that seed is. The prophet says in the next chapter, 'Thy (Israel's) seed shall inherit the Gentiles:' and of these the earliest Jewish translators and commentators understood it. They render, '*a* seed,' not '*his* seed;' 'your soul shall see a long-lived seed [h];' 'these [those cleansed from sin] shall look on the kingdom of the Messiah; *their* sons and their daughters shall be multiplied [i];' 'he sees a noble seed [j].' Later, 'he shall see seed and lengthen days' are united, as expressing the same fact, the prolongation of his life and prosperity [k].

---

[e] The objection that 'seed' cannot mean disciples is first raised by Kimchi (p. 55), followed by Ibn Shaprut (pp. 93, 98), Moses Cohen (p. 123), Lipmann (p. 149), Abarbanel (p. 161), Troki (p. 244), Lopez (p. 348). 'He died unmarried and childless at thirty-three,' Segre (p. 360), Meir b. Shim'on (p. 376), Moses of Salerno (p. 383), Milchamoth Adonai (p. 390). 'How can God have seed?' Buch. d. Verz. (p. 399), Ibn Musa (p. 387), and *t.* (p. 398), Mordekhai (p. 381), Orobio (p. 469), Aaron b. Joseph (p. 571).

[f] Ps. xxii. 27.

[g] Ps. xxii. 30, 31.

[h] LXX., Aq., Symm., Theod. substitute 'his soul' for 'thy soul,' but leave the rest (p. 2).

[i] Jonathan (p. 6).

[j] Saadyah Gaon (p. 18).

[k] Yepheth b. Ali (p. 28), 'I will pay him his reward and he shall see seed,' &c., Rashi (p. 39). Anon. xvi. has 'shall see the king' (p. 65). 'He [God] will heal him and preserve him alive; he will see seed and prolong days, and the pleasure of the Lord, i. e. to do judgment,' &c., xvii. (p. 69), Joseph b. Nathan, as Rashi (p. 74); so Yeshayah b. Mali (p. 77). Mosheh b. Nachman explains it by Ps. xlv. 17 (p. 83). R. Eliyyah Cohen has simply 'see seed,' referring to Is. lxv. 20, 22 (p. 145). Jacob b. Reuben (Karaite) only paraphrases it of prosperity (p. 63), as does David de Rocca Martini (p. 201), Meir Aramah (p. 242), Moses Elsheikh (p. 272). Lanyado simply quotes as one expression of good pleasure, 'will see seed &c.—in his hand' (p. 311). Abraham b. Judah Chazan, 'I will pay him a goodly reward, he shall see seed

The objection is in truth a mere pressing of the primary physical meaning, which practically becomes obsolete. If disciples, not being sons, can be called sons, they may be equally called 'seed.' They are physically neither: metaphorically, they may be called by either name. 'Disciples are called sons, as it is said, "And the sons of the prophets went out,"' says one to whom they are wont to defer[l]. 'It becometh man to take heed to and love his disciples; for they are the sons, who profit in this world and the world to come[m].' 'Honour fathers and the wise; for they are the parents of all[n].' Isaiah himself uses the word in a bad sense, 'seed of evil-doers [much as we should say "brood"] corrupt children[o];' and 'children of transgression, seed of falsehood[p].' Few probably would [with Gesenius] think that 'the seed of the serpent[q]' meant 'the serpent tribe' as propagated naturally, and was not rather like 'the generation of vipers[r]' of whom our Lord speaks. Yet in these cases the word stands with a genitive, 'the seed of:' in this section, as in the Psalm, it stands absolutely, 'a seed.'

In an old comment[s] on 'I will give it to thee and to thy seed,' it is said, 'Thy seed are those like unto thee;' and the proselyte is called 'son of Abraham[t],' and 'Whoever confesseth two worlds' [i. e. this and that to come] 'shall be called thy seed, and whoever confesseth not two worlds shall not be called thy seed[u].' In the Yalkut Reubeni it is said, 'I will grant him children of the law, children diligent in the study and performance of it[v].'

Kimchi raised the objection as to our Lord alone. It would

---

and have long days;' as Ezekiel says, 'I will increase them with men like a flock,' xxxvi. 37 (p. 316). Naphthali Altschuler vaguely, 'He shall see seed in this present world, and prolong' his 'days in the world to come' (p. 322). The older Nizzachon has not the argument (pp. 90, 91), nor Abraham of Cordova (p. 293), nor Salomo de Marini (p. 337), nor Passani (p. 407). Abarbanel paraphrases, 'He shall see the seed of his nation much multiplied' (p. 184).

[l] Maimonides, Yad. Talm. Torah, c. i. n. 2, in Pococke Porta Mosis, c. 8, on this section. Gesenius, who approves of the correction of Maimonides, quotes Schulz (in Paulus Reisen vii. 49), as saying that in the East, Christians are said to be 'of the family (ميلاد) of the Messiah,' Ges. Einl. t. i. p. 125.

[m] Id. v. 12, ibid.

[n] Id. Comm. ad Peah, c. 1, § 1, ibid.

[o] Is. i. 4.

[p] Ibid. lvii. 4.

[q] Gen. iii. 15.

[r] S. Matt. iii. 7.

[s] Bereshith Rabba major in Gen. xiii. 15, in Martini P. F. fol. 302.

[t] Massecheth Bikkurim Hieros., ibid. fol. 303.

[u] R. Yoden b. R. Shallum in Bereshith Rabba on Gen. xxi. 12, ibid.

[v] P. 396.

probably to the Jews involve, that the section should not belong to the Messiah. For with their exalted belief of him, they could not have pictured him as a married man with a large family; still less, that the reward of his suffering should be to have a numerous offspring, like Ahab with his seventy sons.

I have not included under this head of language the objection that 'he was not cut off from the land of the living,' on the ground that 'the land of the living' is Judæa, and the Crucifixion was in Jerusalem. For although some who explain the section of Israel, do interpret 'the land of the living' of its land [w], this is so manifestly an applied meaning, that Lipmann [x] only and one follower [y] use it to swell the list of objections. On the other hand [z], some take it in its uniform primary sense of this life, and deny it to be a fitting saying as to Almighty God [a].

With regard to the word עשיר, as to which moderns, declining to understand 'the rich man' of 'the rich man of Arimathea,' mentioned in the Gospels, have given such wild interpretations contrary to the uniform use of the language, or made conjectures contrary to all authority, it is noticeable, that two only say that it must be interpreted according to the context, all the rest render it in its simple and uniform sense, 'rich.' Of these two, Ibn Ezra shews that he accepted the word in its natural meaning, '[b] את עשיר is like את רשעים, and alludes to the nations who, as compared with Israel, are *wealthy*.' Abulwalid accounts it to signify 'wicked' in no other way than elsewhere 'wise,' i. e. literally neither; but in the one place he must mean that it is used of those who are wicked, in the other of those who are wise: '[c] In (Is. liii) it is not from this meaning, but from the meaning of רשעים who are mentioned with it, and so in "[d] עשירים

---

[w] 'The land of the living' is explained of 'the land of Israel' by Yepheth b. Ali (p. 27), Rashi (p. 38), Joseph b. Nathan (p. 73), de Rocca Martini (p. 200), Naphthali Altschuler (p. 322), Moses of Salerno (p. 383), Man. b. Israel (pp. 439, 445), Clear Fountain (p. 433), Orobio (p. 515), and Ibn Amram (resting on Ezek. xxxii. 24 sqq.), p. 543.

[x] Of 'this life,' Ibn Ezra (p. 46), Jacob b. Reuben, Karaite (p. 62), Ibn Mali (p. 76), Moses b. Nachman (p. 82), Ibn Shaprut (p. 95), Ibn Danân (p. 212), Troki (p. 253), Lanyado (p. 309), de Marini (p. 335), David Altschuler (p. 371), Mordekhai (p. 381), Herz Homberg (p. 402), Passani (p. 410); alternatively of either, Kimchi (p. 53), Aaron b. Joseph (p. 88), Abarbanel (pp. 180, 195), Abraham b. Judah Chazan (p. 316).

[y] P. 149.

[z] Lopez (p. 347).

[a] Mordekhai (p. 381), Milchamoth Adonai (p. 390).

[b] Below, p. 47.

[c] Book of Roots, col. 554 Oxf.

[d] Eccl. x. 6.

set in a low place," he means by it, "the wise[e]," viz. because it is contrasted with סכל "folly."' Salomo ben Melech says of Abulwalid's gloss, 'It is not allowable to abandon the usual signification "rich," merely on account of the parallel clause.'

The object of these remarks is simply defensive, that any who call themselves Christians might not be perplexed in their belief, or confirmed in their unbelief, through this volume, which being the defence of Jewish controversialists for not accepting this section of Isaiah as being fulfilled in Jesus, must necessarily be to a great extent Anti-Christian. Those for whom these remarks are chiefly written would not be benefited by anything said against the prominent misinterpretation in the volume. For they do not believe in it already. To believe in it would involve a belief in prophecy, beginning before the first coming of our Lord, and stretching out nearly two thousand years, and for the most part not yet fulfilled: only they ought not to use Jewish interpretations while disbelieving them. One only thing it may not be without its use to observe, because it illustrates the unique character of the sinless sufferer pourtrayed by Isaiah. Granted all which the Jews say of their sufferings at the hands of the Romans, or old Persian fire-worshippers, or Mohammedans (which fell still more heavily on Christians), or in later times, of Christians, ill-instructed in their religion, in the now past 'iron age of Judaism,' a feature of the picture, very prominent in Isaiah, yet least realised in them, is the meekness of that sufferer. This is not said in the slightest disparagement of them. They expected a Messiah, who should free them by conquest from the yoke of the nations; and so their history was rather like that of their lion-hearted forefathers, the Maccabees, than the silent and patient sufferer pourtrayed by Isaiah.

One thing more may be observed, that the Jewish controversialists, collected here, did not satisfy the Jewish mind by their interpretations. This is implied by the very variety of them. The majority indeed of those who professedly interpret the section, follow Rashi and his followers, Ibn Ezra and the two Kimchis, in interpreting it of themselves[f]. Yet not a few

---

[e] See below, p. 219. The root occurs seventy-seven times in the Old Testament. عثر is not only a different word, but is only used of 'stumbling,' never in a moral sense. The conjectures עשוק (Ewald), עשי רע (Böttcher) only shew that their interpretation did not suit the text.

[f] 'This Parashah the commentators agree in explaining of the Captivity, although the singular number is used in it throughout.' Ibn Crispin (p. 9),

went against the stream. The Karaites only varied the application by interpreting the section of the 'wise of their own sect [g],' on the ground of some persecution which they met with; as some Rabbinic Jews thought it was the righteous among them [h], or any just man [i]; some, that it was Jeremiah [j], or Isaiah himself [k]; some, Hezekiah [l]; one, Job [m]; some, the seed of David in

---

'Rashi, Jos. Kimchi, D. Kimchi, all with one voice explain the entire prophecy of Israel.' Abarbanel (p. 154), 'The majority of commentators, Rashi, Ibn Ezra, D. Kimchi, Abarbanel, agree in holding,' &c., xxxiv. p. 229, 'the correct explanation, as given by D. Kimchi, Rashi, and other expositors.' Lopez (p. 349). Those who follow it are Joseph Kara, R. Jacob b. Reuben, Joseph b. Nathan, Ibn Mali, Ibn Shaprut, Isaac Eliyyah Cohen, Lipmann, Martino, Farissol, xxxiv, Meir Aramah, Troki, Abraham of Cordova, Abraham b. Judah Chazan, Lopez, Segre, David Altschuler, Meir b. Simeon, Mosheh of Salerno (p. 381), Hayyim b. Musa (p. 387), *l.* (p. 391), *m.* (p. 393), Luzzatto (p. 413), Clear Fountain (p. 429), Manasseh b. Israel (p. 436), Orobio (pp. 476–531), Ibn Amram (pp. 532–549), Khozari and its Commentators (pp. 559–563), Gershom b. Nathan (pp. 564–567). The Persian Translation has, 'From the bond of exile and from judgment he was snatched.' The Tataric has, I believe, no indication.

[g] In Yepheth b. Ali (p. 19), Jacob b. Reuben, Karaite (p. 81), Aaron b. Joseph, Karaite (p. 87).

[h] Rashi (p. 37), Meir Aramah (p. 240), R. Abraham b. Judah Chazan (p. 344).

[i] Some in Ibn Crispin, contradicted by him (p. 99); Lipmann (p. 151); 'each individual among the just,' Mosheh Cohen (p. 117); 'a very good man,' Shelomo Levi (p. 275); 'the righteous worshipper of God,' Lanyado (p. 305); 'this good man,' Ibn Janâh (p. 373); 'one, ready to suffer martyrdom for love of God,' Anon. *t.* (p. 398).

[j] Saadyah Gaon in Yepheth b. Ali (p. 19), who says that he lost his senses in so doing; but it is pronounced attractive by Ibn Ezra (p. 43), and Menahem b. Shelomo Meiri (see p. 154), of whom again Abarbanel says, 'What goodness or excellence they see in it, I do not understand.' 'I cannot see a single verse which really points to him' (p. 164); he himself writes against it, (ibid.), as does Herz Homberg briefly (p. 400); Jehuda b. Balaam thought it quite probable (p. 551).

[k] Ibn Ezra ap. Luzzatto, p. 413. And Ibn Ezra himself, according to the reading received by Dr. Neubauer (p. 44 Hebr.), which seems to me the best, 'or my servant will be (הנביא) the prophet, and this is nearer than that,' viz. 'every servant of God who is in exile,' &c. But apart from this reading, Ibn Ezra says at the end of chap. liii, that the subject of chap. liii is the same as that of xlii. 1, xlix. 3, l. 6; but he expressly says on xlii. 1, 'Most commentators say that "my servant" is the righteous of Israel, and the Gaon says that he is Cyrus; and in my eyes it is certain that it is the prophet who speaks of himself, as in xlix. 6, 8.'

[l] Saadyah Ibn Danân, as a revelation to himself (p. 203), and in part by the Rabbis (p. 202), but typically of the Messiah (pp. 202, 205, 206, 216),

[m] Eliezer the German in Luzzatto, p. 413.

exile and the Messiah, so that all the expressions of contempt refer to the seed of David in exile, and all the glorious things to the Messiah [n]; some divided the sufferings and the glory, in like way, between the Messiah ben Joseph and the Messiah ben David [o]; some are divided between two opinions [p]; two think that there is a further reference to the Messiah [q]; one [r], that 'there seems to be considerable resemblance and allusion to the work of the Christian Messiah, and to the events which are attested to have happened to him, so that no other prophecy can be found, the gist and subject of which so immediately applied to him;' some think that it relates to the Messiah and the people together [s]; some suppose it to be an echo of the dissatisfaction expressed by the saying, 'There is a just man and it goes ill with him [t].' Throughout there are those who still interpreted the section of the Messiah [u]; and among them it is remarkable, that Maimonides retained herein the simple faith of his forefathers [v], interpreting of the Messias the words, 'He came up as a sucker,' &c., as well as the glories, 'at Him kings will shut their mouth,' and the prophecy of the Branch in Zechariah, and the coming of the Lord to His temple [w] in Malachi; and

as also Passani (p. 407). Ibn Danân had, at one time, 'not thought it admissible to apply the prophecy to the King Messiah, for reasons which any intelligent man can find out' (probably as too near the Christian interpretation). Hillel said that there was no Messiah for Israel, because they had enjoyed him in the days of Hezekiah. Sanhedrin, quoted p. 294, note a. Moses b. Gecatalia, p. 551.

[n] Karaites in Yepheth b. Ali (p. 19).

[o] Some in Abarbanel (p. 162), in Lanyado (pp. 303–305), in Naphthali Altschuler (p. 321).

[p] Abarbanel, of Israel (p. 168), or Josiah (p. 187); Saadyah Ibn Danân, at one time, Israel or Jeremiah (p. 114); Mordekhai, Israel or the Messiah (p. 379).

[q] Ibn Danân and Passani (note l).

[r] Abr. Farissol, beg. p. 220.

[s] 'When he speaks of the people, the King Messiah is included in it; and when he speaks of the King Messiah, the people is included with him,' Astruc (p. 129); 'including any righteous also,' Sal. de Marini (p. 324).

[t] Mentioned by Farissol (pp. 220, 221), 'I have found some expositors who suppose &c., and others [not the Christians] who apply it confidently to the King Messiah,' &c.

[u] Moses b. Nachman, as a controversialist, of Israel (p. 78), Ibn Crispin (pp. 99, 100), Astruc (p. 129), Moses Elsheikh (p. 268), R. Naphthali Altschuler (p. 319), and the hymn-writer R. Israel Nagara (p. 385); see also Farissol (note t).

[v] In his *Iggeret Teman*, a letter written A.D. 1172 to the Jews in Yemen. See Grätz, vi. 304, note 2.

[w] Pp. 274, 275.

yet that he, idolised by so many, had not apparently the slightest following in this. He held to this faith, although he said that '[x] expectations of the Messiah had always brought misfortune on the house of Jacob,' discouraged all calculation of his coming, mentions three false Messiahs who rose up in forty years, else unknown, yet mentions a family tradition, that prophecy, as a precursor of the Messiah, would burst out anew in 1216.

But manifold and laborious as was their search, they were engaged in an impossible problem, to find any counterpart to this great prophecy, except Him whom it foreshadowed. They were not intellectually second-rate men who felt the difficulty. The sceptical Ibn Ezra, who is described as '[y] a man of remarkable intellectual gifts, vivid, talented, but without warmth,' begins his solution with, '[z] This Parashah is an extremely difficult one. Our opponents say that it refers to their God.' Ibn Crispin complains of '[a] the forced and far-fetched interpretations, of which' others 'have been guilty;' says, that those who interpret the Parashah collectively, '[b] distort the passage from its natural sense,' since 'the singular number is used throughout,' and whereas the prophet calls the people 'Israel my servant,' he here says 'my servant' only. 'These expositors,' he says, 'shut the doors of the literal interpretation against themselves, and wearied themselves to find the entrance.' He himself goes back to '[c] the teaching of our Rabbis, the King Messiah.' R. Isaac b. Eliyyah Cohen, while speaking strongly against the Christian interpretation, says [d], 'I have never in my life seen or heard of the exposition of a clear or fluent commentator, in which my own judgment, and that of others who have pondered on the same subject, might completely acquiesce.' He speaks the judgment of others his contemporaries also. Yet his own interpretation is one of the most forced, and seems only designed to bring into the section forced allusions to our Lord. Saadyah Ibn Danân (a contemporary of Abarbanel [e]), who is praised in other respects [f], says [g], 'I set before myself the notes of those

---

[x] In France, about A.D. 1087; Cordova, about A.D. 1117; Fez, about A.D. 1127; Grätz, pp. 308, 309.

[y] In Grätz, Gesch. vi. 183 sqq. Grätz says of his criticism on the Pentateuch, 'It is a question, *which* was in earnest, his scepticism or his belief?' ibid. p. 192.

[z] P. 43. [a] P. 100. [b] P. 99. [c] P. 100. [d] P. 138.

[e] A.D. 1460–1520; Grätz, viii. p. 327. [f] Grätz, ibid. p. 320.

[g] P. 202.

who had commented upon the Parashah "Behold my servant," and pondered over them, and examined the opinions they contained. But all alike, I found, lacked solidity and soundness.' Farissol apologises for those who interpreted it of the Messiah, '[h] Whatever justice there may be in the expression of our wise men, who applied the prophecy to the Messiah, it should be borne in mind that although they themselves and their words are both truthful alike, yet their object was allegorical.' Moses Elsheikh, 'a writer,' Wolf says[i], 'of much reputation among the Jews,' says[j], 'The verses in this Parashah are difficult to fix or arrange in a literal manner, so that the various parts, from the beginning to the end, may be combined and connected closely together. The commentators I see going up and down among them, and yet neither agreeing on the subject to which the whole is to be referred, nor disentangling the words upon any simple plan.' He himself then in his 'humility, set' himself 'to apply to it a straightforward method, according to the literal sense of the text, such as ought to be adopted by one who would rightly unite the several words and periods, and determine what view is legitimate, what not.' He interprets it of the Messiah; yet, when he comes to verses 9–12, which speak of the death, he says[k], 'These verses are all of them hard, though we shall not touch on everything which might be noticed.' Shelomo Levi says[l], 'Throughout this prophecy, all the commentators exert their utmost on its interpretation, and are at no small variance as to its import.' He expresses himself dissatisfied with all which he had found. Even in later times, R. Naphthali Altschuler[m] expresses his surprise that 'Rashi and R. David Kimchi have not with the Targum applied them to the Messiah likewise.' Herz Homberg argues on the ground of the singular, against Rashi and Ibn Ezra[n]. Passani expresses his surprise at former commentators, and says[o], 'Not one of the explanations is in complete accordance with the language of the text, or succeeds in satisfying us; still less the' Christians. He thinks that, like all other prophecies, most of Isaiah's also point to the latter days, when the Messiah shall have appeared, but exhorts to caution how any so interpret it, 'Take heed, O wise men, in your words, even though the language be meant to be metaphorical and indirect.' R. Tanchum seems to be carefully

---

h P. 223. i Bibl. Hebr. i. p. 808. j P. 259. k P. 269.
l P. 175. m P. 319. n P. 400. o Pp. 406, 407.

ambiguous. He uses the phrase 'any person or nation[p],' but speaks of the subject being 'one of the generation in exile[q]' who had died, yet 'a guide and deliverer[r],' who 'rescues them from captivity and from their enemies generally,' and speaks of 'his hidden nature, the mystery connected with him not being revealed to them.' He concludes with a protest against there being anything 'hyperbolical beyond what is elsewhere permitted[s],' or allegorical[t], and seems to think that the intention of the prophet was, not to be understood. Ibn Amram says[u], 'As relates to the Jews, there is no little difficulty in giving a sense to those most obscure words of Isaiah in the present: they manifestly need a prophetic spirit, whence our older and more recondite masters went apart from one another to different explanations: but,' he satisfies himself, 'each very far removed from the exposition of the Christians.' For error is manifold, truth but one.

E. B. PUSEY.

OXFORD,
December, 1876.

[p] P. 553. [q] P. 555. [r] P. 556. [s] P. 557.
[t] Ibid. and p. 558. [u] Pp. 536, 537.

Brief Extracts, in which the Jewish Commentators write (1) of the vicariousness of the sufferings mentioned in this section, (2) the actual death of the sufferer or sufferers, (3) of his or their continued intercession.

a. *The vicariousness of the suffering.*

'Surely he carried our sicknesses and bare our pains:—but he was wounded for our transgressions, bruised for our iniquities; his destruction is our compensation; and by his stripes we are healed.—God laid upon him the iniquity of us all.—If his soul becomes a trespass-offering for sin—He will bear their iniquities,' Saad. Gaon, pp. 17, 18. 'By the words *surely he hath carried our sicknesses* they mean, that the pains which he fell into were merited by them, but that he bore them instead.—God appoints his servant to carry their sins, and by doing so lighten their punishment, that Israel might not be completely exterminated.—By the Messiah bearing them they would be delivered from the wrath which rested upon them, and enabled to endure it,' Yepheth b. Ali, pp. 23, 24. 'Israel suffered, in order that by his sufferings atonement might be made for all other nations; the sickness which ought to have fallen upon us, was carried by him.—*He was wounded for our transgressions and bruised for our iniquities; the chastisement of* the *peace* that was for us fell upon him, he was chastised that the whole world might have peace—He endured punishment as though he had been a sinner himself, and for the sake of others bare the sin of many,' Rashi, pp. 38, 39. 'They have been carrying sicknesses and pains, which for our iniquities should have been borne by us,' Joseph Qara, p. 42. 'Israel *was numbered with those* who transgressed against God, and *carried the sin of many,* because through his pains the Gentiles had peace; and the sin which they ought to have carried was borne by him,' Ibn Ezra, p. 48. 'The sickness and pain, which ought to have fallen upon us, has fallen upon them, and they are our ransom and the price of our atonement. While they were in exile, we thought that they were smitten by God for their iniquity; but now we see that it was not for their iniquity, but for ours, as it is said, *He suffered pangs for our transgressions,*' Kimchi, p. 52. '*If thou,* Lord, *make his soul,* as it were, *a trespass-offering,* then as every trespass-offering makes some atonement, so the work of this "wise" one will atone for the iniquities of Israel,' Jacob b. Reuben (Kar.), p. 63. '*By his knowledge my servant* Israel *will make many righteous* in a righteous law, and *their iniquities he will bear* in obtaining their forgiveness,' Anon. xvi. p. 65. 'We were thinking, that all these chastenings had fallen upon him because of his own iniquity: now we see that that was not the cause: the sickness that ought to have come upon us, came upon him, and through them atonement was made for us; his chastenings were for our transgressions, and they resulted in our peace: the Holy One did not, as he would have otherwise done, destroy the world for our iniquities; and while Israel was beaten and killed (as in Ps. xliv. 23) for God's holy name, we were healed by his stripes,' R. Joseph b. Nathan, pp. 72, 73. '*He was numbered with the transgressors,* bore chastenings as though he had been a sinner and transgressor himself,' ibid. p. 74. 'It was *our sicknesses* which *he bare*, and which made him sick and pained him.' '*The Lord caused the iniquity of us all* (we all had incurred penalties because of him) *to meet upon him*,' Yeshayah b. Mali, p. 76. '*By his stripes we were healed*, because the stripes by which he is vexed and distressed will heal us: God will pardon us for his righteousness: and we shall be healed both from our own transgressions and from the iniquities of our fathers,' Mosheh b. Nachman, p. 81. 'They thought that the only object of Israel's existence was, as Mohammed said, to bear the pains and misfortunes of the world, and that all their iniquities and transgressions were carried by him as though he had been the scape-goat,' Ibn Shaprut, p. 95; '*he will bear* and atone for *their iniquities*, when the expiation for his own sins and his fathers (by which is meant the exile with its attendant miseries) has been accomplished,' id. p. 96. 'He also *carried the sin of many*; for, besides his own sins, he bore (according to Lam. v. 7) the sins of his fathers and those of his sons as well,' id. ibid. fin. 'It will be as though he had borne all the sicknesses and chastisements which fall upon us. Or, perhaps, *carry* may mean "take away," "forgive" (as Exod. x. 17); from his pity and his prayers for us, he will atone for our transgressions,' Ibn Crispin, p. 108; 'by the weals breaking out on his flesh in consequence of his anxiety for us, God will have mercy upon him, and, by sparing him for the sake of his sufferings endured on our account, heal us,' id. p. 109; 'because we had in our exile incurred the extremest penalty, behold it was as though this penalty, which had been deserved by all of us, had been laid by God upon him,' ibid.; 'his soul will treat itself as guilty, and so receive punishment for our trespasses and transgressions,' id. p. 112; 'will atone for them (for Israel) in the perfection of his nature, until their sins depart from them and they are left guiltless,' id. p. 113. 'All the sufferings and sicknesses, they will say, which we ought to have borne for our iniquities, have been borne by the righteous for our sake,' Mosheh Cohen, p. 117; 'verse 5 applies to each individual righteous man: by the stripes and sufferings which each bore, atonement was made for all Israel,' id. p. 118; 'these righteous ones in Israel were not bruised with sufferings and sickness, except at the pleasure of the Creator, in order that—secondly, they might bear the sins of those who transgressed in Israel,' id. p. 119; 'if the righteous have suffered punishment as though there were guilt in their souls,' ibid. 'Even the transgressors among them will exclaim, that the righteous bore all these sufferings and persecutions in the present world on account of *their* iniquities, that by those sufferings Israel's guilt was atoned for,' id. p. 120. '*The chastisement of our peace was upon him*, because, except for the merits of the righteous, the world had not been preserved, but would have been laid waste by the Holy One for the nations' sins.—*By his stripes we are healed*, for since punishment came upon the righteous without cause, and simply on account of the Gentiles who sinned, therefore the Almighty cuts short the punishment of the Gentiles before the time: thus they are healed by the stripes of the righteous,' Lipmann, p. 150. 'His death was not caused by his own iniquity, but by the wickedness of his generation,' Abarbanel (of Josiah), p. 189; 'the pain and sickness which for our transgressions we ought to have received, were borne by that just one for us,' id. p. 192; 'the blow, which they themselves ought for their iniquities to have received, was made to fall upon Josiah by the hand of Pharaoh Necho,' p. 194; 'he *carried the sin of many*, and died for the iniquities of his people,' id. p. 197. 'Because the troubles which had come to him, and which he had *borne*, were for *their iniquities*,' Martino, p. 201. 'He [Hezekiah] was perfectly just, so that his people were delivered for his merits, and he carried the sins and transgressions, which they had committed in the days of his father,' Ibn Danân, p. 214. 'Now of a certainty we perceive that this servant Israel has suffered the punishment for iniquity which ought to have been carried by us, and borne the pain which for our deeds we ought to have endured,' Farissol, p. 224; 'since he bore the punishment, although unjustly, we are healed, and escape the reward of our iniquities,' ibid.; 'the Lord brought on the *servant* the penalty and retribution which we ought to have paid,' id. pp. 224, 225; 'this happiness will come to him as an equivalent for the penalties he had endured in place of the Gentiles,' id. p. 226. 'If he [the just] is entangled in the iniquity of his generation, repentance is not within his power, and he must die in consequence; hence it is said, *The Lord was pleased to bruise him*, as though for its own iniquities. I notice two things: 1. that he is righteous; 2. that he *sees and is satisfied* with many and sore troubles, and that nothing short of death can secure atonement for him: this being so, it follows that he must suffer, not for his own sins, but for those of the people.—*By his knowledge he will justify the just:* if he does this, however, he will *bear their iniquities*, i.e. bear them on their behalf,' R. Meir Aramah, p. 242. 'The calamities, in which the chastisements of exile consisted, did not come upon him for his own iniquity, but the pains and sicknesses (under which image they are here represented) which ought in justice to have fallen upon us, fell instead upon him,' Troki, p. 251; 'by the clause, *carried the sin of many*, it is signified, that not only was he not wicked, as the Gentiles imagined, but in his righteousness he even bore and carried the sin of many among the Gentiles, as it is said, *And their iniquities he will bear*,' id. p. 256. 'What we had seen before meant nothing except that he was *carrying our sicknesses*, and that his sufferings were for the protection of his generation,' Moses Elsheikh, p. 264; '*he carried our sicknesses*, i.e. he was ready to carry them of his own accord,' id. p. 266. 'The sufferings of the righteous cannot atone for the special sins of the individual, but each man will have to pay his own particular penalty for them after death; *the iniquity of us all*, however, i.e. the iniquity common to our whole race, *the Lord laid upon him*, viz. upon the righteous, who is punished for the iniquity of his own age,' Sh'lomo Levi, p. 282. 'The sufferings of the third kind are such as do liberate a generation from its guilt, and effect atonement for it; and this is what will be the case with the generation of the Messiah.—*The chastisement of our peace was upon him, and by his stripes we are healed*, implying, as it does, that we are entirely free from all iniquity [may allude] to the third, or, in other words, to the generation of the Messiah,' p. 283; 'God here [ver. 12] makes his final declaration respecting the righteous one who is to atone for his generation,' id. p. 286. '*He himself carried our sicknesses and bare our pains*, and by saying *he himself*, the prophet indicates that the righteous, of his own will, was pleased to carry them for Israel.—We thought him stricken of God for his own sins, whereas in reality he was stricken for ours, being himself just and perfect,' Lanyado, p. 306; 'the righteous, voluntarily and of his own accord, bears the sicknesses of his generation, in order to merit the never-ending pleasure of making atonement for them,' id. p. 307. 'Israel suffered in order that by his sufferings atonement might be made for all the wicked,' Abraham Chazan, p. 315. 'Now we see that this was not a consequence of his depression, but that he suffered in order that by his sufferings atonement might be made for the whole of Israel; as it is said of the prophet Micah, that the blood issuing from him made atonement for all Israel,' Naphthali Altschuler, p. 321 (who also mentions the Messiah b. Joseph, and the belief of the present unseen sufferings of the Messiah for Israel, in the Gemara). '*He carried our sicknesses;* for it was we who were really sick and the ultimate cause of his sufferings, and all the punishments spoken of should have come rightly upon us,' Sh'lomoh de Marini, p. 329; '*he will bear their iniquities,* as the righteous bears those of his own generation,' id. p. 338. 'Previously, we [the Gentiles] imagined that sufferings had been sent upon Israel, as a punishment by the Almighty, and therefore thought him "stricken, smitten of God, and afflicted." This was not so however; they were endured by him on our account. Or we may take another line, and suppose that they are words of Israel, spoken by them in reference to the righteous; which case they thoroughly suit. They will then express Israel's confession, that the sufferings, which they ought for their own iniquities to have endured, were borne by the righteous for their sake—*by his stripes we are healed,* by the stripes of the righteous we are forgiven—we followed the stubbornness of our heart, *but the Lord laid upon him,* the righteous, *the iniquity of us all,*' Lopez, pp. 350, 351. 'All these sicknesses and afflictions only befel the righteous, to cleanse them from the iniquity they had committed, and to make atonement for the transgressors in Israel; for the righteous maketh atonement for his generation, as we learn from the case of Josiah,' id. p 352; 'in their death they atoned for the sins of many,' id. p. 353; 'the transgressors in Israel will perceive that all the sufferings of the righteous were on their behalf, that through their death their own sins might be forgiven' &c., id. ibid. '*The chastisement* &c., the sufferings which ought to have come upon us, in order, by blotting out our iniquity, to perpetuate our peace, fell *upon him,* and *by the stripes* which came on him the plagues of our iniquity were *healed,* they were atoned for and so dispersed,' David Altschuler, p. 370. '*He,* either the servant Jacob, or the Messiah who will be king over the seed of Jacob, *was wounded* or *bruised for the iniquity* of the Gentiles, in order that he might receive the penalty on their behalf,' Mord'khai b. Y'hosafah, p. 379. 'The *sicknesses* and *pains* which ought to have fallen to our lot, were *borne* and *carried* by him instead:—*by his stripes,* the stripes which he bore when stricken, we are healed,' Mosheh of Salerno, p. 382. 'Sometimes misfortunes light upon the righteous, not as a punishment, but for the sake of a whole nation, that atonement may be made for it.—God brings sufferings on the just, as a satisfaction for the evil destined to afflict a whole people, that it may thus be averted: as our Rabbis say, "The death of the righteous worketh atonement." When the prophet says, *Surely he carried* &c., he means—they [the sufferings] do not fall upon them [the righteous] for any sin they may have committed, but as an atonement, whether for all the world, or for the entire people, or for some single city,' Yoseph Albo, p. 384. 'They will not at first perceive, that whatever he underwent was in consequence of their own transgression, the Lord having chosen him to be a trespass-offering, like the scape-goat which bore all the iniquities of the house of Israel,' Herz Homberg, p. 401; '*my servant* will be righteous *for many,* adventuring his soul freely for the general good, and not sparing his own life, if others might be benefited through his death, but enduring the burthen of their sins, in order to release them from punishment,' id. p. 404. 'All perceived that he [Hezekiah] *was wounded for* their *transgressions, and bruised for* their *iniquities,* to make atonement for them unto God; for the attribute of judgment, displaying itself before them, *laid upon him the iniquity of them all*, as the text says, *for the transgression of my people*, even *the stroke* which should have fallen *upon them*,' Yacob Passani, p. 409; 'because he bare the iniquities of the age,' id. p. 410. 'In fact it was they themselves [the Gentiles] who had rather been deserving of punishment, and that, through Israel's merits, in acquiescing in their afflictions as just, God had preserved them—until the time of their deliverance should arrive, which would be for the benefit of the whole world,' Luzzatto, p. 423. '*By his knowledge* &c., Israel suffers oppression from the Christians who are healed by those sufferings,' Clear Fountain, p. 432. 'Whereas he suffered the sicknesses and sufferings which we deserved for our sins, his troubles appear to have been the cure of ourselves, the Lord seems to have transferred on him the punishment of us all,' Manasseh b. Isr. Paraphrase, p. 438; 'if he offer his soul as an expiation,' id. p. 439. 'The meaning is that he was prostrated by our sins, and stricken by our offences, just as though he were punished for us. This eminent saint, while bearing the chastisements which came upon him as a trial (since he had committed no sin), attracted to himself, as it were, all the chastisements due to us, and gave us peace for them; thus they came upon him, and *by his stripes we were healed*. We have already explained the possibility of God's acting in such a way, in virtue of a substitution decreed by him,' Y'hudah b. Bal'am, pp. 550, 551; 'any one would think that there was some evil in him, for which he was punished, whereas in fact he was carrying the sin of others,' id. ibid. 'All his afflictions, all the punishment and sufferings of captivity which fell upon him, were for their sins and transgressions, in virtue of the justly merited judgment of God. It is thus that when they have paid the debt which God has adjudged to be due from them, he then sends them a person who will guide them and deliver them,' Tanchum, p. 556. 'His calamities are not the consequence of his own deeds, but on account of the multitude of our sins and iniquities,' Sh'lomoh b. Menahem, p. 561; 'his stripes are healing for us, because he bears what ought to have been borne by us,' id. ibid. 'By the sufferings of Israel atonement will be made for all nations,' Gershom, p. 565; 'the peace which we enjoyed was not owing to our righteousness, but because Israel for their iniquity had received upon themselves the punishment which ought to have come upon us,' id. ibid.; 'the Almighty, unwilling to destroy his world, is represented by the prophet as punishing Israel; for Israel suffered in our stead,' id. ibid.

b. *The actualness of the death.*

'He gave himself over to whatever burial the wicked Gentiles might decree: for the Gentiles used to condemn the Israelites to be murdered and then' &c., Rashi, p. 38. 'Some explain "in his deaths" of those who died in exile,' Ibn Ezra, p. 47; 'all the interpreters say that this verse [ver. 12] alludes metaphorically to those who perished in defence of the doctrine of the Divine Unity,' id. p. 48. 'They were ever killing Israel, while in exile, just as though he had done wrong, although he had done no violence, and although there was no word of guile in his mouth. The meaning of ויתן is that he gave himself voluntarily to death; they were ready to release him, if he would renounce his own law—but rather than do this, he met a voluntary death,' Kimchi, p. 53; 'because in exile he resigned himself to death at the hands of the Gentiles,' id. p. 55. 'And when he reached the gates of death, he made his grave with the wicked: he means to say that he was wicked, and consequently had to meet the death of the wicked, and die in his sin, thereby accepting the sentence passed upon him,' Anon. xvii. p. 69. 'He made his grave at the will of the wicked, gave himself up to be buried at their decree, when the vilest of the people murdered him, because of God's holy name,' Joseph b. Nathan, p. 73. 'The rich in Israel used to kill them,' Y'sha'yah b. Mali, p. 77. 'The stroke had befallen them, and the just had been deprived of life, because of their people's transgression,' Ahron b. Yoseph, p. 88; 'or the sense may be, that they made their grave like men proved to be *wicked* by trial, and sentenced to death, and like the rich man dying in his sins,' id. ibid. 'Whenever they saw a single wealthy Jew, they would seek some mischief against him to kill him,' Ibn Shaprut, p. 96; 'as a reward for his having poured out his soul to die for the sanctity of God's name,' id. ibid. 'Many of the just and pious were slain, and those who buried them *gave* or assigned them their graves *with the wicked*,' Ibn Crispin, p. 111. 'The righteous suffered various forms of death, after the manner in which the wicked condemn those who are judicially condemned,' Mosheh Cohen, p. 118; 'how often did the Israelites resign themselves to death for the holy name,' id. p. 120. 'The prophet uses "deaths" in the plural, because they condemned them to different forms of punishment,' Astruc, p. 134. 'We despised him and pained him still more by slaying him with the sword,' Eliyyah Cohen, p. 143. '*Because he poured out* &c., an allusion to the righteous who died in captivity on behalf of the sanctity of God's name,' Lipmann, p. 151. 'Even after their burial the wicked heathen used to drag them forth from their tombs.—Israel was persecuted by the wicked even to the tomb,' Abarbanel, p. 181; 'while in exile, he poured out his soul to die for the sanctity of the holy name,' id. p. 186; 'his [Josiah's] death is spoken of as his grave or burial; because, inasmuch as every dead man is buried, death itself may be spoken of as burial,' id. p. 195. 'So that those belonging to it would be "drawn and cast out," and not deemed worthy of proper burial,' Martino, p. 200. 'By "giving his grave with the wicked" is signified that he gave himself up to martyrdom for the sake of God's holy name: the expression "with the rich" derives its force from the fact, that the wealthy are murdered for their riches, and not for any wickedness that may be in them,' Sal. b. Melech, p. 219. 'Supposing beforehand that he always made his grave with the wicked, so that his final reward should be "in the underworld beneath," the grave of the wicked being preparatory to the punishment of Gehenna,' Farissol, p. 226. 'The wealthy among them they afflicted and murdered by various kinds of death; "the rich in his deaths" are added because the Gentiles used to murder the Israelites, to secure their wealth,' Anon. xxxiv. pp. 236, 237. 'Nothing short of death can secure atonement for him, so he must suffer' &c., Meir Aramah, p. 242. 'Israel was ready to resign himself to death and burial for the Divine Unity; we [the nations] were incessantly framing fraudulent devices against him to put him to death,' Troki, p. 254. '"He," i. e. Moses, "made his grave with the wicked," for he was buried in profane ground, in order to bring them in with him [into the future world],' Mosheh Elsheikh, p. 271. 'He gave, i. e. allowed his burial and death to take place at the hands of the wicked,' Sh'lomo Levi, p. 284; 'inasmuch as he poured out his soul to die, and in so doing carried the sin of many,' id. p. 287; 'in return for his having "poured out his soul to die," and voluntarily choosing death rather than life,' id. ibid. 'At the time when we smote him [Israel] mortally,' Abraham

Cordov. p. 292. '"He was cut off out of the land of the living," and slain "for the transgression of my people," the stroke intended for them being borne by him instead,' Lanyado, p. 302; 'he was not to be put to death speedily, but tortured by every conceivable method of producing a severe and painful end; and hence it is that the prophet says not "in his death," but "in his deaths,"' id. ibid. 'He resigned himself to whatever form of burial might be decreed against him by the wicked, who were ever condemning the Israelites to be murdered—he consented to be slain according to the will of the wicked, he preferred to meet death for the sake of the Unity of God,' Abraham b. Yehudah, p. 316. 'He resigned himself to be buried in whatever manner the wicked might decree, who were always condemning Israel to be murdered,' Naphthali Altschuler, p. 322; or [if interpreted of the Messiah] 'when the wicked man dies, the Messiah will die likewise,' id. ibid. 'Of the just who were to be found at all periods in Israel, and who were put to death in the cause of truth, not one ever felt anxiety or seemed to be sensible of all that he was suffering,' de Marini, p. 337. '"He made his grave," referring to the righteous who were slain like guilty persons condemned by the sentence of a court' &c., Lopez, p. 351; 'because he poured out his soul to die, by undergoing martyrdom for the holiness of God, as our own eyes see in Spain and Portugal,' id. p. 352. 'We made them buy their sepulchres at a full price—like the wicked who are treated without any consideration' &c., Segre, p. 365. 'He was cut off from the land of life, his sufferings accelerated his death,' David Altschuler, p. 371. 'He made his grave with the wicked, for they spilt their blood—thus they resigned themselves to martyrdom,' Mordekhai b. Yhosafad, pp. 379, 380. 'He made his grave, entrusted his death to the hand of the wicked; he would never comply with false worship, but preferred death,' Mosheh of Salerno, p. 383. 'When he was led to the slaughter, he was taken thither from prison' &c., Anon. *l.* p. 392. 'He died before his time through their slaying him,' Ibn Janâh, as cited by Kimchi, ibid. 'He was put to death without the authority of the government, and without the sentence of a court of judgment; any one that found him murdered him, if he so chose,' Luzzatto, p. 421. '"He made his grave:" Israel, who died for the law and the holy name of God, make their grave with the wicked, which is indeed the case in this long exile,' Clear Fountain, p. 433; 'these passages prove that Israel will be justified by their confidence in God, and by their martyrdom, not by that of the pretended Messiah,' id. ibid.; 'the martyred people poured out its soul unto death,' ibid. p. 434. 'He was buried with malefactors—he gave himself up to death for the sanctification of my name,' Paraphrase of Manasseh b. Israel, pp. 439, 440; 'we have frequently condemned this people to death,' id. p. 446. 'Suffering death with ignominy, and amid the imprecations of the populace,' Orobio, p. 508; 'they judged him, condemned him, and often murdered him,' id. p. 517. 'And why were they slain and expelled from the land of life?' Ibn Amram, p. 543; 'he laid down his life for God and his holy law,' id. p. 547. 'His merits were not known, nor his perfections and excellences described, until after his death, and his departure from the land of the living, i. e. the present world of sense,' Tanchum, p. 555. 'He made his grave with the wicked in an unclean land, and his death with the rich' &c., Sh'lomoh b. Menahem, p. 562. 'Whatever form of death was thus selected for Israel, Israel received it; he endured the death' &c., Joseph Kara, p. 570.

c. *His continued intercession.*

'In virtue of his sufferings—he interceded for the transgressors,' Rashi, p. 39. 'He also interceded for the transgressors, as is said, Jer. xxix. 7, "and seek ye the peace"' &c., Ibn Ezra, p. 48. 'He continued interceding for the wicked who were transgressing against him, and sought blessings on their land from the Lord, cf. Jer. xxix. 7,' Kimchi, p. 55. 'God receives his intercession for the iniquities of us all,' Anon. xvi. p. 65. 'God, for his sake, will receive intercession for transgressors,' id. ibid. 'He interceded for the transgressors, prayed for them to me, that I would have mercy on them, although it was through them that he himself was smitten,' Anon. xvii. p. 70. 'He *prayed* to the Creator *for the transgressors;* for the Jews used to pray for all men, that the Creator would have mercy on his own world, and would not destroy it,' Y'sha'yah ben Mali, p. 77. 'He was punished as though he had been a transgressor himself, whereas in fact he *carried the sin of many*, and made intercession for transgressors,' Ahron b. Yoseph, p. 89. 'Israel interceded (Jer. xxix. 7) for sinners and transgressors,' Ibn Shaprut, p. 96. 'He also interceded for the transgressors (i. e. for Israel); these words explain in what way he carried their sins, viz. by making intercession for them. פגע means to pray or entreat, as lix. 16' &c., Ibn Crispin, p. 114. 'In their death they atoned for the iniquities of the many, and in their lives entreated for mercy upon the transgressors, although oppressed by them,' Mosheh Cohen, p. 120; 'even the transgressors among them will exclaim—that a redeemer would come to them for their sake, seeing that they were ever praying to the Creator, and interceding for mercy on behalf of the transgressors in Israel,' id. ibid. 'He prayed to his God, and God for his merits sent forth healing,' Eliyyah Cohen, p. 142. 'While Israel will be interceding and praying for them,' Martino, p. 201. 'So that, when through his merits and intercession the deliverance was wrought, it was as though he had borne and carried all their sicknesses and pains,' Ibn Danân, p. 209; 'the Lord let himself be entreated by him, forgiving their iniquity and saving them,' id. p. 211; 'he was continually praying on behalf of his generation, and oftentimes God let himself be entreated by him. יפגיע expresses continued action, but Scripture does not mention all the deliverances and wonders which were vouchsafed to him,' id. p. 214. 'Israel used to intercede for the transgressions, as in Jer. xxix. 7,' Sal. b. Melech, p. 220. 'The congregation of Israel was in the habit of praying for the good estate of the kingdom and of the very transgressors who ill-treated them, and for the prosperity and richness of the crops, as we now do,' Farissol, p. 227; 'or, in the days of the redemption they will intercede for the transgressors, that they may be healed and forgiven and be converted,' ibid. '"The chastisement of our peace was upon him," i.e. Israel prayed for our peace, that we might be healed, since we were not ourselves worthy to enjoy it, except through the intervention of the miseries which befel him, and by so doing produced all our present prosperity. This Jeremiah says [xxix. 7],' Anon. xxxiv. p. 235; '"made intercession for the transgressors," as the Psalmist says [Ps. lxxii. 15], "He shall pray for him continually;" for we find פגע used in the sense of interceding, as Jer. vii. 16,' id. p. 238. 'He [Israel] used to intercede with God for our adversities, and God used to hear his prayer, and send forth healing for our wounds,' Troki, p. 252; 'he used to pray to God on behalf of the Gentile transgressors, although they caused him the greatest sufferings, he interceded' &c., at length, id. p. 256. 'He [Moses] made intercession for the transgressors, because in every place that Israel transgressed, he interceded for them,' Mosheh Elsheikh, p. 274. 'Although at the time of his murder he was ranked, in the sentence read out to him, with the generality of other transgressors, yet he took no count of it, knowing truly that he "carried the sin of many," making it, as he did, his constant habit to "intercede for transgressors," in order that atonement might be made for them,' Sh'lomo Levi, p. 287; 'he "interceded for the transgressors," i. e. for the people in the wilderness, who, although continually vexing him, he used to pray might be converted,' id. p. 288. 'He "interceded for the transgressors," to call down blessings upon their land, notwithstanding the fact that they had transgressed against him,' Abraham b. Y'hudah Chazan, p. 317. 'He carried the sin of many, and interceded for the transgressors, praying continually that the world might be restored through the establishment of the kingdom of the Almighty, and that all men might call upon the name of the Lord, to serve him with a whole heart,' Marini, p. 339. 'In their lives they sought for mercy on the transgressors, notwithstanding the oppression which they had endured at their hands,' Lopez, p. 353. 'Though, like David [Ps. xxxv. 13], he was ever making intercession and supplication on behalf of the transgressors who smote him,' Mordekhai b. Y'hosafah, p. 380. 'He will intercede for the transgressors and for those who rise up against him,' Herz Homberg, p. 405. 'He interceded for the transgressors, that the city might not fall into the hands of the king of Assyria,' Passani, p. 410. 'And made intercession for the transgressors (הפגיע as Jer. xxxvi. 25). So Ibn Ezra, Kimchi, Abarbanel.—Israel will be redeemed through their own merits in the endurance of suffering and death, in forgiving their persecutors, and in praying for them, as though to shew that they loved the nations, and, although they rewarded them evil, still bare no ill-will towards them,' Luzzatto, p. 428. 'Israel prays for the welfare of the nations under whose rule they live, as commanded, Jer. xxix. 7. The nations will exclaim, "Who hath believed" &c. that the abased and humiliated people will pray for us?' Clear Fountain, p. 434. 'He bore the offence of many, even praying for the very transgressors from whom he received injuries,' Paraphrase of Manasseh b. Israel, p. 440. 'The prophet attributes four merits to them,—4. having observed the precept of Jer. xxix. 7, and this too so carefully, that in all their prayers, they pray for the health of the prince, and the peace of the kingdom or province wherein they reside, and, what is more, it may be even for the welfare of those from whom they are receiving insult and wrong,' Manasseh b. Israel, p. 448. 'His intercession will avail that the divine justice will pitifully pardon the nations their abominable sins, even those they committed against Israel,—for Israel, full of the love of God and of his divine Spirit, will pray for the rebellious, will be the mediator of peace between the Lord and the nations, praying for them, not with an ineffectual prayer, but one so effectual that his entreaties will always have a happy result in mankind being benefited,' Orobio, p. 531. 'He will pray the Lord for the wicked sons of Israel, transgressors of the law, and daily deprecates for them,' Ibn Amram, p. 548. 'יפגיע *interceded* and prayed for them, as Jer. vii. 16,' Y'hudah b. Bal'am, p. 551. 'He made intercession for those wicked ones who thought evil of him; in his humility he does not hate them for their behaviour towards him, or forsake them and withdraw himself from them, but *interceded* for them (יפגיע like תפגע Jer. vii. 16),' Tanchum, p. 557. 'He will *intercede* with the Almighty that he would bring them forth out of exile for their own merit,' Sh'lomoh b. M'nahem, p. 563. 'Their iniquities he will bear, as happens generally with the righteous, one interceding for others that they may escape unpunished,' Gershom, p. 567; 'for the transgressors who were suffering the prophet interceded with the Almighty, and the Almighty through his means gave prosperity to the world,' id. ibid.

Additional Note on page xxxiv, note [k].

It has been suggested to me, that some might like to see the passage of the Siphra d' Rab as it stands in the printed text, and so to compare it with that which Martini found in his MS. or MSS. (Dr. Neubauer found it for me, xii. 20. In Ugolini's Thesaurus it is in t. xiv, p. dccccxxx). It now runs: 'R. Jose said, If thou art minded to know how great is the reward of the righteous in the world to come, go and learn from the first man, upon whom was laid only one negative commandment, and he transgressed it; see how many deaths were inflicted upon him and upon his generations, and upon the generations of his generations to the end of his generations, and which attribute is greater, the attribute of goodness or the attribute of vengeance? He saith, the attribute of goodness. If the attribute of vengeance be the less, see how many deaths were inflicted upon him and on his generations, and on the generations of his generations unto the end of all generations. He who turneth from the unclean (פגול Lev. vii. 18) and from that which remaineth over [of the sacrifice] (הנותר Lev. vii. 16, 17), and humbleth himself on the day of atonement, how much more does he merit for himself and for his generations, and for the generations of his generations until the end of all generations!' Admitting fully the right of the Jews to adapt their texts for their own private use, and to erase the mention of 'the merits of the Messiah' when they no longer believed them, the omission seems to me to have spoiled the argument. As it stands in Martini, the contrast is clear, between the one sin of one hitherto sinless [Adam] and the merit of the Sinless Sufferer. But since every righteous man has committed many more sins than Adam, there is no contrast between his one disobedience and their observance of a few commands. To me it seems inconceivable, that a mind which could conceive so grand a contrast as that between God's attributes of justice and mercy could have sunk to so poor a contrast, and have imagined (contrary to fact) that two or three ritual observances could have been meritorious for all generations, whereas Ezekiel declares, that the father's observance of the moral law would not avail to the son who habitually broke it. The passage, as it stands in the printed text, seems to me to indicate an omission, such as Martini's text supplies, 'the merit of the Messias' being a known phrase (see note [k]). Again Martini's observation, 'It is much to be noted, that the Targum says, "The Lord says to his Word," when David said, "The Lord said unto my Lord,"' the present text having '*by* his Word,' not '*to* his Word,' is quoted as 'a fair sample of Martini's comments.' Yet

Martini's text, which was also independently that of Hieronymus à S. Fide, and produced in a discussion (c. Jud. i. 8. init. B. P. xxvi. 539), has the advantage, that it *is* a paraphrase, which the printed text is not. In the printed text, there is no Hebrew to correspond to the paraphrase 'by his word,' and no Chaldee to correspond to the words paraphrased 'to my Lord.' In Martini's text, the Hebrew and Chaldee correspond. The idea of the Priesthood of the Word was known to the Jews. Philo says, 'There are, it seemeth, two temples of God. The one is this world, in which also there is a high-priest, His First Begotten Divine Word [a].' I have no doubt that במימריה crept into the modern text as the common phrase, whereas there is no occasion elsewhere for the dative, which is in this place a paraphrase for the Hebrew dative.

---

[a] De Somniis, Opp. i. 653, Mang.

I. THE SEPTUAGINT, AQUILA, SYMMACHUS, AND THEODOTION.

LII. 13 Behold my servant[a] shall have understanding[b], and shall be exalted and glorified[c] exceedingly. 14 In what manner many will be astonished[d] at thee, so dishonoured will thy form be of men, and thy glory[e] of the sons of men[f], 15 so shall many nations marvel[g] at him, and kings shall hold[h] their mouth: because those to whom it had not been told concerning him will see, and those who have not heard will understand.

LIII. 1 Lord, who believed our report? and to whom was the arm of the Lord revealed? 2 We announced [him] as it were a child before him, [he was] like a root in a thirsty land[i]. He hath no form nor glory[j]: and we saw him, and he had no form nor beauty, but his form[k] was 3 without honour and fading away beyond [any of] the sons of men[l]; a man set in a plague, and knowing how to carry sickness[m], because his countenance is turned away from him[n], he was dishonoured

---

[a] A. S. my slave. [b] A. shall be made to possess knowledge. [c] A. S. Th. shall be lifted up and held on high. [d] Th. marvelled. [e] A. his visage .... and his form. [f] S. beyond the sons of men. [g] A. Th. he will sprinkle; S. he will fling away. [h] A. close up. [i] A. he shall come up (or, shall be told of) like a child receiving suck before his face, and like a root out of the impassable land; S. he came up like a shoot before him, and like a root out of the thirsty land; Th. he will come up like a sucking child before him, and like a root in the thirsty land. [j] A. distinction. [k] S. he had no form or reputation that we might know him, neither looks that we might desire him. [l] S. set at nought, and the most insignificant of men. [m] A. a man of pains and known to illness; S. a man full of labour and known to disease; Th. a man of pains and known to sickness. [n] A. his face was as though hidden.

and esteemed not[o]. 4 This man carries our sins, and is pained for us, and *we* thought that he was in labour, and in a plague, and in affliction[p]. 5 But *he* was wounded for our sins, and made sick[q] for our transgressions: the chastisement of our peace was upon him, by his stripes *we* were healed. 6 All we like sheep went astray[r], each man wandered on his own way: and the Lord delivered him over to our sins[s], 7 and *he* by reason of his being afflicted[t] openeth not his mouth: like a sheep he was led to the slaughter[u], and as a lamb dumb before her shearer, so he openeth not his mouth. 8 In his humiliation his judgment was taken away: his generation who shall declare? because his life is taken from the earth, for the iniquities of my people he was led off to death[v]. 9 And I will give[w] the wicked[x] for his grave and the rich for his death: because he did no iniquity, neither [uttered] deceit with his mouth. 10 And the Lord desireth to purify him[y] from his plague[z]; if ye give [an offering] for sin, your[aa] soul shall see a long-lived seed. The Lord also desireth[bb] to take away[cc] 11 from the labour of his soul, to shew him light and form [him] with intelligence[dd], to justify the just that serveth many well[ee]; and their sins[ff] *he* will bear[gg]. 12 Therefore shall *he* have many

---

o Th. and we esteemed him not. p S. Surely *he* took up our sins, and endured our labours: but it thought him to be under the touch [of leprosy] (A. 'touched;' Th. 'beaten'), plagued by God ('by God' also in A. Th.), and humiliated. q A. he was defiled by reason of our defections, bruised. . . . . r A. verged aside; S. turned off; Th. inclined away. s S. and the Lord made the iniquity of us all to meet upon him. t S. he was brought near, and he was obedient. u S. to sacrifice. v S. for he was cut off out of the land of the living, and for the injustice of my people there was a plague upon them; Th. because he was cut off from the land of the living, on account of the defection of my people he touched them. w A. S. Th. he will give. x S. the impious. y S. to have mercy on him. z S. in his wounding. aa A. S. Th. his. bb A. Th. *insert* by his hand. cc S. the pleasure of the Lord shall prosper in his hand. dd A. S. Th. he shall see, shall be filled (S. 'satiated') in his knowledge. ee S. that ministereth to many. ff S. impieties. gg A. shall carry; S. shall take up; Th. took up.

for his inheritance, and shall divide the spoils[hh] of the strong; because his soul was delivered over unto death, and he was numbered[ii] amongst the transgressors[jj], and because *he* bore[kk] the sins of many, and for their transgressions was delivered up[ll].

[hh] A. booty. [ii] A. S. was counted. [jj] Th. held aloof from the impious.
[kk] A. took away; S. Th. took on him. [ll] S. resisted the disobedient.

---

liii. 2. *ἀνηγγείλαμεν.* Cf. the note below on ver. 11 *πλάσαι.* 5. A. *βεβηλωμένος.* The word is regarded as connected with חָלַל, חֹל: we shall find the same view recur in some of the other commentators. 7. *προσηνέχθη*, i. e. נגשׁ for נגשׂ: cf. 1 Sam. xiii. 6 LXX. 8. *εἰς θάνατον.* It is possible, as Frankel conjectures (*Vorstudien zu der Sept.*, 1841, p. 215), that למו, falling perhaps at the end of a line, or having accidentally a stroke after the ו ('למו), was incorrectly taken by the translators as an abbreviation for לַמָּוֶת, i. e. *to death:* Frankel compares Hos. xiv. 3 (*καρπὸν* for פרים), Ps. iii. 8, Num. vii. 88 ('פר or 'פרי resolved wrongly into פרות). 10. *καθαρίσαι.* From the sense attaching to דכא in Aramaic (Chaldee and Syriac), where it is equivalent to the Heb. זכה *to be clear* or *pure.* It is no uncommon occurrence for LXX to interpret a Hebrew word in accordance with the signification borne by a word externally resembling it in the Aramaic dialect spoken at the time when the translation was made. Cf., for example, Ps. vii. 3 *λυτρουμένου*, li. 6 *νικήσῃς*, lx. 10 *ἐλπίδος*, lxi. 8 *τίς*, lxix. 21, civ. 11; Is. xxxviii. 13 *παρεδόθην*; Nah. iii. 8 *ἑτοιμάσαι*; Qoh. i. 17 *προαίρεσις*, ii. 8 *οἰνοχόον καὶ οἰνοχόας*, 12 *βουλή.* 10. *τραυματισμῷ* (S.), החלי being connected with חלל. 11. *πλάσαι.* ישבע (if read as Hif.) might naturally be rendered by *πλῆσαι*: and it was suggested long ago by L. Cappellus (quoted by Schleusner) in his *Notae Criticae* (1689), p. 60 *b*, that the latter was the term actually used by the translators, and that the corruption is to be attributed to the Greek copyists. There are certainly several instances in LXX of corruptions resembling the one before us, which it seems reasonable to assign to this source, especially if, as is sometimes the case, the alteration was in any way facilitated by the nature of the context. In the Psalms alone, for instance, cf. iv. 8 *καρποῦ* for *καιροῦ*, xvii. 14 *ὑείων* for *υἱῶν* (both suggested by the context), xxxi. 16 *κλῆροι* for *καιροί*, xxxix. 6 *παλαιὰς* for *παλαιστάς*, xliv. 13 *ἀλαλάγμασιν* (!) for *ἀλλάγμασιν*, xlix. 9 *ἐκοπίασεν* for *ἐκόπασεν*, lxxviii. 54 al. Cf. also Deut.

xxxiii. 28 ἐπὶ γῆς for πηγή, 1 Sam. ix. 24. Prov. xxxi. 21 etc., and Wellhausen, *Der Text der BB. Samuelis* (1872), p. 8, who cites a curious instance from Judg. v. 8, as well as some of a similar nature from the Peshito. Whether the same explanation can be adopted for ver. 2, ἀνηγγείλαμεν for ἀνέτειλε μέν, is doubtful. μὲν is not a word often used by LXX, and certainly does not seem required there: it seems more probable, therefore, especially as A. has a variant ἀναρρηθήσεται, that their rendering originated in some corruption or obscurity in the Hebrew text which they employed. 12. Θ. ἀπέσχετο, i. e. נמנע.

II. THARGUM OF YONATHAN.

LII. [13] Behold my servant Messiah shall prosper; he shall be
high, and increase, and be exceeding strong: [14] as the house of
Israel looked to him during many days, because their counte-
nance was darkened among the peoples, and their complexion
beyond the sons of men, [15] so will he scatter many peoples: at
him kings shall be silent, and put their hands upon their mouth,
because that which was not told them have they seen, and that
which they had not heard they have observed.

LIII. [1] Who hath believed this our glad tidings? and the
strength of the mighty arm of the Lord, upon whom as thus
hath it been revealed? [2] The righteous will grow up before
him, yea, like blooming shoots, and like a tree which sends
forth its roots to streams of water[a] will they increase—a holy
generation in the land that was in need of him: his counte-
nance no profane countenance, and the terror at him not
the terror at an ordinary man; his complexion shall be a holy
complexion, and all who see him will look wistfully upon him.
[3] Then he will become despised, and will cut off the glory of all
the kingdoms; they will be prostrate and mourning, like a man
of pains and like one destined for sicknesses; and as though the
presence of the Shekhinah had been withdrawn from us, they
will be despised, and esteemed not. [4] Then for our sins he
will pray, and our iniquities will for his sake be forgiven,
although *we* were accounted stricken, smitten from before the
Lord, and afflicted. [5] But he will build up the Holy Place, which
has been polluted for our sins, and delivered to the enemy
for our iniquities; and by his instruction peace shall be

---

[a] Cf. Ez. xxxi. 3.

increased upon us, and by devotion to his words, our sins will
be forgiven us. 6 All we like sheep had been scattered, we had
each wandered off on his own way; but it was the Lord's good
pleasure to forgive the sins of all of us for his sake. 7 He prayed,
and he was answered, and ere even he had opened his mouth
he was accepted: the mighty of the peoples he will deliver up
like a sheep to the slaughter and like a lamb dumb before her
shearers; there shall be none before him opening his mouth or
saying a word. 8 Out of chastisements and punishment he will
bring our captives near; the wondrous things done to us in
his days who shall be able to tell? for he will cause the
dominion of the Gentiles to pass away from the land of Israel,
and transfer to them the sins which my people have committed.
9 He will deliver the wicked into Gehinnom, and those that are
rich in possessions into the death of utter destruction, in order
that those who commit sin may not be established, nor speak
deceits with their mouth. 10 But it is the Lord's good pleasure
to try and to purify the remnant of his people, so as to cleanse
their souls from sin: these shall look on the kingdom of their
Messiah, their sons and their daughters shall be multiplied, they
shall prolong their days, and those who perform the Law of the
Lord shall prosper in his good pleasure. 11 From the subjection
of the nations he will deliver their souls, they shall look upon
the punishment of those that hate them, and be satisfied with
the spoil of their kings: by his wisdom he will hold the guilt-
less free from guilt, in order to bring many into subjection to
the law; and for their sins he will intercede. 12 Then will I
divide for him the spoil of many peoples, and the possessions
of strong cities shall he divide as prey, because he delivered up
his soul to death, and made the rebellious subject to the Law:
he shall intercede for many sins, and the rebellious for his sake
shall be forgiven.

III. THALMUD.

a. Thalmud of Jerusalem.

R. Yonah says, It is written, 'I will allot him a portion with the many:' this refers to R. 'Aqîbha[a], who introduced the study of the *Midrash*, the *Halakhoth*, and the *Haggadoth*[b]. Sh'qalim v. 1.

b. Thalmud of Babylon.

1. The Messiah—what is his name[c]? . . . The Rabbis say, The leprous one [; those] of the house of Rabbi[d] [say, The sick one], as it is said, 'Surely he hath borne our sicknesses,' etc. Sanhedrin fol. 98b.

---

[a] R. 'Aqîbha was one of the most celebrated Rabbis of the school of Jabneh (Jamnia), and a great agitator during the war of bar-Cokhebha (bar-Cozibâ). He is considered by the Jews to have been, like Ezra, a restorer of the law, and is even sometimes compared to Moses. See J. Derenbourg, *Essai sur l'histoire et la géographie de la Palestine*, Paris, 1867, p. 396.

[b] Some account of the meaning of these terms may be found in Smith's *Dict. of the Bible*, iii. 1640; or Neubauer, *La géographie du Talmud*, Paris, 1868, p. xiv.

[c] The other names of the Messiah mentioned in this passage are, 'Shiloh' with reference to Gen. xlix. 10 'until Shiloh come;' 'Yinnon' with reference to Ps. lxxii. 17 'His name shall endure for ever; before the sun [was created] his name was Yinnon;' 'Ḥaninah' in reference to Jer. xvi. 13 'where no Ḥaninah (favour) will be given (יחן instead of אתן of the text, which was the reading of the earliest translators) to you;' 'M'naḥem,' son of Hezekiah, in reference to Lam. i. 16 'the Comforter (M'naḥem) that should restore my soul is far from me.' See for the text of this passage, as well as for some other names of the Messiah according to a Midrash, Wünsche, *Leiden des Messias*, Leipzig, 1870, p. 62 sqq.

[d] Rabbi, 'master,' is the title of R. Yuda the Saint (about 180 A.D.), the redactor of the Mishnah.

B'rakhoth fol. 5ª. 2. Rabbâ[e] states on the authority of R. S'horah that R. Hunâ said, The Holy One bruises with chastisement every one in whom he has pleasure, as it is written, 'And the Lord was pleased to bruise him, he made him to be sick.' It might however be thought, that this was the case even with those who do not accept the chastisement willingly; the words are therefore added, 'If his soul makes a trespass-offering,' for as the 'trespass-offering' implies a knowledge of the sin, so the chastisement to come by the pleasure of God ought to be known by the person who has to receive it. When, then, he had received them so, what is his reward? 'He shall see seed, and lengthen days;' and moreover that the study of the law shall be established by his hands, as it is written, 'And the pleasure of the Lord shall prosper in his hand.'

Sotah fol. 14ª. 3. R. Shimlai[f] established the following Midrash: Why did Moses our Teacher desire to enter into the land of Israel? was it that he wanted to eat of its fruit, or to take his fill of its good things? No: Moses said, Many are the commandments enjoined upon Israel, and only in the land of Canaan can they be performed: let me, then, enter the land, in order that they may all be performed through my aid. So the Holy One said to him, Dost thou seek anything except to receive a reward? I will regard thee as though thou hadst performed them: for thus it is written, 'Therefore will I divide him a portion with the great,' etc.; 'I will divide him a portion among the great,' might bear the meaning like those who come last, not like those who come first; it is therefore added, 'With the mighty he will divide spoil,' like Abraham, Isaac, and Jacob, who were [the first and] *mighty* in the law and the commandments: 'because he poured out his soul to die,' he was ready to die, as it is said, 'But if not, blot me I pray thee,' etc. (Ex. xxxii. 32): 'he was numbered with the transgressors,' for he was numbered with

---

[e] Rabbâ was a Babylonian doctor, who lived about 260 A. D.

[f] R. Shimlai was a doctor of Palestine, who flourished about 230 A. D.

those who died in the wilderness: 'he bore the sin of many,' because he atoned for the making of the golden calf: 'he interceded for transgressors,' because he sought for mercy towards those that had transgressed in Israel that they might turn to repentance—for פגע means merely to *pray* or *intercede*, as Jer. vii. 16.

c. Midrash Rabbah.

Another explanation (of Ruth ii. 14):—He is speaking of the king Messiah: 'Come hither,' draw near to the throne; 'and eat of the bread,' that is, the bread of the kingdom; 'and dip thy morsel in the vinegar,' this refers to the chastisements, as it is said, 'But he was wounded for our transgressions, bruised for our iniquities.' Ruth iv.

I have eaten my honeycomb with my honey (Cant. v. 1): because the Israelites *poured out*[g] their soul to die in the captivity, as it is said, 'Because he poured out his soul to die.' Deut. xxiii.

d. Yalqut.

1. *Who art thou, O great mountain?* (Zech. iv. 7.) This refers to the King Messiah. And why does he call him 'the great mountain?' because he is greater than the patriarchs, as it is said, 'My servant shall be high, and lifted up, and lofty exceedingly'—he will be higher than Abraham, who says, 'I raise *high* my hands unto the Lord' (Gen. xiv. 22); lifted up above Moses, to whom it is said, '*Lift it* up into thy bosom' (Num. xi. 12); loftier than the ministering angels, of whom it is written, 'Their wheels were *lofty* and terrible' (Ez. i. 18). And out of whom does he come forth? Out of David. ii. 571.

2. *I will tell of the institution* (Ps. ii. 7). Already are the words [concerning my servant] told in the institutions of the Pentateuch, of the book of the Prophets, and of Hagiographa: in the ii. 621.

[g] There is a play here on the word יער 'honeycomb,' which, by the similarity of sound, recals the expression הערה 'pour out,' employed by Isaiah.

Pentateuch where are they told? 'Israel is my firstborn' (Ex. iv. 22); in the prophets, where? 'Behold my servant will deal prudently,' and near to it, 'My servant whom I uphold' (xlii. 1); in the Hagiographa, where? 'The Lord said to my lord,' and 'The Lord said unto me' (Ps. cx. 1, ii. 7).

ii. 620. 3. נסכתי (Ps. ii. 6). According to another view this means, 'I have *woven* him[h],' cf. מסכת Jud. xvi. 14: i. e. I have drawn him out of the chastisements. R. Hunâ, on the authority of R. Aḥâ, says, The chastisements are divided into three parts: one for David and the fathers, one for our own generation, and one for the King Messiah; and this is that which is written, 'He was wounded for our transgressions,' etc.

ii 338. 4. Another view[i]. 'Therefore I will divide him a portion with the many,'—Moses will come at the head of every assembly whatever, even that of the masters of the Thalmud, and receive with each of them his reward, as it is written, 'And he came at the heads of the people' (Deut. xxxiii. 21).

According to Raymund Martini.

e. Siphré[j].

R. Yosé the Galilaean said, Come forth and learn the righteousness of the King Messiah and the reward of the just from the first man who received but one commandment, a prohibition, and transgressed it: consider how many deaths were inflicted upon himself, upon his own generations, and upon those that followed them, till the end of all generations. Which attribute is the greater, the attribute of goodness, or the attribute of vengeance? He answered, The attribute of goodness is

---

[h] 'The two verbs משך and נסך are here interchanged,' Wünsche, p. 73. For the rendering 'woven,' cf. Aquila ἐδιασάμην, Jerome *orditus sum*: the verb נסך is treated as though it were connected with סכך.

[i] This passage is preceded by the extract from the Thalmud of Babylon, *b*. 3.

[j] Pugio Fidei, p. 674.

the greater, and the attribute of vengeance is the less; how much more, then, will the King Messiah, who endures affliction and pains for the transgressors (as it is written, 'He was wounded,' etc.) justify all generations! and this is what is meant when it is said, 'And the Lord made the iniquity of us all meet upon him[k].'

f. Thanḥuma[l].

R. Naḥman says, The word 'man' in the passage, Every man a head of the house of his fathers (Num. i. 4), refers to the Messiah the son of David, as it is written, 'Behold the *man* whose name is Ẓemaḥ' (the branch); where Yonathan interprets, Behold the *man* Messiah (Zech. vi. 12); and so it is said, 'A *man* of pains' and known to sickness. Numb. i. 4

According to Hulsius[m].

g. P'siqtha.

The Holy One brought forth the soul of the Messiah, and said to him, Art thou willing to be created and to redeem my sons after 6000 years? He replied, I am. God replied, If so, thou must take upon thyself chastisements in order to wipe away their iniquity, as it is written, 'Surely our sicknesses he hath carried.' The Messiah answered, I will take them upon me gladly.

---

[k] The argument is this: If Adam's guilt entailed such consequences upon all his descendants, and the attribute of vengeance or justice is still not so potent as that of mercy, how much more will the sufferings of the Messiah redound to the advantage of all mankind! Compare the similar reasoning of St. Paul, Rom. v. 15–19, and Delitzsch's note, in his interesting edition of this Epistle in Hebrew (Leipzig, 1870).

[l] Pugio Fidei, p. 664.

[m] Theologia Judaica, p. 328.

IV. ZOHAR.

Section וישב.

He began and said, *Behold my servant*, etc. Happy is the portion of the just, to whom the Holy One reveals the paths of the law for them to walk in! Come, consider the exalted mystery of this verse, as it has been explained before: when the Holy One created the world, he made for it the moon, and caused its light to be small, since it had none of its own at all; it received therefore its light from the sun and through the power of the upper luminaries. During the time that the sanctuary was standing, Israel, the priests, the Levites, and the people never ceased offering gifts and burnt-sacrifices and other rites, tying knots[a], continuing blessings, and keeping up perpetual light. But after the sanctuary was desolated, the light became dark and the moon was no longer illumined by the sun (for the sun was withdrawn and shone no more); nor was there any day over which curses and afflictions and pains, according to the saying of the Rabbis, did not hold sway. Of that time, however, when the day shall arrive for the moon to shine, the passage speaks, which is a mystery of faith, 'Behold my servant shall deal prudently'—my servant, viz. who suddenly wakes and starts up as one who smells a (sweet) savour and rouses himself up to contemplate it. *He will be high*, above the upper light of (all) the luminaries, as it is written, 'He will be *high* that he may have mercy on you' (Is. xxx. 18): *he will be lifted*

[a] This refers to the knots of the phylacteries; see Thalmud of Babylon, B'rakhoth, fol. 6[a].

up above Abraham; *lofty* above Isaac; *exceedingly* above Jacob. Although this passage has been explained [otherwise], still in the mystery of wisdom all is one. At that time the Holy One will suddenly wake up to give her proper light to the moon, as it is written, 'The light of the moon shall be as the light of the sun' (Is. xxx. 26). And because a spirit from on high will be added to it, therefore all the dead who are in the dust will then awake. This is the mystery of 'my servant,' in whose hands are the keys of his lord, as were Abraham's in those of Eliezer (Gen. xxiv. 2), who is called his servant; such also will be the case with the moon, which, as is said elsewhere, is the Metatron [b], the servant sent forth of its lord. . . . These bodies (are those which), as we have said, are appointed to rise first: after they have risen, all the rest in the other countries will rise, and will live in a perfect existence, and be renewed at the renovation of the moon; the world, too, will be made new as at the beginning. It is of that time that the words are written, 'The Lord will rejoice in his works' (Ps. civ. 31): and therefore also it is said here, 'My servant will deal prudently,' in restoring, namely, the soul of each one to its place. He will be high and lifted up and lofty exceedingly, above all the topmost ranks, as we have explained it above.—*As many were astonished*, etc. Come, consider what has been said: when the sanctuary was laid desolate and the Shekhinah carried captive into strange

---

[b] On the 'Metatron' the reader is referred to the Lexica of Buxtorf or Levy, s.v. In one of the two Jerusalem Thargums on Gen. v. 24 it is said that Enoch 'ascended up into heaven by the word of the Lord, and his name was called *Metatron*, the great scribe;' and in the other, Deut. xxxiv. 6, he is said to have been one of the four 'princes of wisdom' who helped to bury Moses. In Rabbinical writings he is spoken of as שר הפנים, the angel who, while others received their commands 'without the veil,' had access to the immediate presence of God, where it was his duty to sit and write down—or cancel—the merits of the people of Israel. Sometimes the word is used more generally of a messenger or guide: and in fact such seems to be the case here.

lands amongst the heathen, what do we find written? 'Behold their strong men cry in the street, the messengers of peace weep bitterly' (Is. xxxiii. 7); all weep for this, and join in lamentation and mourning for the Shekhinah carried into captivity. And as the moon was changed from what she had been, so also her master no longer gave his light, but was changed likewise, as it is written, 'The sun was dark in his going forth' (Is. xiii. 10): and it is to this that the words refer, 'So marred was his countenance beyond man.' According, however, to another explanation, the 'countenance' is that of the servant (the moon), whose form and features were changed from what they once were. And according to a third, it is the heavens that are meant, which after the sanctuary had been laid waste, no longer preserved their original form: and so it is written (Is. l. 3), 'I will clothe the heavens with blackness, and will make sackcloth their covering.'

Section ויקהל.

Happy is the portion of the just in this world and in that which is to come! The souls which are in the garden of Eden below go to and fro every new moon and sabbath, in order to ascend to the place that is called the Walls of Jerusalem. . . . . After that they journey on and contemplate all those that are possessed of pains and sicknesses and those that are martyrs for the unity of their Lord, and then return and announce it to the Messiah. And as they tell him of the misery of Israel in their captivity, and of those wicked ones among them who are not attentive to know their Lord, he lifts up his voice and weeps for their wickedness: and so it is written, 'He was wounded for our transgressions,' etc. Then those souls return and abide in their own place. There is in the garden of Eden a palace called the Palace of the sons of sickness: this palace the Messiah then enters, and summons every sickness, every pain, and every chastisement of Israel; they all come and rest upon him. And were it not that he had thus lightened them off

Israel and taken them upon himself, there had been no man able to bear Israel's chastisements for transgression of the law: and this is that which is written, 'Surely our sicknesses he hath carried.'

Section כי תצא.

In this Parashah, O faithful shepherd [Moses], God speaks of thy gathering to the other world. . . . . But here there is a great mystery, in being buried, namely, in unseemly fashion, in a 'dry land where no water is' ('water' here signifying the law), without form or beauty. Whoever looks at this kind of burial [exclaims], 'We see him, but he has no form that we should desire him:' therefore this prophecy, *Behold my servant*, etc., alludes to him. . . . . Where thy bride is, there thou shalt be united with her, like a true bridegroom. Hadst thou not been buried out of the Holy Land, and far from thy bride, Israel would never have come forth from captivity; and therefore it is said, והוא מחולל—'thou wast made *profane*' [from חל] in thy burial[c] for the transgressions and iniquities of Israel.

Section פינחס.

The children of the world are members one of another. When the Holy One desires to give healing to the world, he smites one just man amongst them, and for his sake heals all the rest. Whence do we learn this? From the saying, 'He was wounded for our transgressions, bruised for our iniquities,' ובחבורתו נרפא לנו, i.e. by the letting of his blood—as when a man bleeds his arm—there was healing for us—for all the members of the body. In general a just person is only smitten in order to procure healing and atonement for a whole generation: and this is the mystery of the saying, There is a just man and it goes ill with him, [a wicked man and it goes well with him[d].]

---

[c] By being buried, namely, away from the Holy Land.

[d] Cf. Thalmud of Babylon, B'rakhoth, fol. 7[a], Wünsche, p. 101.

Section פנחס.

At the time when the Holy One desires to atone for the sins of the world, like a physician who to save the other limbs, bleeds the arm, he smites their arm and heals their whole person: as it is written, 'He was wounded for our iniquities,' etc.

Section כי תצא.

Thy bride [i. e. the law], O faithful shepherd, was given by the Holy One to Abraham . . . . and to Isaac . . . . that she might be true to thee at the time when thou comest to her at the last redemption, as it is written, 'That which was, is that which shall be' (Eccl. i. 9). Because they (Israel) produced and wrought good things for thee, thou hast borne for their sakes ever so many strokes in order that Messiah the son of Joseph might not be slain. . . . . And therefore it is written, 'He was wounded for our transgressions, and by his stripes we were healed.'

Section כי תצא.

. . . . the faithful shepherd, of whom it is said, 'And the man Moses was exceedingly afflicted' (Num. xii. 3), for he bore the weight of the sixty myriads of Israel. Of him, too, it is written, 'From the place of his habitation he looked forth' (Ps. xxxiii. 14). And also, with reference to the generation of the second captivity, 'But the Lord laid upon him the iniquity of us all.'

Section וארא.

Come, consider the congregation of Israel, how it is called a *lamb*, as it is said, 'Like a lamb that before her shearers is dumb.' Why was it dumb? Because while the other nations ruled over it, it was deprived of speech and made dumb.

V. R. SA'ADYAH GAON.

LII. [13]Behold my messenger shall have understanding, and
shall be high and exalted and lofty exceedingly. [14]And as
many will be desolated at him, so will his countenance be marred
beyond any of them, and his form beyond the sons of Adam :
[15]and so will he scatter many nations; at him kings shall shut
their mouths: for they will have seen things such as had not
been told to them, they will consider that of which they had
never heard the like.

LIII. [1]Who hath believed this our report? and upon whom
will the might of God be revealed? [2]Who before this will grow
up like a sucker, and like a solitary root out of the dry ground,
which has no form nor comeliness, and when we see it has
no looks so that we should desire it? [3]So is he despised and
cut off from men; possessed of pains and known to sickness,
and like one before whom faces are hidden; so he is despised
and we esteem him not. [4]Surely he carried our sicknesses, and
bare our pains: and we did esteem him afflicted, smitten of
God, and punished. [5]But he was wounded for our transgres-
sions, bruised for our iniquities; his destruction is our compen-
sation; and by his stripes we are healed. [6]All we like sheep
had gone astray, and every one had turned to his own way;
and God laid upon him the iniquity of us all. [7]He was
tossed to and fro, and he was punished, yet he opened not
his mouth; like a lamb which is led to the slaughter and like a
sheep which before her shearers is dumb, so he opened not
his mouth. [8]From prison and from judgment he was snatched

away, and who shall declare anything concerning his generation?—until he was cut off out of the land of life, and for
the transgression of my people the stroke was upon them. 9 And
he made his grave with the evildoers, desiring to die, and with the rich in his death, although he had done no violence,
neither was there any deceit in his mouth. 10 And God was pleased
to make him afraid and sicken him,—if his soul becomes a trespass-offering for sin, and he sees a noble seed, his time [of life] will be long, and God's pleasure shall prosper in his
hand. 11 And from the travail of his soul he shall see a reward, and shall be satisfied by it, and by his understanding shall the righteous, as also my messenger, justify many, and he will
bear their iniquities. 12 Therefore I will give him a portion with the great, and he shall divide spoil with the strong, because he laid bare his soul unto death, and [was numbered][a] with the transgressors [; and he bare the sin of many, and][a] made intercession [for the transgressors][a].

---

[a] The copyist evidently passed the words between the two فاسقين.

VI. YEPHETH BEN 'ALI.

LII. 13 The commentators differ concerning this section. The *Fayyumi*[a] lost his senses in applying it to the prophets generally, or, according to some authorities, in supposing that it referred to Jeremiah in particular. His explanation is not indeed of a kind towards which any one would feel attracted: and we shall shew the manner in which it may be refuted: for this man attempted the task of interpreting the book of the prophets upon a plan of evolving their meaning out of his own head, and consequently failed to arrive at any consistent view. Some of the learned Qaraites apply the prophecy to the pious[b] of their own sect, resting their view upon two arguments: In the first place, because their history answers to the descriptions given in this section; and secondly, because of the word למו, which is plural. Others of them think the subject of it to be David and the Messiah, saying that all the expressions of contempt, such as 'many were desolated at thee,' refer to the seed of David who are in exile; and all the glorious things, such as 'behold my servant will be prosperous' and 'so shall he sprinkle,' refer to the Messiah. As to myself, I am inclined, with Benjamin of Nehawend, to regard it as alluding to the Messiah, and as opening with a description of his condition in exile, from the time of his birth to his accession to the

---

[a] R. Sa'adyah Gaon of Fayyum.

[b] The early Qaraites applied the term משכילים (Dan. xii. 3) to the members of their own sect, in particular, to those dwelling in Jerusalem; see Neubauer, *Aus der Petersburger Bibliothek*, p. 7.

throne: for the prophet begins by speaking of his being seated in a position of great honour, and then goes back to relate all that will happen to him during the captivity. He thus gives us to understand two things: In the first instance, that the Messiah will only reach his highest degree of honour after long and severe trials; and secondly, that these trials will be sent upon him as a kind of sign, so that, if he finds himself under the yoke of misfortunes whilst remaining pure in his actions, he may know that he is the desired one, as we shall explain in the course of the section. The expression 'my servant' is applied to the Messiah as it is applied to his ancestor in the verse, 'I have sworn to David my servant' (Ps. lxxxix. 4), as we have already explained on Is. xli. 8[c]. The prophet mentions in this verse four grades of dignity which he will rise to successively: 1. ישכיל, which describes his prosperity at the beginning of his career, when he will be victorious in war, a term used also for his forefather David (1 Sam. xviii. 14); 2. ירום, which means he will sit upon the throne of Israel at the time when our lord Elijah will anoint him,—this also is applied to David (Ps. lxxxix. 20); 3. ונשא, referring to the time when he will reign over the entire world, as it is said, 'Let him have dominion from sea to sea' (Ps. lxxii. 8); 4. ונבה מאד, which means he will reach the highest rank possible; hence the addition of the word מאד. In having the last two expressions applied to him, I mean נשא and גבה, the Messiah has the advantage over his ancestor, as we have explained upon Is. ix. 6[d].

[c] On the passage referred to the author says: 'עבדי is employed in Scripture in three senses: (1) for the king, who holds all under his sway, which is the most common signification of the term; (2) for the true worshipper of God, such as Moses (Josh. i. 2); (3) for the servant who has attained a position of such power as to have none his equal; and in this sense Nebuchadnezzar is called "my servant" (Jer. xxv. 9, xxvii. 5). The expression, as used of Israel, embraces all these meanings.'

[d] On this passage Ben 'Ali writes as follows: 'The prophet means that the dominion of the Messiah will be greater than that of any other king of Israel; for David and Solomon ruled over Israel and the kings of

[14] 'As many were desolated' forms here the protasis, of which 'so shall he sprinkle' is the apodosis. His condition is described as being such that any one seeing him would be desolated at him, on account of the sicknesses which had befallen him. רבים signifies the great men who knew him. The prophet explains to them the cause of their desolation concerning him by saying, 'His countenance was marred beyond any man,' i. e. the complexion of his face was so changed as to become like that of a corpse. He adds further, 'And his form beyond the sons of Adam,' i. e. he was so altered in form as to resemble a corpse: and, alluding to the same fact, he says, towards the end of the section, 'For he was cut off out of the land of the living.'

[15] 'So will he sprinkle' is the continuation of 'my servant will prosper,' and intended to describe the reward which he will receive in this world as a return for the many having been desolated at him. '*Blood of*' must be supplied before *nations*. 'At him the kings shall shut their mouth' means that the kings of the world will close their mouth when he lays a command or prohibition upon them. The next words admit of a threefold interpretation: 1. what has not been related in their books and what they have not heard from their instructors; 2. what was not told them by those who brought tidings concerning

---

nations which surrounded them, but the dominion of Messiah will extend over the whole world, as it is written, "Let him have dominion from sea to sea" (Ps. lxxii. 8); "Behold, I have given him for a witness, a prince, and a commander to the peoples;" and again, "Behold, thou shalt call a nation thou knowest not" (Is. lv. 4, 5): accordingly the prophet speaks here of the *increase* of his government. Moreover, although there was peace and tranquillity in the time of Solomon, yet after his death the state of affairs was disturbed and reversed; but in the time of the Messiah there will be peace over the whole world, as it is written, "Nation shall not lift up sword against nation" (Is. ii. 4). And this peace will have no end: for from the days of the Messiah to the end of all generations the whole world will obey God and his anointed, as is expressed in the words, "And of peace there shall be no end."'

him, like the saying of the Queen of Sheba, 'the half was not told to me' (1 Kings xi. 7); the phrase will then intimate that his glorious reign cannot be described; 3. (a word [כמוהו] must here be supplied), what they had never been told *the like of:* there have been indeed in Israel and in other nations kings of whose doings they have heard, but when they witness the reign of the Messiah they will know that there was never any king in the world like him.

LIII. [1]Here begin Israel's words, in justification of the language of the last verse. They ask, in their amazement, Which of the nations believed the report that was amongst us? not one of them; for they all agreed that there would be for Israel no recovery. 'Upon whom has the arm of the Lord been revealed?' i. e. through which nation has the might of God revealed itself; whom nevertheless each one of them boasts to be his master and protector?

[2]Israel turns back now to describe the manner of the Messiah's birth, comparing him to a young twig or sucker because he is one of the children of David, and to a root because he will become a root like his father David. So says Ezekiel (xvii. 22, 23), 'From the top of his suckers I will crop off a tender one . . . and it shall become a goodly cedar.' The expression 'he came up' can be explained in two ways: 1. He came up out of his place like a sucker springing out of a tree: the place intended is Jerusalem; therefore it is said 'before him,' i. e. before the Lord, the pronoun relating to the word 'Lord' in the preceding verse. Or 2. The Messiah came up out of captivity. He then adds, 'And like a root out of the dry earth,' meaning that he resembles a root emerging, sickly and weak, out of the arid soil. This comparison relates to the beginning of his career; and the same is the case with the words 'he had no form nor comeliness,' which in no way refer to the period of his sickness. In this respect he differs from his forefather, who during the time that he was king, when great multitudes gathered round him, and he was consequently well known, had both form

and comeliness. In the next words Israel describes how when they looked at him they saw in him neither majesty, nor comeliness, nor beauty, yet they desired his company, instead of fleeing from it and hiding themselves, as the words in the verse following imply that they did afterwards.

3 He was 'despised,' i. e. humble in rank on account of his poverty, 'holding aloof from men,' i. e. not mixing with them in their banquets and amusements—a natural result of exile, as it is said, 'He sitteth alone and keepeth silence' (Lam. iii. 28)—and 'a man of pains,' i. e. afflicted by them, his sufferings being distributed under two heads: 1. מכאובות, signifying external complaints, like pustules; 2. חלי, i. e. internal ones, such as a fever. 'Like one from whom there is a hiding of faces' may be explained in two ways: 1. like a man who has arrived at such a condition of affliction and mutilation that men hide their faces from him; 2. like one from whom God had withdrawn his mercy, i. e. his blows resemble those with which the wicked are afflicted. The repetition of the word נבזה can also be explained in two ways: 1. despised on account of poverty, and despised in rank; 2. despised in his own eyes, as it is said of the righteous (Ps. xv. 4), 'He is despised and contemned in his own eyes;' and despised in the eyes of others, as they say, 'And we esteemed him not,' i. e. we did not regard him as the expected one.

4 By the words 'surely he hath carried our sicknesses,' they mean that the pains and sickness which he fell into were merited by them, but that he bore them instead: the next words 'yet we did esteem him,' etc., intimate that they thought him afflicted by God for his own sins, as they distinctly say, 'smitten of God and afflicted.' And here I think it necessary to pause for a few moments, in order to explain why God caused these sicknesses to attach themselves to the Messiah for the sake of Israel. We say that God makes known to the people of their own time the excellence of the prophets who intercede for a period of adversity in two ways: 1. whilst Israel's empire lasted, it was

shewn in prayer and intercession, as in the cases of Moses, Aaron, Samuel, David, Elijah, and Elisha, whose prayers for the nation were accepted by God, as it is said, 'They called upon the Lord and HE answered them' (Ps. xcix. 6); 2. in a time of captivity and extreme wickedness, though their intercession left no such traces as these, yet the burden of the nation's sins was lightened; such was the case with Ezekiel when God obliged him (iv. 4) to sleep 390 days upon his left side and 40 upon the right one; he carried on the first occasion the iniquity of Israel, and on the second the weight of that of Judah: it is plain from this how great their iniquity must have been, as in fact it is said, 'The iniquity of the house of Israel and Judah is exceeding great' (Ezek. ix. 9); 'And great is the iniquity of the daughter of my people' (Lam. iv. 6); and in other passages similarly. The nation deserved from God greater punishment than that which actually came upon them, but not being strong enough to bear it (as Amos says, vii. 2, 'O Lord, forgive, I beseech thee; how can Jacob endure, for he is small?') the prophet had to alleviate it. Inasmuch now as at the end of the captivity there will be no prophet to intercede at the time of distress, the time of the Lord's anger and of his fury, God appoints his servant to carry their sins, and by doing so lighten their punishment in order that Israel might not be completely exterminated. Thus from the words 'he was wounded for our transgressions,' we learn two things: 1. that Israel had committed many sins and transgressions, for which they deserved the indignation of God; 2. that by the Messiah bearing them they would be delivered from the wrath which rested upon them, and be enabled to endure it, as it is said, 'And by associating with him we are healed.' God indeed will afflict the Messiah with longer and severer sicknesses than Ezekiel; but this is owing to the period in which he lives and to its requirements, and in giving him the rank of a prophet, he will bring his excellence to light. We have no doubt then that Israel's reward is with God for this world as well as for the next one, as we shall explain on ver. 12. הוא must be explained by *which*, i. e. the sicknesses which he bore were ours, alluding to the words 'known of sickness' in the last verse: the word חלי, which is nearer, is here mentioned first, being followed by מכאובות: he then says with reference to both at once, 'stricken' and 'smitten,' i. e. stricken with sickness and smitten with pains. The expression 'smitten of God' signifies that these sicknesses attacked him by the will of God; they did not arise from natural causes (like humours of the body), or belong to the class of diseases occasioned by change of air: and the word 'afflicted' corresponds to 'despised' in ver. 3, the meaning being that he was afflicted with poverty.

[5] By פשע are denoted great sins, such as sorcery, incest, divination, and similar abominations; by עון [lighter] sins, like theft, robbery, etc. מוסר includes those forms of punishment described in the book of the covenant by the word יסר, as 'I will chastise you' (Lev. xxvi. 28); 'I will chastise thee in measure' (Jer. xxx. 11). I have translated שלומנו 'health,' as Ps. xxxviii. 4, 'neither is there any health in my bones;' for although the word literally means *peace*, it here signifies *health.* Israel says: This chastisement which the Lord has put upon us, and from which he will heal us, is owing to him (עליו). ובחבורתו means that the Messiah, by participating with them in these pains and sicknesses, will be the cause of their being healed.

[6] This verse exhibits Israel's wickedness in not awaking to repentance after God had punished them with his plagues. They are compared in this respect to sheep without a shepherd wandering from the way, and torn by wild beasts, going astray among the mountains, without any to lead them back, as it is said, 'My sheep wander through all the mountains' (Ezek. xxxiv. 6). In like manner Israel in captivity has no one to call him, and lead him back to the right way, and if a guide (משכיל) rises up to them, desiring to bring them back to it, they hasten to kill him, and so cause their captivity to be prolonged. By the words 'we have turned every one to his own way,' they

mean that each is occupied with the necessities of life and with establishing his fortune. And whilst God looks upon their work, and they do not think of their sicknesses, their guilt is thrown upon this guide, as it is said, 'And the Lord laid on him the iniquity of us all.' The prophet does not by עון mean *iniquity*, but *punishment* for iniquity, as in the passage, 'Be sure your sin will find you out' (Num. xxxii. 23). Here the words of Israel end, and the rest of the section contains, as the context shews, the speech of God himself.

7, 8 In these two verses seven things are enumerated which God brought upon the Messiah besides the pains and sicknesses mentioned before: 1. נגש, i. e. the exaction of tribute and fines which were laid upon Israel. 2. נענה, i. e. degradation and defamation—this word follows accordingly נגש. 3. 'He was led like a sheep to the slaughter,' alluding to the times when his life was endangered; the comparison to a sheep is true in three respects: he does not know that they sought to slay him, or that he was being led to the slaughter; he has nobody to assist him by taking up his cause; and he has no power to deliver himself. 4. 'And like a lamb which before her shearers is dumb,' referring to the times both of taxation and of slaughter, when all customary usages are in abeyance; the repetition of the phrase 'yet he opened not his mouth' refers to the double period, both while taxes are exacted from him and he suffers defamation, and also when he is dragged away to violence and execution without any possibility of conciliation. 5, 6. 'From prison and from judgment,' implying that he will be imprisoned, condemned by the judges, and loaded with infamy, as it is said, 'For I have heard the slander of many' (Ps. xxxi. 14). There are thus three couplets, each consisting of two parallel expressions: 1. נגש ונענה; 2. כשה וכרחל; 3. מעצר וממשפט. לקח means that he is liberated from prison by the mercy of God. The words 'and who shall declare his generation' mean, Who can describe the multitude of misfortunes which will befal the Messiah and Israel in this generation? 7. 'He was cut off out of the land of life,' which may be explained to signify either that he despaired of himself on account of the number of these misfortunes, or that he was cut off from the land of Israel, which is the 'land of life' for this nation. And the concluding words of the verse are God's confirmation of what Israel had said, 'he was wounded for our transgressions:' all these seven troubles which came upon him were 'because of the transgression of my people, *for whom* this *stroke was*,' i. e. who deserved it; for למו refers here, as is clear from the context, to Israel.

9 'And he made his grave with the wicked.' This means that he sometimes despaired so much of his life as either to dig for himself a grave amongst the wicked (i. e. the wicked Israelites), or at least desire to be buried amongst them. The general sense is that he resigned himself to die in exile; for those who die at the time of deliverance will not be buried with the wicked, since the latter are to be slain during a period of misfortune, as it is written, 'All the sinners of my people shall die by the sword' (Amos ix. 10). By the 'rich' are meant the powerful men among the Gentiles who are rich while Israel in exile is spoken of as 'poor and needy:' at that time some of them will perish, and the prophet here declares how the Messiah will resign himself to die, and be buried in their tomb. The addition 'because he did no violence' is intended to mark the difference between the Messiah and those wicked Israelites who had perished after perpetrating violence and deceit: he means to say that though he made his grave with them he had still never participated in their actions.

10 It was said above, 'The Lord laid upon him the iniquity of us all,' and the prophet repeats the same thought here, saying that God was pleased to bruise and sicken him, though not in consequence of sin. By the word 'bruise' he points back to the language of Israel in ver. 5, 'he was bruised for our iniquities,' and 'made sick' (החלי) is parallel to 'wounded' (מחלל). The prophet next says, 'When his soul makes a trespass-offering,' indicating thereby that his soul was compelled to take Israel's

guilt upon itself, as it is said below, 'And he bare the sin of many' (ver. 12). Another commentator however understands the phrase as meaning that 'his soul gave itself in place of a trespass-offering,' i. e. he gave himself up freely to be slain. But for myself I prefer the former explanation, which also agrees better with the sense and the spirit of the language. Here the narrative of the state of the Messiah ends, and the account of the rewards given to him begins. In the first place, *he will see seed*[e], . . . and *lengthen days*. The words 'and the pleasure of the Lord will prosper in his hands' embrace three facts: 1. The destruction of the powerful, as it is said, 'He will do his *pleasure* upon Babylon and his arm upon the Chaldeans' (xlviii. 14). 2. Israel's deliverance from exile, and the glorifying of the law and God's name, as we have explained on Is. xlii. 21, 'The Lord is well *pleased* to magnify the Law and make it glorious.' 3. The restoration of Jerusalem and the rebuilding of the temple, as will be explained[f] on the passage, 'For the Lord hath *pleasure* in thee' (Is. lxii. 4). All these three facts will be accomplished by him, in accordance with the promise, 'shall prosper in his hand.'

11 This verse is the complement of the preceding one: there it is said, 'Because he had done no violence;' and here he adds, 'By his knowledge shall my righteous servant make many righteous,' indicating these three things: 1. That he will advance in knowledge till he arrives at truth itself: accordingly the prophet says knowledge, not understanding or wisdom, because it is by knowledge that absolute truth is grasped. 2. That he is a righteous servant, i. e. knowledge and practice in his case coincide, instead of disagreeing as in the case of others (Ps. l. 15). 3. That he will lead others to repent, and make them

---

[e] Marg. note in MS.: 'It seems to me that a word should here follow which has been omitted by the scribe.'

[f] The following is the note referred to: 'חפצי בה means "I have pleasure in her to-day, and do not hate her as before, I therefore cause my glory to return to her;" and this is the meaning of "the Lord hath pleasure in thee."'

righteous. When these three high prerogatives are united in any single man, his position is already sufficiently exalted: how much more so, then, when, in addition, he 'bears the iniquities' of others! The word *many* refers here to the multitude of men who will be present before him. From this use of the word you may learn that the expression 'holding aloof from men' is not to be understood in an absolute sense: the prophet only intends to convey by it the meaning I have assigned to it above: because if he had never associated with any one at all, how could he have been said to 'make many righteous?'

12 The prophet had said in the preceding verse, 'From the travail of his soul he shall see and be satisfied:' and here he proceeds to explain its meaning. In the words 'I will divide him a portion with the great' he points to the portion of land which will fall to the Messiah amongst the tribes, as it is said, 'And for the prince shall there be a portion on one side and on the other of the holy oblation' (Ezek. xlv. 7). 'And with the mighty he shall divide the spoil' refers perhaps to the spoil of Gog, which he will take in company with the Israelites, who are here termed the 'mighty,' because at that time they will be heroes and strong men, as it is said, 'And they shall be like strong men, trampling down their enemies' (Zech. x. 5); and 'When I have made thee as the sword of a hero' (ibid. ix. 13). 'Because he laid bare his soul to die' is analogous to 'he was led like a sheep to the slaughter.' In saying, 'And he was numbered with the transgressors' he means that at the time when God will strike the transgressors of Israel with calamities, the Messiah will be numbered amongst them: this answers to the words in ver. 7, 'he was oppressed and he was afflicted:' in the same way, 'he bare the sin of many' corresponds to 'when his soul makes a trespass-offering.' And the last words 'make intercession for the transgressors' mean that being associated with them in the misery arising from the exaction of tribute and other similar causes, he will pray for their deliverance as well as his own. Observe, that in this section the

chronological order is sometimes reversed: thus, 'Behold my servant will prosper' refers to the latter part of his career, whilst all that follows, liii. 2, 'And he came up before him,' etc., down to 'he shall see seed' (ver. 10), describes his condition during exile. I must here give a compendious account of the whole of the Messiah's career; it is as follows:—His first advent will be from the north, as we have explained upon xli. 25[g], 'I have raised one up from the north and he came;' then with his arrival in the land of Israel the period of affliction and violence will cease from Jacob, and at the same time all the things mentioned in the present section will happen to him. Every good quality will be united in him, but in spite of all this the people will not recognise in him the will of God. For his sake, however, God will deliver Israel from all his afflictions: and when the season of redemption comes, our lord Elijah will appear to the people and anoint him, and from that moment he will begin to be prosperous, as it is said, 'Behold my servant shall prosper.' His forces will then spread in every direction and be victorious, as we have explained on lii. 15; and then at last Israel will dwell in safety. When news of this reaches Gog, they will rush forth and 'gather themselves together against the Lord and against his Anointed;' but when he prays to God in

---

[g] The note is as follows: 'From the prophet's saying, firstly, "from the north," and then "from the sunrising," we learn two things: 1. that we must not imagine the person spoken of in ver. 2 as raised up from the east to be different from the one mentioned here as raised up from the north; 2. that the conqueror who will arrive from the east is identical with the one who is to arrive from the north. The apparent diversity may be explained in two ways: Either his origin will be from the east, and he is then brought up in the north, whence his actual arrival will take place, or *vice versa;* or else we must suppose that the north and east are mentioned together for the purpose of shewing that the point from which he will appear is a distant corner formed by the junction of these two quarters. Another commentator, however, gives it as his opinion that the Messiah will come from the east, but that the prophet speaks of the north because this is a name of Babylon, as it is said (Jer. i. 14), "Out of the north the evil will break forth."'

the midst of his people, God will come to him with deliverance, as his forefather prophesied: 'The Lord answer thee in the day of trouble,' etc., with the rest of the psalm (Ps. xx). And then he will be 'high and exalted and lofty exceedingly;' and afterwards the promise announced by God will be fulfilled, 'Therefore I will divide him a portion with the great;' and last of all he shall 'see seed and lengthen days.' Such is the narrative of his history arranged in due order. And notice how to each of his sufferings and actions a reward or counterpart is assigned, except to the one 'my servant will be prosperous.' Thus, to 'as many have been desolated at thee,' the counterpart announced is, 'so he will sprinkle many nations;' to 'if his soul makes a trespass-offering,' 'he will see seed and lengthen days;' to 'by his knowledge my righteous servant shall make many righteous,' 'I will divide him a portion with the many.' Thus every detail of his history is provided with its counterpart: but to exhibit this fully would occupy us too long. Many of the parallels have been already mentioned by Benjamin of Nehawend in the preface to his commentary on the Canticle[h]. We shall only add that the return to the idea of his death, expressed in the words 'because he laid bare his soul to die,' has two objects: 1. to sum up the scope and object of the whole section; 2. to introduce the final addition 'and made intercession for the transgressors.' Space does not permit us to pursue the explanation of this section in greater detail, as the reader will already have been wearied by its length; we have therefore adhered to the same compendious form adopted in our commentary elsewhere.

---

[h] On Benjamin of Nehawend, see Pinsker, *Lickute Kadmoniot*, i. p. 44; Neubauer, *Aus der Petersb. Bibl.* p. 6; or Grätz, *Geschichte*, vol. v. Only a few fragments, preserved as extracts, have come down to us.

VII. MYSTERIES OF R. SHIM'ON BEN YOHAI[a].

And Armilaus[b] will join battle with Messiah, the son of Ephraim[c], in the East gate...; and Messiah, the son of Ephraim, will die there, and Israel will mourn for him. And afterwards the Holy One will reveal to them Messiah, the son of David, whom Israel will desire to stone, saying, Thou speakest falsely; already is the Messiah slain, and there is none other Messiah to stand up (after him): and so they will despise him, as it is written, 'Despised and forlorn of men;' but he will turn and hide himself from them, according to the words, 'Like one hiding his face from us.'

---

[a] Jellinek, *Beth ham-Midrash* (1855), part iii. p. 80.

[b] Armilaus (perhaps *Romulus*, or the barbarous Greek ἐρημέλαος) represents in Aggadic tradition the great enemy of the Messiah, and according to a late Midrash is identical with Antichrist. See Hamburger, *Real-Encyclop. fur Bibel und Talmud* (1874), ii. p. 73.

[c] On the 'Double Messiah,' see Wünsche, pp. 109 ff., who refers to the exhaustive treatise of J. M. Glaesener, *Commentatio de gemino Judaeorum Messia* (Hildesiae et Lipsiae, 1737). Messiah ben Ephraim (or ben Yoseph) appears in the later Jewish writings as the forerunner of Messiah ben David, who will begin the work of Israel's deliverance and restoration, but before completing it will be slain before the walls of Jerusalem by the formidable hosts (sometimes spoken of as Gog and Magog) assembled against him under Armilaus. Thereupon, the Israelites (as the text says) will *mourn for him* (Zech. xii. 10); but Messiah, the son of David, will continue the struggle, destroy the 'wicked' Armilaus with the breath of his nostrils (Is. xi. 4), and lead Israel victoriously into Jerusalem. The idea of the second Messiah was probably suggested by the language of Zech. xii. 10.

VIII. B'RESHITH RABBAH OF R. MOSHEH HAD-DARSHAN.

According to Raymundus Martini.

And Jacob went forth from Beersheba. This is that which is written, 'I will lift mine eyes unto the hills: O whence cometh my help' (Ps. cxxi. 1)? and, 'Who art thou, O great mountain' (Zech. iv. 7)? The great mountain means the Messiah, and why does he speak of him thus? Because he is greater than the patriarchs, as it is said, 'Behold my servant shall prosper [a].' Gen. xxviii. 10.

I have learnt it from the words of R. Mosheh had-Darshan: The redeemer whom I shall raise up from among you will have no father, as it is written, 'Behold the man whose name is Ẓemaḥ [branch], and he shall branch up out of his place' (Ẓech. vi. 12); and so Isaiah says, 'And he came up like a sucker,' etc. [b] Gen. xxxv. 8

Says R. B'rekhyah, The Holy One said to Israel, You have spoken before me, saying, We are orphans and have no father (Lam. v. 3): the redeemer whom I shall raise up out of your midst will have no father also, as it is said, 'Behold the man whose name is the Branch, and he shall branch up out of his place' (Zech. vi. 12); and similarly by Isaiah, 'And he came up as a sucker before him [c].' Gen. xxxvii. 22.

In the beginning God created the heavens and the earth. This Gen. i. 1.

---

[a] Pugio Fidei, p. 601. [b] Ibid. p. 125. [c] Ibid. p. 594.

is that which is written, 'There is light sown for the righteous' (Ps. xcvii. 11). R. Abba says, 'And with him dwelleth light' (Dan. ii. 22): this is the light of the King Messiah; and so it is said, 'For with thee is the fountain of life, in thy light do we see light' (Ps. xxxvi. 10)—that is, the light of the Messiah. These passages teach how the Holy One watched the Messiah and his generation, and kept them hidden underneath the throne of his glory. Satan said, Lord of the world, this light hidden beneath the throne of thy glory—to whom does it belong? The Holy One answered, To the Messiah and to his generation. Satan said, Lord of the world, suffer me, and I will be an adversary unto the Messiah and his generation. The Holy One said, Thou canst not prevail against him. Satan answered, Lord of the world, suffer me, and I will prevail. The Holy One said, If this is thy intention, I will destroy Satan out of the world, but not a single soul belonging to that generation will I destroy. Forthwith the Holy One began to make a covenant with the Messiah: O Messiah, my righteousness, said he, the iniquities of those who are hidden beside thee will cause thee to enter into a hard yoke: thine eyes shall see no light, and thine ears shall hear great reproaches from the nations of the world; thy nostrils shall smell ill savours, thy mouth taste bitterness, and thy tongue cleave to thy gums; thy skin shall hang upon thy bones, and thy body grow weak in grief and sighing. Art thou willing to accept this? if so, it shall be well; but if not, behold, I drive them[d] from me for ever. Said the Messiah, Lord of the world, I accept it joyfully, and will endure these chastisements, upon condition that thou givest life again to those who die in my days, and to those who died from the time of the first man until now; and that thou savest in my days not these only, but those also whom wolves and lions have devoured, and who have been swallowed up in waters and rivers; and not only these, but such also as were born out of due time;

[d] I. e. the souls hidden under the throne.

nor again these only, but those also whom thou thoughtest to create but who were not created. The Holy One replied, I will do so: and forthwith the Messiah accepted the chastisements of love, as it is written, 'He was oppressed, and he was afflicted[e].'

And Jacob brought her into the tent of Sarah his mother Gen. xxiv. 67.
(Gen. xxiv. 67). This is the King Messiah, who belonged to the generation of the wicked, but rejected them, and chose the Holy One and his holy name to serve him with all his heart, and applied himself to seek for mercy for Israel, and to fast and humble himself on their behalf, as it is said, 'He was wounded for our transgressions,' etc. And when Israel is sinful, the Messiah seeks for mercy upon them, as it is written, 'By his stripes we were healed,' and, 'He carried the sin of many, and made intercession for the transgressors[f].'

---

[e] Pugio Fidei, p. 333 (comp. Yalqut on Isaiah lx. § 359).

[f] Ibid. pp. 430, 671.

IX. LEQAḤ TOBH.

'Let water stream from his buckets[a]' (Num. xxiv. 7)—from the poor who are in Israel: hence they say, 'Be careful with the children of the people of the land [i. e. the poor], because from them doth the law go forth[b].' 'And let his seed be on many waters:' the kingdom of Israel is to be above all the kingdoms of the earth. 'May his king be high above (or, from) Agag:' from the days of Agag, king of Amalek, the kingdom of Israel took its rise. 'And let his kingdom be exalted,' in the days of the Messiah, of whom it is said, 'Behold my servant shall prosper; he will be high and *exalted*, and lofty exceedingly.'

---

[a] There is a play here upon the word מדליו, which is interpreted as though it were pointed מִדַּלָיו.

[b] Thalmud of Babylon, *Nedarim* 81[a].

X. R. SH'LOMOH YIZḤAQI (RASHI).

LII. [13] *Behold* in the latter days *my servant* Jacob, i.e. the righteous who are in him, *will prosper:* [14] *as many* peoples *were amazed* at you when they saw your depression, and said one to another, See how their form is dark and worn beyond that of other men, *so* marred, viz. as we see with our own eyes, [15] *so* now will his hand also be mighty, and Israel shall 'cast down the horns of the nations which have scattered them' (Zech. ii. 4), and *kings* shall *close their mouths* in amazement, for glory *which had not been told them* concerning any man will *they have seen in him and observed.*

LIII. [1] Had we, they will say to each other, had we heard from others what now we are beholding, *who would* ever *have believed it? upon whom has the arm of the Lord* ever *been revealed* as now in splendour and greatness? [2] *Before* such greatness came upon it, this people was in deep depression, and sprang up out of itself like one of the suckers of a tree, or like a root out of the dry earth: from the first it had no form and no comeliness, *and* when *we saw it* without any comeliness *how could we desire it!* (נחמדהו as an exclamation.) [3] *Most despised and forlornest of men.* This prophet speaks constantly of the whole people as one man, as xliv. 1, 2, and above lii. 13 (where ישכיל means *to prosper*, as 1 Sam. xviii. 14). *And* as a result of their shame and depression they were *as* men *hiding* their *faces from us*—like a person stricken [with leprosy], who is afraid to look up, they had their faces bound up that we might not see them: [4] *but*—such is always the signification of אכן—*but* now we perceive that this was not merely a consequence of their own depression: Israel suffered in order that by his sufferings atonement might be made for all other nations: the sickness which ought to have fallen upon us was carried by him. *We* indeed *thought* that he had been hated of God: but it was not so; he was wounded for our transgressions, and bruised for our iniquities; [5]the *chastisement of the peace* that was for us fell *upon him;* he was chastised in order that the whole world might have peace. [6]*All we like sheep have gone astray:* it is now revealed how all the Gentiles have erred. *Yet the Lord* let himself be entreated by him (*asprier*, in French), and propitiated for the iniquity of us all, in that he refrained from destroying his world. [7]*He was oppressed* under oppressors and persecutors, *and answered*, viz. with words of treachery (*surparler*, in French): he endured, *but was silent*, like a sheep led to the slaughter which opens not its mouth, and like a lamb which before her shearers is dumb. The words ולא יפתח פיו belong to the 'sheep.' [8]The prophet here publishes the glad tidings of Israel's release, representing the Gentiles as announcing it in the latter days when they see him *taken from* the *confinement* in which he had been kept by their hands, and *from* the *judgment* or sentence which he had hitherto borne. *His generation*, i. e. the years of weariness and toil which had passed over him, *who could declare? for* from the first he had been *cut off* and exiled *from the land of the living*, i. e. the land of Israel; because *for the transgression of* his *people* the *stroke* of exile had fallen *upon* the just who were among *them*. [9]*He gave* himself over to whatever burial the wicked Gentiles might decree: for the Gentiles used to condemn the Israelites to be murdered and then buried like asses in the bellies of dogs. He agreed, then, to be buried according to the judgment of (את) the wicked, refusing to deny the living God; and according to the judgment of (את) the ruler he gave himself up to any form of death which had been decreed upon him, *because* he would not deny God by perpetrating violence and doing evil, like all the nations amongst whom he was a sojourner: *neither was there any deceit in his mouth*, sc. in consenting to the worship of idols as though they had been God. [10] *But* the Holy One *was pleased to bruise him*, and to lead him back into prosperity: so for this cause he *brought* him *into sickness*. He then says, I will see *whether his soul* is so consecrated and devoted to my holiness as to *return itself* as *a trespass-offering* for all his rebelliousness: if so, I will then pay him his reward, and he shall *see seed*, etc. אשם, as in the history of the Philistines (1 Sam. vi. 3), is the fine or satisfaction which a man gives to one against whom he has committed some offence (in Fr. *amende*). [11] *Of the labour of his own soul* [i. e. of his own work] he ate and was satisfied: he did not plunder or rob other people: *by his knowledge my servant* ever meted out faithful judgment to all that came to be tried before him, and, as happens with the righteous always (as it is said Num. xviii. 1), *bare their iniquities*. [12] *Therefore*, i. e. because he did this, I will divide him an inheritance and a lot *among the great*, sc. with the early patriarchs, *because he poured out* (הערה as Gen. xxiv. 20) *his soul to die, and was numbered with the transgressors*, i. e. endured punishment as though he had been a sinner or transgressor himself, *and* for the sake of others *bore the sin of many*. *And* in virtue of his sufferings—because through him the world received prosperity—he *interceded for the transgressors*.

According to Raymundus Martini.

'Behold my servant shall prosper.' Our Rabbis apply this to the Messiah: Behold, they say, the Messiah was stricken, as it is written, 'He carried our sicknesses and bare our pains,' etc.; and he stood at the gate of Rome amongst those afflicted with sicknesses, as is said in the treatise Sanhedrin, in the section *Ḥeleq*.—'He will be high, and lifted up, and lofty exceedingly.' I have heard that there is a Midrash Aggadah, which expounds this verse as follows: The Holy One will make the Messiah higher[a] than Abraham, of whom it is written, 'I raise *high* my hand to the Lord' (Gen. xiv. 22); lifted up above Moses, of whom it is said, 'As a nurse *lifts up* and carries the young one' (Num. xi. 12); and lofty exceedingly above the angels, of whom it is said, 'Their wheels were *lofty*' (Ezek. i. 18).

---

[a] ירום being used transitively.

XI. R. YOSEPH QARA.

LII. [13] My servant Israel will be high and lifted up: according to the Midrash of our Rabbis, he will be higher than Abraham, of whom it is written, 'I raise *high* my hand to the Lord' (Gen. xiv. 22); lifted up above Moses, of whom it is said, 'As a nurse *lifts up* and carries the young one' (Num. xi. 12); and lofty exceedingly above the angels, of whom it is said, 'Their wheels were *lofty*' (Ezek. i. 18). [14] *So marred was the countenance* of this people: how is it possible that it should be so marred in the manner that we actually see? [15] *So*, viz. according to the measure of their amazement, Israel *will expel* and drive away *many nations. At him kings will shut their mouth*, i. e. will repress their words (Job iv. 2); cf. the phrase (Job xxix. 9) 'to lay the hand upon the mouth.' *For what had not been told them have they seen.* Will they[a] not say that the consolations which the nations then see fulfilled in Israel had never been told them: and that they are discerning in them good things which the ear hath never heard?

LIII. [1] In time past, when Israel were amongst us in depression, *who* ever *believed* that they would come to such greatness? such will be the language of the nations as they see Israel in prosperity. *And* who ever believed that *the arm of the Lord* would be revealed to a people despised as they were? [2] This people that was once despised and 'spoiled' (Is. xlii. 22) has now sprung up like a young twig whose suckers are planted to-day, and to-morrow it springs up and becomes a great tree, or like a root which is put into the earth, and afterwards it lifts

---

[a] Reading יאמרו, which seems required by the sense.

up its branches and produces fruit and becomes a noble cedar: in the same way Israel sprang up *out of the dry earth* of his captivity. *And we gaze upon him;* but the countenance which we see now is *not* like *the countenance* which he had formerly. [3]*He was most despised and forlornest of men;* for you can find no people in the world touched by pains and sickness such as Israel's. Thus in time past, *while* their Creator *hid his face from them, he was despised and we esteemed him not;* [4]*but* now we see that they had served the faithful God, and kept the law of Moses, and observed justice and right, and that they have been carrying *sicknesses and pains* which for our iniquities should have been borne by us; *yet we,* when we saw him smitten, afflicted, and stricken, kept saying that this smiting and this stroke had come upon them *from God,* because they had not adhered to his ordinances and statutes. [5]It was not, however, as we thought: *he was wounded* among the nations *for our transgressions:* for it cannot be supposed that Israel's own iniquities occasioned their devastation, when we now see them high and exalted above every man; since they kept the law of truth, what could have caused them to be *wounded* and *bruised for our iniquities? The chastisement upon him* was *our peace;* i. e. by the humiliation involved in Israel's bearing the yoke of foreign kingdoms, peace was secured for us; because the Holy One created for himself one just nation in the world, which carried on itself all iniquities in order that the whole world might be preserved; *and by his stripes* there was healing for us. [6]*All we like sheep have gone astray:* these are the words of the nations, as they confess, saying, Now we see that we have been keeping a statute of vanity, and have adhered to a law of falsehood . . .[b]

---

[b] Erased in the MSS.

XII. R. ABRAHAM IBN 'EZRA.

This Parashah is an extremely difficult one. Our opponents say that it refers to their God, supposing the '*servant*' to signify his body: this, however, is not possible, for the body cannot 'understand' even during a man's lifetime. Moreover, if their view be correct, what will be the meaning of 'seeing seed?' for he (their God) saw no son; or of 'prolonging days,' which is equally untrue of him; or of 'dividing spoil with the strong?' The proof of its proper meaning lies in the passages immediately before (lii. 12, where 'you' signifies Israel), and immediately afterwards (liv. 1, where 'the barren one' designates the congregation of Israel); similarly *my servant* means each individual belonging to Israel, and consequently God's servant, who is in exile. But many have explained it of the Messiah, because our Rabbis have said [a] that in the day when the Sanctuary was laid waste, the Messiah was born, and that he was bound in fetters (Jer. xl. 1). Several of the verses, however, have then no meaning, for instance, 'despised and forlorn of men,' 'taken from prison and judgment,' 'made his grave with the wicked,' 'will see seed, and prolong days.' R. Sa'adyah interprets the whole Parashah of Jeremiah; and this interpretation is attractive. Jeremiah 'scattered [b] many nations' by the word of prophecy which was in his mouth (i. 9 f., cf. v. 14); he 'came up before him like a sucker,' for when he began to prophesy he was a youth (i. 6); 'the Lord laid upon him the iniquity of us all,' and he 'carried the sin of many,' when he stood before God to speak good for them, and to turn away the wrath from them (xviii. 20); he was 'led like a sheep to the slaughter,' as he says himself (xi. 19); and he 'divided spoil with the mighty,' when the captain of the guard

---

[a] Midrash *Ekha*, i. 16. [b] So Sa'adyah renders יזה: see p. 17.

gave him 'victuals and a portion of meat' (xl. 5). But in my judgment the Parashah is more intimately connected with the context, for what object can there be in mentioning Jeremiah when consolations addressed to Israel form the subject of the prophet's discourse both before and after? In fact, he is simply speaking of each one of God's servants who is in exile; or, which is more probable, 'my servant' may mean Israel as a whole, as in xli. 8.

LII. [13] *My servant shall understand* that he will yet be high again. נשא is Nif'al. [14] שממו as Lev. xxvi. 32: every one who sees the servant of God *will be astonished*. The word *many* alludes to the nations; and after כן the copula must be supplied—'So marred *was*...' משחת is then an adjective; and in form תְּאֳרוֹ [c] resembles רחבו. The phenomenon alluded to is well known: how many nations are there in the world who think that the features of the Jew are disfigured and unlike those of other men, and ask whether a Jew has a mouth or an eye! This is done, for example, in the countries of Ishma'el and 'Edom [d]. [15] כן יזה is the continuation of ירום ונשא: as it was true that his countenance was marred in the eyes of all who saw him, *so* will the time come for him to take vengeance of them and *sprinkle* them, i. e. shed their blood. And then *kings will shut their mouths* עליו, i. e. *because of him; for what had not been told them they will* then *have seen*, because it never entered into the heart of the nations to suppose that there could ever be deliverance for Israel.

LIII. [1] Then they will say, *Who* ever *believed* that things would happen in accordance with this report that we hear? *upon whom was the arm of the Lord ever revealed* as it has been revealed upon these? [2] Each of God's servants belonging to Israel (or the whole of Israel) was *springing up before him like*

---

[c] So our editions: but Ibn 'Ezra, as Friedländer suggests, may probably have read תָּאֳרוֹ, which in fact occurs in a MS. of the Bodleian Library, assigned (see Neubauer, Catal. No. 69) to the 13th century.

[d] I. e. among Mohammedans and Christians.

a sucker (Hos. xiv. 7), or *like a root out of the dry earth* which produces no fruit. *He had no form:* to be explained according to lii. 14. In ונראהו ולא מראה the force of לא extends over the second word as well as that which immediately belongs to it—'he had *no* form, and we did *not* desire him:' so Prov. xxi. 14 יכפה must be understood in the second half of the verse. [3]*He was despised and ceasing from men*, i. e. ceased to be reckoned among men: *a man of pains*, sc. the servant of God; or if עבדי be understood of the nation, then איש will be used to signify 'a being' in general, as Ex. xv. 3 [e]. The expressions pains and sickness allude to the distress occasioned by exile. *And it was as though one hid his face from him:* even to this day there are non-Israelites who when they see a Jew, hide their faces from him; the phrase meaning that they will not look at him for the purpose of saving him. [4]The substance of the verse is as follows:—It was we who caused his sickness; yet he carried it, and bore all the pains wherewith we pained him. *We*, however, thought that he had been *stricken* with the stroke or plague of leprosy (Lev. xiii. 5). מוכה is in *st. constr.:* it was God who smote him and afflicted him because the sicknesses ought to have come upon us, whose laws were altogether vanity, but they came upon Israel instead, whose law was a law of faithfulness. This is proved by the words, 'All we like sheep had gone astray.' [5]מחולל is ptcp. of חולל. *The chastisement of our peace* is that which perpetuates our peace; and this rested *upon him;* as is clear from the words 'and by his stripes we are healed.' By *our transgressions* are meant the sufferings inflicted on Israel by the nations, for which, as Joel says (iv. 21), God will visit them; as to the meaning of *the chastisement of our peace*, it is well known that all the time that Israel is in the humiliation of exile the nations will have peace, for do you not find it written of the time of deliverance that it will be a 'time of distress' (Dan. xii. 1); and again, when those who had been

---

[e] On this passage, compare Friedländer's note.

sent brought back word that the whole earth was 'sitting still and at rest,' that the angel answered and said, 'Until when wilt thou not have mercy on Jerusalem' (Zech. i. 11 f.)? which implies that Jerusalem will not receive mercy during the whole time that the nations are at rest. [6]*All we*, etc.: at last, then, they confess the truth, exactly as in Jer. xvi. 19, 'nothing but lies have our fathers inherited.' The words bear reference to the false supposition of ver. 4. הפגיע is from פגע, Gen. xxviii. 11; and עון is here used in the sense of *penalty* for sin, as 1 Sam. xxviii. 10, Gen. xv. 16, Lam. iv. 6. Others render הפגיע *made to intercede*, cf. Jer. vii. 16, understanding עון in its usual acceptation of iniquity; the sense of the whole will then be that Israel interceded with God, in order that there might be peace in the world, cf. Jer. xxix. 7; but עון in this case agrees but harshly with הפגיע בו. [7]נגש Nif'al. *He opened not his mouth*: there is no need to interpret these words, for every Jew in exile exemplifies their truth: in the hour of his affliction he never opens his mouth to speak, even though he alone is just amongst them all: for he has no care in this world except for the service of God; he knows no prince or dignitary who will stand before him in the breach when men rise up against him (Ps. cvi. 23, cxxiv. 2): he opens not his mouth at any time. [8]*From confinement*, etc.: God, however, will redeem Israel, i. e. the righteous of them. *He was taken*: God took him out of prison, where he was confined under a condemnation of vengeance. ישוחח like שיח Job xii. 8: 'who announced to the men of his generation that it would be so?' *for he was* already *cut off from the land of life*. מפשע עמי: these are the words of each separate nation, 'the stroke that has fallen upon Israel is owing to our transgressions' (like מחולל מפשעינו ver. 5); or, as is more correct, 'for the transgression of my people the stroke will come upon them [f],'—למו being equivalent to להם *for*

[f] I. e. upon the various nations. Ibn 'Ezra considers that, had Israel alone been intended, the singular *upon him* would have been employed.

or *upon them.* [9]Some explain במותיו 'in his deaths' of those who died in exile; but others derive it from בָּמוֹת Deut. xxxiii. 29, i. e. the building erected over a grave: במותיו will then be parallel to קִברו. ואת עשיר is parallel to את רשעים, and alludes to the nations who, as compared with Israel, are wealthy. In my opinion the real meaning of the verse is this: it is intended to describe the distress of the Israelites in exile, which was so intense that, like Samson (Judg. xvi. 30), they desired to die with the nations amongst whom they dwelt—the sense of *and he made* being *and he made* in his own mind, i. e. *purposed to make,* cf. Josh. xxiv. 9. And that this desire arose indeed from their distress is shewn by what follows, *because he did no violence,* etc.; for the Gentiles ill-treated Israel gratuitously, and not on account of any evil deed or word of which they had been guilty—a view which will also accord equally with either signification of ויתן [g]. If it be objected that in במות the *qameṣ* is unalterable (as in בָּמוֹתימו Deut. xxxiii. 29), and that therefore בְּמותיו cannot be derived from it, it may be replied that this word can assume two forms in *st. constr.* like סרים, from which we find both סְריסי (Gen. xl. 7) and also סָריסי (Esth. ii. 21 al.). [10]*To bruise him,* i. e. to chasten him in captivity: דכאו is Piʿel, like דברו (Gen. xxxvii. 4); and החלי is from חלה, but formed after the manner of verbs ל״א, cf. תחלואיה Deut. xxix. 21. *If his soul,* he continues, *puts* its *trespass* before God, i. e. if he confesses his sin—or, in other words, if his soul puts before him the fear of the Lord—he will see sons and prolong his days, so that he and they together will see the salvation of God. The prophet speaks here of the generation which will return to the law of God when the end, the advent of the Messiah, has taken place. *And the Lord's pleasure shall prosper in his hand,* alluding to the Law, when the nations are converted to the true religion. [11]*For the travail of his soul,* i. e. as a reward for what he has endured, *he will see*—either, that is, his desire or prosperity

[g] Namely, either literally *and he made* or *and he purposed to make.*

generally—until he is *satisfied*, because *by his knowledge he will justify many*, viz. the nations whom Israel will teach to fulfil the law. And the meaning of his *bearing their iniquities* is that Israel, acting in a different manner from that in which the Gentiles had acted towards them, will share in the pain suffered by the latter for their sins. Or—and this is, I think, preferable, as the next verse seems to shew—the meaning may be that Israel will pray to God for the Gentiles: in this case, cf. Zech. xiv. 17. [12] All the interpreters say that this verse alludes metaphorically to those who perished in defence of the doctrine of the Divine Unity, רבים (as Esth. i. 8), meaning *the great ones* (i. e. the prophets), and עצומים denoting the patriarchs; the sense accordingly is that those who died in that cause will have a portion with the prophets. Although true in itself, however, such a sense does not agree with the rest of the Parashah, and in my opinion the meaning is rather this: 'I will give Israel a portion of spoil and plunder from many nations (את before עצומים signifying *from*, as Ex. ix. 29), as a reward for his having poured out his soul to die.' Some, however, explain הערה in the sense of *uncover, expose openly*. I prefer the sense here given (cf. Gen. xxiv. 20, although there the conjugation is different), which is also confirmed by Ps. cxli. 8, where עָרָה evidently means *to pour out*. Thus Israel *was numbered with* those who had transgressed against God, *and carried the sin of many*, because through his pains the Gentiles had peace; and the sin which they ought to have carried was borne by him. He also *interceded for the transgressors*, i. e. the Gentiles; as it is said, Jer. xxix. 7, 'And seek ye the peace of the city whither I have caused you to be carried away captives.' I have now explained for you the whole Parashah: in my opinion the expression *my servant* (lii. 13, liii. 11) denotes the same person who is the subject of xlii. 1, xlix. 3; cf. l. 6; and the mystery is to be understood as I hinted in the middle of the book (ch. xl). Thus all these Parashas are connected intimately together.

XIII. R. DAVID QAMḤI.

This Parashah refers to the captivity of Israel, who are here called 'my servant,' as in xli. 8; the prophet says, 'Behold the time will come when my servant will prosper, and be high, and exalted exceedingly.' ישכיל means *to prosper*, as 1 Sam. xviii. 14, and as the word is interpreted by Yonathan[a]. And because the exaltation of Israel is to be very great, the prophet uses a multiplicity of terms to express the idea: ירום ונשא וגבה.

I will now proceed to expound the Parashah as it is expounded by my father of blessed memory in the *Sepher hag-Galuy* and the *Sepher hab-B'rith*, composed by him in answer to the heretics.

14 שמם means *to be astonished*, as Ezek. iii. 15: 'as they were astonished at the extent of thy depression;' and it was natural that they should be thus astonished, for they saw that his countenance and form were marred beyond any man's. The prophet speaks at one moment in the second person, at another in the third, saying 'at *thee*,' but '*his* countenance,' '*his* form;' this is the custom of Scripture in countless passages, as we have elsewhere shewn. The learned Rabbi Abraham Ibn 'Ezra explains the words by pointing out how many nations there are in the world who believe that the features of the Jew are disfigured and unlike those of other men, and remarking that some even go so far as to ask,—in the country of Ishmael or Edom, for example,—whether a Jew has a mouth or an eye. 15 משחת (with Ḥireq under the מ) is an adjective like מבדלות (Josh. xvi. 9), also with Ḥireq. And תארו has Holem, because

[a] In the Thargum: see p. 5.

of the א. יזה has the sense of *speaking*, like הטיף, which means both *to sprinkle* or *drop* (Judg. v. 4) and also *to speak* (Mic. ii. 6). The verb has a causative force, *fera parler* in French. The prophet means to say, As they were astonished at his depression, so will they now be astonished to see his greatness, and will be talking of it continually. *At him kings will shut their mouth*—even to kings, as it is said lxii. 2, will his glory appear in its greatness. יקפצו is either *to open*, as Cant. ii. 8, where קפץ signifies the opening out of the steps in leaping, or *to shut*, as Deut. xv. 7. Either meaning is possible here: the kings may *open* their mouth to tell of his greatness, or *close* their mouth by placing their hand upon it in amazement. *For* they will see then more of his greatness than *what had been told them*, and perceive more of it than *they had heard of*.

LIII. [1] Then the Gentiles will say, *Who* was there that *believed the report* which we heard concerning him from the prophets' lips, or from those who spoke in their name? We never believed what we are now seeing with our own eyes. And *upon whom was the arm of the Lord ever revealed* as it is now revealed upon him? Or על מי may be spoken contemptuously, meaning, Who was he that the arm of the Lord should be revealed upon him? [2] כיונק as Hos. xiv. 7: Israel was like a sucker without beauty springing up out of a root in the dry soil. In my opinion, however, the allusion is rather to Israel's coming up out of exile, which was as surprising and wondrous as for a sucker to spring up out of the dry ground, or for a tree or herbage to flourish there. *Sucker* and *root* are parallel terms for the expression of the same idea; and the meaning of לפניו is that Israel was continually before God, and so nearer to him than any other nation. Yet while in captivity *he had no form and no comeliness*—'form' meaning of course a beautiful form: and *we looked at him, but* he had *no beauty* in his looks; his countenance was deformed and disfigured, unlike other men's. ונחמדהו; the preceding לא stands in place of two: 'we did not desire him,' but rather loathed him.

[3] Not only did we not desire him, *he was* even *despised* in our eyes. חדל אישים; i.e. the *most insignificant* of men, or, perhaps, *forlorn* of men, because they would not associate with him. The *pains* and *sickness* spoken of are the sufferings of exile; and ידוע means that he was *taught* and accustomed to have the yoke of exile pass over him. *And* we were *like men hiding their faces from him;* we would not look at him because of the loathing we felt for him, and we accounted him for nought. [4] The prophet Ezekiel (xviii. 20) says the son shall not suffer for the iniquity of the father, nor the father for the iniquity of the son: *à fortiori*, therefore, one man cannot suffer for another man, or one people for another people; what, then, is the meaning of his *carrying our sicknesses* etc.? What Jeremiah says in his Lamentations, 'Our fathers sinned and are not, and we bear their iniquities' (v. 7), is not parallel; this, firstly, resembles rather Ex. xx. 5, *visiting the iniquity of the fathers upon the children*, i.e. when the children still continue to adhere to the works of their fathers, according to the addition *as regards them that hate me;* for it is a judgment from God when the son bears both his own iniquity and his father's as well: and, secondly, Jeremiah is speaking in the style of mourners, whose words, springing out of the midst of pain and distress, are not regulated by measure and weight. Here the phrases put into the mouth of the Gentiles, such as 'he hath carried our sicknesses' etc., are merely the expression of their own thoughts; it is not asserted that Israel actually bore the iniquity of the Gentiles, but the latter only imagine it to be the case when they see, at the time of Deliverance, that the faith which Israel adhered to was the true one, while that which they themselves had adhered to was the false; accordingly they say (Jer. xvi. 19), 'Our fathers have inherited nothing but falsehood.' Here, then, they ask, What can be the cause of the pains endured by Israel in captivity? they cannot be attributed to their own iniquity, for *they* adhered to the truth, whereas *we* who enjoyed peace and tranquillity, quietude

and security, were adhering to falsehood; it follows, therefore, that the sickness and pain which ought to have fallen upon us has fallen upon them, and they are our ransom and the price of our atonement. While they were in exile, however, *we thought* that they were *smitten* by the hand *of God* for their iniquity; but now we see that it was not for their iniquity but for ours, as it is said, 'He suffered pangs for our transgressions.' [5] מחולל is Po'lel, from the same root and with the same meaning as חיל (Ps. xlviii. 7); for מדכא cf. Ps. cxliii. 3. שלומינו is equivalent to כלנו *the whole of us*, cf. Jer. xiii. 19 הגלת שלומים, i. e. it is carried away, an *entire* or *complete* captivity: 'the chastisements which were to have come upon us, have fallen, the whole of them, upon him.' Others explain שלומנו in its ordinary meaning: 'the chastisements which ought to have come upon us for our sins *while we were at peace* have fallen on him.' בחבורתו is from חבורה (Ex. xxi. 25), only without the *Dagesh*. 'Stripe' like 'stroke,' ver. 8, is used metaphorically of the sufferings in exile. *We were healed*, as Ex. xv. 26; or he may allude to the misfortunes which would fall upon the Gentiles, but prevail only for a time: the Gentiles would then be *healed*, while Israel would be left in calamity. [6] Like *the* sheep, those, viz. without a shepherd; he uses the article to point to the particular kind of sheep who would go astray, those, viz. without a shepherd. Each people *turned* after its own god: but now we see that *all we had gone astray*, while Israel had been in possession of the truth. הפגיע; it is the penalty which *lights upon* them, and it is God who causes it to do so when he sends misfortune upon them. עון means here the *penalty* of sin: so Gen. xv. 16. [7] *He was pressed* (for money, as 2 Kings xxiii. 35, Deut. xv. 2) *and he was afflicted*, sc. bodily (for his body was afflicted with stripes): yet notwithstanding this, he opened not his mouth—was not permitted to cry out and complain at what we were doing to him, but was as a sheep led to slaughter, which does not open its mouth and cry; and as a lamb dumb before her shearers. The simile of the sheep is intended to express his bodily affliction and exhaustion; and that of the lamb to express the extortion he suffered, which is compared to *fleecing;* the prophet likens Israel to a רחל (fem.) and not to a כבש (masc.), on account of his excessive weakness and prostration while in captivity, for with every animal the female is weaker than the male. נאלמה is *Mil'el,* being the perf. Nif'al. *Yet he opened not his mouth,* neither at his bodily sufferings, nor at the loss of his possessions. [8] *From* the *coercion* of exile, in which he was confined, *and from* the *judgment* of captivity when judgments were inflicted upon him, — from all this *he was taken* and redeemed. *And who* was there that *said* or suspected (cf. Gen. xxi. 7) that his generation would attain to such greatness? שוחח means *to speak,* Po'lel from שוח: so Ps. cxliii. 5. *For he was cut off from the land of life,* viz. when he was in exile from his own country, which is called the *land of life,* as in Ps. cxvi. 9. Or the phrase may be explained thus: In exile he was really considered to have been cut off from the land of the living, how then were we to think that such greatness as this would ever be his? *For the transgression of my people.* Each nation will make this confession, saying that in consequence of their own transgression, and not Israel's, had the *stroke* fallen *upon them.* [9] They were ever killing Israel while in exile, just as though he had done wrong, classing him with the wicked whom men put to death on account of their wickedness, although he had done no violence, and although there was no word of guile in his mouth. The meaning of ויתן is that he gave himself voluntarily to death: they were ready to release him if he would renounce his own law and transfer his allegiance to theirs; but rather than do this, he met a voluntary death, cf. Ps. xliv. 23. And *with the rich* also, who are slain for the sake of their wealth: this, and not his wickedness, was the cause of his being murdered. The plural מותיו is employed because they used to be put to death in many ways: some were burnt, some were slain, and others were stoned—they gave themselves over to any form of death for the sake of the unity of the Godhead. [10] Still in his pains and sufferings while in captivity we trace nothing but the operations of the divine *pleasure*: Israel himself adhered to the Law, which is a law of faithfulness (cf. Ps. cxix. 142), and suffered martyrdom on behalf of it; since his pains cannot imply that he was caught in his own iniquities, we must suppose that it was the divine pleasure thus *to bruise and sicken him*: we do not understand all the mysteries of God's purposes. (In החלי the third radical א is wanting: although the verb is generally ל״ה, the word before us is formed and pronounced as though it were ל״א.) Only this do we see clearly, that he will receive a full reward for the misfortune he has endured; *if*, then, *his soul* gives itself in place of *a trespass-offering* (as he says above, 'with the wicked'), *he will see* much *seed*, as the prophet Zechariah says of them (x. 8, 10), and Ezekiel (xxxvi. 37); he will *lengthen days*, as is said at the end of the book (lxv. 22), and by Zechariah (viii. 4); and whereas during the exile it was the Lord's pleasure to bruise him, in return for this *the Lord's pleasure shall prosper in his hand*, for he will multiply him and do good to him exceedingly.—At this point the words of the Gentiles cease, and those of God begin. [11] *For the travail of his soul* which he bore in exile, his reward shall be that he will *see and be satisfied*, i.e. he will see prosperity so as to be satisfied therewith. 'My servant' here still means Israel, as we said at the beginning of the Parashah; and דעתו denotes his knowledge of the Lord, as xi. 9, Jer. xxxi. 33. *My servant* Israel, who will be *righteous* and know the Lord, *will, by his knowledge, make righteous* many nations, as it is written, Is. ii. 3, 'He will teach us of his ways, and we will walk in his paths;' and by his righteousness will *bear the iniquities* of the Gentiles, for by it there will be peace and prosperity in the whole world, even for the Gentiles. [12] The *mighty* and the *strong* are here Gog and Magog, and the peoples who come with him to Jerusalem, as is described by Zechariah (xii. 14). And this glorious fortune will be his *because he poured out his soul to die:* i. e. because in exile he resigned himself to death at the hands of the Gentiles: their wealth will be for his wealth which they had taken, and their soul for his soul, for, as Ezekiel writes (xxxix. 4), 'All the host of Gog and Magog will die there.' הערה is *to pour out*, as Gen. xxiv. 20, but in a different conjugation; and '*with* the transgressors' is like '*with* the wicked,' as we have explained the words in ver. 8. *And he carried the sin of many:* this may be supposed to refer to the time of the captivity; he means to say that Israel *bore* the consequences of *the sin of many*, i. e. of the Gentiles when they sinned against him, and he bore the sufferings which their sin occasioned; cf. Ex. v. 16. Nevertheless, he continued *interceding* for the wicked who were *transgressing* against him, and sought blessings on their land from the Lord; cf. Jer. xxix. 7. The Hif. of פגע is used with the same idea of supplication or prayer in lix. 16, Jer. xxxvi. 25. The reference may, however, be to the time of deliverance: the meaning will then be similar to that assigned to the words, 'He will bear their iniquities,' in the last verse.

I should like to ask the Nazarenes [Christians] who explain this Parashah of Jesus, how the prophet could have said, 'He shall be lifted up and lofty exceedingly?' If this alludes to the flesh, Jesus was not 'lifted up' except when he was suspended upon the cross; if it refers to the Godhead, then he was mighty and lifted up from the beginning [so that it could not be said, He *will* be lifted up]. Moreover, the prophet says *to them* (למו), ver. 8, but then he ought to have said *to him* (לו), for למו is plural, being equivalent to להם. Again he says, 'He shall see seed:' if this refers to his flesh, then he had no seed; if to his Godhead, as the literal sense is inappropriate, they explain the word *seed* as alluding to his disciples, although his disciples are nowhere spoken of as either *sons* or *seed*. He says, too, 'He shall lengthen days;' but in the flesh he did not lengthen days, and if he says of his Godhead that as a reward [for suffering] he will have long life, are not the days of God from everlasting to everlasting (cf. Ps. xc. 2)? Lastly, he says, 'And he interceded for the transgressors;' but if he is God himself, to whom could he intercede?—Our Rabbis[a] explain it of Moses, supposing that he 'poured out his soul to die' when he resigned himself to death (Ex. xxxii. 32), that he was 'numbered with the transgressors' because he was numbered with those who died in the wilderness, that he 'bore the sin of many' when he made atonement for the making of the golden calf, and that he 'interceded for the transgressors' when he sought for mercy on the transgressions of Israel[b].

---

[a] See above, p. 8.

[b] The MSS. continue with the translation of Yonathan (see No. 2).

XIV. R. JACOB BEN REUBEN (THE RABBANITE).

The Apostate:—*Behold my servant . . . and interceded for the transgressors.* You have in these verses, from their first letter to their last, a proof as clear and patent as noon-day that what we assert concerning our Messiah is incontrovertible; there is no need then to say more, and explain how each separate verse reveals some mystery in his life, and declares plainly all the principal actions which he accomplished, or how not a single word fell to the ground of all the testimony which the prophet here presents.

The Unitarian:—You say that this prophecy, from its first letter to the last, is uttered in reference to your Messiah: consider now how many answers can be given to you.

1. You began by saying that the royal Psalmist was addressing him when he spoke the words, 'Thou art fairer than the children of men' etc. (Ps. xlv. 3); you say also that Jeremiah speaks of him similarly as *fair* or beautiful (Ps. xlviii. 3, Jer. xi. 16); and add that all this testimony respecting him is true. And now you go on to assert madly that the words 'so marred was his countenance beyond man' etc. refer to him likewise. But how can this be when you already admit and believe that all the words of the prophets are unfailing and true? you can be only perverting their words and corrupting and falsifying their prophecies if you maintain that when the Psalmist speaks of him as 'beautiful,' Isaiah can come and testify that his countenance and form are 'marred,' or that he is 'despised and

forlorn of men;' or again, that if Isaiah says that he has 'no form nor comeliness,' Jeremiah can call him a 'flourishing olive tree, beautiful with well-formed fruit.'

2. Consider whether the general connection of the verses tends to favour your arguments: it seems to me to go far in the opposite direction. With respect to the meaning of the first two verses, in which the prophet says that the '*servant* shall prosper,' the words 'many were astonished' and 'his countenance was marred' must in accordance with the context refer to the time before his success and the attainment of his kingdom, while the expression 'he will sprinkle many nations,' i. e. will expel them from their kingdoms, must allude to the period following his success. But now when in your argument you assert that this your Messiah is God, and that all the essence of the Godhead resides in him, in what sense can you understand these verses? and how does the prophet announce of him, as a future fact, that he will be 'exalted, lifted up, and lofty exceedingly?' Is not the Godhead (as it is written, Is. lvii. 15) *high and exalted* continually? Who supposes that God could first of all be in a state of depression, affliction, and disfigurement, out of which he would afterwards raise himself, and be exalted above those who knew him? Were this the case, we should no longer be able to recognise him as omnipotent; for although we know that he is represented as saying (Is. xxxiii. 10), 'Now will I arise, now will I exalt myself,' yet we clearly must not suppose the word *now* to imply that he was not exalted previously, because it is the custom of Scripture to use such language repeatedly, as 'Arise, O God' (Num. x. 35), 'Awake, why sleepest thou?' (Ps. xliv. 24.) To express the idea of greatness or might, the Creator is often spoken of in terms strictly applicable only to what possesses a body: but far be it from us to find him described in any passage whatever as being in a condition of depression or disfigurement.

3. According to your view, the prophet declares that he was 'despised and forlorn of men,' a 'man of pains and known

of sickness:' now it seems to me that no one would be called 'known of sickness' or a 'man of pains' except a man who suffered from severe sicknesses continually: and I know, in fact, that you will not find either in your own New Testament, or in the words of the wise men of your own religion who tell you about the Messiah and his deeds, or, in fact, in any book in the world, that he ever had a pain—even a headache—up to the day of his death when he was delivered into the hands of those that smote him: we see then that the very terms themselves which are here employed, 'pain' and 'sickness,' were not realised in his person, and consequently cannot apply to him. The chastisements which he endured in the hour of death would not be spoken of as a 'sickness,' but rather as an 'attack' or 'blow' (פגיעה), as 1 Kings ii. 25, 29. And again, instead of saying he was 'smitten of God,' he should rather have said he was 'smitten of *men*,' as was the fact: only one visited with various kinds of diseases is said to be smitten of God.

4. If these verses refer to your Messiah, who you say is God, then they contain themselves the refutation of your assertions. It is written, 'He was smitten of God:' it follows then—and your own mouth assents against you—that God smites him and he is smitten by God: how then can it be said that he is himself God? Again, it is written that the Lord 'laid on him the iniquity of us all:' as the patient, then, he is inferior to God who is the agent. The same conclusion will be drawn from the words, 'The Lord was pleased to bruise him:' he was the bruised, and God the bruiser; again then he is inferior to God. But you assert that he is God himself; it appears then that the witnesses whom you cite give their witness against you, and attest the contrary of what you affirm.

5. It is said, 'There was a stroke for them' (למו); but if this refers to the Messiah it ought to have been 'for *him*' (לו): for לו is singular, but the prophet uses למו, which is plural. Again it is written אם תשים אשם נפשו, and even though this verse should mean (as you allege it does mean) '*because* he made his

soul a trespass-offering' (אם being equivalent to כי, as Ex. xxii. 24, where, inasmuch as it is a duty to lend, we may render *Because* thou must lend, etc.), yet we know as a fact that he did not prolong his days upon the earth or see seed: rather Ps. lv. 24 was fulfilled in him, for he did not reach half the age usually attained by man, which is seventy years. Moreover, the prophet each time calls him *my servant* (which, as applied to the Godhead, is a term of indignity); understand then and know truly that, as I once replied to you before, when we saw that God appointed his 'servant' as a witness (xliii. 10), so here the same expression is used of no one except Israel, who were 'afflicted and smitten' by the hands of the Gentiles; and of whom, therefore, the whole Parashah is to be expounded unhesitatingly; Israel being called *my servant*, as in xliv. 2, and many other passages.

And so we cannot take your arguments into consideration: your view is not to be substantiated; it has never existed and never been created.

XV. JACOB BEN REUBEN (THE QARAITE).

LII. [13] *My servant*, i. e. the 'wise' (*Maskilim*)[a] who will learn from the mouth of Elijah, *will be high and exalted and lofty exceedingly*, i. e. will rise continually in dignity. [14] *Many were amazed* at thee, i. e. at the sight of thy countenance; and similarly *his countenance*, the countenance viz. of this 'wise' one, *was marred beyond* man. ותוארו, i. e. his likeness, figure. According to another opinion this verse means, As many were astonished at thee, so will his countenance be finer, sleeker, and better favoured than any man's: cf. משחת[b] Lev. vii. 35. [15] Like a man sprinkling water, i. e. casting it out of his hand, so will he cast and drive many nations out of the world. Because what was not told them, i. e. this great glory, have they seen, and wisdom which they had never heard of, have they observed. According to another view, יזה means 'he will *teach* them' wholesome doctrine.

LIII. [1] *Who hath believed?* So the remnant will say to one another. [2] The comparison with a *sucker* indicates that they will be weak and afflicted. *Before him* means in his sanctuary. *Like a root* shooting up *in dry ground*, which has no beauty, so the remnant were devoid of all good counsels, and had no comeliness in their apparel. [3] *Despised* in appearances and *withdrawn from men*, i. e. taking no part in their festivals, or marriage-rejoicings. [4] He was *known* to be sick continually: he was like a leper from whom all *hide their faces*. [5] He was

---

[a] See p. 19, note *b*. [b] Comp. below, p. 67.

wounded, was troubled, and wept for our iniquities, because he was grieved at them. According to another view, *terrified and trembling;* cf. מחולל Prov. xxvi. 10. *The chastisement* for breaking the law, the observance of which would be our peace, fell to his share. ובחבורתו; if he had associated himself with us as he did before [*by his union* with us], he would then have healed us, and delivered us from exile. According to others, if we had associated ourselves with him [*by* our *union with him*], we should have been healed. R. Yonah[c] explains the word as an infinitive with pronominal suffix, 'by bruising him:' compare קחם Hos. xi. 3. [6] הפגיע, i. e. heard his prayer, and took away from us the iniquity of us all. Or, caused to meet, brought upon him, troubles at the hands of the Gentiles for our iniquities. [7] נגש; the rulers oppressed him. והוא נענה; every one cursed him. כרחל; *like a lamb*, because they seized his riches and possessions. [8] The Lord rescued him from the prison-house, and the punishments of revenge. Who is able to tell the years of weariness which passed over him? Who is to be found in his generation to recount the evils which befel him? מארץ חיים; from the happiness and enjoyments of the world. The word למו shews that by the 'wise' (lii. 13) must be understood more than one: the statement cannot therefore be made, as is asserted by some, in view of the Messiah. [9] As he experienced the long duration of the exile, the expectation grew upon him[d] that he would die in captivity *with the wicked.* Whenever the authorities sought tribute of the rich that were in exile, the latter imposed it upon the 'wise,' who thus had to pay as much as the rich themselves did: if then the rich paid one piece of gold each, they paid the same. במותיו means *his bust.* [10] He *bruised*, i. e. humbled him, so that he became as one who was sick. According to others, he bruised himself, viz. in inflicting upon himself sackcloth and fasting. Or דכאו may

---

[c] See his *Book of Roots* (ed. Neubauer, Oxford, 1873), i. col. 208.

[d] Lit. '*he made* or *put* it in his heart that . . . :' cf. above, p. 46.

be an infinitive referring to נפשו; cf. Job xxxii. 2. *If his soul*, the soul of the remnant, *makes* as it were *a trespass-offering* to its Lord—the verb being transitive, and the 'soul' its subject: or, 'if thou, Lord, makest his soul as it were a trespass-offering,' i. e. if the fastings which he undergoes are accepted before thee as a trespass-offering, then, as every trespass-offering makes some atonement, so the work of this 'wise' one will atone for the iniquities of Israel. *He will see seed*, whereas he thought that he would perish in exile, the prophet now declares that he will be in this very different condition: [11] for the affliction of his soul, he will see prosperity and be satisfied with pleasures; and by his *knowledge* or instruction my servant, the just one, will justify the many, and *bear*, i. e. take from them their iniquities. [12] Because of his service and ministry, I will give him a double inheritance amongst the many, as it is said (Is. lxi. 7), *In their land they possess the double.* Or, I will divide him a portion in the midst of the great—he shall receive a possession in the city mentioned in Ezekiel: and *with the mighty he shall divide the spoil* which the Messiah and his sons will take, and some of it will be given to these 'wise' ones. He was numbered with the transgressors, sc. in the penalty which befel them.

XVI.

LII. [13] Behold, my servant the Branch shall go in the right
way, he shall be high and exalted and lofty exceedingly. [14] As the
generations of Israel had been desolated for many years at the
sight of thee, because his looks were marred almost beyond man,
and his form beyond the sons of Adam: [15] so shall he sprinkle the
blood of many nations, before him kings shall shut their mouth
and be dumb; for that which was not told them they have seen,
and that which they had not heard they have observed.

LIII. [1] Who hath believed our report? and upon whom except
us has the arm of God been revealed? [2] And the righteous of
Israel came up like a sucker before him to suck in his knowledge,
and he of them that was firmly rooted in the commandments,
like a tree stretching out its roots to springs of water, out of
the dry ground of the captivity; he had[a] form and comeliness;
we beheld him, and [saw that] he had the look of prophecy,
and found his appearance full of beauty. [3] Despised in his own
eyes, and keeping apart from men, he makes their kings sick,
and by his crying for them causes each to become a man of
pains and known to sickness; God hides his mercy from them
as he hides his face from us in the time of wrath; he makes
every one of them despised and so esteems him not. [4] Surely
for our offences (which were our sicknesses) he has obtained
forgiveness, and our sins, which were the cause of our pains, he
bare in obtaining it; yet we did esteem ourselves to be each of
us bruised for his iniquities, smitten of God, and punished.
[5] He will build our sanctuary, which was delivered up for our

---

[a] The author apparently understood לא in the sense of לו.

offences, and destroyed for our iniquities; the teaching of our
peace, i. e. the instruction of the instructor, is upon him, and
by union with him we are healed. [6] All we like sheep have
gone astray; we have turned every one to his own way, yet
God receives his intercession for the iniquities of us all. [7] When
he draws near to the end of his career, he will be answered
before opening his mouth, his enemies will be delivered before
him like a sheep which is led to the slaughter, and like a lamb
which before her shearers is dumb; but he will not open his mouth.
[8] From confinement in captivity and from judgment every one
amongst us is taken, and who of us can tell in the time of
captivity what God will do with his generation? after the king of
our enemies has been cut off from the land of life, when my people
abandons the transgression which has lighted on them? [9] Each
one of the wicked makes Gehenna his grave, and the rich [makes
it] his high place, so that none of them will have power
to do evil, neither shall any word of deceit find its place in
their mouth. [10] But God was pleased to depress Israel in the
latter end of the captivity, in order that they might repent [and
turn to him] before their king appears, and therefore has he made
them sick; O that thou wouldst take his confession as the sacrifice
of his soul, that so he might see the king, prolong days, and
that the pleasure of God might prosper in his hand! [11] From
the travail of the captivity he shall deliver his soul, he shall
see vengeance on his enemies and be satisfied with the plunder
of their possessions; by his knowledge my servant Israel will
make many righteous [and lead them] in a righteous law, and
their iniquities he will bear in obtaining their forgiveness. [12] As
a reward for this I will divide for him the spoil of Gog who are
the many, and the cities of mighty nations he shall divide as
prey, because he laid bare his soul for death and gave transgressors a share in the law, and obtained forgiveness for the sins
of many; and God for his sake will receive intercession for
transgressors.

XVII.

LII. [13] *Behold my servant*, i. e. those who correct and 'make many wise' (cf. Dan. xi. 33, xii. 3), and 'who sigh and groan' for all the wickednesses of the people (cf. Ezek. ix. 4), *will* in those days *be* very *prosperous*. The expression 'my servant' connects the passage with l. 10; and mention is here made of his affliction and sicknesses, as in Ps. lxxiii. 14, and as you may see in the cases of Elijah, Jeremiah, and, in fact, all the prophets—even Moses (Num. xi. 15). You may see, too, how Daniel endured misery and sickness on account of the destruction of his people, and sought mercy for them with fasting, weeping, and wailing; and all the prophets did the same. And this is what is here meant by the 'stroke,' and the 'stripe,' and the 'chastisement,' and the 'bruising,' and the 'sickness.' The prophets also were despised and of no estimation in the eyes of the nations, and all that saw them mocked at them; even their own people despised them, saying that they were smitten for their own iniquity and sin, and that there was 'no salvation for them in God' (Ps. iii. 3). The Deity here declares that his servant was not smitten and chastised for his own iniquity, but that he sighed and groaned for the wickedness of his people, and suffered humiliation and affliction, and humbled his soul in order to seek mercy for them. [14] *Because many* in the past *were astonished at thee*, because thou wast despised and forlorn of men, a man of pains and known to sickness, and were in wonder at thy form and countenance, because thou wast not like other men, *so* will thy looks be *esteemed* (משחת) above those of the rest of mankind, and *as* many were astonished at thee, and did not esteem thee, but, on the contrary, removed thee from them, *so* now *wilt thou*, too, *sprinkle* and cast away from thee many nations. משחת, as always, means *esteemed and precious*, as למשחה (Ex. xxix. 29); cf. Lev. xxii. 25, Mal. i. 14, in both of which places משחת signifies *fat and precious*, as I have explained in my commentary on those passages, although the form of the word is irregular. A different sense may be obtained by connecting כאשר with the כן which immediately follows it, as Ex. i. 12: *as* they were astonished, viz. in the past, at the humiliation of his countenance, *so* now will his countenance be esteemed and thought great. [15] *At him*—at the terror of him, at his exaltation and regal majesty even *kings will close their mouths:* they will be unable to speak a word or to open their lips; for *what was not told them* by others *they will have seen* from him, and *what they had not heard* from others *they will have understood* from him. The prophet then speaks as follows respecting what is thus told them by him.

LIII. [1, 2] *Who* etc., the language of incredulity or surprise, as Gen. xxi. 7, If it had been said to us that this man was thus prosperous and thriving after he had been despised and forlorn of men, a man of pains and known to sickness, *who would have believed the report? And upon whom was the arm of the Lord* ever *revealed* so as for him to be turned to another man (cf. 1 Sam. x. 6), as it is now revealed upon this one, who, *like the suckers* of a tree *before* God, and *like a root* springing out of the dry earth, *rises up* and grows great out of the midst of sicknesses and chastenings? and who before had no form and *no comeliness and no beauty* when we looked at him, but is now so graceful and comely that we ourselves desire to be like him. [3] *He was despised* by every one, *forlorn of men, and known*, i. e. trained and accustomed, *to sickness*, and was *as though* the Holy One were *hiding his face from him* and chastening him in anger and displeasure. Thus was he amongst us in the past: [4] *but* now we know that he was not smitten for his own iniquity and transgression, but that it was *our sicknesses*—those which for our sins we ought to have endured—that he *carried*, sighing and groaning, and afflicting himself with sickness (as Amos vi. 6) on account of the calamity which was about to fall upon us and the misfortune which was to be our lot. And the pain wherewith we should have let our heart be pained for our misfortune *he bare;* but we laid not our calamities to heart, we abandoned ourselves to luxury and pleasure, 'slaying oxen and killing sheep, eating flesh and drinking wine' (Is. xxii. 13), thinking, like the women in Zion and Samaria (Amos vi. 1), who did not expect evil to come upon them, that to-morrow will be as to-day (Is. lvi. 12), and saying (cf. Jer. xxi. 13), Who shall come down against us? or who shall enter into our habitations? *And* therefore did we esteem him *stricken* and *smitten of God and afflicted*—thought that for his sins the Deity was thus chastening and bruising him. [5]*But he* was just, and *was wounded* (חולל as Is. li. 9) *for our transgressions: the chastenings* which, instead of the peace that as we blessed ourselves in our heart (Jer. xxiii. 17) we looked forward to, we ought to have felt and suffered in sickness for our calamity, *were* all *upon him* and not upon us: he was sick and bruised, we were careless and secure. *And by his stripes* and sickness, which we ought thus to have laid to heart and made our own, *we were healed,* though we did not perceive it; for we kept saying, Peace, peace, when there was no peace (Jer. vi. 14, viii. 11), though the true prophets, who saw what would happen, groaned, stricken down and sick; and hence we were healed. [6]*We all went astray like sheep,* each pursuing after his own advantage; *but the Lord caused the iniquity of us all to meet* (הפגיע as Jer. xv. 11) upon him, in that he afflicted and humbled himself with groanings and sickness on account of our calamity. [7]*He was oppressed* with pains and chastenings, and with the reproaches and contempt and shame and spitting which we heaped upon him; *yet he opened not his mouth,* but accepted the judgment thus passed upon him as deserved. [8] *From the confinement* in which he was kept because of those who reproached and despised him, and sought to take away his life, *and from the judgments* and chastenings and pains which fell upon him, he was almost *taken* out of the land of the living and died : *but his generation* (דור as xxxviii. 12), his seed and descendants, *who could tell of?*—who, while he was still in distress, could think that he would *see seed* and lengthen days? for in the eyes of all that saw him he seemed to have been *cut off*, removed *from the land of the living, because of the transgression of my people,* [because of] *the stroke* which ought to have been *theirs.* [9] And when he reached the gates of death. *he made his grave with the wicked:* he means to say that he was wicked, and consequently had to meet the death of the wicked and die in his sin, thereby accepting the sentence passed upon him. And this, *although he had done no violence,* by which he might justly have incurred a sentence like this: for he might have been rebellious, and reasoned against God's attribute of justice. And if, after it is said that he did no violence and that there was no deceit in his mouth, you ask how he came into such a situation, the reason is given in the next verse. [10] *The Lord was pleased to bruise and sicken him,* in order to try him and prove him and purify him: because, lo, God 'trusteth not his servants' (Job iv. 18), but brings them into temptation so as to prove them: he tries him, because *if his soul lays guilt,* sc. against himself, if it condemns himself and justifies God's sentence of suffering, then he will heal him and preserve him alive: he will *see seed* and *lengthen days, and the pleasure of the Lord,* i.e. to do judgment and justice in the earth, to 'break the teeth of the wicked, and to deliver the afflicted from him that is too strong for him, the afflicted and needy from him that spoileth him' (Jer. ix. 23, Job xxix. 17, Ps. xxxv. 10), *will prosper in his hand;* for he will give him dominion and greatness and strength to judge the afflicted of the people, and bruise the oppressor, to give sentence for his people in

justice and for his afflicted with judgment (Ps. lxxii. 2, 4).
11 Then *for the* chastenings which he thus bore in the past,
he will *see seed*, he will *prolong* and have his fill of life; *by his knowledge he will justify many*, and deliver the afflicted from him that is too strong for him, and *the iniquities of the many*, the sins which one man commits against another, *he will bear*: all will rest upon him; he will carry their 'cumbrance, and burden, and strife' (Deut. i. 12), and upon him will it devolve to order all things, for 'his lips will keep knowledge, and teaching will they seek from his mouth' (Mal. ii. 7). עונותם is *leurs forfaits* in French.
12 *Therefore I will divide him* riches
and honour, *because he poured out* (*esvida*) *his soul to die* for my sake, *and was numbered with the transgressors* in sickness and chastenings, as though he had been really guilty, and had accepted the condemnation passed upon him as just. *But he carried the sin* or guilt *of many* and their pain; and *interceded for transgressors*, prayed for them to me that I would have mercy on them, although it was through them that he himself was smitten.

XVIII. R. YOSEPH BEN NATHAN.

This Parashah is applied by the heretics to the Nazarene. A very learned apostate came once into the presence of the great R. Yoseph B'khor-Shor[a]: How, he asked, canst thou meet the evidence of this Parashah? He replied, O fool, thine ears shall hear that which thou utterest from thy mouth: the prophet calls him his 'servant,' but if he is God, how could he be termed a servant? At once the apostate rent his clothes and rolled himself in ashes and repented [of his apostasy]. Then he speaks of their having seen what 'had not been told them,' i. e. the wondrous and mighty acts of the Deity; but do they possess no record of the Creation as told in Genesis, and of what God did to the generation of the Deluge, and to the generation of the Dispersion, to Pharaoh and the kings of Canaan, and the cleaving of the Red Sea, and all the miracles and mighty acts which were achieved before the birth of the Nazarene? Again he says, 'For the transgression of my people was he stricken;' but did he meet death for any other cause but in order to wipe out the sin of our forefathers in having eaten of the tree of knowledge, for which all were going down into Gehenna? This being so, however, he ought rather to have written, 'For the transgression of *Adam and Eve* was he stricken.' Again he says, 'Although he did no violence:' but if he is God, towards whom could he behave violently? do not all belong to God? 'God is judge: he setteth down one and raiseth up another' (Ps. lxxv. 8).

---

[a] A celebrated French Rabbi of the twelfth century. A commentary composed by him on the Pentateuch is still extant.

The Exposition.

LII. [13]*Behold my servant shall prosper.* He means Israel, who is called God's servant, as xliii. 10, xliv. 1, xlix. 3. ישכיל is *to be prosperous*, as Deut. xxix. 8, 1 Sam. xviii. 14. *He shall be high and exalted*, because their 'horn will be exalted in honour' (Ps. cxii. 9). [14]*As many were astonished*, viz. at Israel's depression, as it is written, 'He hath broken the covenant,' etc. (xxxiii. 8), and *rightly* so (כן as Num. xxvii. 7), *because his countenance was marred beyond man, so* he will *conquer* (cf. lxiii. 3) many nations: [15]*at him kings will close their mouths* (Job v. 16); they will be dumb, and not know what to say; *for what was not told them have they seen*, as though to say, they only knew of the depression of Israel, they had not seen his greatness.

LIII. [1]*Who believed our report?* who was there that believed this prophecy? *and upon whom was the arm of the Lord revealed?* [2]*Like a sucker* or young plant which bursts forth and springs up, and like a flower *rising out of the dry earth*, so was Israel born (lxvi. 8) and sprang up. He had *no form and no comeliness*—he was formerly despised; and *that which was seen in him* had *no beauty.* ונחמדהו Rashi explains 'and can we desire him?' but had Isaiah intended this he would have written ונַחְמְדֵהוּ: נֶחמדהו must mean the most desirable or lovely part of his body, which in Israel was disfigured and had no comeliness; as men say of a person who is plain, The most beautiful part of this man is ugly[b]. [3]*He was despised, and we esteemed him not;* so speak the kings concerning Israel, because he was a *man of pains, and broken by sickness* (cf. ויודע Judg. viii. 16), and because he was *as one hiding his face from us*, by which is meant that he was ashamed of his depressed condition. *Yet we esteemed him smitten of God*—we were thinking that all these chastenings had fallen upon him because of his own iniquity. [4]*But he carried our sickness:* now we see that that was not the cause: the sickness which ought to have come upon us,

---

[b] He treats 'נ as a *ptcp. Nif'al* with suffix.

came upon him, and through them atonement was made for us: [5]his chastenings were for our transgressions, and they resulted in our peace; the Holy One did not, as he would otherwise have done, destroy the world for our iniquities. *And* while Israel was beaten and killed (as it is written, Ps. xliv. 23) for God's holy name, *we were healed by his stripes.* [6]But now we know that *all we like sheep had gone astray, and that the Lord let himself be entreated* and propitiated *by him* for our iniquities; in my opinion, however, הפגיע is *caused to meet* upon him. [7]*He was oppressed* (as Deut. xv. 3, by injurious language: *surparler* in French), *yet* in the gate, the place where the principal people sat (Ruth iv. 1), *he opened not his mouth;* and Israel among the Gentiles was like *a sheep led to the slaughter*, or *a lamb dumb before her shearers.* [8]*From confinement*—from the place in which he was confined by their hands, and *from* the chastening *judgment* which he had endured till now, he was removed (though my own view is that the words mean 'he was taken from *sovereignty*, the *rights* of office;' cf. 1 Sam. ix. 17); and his *generation*—the long years during which weariness and travail befel him—*who can declare?* Or (as I prefer), 'Who would think for how many generations the kingdom was taken from him?' *for he was cut off* and exiled *from the land of life*, i. e. the land of Israel, because *for the transgression of my people this stroke was upon* the just amongst *them.* [9]*He made his grave at the will of the wicked*, gave himself up to be buried at their decree, when the vilest of the people murdered him, because of God's holy name; *and at the will of the rich in his death*, inasmuch as the princes who bore rule over Israel ravished and murdered them. And all this was *because he had done no violence* against the nations in the midst of whom he was a sojourner (or, as I think, 'because he had not *sinned*,' חמס as Prov. viii. 36); and because there was *no guile in his mouth*, he was slain, because, namely, he would not consent to deny the Holy One. [10]*Yet the Holy One was pleased to chasten him*, he therefore made him to be sick; still *if his soul makes itself a*

trespass-offering, if it is given to me for the sanctification of my name—אשם is a *penalty* or *fine,* as 1 Sam. vi. 3, 8—then I too will pay him his reward : he shall *see seed and lengthen days, and the pleasure of the Lord shall prosper in his hand,* so that for having performed well the pleasure of the Lord, he will receive for all his toil a full return.
11 He did not plunder and rob, but ate and *was filled from the labour of his own soul: and by his knowledge he justified the just,* meted out righteous judgment to all who came before him, and *bare their iniquities* (compare Num. xviii. 1).
12 *Therefore,* because of his doing this, *I will divide him a portion or inheritance with the great* (i. e. with the patriarchs), *because he poured out* (Gen. xxiv. 20) *his soul to die, and was numbered with the transgressors,* bore chastenings as though he had been a sinner and transgressor himself, *and made intercession for them :* for, in consequence of these chastenings, there came through his instrumentality prosperity for the world.

XIX. R. Y'SHA'YAH BEN MALI.

LII. [13] *Then* (הנה) Israel *shall prosper* (ישכיל as 1 Sam. xviii. 14): [14] *as many were* at first *astonished at thee*, amazed at the magnitude of thy depression, and *as* the countenance of Israel was *marred beyond man*, etc. The *ḥireq* in מִשחת is in place of *shureq*: for all the vowels are interchangeable. *And his form beyond the sons of men*: his form was altered from what it ought to have been: תֹאֲרו is pointed as the gutturals usually are; פוֹעֲלו (as though for פעולו), Is. i. 31, is similar. [15] *So* now will he shew himself mighty, and *sprinkle many nations*, i. e. expel and scatter them from his land, like a man sprinkling water, without one drop touching another. *At him kings will close their mouth*; they will have no pretext for speaking: *for as it had never been told them* by the prophets of their greatness *have they* now *seen, and what they had not heard* from any man, *have they perceived* and spoken of to one another.

LIII. [1] *Who believed our report*—the report which we were hearing about Israel, that he would be exalted and shew himself mighty over all? *And upon whom hath the arm of the Lord been revealed*, to do wonders and signs for them as he has done for Israel? [2] For Israel *came up like a sucker before him*: like a young shoot which at first is not seen or noticed, but after a little time appears as a great tree; and *like a root* standing *in the dry earth*, which men think to be withered and to have no hope (Job xiv. 7), but which at length shoots up and bears clusters of boughs and branches; so Israel, depressed during their captivity, are now exalted above all. At first he had *no form and no comeliness*, and *we looked at him*, but there was *no beauty* that we should *desire* it, and exclaim, How lovely the beauty of this Jew! [3] *He was despised and forlorn of men*, for every one withdrew from him, and *hid his face* so as not to look at him: *he was despised, and we esteemed him for nothing.* [4] *But* it was *our sicknesses* which *he bare*, and which made him sick and pained him; and this was the reason why he had no beauty. *Yet we esteemed him stricken of God*, thought that it had been his pleasure for him thus to be afflicted: [5] *but he was wounded in our transgressions*, it was reckoned a great transgression on our part by the Creator when we were the occasion of his wounds: *he was bruised in our iniquities*, for when we bruised him, our act was counted an 'iniquity for the judge' (Job xxxi. 28): מְדוּכָא is the same as מְדוּכֵּא, the *qameṣ* being in place of *ṣere*, as in יְבָרֵךְ (Ps. cxii. 2): *our peace was removed* and taken away [from סור] from off him—we gave him no rest; and *in his stripes we were healed*—as we inflicted upon him injuries and blows, it seemed to us as though we had ourselves been healed, so greatly did we rejoice at his calamity. חבורה is like חַבּוּרָה, except that the aspirate is *rafé*. [6] *All we like sheep had gone astray*, each after his own way, and there was none to hold us back: *but the Lord caused the iniquity of us all*—we all had incurred penalties because of him—*to meet upon him* (פגע as Gen. xxviii. 11). [7] נגש והוא נענה; as though it had been נגש ונענה הוא: נענה is Nif'al, the *fem.* occurs lviii. 10. [8] *From sovereignty* (cf. עצר 1 Sam. ix. 17) *and judgment* he was taken away, for his ancestors had been sovereigns and judges: *and* the greatness of *his generation who could tell* (שוחח as Ps. cxliii. 5)? *for he was cut off* (cf. לגוזר Ps. cxxxvi. 13) *out of the land of the living*, and *because of the transgression of my people was this stroke upon them*[a]. [9] *And he made his grave with*, or like, *the*

[a] Some explain this as follows:—*Because of the transgression of my people*, i. e. the sufferings they inflicted on him, *the stroke* was to come *upon them*. [Inserted from another MS.]

wicked, and with the rich in his death—the rich in Israel used to kill them and seize their wealth, *because he had done* us *no violence*, and *no deceit was* found *in his mouth.* [10] *But the Lord was pleased to bruise and sicken him*, and therefore delivered him over into the power of the Gentiles; and so the prophet says, *If his soul makes a trespass-offering*, if it confesses and says, I have sinned, and because of my iniquities have all these things happened to me, then he will *see seed and prolong his days, and the pleasure of the Lord will prosper in his hand.* [11] *For the labour* that he underwent in exile, *he shall see* plentiful prosperity, *and be satisfied*, and I will give him dominion over many nations, so that *by his knowledge he may justify the just; and their iniquities he will correct*—the word סבל being used, as 1 Kings xi. 28[b], of the duty devolving upon a king of correcting and putting straight whatever is crooked. [12] *Therefore will I divide him a portion among many* nations, who will all be subject to him, *and mighty* kings *he will divide* for himself *as spoil, because* in his captivity *he poured out his soul* (Ps. cxli. 8) *to die*, refusing to deny the Creator, and was punished *like the transgressors. But he*, when he was in his own land and by his own sanctuary, *carried the sin of many, and prayed* to the Creator *for transgressors*—for the Jews used to pray for all men, that the Creator would have mercy on his own world, and would not destroy it; nevertheless in exile, he was numbered with the transgressors and was smitten in the same manner as they were.

---

[b] The passage is cited incorrectly, being confused with 2 Sam. xix. 21.

XX. R. MOSHEH BEN NAḤMAN.

הנה ישכיל עבדי. The right view respecting this Parashah is to suppose that by the phrase 'my servant' the whole of Israel is meant, as in xliv. 2, xlix. 3, and often. As a different opinion, however, is adopted by the Midrash, which refers it to the Messiah, it is necessary for us to explain it in conformity with the view there maintained. The prophet says, The Messiah, the son of David, of whom the text speaks, will never be conquered or perish by the hands of his enemies. And, in fact, the text teaches this clearly.

INTERPRETATION.

LII. [13]*Behold my servant shall understand.* For, at the time of redemption the Messiah will perceive and *understand* the end, and know when the period for his coming is at hand, and the time has arrived for him to reveal himself to the congregation of those that are waiting for him. ישכיל is used in the same sense as by Daniel, xii. 9 f., where the meaning is that there will be some among the wicked who will display their wickedness by 'reproaching the footsteps of the Messiah' (Ps. lxxxix. 52) on account of his long tarrying, and by refusing to believe in him at all; thus they will not perceive the end, but will go astray after any one who may claim to be the Messiah: 'those that understand,' on the other hand, 'will be attentive' for the true end, and look for it expectantly. In agreement with the words of Daniel, Isaiah says the Messiah, the servant of the Lord, will *understand:* he will perceive the end, and forthwith will rise up and be exalted, and his heart will be 'lofty in the ways of the Lord' (2 Chron. xvii. 6) to go and gather together the outcasts of Israel, 'not by strength and not by might, but by his spirit' (Zech. iv. 6), trusting in the Lord, after the manner of that first redeemer who came to Pharaoh with his staff and scrip (cf. 1 Sam. xvii. 40), and smote his land with the 'rod of his mouth' (Is. xi. 4). And so it is said in the Midrash, 'He will be higher than Abraham, more exalted than Moses, and loftier than the ministering angels;' the Messiah, that is, will be higher than Abraham, who was an expounder of the belief in God, and, in spite of the opposition of the king, gained proselytes in the land of Nimrod: for the Messiah will do more than he did; he will proselytize many nations. And he will be more exalted than Moses: Moses went in unto Pharaoh, that great and wicked king, who said, I know not the Lord (Ex. v. 2), and, although only a shepherd and the humblest of men, was not afraid of him, but brought forth his people out of the 'furnace of iron' (Deut. iv. 20, Jer. xi. 4). But the Messiah will do more than Moses: for he will stir himself up against the kings of the whole world, so as to bring forth Israel from their hands, and to execute vengeance upon the Gentiles. And he will be loftier than the ministering angels, for although these exert themselves diligently in the redemption of Israel (like Michael, Dan. x. 20, 21), yet the Messiah will achieve more than the whole of them together. And wisdom will accompany this elevation of the Messiah, and his nearness to God: for neither Abraham, whom the glorious and fearful Name speaks of as *his friend* (Is. xli. 8), and with whom also he made a covenant; nor Moses, who was nearer to the Deity than any man; nor the ministering angels, who 'stand round about him on his right hand and on his left' (1 Kings xxii. 19), approach so closely to the knowledge of the Almighty as the Messiah; for of him it is written that he '*came to* the Ancient of days,' and that they 'brought him near before him' (Dan. vii. 13), but of the angels it is only said that 'ten thousand times ten thousand *stood before him.*' And hence Isaiah writes that *he will be high* in the understanding enabling him to comprehend the Deity, and *exalted and lofty* in the knowledge of his blessed name, more than all who were born before him: though to be 'greater than the angels' is said also of others, besides the Messiah, who are righteous. 14 The text continues, referring still to the Messiah, *As many were astonished at thee.* Their astonishment was shewn by mocking him when he first arrived, and by asking how one 'despised,' 'meek and riding upon an ass' (Zech. ix. 9), could conquer all the kings of the world who had laid hold upon Israel, and rescue him from their hand: so acted Pharaoh towards Moses, when he mocked him, as he says (Ex. vi. 12), 'How will Pharaoh listen to me?' 15 As they said, The visage of this man is marred, *so* they will say now that his speech will drop (יזה) upon them, and they will open their mouth wide for the rain of his word (Job xxix. 22, 23). The kings *will close their mouths*, and even in the chamber of their heart (Ezek. viii. 12) will be afraid to speak of him, saying each to his neighbour, Even in thy thought curse not a king (Qoh. x. 20).

LIII. 1 When the report of the Messiah comes among the people, *who* is there among them that will *believe it?* The *arm* is that which he will cause to journey at the right hand of the Redeemer, just as it is said that he 'caused the arm of his majesty to journey at the right hand of Moses' (Is. lxiii. 12). *Upon whom* has this arm been revealed so that he might believe in him? 2 For at the beginning he was *like a small tree* springing up *out of the dry earth*, which never grows great enough to put forth boughs and to bear fruit: he was *despised*, for he had no army and no people, but was 'meek and riding upon an ass,' like the first redeemer Moses, our master, when he entered into Egypt with his wife and children upon an ass (Ex. iv. 20). 3 He was *pained* for the iniquities of Israel, which occasion his tarrying, and hold him back from becoming king over his people; *and known to sickness*, because a man who is sick is continually distressed with pain. חולי is here used of the distress produced by excessive love, as 1 Sam. xxii. 8, 2 Sam. xiii. 2; or it may mean, perhaps, that he will really, as is sometimes the case with men, be made sick by his distress. [4] *Yet he carried our sicknesses*, being himself sick and distressed for the transgressions which should have caused sickness and distress in us, and bearing the pains which we ought to have experienced. *But we*, when we saw him weakened and prostrate, *thought* that he was *stricken, smitten of God.* [5] מחלל; from חולל as Ps. xxix. 9. *The chastisement of our peace* was *upon him*—for God will correct him; *and by his stripes we were healed*—because the stripes by which he is vexed and distressed will heal us: God will pardon us for his righteousness, and we shall be healed both from our own transgressions and from the iniquities of our fathers. רפא as vi. 10, lvii. 19: the metaphor of *healing* is often used with reference to redemption, cf. Jer. xxx. 13. [6] *All we like sheep had gone astray:* he charges Israel with guilt, because during their exile they apply all their attention to the business of this world, and every one devotes himself to the interests of himself and of his own household, when they ought rather to be weeping and praying before God night and day that he would pardon the iniquity of Israel, and speed the time that is to bring deliverance: for with repentance the Messiah will come at once, but without it he will delay until the end arrives, in accordance with the oath (Dan. xii. 7). *And the Lord laid upon him the iniquity of us all*—it lights upon him, because *he* is continually distressed that the wheels of his chariots tarry (Judg. v. 28): *we*, however, pay no attention, but abandon ourselves to our own concerns in the midst of the Gentiles. [7] *He was oppressed and he was afflicted:* for when he first comes, 'meek and riding upon an ass,' the oppressors and officers of every city will come to him, and afflict him with revilings and insults, reproaching both him and the God in whose name he appears, like Moses our master, who, when Pharaoh said, I know not the Lord, answered him not, neither said, The God of heaven and earth, who will destroy thee quickly, etc., but kept silence. So will the Messiah give no answer, but keep silence, and cease not to entreat for Israel, saying to all the kings of the nations, 'Thus saith the Lord, let my people go that they may serve me.' But he, *like a sheep led to the slaughter,* will think in his heart, Even though they slay me, I will perform the mission of my Creator, as it is my duty to do; so said and did Ananias, Mishael, and Azariah (Dan. iii. 18); and in the same way our Rabbis say, 'Whoso gives himself up to die, trusting that a sign will be wrought for him, there is no sign wrought for that man.' Jeremiah speaks similarly of himself (xi. 19), and also the singer Asaph (Ps. lxxiii. 14, cf. lxxxviii. 6). [8] He will think himself *taken away* from ruling over his people, and from being a prince and judge over them, and will wonder *who* there will be to *declare to his generation* the ways of the Lord, and announce that he has been cut off out of the land of the living for the transgression of his people,—an event which will be *a* severe *blow to them.* The passage says in his praise that he will not grieve about his own life, but only for the loss Israel will sustain by his death. [9] נתן is used of *thinking* generally, as Qoh. i. 13, 1 Sam. i. 16, and of *speaking,* as Lev. xvi. 21, Deut. xi. 29. The prophet says, He will *think* in his heart that *his grave* will be *with the wicked* among the Gentiles, for he will say, They will assuredly kill me, and in this place will be my tomb. קברו does not refer to the grave in which he was actually buried, but only the grave in which he expected to be buried: so Is. xxii. 16, Gen. l. 5 (where Jacob speaks of his grave, though he was not buried in it yet). Further, the wealthy Israelites, who take no pleasure in him, will give him many forms of death, for he will expect them to slay him by stoning, or burning, or murder, or hanging, like those who perished during the three days' darkness in Egypt. And this is the reason why מותיו, *deaths,* is plural. Yet *he did no violence,* viz. to the wicked who are mentioned, i. e. to the Gentiles, for he never attempted to rob them of anything that belonged to them; neither was *there any deceit in his mouth* towards the wealthy Israelites. [10] *But the Lord was pleased* to give him happiness through the distress which he endured, so that recognising in himself the presence of guilt and sin, *his soul* might *make a trespass-offering;* but his merit was imperfect, and so all this befel him in order that it might become complete. אם תשים are the words of God, and express his wish: 'If he will only bear all this, and humble himself, so as not to be contentious, and reason concerning my attributes! I will then give him his reward, measure for measure, that he may *see seed,*' etc. אם is used, as Jer. xv. 19, in the sense of *O that . . . He shall see seed:* in him will be fulfilled the promise, Ps. xlv. 17. *He shall lengthen days,* viz. for ever and ever, as it is written (Ps. xxi. 5), 'Length of days for ever and ever;' and so it is said in the *Pirqê* of Rabbi Eliezer, 'As it is written (Ps. lxi. 7), His years shall be as many generations.' *And the pleasure of the Lord shall prosper in his hand:* because he will accomplish the Redemption in which the Lord finds his pleasure, and will teach all the Gentiles to 'understand and know' the Lord: this is what is meant by the *pleasure of the Lord,* as it is written, 'In these is my pleasure' (Jer. ix. 23 [24 Eng.]). [11] *Because of the labour* which he *saw* (experienced) in himself, and because he *was satisfied* with 'shame instead of glory' (Hab. ii. 16), therefore *by his knowledge he will justify the just,* he will know and recognise who are the just that ought to be redeemed; and so in all his judgments he will find out the just, as it is written, He will not judge by the sight of the eyes, etc. (Is. xi. 3, 4, etc.); *and our iniquities,* i. e. those of the *many* who are mentioned, *he will set in order,* viz. by disposing them to repentance: cf. 1 Kings xi. 28, where סבל is equivalent to the disposition or arrangement of affairs (Ex. v. 4). [12] *Therefore I will divide him* a portion *with the many:* because 'the whole of many nations' (Ps. lxxxix. 51) will be his portion and inheritance, *and* from among the Gentiles *he will divide the strong as spoil* for his people and servants, *because he emptied his soul* of everything for death, i. e. he resolved in his mind and resigned himself to die. ערה as Ps. cxli. 8, 'Do not pour out my soul,' i. e. Empty it not of its hope which it longs to see realised: the accomplishment of one's pleasure is spoken of as a *filling* of the soul (Ex. xv. 9), and similarly the frustration of a desire is called its *emptying*. The prophet continues: *And* because *he was numbered with the transgressors*, expected, as I have stated, to be reckoned amongst them, *and carried the sin of many*—what happened to him at that time was not for his own sins, but for the sins of others—*and for transgressors* יפגיע, i. e. (according to what is said above, ver. 6) *allowed* the iniquity of sinners and transgressors *to light* upon himself. There is, however, no mention made in the Parashah that the Messiah would be delivered into the hands of those who hated him, or that he would be slain, or hung upon a tree; but that he should see seed and have long life, and that his kingdom should be high and exalted among the nations, and that mighty kings should be to him for spoil.

Extract from the 'Refutation.'

Friar Paul said, Behold their wise men say that the Messiah will be more glorious than all the angels: this can be realised in none except Jesus, who is God himself, and has fulfilled what is said in the Haggadah, 'He will be high and exalted, and lofty exceedingly—higher than Abraham, more exalted than Moses, and loftier than the ministering angels.'

I replied, But our wise men say this constantly of the righteous in general, affirming them to be greater than the angels[a]. Moses our master said to the angel, In the place where I dwell, thou must not stand[b]: and of Israel as a whole it is said that they are 'more beloved than the ministering angels[c].' The author of that Haggadah, however, meant to say that our father

[a] Thalmud of Babylon, *Sanhedrin*, fol. 93[a].

[b] Midrash, *P'tirath Mosheh* (decease of Moses), according to the *Yalqut*, on Pent. § 940.

[c] Thalmud of Babylon, *Ḥolin*, fol. 91[b].

Abraham gained many proselytes and expounded to the Gentiles the belief in the Holy One, and disputed with Nimrod and feared him not. And Moses did more than Abraham: in his humiliation he stood in the presence of the great and wicked king Pharaoh, and shewed him no favour, but smote him with great plagues, and brought forth Israel out of his hands. And the angels are more actively engaged in the work of redemption than Moses, according to what is said of Michael, Dan. x. 20, 21. But the Messiah will do more than all of them: 'his heart will be lofty in the ways of the Lord' (2 Chron. xvii. 6), and he will enter in and lay his commands upon the Pope and all the kings of the nations in the name of God, saying, Let my people go that they may serve me; not fearing them, but performing in their midst great and destructive signs and wonders; *he* also will stand in their city, even in Rome, until he lay it waste. And if you like, I will go on and explain the whole Parashah.

He would not, however, agree.

XXI. AHRON BEN YOSEPH (THE ELDER).

LII. [13] ישכיל *will be prosperous,* as 1 Sam. xviii. 30. *My servant:* some suppose that the prophet refers here to Israel collectively; but it is better to apply the word to those who are described in ver. 11 as 'bearing the vessels of the Lord:' because the 'wise' [p. 61] suffered more severely in captivity, and resigned themselves to death for the sake of God's holy name: the prophet addresses his consolations to the individual Israelites rather than to the nation as a whole. It is not consistent with the natural sense of the Parashah to refer it to the Messiah: for the Messiah cannot be termed 'forlorn of men.' נשא is *Nifal.* [14] *Upon thee:* the prophet passes from the 3rd to the 2nd person. *So* marred! in mockery and contempt: because the form and features of Israel were disfigured and unlike those of other men. משחת is not an abstract noun or a passive participle, as most except ourselves are of opinion, but is formed like מרשעת, 2 Chron. xxiv. 7, as an adjective: and תוארו resembles פועלו Jer. xxii. 13. [15] *So will he sprinkle* (יזה) the blood of *many nations:* from amazement *kings will close their mouths at him* (cf. תקפץ Deut. xv. 7), *for what was not told them* of old *they see* now in the majesty of the servant of the Lord.

LIII. [1] Israel is the speaker: *Who,* if he had heard it only without having seen it, *would have believed* that the servant of the Lord would be thus exalted? or have imagined on whom the arm of the Lord had been revealed? [2] לפניו; this refers back to מי האמין, viz. who would have believed *before this* that he would grow up like a sucker? others suppose it to mean *before God*, but this is not so natural. 'Who,' the prophet asks, 'could have believed that a root would spring up out of the dry earth?' an allusion to God's delivering his servant from captivity, and bringing him to such wonderful majesty and honour. *He had no form*, viz. previously to this change, *nor beauty*, *that we might desire him:* according to others, however, the negative must be understood twice, so that the meaning will be, 'and we did not desire him.' [3] *He was despised* in consequence of the temptations which beset him in the world, and *without reputation* in the presence of men. חדל is an adjective in *stat. constr.*, like חֲסַר 1 Sam. xxi. 16. *A man of pains*, because of the ill-treatment of the Gentiles, and *known to sickness* (ידוע is in *stat. constr.*), as followed naturally from his life of weariness and toil: the mass of men would not look upon him, because *he was despised and we esteemed him not.* [4] The language of his tormentors: We ourselves were the cause of his sickness and pain, which his piety forced him to endure: yet *we esteemed him smitten of God*, thinking it was God who had been the cause of it. [5] מחלל means *to be made sick.* מדכא is not derived from דכה, for then it would have been pointed מְדֻכֶּא. *The chastisement of our recompense*—the chastisement which was our due—*fell upon him:* and as we inflicted on him stripes and blows (בחבורתו) it became visible to us that *we were healed.* The word בחבורתו ought properly to have Dagesh in the ב. [6] As soon as they recognise the truth, they acknowledge it openly, as in the similar confession (Jer. xvi. 19), 'Our fathers have inherited falsehood.' Others suppose the verse to be spoken by the remnant of the Israelites who had inclined after a well-known belief[a], each following his own choice. הפגיע *made to meet;* cf. פגע Gen. xxxii. 2. עון has here the sense of penalty, as Gen. iv. 13, 1 Sam. xxviii. 10. [7] נגש is *Nifal*, from the same root as נוגש, 'oppressor:' the words 'opened not his mouth' refer to the 'sheep.'

[a] The writer means the school of the Rabbanites, which he refrains from mentioning openly.

[8] עוֹצֶר is a substantive, for he was confined in captivity: *he was taken from confinement* to confinement, *and from judgment* to judgment[b]; *and who could tell* (שוחח as Ps. cxliii. 5) the troubles which befel *the generation* of those that served and feared God? *for he was cut off from the land of life*, i.e. the land of Israel, from which the nation was exiled: and *because of their transgression* did this *stroke* come *upon them.* Or the words may be understood as follows:—Who would speak of their generation (by mentioning them in prayer) after they had been cut off from the land of the living? for the stroke had befallen them and the just had been deprived of life, because of their people's transgression. [9] *He made his grave* את הרשעים, i. e. in whatever manner the worshippers of stars and constellations[c] might condemn any individual Israelite. The idolaters are termed *the rich*, because in their hands Israel resembled the afflicted and needy: מותיו is plural, cf. Ezek. xxviii. 8. Or the sense may be that they made their grave like men proved to be *wicked* by trial and sentenced to death, and like the rich man dying in his sins. [10] *But the Lord was pleased to bruise him* (דכאו like דִּבָּרוֹ Gen. xxxvii. 4), in order to increase his reward, *and sickened him* with long-continued sicknesses (החלי, without א, like החטי Jer. xxxii. 35). *When* (אם as Is. iv. 4) *his soul makes a trespass-offering*, by acknowledging that the chastisements which come upon him are owing to some guilt, and so justifying God, *he will see* his *seed*, when *it prolongs its days:* or the subject of יאריך may be the same as that of יראה [*he* will lengthen days]. [11] *For the labour* which he imposed on himself, *he will see* prosperity, and *be satisfied* with the pleasantness of the Lord (Ps. xc. 17): *and by his knowledge*—the power to grant signs for the confirmation of his words—*he will justify* him that is *just.* The word 'many' is used, in order that no one may

---

[b] He means to say, that he was released from one place of punishment only to be transferred to another.

[c] A Rabbinical expression, signifying *idolaters.*

suppose that he establishes his words only to individuals. Or the meaning may be *for many*, those, viz. of whom it is written, '*Many* shall be made white, and purified and tried' (Dan. xii. 10). *And their iniquities he will bear;* for he will lead them in the way that is good. 12 *Therefore I will divide him* the capital[d] that is to be his in the world to come, *among the great* (רב as Jer. xli. 1), who have died for the unity of God; *and with* (את) *the mighty he will divide spoil, because he poured out* (Ps. cxli. 8) *his soul* in the cause of the Law, and *was numbered with the transgressors*, i. e. was punished as though he had been a transgressor himself, whereas in fact *he carried the sin of many, and made intercession for transgressors.*

[d] See the extract from the Thalmud, *Zebaḥim* 127 *a*, quoted in Buxtorf, *Lex.* s. v. קרן.

XXII. THE OLDER NIZZAḤON.

LII. [13] The whole of this Parashah is interpreted by the heretics of Jesus, who was punished and put to death for their sake, and so forth: but the reply to all this is not far to seek; it is written, 'He *shall be* high and exalted,' which implies that Jesus had not been so before. [14] It is also written that 'his countenance was marred beyond man, and his form beyond the sons of men:' but if he is God, why then did his countenance fall? and if it be answered, Because they smote him and because of the distress he endured, still if he is God, how could his features on this account have suffered disfigurement? [15] If the prophet had meant to say that he would gather many nations to his religion, he should have written יקרב (will bring near or attract), rather than יזה (will sprinkle or scatter). *For what was not told them have they seen:* but do they not affirm that all the prophets prophesied of him?

LIII. [1] *Upon whom was the arm of the Lord revealed?* see then how the work of Jesus had never been revealed either to the wise men or to the prophets! [2] *He had no form*, etc. Do they not declare that these words in the 45th Psalm, 'Thou art fairer than the children of men,' refer to Jesus, whereas here the prophet says of him, 'He was despised and forlorn of men?' And if it be said that during his lifetime he was fair, and that the words *he had no form nor comeliness* refer to his condition at the time of death, the reply is this, that if he were God, what kind of death could have affected him, and what change in the beauty of his countenance could have happened to him? [3] This verse also affords a refutation of the Christians: for every one knows that before Jesus was put to death and hidden from the eyes of creation, men esteemed him for nought, but that afterwards they went astray and followed him, saying he had ascended up to heaven: here, however, the prophet says, If he had not hidden his face from the children of men, we should have esteemed him not. [4] *He hath carried our sicknesses.* To what does this refer? If you say that he carried (*or* took away) their iniquity, was there then no taking away of sin before the birth of Jesus? yet Scripture speaks of sins being taken away and forgiven, as Ex. xxxiv. 7, Num. xiv. 20, and, with reference to the offerings, Lev. iv. 26. And if you still say that by this forgiveness they were delivered, not from Gehenna, but only from [temporal] punishments and chastenings, consider how their punishment cost them their lives (Ex. xxxii. 27 f.), and how it is written, 'And there fell of the people on that day about 3000 men:' it is plain, then, that their forgiveness did not save them from punishment; what object then could it have had except, surely, to deliver them from Gehenna? [5] They assert that all his sufferings were for their iniquities, in order to redeem them from the judgment of Gehenna: but, according to their own teaching, there was no necessity for him to suffer upon this account, for they say that even those men who are free from [actual] transgression or iniquity, go down to Gehenna; it follows then that, unlike the person here spoken of, Jesus cannot have been compelled to undergo death *for our transgressions*, but rather in order to annul the decree that all, good and bad alike, must go down to Gehenna. And if you next assert that he endured all this because of the iniquities committed by the faithful, for which his death atoned, then none of the faithful are bound by the commandment, neither have they any cause to grieve over the commission of robbery, stealing, murder, or adultery, since by his death all crimes are already atoned for. And thus his goodness becomes a mischief and a curse to the whole of creation.

XXIII. R. SHEM TOBH BEN SHAPRUT.

THE TRINITARIAN: In this Parashah it is asserted that just as the exaltation of God's servant had been great, so the humiliation which succeeded it was great likewise (lii. 13 f.); that he was to rule over many nations (ver. 15); that he was despised in the eyes of the Jews (liii. 1–3); that he was God, smitten and afflicted (ver. 4); that by his stripes the sin of Adam was healed for us (ver. 5); that he met death for our sakes (ver. 6); that he met it voluntarily (ver. 7); that there was no one who knew his generation, i. e. his seed, and that death came upon him in consequence of the transgressions of the people (ver. 8); and that he was hung between two thieves (ver. 9). In a word, the whole passage, rightly expounded, bears witness in every line to the history of Jesus our Messiah and to the things that befel him.

THE UNITARIAN: I have five objections to make against the position that this Parashah was spoken with reference to Jesus: 1. You have said that the Psalmist declares of him, 'Thou art fairer than the children of men' (xlv. 3), and Jeremiah also (xi. 16) calls him a 'flourishing olive-tree, beautiful with well-formed fruit,' and now you say that he is alluded to in the words 'so marred was his countenance,' and 'despised and forlorn of men:' these two assertions contradict each other. 2. 'He shall be high and exalted, and lofty exceedingly:' how is this said of God? was he not *high and exalted* from all eternity (Is. lvii. 15)? And think not to refute me by the words, 'Now will I arise,' etc. (Is. xxxiii. 10): it is plain that the prophet there says *now*, because it is a custom of Scripture to use such expressions of God (Ps. xliv. 24): but God forbid that he should be spoken of, in any verse, as enfeebled or disfigured. 3. The prophet calls him a 'man of pains' and 'known to sickness;' but only one on whom disease continually rests is said to be 'known to sickness,' and of Jesus we do not find in any of your books that he was 'sick' except on the day of his death alone, and there is not any passage in which death is spoken of as 'sickness.' 4. He is said to be smitten *of God*, but by your account 'smitten *of men*' would be the right expression to employ: and again, how can he be God? for Scripture calls him *smitten of God*, from which we may see that God is above him commanding him to be smitten: similarly in vers. 6, 10 he is the passive recipient, and God the agent who causes iniquity to rest upon him and is pleased to bruise him. 5. The words 'there was a stroke upon *them*' ought by your arguments to have been 'there was a stroke upon *him*:' if again, as you believe, the words אם תשים וג׳ mean 'when his soul makes a trespass-offering'—אם being=כי as Ex. xxii. 24—then, his soul being liable to such an offering, it is plain that he must have sinned. If now to avoid this conclusion you say that the 'trespass-offering' signified is *death*, then the soul of Jesus died, whereas you assert that the flesh alone died. Again, it is stated, 'He will prolong his days:' but was he not crucified when only thirty-two years old? and if you think that Isaiah alludes to his Deity, since this lives for ever and ever, such a resource is not admissible, because the phrase 'length of days' is only used with reference to the physical world, and is not applicable to life in the spiritual world. Then again, it is said, 'He shall see seed:' but where is his seed? and if you reply that the allusion is to his disciples, in that case the prophet should have written *sons*; for the word *seed* denotes such as are born by carnal generation. It is also derogatory to the Godhead to be called *servant* throughout the passage: the language in xliii. 10 refers to Israel.

The compiler says: Since the Nazarenes make a great point of this prophecy for their religion, so much so indeed that, in my estimation, it seems to be founded upon it, it is my intention to be a little diffuse, and to add four objections of my own: 1. If it alludes to Jesus, how is it that Isaiah says 'he *will* understand?' from this it is evident that previously he must have been devoid of any such attribute: but how can such language be used of God? 2. If the words מוכה אלהים mean, as you say, that he, God, was smitten, then this contradicts the teaching of your own religion: for you assert that only his *flesh* suffered. 3. How can God in any sense be said to be smitten? 4. The expressions in liii. 11, 12 imply plainly that his *soul* endured labour and death: this also contradicts what is taught by your own religion, viz. that only his *flesh* underwent death.

It is evident that the whole Parashah has reference to *Israel*, who were smitten and afflicted by the hands of the Gentiles, and who are called 'my servant,' Jer. xxx. 10, and by Isaiah himself, xliv. 21 and often.

LII. [13] In spite of Israel's being now a people 'foolish' (Jer. v. 21) and despised, a time will arrive when they will rise to great dignity, and *be prosperous* (ישכיל as 1 Sam. xviii. 14). [14] *As* till now the nations had told of Israel's shame, and *as* they had been marred in countenance, and ill-favoured in form, *so* henceforth they will have dominion over their enemies, and many kings—and *à fortiori* the rest of the people—will declare their dignity and honour.

LIII. [2] Their appearance, when returning from exile with disfigured countenances, is compared to that of a young plant which, as it first shoots up, is without form or beauty: yet, in spite of this, the Gentiles will in the future desire them, and say to one another in amazement, This is the people which bare the yoke of exile! [3] We thought that he was *despised and forlorn of men*, etc. The reference is here to the depression of Israel among the Gentiles, and to the manner in which the latter thought of him as a *man of pains,* and *known to sickness,* saying that they were liable to a well-known complaint, viz. emerods[a], as has been already mentioned above, III. 10; at their ignoble and loathsome appearance we, as it were, *hid* our *faces.* [4] They thought also that the only object of Israel's existence was, as Mohammed said, to bear the pains and misfortunes of the world, and that [5] all their iniquities and transgressions were carried by him, as though he had been the scape-goat, and that from him they were to receive *chastisement* or correction, when they were *at peace,* i. e. that they were then to be warned not to sin, lest the same fate should befal them which Israel's sin had drawn down upon him. *By his stripes we are healed:* because they thought that every one who oppressed Israel was healed from his iniquities. [6] This has reference to their belief that *we* slew Jesus because by his death all their iniquities are atoned for, whereas we, by the same death, are loaded with the penalty of them all. [7] The allusion is to Israel who endured their exile with a cheerful countenance, and listened in silence to the reproaches cast upon them. [8] The Gentiles took them and oppressed them and plundered their riches, whether by עצר, i. e. by violence, or משפט, i. e. by unjustly condemning them. And if we had attempted to relate the lot of each separate generation of them, *who would* be able to *recite* the long tale of their weary life up to the time when the final annihilation cut them off from the land of life? *For the transgression of my people,* etc.: either the words of the Gentiles declaring that misfortune would fall upon Israel because of their iniquity, and that therefore it would be their duty to destroy them; or the words of God shewing how all their troubles had come upon

---

a The sense here given, though not the one most usually borne by the Hebrew *Weseth,* seems fixed by the passage referred to, where the author remarks (with reference to Ps. lxxviii. 66), that there were two causes which rendered the Jews peculiarly liable to such complaints, namely, the melancholy produced by constant depression of mind during exile, and their sedentary habits.

Israel (who are the Lord's *people*) because they had sinned and transgressed, and therefore he had hidden his face from them; otherwise, indeed, the Gentiles would have had no power over them, as it is said (Deut. xxxii. 30), 'Except their rock had sold them,' etc. Ver. 10 speaks to the same effect: All their misery, it says, was the Lord's doing as a chastisement for their transgression. The first of these two explanations seems to me preferable. [9] The manner of the Gentiles was to adopt towards the Jews a course of persistent wickedness, so that whenever they saw a single wealthy Jew they would seek some mischief against him, in order to kill him and secure his riches, although there was no violence in his hands, or deceitfulness in his mouth. After this he would be buried in the graves of the wicked, like men executed for some crime. They would do the same even to such as were not wealthy, declaring that they were wealthy, and must possess riches. [10] *The Lord*, then, *was pleased to bruise him;* [11] yet for the labour which he endured in exile and accepted cheerfully, he *will be satisfied* with the portion allotted to him, knowing, as he does, that in virtue of it he will *justify many* so that they will 'behold the pleasantness of the Lord, and meditate in his temple' (Ps. xxvii. 4): *he will bear* and atone for *their iniquities*, when the expiation for his own sins and his fathers' (by which is meant the exile with its attendant miseries) has been accomplished. Cf. Lam. iv. 22 (which is the reverse of Gen. xv. 16); and for the sons *bearing the iniquities* of their fathers, Lam. v. 7. [12] He will be worthy to *divide* the *spoil* of his enemies, as a reward for his having *poured out his soul to die* for the sanctity of God's name. And he was *numbered with the transgressors,* viz. when condemned by the Gentiles, as is described in ver. 9: he also carried the sin of many, for besides his own sins, he bore (according to Lam. v. 7) the sins of his fathers and those of his sons as well, *and interceded for transgressors:* Israel interceded (Jer. xxix. 7) for sinners and transgressors; cf. Ps. xxxv. 13. ל here means *for the sake of* . . . , as Gen. xx. 13.

Questions propounded by Maestro Alphonso the Apostate, on the book of The Wars of the Lord, *with the author's reply.*

The Trinitarian:—Why do you raise an objection on the ground of the words 'his countenance marred beyond man?' No argument can be derived from what Jeremiah says (xi. 16), because, as a man's circumstances change, so is he himself changed likewise. The words have reference to Christ's *manhood:* and in this respect God is really superior to him. Then the expressions, a 'man of pains' and 'known to sickness' allude to the time when they set him at nought before his death, and were known to be true to all Israel who went up to the feast. He is called 'smitten of God,' because the foolish and wicked men who condemned him thought they were punishing his transgressions in accordance with the law. 'The Lord was pleased to bruise him,' viz. in respect of his manhood: 'because of the transgression of my people,' etc.; this resembles ver. 11, 'their iniquities he will bear,' because the murderous death which they wreaked upon him is 'a blow for them,' inasmuch as in consequence of it, they will be in perpetual exile, as the Scripture says, Ps. lxxxi. 16. Lastly, by *seed* are signified his disciples, who will prolong their days for ever; and by the expression 'poured out his soul to die' the prophet means to indicate his yielding up of the ghost.

The Unitarian:—Your argument, founded on the fact that, owing to sickness and trouble a man changes himself as his circumstances change, comes to nothing, because the words 'He came up as a sucker' etc. shew that Isaiah is speaking of the *beginning* of his appearance: if now he was even then 'despised and forlorn of men' and devoid of form or beauty, when was he ever like a 'flourishing olive-tree, fair with well-formed fruit?' Again, the expression 'known to sickness' cannot allude to the time when the soldiers smote him, because this was immediately succeeded by his crucifixion, as it is stated, Mat. xxvii; in that case, then, there could have been no time for his blows to produce *sickness*. Nor, in fact, is it ever asserted in any of the Gospels that he did sicken from them, or that he was even smitten severely, but only that they struck him on the face by way of insult: moreover, by your argument, the expression ought rather to have been 'known to *smitings*.' And if, as you assert, the words 'stricken and smitten' refer to his condemnation and punishment, the prophet ought rather to have written 'slain and put to death;' for the penalty he then paid did not consist in oppression or smitings, but in death. Again, if the 'transgression of my people' means their transgression in killing him, he ought not to have called them *my people*, because he must have counted them as his enemies: he ought rather to have said '*the* people' absolutely [or his people], cf. Ex. xxxii. 7 (Deut. ix. 12). Moreover, since even after the transgression which they had committed, he still calls them his people, it is plain that Israel's name did not perish, as you say was the case. And your assertion that his *seed* means his disciples is untrue, because the word is invariably employed in connexion with carnal birth: as I have stated in its proper place, it is impossible that the prophet should designate the disciples as *sons* . . . .

XXIV. R. MOSHEH KOHEN IBN CRISPIN.

A.

This Parashah the commentators agree in explaining of the Captivity of Israel, although the singular number is used in it throughout. The expression *my servant* they compare rashly with xli. 8, 'thou Israel art my servant,' where the prophet is speaking of the people of Israel (which would be singular); here, however, he does not mention Israel, but says simply *my servant;* we cannot therefore understand the word in the same sense. Again in xli. 8 he addresses the whole nation by the name of their father Israel (or Jacob, as he continues, '*Jacob* whom I have chosen'), but here he says *my servant* alone, and uniformly employs the singular, and as there is no cause constraining us to do so, why should we here interpret the word collectively, and thereby distort the passage from its natural sense? Others have supposed it to mean the just in this present world, who are crushed and oppressed now, but who in the future will have understanding, and 'shine as the brightness of the firmament' (Dan. xii. 3): but these too, for the same reason, by altering the number, distort the verses from their natural meaning. As then it seemed to me that the doors of the literal interpretation of the Parashah were shut in their face, and that 'they wearied themselves to find the entrance,' having forsaken the knowledge of our Teachers, and inclined after the 'stubbornness of their own hearts,' and of their own opinion, I am pleased to interpret it, in accordance with the teaching of our Rabbis, of the King Messiah, and will be careful, so far as I am able, to adhere to the literal sense: thus, possibly, I shall be free from the forced and far-fetched interpretations of which others have been guilty. In the course of my exposition, I shall allude to the phrases in it which will convince the man of intelligence that it cannot (as is done by our opponents) be explained with reference to God; thus, in addition to the exposition itself, I shall be enabled to offer a reply to their objections.

My servant. I may begin by remarking that we find this term used in Scripture of an individual prophet, as Moses (Num. xii. 7), and Job (i. 8), of all the prophets generally (Amos iii. 7), and of the whole of Israel (Lev. xxv. 42). In each of these cases, it is plainly applied to the sons of men born of human parents; but we do not find it used of angels, known clearly to be such, because it is only applicable to one who enslaves himself assiduously to the service of God, and directs both his person and his thoughts 'to serve him with all his heart and with all his soul' and with all the members of his body (for this is the meaning of 'all his strength'), like the faithful servant of whom it is said, 'With all my strength have I served your father' (Gen. xxxi. 6), who keeps himself aloof from serving any besides, and who therefore, because it is his own choice to serve him, is called the servant of the Lord. This service is implanted in the heart, as it is written (Deut. xi. 13), 'And to serve him in all your heart:' it cannot, therefore, be predicated of an angel, i. e. of any of the abstract intelligences, for it has its seat in a bodily organ, in the *heart*, and nowhere else, and an angel has no body or bodily strength. *À fortiori*, then, the expression cannot possibly be applied to the substance of the Creator himself, as is done by our opponents in their theory of the Trinity, according to which, this man was of the substance of the Creator. For they hold that the whole [Godhead] is of one substance, but that it is divided into three persons, the Father, the Son, and the Spirit, that the Son took flesh and came down to the earth: now, even granting all this, which, though it is impossible to speak about, still less to conceive, you nevertheless maintain, how could he describe himself as 'my servant,' i. e. as one who devoted himself to serve 'me,' i. e. to serve himself? since, for a man to be called his own servant is a palpable absurdity. *He shall be high*, etc. These words afford likewise an answer to our opponents; for they refer exclusively to the *future*. The prophet says, 'He *will* be high and exalted, and lofty exceedingly;' and this language clearly cannot be applied to God; for how could it be said of him that, like a mortal man, he will at some future time be high and exalted, as though he had not been so before? yet, if God is God, he is the same in the past as he will be in the future. If, now, they say that the word *servant* denotes the flesh in which he became incarnate in the world, a twofold answer is close at hand: 1. from the prophet's saying, 'My servant shall have understanding,' it is clear the term is connected expressly with something possessing intelligence; it is, however, well known, that the intellectual powers reside, not in the body, but in the soul: 2. he says that he will be 'high and exalted;' but during the whole time that he is reported to have been incarnate, we do not find that exaltation or supremacy ever fell to his lot, even to the day of his death.

I will now proceed to my exposition. [13] *Behold my servant shall have understanding.* From the prophet's saying 'understanding,' it may be seen that all the lofty predicates which he assigns to him have their source in this attribute; in virtue of his comprehensive intelligence he will attain to an elevation above that even of the most perfect men in the world. *He shall be high and exalted, and lofty exceedingly.* According to the Midrash of our Rabbis; 'he will be *higher* than Abraham, *more exalted* than Moses, *loftier* than Solomon, *exceedingly* above the ministering angels.' He will be *higher* than Abraham, who was first of all a 'high father,' and afterwards the father of a multitude. He will be *more exalted* than Moses, who was 'exalted[a] above the exalted ones of Levi' (cf. Num. iii. 32), who was a prophet such that 'none arose like him in Israel' (Deut. xxxiv. 10), who 'saved' Israel 'with a great salvation' (cf. 1 Chron. xi. 14) when they came out of Egypt, and the report of whom spread into all places until 'the dukes of Edom were confounded' before him, and 'trembling seized the mighty men of Moab, and all the inhabitants of Canaan melted away' (Ex. xv. 15). But this one will be exalted far above Moses: for when he gathers together our scattered ones from the four corners of the earth, he will be exalted in the eyes of all the kings in the whole world, and all of them will serve him, and will exalt him above them, as Daniel prophesies concerning him, 'All nations, peoples, and tongues shall serve him' (Dan. vii. 14, 27). He will be *loftier* than Solomon, whose dignity was so lofty that he is said to have 'sat on the throne of the Lord' (1 Chron. xxix. 23), and our Rabbis say[b] that he was king over both the upper and the nether world. But the King Messiah, in his all-comprehending intelligence, will be loftier than Solomon. *Exceedingly* above the ministering angels, because that same comprehensive intelligence will approach [God] more nearly than theirs. For it is an exceedingly high privilege, that one whose nature is compound and material should attain to a grade of intelligence more nearly Divine than that which belongs to the incorporeal; and so it is said of him that 'his strength is greater than that of the ministering angels,' because these have no impediment in the exercise of their intellect, whereas that which is compound is continually impeded in consequence of material element in its nature. Accordingly the grade of his intelligence being such as this, he is said to be 'lofty exceedingly,' and his strength to be 'greater than the angels.' It is probable, however, that this Messiah will not be

[a] A. V. 'chief over the chief,' but the word rendered *chief* (elsewhere also *prince*) means properly 'one lifted up or exalted.' In the text the phrase is applied to Eliezer, not to Moses.

[b] Thalmud of Babylon, *Sanhedrin*, fol. 20[b].

born in the midst of the captivity of Israel, in one of the many places all over the earth where they are bowed down beneath the Gentiles, because there, being in such a state of subjection, it would be impossible for a man to be born who would attain to this high elevation; but there are, perhaps, spots in the world, where Israel dwell in tents (Jer. xxxv. 7) in the midst of the wilderness, far away from the dominion of the nations though still in exile from their own land; and these may represent a part of the Israelites whom Sanhérib, king of Assyria, carried away captive to Chalach and Chabor (2 Kings xviii. 11), and who were afterwards joined by the families of the house of David, and, in particular, by that pure tribe out of which the King Messiah is destined to arise. And when this 'servant of the Lord' is born, from the day when he comes to years of discretion, he will continue to be marked by the possession of intelligence enabling him to acquire from God what it is impossible for any to acquire until he reaches that height whither none of the sons of men, except him, have ever ascended: from that day he will be counted with his people Israel, and will share their subjugation and distress; 'in all their affliction' (Is. lxiii. 9) he will be exceedingly afflicted; and because of their being outcasts and scattered to the ends of the world, his grief will be such that the colour of his countenance will be changed from that of a man, and pangs and sicknesses will seize upon him (for great grief, as physicians know, by producing melancholy, subjects a man to many diseases); and all the chastisements which come upon him in consequence of his grief will be for our sakes, and not from any deficiency or sin on his part which might bring punishment in their train, because he is perfect, in the completeness of perfection, as Isaiah says (xi. 2 f.). Truly all his pains and sicknesses will be for us; continually will he be prostrating himself, and stretching out his hands to God on our behalf, and praying him to hasten the time of our redemption, until in compassion upon him, and in order to shorten the intense grief felt by him for us,

the Creator 'speeds' the time of our deliverance. This is what the prophet means when he says (lx. 22), 'In its time, I will *speed* it:' he will *speed* to redeem us, before the time comes; and that because of his compassion on the 'affliction' wherewith 'he was afflicted' for our sakes. And so great will be his grief and pain endured thus on our behalf, that those who see him will despise him, thinking that in consequence of his many deficiencies and sins God brought all those chastisements upon him, or else that they were intended as chastisements of love; for they will never believe that such sufferings could be caused merely by grief. And because of their attributing them to these deficiencies and sins, he will be despised in their eyes, and they will count him as nothing, not perceiving the great perfection that is in him, who will be a compassionate father to have compassion on us, even more than Moses our master, and in the multitude of his compassion for us will draw to himself all those sicknesses and chastisements, until the Creator hears his prayer, and looks upon all his pain, and has compassion on us for his sake, and speeds our redemption, and sends him to redeem us. And then at last the Creator will assign him his reward for all the grief which he bore for us, and will 'multiply his seed, and prolong his days, and divide him a portion in the earth among the great, and give him the spoil of mighty nations.' Such is the meaning of the Parashah as a whole: I may now explain each verse separately for itself.
14 *As many were desolated at thee:* he means Israel who are sitting in desolation on account of the delay which hinders the approach of the Messiah. *So marred was his countenance beyond man:* i. e. so much was he himself also pained and grieved at the delay in his coming to redeem us, that his countenance grew disfigured beyond any man's, and his form, from the same cause, more than the forms of other men. The prophet begins in the 2nd pers. *at thee*, and then proceeds to speak in the 3rd *his countenance:* he ought properly to have used the 3rd pers. from the first, *at him*, but it is customary

for the two persons to be thus combined in a single verse, as 'Hear peoples, all of them!' (1 Kings xxii. 28, Micah i. 2), where it ought to have been *all of you;* and so 'All of them, return!' (Job xvii. 10), and often. [15] *So will he sprinkle many nations,* i. e. *as* his countenance is marred beyond man when he comes to redeem us, *so* he will scatter many nations and disperse them to the ends of the earth, like one who *sprinkles,* i. e. who scatters blood. The expression *sprinkle* means that he will scatter them without difficulty, like one who sprinkles blood, just as previously (xi. 4) it is predicted that he will 'smite the earth with the rod of his mouth:' and so I find Yonathan interprets the word. *At him kings will shut their mouth:* because from the vastness of his might and the number of his miracles and the greatness of the terror cast upon them, when he 'smites the earth with the rod of his mouth, and with the breath of his lips slays the wicked,' they will be so amazed at his rebuke as to close their mouth, and not to speak from amazement at what he does. *For that which was not told them they have seen:* for although much of his work was told them, what they have seen has been far more. *And that which they had not heard have they observed:* what they had never heard before about his high dignity, and great wisdom, they will find in him when they observe his work; and therefore they are amazed so that they cannot speak. Upon this explanation קפץ means *to shut* (as Deut. xv. 7, Job v. 16): it may, however, mean *to open* (as Cant. ii. 8, of the legs *opened* or extended in leaping); in the latter case, the prophet says they will *open* their mouth to tell of his greatness and dignity. There are some, too, who explain נזה in the sense of *speaking*—the force of the Hif'il being 'he will make others speak:' for a speaker sprinkles and scatters his words towards his hearers, and accordingly we find נטף *to drop* used both of the clouds *dropping* water (Judg. v. 4), and of speech (Micah ii. 6); since the two actions are spoken of by a single term, we learn that there is some feature common to both. If *sprinkle* be understood in the same sense here, it will mean that, as his countenance was marred beyond man, he will make many nations speak of it, when he comes forth to redeem us, and they will ask, 'Will a man whose form and countenance is thus marred, come to save and redeem a people so numerous as Israel who are dispersed in every corner of the earth?' but afterwards, when he comes to fight against the kings and to redeem Israel from their power, and when they behold his might and the miracles he will perform, they will *shut their mouth* in silent amazement, seeing in him marvels which had never been told them, and discerning high attributes which before they had never heard of. (Or, upon the other view, they will *open their mouth*, in order, viz. to tell of his greatness, as I have explained.)

LIII. [1] *Who hath believed our report?* who was able to believe the report which we heard of him, when they said to us that, as the prophets had announced, he had at last come to redeem Israel 'with a mighty hand, and stretched-out arm,' until we saw the matter with our own eyes? *And the arm of the Lord, upon whom has it been revealed?* The arm, being the principal and strongest limb, is used metaphorically for *strength*, as Ps. lxxxix. 14, 'Thine is an arm with might!' The meaning thus is, Upon whom of yore was the might of the Lord revealed, so as for him to rule by means of it over all the sons of men, as it is now seen upon this Messiah, and as it has never been seen upon any besides him? [2] This verse states how the servant of the Lord grew up, viz. like a branching tree which had sprung up out of the dry earth and come to maturity *before him*, i. e. before his appearance, and which, as the branches rose out of the roots, we perceived had sprung up in deficiency of water. Or, perhaps, he may be compared to both the branches and to the root separately, each of which sprang up out of the dry ground, and without either form or comeliness. The King then, through the grief and sorrow which he bore on our account from the time of his coming to years of discretion, and which clung to him until it left him no form or comeliness, resembles either the branching tree coming up out of a root planted in the dry earth, or both the branches and the root together, which sprang up out of the dry soil. *Sucker* is used for the boughs and branches of a tree, as Ps. lxxx. 12. The passage must be understood as if it had run thus:—And he came up like a sucker and like a root out of the dry earth, before him (i. e. which we noticed growing up before he appeared), which had no form and no comeliness; the comparison is thus between the servant of the Lord and these. *And we shall see him*, etc., i. e. from the moment when *we see* that he is come to redeem us, although his countenance is unlike that of other men, because of the changes marked upon it by his grief (as we have already explained), yet on account of his mighty wonders, the great and desirable deeds he will perform, and the salvation with which he will save us, *we shall desire him*—desire to draw near to him and behold him. Others suppose that the two clauses are parallel, the force of the negative extending over both the last words 'we shall see him, but there will be no beauty that we should desire him:' on account of his marred and altered countenance we shall not desire to look at him. [3] *Despised, and forlorn of men:* despised, namely, in the eyes of the world because of his loathsome appearance. *Forlorn of men* means either forlornest, i. e. the most insignificant of men, or else forsaken by men, who will refuse to associate with him for the reason just given. *A man of pains and known to sickness*, i. e. possessed of pains and destined to sicknesses: so all that see him will say of him. They will also, it continues, on account of his loathsome appearance, be *like men hiding their faces from him:* they will not be able to look at him, because of his disfigurement. And even we, who before were longing to see him, when we see what he is like, *shall despise him* till we no longer *esteem him*, i. e. we shall cease to think of him as a Redeemer able to redeem us and fight our battles because of all the effects which we see produced by his weakness. [4] *Surely our sicknesses he hath carried.* These words explain the cause of his sufferings; they all come upon him on account of the grief and sorrow which he will feel for the sicknesses caused by our iniquities: it will be as though he had borne all the sicknesses and chastisements which fall upon us. Or, perhaps, 'carry' may mean *take away, forgive,* as Ex. x. 17; from his pity and his prayers for us he will atone for our transgressions: *and our pains he hath borne,* viz. as a burden upon himself, cf. 1 Kings v. 29; i. e. all the weight of our pains he will carry, being himself pained exceedingly by them. *And we esteemed him stricken, smitten of God, and afflicted.* We shall not believe that there could be any man ready to endure such pain and grief as would disfigure his countenance, even for his children, much less for his people: it will seem a certain truth to us that such terrible sufferings must have come upon him as a penalty for his own many shortcomings and errors: and therefore we shall account him 'smitten of God;' in other words, we shall consider them to have been sent upon him directly from heaven. 5 But it is not so; they are not a penalty sent from God, but *he was panged for our transgressions* (מחולל from חיל, Ps. xlviii. 7 al.)—pangs, as of labour, will seize him for the distress that has come upon us for our transgressions. *He was bruised for our iniquities,* i. e. crushed and broken, as Ps. cxliii. 3, 'He hath bruised my life down to the ground,' Lam. iii. 34, Is. lvii. 15: his grief for our misery will be so great as quite to break him down. *The chastisement of our peace:* some render 'the chastisement *of the whole of us,*' understanding שלום in the sense of *completeness, entirety,* cf. 1 Kings vii. 51, Gen. xv. 16, xxxiii. 18, Deut. xxv. 15: others, however, adhere to the meaning *peace,*—the chastisements which ought to have come upon us while we were at peace have as it were fallen upon him. *And by union with him we are healed,* i. e. although he is in the utmost distress from pain and sickness, yet by union and nearness to him, we are healed from all the diseases to which our afflictions give rise. Others explain

חבורה as identical with חבּורה (with loss of the Dagesh, as חברברות Jer. xiii. 23, of the *dark stripes* on a leopard, which resemble the dark stripes on a man's flesh): upon this view חבורה means an *incision* or *slit*. Our Rabbis explain it as signifying a blow which causes the blood to coagulate beneath the skin, in accordance with their saying[c], 'What is a חבורה which never disappears? It is a bruise where the blood, though it does not break out through the skin, nevertheless coagulates beneath it:' the meaning will then be, that by the weals breaking out on his flesh in consequence of his anxiety for us, God will have mercy upon him, and, by sparing him for the sake of his sufferings endured on our account, heal us. [6] Like sheep which have no shepherd, and which wander hither and thither on the plain, so were we wandering in our own works and ways, each going after his own business, and none caring for the service of God: our iniquity was 'too great to be forgiven,' and because in our exile we had incurred the extremest penalty, behold it was as though this penalty, which was deserved by all of us, had been laid by God upon him. [7] This verse describes the penalty thus mentioned as seemingly laid on him by the Creator, when the sufferings come upon him, which (as I have explained) he will cause for himself: in his distress he will then resemble a man whom his creditors *press upon* in order to take from him what he has. נגש is applied to the extortion of money, as Deut. xv. 2. ענה is used with reference to the body; while enduring his sicknesses and pain, he is like one whose body is being afflicted with stripes and other humiliating punishments: all these he acquiesces in, and accepts with a cheerful countenance. He is *like a sheep* in not opening his mouth to cry; and is further compared to a lamb (*fem.*), because the female is always weaker than the male. [8] His altered countenance makes him look like one who has been long confined in prison, and whose continual

---

[c] Thalmud of Babylon, *Shabbath*, fol. 107[b].

anxiety whether he will be brought out to execution, has caused his complexion to change. In the same way, he is like one who stands at the bar before his judges, and they condemn him to death so that his features alter at the prospect. Thus the words מעצר וממשפט לקח mean '*he is like* one taken out of confinement, and from the place of judgment (and led away to execution).' עָצַר is *to detain*, or *confine*: and so עֹצֶר is the place where men are detained and prevented from going out: cf. Judg. xiii. 15, 1 Sam. xxi. 8 (where נעצר means that Doeg was detained before the Lord to pray), Jer. xxxiii. 1, xxxix. 15. ישוחח signifies *to tell*, as Ps. cxliii. 5: 'who will be able to tell of all the greatness and the glory which will be shewn to his people by his means in his generation?' the expression is hyperbolical, resembling Gen. xxi. 7. *For he is cut off*, etc. The nature of this Messiah is exceeding wondrous: it is composed of two contradictory elements. His *soul* is 'cut off from the land of the living;' in other words, it is derived from the living angels who exist for ever, i. e. from the abstract intelligences: these form the source from which his own intelligence emanates, and gradually, in virtue of its comprehensive wisdom, ascends to an elevation, which, as we have explained above, none else has ever attained. His *body*, on the other hand, is composed of griefs and pains and sicknesses—of grief *for the transgression* and affliction *of his people* (which was so great as to disfigure his appearance), and of pains and sicknesses greater than those of other men. And it is an indication of his perfection that he does not care for the pain of his own body; for he recognises its proper rank, and its deficiencies, in this nether world—a world which has no permanence and continueth not in one stay, but is ever changing from one nature to another. Such a merciful father is he to us that, as he sees us in the misery of exile, the vigour of his body forsakes him, and for our sake he 'enters into the thickness of the beam[d]' to grieve

[d] A phrase signifying 'to do the impossible.'

for us and to pray for us, until he redeem us from our exile. And, therefore, all that hear of him, or know him, will marvel at him exceedingly, because never in the world had a prophet or wise man been heard of who was compounded of two natures such as these. In this exalted perfection he will continue till for his merits, and in compassion for his grief, and because of his wondrous nature, the Lord *hastens* the time of our redemption, according to the words which I have explained, 'I the Lord, in its time, will speed it,' i. e. 'when its time approaches, before the day when it should actually arrive, I will hasten its advent.' Thus the text states the reason why none can *declare his generation*, because, namely, he is 'cut off,' or derived, from the land of the living and from the transgression of my people. The last word למו refers to 'my people :' 'from the transgression of my people, (which was) a blow to them,' since in consequence of it, many plagues fell upon them. [9] Here it is stated what these plagues were: many of the just and pious were slain, and those who buried them *gave* or assigned them their graves *with the wicked*. And you can think of no heavier blow to fall upon my people than that they should be buried 'with the wicked' as though belonging to their company; as it is said of Abner, 'Was Abner to die as a fool dieth?' (2 Sam. iii. 33.) In the same way the *rich* are spoken of, as slain miserably by various kinds of death, and afterwards buried in contempt with the wicked, neither their riches nor their honour profiting them anything. The whole phrase will thus mean, that the grave of my people was with the wicked, and that the rich also among them were assigned at their death a burial-place with the wicked as well. And all this was inflicted upon them *because they had done no violence, and there was no deceitfulness in their mouth.* [10] The reference is now again to the King Messiah, of whom the prophet had been speaking at the beginning: we cannot, he says, attribute the sicknesses and pains, which befel him after his perfection was known in the world, to any inherent defect in himself; they are the chastisements of love wherewith *the Lord was pleased to bruise him* by the agency of *sickness*[c] (or perhaps, *and to make him sick*—החלי being written defectively for החליא). Where mention is made of 'the Lord's pleasure,' we cannot arrive at the full meaning; God's own will none but himself can completely comprehend, though *we* attribute the pains and sickness spoken of to this cause, because we cannot credit that a man should ever for his own people, or even for his sons, be sufficiently distressed to bring them upon himself. *If his soul makes itself into a trespass-offering*, implying that his soul will treat itself as guilty, and so receive punishment for our trespasses and transgressions. *He shall see seed*, etc.: as though the Creator said, 'If he has done this for my people, behold his reward is with him, *he shall see seed, he shall lengthen days*:' in opposition to what the world thought of him, who imagined from his prostration that he was destined to have no seed, and that it was impossible for him to have long life, the Creator, whose thoughts are not as our thoughts, promises that 'he shall see seed, and prolong his days;' he will restore him to the days of his youth, and he will give him his seed and lengthen his days. *And the pleasure of the Lord, he shall prosper with his hand*, i. e. 'the pleasure of the Lord *is that* he shall prosper in all the work of his hands:' the reward for all the afflictions which he imposed upon his body for the Lord's people is, that he will recover strength and vigour so as to have seed, and enjoy long life, and prosper in whatever he sets his hand to. This verse affords a cogent reply to our opponents, shewing convincingly that the Parashah does not speak of God, as their arguments assert that it does; even if it be urged that God's people are called *sons* (as Deut. xiv. 1), and similarly that the prophets' disciples are called the *sons* of the prophets (2 Kings ii. 3 al.), although this argument might be valid if the same term *sons* had been used here as well, it is nevertheless impossible that 'seed' can be employed with

[c] החלי being taken as a noun, 'with sickness.'

reference to God, for God has no seed. Moreover, the expression 'shall prolong his days' evidently has reference to a limited space of time: but there are no limits to God's infinity; and had the prophet been speaking of God he must have said, 'He will endure *for ever and ever*' (like Ex. xv. 18, Ps. ix. 8, and often similarly): it is, however, certain that the Parashah alludes to none but a mortal man, born beyond reach of doubt of human parents. [11] *Because of the labour* and distress which he brought upon *his* living *soul*, and upon his body, for the sake of the people of the Lord, *he will see* all prosperity so as to be *satisfied* with it. *By his knowledge*, etc. He proceeds to tell of his high perfection, how *in his* unfaltering *knowledge* he will *justify the just*, and stand in defence of the truth, without the need of witnesses or proof, solely in virtue of the truthfulness of clear and complete perceptions. And my servant will do this לרבים, i. e. *before the eyes of the many*, viz. Israel, of whom Isaiah spoke at the beginning of the Parashah, 'As *many* were astonished;' for Israel multiplied and were more numerous than the other nations (Ex. i. 7, Num. x. 36). *And their iniquities*, i. e. those of the many, of Israel, *he will bear*, and will atone for them in the perfection of his nature, until their sins depart from them and they are left guiltless. [12] *Therefore*, etc., 'after he has done all this and delivered the multitudes of Israel, *I will allot him* a large portion in their midst:' for the Creator will assign him a portion in the land of Israel, as our Rabbis say (*Babhâ Bathra*, fol. 122 [a]), 'The whole land of Israel will be divided into thirteen portions.' In the same place it is explained for whom the thirteenth is intended, viz. for the prince who will be among them, as it is said in Ezekiel (xlviii. 19) that there will be a portion for the prince, etc.—a verse which refers to the King Messiah. *And the mighty*, i. e. the mighty nations, Gog and Magog, who come to attack him, *he*, and Israel 'the many,' *will divide as spoil, because he poured out* (Gen. xxiv. 20) *his soul to die*, i. e. brought it 'nigh to the gates of death' in consequence of the grief and pain which he bore for Israel, and also, the prophet adds, for himself, the punishments which came upon him being such that those who saw him imagined him to be like the transgressors and counted him among them: all this befel him because of the greatness of his love and compassion for his people Israel. *Yet he* in his perfection *carried the sins* of Israel *the many*, until he made expiation for them and removed their sins from off them. *He* also *interceded for the transgressors* (i. e. for Israel): these words explain in what way he 'carried their sins,' viz. by making intercession for them. פגע means *to pray* or entreat, as lix. 16, Gen. xxiii. 8, Jer. xxxvi. 25. This prophecy was delivered by Isaiah at the divine command for the purpose of making known to us something about the nature of the future Messiah, who is to come and deliver Israel, and his life from the day when he arrives at discretion until his advent as a redeemer, in order that if any one should arise claiming to be himself the Messiah, we may reflect, and look to see whether we can observe in him any resemblance to the traits described here: if there is any such resemblance, then we may believe that he is the Messiah our righteousness; but if not, we cannot do so.

The explanation of this Parashah, referring to the Messiah speedily to be revealed in our own days, is now completed.

Says Sa'adyah [Ibn Danân], the scribe: I have here transcribed an exposition of this Parashah: perhaps an answer may be found in it against the heretics who interpret it of Jesus. It is my intention to keep myself continually at the doors of the learned; and, so far as my ability can command, I shall follow the saying of our Rabbis, 'And know now how to reply to Epicurus[f],' though it does not seem to me to be right or permissible to apply the prophecy to the King Messiah (for reasons which any intelligent man will easily find out): it must, in fact, be referred either to Israel as a whole, or to Jeremiah.

[f] *Aboth*, § ii. On 'Epicurus,' the general title for those who reject and despise the Jewish faith, see Buxtorf, *Lex.* s. v.

B.

Says the Apostate: Although you are seeking and searching after me to refute the arguments which I bring against you concerning the coming of Jesus our Messiah, I will now adduce some clear proofs from the prophecy of Isaiah, shewing how he is come and how he underwent great sufferings, and was afterwards condemned to death for the redemption of his creatures who were in Gehenna, and how he saved them from the power of their well-known adversary [Satan] (as I have said above), into which they had fallen in consequence of the 'original' sin committed by Adam and Eve, which could not be atoned for except by the agency of one greater than our first parent. And it is impossible that there can be any greater than Adam except Jesus our Messiah, who is man and God. If, therefore, you will confess the truth, you will have no valid answer to the proofs I shall bring forward.

LII. 13 The first verse of the Parashah your learned men in the Thalmud expound thus: 'He will be higher than Abraham, more exalted than Moses, and loftier than the ministering angels.' Who, now, is greater than Abraham, more exalted than Moses, and loftier than the angels, except Jesus our Messiah, who is both man and God? 14 *As many*, etc.; i. e. As his greatness was wonderful, so marred was his flesh and his form from the sufferings and death at the time when they crucified him, so will he rule over many nations, and kings will close their mouths at him, because (as was indeed the fact) the miracles and wonders which they saw him perform had never been told them.

LIII. 1 לשמועתנו is to be taken in its ordinary sense. 2 He had no form, and we esteemed him not, for he was despised in the eyes of the Jews, and was a man of pains and known to sickness; by these are signified the sufferings which the Jews inflicted on him. 3 God himself, then, was *smitten and afflicted*, viz. by bearing our iniquities for our advantage. 4 Through his death, the original sin, in consequence of which [even] the righteous were delivered to Gehenna, was *healed to us.* [5] Before he came, the children of the world were wandering about like sheep without a shepherd: each had turned after his own way, to do what was right in his own eyes; they were like blind men groping for a wall (Is. lix. 10). But *the Lord laid upon him the iniquity of us all,* he was delivered up to death to atone for our sins: and (ver. 6) he met death willingly for the redemption of our souls: there was none (ver. 7) who could discern any seed which came from him, and for the transgression of my people death fell upon him; lastly, at his crucifixion (ver. 8), two malefactors were hung beside him. Now see in what way this whole Parashah from beginning to end has reference to Jesus our Messiah; for you cannot deny that every single word in it was fulfilled in him, both generally and in particular.

The author answered: You think in your heart that none of the proofs which you have brought forward to shew that the Parashah was spoken with reference to Jesus your Messiah admit of any answer; but do not the portions preceding and following it, as well as what it contains itself, make your reasoning valueless, and prevent its standing or being confirmed?

Again the author answered: Do not condemn me if I protract my reply here: I am forced to do so, because in this Parashah they press their objections upon us more closely than in any of their other refutations; I would urge, then, the following thoughts. Do not the preceding verses allude to the gathering in of our exiles in the future (lii. 12, 'For not in haste,' etc.), and the consolations of Jerusalem? and is it not written afterwards, 'Rejoice, O barren woman,' etc. (liv. 1, 2, 3–8)? and again, 'This is as the waters of Noah,' etc. (liv. 9, 10)? in the middle, then, the prophet describes what the nations will say of Israel generally at the time when this gathering takes place, and what the nations and the multitude of Israel will say of the righteous in particular, when they see them invested with dominion and greatness; for then they will 'be astonished at' them, because before they had seen them despised and depressed among the peoples (as it is written, xlix. 7), but now 'kings will be their nursing fathers, and queens their nursing mothers' (xlix. 23); and at that time, as Daniel writes (xii. 3), the righteous in particular will have illimitable greatness. Such is the simple and literal interpretation of the Parashah.

LII. 13 *My servant.* This is said of each individual among the just, exactly as in Jer. xxx. 10, xlvi. 27 f., also Is. xliv. 2: in the same way the prophet says here, 'Behold my servant will prosper' (ישכיל as 1 Sam. xviii. 14). 14 All the nations were in astonishment and wonder at the depression of Israel in captivity, when their countenance and form were marred beyond those of other nations: for when any one of you wishes to indicate that a person is held in some contempt, he calls him a Jew. 15 *As* they were thus depressed and despised, and *as* many marvelled at their prostration, *so* will they rule over many nations: like a man sprinkling blood with his finger who can scatter it in whatever direction he pleases, so will they do what they please with many nations. *At him kings will shut their mouths*, i. e. in astonishment, when they see all their dignity and dominion; for *what had not been told them have they seen*, viz. such greatness as they had never heard of as appertaining to any nation before.

LIII. 3 All Israel were continually smitten and afflicted among the Gentiles: and the more they were afflicted, the more were they despised in their eyes until they hid their faces so as no longer to gaze upon them.—Up to this point it is the Gentiles who speak: what follows is supposed to be spoken by the multitude of Israelites as they look upon the exaltation of the righteous. 4 All the sufferings and sicknesses, they will say, which we ought to have borne for our iniquities, have been borne by the righteous for our sake. *He was* מוכה אלהים, i. e. smitten *from* or *by* God; cf. Deut. xxi. 23, Job i. 16, Prov. xxv. 2; in all these passages and many besides the genitive signifies *from* God. 5 This verse (as I have explained above) applies to each individual righteous man: by the stripes and sufferings which each bore, atonement was made for all Israel. [6] The transgressors in Israel are here represented as saying, All we like sheep have gone astray after 'the obstinacy of our own heart;' but the blow and the sufferings which ought to have come upon us, have been all laid by the Creator upon him: for the righteous are always involved in the iniquity of the generation [in which they live]. [7] A description of the pious Israelites among the Gentiles: oppressed and afflicted, many of them were slain, and others ill-used by condemnation and persecution, and men were devising against them to blot out their name from the world, except for the mercy of God who would not abandon them to their power, and to the terror of the kings, as it is written, 'For thy sake are we slain all the day long, though we have not dealt falsely with thy covenant' (Ps. xliv. 23, 18): this fidelity is alluded to in the words, '*he opened not his mouth*,' viz. for the purpose of casting forth words of impiety against heaven. [8] All day long the Gentiles kept them in confinement, or condemned them by cruel sentences: *who*, he continues, *can tell* of all the weary vexations and sufferings which each *generation* of them endured in exile for the sacredness of Heaven? how many of the righteous were murderously slain, and *cut off* in the midst of their days! for the *strokes* which ought to have come upon us for our transgressions fell upon them! למו is plural, as by the help of God I shall explain further on. [9] The righteous suffered various forms of death, in accordance with the manner in which the wicked kill those who are judicially condemned, and whose only burial is to be cast forth for the dogs. If you ask, Is it not plain from the expression *his grave* in this verse that they buried them? how then do you assert that they were not buried? I will shew you a verse like this [in which the word *burial* is used improperly], Jer. xxii. 18, where it is said of Jehoiakim that he 'shall be buried with the burial of an ass, drawn and cast forth beyond the gates of Jerusalem.' Or we may interpret the words differently, and suppose that the Gentiles treated the murdered Israelites as it is the custom to treat malefactors condemned to death by a judicial sentence; in other words, that instead of burying them in the sepulchres of their fathers, they threw them by themselves on to dunghills, in order that they might not render the ground pestilential and offensive. *And with the rich in his death:* the righteous Israelites thus murdered were treated like the rich and wicked man who dies without repenting during his lifetime, and every one then curses both him and his age; so they did to the Israelites, and therefore it is said, With the rich *in his death*—comparing Israel to the rich in his *death*, and not in his *burial*, for the rich are mostly buried in pomp. And so, in spite of their having *done no violence*, they inflicted on them all the harm possible, which it was in the power of their hands to effect. [10] Yet these righteous ones in Israel were not bruised with sufferings and sickness except at the pleasure of the Creator, in order that, firstly, retribution might be exacted from them for the few iniquities which they had committed; secondly, that they might bear the sins of those who transgressed in Israel (because, as we learn from the case of Josiah who, though perfectly righteous, was slain in the iniquity of his own generation, the righteous are implicated in the sin of their own age); and, thirdly, that they might attain future greatness and dignity in the present world in the eyes of the Gentiles, and also as their 'exceeding great reward' in the world to come. Elsewhere, also, the prophet speaks (Amos iii. 2) of those whom the Lord honours and cares for as being 'visited;' and similarly Solomon says (Prov. iii. 12), 'Whom the Lord loveth, he correcteth.' *If his soul*, etc.; i.e. If the righteous have suffered punishment as though there were guilt in their souls, to compensate for this they will, each one of them, *see seed*, etc.; [11] and in return for *the travail of his soul*, and because he *bears their iniquities*, each shall *see and be satisfied*, etc. [12] Then, because of all this, *I will give him a* goodly *portion* out of the spoil of *many, and the mighty he shall divide as spoil*, viz. all the nations who will advance in battle (Zech. xiv. 2) against Jerusalem, the people of Gog and Magog, whom they will 'spoil and plunder' (as is described in Ezek. xxxix. 10), *because he poured out his soul to die*—how often, namely, did the Israelites resign themselves to death for the sake of the Holy Name! *And he was numbered with the transgressors*: for the pious in Israel were punished and treated as offenders. *And made intercession for transgressors*: in their death they atoned for the iniquities of the many, and in their lives entreated for mercy upon the transgressors, although oppressed by them; as we may see from the case of David, who says with reference to those who were seeking his hurt, 'Instead of my love, they hate me, but I give myself up to prayer;' and, 'As for me, when they were sick, my clothing was sackcloth,' etc. (Ps. cix. 4, xxxv. 13). Here then you have a series of clear proofs that the whole of this Parashah, from beginning to end, refers to the recompense of good with which the Creator will in the future reward Israel for the chastisement and stripes endured at the hands of the Gentiles in this world: the honour and greatness which he will then give them to inherit will be such that all the nations, with the rest of the mass of the Israelites, will be astonished at their dignity and rank, as it is written (Dan. xii. 3); while even the transgressors among them will exclaim that the righteous bore all these sufferings and persecution in the present world on account of *their* iniquities, that by those sufferings Israel's guilt was atoned for, that a redeemer would come to them for their sake, seeing that they were ever praying to the Creator and entreating for mercy on behalf of the transgressors in Israel. And this is the simple, literal sense borne by this Parashah.

Your own position, on the contrary, which affirms that the Parashah alludes throughout to Jesus your Messiah, is untenable in ever so many respects. Did I not point out to you above, how immediately before the Parashah begins (lii. 12), the prophet had predicted the gathering together of our exiles, and how at its conclusion he at once commences to address consolations to Jerusalem, telling her how the Creator will cause Israel to dwell in her midst as at the beginning (liv. 1, 3, etc.), while in the intermediate portion he makes mention of the greatness and dignity which will at that time accrue to the nation? And if this be so, then are you building the foundations of your argument upon an unsound basis; and as soon as the foundation, having no solidity or substance, is torn up, the house built upon it will fall to pieces. Now are not the very first words of the Parashah, 'Behold *my servant* will prosper?' how then can you assert that this is said of your Messiah, and not be ashamed to call your God a 'servant?' Does not your Gospel bear witness that the Father, the Son, and the Spirit are three in Person, but one God in *Substantia*, *Potentia*, and *Habitus*? how then can you make the King of kings, even the Holy One, into a servant? And if you reply that he was a servant during the time that he took the form of a man, and that it was after his death that he was made God and King, is not then the verse fulfilled in him which says, 'Beneath three things the earth trembleth .... *beneath a servant when he becometh king*' (Prov. xxx. 21 f.)? Moreover, you attribute to him change and accident, such as are not found in the Creator, as it is written, 'I am the Lord, I change not' (Mal. iii. 6). In the same way you cannot bring him under the definition of 'accident,' because God belongs to the category of 'substance.' Thus the very outset of your argument refutes all the proofs which follow. To continue, however. You said that the words, 'Thou art fairer than the children of men,' etc., have reference to him: but now you assert the reverse, appealing to the words 'he had no form' etc., and 'known to sickness,' a phrase implying that he was a sufferer all his lifetime. It is said also that he was 'smitten of God:' but if he was God himself, how did God smite him? and if you answer that the words mean 'God, smitten and afflicted,' viz. at the crucifixion, are you not attributing to your God something accursed?

for it is written, 'He that is hanged is accursed of God' (Deut. xxi. 23). 'And his generation who can tell?' You say that this means there is no one who can discern any seed sprung from him: here your own mouth shall condemn you, and not I; for it is written of him immediately afterwards, that 'he shall *see seed*.' The word *dôr*, however, which you explain 'generation,' does not signify 'seed,' but is used to denote the men belonging to any particular period, as Qoh. i. 4 (the men of each age pass away, and are succeeded by those belonging to the next), Deut. i. 35, Ps. lxxii. 5, and often. Again, if, as you say, he rose again the third day, and ascended up into heaven, and is equal with the Father, and lives for ever and ever—for you say that he is 'very God'—how is it that he was cut off from the land of the living, i. e. from the land of glory, which is similarly styled the 'land of the living' in Ps. cxvi. 9? Again, at the end of the verse, for למו (which is plural, Lam. i. 22), Isaiah ought to have used the singular לו: and if you reply that in adopting the plural he means to allude to the manhood and the Godhead of your Messiah (which you call his humanity and divinity), you destroy your own argument, because it is a great point in your religion that the flesh only, and not the Godhead, endured sufferings and death. The next verse also nullifies your assertion, that he came of his own accord, and by his own pleasure, to meet death for the redemption of his creatures: if this had been the case, the prophet must have said, 'Yet *he* was pleased to crush himself;' but it is plain, on the contrary, that the 'pleasure' was not in him, but in the Creator. And, if he is God, how can you attribute any 'trespass' to him? If you say that the phrase, 'to make his soul a trespass-offering,' means merely that he was put to death, 'body' or 'flesh' ought to have stood in the place of 'soul,' because you yourselves maintain that his soul was the Godhead within him, which in this case must have suffered death; and if you say that אשם, after the manner of Scripture, signifies the 'sin' itself, then his Godhead is no longer free from sin. Again, how are the words 'he shall see seed' fulfilled in him? where is the seed which he saw? If the sense be that you yourselves, being his children, are the 'seed' spoken of, then the prophet ought to have said 'children' and not 'seed:' for the word *seed* is only used in its literal and primary signification, of what in your language is termed *esperma;* and how, in this sense, can your God be said to have seed? Moreover, in what way did he 'prolong his days,' when you yourselves assert that he was put to death when but thirty-three years old, when, therefore, he had not reached the half of his days? If it be supposed to be his Godhead, which, living for ever and ever, 'prolongs its days,' it must be recollected that 'length of days' is an expression applicable only to flesh and blood, which lives for many days, and then dies, as it is written, 'That he may prolong days *in his kingdom*' (Deut. xvii. 20); and again, *upon the earth* (xi. 9); and in the law about birds' nests, xxii. 7, cf. Josh. xxiv. 31: in all these passages, as it seems, the expression is used only of persons liable to death, but how can you say of him who lives for ever, that he will *prolong* his days? And from the words, 'the pleasure of the Lord shall prosper in his hand,' it is plain that he was not the Lord himself. Nor can ver. 11 refer to him: you yourselves declare that he never endured travail or pain: it was only his flesh that suffered, and not the soul, which you say is the seat of his divinity. And if it is true that the next words were spoken of your Messiah, when was it that he 'divided spoil with the many?' If it was while he was in the flesh, in the form of a man, tell me what was the battle that he fought, and who were the 'many' and the 'mighty' with whom he divided it? you will not find it so stated anywhere, either in the Old Testament or in the Gospel. And if you say that it was after his death, when he was God, that he divided spoil, how can you use such an expression of God? and who could have 'divided him his portion,' because, by your arguments, he is himself God? The Creator certainly putteth into possession and maketh rich, and giveth in abundance and divideth spoil to a man as it seemeth right in his eyes, but how could you say that the Creator supports or assists himself by such a process? woe to the man who believes at all in a thing like this, for there is no intelligent person in the world who can tolerate it. And how can you assert that Jesus 'poured out his soul to die,' or met death voluntarily and without any coercion, for the redemption of his creatures, when your own Gospel testifies the reverse? for it says that he was in fear and dread of death, *Tristis anima mea, luctavit* [?] *et timuit de morte;* and again, in the same place, that he prayed to his Father, saying, 'Father, let this death pass from me, yet not my will but thine be done' (Mat. xxvi. 37–39), as though it were not in his own power to cause it to do so. Besides, at the time of his crucifixion, it is said in the Gospel that he was 'grieved even unto death,' saying, 'My God, my God, why hast thou forsaken me?' etc.: how then can you maintain that he gave up his soul to die voluntarily? How, in fact, can you say that his *soul* died at all, when, according to your creed, it was not his soul (i. e. his Divinity) which was afflicted by death, but only his body? And, lastly, as to the Haggadah, 'He shall be higher than Abraham, more exalted than Moses, and loftier than the ministering angels,' to which you refer, alleging that such titles of rank and dignity cannot be predicated of any man in the world except Jesus, who was both God and man, although you adduced it at the beginning, I have postponed replying to it till now, because I thought it of the highest importance to answer you first on the point of the literal sense of the prophecy, since the Haggadah, as the name implies, *Romance* in French, does not offer any basis for a reply. And had I wished it, I should not have answered it at all: because our doctors say, Men do not reply to a Haggadah; for what we believe in the Thalmud to contain the basis of our faith, are such ordinances as those relating to marriage (*Qiddushin*), divorce (*Gittin*), the Levirate (*Y'bhâmoth*), with the rest of the ritual regarding clean and unclean, etc., which has been laid down for us by the Rabbis; these, therefore, we are all bound to observe according to their prescription, because at their mouth we live. These alone constitute the Thalmud, the basis of our belief: and this Halachah has been fixed by the most famous Rabbis, after repeated and minute discussion, in accordance with the opinion which seemed to be most strongly supported by clear and convincing proofs. The Haggadahs of the Rabbis, on the contrary, it is well known that we do not use in the same way, because each of these expresses simply the opinion of an individual, who would sometimes, for example, tell his disciples a Haggadah to amuse them; at other times, if they were sleepy, would recite them some strange story to rouse them up. Thus we hear that while Rabbi [Yehudah], the Saint, was once expounding to his pupils, some of them being asleep, he said to them in a loud voice, There once lived a woman in Egypt who bore sixty myriads in her womb: upon hearing this marvel, they at once awoke, exclaiming, O master, how was that possible? He replied, Jochébed bore Moses, who was reckoned as equivalent to all Israel, and Israel numbered sixty myriads. Upon other occasions the teacher, wishing to enunciate some doctrine in philosophy, but not to proclaim it publicly to the world at large, would express it in the form of a Haggadah or proverb (as in the book Kalilah and Dimnah [a]), in order that any other wise man reading it might understand its import, and that the multitude might be amused by it, regarding it as a romance: in fact, this was the design of king Solomon in the Song of Songs. At other times, again, the master would affirm something hyperbolical, which could not possibly have occurred, being preternatural, as in the story about 'Og, king of Bashan, which is as follows: 'Og said, The camp of the Israelites measures three parasangs, I will take up a rock of the same size, and cast it upon them. So he uprooted a rock covering three parasangs, and held it over his head with the intention of flinging it at

[a] The title of the Arabic translation of the famous collection of Sanskrit fables called the *Pañchatantra*: see Max Müller, *Chips*, etc., ii. p. 230; or, in greater detail, the Introduction to Th. Benfey's translation (Leipz. 1859).

them. The ants, however, came and ate a hole through the rock so that it fell down upon his neck, and upon his attempting to throw it off, it broke his teeth: this is that which is written (Ps. iii. 8), 'The teeth of the wicked thou hast broken' (where for שברת *hast broken*, read שרבבת *hast caused to hang down*). How, now, is it possible to accept this Haggadah in its literal sense? there is no one in the whole world so simple as to believe that any man born could pluck up a mountain extending over three parasangs, and raise it above his head. We can only suppose, therefore, one of two things. We may suppose, firstly, that the author of this story spoke hyperbolically: 'Og may possibly, for the purpose of killing some of the Israelites, have taken up some huge stone, although not so large as the twentieth of a parasang, and flung it at them: even then, however, the hyperbole would be excessive. In the same way our Rabbis tell us that in both the Law, the Prophets, and the Writings, hyperbolical passages are to be found, which cannot be interpreted literally: thus in the Law we read of 'cities *built up to heaven*' (Deut. i. 28); in the Prophets, how 'the earth was cleft at the voice of them' (1 Kings i. 40); in the Writings, that 'the whole city was moved at them' (Ruth i. 19). Similarly, also, in the Thalmud, in the account of the veil of the Temple, we read how 300 priests used to wash it (*Thamid*, fol. 29 [a, b]); and we hear besides of the enormous size of the golden vine which Herod placed in the sanctuary, and of the apple-tree which stood in the midst of the altar, respecting which there is a hyperbolical saying by Rabba. In *Babhâ Bathra* Rabba says, I once saw a frog as large as Acra Hagroniae[c]. How large was Acra Hagroniae? As large as sixty houses. But a serpent came and swallowed up the frog, and then a she-raven came and swallowed up the serpent, after which she flew away and settled on a tree. Come, consider how great must have been the strength of this tree.

---

[c] See Neubauer, *Géogr. du Talmud*, p. 347.

Again, Rabba, the grandson of Ḥannah, said: Once upon a time, as we were travelling on board ship, the ship was for three days and three nights between the two fins of a fish,—the fish moving against the wind, and the ship with it. If you think that it did not go fast, listen to what R. Dimi said: We went sixty parasangs during the time it takes to boil an egg; and a horseman having shot an arrow, the ship kept ahead of it. Another story by the same Rabba is this: We were once journeying on shipboard, when we saw again a fish, in the ear of which a small insect had settled: the fish died, and was thrown on shore by the sea: it then, firstly, laid waste sixty cities; next, sixty cities ate of it; and, lastly, sixty cities preserved it in salt, and from the ball of its eye extracted three hundred flasks of oil; when, after a twelve-month, we came there again, we found that its bones had been sawn up, in order to build with them sixty cities. And there are many Haggadahs such as these. Or, secondly, it is possible that in the Haggadah alluded to, the design of its author may have been to hint at some other meaning: it is said, for example, that ʻOg was Eliezer Abraham's servant, and we may suppose that he was desirous of going to fight against Israel, trusting in the merits of the three patriarchs, who are called mountains, as in Micah vi. 2, 'Hear, O *mountains*, the contention of the Lord;' and that the prayers of Israel are likened to ants, because their power lies in their mouth and is weak elsewhere, while the merits of ʻOg were owing to the service which he had done to the patriarchs. And in the same way, the language of our wise men may be no less hyperbolical, when they say, He will be higher than Abraham, more exalted than Moses, and loftier than the angels: they may mean to imply that the elevation and dignity of the just in Israel, in the days of the Messiah, will be so immeasurably great that, hyperbolically, it can be spoken of in these terms.

And since you have adduced a proof from the sayings of our wise men of blessed memory, I also will adduce one from the same source, to shew that this Haggadah refers to the righteous in Israel (*Sanhedrin*, fol. 93[a]). Says R. 'Acha, The righteous are greater than the ministering angels; this is clear from the verse of the Law, 'And he wrestled with the angel and prevailed' (Hos. xii. 5, cf. Gen. xxxii. 29). We may accordingly reasonably infer, that the dignity of the righteous is superior to that of the angels, because, man having been created out of the four elements, the evil imagination originating in matter and the affections of the animal soul shew themselves within him: he, however, subdues his imagination, and keeps his desires in subjection, fortifying and strengthening his intelligence against the material element in his nature, and devoting himself to intellectual study and the service of his Creator. Now is not the righteous man who acts in this way greater than the angels? for the angels are not made of matter, and there is no cause for surprise in their being free from sin. The same Rabbi appeals afterwards to the prophecy of Zechariah (xii. 7, 8), who says similarly, 'The house of David shall be as God, as the angel of the Lord before them.' You have now, in this verse, a confirmation of the Haggadah which says they will be 'loftier than the angels;' and also proofs from the Thalmud, as well as by logical reasoning, that both it and the Parashah under discussion, refer to the exaltation and honour which will accrue to Israel in the time of our Messiah, whereas your own arguments are left without anything to rest on.

Says the transcriber: Although all these arguments are clear to him who understands, and are sufficient as a reply to Epicurus, I see that the old fathers have still left space for any man of an intelligent and an inquiring mind to gain renown in. For, with respect to this Haggadah, I feel there is something attractive and satisfactory in the explanation given by the greatest among the wise men of our nation, and one whose name is known in Israel, the wise and perfect Don Isaac Abarbanel: I think, therefore, that now is the time to mention it here, in order that 'he that reads may run through it.' It is as follows [see p. 165].

XXV. R. SH'LOMOH ASTRUC.

An Exposition of the Parashah, 'Lo, my servant shall prosper,' *by the holy En Sh'lomoh Astruc.*

LII. 13 *My servant shall prosper*, or *be truly intelligent*, because by intelligence man is really man—it is intelligence which makes a man what he is. And the prophet calls the King Messiah *my servant,* speaking as one who sent him. Or he may call the whole people *my servant,* as he says above *my people* (lii. 6): when he speaks of the people, the King Messiah is included in it; and when he speaks of the King Messiah, the people is comprehended with him. What he says then is, that my servant the King Messiah will prosper. Our Rabbis declare that he will be *higher than Abraham,* because Abraham possessed nothing except seventy souls, but the King Messiah will turn to the service of God 'many peoples,' i. e. the whole world: *more exalted than Moses*, for Moses drew but a single nation to the service of God, but the King Messiah will bring to his service 'many peoples,' and will restore peace between many kings: and *loftier than the angels*, for his sway will extend even over the heavens, whose movements he will miraculously change. Or we may say that he will be *high through* [lit. *from*] *Abraham*, because his elevation will owe its origin to the righteous merits of Abraham and to what he will inherit from him in the knowledge of the unity and sufficiency of God: *exalted through Moses*, because it will be a consequence of his establishing and cleaving to the law of Moses: and *lofty through the angels*, in that it will depend on the intelligent powers which belong to him and are his ministers, and which tend to attach themselves to God, so that he will be like the angel of the Lord of hosts. Of him, also, it is said, that 'his angels he will appoint for thee to keep thee in all thy ways' (Ps. xci. 11). [14] The prophet, speaking of Israel as a whole, says, Just as all who saw thee were amazed at the greatness of thy distress, and said, What is the heat of this fierce anger (Deut. xxix. 24) that is upon this people more than upon any other people? and, Is this the city which men used to call the perfection of beauty (Lam. ii. 15)? [so will they now be amazed at thy glory]: for as before the Lord gave full measure in smiting thee, so will he now give thee full measure of prosperity, so that the dignity of this Anointed One, when he is anointed, will surpass that of all others who are anointed, by the radiancy of his countenance which will shine like that of Moses (Ex. xxxiv. 30). By 'his *form*,' i. e. κατ' ἐξοχήν, his beautiful form, he means the form of his garments, which will be more beautiful than those of any who came before him; or perhaps by 'form' he may intend to signify intelligence. [15] *As* the Gentiles 'gnashed the teeth, saying, We have swallowed them up' (Lam. ii. 16), and *as* amazement seized some of them as they saw their distress and asked whether this was the city which was called the perfection of beauty, *so* will the Lord abundantly *cause many nations to speak* of the dignity of the people and his Messiah. יזה is from a root signifying 'to speak,' and is equivalent to the Spanish *fará parlar;* the meaning is, that God will force them to speak about the Messiah. *Kings*, he continues, *will close their mouths* (קפץ as Job v. 16), so as no longer to tell of their own dignity, but only of the dignity of the Messiah: they themselves will be as if they had never been born. Or קפץ may mean 'to strengthen oneself,' as in Cant. ii. 8; the sense will then be, 'they will *exert themselves* so as to speak of the dignity of the Messiah.' After this, the prophet gives a reason why the kings and nations should thus speak, viz. because *that which had not been told them they have seen*, i. e. they have seen in this Messiah what had never been told them of any man born: and *that which they had never heard of* as belonging to any created being, *they have perceived* in him. Such are the words of the Gentiles and their kings.

LIII. [1, 2] A continuation of the words spoken by the Gentiles and their kings: *Who*, at the time when our exaltation and prosperity seemed secured to us, would have believed this *report* brought *to us*, who are now in utter depression and disgrace? such a wondrous change could indeed have been anticipated by no one. *And upon whom was the arm of the Lord ever revealed* to raise him to such dignity as this Messiah? who *came up like a sucker* in pride and strength, as though it had roots in spite of the *dry ground* in which it grew, and notwithstanding that till then it had been devoid of *form and comeliness*. For when *we looked at him*, and gazed upon his countenance, *it had no beauty, and we did* not *desire him*. ונחמדהו ought strictly to have been ולא נחמדהו: he means to say that there was nothing in him calculated to cause us to desire him. Or, the meaning may be, 'and *now* we desire him,' viz. on account of the many desirable qualities which he possesses. [3] *He was despised and forlorn of men*, i. e. he was not permitted to enter the society of men, because he was *a man of pains*, and *broken by sickness*. ידוע as Jud. viii. 16; or perhaps the word denotes that he was so well known generally for the sicknesses which he endured, that in imprecations men would say, May such a one be like him! The next words assign the reason why Israel was thus rejected and cast aloof and hated in their eyes: they say, 'When we saw *the face-hiding*, i. e. the manner in which God hid his face *from him*, and carried him far away captive among the Gentiles, he *was* then *despised* and cast aloof by us, *and we esteemed him not*—he had no value in our eyes.' Or, '*We did not think of him* that God would again open his eyes and have mercy upon him, after having thus rejected him and removed him far from his own territory; and therefore this prosperity and greatness, which is now his, is "wonderful in our eyes."' [4] The nations and their kings are still the speakers: '*We* will atone for their blood; the pains and distresses which have befallen them are owing to our transgressions' (in accordance with the confession, *All we like sheep have gone astray*): the prophet's object is to shew beyond reach of doubt, when the various nations are given up each to its appointed fate, whether to the sword, or to famine, or to battle, and when Israel are settled in their midst, and do not deserve to be delivered by a special providence, that they will be involved in the calamity on *their* (the Gentiles') account. And so the next verse says, [5] *He was wounded for our iniquities*, etc., i. e. his being wounded and bruised by the pains which we caused him was a penalty upon him, and after that, his iniquities and transgressions became ours, according as it is written, 'All those that eat him will be guilty' (Jer. ii. 3). Our Rabbis say also, 'He desires to lay waste his house, and to wash his hands on that man[a].' The verse continues, מוסר שלומינו עליו, i. e. either the *peace* that was for us *was removed* and taken away from them; or [*the removal of our peace is upon*, i. e. is to be attributed to, *him*], 'all the time that our peace was taken away from us, and this affliction came instead, we kept complaining of him, and saying that *he* was the cause and occasion of the harm which befel us.' *By his stripes we are healed:* they thought that if they were to inflict upon him

[a] *Gittin*, fol. 56. The context relates to the destruction of the Temple: 'God sent against them Nero Caesar: when he arrived, he shot an arrow towards the East, it fell in Jerusalem; he shot one towards the West, it fell likewise in Jerusalem; he shot towards the four winds of heaven, and each time it fell in Jerusalem. He said then to a child, Repeat me your texts. The child answered: "And I will lay my vengeance upon Edom [Rome] by the hand of my people Israel" (Ezek. xxv. 14). Nero said, The Holy One (blessed be He!) *wishes to destroy his temple, and to wash his hands upon the man* who does it; so he fled away, became a Jew, and from him R. Meir was descended. He then sent against them Vespasian,' etc.

bruises and stripes, it would be healing for themselves: there was no healing, then, or rest of spirit for them, except by smiting and bruising Israel. Or, perhaps, they may mean to say, 'Contrary to what we expected, at the time when our peace was destroyed and injury came upon us on his account, we now see that it is rather healing which has come to us: and this, because, when he was injured and smitten in consequence of his union and connexion with us, he prayed to God, and God removed the blow,' as I shall further explain on ver. 7. It is thus through *his union* with us in the calamity referred to that the healing is near at hand. Or both meanings, 'stripe' as well as 'union,' may perhaps co-exist in חבורה: 'when he was smitten in company with us, he prayed that our misfortune might be removed, and so we were healed.' 'He was wounded for our transgressions' is parallel both to 'He carried our sicknesses,' and to 'We accounted him smitten, stricken of God, and afflicted:' the prophet then adds מוסר שלומינו עליו to introduce what follows, and to explain how, in opposition to what they had anticipated, viz. that Israel would injure them, their own healing was, in fact, owing to him. And so, to corroborate this, and to shew that Israel's calamity was accidental, and that they themselves were the transgressors upon whom it ought to have fallen, they continue, [6] *All we like sheep have gone astray*, thereby confessing that they were the erring ones in religion and conduct, and that what had befallen Israel was merely the consequence of the punishment inflicted on the Gentiles, and had thus befallen Israel accidentally,—either because they were connected with them, or in order to punish the Gentiles as the Egyptians were punished; for even when it was God's will to correct Israel, he himself was angry but a little, while the Gentiles helped on the misfortune, even going so far as to inflict upon the people 'double for all their sin.' [7] *He was oppressed, and he was answered*, etc. The Gentiles still continue speaking; their words assigning a reason for the preceding 'by union with him we are healed.' The meaning, therefore, is that, when the healing effected by Israel has arrived, they will speak and say that when *he was oppressed* and afflicted and prayed to God, *he was answered* and his prayer for the removal of the calamity heard and accepted, but that nevertheless 'when we condemned him he was dumb, *and, like a sheep led to the slaughter, opened not his mouth.*' Or the passage may describe the evil they did to Israel, how he was *oppressed and afflicted* and bruised, and could not *open his mouth:* the following words then assign a reason for this depression of Israel, and for their being debarred from speaking. [8] An avowal of their wickedness in having depressed Israel, and exalted themselves: now, however, they repent of what they had desired, and their words assign the reason why Israel had been dumb before them, and why they had despised them, viz. because they saw that the people were *taken away from sovereignty and judgment.* עוצר is from the same root as יעצור 1 Sam. ix. 17. The next words describe what they will say when they see the prosperity and success of this Messiah: '*Who would tell* of him, as we did, that he would be *cut off out of the land of the living,* i. e. out of the future world, or that *the stroke* of exile, which fell *upon them,* was caused by their *transgressions against my people,* and against our Saviour who rescued the souls from Gehenna?' Or, Who will say now what we said to them whilst they were in exile, when my people attributed to them (as they then believed) transgression in having condemned this man [i. e. Jesus]? [9] They declare here how the people of the King Messiah *were buried* in the same place *with the wicked* who are condemned to death by the sentence of a court, and how they were *with the rich in their death,* being slain without any ground of justice, like a rich man murdered, because envied, for the sake of his wealth. And the prophet uses 'deaths' in the plural, because they condemned them to different forms of punishment—all, however, unjustly, since, as the prophet adds, *he had done no violence, neither was there any deceit in his mouth.* Or the last words may close the confession of their own machinations, in condemning Israel '*because he had done no violence*:' for what they did to him was done with an observance of the usual forms of justice. [10]After that they add, 'The sicknesses which God sent upon Israel were because he desired *to bruise him*, and correct him, in order that, if he *laid the guilt upon his soul*, and returned to the Lord, he might have mercy upon him, and give him seed and length of days, and make him prosper in all his pleasure:' these are still the words of the Gentiles and their kings. Or [if תשים be the 2nd pers.], they may be supposed to address one another, 'If you think now as you thought before, and still intend to lay a trespass-offering upon the soul of this people, believing that it is guilty in itself, and that it will have no reward but that its soul will perish—if all this be so, how then has God exhibited towards him such providential care, permitting him to *see seed*, and *prolong his days*, and *prosper in the Lord's pleasure*, as he is doing now? We see surely that it is for his own good that his heifer has been hurt[b], and that he has borne all his misfortunes for the perfecting and correction of himself.' And this is what is meant by the next verse: [11]Israel, the Gentiles here declare, will enjoy prosperity, and *be satisfied with* the perfection of *his soul*: for *my servant*, this Messiah, *will justify him that is* truly *just*, as they say, 'Until Elijah come,' and will proclaim to *the many* his righteousness. *Their iniquities* also *he will bear*: as he says, 'I will *bear* and put in safety' (Is. xlvi. 4), in order for men to know that the Lord corrected him and delivered him because he loved him. Having now finished his account of what the kings and nations will say when they see the success of the Messiah and of the people, the prophet passes back in order to complete what God had said above, 'He shall be high, and exalted, and lofty exceedingly,' by the addition of ver. 12, which says, [12]*Because he poured out his soul to die*, i. e. to endure afflictions—people in distress are

[b] Comp. Ex. xxii. 10: a particular instance is chosen for the purpose of typifying the various forms of loss and damage to which Israel was exposed.

called 'sons of death,' Ps. lxxix. 11, cii. 21—and because he carried the sin of many (as he says, 'I have done it, and I will *carry*,' Is. xlvi. 4), viz. the sin of the Gentiles, as was said above (ver. 5), and was numbered with the transgressors, *therefore I will* grant to him that he may *divide spoil with the many*, i. e. with Gog and Magog, who are a people *mighty* in number (as David says, Ps. iii. 2). The meaning of 'he was numbered with the transgressors' is that he was among their number at the time of their punishment, and that 'in all the distress' of the Gentiles 'he was distressed' (lxiii. 9); or, perhaps, that the Gentiles considered Israel to belong to one class with the transgressors who perish. It is said, lastly, לפושעים יפגיע, i. e. either that in the eyes of the transgressors he was smitten terribly; or that he was constantly begging and praying for mercy at the hands of the transgressors, i. e. of the Gentiles who were ever afflicting him; or, thirdly, that by his prayers he was making intercession even for them, although they had transgressed against him, and done him injury. Or the prophet may mean that now the Messiah will devote himself to shewing mercy to the Gentiles, and will be anxious to pardon them and restore them to prosperity. יפגיע either means he will *intercede for the* transgressors; or it may have a transitive force, as though to say he will compel them to 'return upwards' (cf. Hos. vii. 16, xi. 7), and pray to him, as he says, 'For then will I turn to the people a pure language, that they may all call upon the name of the Lord, to serve him with one consent' (Zeph. iii. 9): O then may our eyes behold and our heart be glad! Amen and Amen.

XXVI. R. YIẒḤAQ 'ELIYYAH KOHEN.

A Commentary on the Parashah, 'Lo, my servant shall prosper,' *by the wise and perfect master, Yiẓḥaq 'Eliyyah.*

To those who wait there will 'come up saviours' and consolations in Zion: these are the honied words of this prophecy: O may the lips of the priest 'drop with honey!'

Says Isaac the priest: The glorious Lord hath stirred up my spirit to publish to the world an interpretation of this Parashah: I will take hold upon him, for he will guide me to expound it rightly; and I shall receive a reward for my explanation, because I have been 'very jealous' against our objectors who by their own shortsightedness and the shortsightedness of those who translate them into their own tongues, 'turn to wormwood' (Amos v. 7) the right sense pertaining to the prophets' expressions; and perverting what is straight, 'make corrupt and abominable' their pleasant words. All day long do they dispute with us, sitting openly in public places and defending the belief that is planted in their hearts respecting the fundamental truth, Whether or not among the 'vanities' of the Gentiles there are any that can become incarnate [a], and gaining confirmation for their convictions whenever they see individuals from amongst ourselves associating in their ranks. With a high hand they go forth, 'swallowing up the way of their people's paths,' and 'making their leaders err' (Is. iii. 12); nor

---

[a] A play upon the prophet's words, Jer. xiv. 22, depending on the double sense attaching to the root גשם; in Biblical Hebrew *rain*, in later Hebrew and in Aramaic *body*: hence as a verb, *to become incarnate*.

are they ashamed even to speak with us in the ears of the people in the language of both Jews and Syrians[b]. We hear but are silent, in all assemblies and concourses flattering them; yet they reproach and revile us before the eyes of all, but we are not abashed or put to confusion, either 'at themselves or at the noise of them' (Ezek. vii. 11), for we know that, since they are not in the least degree assured firmly of the truth of their belief, it is impossible that they can have set their mind to make their heart and their mouth agree. And inasmuch as I have never in my life either seen or heard of the exposition of a clear or fluent commentator, in which my own judgment and that of others who have pondered on the same subject might completely acquiesce, I have resolved, with 'the help of my God upon me,' to discover and publish the true sense for the benefit of every one who possesses the intelligence to understand; and to shew that it is as widely removed as possible from the strange conception alluded to, which only seemingly approximates to it, in order that the reproach and nakedness of its advocates may be made the more evident.

LII. 13 The prophet, speaking in God's name, calls Israel *my servant*, as above, xli. 8, xliv. 1, and as we often find him called elsewhere, both by Isaiah himself and by other prophets as well. Here he declares that, although at the time spoken of, Israel is in great depression, and his exertions unsuccessful, yet the days will come when he *will prosper* (ישכיל as 1 Sam. xviii. 14) in all that he sets his hand to. *He will be high, and exalted, and lofty exceedingly.* Inasmuch as the three words employed all represent variations of the same general idea of laudation, our doctors expound each minutely, saying, 'He will be high above Abraham, exalted above Moses, lofty above the ministering angels.' By this, however, they give occasion to error on the part of the heretics, who exclaim that such expressions are sufficient, pointing, as they evidently do, to the Godhead, which the

---

[b] Is. xxxvi. 11: he means to say in both Hebrew and Spanish.

Christians conceive to have been united to the body of the Messiah, who was 'higher than the angels.' But God forbid this to have been the intention of our Rabbis: the *Mem's* denote [not comparison or superiority, but] derivation, and must accordingly be rendered by '*from*.' Elevation and dignity, it is meant, will come to Israel 'from Abraham' and Abraham's merits, who was the *high* father of a 'multitude of nations,' and our father in particular, and the imprint of whose nature should be discernible in us all. He will be exalted 'from Moses,' because from Moses, who *exalted* himself over Pharaoh and Egypt, over Sihon and Og, and over the kings of Midian, he will receive the power of triumphing over his enemies. And he will be lofty 'from the angels,' because these will raise him up and help him, as they helped him in the days of old, and both when he came forth out of Egypt, and at other times, wrought for him, at God's good pleasure, marvellous signs and wonders, as we believe, through God, they will work for us likewise. 14 *They were astonished at thee,* O my servant, and their wonder at thy depression was so great that they exclaimed, *His countenance is marred beyond man, and his form beyond the sons of men:* in these words they give vent to their surprise at Israel's marred and disfigured form. By the word *form,* the notion is conveyed of the qualities or attributes of the soul, by which human society is preserved: the meaning being, that in Israel these attributes are marred and distorted more than in any other men. 15 The prophet means to say that his appearance and form, and the wonderful expression which he will wear at the time of the deliverance, when the destined period of unequalled prosperity has arrived for him, will cause the nations to proclaim his dignity and praise. רבים means *nobles,* as Jer. xxxix. 13: and the 'nations' are those collected from among all peoples, their residuum, so to speak, who cannot trace their descent from any single ancestor. To these, and especially to their kings, Isaiah's predictions, as I shall presently shew, may be referred: for these nations in particular have always hated us, and made us wanderers upon the earth; and their chief, the Caesar of the Roman empire, laid waste our Sanctuary, and led us captives from our land, their hatred of us increasing still more, after they had accepted for themselves and for their seed, the belief alluded to [i. e. Christianity]. יזה has a causative force, being formed from נזה, and applied metaphorically in the sense of *sprinkling* or dropping *words;* it is thus equivalent to *fará parlar* in Spanish. *At him kings will shut their mouth,* i. e. the kings of this people: the gesture being that of one who feels astonishment or surprise at what is wholly above his comprehension, and who at first closes his lips forcibly and contorts his whole countenance and expression in amazement, but afterwards speaks out. In the same way these kings will close their mouths in astonishment at the marvellous and splendid prosperity which will then be visible amongst us. *For,* he continues, their eyes will suddenly *behold* such a degree of exaltation as *had never been told them,* because, had they heard of it previously, they would have had a foretaste of what it would be like, and would not have felt such wonder when they actually saw it. The *hearing* spoken of in the next words does not mean the hearing of the ear, but (as Ex. xxiv. 7 and often) the reception and understanding of the heart: what had never entered into their hearts to imagine or conceive, they will then understand.

LIII. [1]Here the kings commence speaking: *Who,* they ask, *can credit* this *report* which we now hear and understand? and, *Who* ever *believed* that *the arm* or might *of the Lord* would be revealed upon him to whom it has now disclosed itself just at the time when he was laid low in complete exhaustion and insignificance? The revelation is the one alluded to above (lii. 10), where it is said, 'The Lord hath *laid bare* his holy arm before the eyes of all the Gentiles,' etc. [2]And who of the children of men would believe that one who *before it,* i. e. before this, was *like a sucker,* would *spring up,* and rise to such dignity? for a young shoot may be planted in such a way as never to thrive and acquire the power of producing leaves or bearing fruit [c]. *And as a root out of the dry ground:* for at that time he was like a root in a dry and arid soil, which will never put forth any shoot. *He had no form and no beauty*, so that it might be thought possible for him ever to attain prosperity; *and we despised him*, but he bore the contempt in silence, and answered not a word, *neither shewed* us what there was in him worthy to be desired, for fear lest, if he were to do so, our own shame might be revealed, because we should then no longer despise him, but begin to long for and desire him. ראה means *to look down upon*, as Cant. i. 6; and מראה is a partic., as Ex. xxv. 9. [3] The prophet now states the nature of this contempt,—how *he was despised* in his own eyes, and *separate from* all *men* by reason of his insignificance; how, further, he was like a man tried by such a continued succession of pains that they became natural to him, and he felt them no longer; how also he was *broken* (Jud. viii. 16) by severe sickness, and was *as one who*, in order to learn his shortcomings and his shame, seeks to *hide his face from us.* So was he esteemed in our eyes; *he was* therefore *despised, and we esteemed him not:* [4] *but* now we perceive that this his disfigurement resulted because *he carried our sicknesses and bore our pains*, viz. the sicknesses of our soul (notice that *pain* is parallel to *sickness*). By these are signified false beliefs, which press more heavily on a man than anything else. For there is no pain greater than the pain of the soul; and, therefore, when one of our wise men was asked, Why is a heavy man heavier than a heavy burden? he replied, Because the former is heavy both in body and soul, but the latter in body only. *We*, however, the prophet continues, *thought him smitten and afflicted by God* for his own transgressions: but in fact he was smitten solely by the unwarrantable opinions and reasonings which he heard

---

[c] He intends the verse to be rendered, *For* [what was] *before like a* [stunted] *sucker, sprang up*.

from our lips, and was compelled by terror to endure. Or, more probably, the meaning may be, that we thought him stricken for the transgression and blow inflicted by him (as we conceived) upon God, crucified, smitten, and afflicted at his hands. [5] Not only, however, was he *wounded for our transgressions*, i.e. wounded by bearing them, and *bruised by* the weight of *our iniquities* (as is stated): we went on to pain him still more grievously than before; for ever and anon, when *peace was removed* from us, we laid the blame of its removal *upon him*, saying that our distress all came upon us in consequence of his iniquity and because he dwelt in the midst of our land. But it was not as we imagined: our peace did not depart from us on his account; on the contrary, *because of his union* with us, and because we threw the blame of our calamities upon him, and he was smitten by us both in word and deed, he prayed to his God, and God for his merits sent forth healing. And this is what the nations say here, *And by union with him we were healed.* חבורה is a mixed form, derived from חברה (Job xxxiv. 8) and חבורה, like משתחויתם (Ezek. viii. 16), which is formed similarly from השחית and השתחוה. [6] *Like sheep* without a shepherd *we have all gone astray* in a 'work of errors' (Jer. x. 15, li. 18): yet it is not after the proud (Ps. xl. 5) that we have gone, but *we have all turned after the way of the 'man,'* whose end was that God *caused the iniquity of us all to meet upon him* by the judgment of an earthly court. The prophet alludes here to the death [of Jesus], whose religion was such as to be a source of great 'iniquity' to us all. The expression must thus be referred to the *Godhead*, its incarnation, sufferings, and death: for it is impossible that *every man*[d] should turn after his own way, and do what is right in his own eyes, in a place where there are kings ruling and punishing the evil doer: and this is a proof that

[d] Instead of the usual translation, We turned every man after his own way, R. 'Eliyyah, for the reason here assigned, prefers to construe differently, 'The man [i.e. Jesus] we have turned after his way.'

it is the kings themselves who are here speaking. We must therefore suppose that the pronoun in '*his* way' points to the well-known 'man' [Jesus], a supposition which is confirmed by the fact that the number of the letters in האיש ['the man'] is the same as the number formed by the letters of his name (ישו), the letters themselves being also identical in the two cases, ה with א being treated as equivalent to ו; and just as our wise men take off one letter from his name, saying, 'There is no salvation for him[e],' so the prophet omits ה [in האיש] in order that no one should think it possible for man to be ever associated with God. The intelligent will understand[f]! [7] Nor was it enough that *he was oppressed and afflicted* by bearing our sicknesses, and that *he opened not his mouth:* we despised him, and pained him still more by smiting and slaying him with the sword, and plundering him of all his riches. Accordingly it is said, *He was led like a sheep to the slaughter, and like a lamb*, etc.; as though to say, At one time he suffered by being butchered like a sheep, at another by his wealth and possessions being taken from him [like wool from a lamb]. Notwithstanding this, *he never opened his mouth* to complain of his wrongs before any of the judges or the king, because even the authorities took pleasure in the wiles of the transgressors against him, thinking that the hope of his soul had perished. [8] *He was taken away from* the *coercion* of the coercer (i.e. the king), *and from* the *judgment* of the judge: for, since the Christians are accustomed in general to be subject to two kings, the king and the priest—the former having power over the body, and being called the 'coercer,' as 1 Sam. ix. 17; and the latter having to deal with the soul, and being termed the 'judge'—the prophet here speaks with reference to each of these offices at once, saying that he was removed from both. The *kings* are the same as those

[e] Ps. iii. 3: the spelling ישו, in lieu of ישוע, seemed to our author to have been selected intentionally for the purpose of severing all appearance of connexion between the name of Jesus and 'salvation' (ישועה).

[f] I. e. φωνᾶντα συνετοῖσι.

alluded to in Is. lii. 15. Of the men of *his generation*, he next asks, among all nations of the earth, *who* or where was the man that *could* intelligently *conclude that he had been cut off out of the land of the living?* The *transgression* of my people consisted in their entertaining an opinion the reverse of the truth: it thus caused a *stroke* to fall upon them, because he 'is the righteous, and I and my people are the wicked' (Ex. ix. 27). And 'the land of the living' is the world of spirits, as David writes, 'I shall walk before the Lord in the lands of the living' (Ps. cxvi. 9), and I have done good in my works in order that I may walk there, because 'I make men believe when I speak,' i.e. I justify many and inspire them with right beliefs by my words—האמנתי being here causative—'I have sung aloud' (ענה as Ex. xv. 21 or Is. xxvii. 2 of *praise*), as though to say, I have composed songs and antiphons many in order that men may use them for prayer and praise: 'I said in my alarm'—if I was seized with alarm because of my distress, I put my trust solely in the Lord, that he might deliver me, and said, 'All men are liars,' and, 'Vain is the help of man.' [9] The subject of ויתן is 'my people' (ver. 8): not only did we beset him all his life long with persecution, vexation, and contempt: *he gave up* his own body to be buried in the tomb of *the wicked*, judging himself to be a wicked man, 'poor and lightly esteemed' (1 Sam. xviii. 23), who for his deceitfulness and violence ought not to receive any honour. But when one of his own people died, he treated him as a *rich* and honourable man, shewing him respect and burying him in a distinguished spot, prepared beforehand near himself. And all this contempt was heaped upon him *because he had done no violence, and* because *there was no deceit in his mouth* in all his behaviour toward the person who is here hinted at [Jesus]. Up to this point are the words of the kings, confessing their transgression, and speaking on behalf of themselves and their people: in the next verse the prophet makes a change, and begins to speak in the name of God. [10] *But the Lord was pleased to bruise him* and *to sicken him* with the rod of exile,

in order to try him: *but if his soul makes a trespass-offering* for itself, and acknowledges that for its iniquities and guilt it deserves such suffering, and so justifies the Lord for sending it, then for its merits in doing this *he shall see seed* in the latter days, and the time will draw near of which the prophets spoke, saying, 'As the days of a tree are the days of my people, and the work of their hands shall my chosen ones use up' (Is. lxv. 22); and again (ver. 20), 'The youth shall die a hundred years old.' Then also *the Lord's pleasure*, i. e. adherence and devotion to his law, *shall prosper in his hand* in such a manner that there will not come forth against him any adversary or oppressor such as he had over him while he was in the pit of exile.
11 *From the labour of his soul*, viz. the spiritual labour which he bestows upon the law, *he will see and be satisfied*, i. e. attain to it and be satisfied from it: *by his knowledge* and intention he will make it his aim *to justify the just*—my servant will be able to justify *many*, though all will not like him reach such dignity and wisdom as to merit the prerogative and office of judge, and those who thus fall short of it will, as it is said in Daniel (xii. 3), 'shine as the brightness of the firmament' [and not, like those who 'turn many to righteousness,' as 'the stars for ever and ever']. *And those whose iniquities he bare*, i. e. even those whose iniquities he was bearing throughout the whole of the exile, he will teach righteousness, and bring them back to the truth. יסבל is future instead of past, like יעשה (Job i. 5). Or, possibly, the phrase 'making many just' may allude to the King Messiah, of whom it is said (Jer. xxiii. 5, cf. xxxiii. 15), 'I will cause a righteous Branch to flourish for David, and a king shall reign and prosper, and shall execute judgment and *justice* in the earth.'
12 *Therefore I will divide him* a portion and inheritance *with nobles* and princes, *and with the mighty he shall divide* the *spoil* of the enemy, *in return for* his having *prepared* and appointed *his soul to die* for the glory of God, *and* because *he was numbered with the transgressors* and the wicked (for now he will be numbered with just and honourable princes, with the

great and 'noble who are in the earth'), and *carried the sin of many.* For all this will be so no more: he will no longer be afraid of them as he was once, but will *fall upon* them and destroy them out of the world, rendering their desert upon their heads, if they do not return to what is good, but cleave still to their wickedness. Thus will Israel 'rejoice in their king' (Ps. cxlix. 2); and 'joy and gladness shall draw near' (Is. xxxv. 10). Then thou shalt tell how that belief is finally destroyed and swallowed up, which teaches that the Living, the Self-subsistent, and the Eternal, consented to undergo change and death so as for men to make his death a cause of weeping year by year throughout their generations[g]. Then, too, we shall not ourselves weep any more over the desolation of our glorious sanctuary, which was built to last for ever, nor be a reproach and proverb to the Gentiles: as it is written (Is. xxv. 8), 'He hath swallowed up death for ever, and the Lord God will wipe away tears from off all faces!'

[g] Alluding, of course, to the observances connected with Holy Week.

XXVIII[a]. R. LIPMANN OF MÜHLHAUSEN.

LII. [13] At this point the Christians 'open their mouths without measure' (Is. v. 14), and explain the Parashah of the Nazarene: their position can, however, be refuted both from the contents of the Parashah itself and also from what precedes and follows it. The preceding context speaks of the redemption of Israel, of gathering them from exile, and bringing them to their own land, Is. lii. 1, where the words 'uncircumcised and unclean' point, as I have explained above (§ 228), to the days of the Messiah; for how can it be said that the 'uncircumcised and unclean' do not come there now? is not Jerusalem at present filled with all the heretics in the world? Then he continues, 'Ye were sold for nought,' etc. (Is. lii. 4 f.), alluding to the Israelites who went down into Egypt, and to those who were led captive to Chalach and Chabor by the king of Assyria, as is narrated in the book of Kings (II. xvii. 6, xviii. 11). These and the following verses down to lii. 12 make it plain to every one to whom God has given eyes to see and a heart to understand, that the Parashah beginning with the next verse must refer likewise to Israel's redemption from captivity. And this conclusion is confirmed by the words immediately succeeding it, 'Shout, O barren one,' etc. (Is. liv. 1), all of which refer to the same occasion when the re-gathered exiles will be 'many:' for how can the passage be explained of the mother of the Nazarene? is it not written, 'The woman that hath not borne,' whereas all admit

---

[a] For XXVII see the preface.

that the mother of the Nazarene did bear? In the same way, the 'desolated cities' (ver. 3), 'thy redeemer' (ver. 5), etc., down to 'the waters of Noah' (ver. 9), all point in the same direction, and allude to the days of the Messiah, as, by the help of God, I shall explain below, § 237, on Is. liv. 17. Again, at the beginning of the Parashah, the expression *my servant* occurs, and still they assert that there is only a Trinity in the Godhead, viz. the Father, the Son, and the Spirit; but if at one time they make the second Person into a servant, and at another into a son, then the Godhead is not threefold but fourfold; and is it not also a dishonour for them that he is called 'servant?' for the servant is not of the same species with the man, as the son is with the father. Then, after having interpreted the term 'servant' of the Nazarene, they are, in consequence, reluctantly compelled to explain it further of his carnal body; and this involves the error of supposing that the body 'has intelligence' (ישכיל), for it is not the flesh, even in a living man (as is well known to all educated persons), but rather the intelligence within it, that is the seat of understanding. They next have to admit that this intelligence of his is what they call the Father; for if they allowed it to be something different, and separate from the intelligence of the Father, then the Unity of the Godhead would be lost, and all their belief about the Trinity being one, and not two or three, would be overthrown. It is, moreover, surprising that he is termed 'despised and forlorn of men,' and 'stricken,' i. e. with the plague of leprosy: for how can they apply such expressions to their God? And by explaining the second verse of the Parashah with minute exactitude, in which the prophet says *at thee* rather than *at him*, we may see that, as I shall immediately shew, he was addressing those to whom the prophecy relates, i. e. Israel. Then he says 'smitten of God,' because the subject spoken of had been smitten by him: whereas to support the erroneous view of those who apply the phrase to their God, the order of the two words must have been reversed: it must have been 'smitten God' rather than 'God-smitten.' Next it is said, 'He was cut off out of the land of life:' this means the land of Israel, which is so called from its being a goodly land and filled with every provision for life (מחיה), 'flowing,' to use the words of Scripture, 'with milk and honey:' in Ps. cxvi. 9 and Ezek. xxxii. 23 the expression occurs in the same sense (I have given it, however, another signification in the Parashah ויחי [Gen. xlvii. 28 to l. 26] above, § 42). Now how can this be explained of the Nazarene? did not he die *in* the land of Israel? if the verse refers to him it ought to have run, 'He was cut off *from life:*' for what was the *land* from which he was cut off? It is strange also that, though they have eyes, they still do not see the force of what is written in ver. 10: for how could his happiness depend upon a condition (*if* his soul ...)? and how does the receiving a reward accord with his nature? Who is the madman that can say such things of God? are they not inapplicable to any except men? And when it is said, 'He shall see seed and lengthen days,' did either he or his seed have long life? And if they answer that the Nazarene had seed, then he must have begotten for them a plurality of deities: for 'seed' cannot be interpreted to mean *disciples*, and you will not find in the whole twenty-four books of the Bible that disciples are called anything but 'sons' (as, 'Ye shall teach your sons,' Deut. xi. 19; 'the sons of the prophets,' 2 Kings ii. 3 al.; 'my son,' Prov. i. 8 etc.): but the *seed* of the Messiah can, beyond question, signify only his physical offspring. And therefore we cannot, as some have done, conclude that the 'servant' indicates a single person: it must denote a whole, comprehending a multitude of individuals. Observe, too, that he does not say *death*, but *deaths:* yet a single man cannot die more than once; and that the end of the Parashah (liv. 17) indicates likewise a plurality, speaking of the *servants* of the Lord in the plural. In the same way Isaiah frequently speaks of Israel collectively in the singular under the designation of 'servant,' as in the Haftarah to [the Parashah] לך לך [Gen. xii. 1–xvii. 27], Is. xli. 8; so also, when addressing him by the title expressive of his lowliness, as a *worm* (xli. 14). The exile he speaks of elsewhere under the imagery of 'stripes' and 'blows:' cf. above, xxx. 26, and at the beginning of the book, i. 6: the expression must therefore be understood here in the same sense.

It is an established usage for Israel to be called 'my servant,' in the singular, as I have explained, though the term does not include *all* Israel, but only the righteous amongst them: because the wicked, not doing what is right, are not in general God's servants. The prophet addresses Israel and says that *as* the nations, of whom there are *many*, saw what a multitude of great and just ones were brought low in exile, *so* at the hour of redemption they will be amazed at them and will say, We thought them to be guilty of transgressions themselves, but, on the contrary, they bore ours: because when the Holy One sent pestilence and famine and his other judgments into the world for the sins of the Gentiles, the righteous who had not offended were struck in consequence (as I have explained under the Parashah האזינו [Deut. xxxii. 1–52], § 106). They will say further, *The chastisement of our peace was upon him*, because, except for the merits of the righteous, the world had not been preserved, but would have been laid waste by the Holy One for the nations' sins: their tranquillity, then, has its basis and support in the merit of the righteous. *By his stripes we are healed*, for, since, as I have explained, punishment came upon the righteous without cause, and simply on account of the Gentiles who sinned, therefore the Almighty cuts short the punishment of the Gentiles before the time: thus they are healed by the stripes of the righteous. *All we like sheep have gone astray:* because it will become clear to them that their own belief has been an error, and they will come round to ours, as it is said, 'In that day the Lord God will be one, and his name one' (Zech. xiv. 9), which, with the help of God, I shall explain in § 259, on Zephaniah. *He*—viz. the servant, i. e. the righteous—*was oppressed*, and was *like a sheep led to the slaughter.* Up to this point the prophet describes how the Gentiles will speak in the future: he now begins to speak in his own person. *Who will declare his generation?* i. e. who can tell all the sufferings of the generation of this servant, and his persecution during the captivity? *And for the transgression,* etc. The conjunction[b] adds a fresh reason for what had occurred: he means to say, that not merely because of the Gentiles did punishment fall upon the righteous, but also for the transgression of my people was there a stroke upon them—the transgressions of the wicked [amongst them] were partly also the cause of the righteous being in exile. The 'servant,' he goes on, *made his grave with the wicked,* i. e. in accordance with their plan and judgment[c]; *and with the rich,* as though to say, not by the judgment of kings and princes only, but even by that of ordinary wealthy men, who likewise exercised authority over him. *His death* is parallel to *his grave:* he gave himself up into their power, not only for burial but also for death. *He shall see seed, and lengthen days.* These words are a proof that by the 'servant' are designated the righteous in the days of the Messiah. *Because he poured out his soul to die.* An allusion to the righteous who died in captivity on behalf of the sanctity of God's name: because he 'keepeth mercy for thousands' (Ex. xxxiv. 7).

The Parashah is also allegorically expounded of the Messiah; but I have endeavoured to explain it in its natural sense. Its Midrash is as follows:—'He shall be higher than Abraham, more exalted than Moses, loftier than the ministering angels.' The misbelievers, however, err, asserting that there is none higher than the angels save God alone: but this objection is met by R. Mosheh of Coucy (with whom common sense agrees), who points out that the just and perfect man is in every respect superior to the angels: because the angels are perfect through

---

b R. Lipmann is quoting from memory; there is no *and* in the Hebrew.

c Comp. above, pp. 38, 73, 88.

being devoid of all evil passion, whereas any one who suffers from evil passions, and is nevertheless perfect in spite of them, is altogether better than they are. Nor is there any occasion to object, that the perfection of a man cannot resemble the perfection of an angel: because in Joshua (v. 14) it is said, 'I am the captain of the Lord's host: now am I come,' which is explained by our Rabbis thus, '*Now I am come:* but Moses thy master had no pleasure in me, as it is written (Ex. xxxiii. 15), If thy [God's] presence doth not go, take us not up hence[d],' which they further explain by saying that Moses himself took the place of the Metatron[e]: since then the Messiah is more exalted than Moses, it is evident that he is also loftier than the angels.

---

[d] Cf. Qamḥi: דרש אחר. עתה באתי שני פעמים אני הוא שבאתי בימי משה רבך שנא׳ הנה אנכי שולח מלאך (Ex. xxiii. 20) וראה אותי ולא רצה שאלך עמו שאמר להקב״ה איני הפץ אלא בך מיד. The argument is this: The angel who appeared to Joshua was the same who had been 'sent' (Ex. xxiii. 20, cf. xxxiii. 2) to accompany Moses: Moses, however, rejected him, desiring God's own presence instead; a distinction is thus shewn to exist between God and the highest angels, which renders it possible for the perfection of the latter to be reached approximately by man.

[e] Comp. above, p. 13.

XXIX. DON YIẒḤAQ ABARBANEL.

The thirtieth prophecy begins with the words, *Behold my servant* . . . , and extends as far as, *Shout, O barren one* (liv. 1), thus occupying an entire Parashah. I intend to ask six questions respecting it.

1. The *first* question is to ascertain to whom it refers: for the learned among the Nazarenes expound it of the man who was crucified in Jerusalem at the end of the second Temple, and who, according to them, was the Son of God, and took flesh in the virgin's womb, as is stated in their writings. But Yonathan ben Uzziel interprets it in the Thargum of the future Messiah; and this is also the opinion of our own learned men in the majority of their Midrashim, although one of the verses in it, 'Therefore I will divide him a portion with the many' (liii. 12), is referred, as will be there shewn, to Moses our master. In the same way I see in the exposition of R. Mosheh ben Naḥman that he explains the prophecy of the King Messiah. The Ga'on, R. Sa'adyah, however, interprets it entirely of Jeremiah, understanding *he will sprinkle* (lii. 14) in the sense of *dropping words*, because Jeremiah prophesied about many peoples; pointing out also that the word *sucker* is an allusion to his 'youth' (Jer. i. 6), that he 'bare the sin of many' when he 'stood before' God 'to speak good for them' (xviii. 20), that he was 'like a sheep led to the slaughter,' as he says himself (xi. 19), and that the words 'I will divide him a portion with the great' have reference to the provisions with which he was every day supplied (xl. 5). And R. Abraham

'Ibn 'Ezra, as also R. Menaḥem [ben Sh'lomoh] Me'iri, speaks of this interpretation as 'excellent;' though what may be the goodness or excellence that they see in it, I do not understand. Rashi, however, and R. Joseph Qamḥi, and his son, the great R. David Qamḥi, all with one voice explain the entire prophecy of Israel. We ought, therefore, to ascertain at the beginning of our exposition the true purport of the prophecy, as regards the subject to whom it refers.

2. The *second* question is to inquire into the meaning of the Midrash on the first verse, 'He shall be higher than Abraham, more exalted than Moses, and loftier than the ministering angels;' for although this is explained of the King Messiah, it is extremely difficult to understand how any child of man can be exalted above Moses, of whom the Law bears witness, saying, 'No prophet ever arose in Israel like him' (Deut. xxxiv. 10); still more so, then, how any one 'born of woman' can assume a position higher than the angels, whose substance admits of nothing above it except the substance of the First Cause: from the latter expression, in fact, Christian teachers have attempted to establish their doctrine of the Divinity of the Messiah. Nor can the difficulty be met as was attempted by the learned En Bonet[a], who explained 'ministering angels' to mean *the learned*, saying, 'Who are the ministering angels? Our Rabbis:' for how could it ever enter any one's thoughts to speak of their dignity as above that of Abraham and Moses? And the view cannot be supported by what is alleged in proof out of Scripture: for the ver. Ezek. i. 18 speaks simply of the host of heaven; how then can it be used as an argument for the signification *Rabbis*?

3. The *third* question is this: If, as the expositors say, the prophecy is intended to apply to Israel, why is Israel described as a man—e.g. '*his* countenance,' '*he* was despised,' '*a man* of pains?' because, although a whole people, as constituting a single unit, is frequently spoken of in the singular, yet it is not

[a] R. Y'dayah ha-Penini, of Béziers.

termed a 'man;' for a man would be one of the individuals specified, and the term by which a particular part is described is different from that which must be used to describe the whole.

4. The *fourth* question is concerned with the expressions which speak of some one as bearing the sins and iniquities of others. If these refer to Israel, viewed in relation to the other nations, then a great difficulty arises in connexion with the divine government of the world, in accordance with which, to adopt Ezekiel's words (xviii. 20), 'a son shall not bear the iniquity of the father, and a father shall not bear the iniquity of the son:' how much less then can one nation bear the iniquity of another! Nor can Israel even be said to have borne the sins of the nations while in captivity; for what Jeremiah says (Lam. v. 7), 'Our fathers sinned, and are not, and *we* bear their iniquities,' will not apply here, but resembles rather Ex. xx. 5, 'visiting the iniquity of fathers upon children,'—visiting it, namely, if and while the children persevere in the deeds of their fathers.

5. The *fifth* question. When the prophet says, 'But we *thought* him stricken, smitten of God, and afflicted,' as though he were not so really, how can this be applied to Israel? for in the captivity, when the people were punished for their iniquities, Israel was indeed 'stricken, smitten of God, and afflicted.' How then can it be implied that this was not the case? The prophet adds, *If his soul makes a trespass-offering;* as though it were doubtful whether Israel was punished for his sins; yet that this was the case is evident from the testimony and warnings of the prophets. So also in ver. 8 it is said, *For the transgression of my people was he stricken,* but Israel's stroke was for their own transgressions, and not for those of other nations.

6. The *sixth* question relates to ver. 11. It is clear that there is nothing in the whole passage to determine what 'seeing' has to do with the 'labour of his soul,' or what connexion there is between 'being satisfied' and 'seeing,' or of whom it is said that he will 'justify many.'—Our conclusion must be that the

text requires to be handled with the greatest care. For my own part, I shall endeavour throughout to explain the prophecy in such a manner as to answer the six questions just propounded. The purport of the prophecy, as a whole, will be discovered if we can ascertain the true meaning intended by the prophet, not allegorically, but in accordance with what its natural sense suggests to a fair and straightforward judgment. We must therefore examine each of the opinions mentioned under the first head, and inquire whether they agree with the literal sense of the words, and with the general tenor of the whole Parashah.

The opinion held by the learned among the Nazarenes, then, is that the prophecy refers to Jesus of Nazareth, who was put to death at the end of the second Temple: that to him the words apply, 'He shall be high, and exalted, and lofty exceedingly'—according to the Midrash, 'Higher than Abraham, more exalted than Moses, loftier than the angels'—words which cannot be true except of the First Cause, who (Eccl. v. 7) is 'loftier than the loftiest:' that of him it is said, 'He was stricken, smitten,' etc. because he was God, and was also stricken, smitten, and afflicted: and that, because he cancelled the penalty resting upon human souls for the sin of the first man, he is spoken of as 'bearing their iniquities,' and 'carrying the sin of many,' and 'interceding for transgressors,' as is explained at great length in their commentaries. This opinion, however, if properly examined, possesses many weak points. 1. It is asserted that our first parent, in agreement with his sin, was punished spiritually by his soul descending to Gehenna, and remaining there for ever; but this is nowhere stated in Scripture, either at the time when the commandment was given to him, or in the narrative of his punishment and curse. And the proof adduced for it from the words, 'Thou shalt surely die,' can be shewn to have no force, from the parallel place where Nathan says to David, with reference to the affair of Bathsheba, 'The son that is born to thee shall surely die' (2 Sam. xii. 14)—

as he actually did die (ver. 18): there can be no doubt, however, that Nathan did not sentence the child to Gehenna. Abimelech, too, uses the same expression (Gen. xxvi. 11), but without condemning to spiritual death in Gehenna (for he was not God, to do that): 'thou shalt surely die' is like 'thou shalt surely eat,' 'thou shalt surely remember' (Deut. vii. 18), etc., the verb being doubled to add emphasis to the sense. 2. It is admitted that Adam was punished spiritually for his sin; but what have the rest of mankind, who come after him, done that they also should be liable to Gehenna? They have not sinned themselves, and the soul of the son cannot bear the iniquity of the mother, for although a man is in his body the son of his father and his mother, yet his soul was not begotten by his father's soul: rather, as is said by the prophet in the name of God, 'As the soul of the father, so is the soul of the son: they are mine' (Ezek. xviii. 4). If then the soul of Adam did wickedly, while the soul of Abraham did just the reverse and clave to God, how could the divine justice punish both together, so as for the 'righteous to be as the wicked,' though each was at its birth pure and free from every uncleanness? 3. Even though it be agreed that the penalty was a spiritual one, and that it embraced Adam's descendants, still, if it is in God's pleasure to pardon and to forgive, is his arm, endowed as it is with infinite strength, 'shortened' so as to be unable to save except by his clothing himself with flesh and undergoing sufferings? Besides, 'the soul that sinneth, it shall die' (Ezek. xviii. 4) and be punished: it cannot accord with the order of justice, that one against whom others have sinned, should receive punishment rather than the sinner himself. And if it be replied that it was fitting that an isolated individual belonging to our race should undergo the penalty in order to atone for all the rest, then it was also fitting that a man like ourselves—some prophet or wise man—and not the First Cause, the Blessed One, should undergo it and suffer. For even if it were true that the First Cause had taken flesh, he would not have been a man like one of us: how much more then is the supposition self-contradictory—as in fact is the normal case with the generality of their arguments—that the Deity should become incarnate? For it is impossible that the First Cause, who is infinite power, should take flesh, and so become finite, to cancel a spiritual penalty not mentioned in Scripture, whilst the penalties which are mentioned there, should continue to be inflicted upon mankind. Many other weak points could also be charged against the above-mentioned strange idea, as in fact has been shewn in the amplest way by R. Ḥasdai in his Spanish work on the controversies of religion, a work which has been already translated into Hebrew. Now, if the fact [of the incarnation] is impossible in itself, how can the prophet's words be supposed to refer to it?

In addition to this, however, the simple sense of the words themselves will not bear the interpretation put upon them. And this for several reasons. 1. How could the prophet say of God, ישכיל? If this means 'to acquire knowledge' or 'intelligence,' then God, just because he is God, knows from all eternity even that which is shrouded in darkness: how then can the prophet testify of him, 'he *will be* intelligent,' as though he were devoid of intelligence now, but that the time would come for him to acquire it? And if the word signifies 'prosperity' or 'success' (as 1 Sam. xviii. 14), what was the success which came to him as something new? was it in things carnal or in things spiritual? for 'successful' and 'not successful' are terms which cannot be rightly predicated of the First Cause. Moreover, so far as the *manhood* [of Jesus] is concerned, it is evident from the history of his last moments, that he did not have success. 2. He is called 'my servant.' Now how could God call one who was of the self-same substance with himself, his 'servant?' because 'master' and 'servant' are two distinct terms, each exclusive of the other. And it cannot be replied that the word is used relatively to his manhood, because both the 'prosperity' named previously and the 'exaltation' mentioned directly afterwards are attributes applicable to him only in so far as he is (as the Christians think) God: the expression 'my servant,' therefore, which stands between the two[b], must perforce be understood in the same sense. An object is, moreover, not defined or described except by its 'form;' a 'man,' for example, is so called not on account of his material body, but because of his rational soul: even therefore, from the point of view of those who assert that God became incarnate, he could never be termed a *servant;* his name would, on the contrary, always be one in some way connected with his ultimate form[c]. It has also already been pointed out by R. Abraham 'Ibn 'Ezra that 'servant' cannot well denote the body, because the body, even whilst living, possesses no 'prudence' or 'intelligence.' 3. Isaiah says, He will be 'high and exalted,' the verbs being, as you know, all future. I wish I could learn whether this 'exaltation' was to shew itself in things pertaining to the body (relatively to his manhood), or in those pertaining to his Godhead: for, in so far as his manhood was concerned, he enjoyed no exaltation or dignity, but rather suffered humiliation and death—which, in fact, the Christians say themselves is foretold in this very prophecy; while if, on the other hand, the words relate to his Godhead, then the announcement is an idle one, for God, just because he is God, is for ever 'high and exalted, and inhabiteth eternity' (lvii. 15): how then can a period be predicted when he will *become* high and exalted afresh? 4. He says that his 'countenance was marred beyond man;' and again, that 'he had no form or comeliness,' etc. Such phrases shew that he was troubled naturally by melancholy, and was also of weak constitution, and a feeble frame. This account of him, however, though in agreement with what is stated here, is not in accordance with fact: for Jesus was young and hand-

---

[b] In the Hebrew the order is, 'Behold prosperous-shall-be my servant, he-shall-be-high,' etc.

[c] I.e. with his εἶδος as God, rather than with his ὕλη as man.

some,—even their own teachers saying that his constitution was of a normal state. And if the words have reference to his death, every one's countenance is altered when he is dead: he could not, then, on this account alone, be spoken of as 'marred beyond men.' In the same way the words 'no form and no comeliness' would be used of one who is yet living, and who[d] is ordinarily called 'a man of pains' and 'known to sickness,' by which are meant the pains and sicknesses which he was accustomed to, and which he habitually bore: of such, however, the records about Jesus do not say a single word. 5. He says, 'He hath borne our sicknesses and carried our pains.' These expressions cannot be understood of the sufferings borne by the souls of the just in Gehenna for the sin of their first parent, from which Jesus released them: because a spiritual penalty is never called 'sickness;' and still more, because it is said that he 'bore' and 'carried' them—for even the Christians do not venture to affirm that the Godhead bore the pains of Gehenna. The natural sense of the words is that he took upon himself the sicknesses which he removed from them; accordingly it is said, 'We thought him smitten, stricken of God, and afflicted'—he was not stricken and smitten himself. If, again, the words be understood of the sufferings inflicted upon Jesus at the time of his death, then the terms themselves present a difficulty, for the death brought about by the Jews did not consist of 'sicknesses' or 'pains;' and the last clause, 'by his stripes,' etc., a greater difficulty still—as though such sicknesses and pains had been theirs, but he had taken them upon himself, and so they had been healed! 6. How can it be asserted that the prophecy refers to Jesus of Nazareth, and that the words 'he was cut off out of the land of the living' allude to his death, when we find it said, 'For the transgression of my people, there was a stroke upon *them?*' למו is plural, and indicates that the Parashah alludes not to an individual,

---

[d] Reading והוא and היינו for ההמה and היו respectively.

but to a multitude; otherwise, it must have been לו 'upon *him*.' You ought also to know that the Nazarene translators, in order to escape this difficulty, render למו by the *singular;* this, however, is not correct. 7. He says, 'And he made his grave with the wicked.' This is referred by the Christians to Jesus of Nazareth, whose death was accomplished by the hands of the wicked, i. e. the Israelites; but according to their view, it ought to have been 'made *his death* with the wicked,' not *his grave;* for by their own accounts he suffered no ill-treatment at his burial, but only at his death. The following words, 'And the rich in his death,' have plainly nothing to do with him. 8. 'The Lord was pleased to bruise him.' Now, if he had been God, and had consented to endure these sufferings in order (as the Christians hold) to rescue the souls of the saints from the pit, how could it be said to be *God's pleasure* thus to bruise and sicken him? moreover, what is done without any assignable cause is attributed to 'pleasure,' and not what is done for some definite purpose. Still less can the next words be understood of God: how could guilt or 'trespass' be attributed to his 'soul,' i. e. to the pure and absolute Godhead? 9. 'He shall see seed, shall lengthen days.' Yet, according to what is related of his life, Jesus died in youth, and had neither son nor daughter. Or, if 'seed' be explained of those who followed his doctrine, then such as these are never in the whole of Scripture so named: nor is justice done to the expression 'he shall *see*,' which means properly 'he shall see *in his own lifetime* his own and his children's sons.' And, if it be supposed to refer to God, it is well known that God sees and observes both the future and the past: how, then, can it be said that he '*will* see seed,' as though such 'seeing' were something new for him? And if Jesus died in his youth, when not more than thirty-two years old, where are his 'long days?' As to the phrase, 'The Lord's pleasure shall prosper in his hands,' there can be no doubt that it describes how a man performs his pleasure *through some one else*, and does not denote what he does in his own person [:

'his,' therefore, cannot refer to God]. 10. He says, 'Therefore I will divide him a portion with the many;' but even if this be explained of the many nations who have accepted his doctrine and religion, what can be done with the clause which follows? did this man ever carry on war and divide plunder or 'spoil?'

It will be clear now from these ten considerations, each drawn from the words of Isaiah themselves, to say nothing of others derived from the same source, that, in accordance with its simple and straightforward sense, and as rightly understood, this prophecy cannot possibly be interpreted as is done by Christian expositors. Such is the first part of the interpretation of the Parashah.

As regards the course taken by Yonathan and our other wise men, who interpret it of Messiah our righteousness, I do not know whether in saying this they mean Messiah the son of Joseph, who they believe is to come at the commencement of the deliverance, or whether they intend Messiah the son of David, who is to arrive afterwards. In either case, however, the natural sense of the words will not admit of such an explanation. Of Messiah the son of Joseph, who is to die at the outset of his career, it could not be said that he would be 'high and exalted, and lofty exceedingly;' such dignity as this he would never even acquire, still less maintain. The subject of this prophecy is further spoken of as having a countenance 'marred beyond men,' as being 'despised,' 'a man of pains and known to sickness:' yet all this forms no part of the description of the Messiah as given by our own Rabbis: why, indeed, should it? The meaning of 'with the rich in his death' is also not to be ascertained. And how could it be said of him that he will 'lengthen days,' when he was to die at the beginning of his career? If, on the other hand, our Rabbis have in view Messiah the son of David, then a difficulty arises from the words 'marred beyond man,' 'without form or comeliness,' for Isaiah himself, so far from calling him 'despised' or 'forlorn of men,' describes him as God's 'chosen one, in whom his soul delights' (xlii. 1), and as the 'rod out of the stump' of Jesse, upon whom 'the spirit of the Lord rests' (xi. 2), and unto whom 'the Gentiles will seek' (ver. 10). Then again, how could he be said to have 'borne our pains,' or to be 'stricken and smitten?' rather, he is to be a righteous king—not 'stricken and smitten,' but 'righteous and victorious' (Zech. ix. 9). And if this is the case, what can be the sense of the verses which teach how he will bear sufferings and death for Israel's sake? A further difficulty is caused by ver. 8; for Messiah, the son of David, will possess 'sovereignty and right,' instead of being 'taken' from it: nor will he be 'cut off out of the land of life,' but rather reign there: the plural למו 'upon *them*,' ought also to be the singular לו 'upon *him*.' And, lastly, the words, 'made his grave with the wicked,' are contradicted by what the prophet says above (xi. 10), 'and the place of his rest shall be glorious.' In a word, the interpretation of Yonathan, and of those who follow him in the same opinion, can never be considered to be the true one, in a literal sense, because the character and drift of the passage as a whole will not bear it: these learned men were only concerned with allegorical or adventitious expositions, and hence merely applied the traditions they had received respecting the Messiah to the present passage, without in the least imagining such to be its actual meaning. For although our Rabbis explain the first verse, 'Behold my servant will deal prudently,' etc., of the King Messiah, yet the verses which remain they apply exclusively to Israel; and the same thing is done also by Yonathan, who interprets the first few verses of the Messiah, and the rest of the chosen just ones. This transition is the less difficult, since many of them expound the words, 'I will divide him a portion with the many,' of Moses, our master, who died with the generation of the wilderness: but they do not on this account affirm that the whole Parashah relates to him. And R. Mosheh ben Naḥman, although he explains it of the King Messiah, states that in his opinion it was uttered originally with reference to the congregation of Israel.

As to the opinion of the Ga'on, who supposes the prophecy to allude to Jeremiah, I cannot in truth see a single verse which really points to him. How is it possible to explain of Jeremiah the verse, 'He shall be high and exalted, and lofty exceedingly,' or, 'Kings will shut their mouths at him?'—for at the time when he lived the appearance of a prophet was nothing unusual. Or how could it be said of him, that he 'bare our sicknesses,' or that 'by his stripes we were healed,' or that the iniquity of us all was 'laid upon him,' as though he suffered the entire penalty, and Israel escaped free? Nor do we read in his history anything of his being stricken 'for the transgression of my people, or of his 'making his grave with the wicked,' still less of his 'seeing seed,' and having long life, or 'dividing spoil with the mighty:' not a word of all this can be substantiated from the history. I indeed wonder greatly who can have led the Ga'on into this opinion, and am surprised both at him and at the scholars who applaud his exposition. We conclude, then, that all these methods of interpretation are alien to the subject, and have no basis or support in the words of Scripture.

The opinion which ought to be adhered to, as being the true one, is to be found by one of two courses. The *first* is in harmony with the view which refers the prophecy to Israel, who is called God's servant, as xli. 8, xlv. 4. This course is at once suggested by what is said above, 'For the Lord goeth before them' (lii. 12), which must necessarily allude to Israel, and by what follows afterwards, 'Shout, O barren one' (liv. 1), which alludes to Israel likewise: this being so, the intermediate portion cannot but be explained in the same way, and allude to Israel as well, exactly like that which immediately precedes and follows it. The Parashah may then be divided into three parts. In the *first*, extending from lii. 13 to lii. 15, the prophet describes the prosperity of the people of Israel, and explains how it will be one of the consequences of their subjection and depression during captivity. The *second*, extending from liii. 1 to liii. 9, contains the confession to be made by the Gentiles at the time of deliverance, of their transgression and sin for having, in many different modes, harmed and afflicted Israel. The *third*, from liii. 10 to the end, consists of the prophet's own words, explaining the cause why these sufferings had fallen on the nation, and leading them to hope confidently for the reward which would ultimately arrive for them. The *second* course is one which has suggested itself to me, of supposing the whole prophecy to have reference to Josiah, king of Judah. And now, the general purport of the Parashah having been ascertained, and our *first* question accordingly solved, I shall proceed to explain it literally, as well as I can, according to each of these two methods.

With respect to the Midrash, 'He shall be higher than Abraham, lifted up above Moses, loftier than the ministering angels,' the Rabbis do not, in saying this, intend to refer to Israel, but, as their manner is, to expound the verse in which the words in question occur, of the King Messiah. The exposition itself occurs in the Midrash of R. Tanchuma[e], as follows:—'*Who art thou, O great mountain?* (Zech. iv. 7.) And why does he call him "the great mountain?" because he is greater than the patriarchs, as it is said, "My servant shall be high and exalted, and lofty exceedingly:"—he will be higher than Abraham, who says, "I raise *high* my hands unto the Lord" (Gen. xiv. 22); lifted up above Moses, to whom it is said, "*Lift* it up in thy bosom" (Num. xi. 12); loftier than the ministering angels, of whom it is written, "Their wheels were *lofty* and terrible" (Ez. i. 18).' Although, however, their words, as I have quoted them, refer to the Messiah, and I am about to interpret the Parashah of Israel, I must not shrink from explaining the saying, lest otherwise the heretics come and shelter themselves beneath it. One theory I have seen[f],

---

e Cf. above, p. 9.

f Cf. above, p. 139.

which accounts for the *Mem* before 'Abraham,' 'Moses,' and 'the Angels,' by asserting that it is not the *Mem* of superiority or comparison ('above' or 'than'), but the *Mem* which indicates the cause or source, from which the predicate named proceeds, and that the intention of the Rabbis was thus to express how three kinds of perfection would be united in the King Messiah; firstly, the natural perfection which descended upon him from Abraham; secondly, the perfection acquired by habit, and derived from Moses, in whose law he would be well versed; and thirdly, a divine perfection to be shed down upon him in great abundance from the Lord out of heaven. But with this explanation, the words of the Midrash itself do not accord. I have already stated my own view in the treatise which I have composed, entitled, 'The Salvation of his Messiah' (II. II. 1), and will here repeat for you the substance of it. 'Our wise men magnify the dignity of the Messiah under three aspects. 1. In relation to *God*, they affirm that he will love him, and walk after him, and cleave to him, and direct all his actions to his service, declaring that in these respects the Messiah will attain a higher eminence even than Abraham our father, who forsook "his land, and his kindred, and his father's house," in order to follow after God, and who received the seal of a holy covenant, saying, "I am the Lord's" (Is. xliv. 5), who to perform the Divine command proceeded to bind his only son, and who, after the victory over the kings, was not penetrated by any feeling of pride, or a thirst for the glory achieved by their conquest, or any desire of their spoil, but said, "I raise *high* my hands unto the Lord, that I will not take," etc. (Gen. xiv. 23), thereby implying that the glory he loved was not carnal or material. The King Messiah, however, will be higher in the fear and love of God even than Abraham: as the prophet says (Is. xi. 2, 3, 5), "The spirit of the Lord shall rest upon him, the spirit of knowledge and the fear of the Lord, and his delight shall be in the fear of the Lord," and "righteousness shall be the girdle of his loins," etc. 2. In relation to the *people*, whom the Messiah, being "mighty to save" (lxiii. 1), will redeem and rescue, it is affirmed that he will be "lifted up above Moses"—not, however, in virtue of his rank as a prophet, or lawgiver, or of any of the other offices by which that lord of the prophets is elevated above the rest of mankind, but from the fact of his collecting together the several captivities of Israel, and then redeeming and conducting them into their land. For although Moses, our master, brought Israel forth out of Egypt and carried them to the land which the Lord had sworn unto their fathers "as a nurse *lifteth up* and carrieth a sucking child" (Num. xi. 12), yet the future deliverance will be greater even than this: because in Egypt, the Israelites were at least all collected on one spot, and near to their own land, whereas the King Messiah will gather together the outcasts of Judah and Israel, who are scattered abroad, from one end of heaven to the other. In view of the perfection thus to be exhibited relatively to the people, they say, "He will be lifted up above Moses," appealing in proof of the Midrash to the words addressed to him (*l. c.*), "*Lift it up* in thy bosom, as a nurse *lifteth up* a sucking child," which refer to the deliverance of the nation, and their guidance to the promised land. 3. In relation to the *Gentiles*, it is asserted that he will prevail over them and destroy them; for although their heavenly "princes" (Dan. x. 13, 20, 21) will pour down all blessings upon them, still the hand of the King Messiah will prevail, till the armies of the sky are annihilated before him. And so our Rabbis say, "The Lord doth not avenge himself upon any nation until he has avenged himself upon its God[g]." The King Messiah will be in the midst of his people as one of the host of heaven, or as one of the princes who protect the various nations upon earth; for just as these heavenly princes receive abundant power according to their rank, and shed it down upon the nations they protect, and just as their own strength joins battle with that of the

[g] See *Mekhilta*, on Ex. xv. 1.

other princes who come to oppose them (as is described in Daniel, x. 20, xii. 1), so the King Messiah will receive power from the First Cause in abundance, and will pour down upon his people prosperity, glory, and continual peace, putting to nought the forces of all those princes who oppose him. And, therefore, they rank the Messiah together with the ministering angels, meaning by these, the guardian princes of the various nations, upon each of whom are conferred abundant blessings by the Creator, but who will be inferior in dignity to the Messiah. And this upon two accounts; firstly, because the abundance destined for the Messiah is sent down upon him directly from God, whereas, in the case of the other princes, it is transmitted through a series of intermediate agencies; and secondly, because when the crisis comes, the strength of the other nations will be destroyed and avail them nothing—the cord of mercy being severed which had before been extended to them out of heaven, while the strength of the Messiah, on the contrary, will increase and be confirmed, God pouring out upon him "a spirit from on high" (xxxii. 15). And so, because the Messiah as he fights with the other nations will annihilate the powers of heaven, they say that he is "loftier than the angels."'

Such is the explanation of this Midrash, which commends itself to me, when the first verse is expounded of the King Messiah; and with it our *second* question receives its solution. After these preliminaries, we may proceed to the exposition of the text, in accordance with the first method mentioned above, which supposes it to allude to the congregation of Israel.

LII. 13-15 These verses form the first subdivision of the whole Parashah, in which the prophet relates the successes which will attend the nation at the time of its redemption: the promise of redemption had been just given (ver. 12), and here the exalted titles are described, to which the people of Israel will possess a claim at the period of its fulfilment. Israel is addressed as *my servant*, because of the many grievous years of exile which it endured for the honour of God, without forsaking his ordinances and his service, like a servant true to his master. The prophet says that, during the captivity, the people were despoiled of *four* great privileges which they had previously enjoyed while the 'friendship of God was over their tents' (Job. xxix. 4). The *first* privilege was wisdom and knowledge; for whereas before they had been 'a wise and prudent people,' after they had gone into exile 'the wisdom of their wise men perished, and the prudence of their prudent ones was hidden;' or, as the Psalmist says, complaining of the loss (Ps. lxxiv. 9), 'With us there is none that knoweth how long.' The *second* privilege was the possession of royal power; instead of being 'higher than the kings of the earth' in dominion and power, during captivity they 'sat on the earth in silence' (Lam. ii. 10), and passed from the extreme of glory and power, to the extreme of humiliation and decay. The *third* privilege was the gift of prophecy: whereas, formerly, there had been amongst them 'an assemblage of prophets,' and, in consequence of the presence of the Ark and of the Sh'khinah in their midst, the power of prophesying had grown great and manifested itself every day, when they went into exile they 'found no vision of the Lord' (Lam. ii. 9); or, as the Psalmist says in his complaint, 'There is no prophet left' (Ps. lxxiv. 9). And the *fourth* privilege was the possession of the Sh'khinah, for by its mediation they were able to adhere to him who is 'loftier than the loftiest' (Qoh. v. 7), as he testifies, 'And I have brought you to me' (Ex. xix. 4), but when they entered into captivity, he hid his face from them, the Sh'khinah departed from them, and stood far off[h], and whereas before they had been cleaving upwards, he now cast down the beauty of Israel from heaven upon earth, and removed them from him: Isaiah promises, however, that at the future time of deliverance, the nation will again become fully worthy of these four privileges. With reference to the first he says, 'Behold my servant *shall be prudent:*' although

---

[h] Literally, 'ten stations:' see Talmud of Bab., *Rosh hash-Shanah*, 31[a].

now, while in exile, it is like a 'foolish people,' like a 'silly dove without sense,' yet, at the time of redemption, it will acquire knowledge, or, as the angel says to Daniel (xii. 10), 'They that are prudent, shall have understanding.' With reference to the second he says, *he shall be high:* this relates to his rising up out of the affliction and depression of exile, and advancing to the royal throne. The verb *to be high* is used of the subjugation of territory and elevation to the throne, as Ps. xxxvii. 34, 'He will raise thee on *high* to inherit the earth;' and xcii. 11, 'My horn is *high*, like the horn of a buffalo:' it is as though the prophet had said, 'This people, which hitherto has been in the deepest depression, will at that time attain to royal power, and be exceedingly exalted.' With reference to the third he says, *and lifted up*, which alludes to prophecy, as in 2 Kings ix. 25, 'And the Lord *lifted up* against him this burden,' as though to say, that although Israel had continued ever so many years in exile without any prophet, yet you will see the time come when he will again begin to prophesy, and to receive and *lift up* the burden from God. And with reference to the fourth he says, *and lofty exceedingly*, i. e. although in captivity Israel were far removed from their God, at the time of the deliverance he will raise himself aloft. The word *lofty* is not correctly used except in reference to the elevation arising from adherence to God, according to the use of the term Job xxii. 12, 'Is not God's the loftiness of heaven?' Ps. cxiii. 5, 'Who maketh lofty his dwelling;' Qoh. v. 7, 'Loftier than the loftiest.' Thus, in concise language, the prophet announces the four promised privileges of which the future nation will be deemed worthy.
14 In this verse there is an instance of what I have often named to you, the habit of the prophets to speak at one moment in the second person, and at another in the third: so here, Isaiah, addressing Israel, says *at thee*, though the rest of the Parashah is in the third person,—'*his* countenance,' '*he* will sprinkle,' etc. The answer to 'As they were astonished,' is not *so marred* . . . , but *so will he sprinkle*, the meaning (as the commentators

explain) being this, that *as* many nations were astonished at thee (according to the prediction of Moses, our master, in his imprecation, Lev. xxvi. 33), astonished, namely, at thy depression and evil destiny, and the attacks of thy enemies (and this, too, not without reason, *so marred* was Israel's countenance beyond man, and his form beyond the sons of men), [15] *so*, in spite of being thus minished, he will *scatter* and conquer *many nations:* in other words, the exaltation of Israel at the latter end will be in exact proportion to their previous humiliation and decay. יזה, however, may perhaps have the same force as lxiii. 3, and signify that he will shed or 'sprinkle' their blood. R. David Qamḥi and his father explain the word, like יטיף 'drop,' Amos vii. 16 etc., of *speech*, the meaning then being, that he will cause them to speak about himself, from astonishment at his sudden elevation. This view is suggested by the following יקפצו i. e., properly, 'they will speak with great bounds or leaps' respecting him, and by the words, *what had not been told them they have seen*, i. e. what had never been told them at any time, as having happened to any other people, they now see realised in Israel, and *what they had not heard of* as having ever occurred before, *they* now *perceive* in his case—the last clause repeating the former in different words. It would be more correct, in my judgment, to explain 'what had not been told them have they seen,' of the privileges granted to Israel while the first Temple yet stood, and 'what they had not heard of they have perceived,' of the new life they entered on at the time of the second Temple. And this is the only suitable way according to the literal sense of the verses, though Rashi supposes the meaning to be, that the kings will *close* their mouths in amazement. In case, however, you do not like to assume this transition from the second to the third person, you may explain the words *at thee* as not referring to Israel at all, but to the nations; for having just before (lii. 11) said, 'Touch not that which is unclean,' meaning by this the Gentiles, whose corruption will cause them, at the time of their destruction and fall, to be treated as unclean, the prophet here continues, *As many were astonished at thee*, i. e. 'As many, O thou unclean enemy, were astonished at thee in thy fall, so was his countenance—the countenance of Israel my servant'—whom he has just mentioned—'marred beyond men; and as thou didst corrupt Israel, it is only just that *so* he should sprinkle many nations, in order that what thou hast done to others should be done to thee, and that thy dealings towards them should come back upon thy own head.'—Here the first subdivision ends.

LIII. 1-9 This forms the second subdivision, in which the prophet narrates the language of the kings as they cry out in their amazement: *Who*, they say, *hath believed our report? and upon whom is the arm of the Lord revealed?* The question relates to the occurrence of two new and marvellous facts. The first of these is the ruin of high and mighty nations who have fallen from heaven so that the fire consumeth them: *who believeth the report* of our exaltation and imperial power, now that we are like fish caught in a net, or like the cities which God overthrew in the day of his fierce anger? (cf. Deut. xxix. 22.) R. Abraham 'Ibn 'Ezra, however, explains the first part of the question thus:—Who ever believed this report which we now hear of the success and prosperity of Israel? The second of these new facts is the revelation of the arm and power of the Lord—*upon whom?* It might have been expected that it would be revealed upon the possessors of some exalted or kingly office, but the Lord chose rather 'a people spoiled and despised' for it to be revealed to. This, then, is the second wonder, that, after the Holy One had willed to 'create a new thing in the earth,' and to shew forth his infinite power, the revelation was made to a people depressed and despised. Another explanation is, however, also possible: inasmuch as, at the time alluded to, all the inhabitants of the world will recognise that 'the kingdom is the Lord's,' and that the law of Moses is the truth, they will repent and give up their old convictions, confessing that their 'fathers have inherited vanity' (Jer. xvi. 19), and wondering at their predecessors, who, being possessed of knowledge, nevertheless persuaded them to trust to the false beliefs promulgated by themselves. By way of reproof for this, they here ask, *Who hath believed our report?* i. e. Who is there that has given his adherence to the words expounded and accepted amongst us? 'For,' they continue, alluding to Moses, of whom it is said, that God 'made the arm of his glory [i. e. the law] journey at his right hand' (lxiii. 12), 'the arm of the Lord and his majesty was already, in the days of old, revealed upon one, viz. upon Moses; and if so, who is the man, and where is he, that has established our beliefs! and who hath believed the report which we received from him!' [2] At the redemption of Israel they will say, *And he came up like a sucker before him, and like a root out of the dry earth.* The two comparisons are dissimilar in character; a 'sucker' is the name for a young child sucking his mother's breasts—or if the word denotes a *shoot*, as Hos. xiv. 7, it is still used of something as it begins to shoot up—whereas a 'root' is different, being spoken of as 'waxing old in the earth' (Job xiv. 8). This being so, a 'sucker' is the opposite of a 'root,' and it is difficult to understand why the two similes should both have been selected, being so different in themselves. The meaning of the verse is, however, this: Do you not see, they will say, how the people of Israel sprang up before him as a suckling—i. e. like a child for him to play with, and so quick was its growth, that it was like a people whom he had just chosen for himself (as was the case with those who came out of Egypt), and upon whom, therefore, he multiplied wondrous blessings? (Here יונק is used as in the passage from Hosea.) It is not so, however, now: now they are like a root out of the dry earth, because, after the many thousand years he has caused them to spend in captivity (the 'dry earth'), so that they are no longer a young child to be played with, but an old root, they are dried up like an aged tree, and cease to possess any more the beauty which is peculiar to children, and which makes men love to play with them; for *he has no form and no comeliness,* i. e. no fair or beautiful form, *and we looked at him,* and can therefore attest ourselves that this is so, and that no superiority or perfection can be discerned in him. If, then, it is the case, that *he* thus *has no beauty, could we* be expected to *desire him,* being such a child as he is?—All this is intended to emphasize their first expression of wonder, *He came up like a suckling before him.* 3 They will further say, *He was despised and forlorn of men,* i. e. despised by other nations, and deserted by men, viz. by men of valour, so that none were left in his midst. The phrase חדל אישים may, however, also be interpreted *ceasing from men,* in allusion to the edicts by which the Gentiles expelled Israel from their lands, each king and city saying, Rise up, and go forth out of the midst of my people; such expulsions would be included in the expression, because, when they took place, Israel *ceased* to dwell amongst men. It is, then, as though they had said, Not only has Israel no form or comeliness that we should desire him, but we even despise him and expel him from our lands, because he is *a man of pains and known to sickness.* R. Abraham 'Ibn 'Ezra maintains that the 'pains' and 'sickness' intended are the miseries of the captivity. It is more correct to say, that on account of the severity of the captivity and its attendant miseries, the Jews, more than other men, laboured under a continual succession of sicknesses—whether melancholy or emerods[1] (to which they are said to be especially liable), or fevers attended by fits of perspiration, which we also know from experience attack them: to all these the Jews were so much exposed, and suffered so much more from them than other nations, that it is said, 'The Lord shall make the pestilence *cleave* to thee' (Deut. xxviii. 21), in allusion to the persistent character of such diseases. And, therefore, the prophet applies to them the term

---

[1] אם הטחורים seems to have dropped out after השחורה.

'man of pains:' and these pains were such, that we *hid our faces* from him in order not to see him, because *he was despised and we esteemed him not.* Or, perhaps, the meaning is, that the pious among them were hiding their faces, so as not to look upon the features of a Jew: for this would have been accounted by them as 'iniquity for a judge.' The Nazarene expositors reject the idea that איש ('man') can be used of a *people*, alleging that it denotes some definite individual, and not a whole species or genus; in truth, however, this objection arises from nothing but their slender acquaintance with Scripture; for, is it not written, 'And the men[k] of Israel were mustered' (Judg. xx. 17), 'And the men of Israel went out' (ver. 20), and similarly vers. 22, 38, xxi. 1, 1 Sam. xiii. 6, xiv. 24, xvii. 2, and often? And who can exclude the expression here from the same category? Israel having been throughout the Parashah spoken of, as by a parable, in the singular, this fact, of itself, causes him necessarily to be treated as an individual man. Or, perhaps, we may say that איש is not used in the Parashah with reference to Israel at all: in lii. 14, 'beyond *men,*' other people are clearly intended, and in the present verse the meaning may be that not only was he despised and forsaken by all the noble, handsome, and robust men among the Gentiles, but even the man who, in his own person, and by natural constitution, was disfigured and loathsome from the impurity of illness, was *like one hiding his face from* Israel: an unclean alien, who could be designated as a 'man of pains and known to sickness,' was, nevertheless, as one who hid his face from him. ו before כמסתר will then be equivalent to והיה, as in the many parallels adduced by R. Yonah[l].—The prophet next names, similarly, 'the despised,' i. e. the man of no reputation and of insignificant rank,

---

[k] Lit. 'and the *man* of Israel,'—the verb being indifferently either sing. or pl. This peculiarity of the Hebrew idiom is sometimes preserved literally in the LXX, as καὶ ἀνὴρ Ἰσραὴλ ἐπεσκέπησαν, Judg. xx. 17, etc.

[l] See the *Riqmah*, p. 22 (ed. Goldberg).

in order to indicate that there were such among the Gentiles, who, though poor and afflicted themselves, still held Israel in no estimation whatever. He says, '*We* esteemed him not,' in the plural, to shew that he desires to embrace the whole of them; as though he had written, 'Small and great alike, we held Israel in no esteem.' Or 'despised' may be explained as referring to Israel; the complete sentence will then run thus:—He was despised and forsaken of men, and even the man of pains and known to sickness hid his face from him, because he (i. e. Israel) was despised amongst us, and we esteemed him not. According to Rashi, the words כמסתר פנים mean that Israel, when he saw himself despised and depressed, stricken and afflicted, *hid* and concealed *himself* from the eyes of the Gentiles, in order that they might not look at him. And this view is correct. [4] The kings now enumerate, in their discourse, the various kinds of calamity and misfortune which Israel suffered in captivity: these are four in number. The *first* comprises the bodily hardships which the Gentiles imposed upon them: of these it is said, *He hath carried our sicknesses, and borne our pains.* The true explanation of these words, in my opinion, is not, as is done by the commentators, to refer the pronoun to the *nations*, as though the sicknesses and pains were to be felt by them; for a state or condition may be spoken of as belonging to the *agent* who is instrumental in creating it, no less than to the *recipient* upon whom it is produced. Accordingly it is said, 'I have heard thy prayer' (Is. xxxviii. 5), 'A prayer by the afflicted' (Ps. cii. 1), where the person praying, or in affliction, is the author of the prayer; but also, 'I will make them glad in the house of my prayer' (Is. lvi. 7), where the prayer is attributed to God as being its recipient: and similarly, 'Thou art my king, O God' (Ps. xliv. 5), i. e. the king who reigns over me, but, 'I have set my king' (ii. 6), viz. the king whom I have appointed as my deputy. So, again, the destruction of Sodom and Gomorrha is sometimes assigned to God who brought it to pass, as, 'Like God's overthrow of

Sodom and Gomorrha' (Is. xiii. 19); and sometimes to the cities as its recipients, as, 'Like the overthrow of Sodom and Gomorrha' (Jer. xlix. 18). In the same way, in the expressions '*our* sicknesses,' '*our* pains,' it is possible that the pronoun may indicate the patient who experiences the sicknesses and pains; but it is also possible that it may indicate the *agent* who is their cause. And inasmuch as mention has just been made of Israel's being 'a man of pains and known to sickness,' it seems probable that the kings and others who are here speaking would state who was the author of their suffering thus in exile: and so the prophet says, 'Surely he has carried our sicknesses' etc., i. e. Of a truth the sicknesses carried by him in exile were caused by us, and the pains which he there bore were *our pains*, i. e. proceeding from us, and passing on to them. Yet *we did esteem him stricken, smitten of God, and afflicted*, we thought that these sicknesses and pains proceeded from God for their punishment, but it was not so; they proceeded from us, and we were their cause. [5] After mentioning this first class of bodily hardships, the pains and sicknesses which came by natural agency, they pass on to speak of those which they themselves inflicted upon them purposely while in exile, 'blows, and stripes, and fresh sores,' saying, 'He was wounded for our transgressions,' etc., i. e. 'Israel also received other indignities, being wounded and bruised for our wickedness and iniquities: for in the malignity of our purpose, and the multitude of our transgressions, we were ever wreaking destruction in their midst.' The following words are explained by R. Abraham 'Ibn 'Ezra as signifying that the chastisement which was to guarantee the perpetuation of our peace was *upon him*, i. e. acted destructively against him, for *by his stripes we are healed*—so long, viz. as the Gentiles are in prosperity, there is trouble for Israel, but when God delivers Israel, there will be a time of distress for the Gentiles, and therefore it is said that 'through Israel's stripes there is healing for us.' In my judgment, however, the kings and Gentiles rather speak thus:—

We inflicted all this misfortune upon Israel, because by the fault of those who were our teachers, and who expounded and determined for us our law, all the *instruction* (correction) which they imparted *for* the perpetuation of *our peace* was directed *against him*, i. e. against Israel: they taught us, namely, incessantly that *by his stripes we were healed;* in other words, that when the 'stripes of a wound,' which are the 'clearing of an evil' (Prov. xx. 30), were inflicted on him, there would be healing and peace for our souls: on this account, therefore, we were desirous for his destruction. [6] In spite, however, of the nations being various, Edom, Ishmael, etc., and their religions different, there was still one point common to them all—they had all set their heart to do evil to Israel; accordingly, the kings are represented as saying, 'In our laws and religions, all we like sheep have gone astray,' or, in the words of the prophet (Jer. xvi. 19), 'Our fathers have inherited nothing but vanity.' *And the Lord hath laid upon him*, etc., i. e. Israel received the wickedness of them all upon himself: the 'iniquity of us all' is like 'our iniquities' just above, for עון is not used of the penalty of sin (as the commentators allege), but rather of the foul and wicked deeds wrought against Israel. By the words *the Lord laid upon him*, these are here attributed to the Deity, in order to indicate that God has 'ordained' Israel 'for judgment, and established him for correction' (Hab. i. 12) in captivity, and so to endure punishments at the hand of the Gentiles; or, perhaps, they may be designed as the expression of their own conviction that the misfortunes which fell upon Israel, whether natural or accidental, were all sent by Providence for the evil of their deeds and their false religion, and not for the wickedness of the Gentiles themselves, in accordance with what they say above, 'But we esteemed him stricken *of God* and afflicted.' It is plain from this passage, that the sicknesses which ought to have fallen upon the Gentiles, were carried by Israel instead: it is not, however, said that Israel received the penalty which ought to have fallen on the Gentiles for their *sins* (although this is what the Christians believe to be the opinion held by the Jews), for it does not appear to have been the prophet's intention to speak about this: rather, as I have explained, the sicknesses and pains are not referred by him to their author, but are treated as belonging to the recipient in whom they reside. And by this observation, the *fourth* question, proposed above, is closed. [7] The first class of Israel's misfortunes, those viz. affecting the body, being now concluded, the prophet proceeds to the *second* class, affecting their property, and comprising oppressive tribute and taxation, with other forms of spoliation and plunder, from which Israel suffered continually. Of this he says, *He was oppressed and he was afflicted*, where 'oppression' (נגש) signifies the extortion of money, as 2 Kings xxiii. 35, Deut. xv. 2; if so, however, the two forms of persecution are conjoined, that, viz. affecting his body, and that affecting his substance, so that the meaning is, 'He was oppressed or plundered of his riches, *while* or *though*, at the same time, *afflicted* in his body.' Still, in spite of this, he *opened not his mouth*, but was *as a sheep* which men lead off to slaughter, but which emits no cry: in the same way, the Israelites bore in silence the violence done to their bodies. Of those touching their substance he continues, *And as a lamb*, from whom her shearers remove the wool, so was Israel dumb, and opened not his mouth before those who spoiled him. And because *two* comparisons are here instituted, one relating to the deprivation of life, and the other to the deprivation of substance, the words 'he opened not his mouth' are repeated twice. It is possible, however, to interpret the opening part of this verse, 'He was oppressed and he was afflicted,' entirely of the plunder of his substance, understanding it to mean that the Israelites were afflicted by imprisonment and chains until they gave up what was required of them. [8] In this verse the *third* kind of misfortunes are described, how, viz. while in exile, Israel possessed neither kingly power, nor the staff of judgment, nor authority to create or maintain courts of justice, such as they possessed before in their own land; and therefore the prophet says truly, *From coercion*, i. e. from sovereignty (1 Sam. ix. 17), *and from judgment*, i. e. from the Sanhedrin and the divine right conferred by the law, Israel *was taken away*. And because it might occur to an objector to ask how he can say *taken away*, as though previously Israel had enjoyed both, whereas, in fact, they had been for long years in exile, without the prerogatives of either sovereign or judge, subjected to the laws of the Gentiles, he adds, *And his generation who shall declare?* i. e. Who indeed can tell of the dignity and privileges which belonged to Israel's generation in the former days, now that he is *cut off from the land of life*, i. e. the land of Israel, where once he enjoyed the rights of 'sovereignty and judgment?' is he not of a truth shorn of them all through the wickedness of the nations who came up against him, made havoc of him, and seized his land? He continues, *On account of the transgressions of our nations*, i. e. Babylon and Edom, who cut Israel off from the land of life, *the stroke* of devastation and deprivation of rights passed over *them*, i. e. Israel: for although the prophet in this Parashah generally addresses Israel in the singular, yet here he makes it his aim to characterize them by the plural term למו, in order to render it clear that the individual mentioned throughout is not some isolated man, but the whole nation collectively. Or, perhaps, למו is used for the purpose of alluding to the *double* destruction which befel Jerusalem and the Temple, the first [under Nebuchadnezzar] and the second [under Titus]. Rashi explains *his generation* etc. as follows: 'The years during which Israel remained in captivity, and the wearying vexations which came over him, when cut off from the land of life, who can tell? for they are more in number than the locust, and cannot be counted.' And here ends the enumeration of the third class of misfortunes. 9 The prophet now passes on to the *fourth* class, describing how, even in their death, they had no security or freedom from the wickedness of the Gentiles: the Psalmist indeed says, 'Free among the dead' (Ps. lxxxviii. 6), but the Israelites were not *free among the dead,* for even after their burial the wicked heathen 'in the pupil of the night and darkness' used to drag them forth from their tombs, in order to plunder their grave-clothes, and to insult and abuse their bodies, especially if the dead person was sufficiently wealthy for them to imagine that his 'glory' and riches might 'descend after him.' And so they would cast him out of his sepulchre, like a 'carcase trodden under feet,' and expose him naked before the sun, as has happened in our lands oftentimes. It seems to me, therefore, to be beyond doubt that by the words *made his grave with the wicked,* it is meant that Israel was persecuted by the wicked even to the tomb; and by *the rich in his death* that, if a Jew was wealthy at the time of his death, his tomb was so much the more likely to be given over to their clutches. And since at this point the nations who have been speaking, close their description of Israel's misfortunes during exile, they add, *Because he did no violence* etc., as though to say, All that we have mentioned came upon him, because he would not perpetrate any deed of violence, or utter falsehood, for which he might deserve it. The words are spoken from the point of view of the Gentiles, not that of the prophet: because it is quite clear that during the captivity there were transgressors in Israel, men of violence, deceitfulness, and fraud,—so much so, indeed, that it is promised that in the future 'the remnant of Israel shall not do iniquity, nor speak lies, neither shall there be found in their mouth a tongue of deceit' (Zeph. iii. 13): this immunity from crime could not, therefore, have existed previously, but is assumed by the Gentiles, because their design is to shew how Israel had endured the calamities of exile unjustly. Rashi, however, interprets thus:—Israel gave himself up to be buried in whatever place might be determined by the wicked heathen, who used to murder them in every way possible, and then bury them like asses; and if there was any one wealthy among them, his wealth alone, though he had done no wrong, might be the occasion of his death. Others, seeing that Israel was in captivity under Edom [Rome], suppose that all these misfortunes were occasioned by the murder of the man who was put to death towards the end of the second Temple: the Jews acted then in accordance with justice, and *because they did no violence* by perverting judgment and rescuing him after he had been justly condemned, many troubles and misfortunes came upon them. Calamities befel them also amongst the Ishmaelites [Mohammedans] because they would never acknowledge the fundamental truths of their law, or accept the doctrines of their religion. The meaning of the whole will then be, *Because he did no violence* when Jesus of Nazareth was put to death, he was persecuted by Edom; and *because there was no deceit in his mouth*, by uniting with the Ishmaelites in their religion, he experienced at their hands subjugation and ill-usage. 10-13 These verses form the *third* subdivision of the Parashah, and contain the words of the prophet himself. For the interpretation of the first verse, the methods adopted by the commentators not commending itself to me, three different courses have suggested themselves: the first two of these, for reasons which will be explained, I do not adhere to; the third I have 'taken hold of, and will not let it go.' The *first* course is to assume an inversion, and to connect the conditional particle 'if' with what precedes: the sense will then be, '*If* the Lord is pleased to bruise him, i. e. to punish him with exile, his soul will make a trespass-offering.' In other words: Know and believe that all this proceeds only from Israel's sin and the guilt of his own soul: there are no chastisements without iniquity; if, therefore, the Lord is pleased to bruise Israel, and to sicken him by plagues of every description, do not, like the Gentile kings, think that all this came upon him because he had done no violence, and there was no deceit in his mouth; on the contrary, his soul will make a trespass-offering, and we must believe that he endured the sufferings of exile for his sins. And then it is added, after his iniquities have been blotted out by these sufferings, *he shall see seed*, at the time, viz. of deliverance, when their seed will be multiplied exceedingly, as Ezekiel (xxxvi. 37) and Zechariah (x. 8, 10) both declare, *and lengthen days*, as Isaiah says (lxv. 22), 'As the days of a tree shall be the days of my people,' and (ver. 22), 'The youth shall die a hundred years old;' and *the pleasure of the Lord shall prosper in his hand*, because by his means the kingdom and power of God will be manifested in the world. But I have abandoned this interpretation, because it is not in accordance with the accents, which connect 'if' with the word following it by *Maqqef*. The *second* course is to derive החלי not from חלה *to be sick*, but from the same root as תחלימני (xxxviii. 16) *to be plump and healthy*, as though the prophet said, *And the Lord, who was pleased to bruise* Israel in exile, restored them again to life and health by delivering them: and therefore (so the next words imply), although much guilt and sin attaches to him, he will still be worthy of great and long prosperity. But this interpretation likewise is unsatisfactory, because the root of תחלימני is חלם, whereas that of החלי is חלה: החלי therefore cannot have the meaning of חלם, since if this were the case, the Mem being radical, it must have been written החלים. The *third* course seems to me to be the correct one. The prophet, as though replying to the kings, says:—Israel's exile, although we concede that it is caused by his sins, is not perpetual; the Lord will not make a full end of his people and his inheritance, so as to remove them from his face for ever: it is rather for the purpose of chastising him 'as a man chastiseth his son;' which is what is meant by the words, 'The Lord is pleased to bruise him.' And these chastisements do not take the form of death, as they often do with a man who in his vexation slays his neighbour, but take the form of sickness with an abundance of remedies and cures: for, as the Psalmist says, 'It is my sickness, the years of the right hand of the Most High' (Ps. lxxvii. 8–11), by which he means that it was not complete and simple annihilation which had come upon him, but that he had merely 'become sick' (Dan. viii. 27), even though his sickness might seem inveterate and more protracted than the 'years of the right hand of the Most High,' i. e. years as numerous as his power could bring forth; so here, by *making him sick*, the prophet implies that it was sickness and not annihilation which God had decreed against him. And therefore, 'although his soul makes a trespass-offering,' i. e. although Israel is sinful and guilty, he will, nevertheless, be healed of his sickness, and *see the seed* of his nation multiplied, *and lengthen days* throughout a life of continued prosperity; and, in addition to this, *the pleasure of the Lord*, which is, that all the children of the world shall come, as Zephaniah says (iii. 9), to recognise his Godhead, *shall prosper in* Israel's *hand*, because 'out of Zion shall go forth a law, and the word of the Lord out of Jerusalem' (Is. ii. 3). The great R. Abraham 'Ibn 'Ezra explains the verse as follows:—The Lord was pleased to bruise and sicken him through exile; but if Israel will make his soul a trespass-offering and confess his sin, saying, like Joseph's brethren (Gen. xlii. 21), 'Truly we are guilty, and therefore all this distress hath come upon us,' then, after this repentance, God will redeem him, and he shall see seed, and lengthen days. But the explanation which I have given is more correct. It is now plain (1) that the words, 'But we esteemed him smitten of God and afflicted,' and, 'For the transgression of my people there was a stroke upon them,' express the ideas of the Gentile kings who do not know the ways of the Lord; and (2) that the words, 'If his soul' etc., are unquestionably spoken in the prophet's own person, meaning, that if he attributes guilt to his soul, truly even after having had his iniquities blotted out, he will see seed and have long life. And if all this be true, then our *fifth* question will have been solved. [11] Here the prophet states by what merits Israel's guilt will be atoned, so as for him to *see seed* and *lengthen days, and* how *the Lord's pleasure*, the instruction of the Gentiles and their being brought under the wings of the Shekhinah, *will prosper in his hand*. The three verbs יצדיק, ישבע, יראה do not, in my opinion, refer to the future, but relate what took place during the captivity—how Israel *was* seeing, *was* satisfied, *was* justifying. The prophet, in short, describes three great merits which then belonged to Israel. The *first* of these, adduced in view of what had just been said respecting Israel's guilt, is, that *for the mischief of his soul he saw*, i. e. he perceived and *saw* the guilt and iniquities of his soul, in order to turn from them: עמל ('mischief') is already used of sin or guilt, Ps. vii. 15, Hab. i. 13. The *second* is, that *he was satisfied in his knowledge*, implying that although while in exile, when 'terrors' came about him 'like water' (Job xxvii. 20), he was hungry and thirsty and in want of everything, still in his own eyes he was contented and rich, and grew great in himself by his knowledge of the law of God, which told him how 'the man that is satisfied continueth, without being visited of evil' (Prov. xix. 23), and does not care for any trouble which he may incur on account of the 'statutes of the Lord' which 'rejoiced his heart.' The authorities who inserted the accents have, however, placed *Zaqef* on יִשְׂבָּע, in order to separate it from בדעתו, and the ב is pointed with *Qameẓ;* if this punctuation be adhered to, the meaning will be that he *was satisfied* and rejoiced in himself, the cause and ground of his satisfaction being added afterwards, viz. *through his knowledge.* Rashi's explanation is, that he saw and was satisfied by his labour, without committing any robbery. Israel's *third* merit is, that, although in the midst of enemies and in exile, he yet 'kept no bridle on his mouth' in the matter of his own religion and law, and made no acknowledgment of their creeds for the purpose of flattering them: but Israel, the faithful servant, was ever justifying publicly amidst the multitude the knowledge that was truthful and just, in spite of the many misfortunes he thereby endured from the wickedness of the Gentiles. And so it is said, how *the just one, my servant* Israel, *justified to many* of the Gentiles his knowledge (the knowledge mentioned immediately above), although, in consequence of doing so, he *bare their iniquities.* It is also possible to explain the verse of the future—the three verbs here corresponding to, and expanding the three promises of ver. 10. Thus, as there it was promised, 'He shall see seed,' so here it is added, *More than the travail of his soul* which he experienced in exile (the מ being the Mem of superiority or comparison, as Eccl. vii. 1, Prov. viii. 11), *he shall see* seed at the time of deliverance: as there it was said, 'He shall lengthen days,' so here it is added, *He shall be satisfied,*—shall always die an old man and full of years (lit. *satisfied* of days); and as there it was predicted that 'the Lord's pleasure,' i. e. the bringing in of the Gentiles to call upon his name, should 'prosper in his hand,' so here it is added that *by his knowledge* and wisdom, Israel *my servant, the righteous one, shall make many righteous* by turning them from their own lying beliefs, and leading them to 'everlasting righteousness' (Dan. ix. 24), not desisting on account of the ill-treatment received at their hands during exile (for such is the meaning of the last words, viz. *although* now, during the exile, *he bears their iniquities*). The sense of this difficult passage will by this time have been made clear, and so the *sixth* question is solved. [12] The first part of this verse is assigned by the commentators to God, or to the prophet speaking in his name: but it is better to regard it as the prophet's prayer entreating God to *divide him* (חלק as xxxiv. 17) *a portion with the many*, i. e. that Israel may rule over many nations among the Gentiles, and that God may give them to him as an inheritance. So, too, by the *mighty*, are meant the mighty nations who will come up against Israel in the days of Gog and Magog, and whose spoil the Holy One will give into the hands of Israel. Four causes are then assigned for Israel's being worthy of these favours. The *first* is, that while in exile he *poured out* (Gen. xxiv. 20) *his soul to die* for the sanctity of the Holy Name: the *second* is, that the Gentiles, at the same time, then classed him *with the* generality of *transgressors* and renegades, with 'plenty of indignation and contempt' (Esth. i. 18), and therefore his reward will be that he will rise to greatness:

the *third* is, that he *carried the sin of many*, i. e. not that he atoned for their sins, but that in receiving injury from the Gentiles, he took upon himself their wickedness and evil deeds which are the 'sins' and 'iniquities' spoken of: and the *fourth* is, that when he was in captivity, he *made supplication to the transgressors*, and entreated them like servants whose 'eyes are towards the hand of their master;' and therefore it is in the order of justice that in the same place where formerly he fell down at their feet in supplication, he should now rule over them, and divide their spoil. יפגיע has the same force as in Jer. vii. 16, viz. *to entreat.* Perhaps, however, the meaning may be, that in captivity Israel *interceded* with God *for* the peace and prosperity of the Gentiles, as it is said in the Prayer of the *Mussaf*[m] for the New Year, 'And let all the children of the flesh call upon thy name, to turn to thee all the wicked of the earth: let all the inhabitants of the world acknowledge and know that to thee every knee shall bow,' etc.; and similarly by Jeremiah (xxvii. 9), 'And ye shall pray for the peace of the city.' Others explain יפגיע from 1 Kings ii. 31, supposing the meaning to be, that he *slew* and made havoc of the transgressors among the Gentiles; but this view is not correct. Such is the explanation of this Parashah, according to the first method, which applies it to Israel; and the questions arising in connexion with this view have been now answered.

The *second* method is to refer the entire prophecy to Josiah, king of Judah, who 'did that which was right in the eyes of the Lord,' and like whom 'there had been no king before him' (2 Kings xxii. 1, xxiii. 25), and who, when Phar'oh Necho, king of Egypt, came up to fight against the king of Assyria, would not allow him to pass through his land, but went out against him to battle, and was slain by the archers (2 Chron. xxxv. 23), and to whom Jeremiah (Lam. iv. 20) alludes as having perished

---

m The *Mussaf* (lit. 'Addition') consists of the devotions which follow morning prayer (*Shaḥrith*) on the Sabbath and certain festivals.

in the iniquity of his generation. And because, in view of the integrity of his life, his death was strange and surprising, the prophet utters over him this Parashah, for you will find below, in the Parashah צופיו עורים (lvi. 10–lvii. 2), how he alludes again to Josiah, saying, 'The righteous hath perished, and no man layeth it to heart,' etc. (lvii. 1); and in the book of Lamentations, he laments over him in the words (iv. 20), 'The breath of our nostrils, the Lord's anointed, is caught in their pits,' etc. Nor is there anything remarkable in this prophecy coming in the midst of a series of promises of the future redemption; for the prophecies in this book are not all of them connected or related to one another, but each separate prophecy and each separate promise uttered by the prophet stands by itself, as may be seen from their contents. Even were it otherwise, however, it might be reasonably supposed that after he had said above (lii. 1), 'There shall no more pass through thee the uncircumcised or the unclean,' and warned the nations (ver. 11) to 'go out from thence, and touch not that which was unclean,' the prophet was here shewn the great calamity which would accompany Phar'oh Necho's passage through the land of Israel at the time when Josiah was slain, in order to have an opportunity of declaring that nothing like it should occur again at the time of the future redemption, because then none uncircumcised or unclean should pass through any more. [13] The prophet begins by describing in the first verse, in the name of God, the integrity of the king; in the next verse follows the account of his death; and in the third the manner in which he was avenged. He relates, firstly, how Josiah was a *servant* of the Lord in all his deeds, as it is said in the Chronicles (xxxiv. 33), 'And Josiah took away all the abominations . . . , and made all that were present in Israel to serve the Lord their God, all his days;' and describes how he *had understanding*, i. e. was wise and learned in the ways of God and in the book of the Law, as is told in the narrative. And since David, too, is called 'the servant of the Lord' (2 Sam. vii. 5 al.), and is stated to have 'had understanding in all his ways' (1 Sam. xviii. 14), and Josiah also is said to have 'walked in the ways of David his father' (2 Chron. xxxiv. 2), the prophet, wishing to suggest the comparison, speaks of him in the same terms, 'Behold *my servant* shall *have understanding.*' Then in consideration of his regal power, as king of Judah, he continues, *he shall be high;* and inasmuch as besides reigning over Judah, he reigned likewise over those amongst the ten tribes whom Jeremiah converted to the truth (as it is said, 2 Chron. xxxiv. 5 f., 'In the cities of Manasseh and Ephraim and Simeon, even unto Naphtali,' which shews that his authority extended over these as well, and as our Rabbis say in the last section of the treatise *'Erubin,* 'Jeremiah converted them, and Josiah was king over them'), adds further, *shall be exalted.* Lastly, he concludes, *and shall be lofty exceedingly,* intimating thereby how all his thoughts and deeds were directed upwards, to the service of God, who is 'loftier than the loftiest' (Eccles. v. 7), and not to the sun or the moon, as were those of his fathers Manasseh and Amon. Or we may suppose that the words *shall be high* are an allusion to the dignity of the kingdom, *exalted* to the dignified attributes for which he was eminent, and *lofty exceedingly* to the excellency of knowledge and adherence to God, which in him were super-eminently conspicuous. [14] After the account of his high perfection follows that of his death, which was not caused by his own iniquity, but by the wickedness of his generation; and, therefore, addressing Israel (to whom the preceding discourse, ver. 12, is directed), the prophet says, *As many were laid desolate,* etc., i. e. As thou, Israel, wast the cause of death and desolation to many honoured prophets and pious men of old, who died through the wickedness of their own generation, such as Moses and Aaron, and to many besides no less honoured than they were, *so at thee,* and on thy account, *was his countenance,* the countenance, viz. of my servant Josiah (who is here spoken of), *marred by man*—for Josiah's face was disfigured by the hand of man, i. e. by Phar'oh Necho—*and his form by the sons of men*, i.e. by his mighty men of valour, and the archers who shot him. The verse thus means, that his death did not take place (as such perfect piety might have seemed to require) at the hands of heaven, but that he was marred and slain by the hands of men for the sin of his people. [15] After relating his death, the prophet announces the promise of vengeance to be executed by God upon Phar'oh and upon Egypt, saying, *So shall he sprinkle many nations*, i. e. As these sons of men, these Egyptians, shed the blood of Josiah, so shall God for his sake sprinkle the blood of many nations: for although 'blood' is not expressed in the text, it is, nevertheless, virtually contained in the word 'sprinkle,' which involves the idea of sprinkling blood. Turning next to Phar'oh Necho, the 'man' by whose hands the countenance of Josiah was marred, Isaiah says, *At him kings will shut their mouths*, etc., alluding to the great destruction wrought by Nebuchadnezzar and the kings who were with him upon Phar'oh and all Egypt shortly after Josiah's death (2 Kings xxiv. 1, 7, 10); and because the 'kings' of the earth did not believe that the realm of Egypt would be completely and utterly destroyed, he therefore adds, *For that which had not been told them have they seen, and that which they had not heard they have perceived.*

LIII. [1] After this, the prophet begins in the name of Israel to complain for the death of Josiah, saying, *Who hath believed* this evil *report* of the death of Josiah? for there is no one who can believe that Israel would have 'turned their neck in the presence of their enemies,' or that 'their king' would have died 'before them' (cf. Mic. ii. 13). It is, however, possible to suppose that the ל in לשמועתנו assigns the *cause*: Who is there that believes in the reality of this great misfortune? No one believes in it, *because of* the report we had of the integrity, the justice, the purity, the piety, and the religion promoted by his hands; for by reason of all this, God should rather have rescued him 'from the snare of the fowler,' and let him 'be mighty over his enemies,' and 'trample the young lion and the adder under foot;' but, in fact, the reverse happened, and the arm, i. e. the power, of the Lord became a help to Phar'oh Necho, so that Josiah was slain. Such, namely, is the meaning of *And the arm of the Lord, upon whom has it been revealed?* in other words, Was Phar'oh Necho so much juster and more upright than Josiah that the arm of the Lord was revealed upon him?—the contrast between the perfection and goodness of Josiah, and the inferiority and wickedness of Necho suggesting a complaint over the harshness of divine Providence which ordained that Josiah should be righteous, but that it should go ill with him, Necho be wicked, but that it should go well with him. [2] This righteousness is now described: from his youth, from the time when he was a sucking child, he directed himself unswervingly to the service of God, 'to walk before him in the integrity of his heart,' as it is related in the Chronicles (2 Chron. xxxiv. 3) how, while yet a lad, he began 'to seek the God of his father David.' The prophet dilates upon his perfections, saying how he was *like a root out of the dry land*, because his fathers Amon and Manasseh were evil, and sinners before God exceedingly, so that when Josiah became king, the land was all drought and darkness, filled with idols and strange worships; Josiah, however, came forth as 'a lily amongst the thorns' and as a 'root out of the dry land,' but now, when the misfortune comes home to him, and the terrors of death fall upon him, he has *no form and no beauty*, i. e. 'the complexion of his face is changed,' he has no longer any form, or the regal majesty which before had rested on him, and when we see him, we shall not behold in him the countenance he had before (as he says above, His countenance and form were *marred*), yet, because he is beloved of his people, he adds, *and we shall desire him*, because after his death men's desire for him became great. And observe that, while in the book of Kings the account of his death is given briefly, in the Chronicles (2 Chron. xxxv. 24) it is related that it did not take place immediately after he was wounded, but that he was carried to Jerusalem *stricken and smitten*, and *marred* in countenance and form, and there died. [3] After describing the perfections of Josiah, the prophet then depicts the insignificance of the man who caused his ruin, Phar'oh Necho. In view of his bodily defects he says, *He was despised and forlorn of men:* for Necho was not a valiant man 'mighty in deeds' (2 Sam. xxiii. 20), but lame[n] in his feet from gout; and as above (lii. 14) he speaks of him as a 'man,' so here he terms him 'a *man* of pains.' For this cause he was the more despised and lightly esteemed in our eyes, so that we *hid our faces* from him and did not listen to his words when he sent to Josiah, saying (2 Chron. xxxv. 21), 'What have I to do with thee, O king of Judah?' etc., but refused his counsel, because *he was despised and we esteemed him not.* [4] Yet it was not Necho's hand which fell upon Josiah to slay him: it was *our sicknesses* which he carried—we, and not Necho, caused the pain and sickness which he bore. In the expressions '*our* sicknesses,' '*our* pains,' the pronoun indicates the source from which the sicknesses and pains proceeded, the meaning being that their sins, and not the power of Phar'oh, occasioned his death. Or the pronoun may point back to the possessor, as though to say, The pain and sickness which for our transgressions we ought to have received, were borne by that just One for us, and therefore *we thought that he was smitten* and put to death by the hand of God, and not by the hand of Phar'oh Necho. [5] Thus, because he was *wounded for our transgressions, bruised for our iniquities*, so that his death was for the wickedness of his generation, God, who judges the whole earth, and not Phar'oh Necho, was the real agent in it, Phar'oh was but the instrument, like the sword in the hand of the executioner. The proof of this lies in the words *our peace* [which rested] *upon him was removed*, i. e. by his death the peace and the confidence which we reposed in him while he was still alive came to an

[n] Probably an inference from the name *Necho*, which differs but slightly from the Hebrew word here rendered 'lame,' viz. *nechê*, lit. *smitten*.

end. Or עליו may mean *by* or *through* his death, in consequence of which their peace was removed. This was a result which actually happened; for after his death, Jehoahaz was king for three months, and Phar'oh Necho threw him into chains at Riblah, and imposed a great fine on the land, and made Jehoiaqim king in his stead (2 Kings xxiii. 33 f.), whereupon Nebuchadnezzar came up instantly against him, and bound him in fetters to take him to Babylon (2 Chron. xxxvi. 6), and he died on the road amid contumely and contempt. After Jehoiaqim, Jehoiakin was king for three months till Nebuchadnezzar came up against him likewise, and carried him away captive with all the vessels of the Temple, and many of the princes of Jerusalem, and men of valour, and the craftsmen and smiths (2 Kings xxiv. 14), and made Zedekiah king, in whose days the city was laid desolate, and the sanctuary burnt, his sons slain before his eyes, and he himself blinded and carried off to Babylon (2 Kings xxv. 7). These facts will make it clear to you how, from the day of Josiah's death, all the *peace* of Judah and Jerusalem *was removed;* and how the nation, unable to resist its persecutors, passed from one misfortune into another, till after a brief interval of twenty-two years of affliction and hard service, Judah was carried away captive: and so it is said with justice, *Our peace was removed because of him*, because, namely, the peace and prosperity of the people departed with his death. But the reverse of this is depicted in the concluding words of the verse, which relate how *by* his *union with us* while alive *we were healed;* he was our protector, and by him there was complete healing for all the sicknesses produced by our transgressions and distresses, or, as Jeremiah says in entire accordance with the expressions here employed, 'The breath of our nostrils, the Lord's anointed, is caught in their pits—he of whom we said, In his shadow shall we live amongst the nations' (Lam. iv. 20). [6] Since, however, some might object on the ground that the men of Judah were just and good in the days of Josiah, and wonder, therefore, how it could be said that he was *wounded for our transgressions*, to obviate this objection it is added, *All we like sheep did go astray*, etc., i. e. although Josiah removed the high places and the strange idols from the land so that the people no longer worshipped them generally and in public as in the days before, yet in particular cases and secretly the worship of them was still practised, as our Rabbis say in *Ekhah rabbâthi*[o]. *And the Lord made to meet* (or, *impinge*) *upon him the iniquity of us all;* the blow which they themselves ought for their iniquities to have received, was made to fall upon Josiah by the hand of Phar'oh Necho. [7] The next point related in this dirge concerning the patience of Josiah is how, notwithstanding that he saw himself *oppressed*, i. e. externally beset by perils during the war, as well as inwardly *afflicted*, stricken, and smitten, he still *opened not his mouth* to 'curse his day,' neither out of his anguish 'ascribed foolishness to God,' but in his patient endurance was *as a sheep*—the male of the flock—which, while led to the slaughter, in addition to its own fate, sees *the lamb*, its mate, *dumb before her shearers*, yet being naturally a patient animal, utters no cry, either for its own impending slaughter, or for the fleecing of its mate. In the same way Josiah saw his people and his camp *oppressed*, pursued, and spoiled by their enemies like the shorn lamb, and beheld himself *afflicted* and stricken, and brought to die in Jerusalem after the manner of the sheep led to the slaughter; nevertheless *he opened not his mouth* to complain of the divine dispensation. Upon this explanation the words *opened not his mouth* will refer the first time to Josiah, and the second time to the male sheep; and the כ in כרחל will not be the *Caph* of comparison, but the *Caph* which indicates time, as Ex. ix. 29, 1 Sam. ix. 13. [8] The prophet still continues his complaint, saying, *From sovereignty and from judgment he was taken away*, because at his death he ceased to be king and to exercise judgment and justice; and when God had deprived him of these

---

[o] Not to be found in our editions.

prerogatives, *who could* then *pray for* and protect *his generation?* Or, *who could declare* and teach them the knowledge and fear of the Lord, *after he had been cut off out of the land of the living?* Therefore also it is added with truth, that *for* this *transgression of my people* (which was the cause of his death) *the stroke* came *upon them*, viz. upon Israel themselves, because it was they who were 'stricken' by his death even more than he himself; for Josiah experienced no further harm except that God [9] *assigned him his grave with*, and through the instrumentality of, *the wicked* Egyptians. His death is here spoken of as his 'grave' or 'burial;' because, inasmuch as every dead man is buried, death itself may be spoken of as burial. Or the meaning may be, that God made the wicked Egyptians to be the instrument and cause of his burial taking place: they were in the position of men who cause the dead to be buried. Or the words may be explained of the burial of the body of Josiah by the side of Amon, and Manasseh, and his fathers, who were *wicked*, or of the children of Judah and men of Jerusalem, who were worshippers of false idols. God also made Phar'oh Necho, *the rich*, who ruled over the treasures of Egypt, the instrument and mediate cause of his death, as is signified by the words, *the rich in his death;* since, owing to his insignificance, the prophet does not term him 'king' or 'mighty man' (because he did not achieve his conquest by the sword), but *rich*, which is a name applied to a king, as by Solomon, Eccl. x. 20. The last words, *because he did no violence*, etc., allude to Josiah's being 'perfect and upright, a fearer of God and removed from evil.' [10] Josiah, however, did not die for his own iniquity, but because God *was pleased to bruise him*, as it was he, rather than the archers, who caused him his sickness. It may be observed that the same word [החלי *to be sick*] is used by Josiah in speaking of himself at the time when he was wounded, 2 Chron. xxxv. 23, 'Take me away, for I have been *made sick* exceedingly.' The whole force of the complaint lies in the fact that his death took place, not by judgment and justice, but at the pleasure and will of the

Most High; and in order to intensify it yet more, there is added, *If his soul*, etc., i. e. since Josiah, though well-seeming with both God and man, was thus bruised by the Almighty, it will follow that *if*, on the contrary, he had been a man of guilt and sin (for this is the meaning of, *If his soul were to make a trespass-offering*), his days would not have been shortened, but *he would see seed and lengthen days*, i. e. would have seen children's children, and lived to old age and hoary hairs, and the Almighty would not then have been pleased to bruise him, as he actually did; rather, through his being sinful and guilty, it would be *the Lord's pleasure* that Josiah *should prosper by his hand*, and conquer his enemies instead of being conquered by them, and slay them in the same manner in which, in fact, he was slain himself. All this is said in irony, which is the habitual resort of indignant lamentation, as in Job's complaint at the prosperity of the wicked, xxi. 7–9.
11 Having now finished his account of Israel's complaint, and their murmurings against the Lord for the slaying of Josiah, Isaiah proceeds to give the words of the Almighty's reply. *For the travail of his soul*—the travail, viz., which resulted in his death—this will be his reward, *he shall see and be satisfied*, i. e. *shall see* the 'light of life' (Ps. lvi. 14), and *be satisfied* with a 'satiety of joys' (Ps. xvi. 11), the entire phrase being an allusion to the soul's spiritual reward in the future world (as he proceeds at once to describe). Josiah, he says, deserved rightly this reward of the Most High, because, *by his knowledge* and understanding, *my servant* Josiah, when stricken and smitten at the hour of his death, *justified the Just One* of the world *to many*, i. e. publicly, and in the presence of many people, justified the judgment against himself, so as to preserve inviolate the sanctity of God. For, as our wise men say in the treatise *Ta'ainoth*[p], when Josiah was brought, stricken down, to Jerusalem, Jeremiah directed his ear towards him so as to

[p] Fol. 22b.

catch what he might say, and heard him repeat the words, 'The Lord is just; for I have rebelled against his command.' And therefore it is said with truth that he *justified the Just One*, although it was only out of piety and humility that he spoke in such terms; for in reality the case was different, *and he was bearing the iniquities* of Israel, who were the occasion of his death. [12] *Therefore I will divide him a portion with the great*—he will have his portion with the holy patriarchs, as Rashi explains, for the 'giants who were of old' are, from their exalted rank, called *great ones:* further, *with the mighty he shall divide spoil,* because at the time of the resurrection, when the just in Israel will be brought to life, and return to their own country, Josiah, in company with the mighty, and the perfect who will then rise from the dead, will divide the spoil of this corporeal world, and make them worthy to enjoy the land of Israel, and the good things which it will produce. This will be a recompense for his having *laid bare* his soul, in order to consecrate it to God, when *about to die*, and being *numbered with the transgressors,* viz. in suffering himself to be reckoned amongst them by justifying God's judgment against him, and confessing that he had 'rebelled against the command,' although in reality it was not so: because he did not die for his own sin, but *carried the sin of many,* and died for the iniquities of his people; and *because of the transgressors* in Israel, Phar'oh Necho *caused* the final blow *to fall* upon him (יפגיע with the same force as in ver. 6) at the hands of the archers. And now the whole Parashah has been explained; the questions arising out of it have been solved in accordance with the second scheme as well as the first, and we have freed ourselves from the murmurings of the learned men of Edom with their perverted interpretations.

XXX. R. DAVID DE ROCCA MARTINO.

LII. [13]This Parashah may be divided into three parts: the first extending from lii. 13 to lii. 15, the second from liii. 1 to liii. 9, the third from liii. 10 to the end.

The *first* of these parts is spoken entirely by the prophet, and falls into two subdivisions. Of these, the first contains the promise of the future prosperity and exaltation of the afflicted congregation, addressed as in xliv. 2 by the title of *servant:* this is comprised in the first verse. The second subdivision announces the nation's success in terms of a proportion, declaring that this success will be in the exact ratio of its previous depression and distress; moreover, precisely as the depression was infinitely great, so will the subsequent prosperity be infinitely great likewise. This is included in the next two verses, 14, 15.

The *second* part contains the confession and acknowledgment which will be made by the kings of the Gentiles when they see the success and safety of Israel: this part falls into three subdivisions. In the first, consisting of three verses (liii. 1–3), the astonishment of the kings is described when they see how the 'dry bones' revived and received from God prosperity. The last words, *He was despised, and we esteemed him not,* exhibit in a summary form how severe were their humiliation and sufferings, and how great the contempt in which they were held: nevertheless *the arm of the Lord was revealed* upon them in a mysterious and wonderful manner. The second subdivision, consisting of verse 4, recounts the confession of the kings, when they exclaim, We are verily guilty, in that we saw their anguish; it is we, and not, as we imagined, they, who have sinned. The third subdivision enumerates in detail the various forms of distress and affliction which befel them. These are four in number: 1. those affecting the body, i. e. martyrdom; 2. those affecting property, viz. tribute and taxes; 3. deprivation of the rights of government and execution of justice; 4. contempt shewn for the dead by forcing open their sepulchres. The first of these four is described in verse 5, 'he was wounded for our transgressions,' alluding to those who were put to death, and endured blows and stripes for the sake of God's holy name, 'the chastisement of our peace was upon him,' alluding to the sufferings which fell on them; for while the Gentiles enjoyed peace and tranquillity, Israel were in 'sighing and great distress,' the *stripes* being those of men smitten and bruised by exile. And because their distress was so keen, they seize the opportunity of confessing (as Joel says, iv. 21, 'I will hold guiltless their blood, which I held not guiltless before'), *All we like sheep*, etc., excusing themselves and craving for pardon, saying, O let us not perish for the life of these men; for thou, O Lord, hast only done that which it was thy pleasure to do. The second form of distress, which affected their possessions, is mentioned in verse 7, where the words, *He was oppressed, and he was afflicted*, are an allusion to their being seized and thrown into prison until they had paid the tributes and burdens imposed upon them. The prophet adds, *Like a sheep*, bound by its feet when led to the slaughter-house, they led him off to prison until a 'present' for his redemption should be 'brought to him that is to be feared;' and *like a lamb which before her shearers is dumb*, in allusion to those who incessantly year after year laid burdens upon them, leaving them robbed like a shorn lamb. The first of the two clauses will thus refer to unusual or extraordinary burdens. The third form of distress follows in verse 8. The authority and functions of government were taken away from him; he had no power to make new laws, or alter the judicial procedure, or dispose anything afresh in the presence of his contemporaries, owing to the fact that he had been expelled and cut off from the land of life in which was the Polished Hall[a], where laws were given and judgment announced to Israel: since, further, this exile from the land of life was notably and principally caused by a great blow which befel the nation at the same time, the final confession is appended, 'For the transgression of my people, (which was) a blow to them [to Israel].' The fourth form of distress, relating to the mode of burial, is described in verse 9; at times it would be the lot of the nation, or 'despised' 'servant,' here spoken of, to be ranked with the wicked, and 'the rich who answereth roughly' (cf. Prov. xviii. 23), so that those belonging to it would be 'drawn and cast out' (cf. Jer. xxii. 19), and not deemed worthy of proper burial. Here ends the second part of the Parashah.

The *third* part, verses 10–12, is occupied by the words of the prophet, and falls into three subdivisions. The first of these, comprised in verse 10, announces how the 'servant' will accept his chastisements in love, and justify the judgment passed upon him, because *the Lord was pleased to bruise* and afflict him, though not so far as to annihilate him, or utterly annul his covenant with him; then, after his wisdom has thus decreed, he will naturally find his delight in *the Lord's pleasure*, so that [instead of bringing any more affliction on him] it will now result in his prosperity and freedom. For God 'killeth and maketh alive, he bringeth low and also lifteth up' (1 Sam. ii. 7, 8), and 'healeth the stroke of his wound' (Is. xxx. 26). The second subdivision, consisting of verse 11, describes how the 'servant,' so soon as he realises his deliverance and freedom, will begin to proclaim his righteousness in public before the eyes of the nations: for just as before the latter had condemned themselves, confessing that they had 'all gone astray like sheep,' so now the servant, who is the subject of the prophecy, will main-

---

[a] The building in which the great Sanhedrin held its sittings: see Neubauer, *Géogr. du Talmud*, p. 144.

tain before *many* the justice of his cause, declaring that he is 'just in his speaking, and clear when he is judged,' because the troubles which had come to him and which he had *borne*, were for *their iniquities*. In the third subdivision, occupying verse 12, the prophet solemnly assures the 'servant' that he will be rewarded sevenfold for all that had been taken from him (in the same way that it is said, Gen. xv. 14, with reference to the subjection in Egypt, 'And afterward they shall come forth with great substance'): this is alluded to in the words, *With the mighty he shall divide spoil*, viz. in return for his servitude and endurance. The reward will come to him from the Gentiles, as a ransom or offering for their transgression, in accordance with the prophets' declarations, 'The multitude of camels shall cover thee,' etc. (Is. lx. 6), and that they will bring their offerings into the sanctuary (as he continues, verse 7, 'All the flocks of Kedar, etc.), whilst Israel will be *interceding* and praying for them.

THE EXPOSITION IS ENDED: PRAISE BE TO GOD!

XXXI. R. SA'ADYAH IBN DANÂN.

Says Sa'adyah, son of R. Maimun, Ibn Danân: Behold in the Lord's compassion on me, he hath put in my heart intelligence and knowledge to comprehend and understand the words of the wise who expound the Scriptures, to consider attentively things secret and sealed up, and to solve hard and difficult problems: he hath also brought me forth and set me outside the city of chatterers and praters, and of all them that are perplexed and confused. And my mouth and tongue have resolved not to utter words without sense, or to raise their voice 'in storm and tempest,' or exhibit an angry countenance; but, like the wise (Eccles. ix. 17), that I should publish my words 'in quietness,' and of the 'uprightness of mine heart' (Job xxxiii. 3) address my companions and friends.

I was perusing the book of the prophet Isaiah, and when I came to the Parashah *Behold my servant*, I set before myself the notes of those who had commented upon it, and pondered over them and examined the opinions they contained. But all alike, I found, lacked solidity and soundness: as was the more palpable, since each differed from the rest in the subject to whom he supposed it to refer, some expounding the Parashah of the congregation of Israel as a whole, and others, in one way or another, of the King Messiah, who will speedily be revealed in our days. This, in fact, is done by our Rabbis, who, in the section *Ḥeleq*[a], on the words *To the increase of government* (Is. ix. 7), expound as follows:—The Holy One sought to make

[a] *Sanhedrin*, 94[a].

Hezekiah the Messiah; and [to make] Sanherib, Gog and Magog: and the heretics explain it of *their* Messiah, by their method of interpretation discovering in it arguments relating to his passion and death, and their false belief in him, which, however, have been refuted oftentimes with unequivocal proofs by learned Jews. One of these, R. Joseph ben Kaspi, was led so far as to say that those who expounded it of the Messiah, who is shortly to be revealed, gave occasion to the heretics to interpret it of Jesus. May God, however, forgive him for not having spoken the truth! our Rabbis, the doctors of the Thalmud, deliver their opinions by the power of prophecy, possessing a tradition concerning the principles of interpretation, so that their words are the truth. The principle which every expositor ought to rest upon is never to shrink from declaring the truth; in order that such as are foolish may not err: for our God will not destroy anything out of his world for the sake of fools who worship his creatures. And now I will make known what has been communicated to me from heaven, how, namely, the Parashah was originally uttered with reference to Hezekiah, king of Judah and Israel, but, being 'a word spoken deftly[b]' (Prov. xxv. 11), nevertheless alludes covertly to the King Messiah. In this respect the Parashah *Balaam* (Num. xxii. 1—xxv. 9) forms a parallel to it, speaking, as it does, ostensibly of king David, but alluding covertly to the Messiah. And, similarly, there is no doubt that the building of the temple in Ezekiel refers to the third Temple as well as to the second; for though our Rabbis, in the tract *Middoth*[c], adduce from it a proof respecting the construction of the latter, the gathering together of all the tribes, the division of the land into thirteen parts (Ezekiel xlviii), the gates named after the twelve tribes (xlviii. 31), and the installation-offerings which are spoken of (chap. xlv), have hitherto neither existed nor been created. It is beyond doubt, then, that this prophecy, being

---

[b] And accordingly capable of a double meaning. [c] ii. 5.

likewise 'a word spoken deftly,' while it refers directly to the second Temple, is at the same time intended to point covertly to the third: because, though the hopes and expectations of the generation in which Ezekiel lived were centred in the former, yet the aim of the prophet and the scope of his predictions extended to the latter; and God forbid that, when promising prosperity, a prophet should assume an extravagant or hyperbolical style, which in general is only adopted by them for proverbial sayings, or in declarations of terror, or rebuke. The central idea in the Parashah is the greatness of king Hezekiah, his prosperity, his righteousness, the merits which accrued to him therefrom at the time when he and his people were delivered from the hand of Sanherib, and the troubles which came upon him subsequently from Sanherib and his hosts. Now Isaiah's prophecies were composed with the view of describing the fall of Sanherib and of his army. From the Parashah *Ho Assyria!* (Is. x. 5 ff.) to the Parashah *Sanherib* (xxxvi. 1 ff.), he treats of various events connected with his history, according to the visions received by him on different occasions; at one time speaking of the fall of Sanherib himself; at another, of the fall of Babylon with him (for Babylon was contiguous to Assyria, and, at the time in question, under the dominion of Sanherib); then again of the greatness and goodness of Hezekiah; then of the exile of the ten tribes; next of the events of the Babylonian captivity. After all this he annexes the Parashah *Sanherib* (Is. xxxvi. 1 ff.) for the purpose of exhibiting how, in the destruction of Sanherib and his host, his own predictions had been fulfilled, together with an account of Hezekiah's sickness, of the miracle which was wrought when the sun went back, and of the prophecy uttered by himself at the time when the embassage from the king of Babylon came to Jerusalem. Then follow chaps. xl. 1—lii. 12, relating similarly to different subjects, according to the visions received by the prophet, some describing the prosperity and tranquillity during the days of Hezekiah, and others (as I believe) announcing the salvation which was to come to pass at the building of the second and third Temples. And so we thus arrive at the Parashah now before us, couched in a highly concise and elegant style, and embracing a history of Hezekiah, but at the same time pointing distantly (as I have said) to the King Messiah (who is speedily to be revealed in our own days). And if you object that the various Parashahs and prophecies of Isaiah follow a definite order, and wonder therefore why this one, which ought to have preceded the Parashah *Sanherib*, is placed so late, we shall reply that Sanherib's fall had already been described before the Parashah which bears his name, that the principal idea in the prophecy before us is the prosperity and greatness of Hezekiah, which belong to a later date, and, moreover, that it alludes besides to the Messiah.

LII. [13] The prophet begins, *My servant* ישכיל, meaning thereby to say that Hezekiah, who *had prudence* and understanding, and adhered to the Law and commandments of his God, not dealing foolishly like his father, who transgressed and served false gods, *shall prosper:* for השכיל means both *to be prudent* and *to be prosperous* (as 1 Sam. xviii. 14). In the same way, learned men interpret שמע, in Deut. vi. 4, '*Hear*, O Israel,' to signify not merely that they are to hear and *receive*, but also that they are to hear and *understand*. *He shall be high*, etc. Our Rabbis expound this in a Midrash of the King Messiah, saying, 'He shall be higher than Abraham, exalted above Moses, and loftier than the ministering angels.' Similarly it is said of Hezekiah that he was the Messiah of his generation, because the miracle wrought for him at the destruction of the Assyrian camp was greater than the battle of Abraham against the four kings, when he said, 'I raise *high* my hand unto the Lord' (Gen. xiv. 22). Greater, too, than the battle of Moses against Sihon and Og, when the Holy One *exalted him* by smiting them, saying (Deut. ii. 25), 'This day will I begin to put the dread of thee and the fear of thee before the face of all nations.' Greater, lastly, than the overthrow of Sodom and Gomorrha by the angels, when 'brimstone and fire' descended upon their inhabitants out of heaven, so that all were burnt up; for in the case of the Assyrian soldiers, while their spiritual nature was consumed, their bodies were preserved alive. And so our Rabbis expound Is. x. 16, 'Under his glory he shall kindle a burning,' of a conflagration of the soul but preservation of the body[d]. But the simple sense of the text is this, that he would be *high and exalted* on account of his success, *and lofty* at his latter end *exceedingly*: and so it is written in the book of Chronicles (II. xxxii. 25) that 'his heart *was lofty*' and elevated after he had been cured of his sickness and was confirmed in prosperity. [14]The Holy Spirit tells the prophet—or else the prophet says so to himself—how *many* of the people *were astonished* and surprised at the promise of Sanherib's fall before Jerusalem, because he had taken all the fenced cities of Judah, and laid siege to the capital (Is. xxxvi. 1), so that they would not believe Isaiah's words. Or, according to another explanation, the people expected that the prophet's intercession would deliver them, so that the wicked amongst them *were astonished at* Isaiah, saying, What do we care about a prophet who will not rescue us from this distress? In a similar strain, Jehoram, son of Ahab, exclaims (2 Kings vi. 31), 'If the head of Elisha, son of Shaphat, shall stand on him this day!' because he thought that Elisha, if he chose, could raise the siege, and so liberate him. *So marred*, etc. The countenance of the 'servant' (i. e. Hezekiah) was marred, and his form disfigured, on account of the trouble and pain endured by him, and the fasting and affliction which he underwent; for the iniquities of the people, and their deeds in the days of his father, filled him with fear, lest perhaps they might have caused the fatal decree to be passed against them. Scripture states, however, that his prayer was accepted (Is. xxxvii. 21 ff.), and that his righteousness stood him in good stead, although the people attributed his success to the merits of David his father. [15]The promise to

---

[d] *Sanhedrin*, 94[a].

Hezekiah, how, for his merits in the endurance of distress, and in trustful dependence upon his God, *he should declare to many nations* and kings, when they ask him about the miracle which 'was done in the earth' (and which they will know of, since it 'made the earth to tremble and kingdoms to quake'), the providence of his God towards him, and the signs and wonders which he wrought. Or כן יזה may mean, He will *make them ask* about the miracle, for both he himself and the prophets with him had the reputation of possessing great wisdom; and just as the king of Babylon sent to enquire concerning it (2 Chron. xxxii. 31), so other kings and princes will enquire likewise. Those *kings*, however, who have the design of going up against his land, and fighting against him, *will close their mouths*, and desist from speaking *against him*, in alarm, lest that which happened to the army of Sanherib should happen also to them; *for that which had not been told them have they seen*—they saw the going back of the sun, before they had been told of the miracle vouchsafed to Hezekiah, *and that which they had not heard they have perceived*—the destruction, without sword or battle, of such a vast host as that of the Assyrians, had never been heard of, though now they knew that it had taken place. Or both clauses may be parallel, intimating that the fall of Sanherib *had not been told them*, and that *they had not heard* of it.

LIII. [1]But even if what had happened in the former days (i. e. the fall of the Assyrian) were told them, *who would believe a report* such as that would be? or *upon whom* of the nations *was the arm of the Lord* ever *revealed* to work for them a miracle so great as this? [2]*And he came up as a sucker before him*, for through the merits of the righteous shepherd [David] he flourished like a blooming tree; and so it is written, 'There shall come forth a rod out of the stump of Jesse, and a branch out of his roots shall be fruitful' (Is. xi. 1). *As a root out of the dry earth:* because Hezekiah was just, and pious, and wise, and followed after the Law and the commandments diligently, notwithstanding that he had been brought up in the house of his father, the wicked renegade Ahaz; for he rejected all his father's deeds, and from his youth accustomed himself to adhere closely to the law of the Lord. The righteous is spoken of as a *sucker* and *root*, and the wicked and his house as the *dry earth*, after the manner of Deut. xxix. 18. He had *no form or comeliness*, because during his youth he was in such constant grief and distress on account of the deeds of his father that this, coupled with the fire which his father made him pass through when he was small, caused him to be ailing. Our Rabbis have, in fact, a tradition to the effect that he was anointed by his mother with the oil of the salamander[e], and so preserved from the flames, while all Ahab's other sons perished in the fiery oven which he made them pass through in honour of the idol; and that when elevated to the throne he had none of the majesty generally possessed by a king's son, because he had always been disputing with his father. *And* now, Isaiah continues, *we see him*, but do *not* fill our eyes with the *sight* of him, because, in our love for him, the desire of our heart is that no evil eye should gain power over him: therefore *we see him and desire him*—we have no wish except that he may enjoy long life, and that our sons may resemble him in being righteous, and prudent, and good. [3] *He was despised*, viz., by Sanherib and Rabshakeh, who treated with contempt his kingdom, his worship, and his confidence in his God, saying, 'Where are the gods of Hamath and Arpad?' (Is. xxxvi. 19); and, 'Where is the king of Hamath and the king of Arpad?' (Is. xxxvii. 13); 'Give pledges to my master, and let not Hezekiah deceive you' (vers. 8, 14), etc.; *and ceasing from men*, because he desisted from fighting, and relied upon prayer, although in the eyes of Sanherib he seemed to be entirely destitute of strength, for he speaks of him (ver. 14) as not being able to deliver them. *A man of pains and known to sickness*: because he was pained in heart and distressed at the reproaches cast at him by the 'attendants of the king of Assyria'

---

[e] See Buxtorf, s. v. סלמנדרא.

(ver. 6), and sick in body from lamentation and grief. And so there is a Midrash to the effect that Hezekiah had an illness previous to the one in which he was 'sick unto death' (Is. xxxviii. 1)[f], the addition *unto death* implying that another sickness had preceded—perhaps during the siege of Sanherib—which was not unto death. *And as one hiding his face from us:* for he heard himself reproached by the people and their captains, who advised submission to the Assyrian, and declared that Hezekiah the king was attempting to entrap them: he acted, however, like one who hid his face from them, and as though he neither heard what they said nor knew their thoughts. So there is a Midrash in which our Rabbis say that Shebna the scribe wrote on a leaf, 'Shebna submits and Hezekiah rebels,' and winding it round an arrow, shot it into the camp of the king of Assyria[g]. *He was despised and we esteemed him not:* even some of his own people despised him, not thinking him to be so just and pious, or worthy to have such a great miracle wrought for him as the deliverance proved to be. [4]*Surely he carried our sicknesses,* etc. Hezekiah was a mighty man of valour both in heart and in body, and although anxiety and fear lest the transgression of his people might cause them some mischief had distorted his countenance and form, yet he exhibited no terror or alarm before Sanherib, but 'comforted' and encouraged the people to such a degree as to remove the sickness and pain produced in their hearts by fear. Accordingly he says (2 Chron. xxxii. 7), 'Be strong and courageous, be not afraid;' and (ver. 8), 'With him is an arm of flesh, but with us is the arm of the Lord our God to help us:' so that when through his merits and intercession the deliverance was wrought, it was as though he had borne and carried all their sicknesses and pains. The people, however, still *thought* he would be taken by the king of Assyria, and *smitten and afflicted* by his hands—contrary to what actually happened; for his righteous-

---

[f] *B'reshith Rabbâ*, c. 65.

[g] Thalm. Bab., *Sanhedrin*, 26[a].

ness and prayers protected both himself and them; but the people did not possess his faith, or have confidence in his righteousness and devotion to God, for amongst them still lingered some wicked ones from the days of Ahaz. By '*smitten of God*,' the prophet means to say smitten *severely*: the Divine name is added for the purpose of intensifying the meaning, as in the expressions 'flame of Jah' (Cant. viii. 6), 'mountains of God' (Ps. xxxvi. 7). [5] But *he was panged and bruised* for the iniquities and transgressions committed in the days of his father, when they forsook the Law and the service of God: *the instruction of our peace*—i. e. of the Law and the commandments—*was upon him;* he undertook the office of instructor, and by his constant efforts brought back the nation to goodness, establishing a multitude of schools in which the Law was taught and enforced. Our Rabbis thus expound as follows:—'*And the yoke shall be destroyed because of fatness* (Is. x. 27), i. e. the yoke of Sanherib by the fatness of Hezekiah. What did he do? He affixed a sword at the entrance to every place of study, saying, Every one who does not occupy himself with the Law shall be pierced through with this sword. They sought, therefore, from Dan to Beersheba,' etc.[h] *And by his associations we were healed;* by the companies which he brought together in the different schools for the study of the Law, those who attended them were healed for their transgressions (as Is. vi. 10), as though to say, Through their study of the Law, to promote which Hezekiah thus forcibly associated them, they received pardon for their iniquities, being made aware that they had been healed (i. e. forgiven), by the great deliverance from Sanherib. [6] *All we like sheep had gone astray*—all had erred in their counsels, one saying, Let us serve the king of Assyria! another, Let us go out and fight! a third, Let us go out and escape! *Each had turned after his own way*, i. e. the way suggested by himself. Or, according to another view, the expressions

[h] *Sanh.*, 94[b]. The quotation continues, 'and none was found ignorant of it.'

have reference to the days of Ahaz, before Hezekiah had converted them to the way of the Lord, when they *went astray like sheep, each to his own way*, doing what was right in his own eyes, and not enquiring of the Lord. *Yet the Lord through him condoned the iniquity of us all*—let himself be entreated by him, and received his prayer, forgiving their iniquity and saving them. הפגיע means *to receive prayer*, just as פגע means *to pray* (Jer. vii. 16); the same difference existing between them as between נעתר and עתר[i]. And בו signifies *for his sake.* [7] *He was oppressed*, viz. by Sanherib, *and he was afflicted* by the reproaches of Rabshakeh, *yet he opened not his mouth* to answer them, as it is written, 'For the king's commandment was, saying, Ye shall not answer him' (Is. xxxvi. 21): *as a lamb he was led to the slaughter*, for, like Zedekiah who rebelled against Nebuchadnezzar, he had been destined to be delivered into the hands of the king of Assyria, and would indeed have been delivered to him except for the salvation of the Lord. And possibly also the wicked among the people spoke of him as being thus about to be delivered up, and slain by Sanherib for having rebelled against him. *As a lamb dumb before her shearers, so he opened not his mouth:* his captains and servants kept devouring his substance, and wished to submit to the king of Assyria; but Hezekiah, though he knew of it, was silent, trusting with all his heart in his God. It is the custom of kings during war or a siege to double and even quadruple their soldiers' pay. [8] *For his sovereignty and judgment he was chosen.* עצר has the sense of *regal power*, cf. 1 Sam. ix. 17, and לקח signifies *to take* or *choose*, as Deut. iv. 20: the meaning of the phrase being that because Hezekiah attended to the laws of the realm, and observed the judgment of the Law, to do what was good and right in the eyes of the Lord, God had chosen him and raised him to power; for Hezekiah was both king and a father of the Court. *And who could teach his generation* the Law, as

---

[i] See, for example, Gen. xxv. 21: comp. Qamḥi, s. v. עתר.

Hezekiah could, *if he had* succumbed to his sickness and *been cut off out of the land of the living?*—as he says, 'Jah, Jah, in the land of the living I shall not behold!' (Is. xxxviii. 11.) שוחח is a transitive verb with a double object: *to make* others *meditate* in the words of the Law. *For the transgression*, etc.: as though to say that for the people's transgression he was sick and in danger of death, and that for their iniquity a just ruler, such as he was, was nearly lost to them: the sense thus resembles that of Is. lvii. 1, 'Because of the wickedness, the just is taken away.' The prophet says, A 'stroke[k]' upon *them*, because the boil from which he suffered would have injured them still more had he died from it: since for the death of this 'just' one they would have been exposed to terrible calamities, and to the liability of having their iniquities visited upon them. [9] Already had great distress come upon him when he was first besieged in Jerusalem, and when he seemed to be buried in the midst of *the wicked* hosts besieging him, i. e. the Assyrian army. Hezekiah's tomb is [spoken of by anticipation] like Shebna's (Is. xxii. 16)[l]. *And the rich*—i. e. simply the king, as Eccles. x. 20—*was on his high places:* through fear of Sanherib, Hezekiah was constantly offering prayer and supplication in his high places, i. e. in the Sanctuary and the School. The form of the Temple was that of one hall rising above another, like so many high places. And all these troubles, arising from Sanherib's presence and Hezekiah's sickness, were *not owing to* any *injustice which he had committed* while giving judgment in his court, *or* to any *deceitfulness in his mouth*, declaring itself in the laws of his realm; [10] but happened because *the Lord chose to bruise and sicken him* for his refusal (as our Rabbis relate[m]) to 'be fruitful and multiply;' since, although his intention was excellent, viz. that no wicked son might proceed out of his

[k] The word is used technically of the 'stroke' of leprosy, Lev. xiii. throughout (A. V. 'plague').

[l] Comp. above, p. 82.

[m] *Yalqut*, Kings, § 242.

loins—yet, inasmuch as it involved a frustration of the Divine command, the Almighty brought punishment upon him so as to slay him, rewarding him measure for measure; for God 'created not the earth for a waste, he formed it to be inhabited' (Is. xlv. 18). *If*, however, *his soul makes a trespass-offering*, and atones for its sin by obeying the commandment, he will then have seed, *and lengthen days* (as the prophet promises, Is. xxxviii. 5, 'Behold I add to thy days fifteen years'), *and the pleasure of the Lord*, his position as king and judge, *will prosper in his hand:* accordingly the promise runs on (ver. 6), 'And from the hand of the king of Assyria I will deliver thee, and this city,' so that Hezekiah would have tranquillity and peace for carrying on the government, and executing judgment in the Law of the Lord, and in obedience to what was right in his eyes. 11 *For the labour of his soul*—the labour exerted by it in studying the Law—*he will see* the truth, win the favour of his Creator, *and be satisfied* with prosperity: every one capable of being *just* and wise *will my servant make righteous* so as through him to bring advantage to many *by his knowledge* and wisdom, and devotedness in teaching them the Law; *and their iniquities* which were resting upon them, by his righteousness and wisdom which he taught them, *he will bear*—he will protect the generation in which he lives, so that no evil thing may be found in it, but only peace, happiness, and wisdom, as he says himself (Is. xxxix. 8), 'There shall be peace and truth in my days.' 12 *Therefore I will divide him* a portion *with the many:* for God awarded him both riches and honour, and lifted him up in the sight of all nations, as is recorded, 2 Chron. xxxii. 23. *And the mighty he shall divide as spoil*—for he was given the plunder of Sanherib's army: in 'the mighty' there is an allusion to the plunder of the ten tribes, which had been in the possession of Sanherib's host, but was then recovered by Hezekiah; and the expression 'he shall *divide* spoil' is employed, because it was customary for half of it to belong to the king, and half to the army. But just before, 'divide' has a different sense: there the allusion is to the presents sent to him by the kings and captains; because after the great miracle had been wrought for him he became amongst them as a 'prince of God[n]:' חלק, like חצה, is thus used of division into either equal or unequal portions. *Because he poured out his soul to die:* when the siege was first begun by the king of Assyria, some of Hezekiah's captains treacherously formed the plan of winning Sanherib's favour at the price of their master's head; Hezekiah, however, reasoned that if a miracle were wrought for him, all would of course be well, and if his sin caused events to take a different turn, he would die in the service of his God: he thus, so to speak, 'poured out his soul to die.' *And he was numbered with the transgressors,* viz. when Sanherib put him into the same category with the kings of Hamath, Arpad, and Sepharvaim (Is. xxxvii. 13), and when Rabshakeh accounted him a transgressor, saying (ver. 7), 'Is not this he, whose high places and altars Hezekiah hath taken away?' *But he bare the sin of many*—he was perfectly just, so that his people were delivered for his merits, and he carried the sins and transgressions which they had committed in the days of his father: contrary, therefore, to what Sanherib and Rabshakeh expected, the people were not on his account involved in any disaster. *And made intercession for the transgressors*—he was constantly praying on behalf of his generation, and oftentimes God let himself be entreated by him: יפגיע expresses continued action, but Scripture does not mention all the deliverances and wonders which were vouchsafed to him. After the fall of Sanherib, and victory of Hezekiah, numbers belonging to Israel gathered themselves together from distant parts, and coming to the land of Israel and Jerusalem, united themselves with the poor of the people whom Shalmanezer had left, and thus the whole country from Dan even unto Beersheba (which, as appears from 1 Sam. iii.

---

[n] To whom, therefore, it was fitting that presents should be given: cf. Gen. xxiii. 6.

20, are its boundaries) became consolidated and settled. And so it is related how Hezekiah 'sent to all Israel and Judah' (2 Chron. xxx. 1, cf. 5). Our Rabbis say in the section Ḥeleq[o], that in the days of Hezekiah search was made from Dan unto Beersheba, and lo, he reigned over both Israel and Judah like David his father, and that this is the reason why Isaiah has annexed to this Parashah the one beginning *Shout, O barren one*; where Jerusalem is thus addressed, because a vast multitude from Israel were collected in her, so that the city was firmly and compactly established, and her inhabitants were more numerous than those of the kingdom of Samaria. For this reason the prophet bids her *shout and be glad* at her populous condition, like *a barren woman*, because she had not brought forth the crowds which peopled her, but they had come to her from other cities: 'break forth into singing and cry aloud' is then parallel to 'shout,' being added with the view of intensifying the meaning. *For more* are *the children of the desolate*—the children of Samaria, whose kingdom was laid desolate, and whose 'king went into captivity,' are now more numerous in Jerusalem than the natives of the capital. *The children of the married one* are here the people of Jerusalem, who were victorious and in tranquil prosperity, under Hezekiah, their 'just' and 'successful' king. In this comparison, the people or city is likened to a woman, and its king to her husband, while the nation whose head and sovereignty have both perished is likened to a desolate widow. In the succeeding verses, the prophet describes the settling of the rest of the land; but the remaining portions of the book relate mostly to the third Temple, to be built speedily in our own days.

Says the author: Behold, we have explained the several parts of this Parashah in an elegant and plausible manner; and the interpretation here given is the one that is revealed and open to all, but there is a secret one, sealed and treasured up in its

---

[o] Above, p. 210.

midst, which sees throughout allusions to the King Messiah (who is assuredly to be speedily revealed in our own days). And in the same sense it is expounded by our Rabbis: we cannot, however, interpret each individual detail in it of the Messiah, because we do not know all the incidents of his advent, or the precise manner of the redemption which he will then accomplish for Israel. Still, what our Rabbis teach in this respect, we must accept, for, like all their other opinions, it will be true and right; but any one who imagines himself able to apply every single particular in the Parashah to the Messiah, is in error, and feeling after darkness rather than light, as is the case with the heretics who struggle vainly to refer it to their Messiah in detail. We see then their error and delusion, which has already more than once been sufficiently replied to by our wise men. May God, for his name's sake, lighten our eyes with the illumination of his Law, and bring us forth out of darkness into light, and redeem us with a perfect redemption!

XXXII. R. SH'LOMOH BEN MELEKH.

LII. [13]ישכיל *will prosper,* as 1 Sam. xviii. 14, and as the word is rendered in the Targum of Yonathan. [14]שממו *were astonished,* as Ezek. iii. 15. משחת, from the Hif'il, with *Ḥireq* in place of *Qameẓ*. Or it may be an adj., like מִבדל, Josh. xvi. 9, with *Ḥireq* under the *Mem.* תֹּארו, with the *Ḥolem* retained, contrary to custom, on account of the א: otherwise, it ought to be תָּאֳרוֹ. Cf. פּוּעֲלוֹ, Jer. xxii. 13. [15]יזה; used here in the sense of *speaking,* like נטף, which similarly bears the double meaning of *dropping* or *sprinkling,* Judg. v. 5, and also of *speaking,* as Mic. ii. 6. The word is Hif'il, with a transitive force, *fara parlar* in Spanish. גוים; the *Yod* of the plural is dropped in writing, but preserved in pronunciation. יקפצו *to close* or *refrain;* but whether the word be interpreted in the sense of *opening* (as Cant. ii. 8, where it is used of the legs extended in leaping), or in that of *shutting* (as Deut. xv. 7), either explanation will be admissible here: the kings will either *open* their mouth to tell of his greatness, or *close* it by placing their hands upon it in amazement.

LIII. [2]יונק, as Hos. xiv. 7: young and tender plants are called *suckers,* just as a young child is called a *suckling.* ונחמדהו *and we were not desiring him,* but, on the contrary, abominated him: the negative must be supplied from לא מראה. [3]חדל, an adj., in *st. constr.:* the word denotes him as the most insignificant of men. ידוע *known*[a]: the sense being that it was known to all as an established fact that he was a sufferer from

[a] Not, as some commentators explain, in that of *broken.*

sickness. מסתר, a substantive. ולא חשבנוהו, the verb means *to esteem:* we did not in the least appreciate or value him. [4]חלינו, a subst., with the *Yod* of the plural dropped. סבלם, the burden and weight of the pains pressed heavily upon his shoulder. [5]מחלל, a partcp. of the quadrate form [Poʿel], from a verb ע״ע, signifying *wounded;* or possibly from a verb ע״ו, in the sense of *panged,* cf. חיל, Ps. xlviii. 7, etc. מדכא, as Ps. cxliii. 3. שלומנו *our peace,* as though to say, The chastisement which should have come upon us while we were in peace fell upon him. But R. Yoseph Qamḥi explains it to mean *the whole of us,* like הגלת שלומים, Jer. xiii. 19, i. e. a whole or complete captivity: the sense will then be, that the chastisements which should have come upon us fell wholly on him[b]. ובחבורתו, like חבורה, Ex. xxi. 25, except that the *Dagesh* is omitted: it signifies a *slit* or *cut,* the same root being used in the Jerusalem Targum for התגודד, Deut. xiv. 1. From the language of our Rabbis it would appear that a stripe or wound is called חבורה, when the blood coagulates underneath, without breaking out; for they say, 'What is a חבורה which never disappears? It is a bruise where the blood, though it does not break out through the skin, nevertheless coagulates beneath it.' It is called a חבורה, because the blood is *collected together* in the wound itself[c]. We were *healed*—in the same sense as Ex. xv. 26. [6]כצאן (with *Pathaḥ*); like *the* sheep, viz. the sheep which are without a shepherd: the definite article is therefore inserted, because the sheep which have no shepherd are those which go astray. הפגיע, it is the penalty which lights upon them, and God who causes it to do so, viz. when he sends misfortune on them: עון means here the penalty for sin, as Gen. xv. 16. [7]נגש *to oppress,* viz. for money, as 2 Kings xxiii. 35, Deut. xv. 2. נענה *was afflicted* in the body—alluding to the stripes he used to undergo. נאלמה,

[b] Comp. above, p. 52.

[c] Above, p. 109. The author's words agree closely with those of Qamḥi, *Book of Roots,* s. v. חברברה.

Mil'el, being perf. Nif'al. [8]עוצר, the place where he was *confined*, by which the prophet means the captivity. משפט, i. e. the exile, when *judgments* were inflicted upon him: from all this he was *taken* and redeemed. ואת דורו וג' *who* was there that *said* his generation would ever attain such greatness? cf. Gen. xxi. 7. שוחח is *to tell* or *declare*, as Ps. cxliii. 7: in both places the form is Po'lel, from שוח. *My* people: each separate nation is supposed to say this; the stroke had fallen upon Israel, not for their own transgression, but for that of the nations. [9]עשיר, considered by R. Yonah [d] to be equivalent to רשע *wicked;* but it is not allowable to abandon the usual signification 'rich,' merely on account of the parallel clause. The prophet says that through being slain because there was 'no violence in his hands,' he died before his time, like the wicked, who (Ps. lv. 24) 'do not live out half their days,' being put to death for their wickedness. In the same way, the words *with the rich in his death* mean that he perished like the rich who are murdered for the sake of their wealth. By *giving his grave with the wicked* is signified that he gave himself up to martyrdom for the sake of God's holy name: for if he had denied his own Law, and transferred his allegiance to theirs, they would have released him: and the expression *with the rich* derives its force from the fact that the wealthy are murdered for their riches, and not for any wickedness that may be in them. מותיו, plural from מָוֶת, the *Waw* becoming quiescent: the plural number indicates how death was sometimes produced by repeated stabbings, sometimes by severe tortures; in time of persecution, too, some were burnt, others murdered, others stoned: they were ready to meet any form of death for the Unity of God. [10]החלי, pronounced like a verb ל״א, with the third radical dropped in writing, although the root is in general ל״ה. יאריך *will make* others *prolong*, with a causative signification, for their long life will be owing to him and his obedience to the commandments:

[d] *Book of Roots*, col. 554 (see below, Note *b*).

see the root. [11]יראה ישבע, i. e. *he will see* prosperity, so as to be satisfied with it. הערה *to pour out*, as Gen. xxiv. 20, though in a different conjugation. [12]יפגיע *to intercede* or *entreat*, as lix. 16, Jer. xxxvi. 25, similarly in Hif'il. The meaning is that Israel used to intercede for the transgressions, as it is said (Jer. xxix. 7), 'And seek ye the peace of the city whither I have led you away captives.'

XXXIII. R. ABRAHAM FARISSOL.

Inasmuch as in this Parashah there seem to be considerable resemblances and allusions to the work of the Christian Messiah, and to the events which are asserted to have happened to him,—how, e. g., he came and bare the iniquity of the Church,—so that no other prophecy is to be found the gist and subject of which can be so immediately applied to him, it is essential that we should discuss and explain it with care; thoroughly and clearly examining each separate verse, and exhibiting its connexion with the rest, in order that 'he who runs may read.' In the first place, then, we may mention that this Parashah also is divided in two by Hieronymus, the learned Christian translator, who makes a division in the course of the Parashah, separating the first three verses from what follows, and commencing the fifty-third chapter at the verse *Who hath believed our report?* From this point onwards, through the whole length of the Parashah, Christian commentators explain whatever they desire of the sufferings specially attributed to their Messiah, on the ground that he came to die, and to carry and atone for the iniquity of the Church. For our own part, however, we shall start at the proper opening of the Parashah, *Behold my servant*, etc., endeavouring first of all to elicit the intention of the prophet, and to ascertain who the 'servant' is to whom he appropriates the Parashah: by this method we may hope afterwards to discover the drift of the whole, and avoid deducing from it any idle inferences.

I have found, then, some expositors who suppose the Parashah to be an echo of the murmur of dissatisfaction expressed by the saying, 'There is a just man and it goes ill with him[a]:' and others who apply it confidently to the King Messiah, who will be equally a servant of God and the Messiah—an opinion shared by our Rabbis in the Midrash, when they say, alluding to his dignity and greatness, 'He shall be higher than Abraham, more exalted than Moses, and loftier than the ministering angels.' We shall ourselves, however, with no less confidence, suppose that it refers properly to the congregation of Israel, which the prophet addresses by the term *servant*, in the singular number, exactly as we find him doing, by habit and preference, in many of his previous prophecies. Thus he says above, 'Remember these things, O Jacob, and Israel; for thou art my servant: I have fashioned thee, thou art my servant'—language which shews, beyond the possibility of doubt, both that the prophet is addressing the congregation of Israel, and that he applies to it the name of *servant*: the verse so adapted to establish this occurs in the forty-fourth chapter of Isaiah [ver. 21]. In addition, however, to this passage, which has been shewn to be so important for proving that Israel is spoken of by the particular and individual term *servant*, many others can also be found, likewise preceding the Parashah at present under discussion, in which, adopting the same standpoint, he adopts naturally the same appellation. For instance, 'But thou Israel art my servant' (xli. 8); 'Now, therefore, hear, Jacob my servant' (xliv. 1); and a little below the verse just quoted (ver. 21), 'I have formed thee, thou art a servant to me, O Israel, thou shalt not be forgotten by me: I wipe out as a cloud thy transgressions,' etc. (by which he means to say that the iniquities of the congregation will be pardoned); and immediately afterwards (ver. 23), 'For the Lord hath redeemed Jacob.' Under these circumstances, it having become clear from the prophet's own words that the subject of the Parashah is the

[a] Above, page 15.

congregation of Israel, we are necessarily bound to interpret it accordingly, in agreement with what was his real design. And so, when at the end he says, *My servant* shall justify many, we must not force ourselves to the belief that a different subject is referred to. Whatever justice there may be in the expressions of our wise men who applied the prophecy to the Messiah, it should be borne in mind that although they themselves and their words are both truthful alike, still their object was an allegorical one. But for ourselves we shall explain it wholly of Israel, who is called a *servant*, because their distress and the length of their captivity are the subject of complaint: we shall also discover in it the language of the Gentiles after the redemption has arrived, when they will begin to express the utmost amazement at the pains and calamities we had previously endured, saying that they, rather than Israel, ought to have undergone such penalties and punishments as those. In this way we shall succeed in avoiding a long exposition.

LII. [13] The prophet, speaking in the name of God, says, *Behold my servant*, i.e. my servant Jacob and the congregation of Israel, *shall prosper: he shall be high and lifted up*, viz. in the future exaltation. [14] *As many* peoples and kings *were astonished at thee*, O congregation of Israel, and amazed that the countenance of God's servant should be *marred beyond man, and his form beyond the sons of men*, saying in contempt, as they still do continually, when they see a Hebrew, 'He has the face of a Jew!' [15] *so* the time will come when many nations will *speak* of him—יזה being Hif'il and applied to *speaking*, like הטיף, Mic. ii. 11—and *kings* express amazement with their lips at the mighty salvation vouchsafed to him; *for that which had not been told them*—how, namely, such good fortune would one day really be theirs—*they* now *have seen, and that which they had not heard they have perceived*, for the Gentiles and their kings have never heard or imagined, neither do they believe, that Israel will ever be saved.

LIII. [1] The Gentiles and kings now say, *Who hath believed* this *report* which we hear? *and upon whom hath the arm of the Lord been revealed?* upon this servant, who before was despised, dispersed, and rejected, [2] but now grows up in prosperity, *like a root* springing up in exile to 'produce fruit upwards,' although before he had *neither form nor comeliness*, nor the exquisite beauty of a man *that we should desire him.* [3] *He was* in truth *despised and forlorn of men*, exposed to accidents and sickness: in his depression he kept his face unceasingly *hidden* from us; he was despised and we accounted him for nought. All this is supposed to be spoken by the Gentiles: [4] then, when they see the salvation of Israel, and their peace budding forth, they continue, *Surely he hath carried our sicknesses*, etc., i.e. now of a certainty we perceive that this servant Israel has suffered the punishment for iniquity which ought to have been carried by us, and *borne the pain* which for our deeds we ought to have endured: *yet we*, while he was in exile in our midst, thought that all his calamities and sufferings were occasioned by his being *stricken, smitten of God, and afflicted* with troubles proceeding from the Lord out of heaven. [5] *But he*—the nations are still speaking, as in the preceding verse—*was made sick* and punished in our stead: *the correction of our peace*, i. e. the sentence of peace obtained by us, should properly have rested *upon him*—he ought to have continued in peace and happiness rather than we; *but* now, since he bore the punishment, although unjustly, *we are healed*, and escape the reward of our iniquities. For, since it is clear from their having attained such prosperity, that, in spite of their sufferings, they were nevertheless right in their beliefs, we perceive that we, and not Israel, were the guilty: that we transgressed and were rebellious in the subjection wherewith we subjected them, although we still received no retribution at their hands. Of a truth, they will then continue, *all we like sheep have gone astray* in our false opinions concerning him; as Jeremiah says (xvi. 19), 'To thee will come nations from the ends of the earth, and say, Our fathers have inherited nothing but vanity:' but the Lord *laid upon him the iniquity of us all*—

brought on the 'servant' (as implied above, in the words, Surely he hath carried our sicknesses) the penalty and retribution which we ought to have paid. [7] [b]The [Christian] translator has rendered this verse as though it were an exposition of the ideas held by Christians, applying it to the atoning death of their Messiah; for ourselves, however, we explain נגש from Ex. v. 13, and suppose the nations to be describing[b] how the 'servant' is *oppressed* and crushed by adversity together with themselves, and also at the same time *bowed down* beneath the yoke of affliction, calumny, and persecution that was laid upon them (the nations), unable, for the terror they caused him, to *open his mouth*, and resembling rather *a sheep led to the slaughter*. [8]At this juncture, when they see his final exaltation, they will say, *From* the *confinement* of captivity, *and* the *judgment* of retribution which he endured, *he has been taken* away, to come forth into the light; *and who would* ever *have told* the men of his generation that he would be delivered from all the troubles which surrounded him? *for*, so they thought, he *is cut off out of the land of life*—he will not be counted worthy of the happiness reserved for the world to come: *for the transgression of my people*, says each of the kings, and for their sins, *there is a stroke upon him*, viz. upon the 'servant' who is all along spoken of, [c]as in ver. 5, 'He was wounded for our transgressions[c].' למו will then be equivalent to לו, as Ps. lv. 20, and often. Otherwise, however, we may explain as follows: *For their transgression* in injuring the congregation of Israel, *there is a stroke for them*—the children of my people will receive retribution, and a stroke will fall upon them from heaven, as it fell on Pharaoh (Gen. xii. 17). [d]In this case the word למו will retain

[b] In B:—The translator Hieronymus alters here the meaning of the words: the general sense, however, remains almost the same; for there are copies in which the ש is pointed on the left (שׂ), so that נגש must be explained from Ex. v. 13, the prophet describing, etc. [Jerome's version is, *Oblatus est quia ipse voluit*. etc.]

[c] Only in A.

[d] Only in B.

its regular plural force, being equivalent to להם. Or למו *them* may refer back to *Israel*, according to the sense of ver. 4, 'He carried our sicknesses[d].' [9]As, above, the nations are represented as supposing him to have been 'cut off from the land of life,' so here they are represented as supposing beforehand that he always *made his grave with the wicked*, [e]so that his final reward would be 'in the underworld beneath'—the grave of the wicked being preparatory to the retribution and punishments of Gehenna: now, however, they perceive their supposition to have been false, *because*[e] *he did no violence, and there was no deceit in his mouth.* [10]At this point the truth is stated in the prophet's own words: *The Lord was pleased to bruise and sicken him*, so as to see whether he would *make his soul a trespass-offering*—in other words, whether the 'servant' would justify the judgment passed upon him, in order that he might be worthy to *see seed*, i. e. to see his children live long, even in exile, and *lengthen days*, without being cut off for ever in captivity, *and* that at last *the Lord's pleasure*, his holy Law, *might prosper in his hand.* [11]*For the travail* which his soul had experienced in exile, *he will* now *see* happiness *and be satisfied* with his prosperity and the *knowledge* in which he will grow great and wise, multiplying understanding, as it is said, 'The earth shall be filled with the knowledge of the Lord,' so will my servant (the same servant mentioned above) *make many righteous, for their iniquities did he bear.* The last words shew that this happiness will come to him as an equivalent for the penalties he had endured in place of the Gentiles: cf. ver. 4, 'Our sicknesses he hath carried.' [12]*Therefore*, says the prophet in the name of God, because of the calamities he has endured, [f]*I will divide*

---

[e] In B: i. e. that he had to endure the penalty and reward of the wicked; *and*, moreover, was *with the rich in his death*, i. e. that the portion of his soul would then be like that allotted to wealthy robbers: this opinion concerning him was false *because*, etc.

[f] In B simply: *I will divide him* spoil and plunder *with many, even with* great and *mighty* kings; and this shall be the portion of the 'servant.'

him the spoil of Gog and Magog, together *with many mighty* kings: and this will be accomplished for him in the latter days[f], *because he poured out his soul to die*, and received chastisements [g]of love[g], *and* moreover *was numbered* by the Gentiles *amongst the transgressors* and the wicked, *and carried the sin of many* (as is said above) *and interceded for the transgressors;* for not only did the congregation of Israel bear the retribution which properly and rightly should have fallen upon others, who had ill-used them and kept them in subjection, but they were in the habit of praying for the good estate of the kingdom [h] and of the very transgressors who ill-treated them, and for the prosperity and richness of the crops, after the manner of the general prayers which we still use daily in captivity. Or the meaning of the last words may be this, that [i] in the days of the redemption[i], they will intercede for the transgressors [j] in order that they may [k] be healed, and forgiven, and [k] be converted. Such, then, [l]is the right method of exposition to pursue in the present Parashah, to pay, namely, close attention throughout to the prophet's meaning, for the purpose of ascertaining who is the 'servant' that will instruct them: the servant is the nation, suffering and smitten [l] for their sins more than any other people, by whose stripes and blows it appears [m] clearly [m] that the Gentiles will all be healed, and escape altogether the penalty which their rebellion deserves. And so they say of the Mahometans, the whole tribe of Arabs and Turks, that they will never receive any penalty for their rebellion, but will always dwell [n] securely in the world, enjoying every blessing from the host of heaven [n]. Hence also it becomes plain that Israel alone was destined for punishment—possibly because through their being

---

[g] Only in A. [h] *Abhoth*, iii. 2. [i] after the captivity, A.

[j] B *adds*, who ill-used them. [k] Only in A.

[l] is the preferable view. At that time, too, the nations will be amazed at the blow of exile and the other calamities which perpetually befel Israel, B.

[m] even at the present day, B.

[n] peacefully, with 'no breaking in, and no complaining in their streets,' B.

smitten others are to be healed. This exposition has already been hinted at by the authors of our traditions, as also in the learned Cuzari[o], who explain that it is a natural and regular ordinance of God for the most precious, the most indispensable, and the most active member of the body to be smitten and require curing: and hence that in any complaint, [p]the most vital parts, and, in particular, the liver (which is the fountain of a man's life blood), suffer[p] most quickly and most severely, and must therefore be bled and purged, in order that the other members may be healed. Whoever, then, understands in what way Israel, the 'people near unto Him,' is the heart of the whole world, and Israel's territory the fountain of all lands (because from its sufficiency the whole world drinks), will also understand this, and perceive how *by their stripes* all besides *were healed*. We have already explained above the principal reason why Israel suffered more than other nations, viz. because they had received the commandment, and because, in fact, they existed for the purpose of obeying the Law—a law, which was given to us, and not to any other nation; as it is written, 'An inheritance to the congregation of Jacob' (Deut. xxxiii. 4); and, 'Who declareth his words unto Jacob' (Ps. cxlvii. 19). Hence for their perverseness they were punished beyond any other people who had not received any such law: and accordingly Amos says, 'You only have I known out of all the families of the earth; therefore I will visit upon you all your iniquities' (Amos iii. 2).—May the Lord purify us and save us!

---

[o] Yehudah ha-Levi, *Cuzari*, ii. 36.

[p] In B: the great monarch, the heart, suffers.

XXXIV.

You already know that the majority of commentators, Rashi, R. Abraham 'Ibn 'Ezra, R. David Qamḥi, and Abarbanel, agree in holding that this prophecy refers to the Israelitish nation. The same opinion commends itself also to me, since in many of Isaiah's other prophecies we have observed likewise how the people are designated by the term *my servant*, as xli. 8, 9, xliv. 21, and often besides: in Leviticus, also, God exclaims (xxv. 55), 'For unto me are the children of Israel *servants*.' It follows, then, that the 'servant of the Lord,' when used absolutely, must signify Jacob and his children, the peculiar people. And do not object to me on the ground that our wise men have expounded the prophecy of the King Messiah (as we find it said, He shall be higher than Abraham, more exalted than Moses, and loftier than the ministering angels); because our belief is that the King Messiah is flesh and blood, even one of the righteous kings of Israel, as R. Mosheh Maimuni [Maimonides] writes[a] in the part *M'lâkhim*, 'From the greatness of the king may be inferred the greatness of the nation, exactly as from the greatness of the nation can be understood the greatness of the king:' hence the promises uttered respecting the King Messiah belong also to Israel, just as those which have reference to Israel have reference to the Messiah likewise. Nor did our

---

[a] *Yad ha-ḥ^{a}zâqah*, § *M'lâkhim*, c. xi.

Rabbis intend by their Midrash to imply that he would be greater than Moses and the angels: there is no need to suppose that the *Mem* must denote superiority or comparison; it may in this place signify *from*, as 1 Chron. xxix. 14. Their meaning would thus be that his princely nature would owe its origin to his being of the seed of our father Abraham, his power of prophecy to his being a disciple of Moses our master, the permanency of his law and the penetration of his intellect to the angels being amongst the members of his household.

LII. [13] The prophet says that the nation ישכיל. This word we find used both of 'understanding,' as in Isaiah himself, xli. 20, and also of 'prosperity' or 'success,' as 1 Sam. xviii. 14. In the present place you can interpret it in whichever way you prefer; since we find both promised to the nation in different passages: Jeremiah, for instance (xxxi. 33), says, 'All of them shall know me;' and Isaiah (xlviii. 15), 'He shall make his way prosperous.' *Shall be high:* this word is used of victory over enemies, as Mic. v. 8: accordingly it is here promised that the nation shall be high above its enemies and shall subdue them. *And exalted:* the good name that travelleth afar is thus designated: Scripture, for instance, says of Hezekiah (2 Chron. xxxii. 23), that 'he was exalted in the eyes of all the earth;' and in the same way the prophet here promises that the nation will be exalted in the eyes of every one, and that its name will go forth into all the world: the same promise occurs often besides, as Jer. xvi. 19. *And lofty exceedingly:* the man who does not turn to the vanities of this world, but fixes the desire of his soul wholly on intellectual studies, and directs his intelligence upwards is said to be *lofty:* thus Scripture says of Jehoshaphat, king of Judah (2 Chron. xvii. 3–6), how 'the Lord was with him,' etc., and 'his heart was *lofty* in the ways of the Lord;' and so it is promised here that Israel will not 'turn towards the proud, and such as incline after lying' (Ps. xl. 5), but will elevate his intelligence upwards so as to gain understanding and knowledge of the ways of the Lord. [14] Isaiah says that at the time of the captivity all who saw them *were astonished* and confounded at their fall; so it is written (2 Chron. xxix. 8), 'And the Lord's anger was upon Judah and Jerusalem, and he delivered them to trouble, astonishment, and hissing,' in accordance with the prediction delivered by Moses (Deut. xxviii. 37), 'And thou shalt become an astonishment, a proverb, and a by-word,' etc. And this astonishment, he goes on, arose from their *form* being *marred*, in the words of the Mourner (Lam. iv. 8), 'Their form is become darker than the Nile, they are not known in the streets.' [15]The verb הזה, analogously to נשל, is used of anything moved forcibly and irregularly from place to place: thus, Is. lxiii. 3, 'And the juice of them *was shaken* upon my garments;' 2 Kings ix. 33, 'And some of her blood *was shaken* upon the wall;' נשל occurs in a similar signification, Deut. xix. 5, 2 Kings xvi. 6. Here the prophet says that as during the exile men had been astonished at Israel, so now their greatness, extending as it does from one end of the earth to the other, will expel many nations from the places of their abode. It is possible that this term הזה, which is most frequently applied to blood, is chosen with the view of indicating that the expulsion will be attended with bloodshed. *At him kings will shut their mouth:* when they hear of Israel's greatness, the kings of the earth (as Micah says, vii. 16) 'will be confounded and put their hand upon their mouth.' *For that which was not told them*, etc.: the prophet himself says (lxvi. 8), 'Who hath heard such a thing as this? who hath seen things like these?' on account of all these things they will *shut their mouths*—they will have no mouth to speak with, after seeing what they had never, during their whole lives, imagined that they would behold.

LIII.[1] Then they will each say to himself, *Who* ever *believed* that we should hear a report such as we are hearing now? So Habakkuk says (i. 5), 'Behold among the Gentiles, and regard, and wonder marvellously: for I work a work in your days, which ye will not believe, though it be told you.' And this amazement will be increased amongst them when they perceive how *the arm* and might *of the Lord had been revealed* to 'a people despised and plundered,' as Isaiah himself declares (xlix. 7) had been the case with Israel hitherto. [2] For wonderful to tell, he had suddenly begun to flourish *like a sucker*, i. e. like a twig from a tree planted in the earth, *and like a root out of the dry earth*, i. e. like the root which remains concealed in the ground when the tree is pulled up, so that the passers-by cannot see it, and do not suppose it to be there, though presently it puts forth its shoots and becomes a great tree: such will be the language used of Israel, when, after having been long dried up, it has again produced fruit upwards. You find Hosea speaking similarly (xiv. 6), 'I will be as the dew unto Israel: let him flourish as the lily, and cast forth his roots as Lebanon! let his suckers spread, and his beauty be as the olive!' *He had no form and no comeliness:* these words allude perhaps to the wise men of Israel and the Sanhedrin; for the glory of a nation consists in its wise men. Our Rabbis have this Midrash: While a righteous man is in a city, he is its glory, its ornament, and its splendour: when he leaves it, its glory leaves it, its ornament leaves it, its splendour leaves it[b]; and so you find that when Israel was carried captive from their land, the Mourner says (Lam. i. 6), 'From the daughter of Zion all her splendour is departed,' where our Rabbis say, This refers to the Sanhedrin, which went into captivity[c]. *And we saw him, but there were no looks* [to gaze at]. These, too, are the words of the Gentiles and their kings, saying that 'during the exile we did not gaze at him, because he was despised in our eyes: now, however, *we desire him*, and long to be as he is.' So Balaam says (Num. xxiii. 10), 'May my last end be like his!' and the Psalmist (Ps. cxii. 10), 'The wicked shall see, and be vexed: his teeth he will gnash and melt away: the desire of the wicked shall perish,'—for this Psalm relates to the heathen who are devoted

---

[b] *B'rêshith Rabbâ*, § 68. [c] *Ekha*, i. 6.

to idolatry, describing how the wicked at the time of the redemption will be so vexed when he sees the successes of this nation that he will gnash his teeth at finding himself unable to arrive at prosperity like theirs. And Haggai says (ii. 7), 'To the desire of all nations shall they come,' meaning that Israel will advance to such a position that all nations will desire to be like them; [but in vain,] for their hopes will perish, and they will not be able to overtake them. [3] *He was despised:* the nations will declare how hitherto Israel had been despised and depressed, as the prophet himself states above, xlix. 7; so Nehemiah (ii. 19) relates that they were 'mocked and despised' when they began to build the walls of Jerusalem. *A man of pains:* Isaiah describes how the nation was incessantly in a state of pain, as the Mourner complains, when he asks, 'Is there any pain like unto my pain?' (Lam. i. 12.) And, similarly, Jeremiah says (xv. 18), 'Why is my pain perpetual and my plague incurable?' and again (xxx. 15), 'Thy pain is incurable.' *And known to sickness:* they were exposed to every description of malady, as Scripture predicts (Deut. xxviii. 59, 61), 'Every plague and every sickness, and sicknesses sore and of long continuance, will he bring upon thee;' and, similarly, Isaiah (i. 5), 'The whole head is sick;' and Jeremiah (iv. 31), 'I hear a voice as of a woman in sickness, and anguish as of her that bringeth forth her firstborn.' וכמסתר פנים ממנו; the commentators explain this as signifying that the Gentiles hid their faces from Israel: perhaps, however, the meaning is rather that they imagined the Almighty had hidden his face from them; for is not the expression '*as though* hiding' an objection to the former view, which would require simply '*hiding?*' The fact is that the prophet adds *as though*, because he speaks of the Almighty's hiding his face, which can be true only metaphorically. In similar terms the Mourner (iv. 15 f.) exclaims, 'They say amongst the heathen, no longer will they dwell in the presence of the Lord; he hath divided them, he will no more regard them.' [4] The Gentiles continue speaking. Israel, they say, has done excellently in accepting the chastisements which we laid upon them and which they bore—for '*our* sicknesses' does not denote the sicknesses borne by the nations, but the sicknesses which they inflicted upon others: the pronoun sometimes indicates the agent, as 'my blows' (Ex. ix. 14), and 'my bruise' (Gen. iv. 23), where the agents are God and Lamech respectively. In the same way the Psalmist says (xxxix. 11), 'Remove thy stroke from off me,' meaning the stroke which thou hast brought upon me; and so here the nations are the agents, and declare how Israel bore the sicknesses which they themselves had occasioned. So Jeremiah says (x. 19), 'Woe is me for my hurt! Truly this is my sickness, and I must bear it;' and the Psalmist (lxix. 8), 'For thy sake I have carried reproach, shame hath covered my face.' *Yet we*, they continue, *thought* that the calamities which befel him in exile at our hands [were sent of God[d]], for seeing him *stricken*, we conceived him as being without hope: so the Psalmist says (lxxxviii. 5), 'I am esteemed as those that go down into the pit;' and again, speaking in the name of the nation (cxl. 2), 'Deliver me, O Lord, from the evil man, from the man of violence preserve me, who imagine mischief in their heart.' [5] *For our transgressions.* The word *transgression* is used, as by Jacob, Gen. xxxi. 36, or Joseph's brethren, l. 17, of a trespass or offence committed by one man against another: the Gentiles therefore say, We now recognise that he was wounded by us; for though we did not suspect it before, in wounding him we 'transgressed and rebelled.' And so Jeremiah says (l. 7), 'All that found them have devoured them: and their adversaries say, We are not guilty, because they have sinned against the Lord.' It is well known also how many our sufferings in exile were: the Psalmist says (lxix. 27), 'Him whom thou hast smitten they persecute, and tell the pain of those whom thou hast wounded.' *Bruised for our iniquities;* for if we bruised him, then iniquity came upon us: the Psalmist

---

[d] Some such words as these seem to have dropped out in the Hebrew.

says, 'Thou hast bruised us in the place of dragons' (xliv. 20); and, 'They bruise thy people, O Lord, and afflict thine heritage' (xciv. 5). And *the chastisement of our peace,* continue the nations, meaning the chastisement they had inflicted upon Israel, was *upon him;* i.e. Israel prayed for our peace, in order that we might be *healed,* since we were not ourselves worthy to enjoy it except through the intervention of the miseries which befel him, and, by so doing, produced all our present prosperity. For while they were in exile, the Israelites used to pray for us, as they were commanded to do by the prophets: this Jeremiah says (xxix. 7), 'Entreat for the peace of the city whither I have taken you captives, and pray for it unto the Lord:' you know also the saying of our Rabbis, 'Tyre was not filled until after the desolation of Jerusalem[e].' 6 The prophet predicts how in those days the Gentiles will acknowledge their error, and confess it with their lips. And Isaiah says (ii. 20), 'In that day a man shall cast his idols of silver, and his idols of gold,' etc.; and again (xxix. 24), 'They that erred in spirit shall come to understanding.' *But the Lord,* etc.: as though to say, Now we see that it was God's will that we should all sin against them, though far be it from us to say that God was himself the cause of their thus sinning, as Job says, 'Why hast thou set me as a mark[f] for thee?' (vi. 20.) 7 Here a fresh class of the calamities inflicted upon Israel is described by the Gentiles: how, namely, they oppressed him day after day by the imposition of taxes and other burdens, as Scripture says, 'They devour Israel with their whole mouth' (Is. ix. 11); and, 'Thou makest us like sheep to be eaten' (Ps. xliv. 11); for Israel was oppressed and afflicted by them, without opening his mouth. *As a sheep.* The nation is frequently spoken of as a sheep; for example, by Jeremiah (l. 17). Here the Gentiles declare that in spite of the misery they had occasioned to Israel, the latter had no

---

[e] Cf. Ezek. xxvi. 2.

[f] Lit. *a meeting-place* for the arrows,—the substantive corresponding to the verb in the text, *caused to meet.*

mouth wherewith to cry out against it—in the words of the Psalmist, 'I am dumb, I open not my mouth' (xxxix. 10); and, 'I am become as a man that heareth not, and in whose mouth are no reproofs' (xxxviii. 15). [8] The king who rules over a people is called a *coercer* (עוצר), as when the Lord says to Samuel, 'This same shall *reign over* my people' (1 Sam. ix. 17). Here it is described how Israel was deprived of sovereign and judicial power, i. e. of the judges and rulers appointed by their Law, in accordance with the prediction, 'And there is none coerced or released' (Deut. xxxii. 36). And so the Psalmist says (lxxxix. 45), 'Thou hast made his purity to cease,' i. e. removed the priest who judges and purifies [i. e. acquits], 'and cast his throne down to the ground,' i. e. cast down their throne so that they are without a king. *But* now *who is able to tell of* the greatness of *his generation?* because, in the eyes of the nations, he seemed to have been *cut off out of the land of the living*. So Isaiah writes (lx. 15), 'Whereas thou hast been forsaken and hated, etc., I will make thee a joy of many generations;' and the Psalmist (xlviii. 14), 'That ye may tell it to an after generation;' and Joel (iv. 20), 'But Judah shall dwell for ever, and Jerusalem to all generations.' *For the transgression of my people.* The kings of each nation of the earth confess that the blows wherewith they had smitten Israel arose from the transgression of their own people, and not from any offence on Israel's part: this has been already intimated by Isaiah himself (xlvi. 8), 'Remember this, and shew yourselves firm; bring it again to mind, O ye transgressors!' and in another place (i. 28), 'The destruction of transgressors and sinners.' [9] Another of the calamities which the nation endured was being buried in a foreign land. Amos says to Amaziah (vii. 17), 'Thou shalt die in an unclean land;' and the prophet Hosea (ix. 6), 'Egypt shall gather them up, Memphis shall bury them.' And *the wealthy* amongst them they afflicted and murdered by various kinds of death, in order to devour their riches, as Zechariah says (xi. 4 f.), 'Whose possessors slay them, etc., and their own shepherds pity them not.' The words *and the rich in his deaths* are thus added because the Gentiles used to murder the Israelites for the purpose of securing their wealth. *Because he did no violence;* i. e. because we had not sinned against them, or as the Psalmist says, speaking in the name of the people (lxix. 5), 'What I had not robbed, I then restored.' *And there was no deceit in his mouth,*—in the words of the prophet Zephaniah, when alluding to the same period (iii. 13), 'The remnant of Israel shall not do iniquity, neither shall a deceitful tongue be found in their mouth.' [10] Here the prophet begins to address the nation, reminding them that the decree to bruise them was from the Lord : in the words of the Mourner (i. 5), 'The Lord hath made her to grieve,' or of the Psalmist (xliv. 20), 'Thou hast bruised us in the place of jackals.' *If,* however, *his soul makes* itself *a trespass-offering* (as the prophet Ezekiel says, xliii. 10, 'That they may be ashamed of their iniquities), *he shall see seed, shall lengthen days*—alluding to the multiplication of their children, and length of their lives, which are both predicted by Hosea (i. 10) and Isaiah (lxv. 20)—*and the pleasure of the Lord,* i. e. whatever he desires, *shall prosper in their hand,*—as Isaiah himself says (lxii. 4), 'Thou shalt be called Hephzibah, for the Lord hath pleasure in thee.' [11] *For the travail* and weariness which came upon them, they will now *see and be* proportionately *satisfied* with 'fulness of joys:' in the words of Joel (ii. 25), 'I will restore to you the years that the locust hath eaten, the cankerworm, and the caterpiller, and the palmerworm; and ye shall eat in plenty and be satisfied, and my people shall never be ashamed,' where the prophet promises that all which the four kinds of locust, i. e. the four kingdoms, have devoured, will be restored to us by the Holy One, until we are again able to eat in plenty and praise his name. Similarly, it is foretold here how Israel will rejoice after the travail of captivity, and be satisfied with the fulness of joys prepared for him by the Almighty in the future redemption. In those days, he adds, the land will be so filled with the knowledge of the Lord that every one *by his knowledge will justify the just;* and this, not merely amongst those of his own people, but *amongst many*, exactly as Micah also proclaims how the nation will 'judge amongst many peoples, and rebuke strong nations' (iv. 3). *And their iniquities*, those, namely, of the 'many,' *he will bear*, i. e. each individual member of the nation will bear its iniquities for himself; they will no longer need God to take away their iniquities as he had done hitherto (for one of his blessed attributes is his readiness to forgive sin): accordingly Ezekiel writes (xxiii. 49), 'And they will put your lewdness upon you, and the sins of your idols shall ye bear.' [12] The prophet now proclaims how the reward for all the travail which had passed over them during exile, is with the Lord; for he will give them the wealth of the Gentiles,—as the prophet Zechariah foretells (xiv. 1), 'Thy spoil shall be divided in the midst of thee;' and Isaiah (lx. 16), 'Thou shalt suck the milk of the Gentiles, and shalt suck the breast of kings.' And all this will be awarded to them because each one of them had given himself up to die for the service of God,—as the Psalmist says (xliv. 23), 'For thy sake we are slain all the day long, we are counted as sheep for the slaughter.' *He was numbered with the transgressors;* for all the Gentiles ranked them in the same category with the wicked: go and learn how the 'adversaries of Judah' 'wrote an accusation,' and sent it to the Persian monarch, requesting 'search to be made' in the records of the state, in order that it might be discovered how the city had ever been 'rebellious, and hurtful to kings and provinces' (Ezra iv. 1, vi. 15): you see from this that our nation was always considered, by those who knew it, to be rebellious and apt to transgress from its allegiance. Now, therefore, the reward is promised, *I will divide him a portion with the many. And made intercession for the transgressors*, as the Psalmist says (lxxii. 15), 'He shall pray for him continually: for we find פגע used in the sense of *interceding* (as Jer. vii. 16). It may also, however, signify to *strike* or *slay* (1 Kings ii. 29, and often): in the latter case the meaning will be that he will slay the transgressors, as Isaiah, speaking as one bringing glad tidings to the nation, says (xxx. 25), 'And there shall be upon every lofty mountain rivers, streams of water, in the day of the great slaughter, when the towers fall.'

XXXV. R. MEIR ARAMAH.

LII. [13] *My servant.* In a preceding chapter (li. 19) the prophet (using the singular number) had made the announcement to Israel, 'Two things are come unto thee,'—the first, affecting their possessions, being desolation and destruction; the second, affecting their body, being the famine and the sword; and such is their lot to-day: [a] but afterwards he declares that their condition will be turned into one of joy and gladness, saying (lii. 7), 'How beautiful upon the mountains,' etc. He explains, however, that this will only take place after the lapse of long years: meanwhile the people need watching and warning not to mingle with the heathen; and hence the command (ver. 14), 'Depart ye, depart, come forth thence; touch not the unclean,' with the explanation, 'For ye shall not come forth in haste.' Here the prophet foretells that, as the whole nation are to meet with contumely and reproach among the Gentiles, so, or rather to a greater degree, will the wise meet with contumely and reproach in Israel itself—whether as affecting their substance or their persons: it will, however, as he explains, redound to their advantage; and accordingly Israel may hope one day to obtain authority over the Gentiles. And this is the sense of 'Behold my servant shall prosper;' but what follows[a], [14] *As many were astonished at thee,* refers to Israel, when he was despised and rejected in their eyes. [14]–LIII. [3] *So marred,* viz. as compared with other men, *was the countenance* of this 'wise' one: you know the conditions under which he lived: 'Thou shalt eat a morsel with salt, and drink water by measure; thou

[a] See the addition, p. 387 (Hebrew text).

shalt sleep upon the ground, and live a life of pain[b].' Who under such conditions as these, which actually fell to Israel's lot, could live the ordinary life of a human being? *So will he scatter many nations*, and by his knowledge hold sway over them, and gain admittance to the table of kings; for they will *hear* from his lips, after the *arm of the Lord has been revealed* upon him, *what had never* before *been told them*. Although, however, in consequence of these conditions of life, their manners are poor (for they are generally intractable), we nevertheless *shall desire* them, because of their intelligence. 4 The prophet now proceeds to state a striking truth, pointing out how, when chastisements fall on one like this just one, the worshippers of stars and constellations[c] are led by them to infer the wickedness of their belief, according to the saying[d], 'There is a just man and it goes ill with him:' not understanding that 'the just perisheth and no one perceiveth that he is carried away from misfortune (to come):' for a righteous man is 'like the lamp of God before the people,' which, however, by being wicked and sinful, the people extinguish; and this being the case, their death is a proof of the people's sin, rather than (which God forbid!) of the Almighty's injustice. Accordingly, the prophet says, *Surely he carried our sicknesses and bare our pains; but we thought him stricken and smitten of God*, in consequence of an uneven dispensation of Providence. 5 There are two kinds of chastisement which may possibly fall upon man, the chastisements of love, and the chastisements of sin; and both these came upon Israel on our account. For of this people it is said, *He was wounded for our transgressions, bruised for our iniquities;* and again, *The chastisement of our peace*, i. e. which resulted in our peace, rested likewise *upon him*. 7 The two kinds of penalty mentioned above as having been imposed upon the nation collectively by the Gentiles are here further described: they affect his person and his property respectively, the former

---

b *Abhoth*, vi. 4. c I. e. the heathen. d Above, p. 15.

being indicated by the words *Like a sheep led to the slaughter*, the latter by those which follow, *As a lamb which before her shearers is dumb.* [10]A demonstration that by comprehending the meaning of sufferings falling on the just for his sins (for there is none so just as never to commit sin) we can understand those which fell upon him for the sin of the people that is here spoken of. The prophet declares that the former will not issue in death: for every one is aware that a righteous man repents and confesses his guilt; and when he does this, he receives mercy from heaven, like Hezekiah, and lives. But if he is entangled in the iniquity of his generation, repentance is not within his power, and he must die in consequence; hence it is said, *The Lord was pleased to bruise him*, as though for its own iniquities (as we have just explained); when, then, *his soul lays a trespass-offering*, viz. upon itself, and recognises its guilt, it will of necessity *see seed and lengthen days*, for *the pleasure of the Lord will prosper in his hand*, so as to make atonement for him. For myself, however, I notice two things: 1. that he is righteous, 2. that he *sees and is satisfied* with 'many and sore troubles,' and that nothing short of death (as I have said) can secure atonement for him: this being so, it follows that he must suffer, not for his own sins, but for those of the people. [11] Accordingly the next verse says, *Of the travail of his soul he shall see and be satisfied*, referring to the misfortunes spoken of; and, *By his knowledge he will justify the just:* if he does this, however, he will *bear their iniquities*, i.e. bear them on their behalf. [12]An explanation that the sufferings are no crime in him; for in a world that is wholly good the Lord will pay him his reward *amongst the mighty* and *the strong*, because his deserts will be great: he then (as they say) will be 'higher than Abraham, more exalted than Moses, and loftier than the ministering angels,' for there is no dignity more elevated than that of him who sanctifies the name of Heaven, by being involved in, and suffering for, the iniquity of his age.

XXXVI. YIZḤAQ TROKI.

LII. [13] From this verse, as also from liii. 1, with those which follow as far as liii. 12, the Nazarenes argue to prove that Isaiah predicted of Jesus of Nazareth: of him, they affirm, he says, He shall be high and exalted, and lofty exceedingly, for the language here employed is applicable to him alone and none besides. In the same way they suppose him to be referred to in the words, He carried our sicknesses, etc.; and, He was wounded for our transgressions: because Jesus suffered affliction for their sakes to save their souls by his death from the power of Satan, who ruled over them. In reply it may be shewn that their argument is not valid: for whereas the text says, 'Behold my *servant*,' how can they apply this to Jesus of Nazareth? since they themselves, according to their own absurd tenets, assign to him Deity; and how could God in any prophecy be called a *servant?* If now the objector maintains that he is termed a 'servant' in respect of his material body, and 'God' in respect of his nature as a spirit, we must reply that it has already been irrefragably demonstrated in § 10 that even from the point of view of the gospel Jesus of Nazareth is not God, and still less so from his own standpoint: he never in any place speaks of himself as God, as will be further shewn in the second part of this treatise, by a detailed examination of the individual expressions used by the Evangelists. It must in addition be remembered that the words, *He shall be high*, etc., were not fulfilled in him: since he was condemned to death like any other common man among the people. Nor was the prediction, *He shall see seed, shall lengthen days*, ever fulfilled in him: he had no seed; and it cannot be said that his disciples are here meant by his 'seed,' for we never find disciples termed *seed* but only *sons*, just as teachers are spoken of as 'fathers:' the term seed is restricted to the descendants of a man, who come forth out of his loins. Similarly we do not find that he 'had long life;' for he was put to death when thirty-three years old. And they cannot legitimately refer this expression to the Godhead; because the Deity is not determined by length of days: he is the first, and he is the last, and his years have no end. Then, again, of whom will they interpret the verse, *Therefore I will divide*, etc.? who are the many and the mighty that are made his equals, and with whom, as they imagine, he is to divide spoil? And when it is said, *And made intercession for transgressors*, to whom did he intercede for them if, as their fond belief will have it, he was God himself? And there are many places similar to these. The truth is, the whole Parashah, down to liii. 12, was spoken prophetically to Isaiah with reference to the people of Israel, who were enduring the yoke of exile, and who are called 'my servant,' in the singular, as frequently elsewhere, Is. xli. 8, 9, xliv. 1, 2, 21, xlv. 4; and as we find also to be the case in the prophecy of Jeremiah, xlvi. 27, 28; and in the Psalms, cxxxvi. 22. You see that in all these passages Scripture designates the Israelitish nation as a servant, or as God's servant, in the singular. And so when the Ten Commandments were given we observe that the Almighty spoke to 600,000 men in the singular number ['I am the Lord, *thy* God,' etc.] If now they argue from the text, *Surely he carried our sicknesses*, etc., and assert that it was never at any time either seen or heard of that the people of Israel bore sickness or pain, or received stripes for the iniquity of other nations (for even the calamities and chastisement which they did endure were for their own sins, and not for those of other people), the reply is clear that it is a common custom in the mouth of the prophets to describe the miseries and humiliation of the captivity under the image of sickness or wounds, as Is. i. 5, 6, xxx. 26,

Hos. vi. 1, Lam. ii. 13, Jer. x. 19 (where the prophet explains what the 'hurt,' and the 'wound,' and the 'sickness' are, by adding, verse 20, 'My tent is wasted, and all my cords are broken,' etc.), xxx. 12–17 (the next verses shew what the 'bondage' and 'healing' denote, 'Behold I bring again the captivity of Jacob's tents,' etc.), xxxiii. 6 (explained by verses 7 f. to the end of the Parashah). From all these passages it is plain that Scripture speaks of the exile, with its attendant misery and weariness, as a sickness, a wound, a breach, a stripe; while redemption, freedom, and deliverance are described under the metaphor of healing or medicine. The general design, then, of the prophecy contained in this Parashah is to confirm and encourage us in the assurance that although by our exiles we are exceedingly depressed and brought down, even to the dust, there is still hope for us hereafter, that through the Lord's compassion on us we may again be 'high and exalted,' and that from the time of redemption onwards our position may rise until the nations of the world and even their kings, when they see the salvation of Israel and their elevation to the highest conceivable pitch of dignity and greatness, become astonished and awe-struck at the spectacle: for just as before they had marvelled at our depression in exile, when every nation on the face of the earth looked down upon us and despised us, so they will then marvel in like manner at our exaltation, and speak of it continually, saying one to another, Lo, now we perceive clearly that all we like sheep without a shepherd have gone astray, we have turned each after his own way: 'our fathers have inherited lies and vanity, wherein there is no profit' (Jer. xvi. 19), neither is there any divine law, or true religion, in any nation of the world except in Israel. From this we see further that the chastisements and calamities borne by Israel during their captivity did not fall upon them for their own iniquity; it was we who for the multitude of our sins had rendered ourselves liable to endure them, but the sickness and the pain which ought to have been ours came upon them, in order to make atonement for our guilt in treating them as our slaves; and, indeed, they were ever praying and interceding for our peace and the prosperity of our kingdoms: we however, on the contrary, thought that these troubles had fallen upon them because of the greatness of their iniquity (i. e. the murder of the Messiah and of God). Thus far extend the words of the Gentiles.

To this it may be added that the nations of the world, being as insignificant in the eyes of the Creator as the animals, do not have their sins providentially visited upon them from heaven, except when they either do harm to Israel, while engaged in executing God's pleasure, or perpetrate some great enormity, such as was committed by the generation of the Flood, or by Sodom and Gomorrha: in such cases the Almighty visits their iniquity, and consumes them utterly. Israel, however, is treated differently: in his love for us, God demands the penalty for our offences in this life little by little, by means of exiles and partial punishments, without making a full end of us; as he assures us, when he says by the mouth of his prophet (Jer. xxx. 11), 'I am with thee, saith the Lord, to save thee: I will not make a full end of thee; but I will correct thee in measure, and will not hold thee altogether guiltless;' and similarly in Amos (iii. 2), and the Proverbs (iii. 12), 'Whom the Lord loveth he correcteth.' The reason of this is that Israel is the choicest of human kind, just as the heart is the choicest organ in the body[a]; when, therefore, they are in exile in the midst of the nations, like the heart in the midst of the other organs, they bear all the calamities which fall upon the Gentiles in whose midst they are, exactly as the heart bears the bitterness and anguish of all the body in the centre of which it resides. And so it is written (Ps. cvi. 35 f.), 'They were mingled with the Gentiles, and learned their works,' etc.; and again (Prov. xiv. 10), 'The heart knoweth the bitterness of its own soul.' As, moreover, in time of trouble it is the heart alone which experiences the anguish of

---

[a] Compare above, p. 228.

grief and distress, so in time of prosperity it is the heart also which alone experiences the delights of gladness and joy; and this is what is meant when in the verse from the Proverbs it is added, 'And no stranger mingleth in its joy.' Further, as the heart is the most important part of the body, so is Israel the most important of all the nations; and as by bleeding some vein which originates in the heart the whole body is healed, so by union with Israel healing is secured for all nations, so soon as they come after us and join themselves to us, as it is written (Is. xiv. 1), 'And strangers shall be joined with them,' etc. And it is admitted that God chose Israel to be his peculiar people (Ex. xix. 5): he therefore gave them his law to teach them the way in which they should walk, and the deeds they should do; he also (because 'his mercy is over all his works') put it in their hearts to instruct the rest of the world, as he says in the same passage, 'Ye shall be to me a kingdom of priests;' and again (Is. lxi. 6), 'Ye shall be named the priests of the Lord.' Scripture thus addresses the whole Israelitish nation by the title of priests, in order to teach us that as the priests and Levites used to give the people instruction in the Law and the Commandments (as it is written, Deut. xxxii. 10, 'They shall teach Jacob thy judgments, and Israel thy law'), so Israel will be the teachers and instructors of the nations, amongst whom they are dispersed, in the words of the living God; as it is written (Ps. xcvi. 3), 'Tell his glory amongst the heathen;' and (cv. 1), 'Praise the Lord, call upon his name; declare his doings amongst the peoples:' and as the Levites and priests were supported by the offerings and tithes of the Israelites, so will the people of Israel be supported in the future by the gifts of the Gentiles, in recognition of the services done to them while in exile, and as a reward for their instructions; and this is what is meant when in the same passage from Isaiah it is said, 'Ye shall eat the riches of the Gentiles, and in their glory shall ye boast yourselves.' From this it follows that no blessing or spiritual progress can possibly accrue to the nations of the world, except through the mediation of Israel, as it is written, 'And in thy seed shall all nations of the earth be blessed' (Gen. xxii. 18, xxvi. 4); and again, 'In thee and in thy seed shall all kindreds of the world be blessed' (xxviii. 14); and as we have explained in § 13. You see, then, that this people was chosen by the Almighty to be his portion and his inheritance, as it is written, 'For he hath chosen Jacob unto himself, and Israel as his own possession' (Ps. cxxxv. 4); and, 'For the Lord's portion is his people, Jacob is the lot of his inheritance' (Deut. xxxii. 9); and, in addition, to be likewise a guide to other nations, instructing them in the way of the Lord: accordingly, 'to them alone was given' the divine law to shew them the right way, for when the leader walks on the good road, then all those who follow after him will attain the 'haven of their desire;' while those who do not follow him, or are forsaken by him, will most certainly go astray. Whoever, therefore, wishes to go on the right way must take hold of the skirts of the leader's garment, in order not to be deserted and left to wander away from the path intended by God to be adhered to. And this is what is described by Zechariah in his prophecy concerning the future (viii. 23): 'In those days shall ten men out of all languages of the nations take hold of the skirt of him that is a Jew, saying, We will go with you, for we have heard that God is with you.' Moreover, of the goodness which the Lord will then bestow upon the guides, he will bestow also by their mediation upon those that follow them, as it is written, 'And it shall be, if thou go with us, that what goodness the Lord shall do unto us, the same will we do unto thee' (Num. x. 32),—a promise which we find fulfilled in Jethro's seed (Jer. xxxv. 19): 'Thus saith the Lord of hosts, the God of Israel, Jonadab the son of Rechab shall not want a man to stand before me for ever,' a declaration resembling the assurance made to Israel (Is. lxvi. 22) that, like the new heaven and the new earth, their seed and their name should stand before God for ever. Similarly, various vexations and accidents of the road will befal the leaders travelling in the front, especially in a host marching to battle, when those in the van are exposed to wounds and blows and bruises; nevertheless, when they defeat their enemies and divide the spoil, then those who follow after them have a share in the booty without having suffered anything; and this is what Isaiah alludes to when, speaking of the future under the form of a parable, he says, *He is wounded for our transgressions, bruised for our iniquities, and by his stripes we are healed;* and in the other passages resembling this. And as those who advance first to battle receive more wounds than those who come after them, so they also obtain a larger amount of spoil; as the prophet says, *Therefore I will divide him a portion with the many,* etc. It is also clearly evident, from the verses contiguous to this section, both before and after, that the text relates solely to the calamities and depression of the nation while in exile, and to their elevation and high honour from the period of redemption onwards: it is evident from those which precede it, as, for example, from lii. 1, 'Awake, awake,' etc., with the subsequent verses as far as verse 12, 'Ye shall not go out with haste, nor go by flight,' etc., which is immediately succeeded by the Parashah itself; it is evident also from those that follow it, as liv. 1, 'Shout, O barren,' etc., with the verses following, which all attest and announce the future deliverance, and declare that after it the people shall never again go into exile, as he states in one of the previous Parashahs (li. 22), 'Thou shalt no more drink it again;' and similarly (lii. 1), 'Henceforth there shall no more come into thee the uncircumcised or unclean;' and below (liv. 9), 'For this is as the waters of Noah unto me,' etc. Such, then, is the general import of this Parashah: we shall now proceed to explain each separate verse of it by itself in the name of Him whose name is blessed.

LII. 13 ישכיל signifies *to prosper,* as 1 Sam. xvii. 14; the meaning being that Israel will prosper when he comes forth from the captivity of Edom and Ishmael[b], who are spoken of

[b] I.e. Rome and Islam.

above (lii. 1) as the 'uncircumcised and unclean:' from that time onwards *he will be high and exalted, and lofty exceedingly:* the idea of elevation is expressed in every form in order to indicate that our future exaltation will be the highest possible or imaginable even for the choicest of the human kind. [14] שמם is *to be astonished,* as Ezek. xxviii. 19: '*As many were astonished at thee,* because of thy depression and the length of thy captivity, until they said one to another, Of a truth (כן as Num. xxvii. 6) his countenance is marred beyond that of any other man, and his form more than the rest of the children of men (for it is a custom of the Gentiles, when they see a man very much disfigured, to say, This man is as ugly as a Jew[c]), [15] *so* will they then be astonished at the greatness of our exaltation, commenting upon it amongst themselves, and saying, Who hath believed our report? etc. (liii. 1, with the verses following), while their *kings,* amazed equally at our success, *will close their mouth,* and put their hand upon their lips! יזה has a causative force, and signifies *to make to speak,* from נטף, Mic. ii. 6. And the meaning of קפץ is *to shut* or *close,* as Job v. 16. The idea of the whole is similar to that expressed by the prophet Micah (vii. 10), 'The nations shall see and be confounded at all their might; they shall lay their hand upon their mouth,' because they will *see* in our exaltation more than *what had been told* them from our lips, *and perceive* in our greatness at that time more than *what they had heard* from the prophets' words.

LIII. [1] When the Gentiles behold the prosperity of Israel they will say, *Who* of us *believed the report* which we heard of him from the prophets? yet now we are seeing with our own eyes more than we then heard. And even what we heard we did not believe, how, namely, *the arm of the Lord* would be *revealed* upon him; because he seemed in our sight to be insignificant and despised. [2] But it is not to be wondered at, if we failed to believe: his ascent to the elevation he now holds was

[c] Compare above, pp. 44, 49.

not accomplished by a natural process; but in a marvellous and miraculous manner, like the growth of a sucker out of *a root in the dry ground:* while he was in captivity, there was no one who conceived the possibility of his ever emerging from it: to the eye of human intelligence it seemed impracticable, because he had no form or comeliness, and no beauty of face, but was marred and disfigured beyond all other men. Therefore we had no desire or longing to look upon him, but *despised him*, and held him in abhorrence. [3] How indeed could we do otherwise, when he was *the most despised and insignificant of men?* for it was his lot to be enduring continually every mental suffering and every bodily wrong—such were the chastisements of the captivity, here spoken of metaphorically as *pains* and *sickness*,—and in his humiliation and depression we would not look at him, but spurned and depreciated him, till we would esteem him for nought. [4] The nations continue declaring their conviction: Since we now have it confirmed by ocular proof that the truth is with Israel, and that all we like sheep have gone astray, it follows that the calamities in which the chastisements of exile consisted did not come upon him for his own iniquity, but that the pains and sicknesses (under which image they are here represented), which ought in justice to have fallen upon us, fell instead upon him. *We, however, thought that he had been stricken, smitten and afflicted by God*, for his unbounded spirit of rebellion against him; but it did not happen to Israel thus: they were smitten (as the next verse states) for our iniquities and transgressions, not for their own. [5] מחולל; this is the passive partic. Po'lel from חיל (Ps. xlviii. 7 al.) The meaning of *the chastisement of our peace was upon him* is this: The present world is a world of alteration and change, and its goodness is not perfect or complete; it has no peace that is free from suffering, no prosperity unruffled by vexations and strife, no joy untouched by sorrow and sighing; all its happiness and all its delights are commingled with misfortune and grief. So we, they say, saw that while the peace fell to our lot, the chastisement attending it fell upon him: he received bruises and stripes, i. e. the penalties of exile, and we received medicine and healing,—in other words, prosperity and power. רפא has the same sense as in Ex. xv. 26, 'I am the Lord that healeth thee,' as he had said before, 'Therefore I will put none of these diseases upon thee, which I have brought upon the Egyptians.' And חבורה is to be explained as Is. i. 6, except that there the word has *Dagesh*, while here this is omitted. It is possible, however, to derive it from חבר with the sense appertaining to the word in Hos. iv. 17: חבורתו will then be a substantive with suffix of the third person, formed like גְּבוּרָתוֹ; and the meaning will be that by being in one *union* and fellowship with us, he used to intercede with God for our adversities, and God used to hear his prayer and send forth healing for our wounds. [6] In this verse the Gentiles all confess their iniquity, which is at last revealed before the sun, saying, Now we are sure that the truth has been all along with Israel and not with us; for *all we like sheep* without a shepherd *have gone astray, we have turned each after his own way*, i. e. each has turned to its own gods, but now we know that these were no gods, as it is written, 'Unto thee will the Gentiles come from the ends of the earth, and will say, Our fathers inherited nothing but lies' (Jer. xvi. 19); and immediately afterwards, verse 20, 'Shall a man make gods unto himself, and they are no gods?' For this we had been liable to an infinite penalty, had not the Almighty *caused the penalty of us all to meet upon him*. Accordingly till now he has performed our service for us, carried our yoke, and borne our pains; but henceforth it is we who, voluntarily and heartily, shall have to do work for him, as it is written (lxi. 5), 'Strangers shall stand and feed your flocks;' and (xlix. 23), 'Kings shall be thy nursing fathers, and queens thy nursing mothers,' with many other passages of similar import. [7] When he was under our power in exile, he was unceasingly *oppressed and afflicted;* we oppressed him for money, exacting from him 'tribute, and excise, and way-tolls' (Ezra iv. 13), and much in addition by every description of fraudulent device;

and we afflicted his person with divers forms of violence: yet, in spite of all this, he never opened his mouth to cry out or complain of what we did to him, but endured everything *like the sheep* which cries not while being led to the slaughter, and *like a lamb* which, while men are shearing it, is silent and dumb, and which does not even quiver[d] like a ram by reason of its weakness (for in every species the female is weaker than the male). In the same manner, Israel was weak and prostrate in captivity; and therefore he opened not his mouth, because there was no one to deliver him out of our hands, as the Psalmist says (xliv. 12), 'Thou givest us as sheep to be eaten;' and again in the same Psalm (verse 23), 'We are counted as sheep for the slaughter;' and similarly Jeremiah (l. 17), 'Israel is a scattered sheep: first the king of Assyria hath devoured him; and last this Nebuchadrezzar king of Babylon hath broken his bones.' 8 *From the coercion* of the exile, and the bond of captivity and slavery, in which he was held confined by our hands, he is now delivered and escaped; *and from judgment*, i. e. from the fraudulent devices whereby we inflicted sore judgment upon him, *he is taken* and redeemed; *and his generation*, in which during the exile he suffered many chastisements and divers forms of death, *who is able to declare?* or who can tell of all the trials which befel Israel during the same period, how again and again he was cut off out of the land of the living and put to death by every mode of torture for the Unity of God? Yet we thought that all this was devised against them on account of their own transgressions; but it was not so; the stroke fell upon Israel *for the transgression of my people.* Chastisement and death are here spoken of as a *stroke;* because one who is 'stricken[e]' is counted as dead, as Aaron speaking of Miriam (Num. xii. 12) says, 'Let her not be as one dead!' By the expression '*my* people,' the prophet means

[d] Viz. after slaughter: the term is applied to denote the tremulous muscular movements which sometimes exhibit themselves in an animal immediately after it has been slain.

[e] Namely, with leprosy; see p. 212.

to indicate that each separate nation will use this language, in order to indicate that the stroke came upon Israel for its transgression and not for theirs. [9] Israel was ready to resign himself to death and burial for the sake of the divine Unity, as it is written (Ps. xliv. 23), 'For thy sake we are slain all the day long;' we were incessantly framing fraudulent devices against him to put him to death, just as the wicked are put to death for their crimes: similarly we were in the habit of murdering *the wealthy* by various contrivances for the sake of his riches; and even the poor Israelite was invested by us with the reputation of being rich, and tortured cruelly for the purpose of forcing him to disclose where his money was secreted. And all this occurred, *although he had done no violence;* he was not put to death for any wickedness that he had committed, but simply in order that we might secure his wealth; and also because he would not confess to our lying belief, nor by acknowledging it utter *deceitfulness with his mouth*, at a time when a single word —though spoken in deceit, and though his heart might not be in accordance with the declaration of his lips—would have been sufficient to release him from any one of the varied forms of death to which we might have sentenced him. [10] Since, then, he thus maintained his adherence to the divine law, and evinced his willingness to meet death under whatever form, we can assign no cause for his pains and calamities in captivity, except that God was in this way *pleased to bruise and sicken him*, in order to humble and try him, that it might be 'well with him at his latter end,' i. e. at the time of redemption, as we now see to be the case: *if* therefore *his soul gives* itself in place of *a trespass-offering* (as the prophet said, *made his grave with the wicked*), as a reward for doing this, *he will see seed* (i. e. *much* seed, just as *stature*, Num. xiii. 32, means *large* stature); and this is what Zechariah alludes to when he says (x. 8), 'I will hiss to them, and gather them, and they shall increase as they have increased;' and (verse 10), 'I will bring them into the land of Gilead and Lebanon, and place shall not be found for them;'

and again (Ezek. xxxvi. 37), 'I will increase them with men like a flock.' In the same way it is promised that he shall *lengthen days*, as it is said in this very book (lxv. 22), 'As the days of a tree shall be the days of my people;' and by Zechariah (viii. 4), 'Each with his staff in his hand for very age.' If so, then, *the pleasure of the Lord*, who had thus bruised Israel in exile in order to do good to him at the time of redemption, is that *he shall prosper with his hand:* for God will multiply him, and bless him exceedingly, as it is written, 'And he will do thee good, and multiply thee above thy fathers' (Deut. xxx. 5).—Here the words of the Gentiles terminate, and the Almighty commences speaking. [11] *For the travail of his soul*, which he endured in the captivity, he will receive a goodly recompense, which *he will see, and be satisfied* therewith; as also *by* his *knowledge of me* (as it is written, Jer. xxxi. 33, 'All shall know me, from the smallest to the greatest'), *the righteous*, i.e. *my servant* Israel, *will justify many nations*, as it is said (Mic. iv. 2), 'He will teach us of his ways and we will walk in his paths:' *and he* in his righteousness *will bear the iniquity of many* nations, for through it there will be peace and prosperity in the world, including even the Gentiles. [12] *Therefore I will give him* his lot and portion with my servants, the famous ones of the earth, i.e. with the patriarchs and holy prophets; by this is meant his spiritual welfare, which is placed above the temporal; and רבים must be explained as Gen. xxv. 23, 'The *greater* shall serve the smaller.' Afterwards, he will enjoy temporal welfare, in accordance with what follows, *and the mighty he shall divide as spoil*, where the 'mighty' are Gog and Magog and the nations accompanying them, who will come up to fight against Jerusalem and there perish themselves by various forms of death, as a punishment for those which they had inflicted upon Israel. And so it is written, 'I will plead against him with pestilence and with blood; and an overflowing rain, and great hailstones, fire, and brimstone will I rain upon him and upon the many peoples that are with him' (Ezek. xxxviii. 22). And after this Israel will *divide their spoil* and take of their wealth, in return for what they had taken from him during the captivity; as Scripture says, 'And they shall spoil those that spoiled them, and rob those that robbed them' (Ezek. xxxix. 10); and, 'The wealth of all the heathen shall be gathered together, gold and silver and apparel in great abundance' (Zech. xiv. 14). This, then, will be Israel's recompense for his readiness to meet death at the hands of the heathen; their soul shall be for his soul, and their wealth for his wealth (which they had robbed him of), *because*, as the prophet says, *he poured out* (ערה as Gen. xxiv. 20) *his soul to die*, and because he was *numbered with the transgressors* (as is said above, 'And gave his grave with the wicked'), viz. through the Gentiles holding him in the estimation of an evil-doer, hated by God. And therefore there would be given him an ample share in that rich and copious portion reserved for those that fear the Lord, and esteem his name, as did the holy patriarchs and many also of the prophets, the worthies of the nation. By the clause, *carried the sin of many*, it is signified that not only was he not wicked, as the Gentiles imagined, but in his righteousness he even bore and carried the sin of many among the Gentiles, as it is said, 'And their iniquities he will bear.' In like manner, he used to pray to God on behalf of the Gentile transgressors: although they caused him the greatest sufferings, he nevertheless interceded and supplicated for their peace and the prosperity of their kingdoms, entreating the Almighty to give the rain of their land in its season, as the inspired prophet enjoins, 'And seek the peace of the city whither I have led you away captives, and pray for it unto the Lord' (Jer. xxix. 7); and our Rabbis, Ho, thou that prayest for the peace of the kingdom[f], etc.; and as we Jews repeat continually in our prayers, O our God, that art in heaven, give life and peace to the King our master; O our God, that art in heaven, give peace in the earth; O our God, that art in heaven, give peace in the kingdom; O our God,

[f] See *Abhoth*, iii. 2.

that art in heaven, give dew and rain for a blessing in due season upon the earth; O our God, that art in heaven, give seed to the sower and bread to the eater;—as it is laid down in the Order of Prayer according to both the Spanish, and many other uses.

And now our answer, and this argument also, is completed—a true answer in accordance with the words of the text, which no one will be able to repudiate, except such as deny altogether the words of the living God.

XXXVII. R. MOSHEH EL-SHEIKH.

LII. [13] The verses in this Parashah are difficult to fix or arrange in a plain and literal manner, so that the various parts, from the beginning to the end, may be combined and connected closely together, 'the head with the legs and the inwards thereof.' The commentators I see going up and down among them, and yet neither agreeing in the subject to which the whole is to be referred, nor disentangling the words upon any simple plan. I therefore, in my humility, am come after them; not with any sense of the wisdom that I am about to utter, but merely with the object of applying to its elucidation a straightforward method, in accordance with the literal sense of the text, such as ought to be chosen by one who would rightly unite the several words and periods, and determine what view is legitimate and what not. I may remark, then, that our Rabbis with one voice accept and affirm the opinion that the prophet is speaking of the King Messiah, and we shall ourselves also adhere to the same view: for the Messiah is of course David, who, as is well known, was 'anointed,' and there is a verse in which the prophet, speaking in the name of the Lord, says expressly, '*My servant* David shall be king over them' (Ezek. xxxvii. 24). The expression *my servant*, therefore, can be justly referred to David: for from what is explicit in one place we can discover what is hidden or obscure in another. Although now we shall not call attention to everything in the text that might deserve it (since much is already before the eyes of all), no one will fail to notice, how in the introduction the prophet says at once, *Behold my servant shall prosper,* instead of employing the phrase, 'Thus saith the Lord,' as at the beginning of every other Parashah. Our Rabbis say that of all the suffering which entered into the world, one third was for David and the fathers, one for the generation in exile, and one for the King Messiah[a]. If we examine the meaning of this saying, we shall see that there are punishments for iniquity, and also punishments of love, the latter being endured by the righteous for the wickedness of his own generation. Now those who do not know how far the reward of the righteous really extends feel surprised at this, asking, Is it the Lord's pleasure that either one man should sin, or a whole generation? and wondering whether it can be true that he will be wroth with a just and perfect man who never sinned, and heap on him the iniquities of all wrong-doers, in order that they may rejoice, and he, the just, be pained; that they may be 'stalwart in strength,' while he is stricken and smitten; that they may exult at his calamity, and mock during their feasts at his distress, while he is smitten for their sakes. In order to put an end to the 'fear from this thing,' God declares in these verses how far the merits of those who thus suffer for the sins of their own age extend their effects, adducing a proof from the case of the Messiah who bore the iniquities of the children of Israel, 'and behold his reward is with him.' The Almighty argues with Israel (whom he has hitherto been addressing, lii. 11 f.), saying to them in tones of love (and, like one talking with a beloved son, using the singular number): Did I not promise that the Lord would go before you, and the God of Israel be your rear-ward? and will ye not marvel that all your sins have not been 'scoured and flooded away' to the extent of really deserving such great blessings? O that we had been counted worthy to walk in affliction, and after that to build for ourselves the sanctuary (as were those who built the second

---

[a] Compare p. 10; Wünsche, p. 73.

Temple by the permission of Cyrus): but look and learn how great is the power of the man who suffers for a whole generation; you shall then see from the exaltation which I shall confer upon the King Messiah how vast are the benefits of the chastisements of love to him that endures them. *Behold my servant* (i. e. the Messiah) *will prosper*,—for this is the meaning of ישכיל in this passage, as 1 Sam. xvii. 14,—and this prosperity of his will extend through four worlds, viz. the lower world, the world of angels, the world of stars, and the highest world of all, in each of which the same prosperity will attend him. He will be *high* in this world; *exalted* in the world of stars—as was Joshua, when he said, 'Sun, stand thou still upon Gibeon,' etc. (Josh. x. 12); and *lofty* in the world of angels, who will 'have access to his audience' (for he will not be inferior to king Solomon, as the Rabbis say [b], Why was not Solomon reckoned amongst those who ruled over the world? Because he was king over the powers that are on high, i. e. over the angels, as it is written, 1 Chron. xxix. 23, 'And Solomon sat on the throne of the Lord'); *exceedingly*, because prosperity will accompany him in the uppermost world as well, in the presence of God, according to the saying of the Rabbis on Ps. ii. 8, that he will be 'like a dear son, delighting himself before his Creator [c]:' he says therefore, *Ask of me*, etc., because of the good fortune which is to be his in each of these four worlds. Such is the meaning of this first verse of the Parashah, the last four words of which, as has now been explained, correspond to these four spheres of power.

Our Rabbis say further, 'He shall be higher than Abraham, of whom it is written (Gen. xiv. 22), "I raise *high* my hand to God;" lifted up above Moses, of whom it is written (Num. xi. 17), "And they shall *lift* the burden of the people with thee;" and loftier than the ministering angels, of whom it is said (Ezek. i. 18), "Their wheels were lofty."' It is not without a purpose that Abraham, Moses, and the angels are here mentioned: though

---

[b] Thalm. Bab., *Megillah*, 11[b].

[c] Compare Buxt. s. v. חטא.

to be 'lifted up above Moses' is indeed impossible; for whom have we greater than Moses? The Rabbis say[d], on the verse Gen. xiv. 17, that all the nations of the world agreed among themselves to make Abraham their king, erecting for him a high throne, and setting him upon it, and then shouting before him, Thou art our king! Let us examine now the meaning of this Midrash, according to the method we have prescribed ourselves. He will be higher than Abraham in the earth; for as all nations acknowledged Abraham's sovereignty (in the manner described), so, and more also, will the Messiah be exalted. Next, as Moses ruled even in the world of stars—the Rabbis say[e] that for this reason the hail, the locusts, and the grasshoppers were sent through his instrumentality, and that hence also he is bidden, Ex. ix. 22, x. 21, cf. x. 12, to stretch out his hand toward heaven—so, and even more fully, will the Messiah hold sway there likewise: this, and this only, is the meaning of the phrase *loftier than Moses;* it does not imply that he will be superior to him in wisdom or in prophecy, nor, again, that at the time alluded to Moses will not in every respect be the greater (indeed anything different from this will not be credited by those who have real knowledge), but only that he will be more exalted than Moses was previously, in his own lifetime. He is, thirdly, to be loftier than the angels, according to the text (Ezek. i. 18); for these had 'loftiness *and fear*,' i. e. in spite of their high position, they still stood in awe of the Almighty, not venturing, like the righteous one who 'played before him, as a son before his father,' to make requests of their Creator. Such, then, is the meaning of the phrase *lofty exceedingly above the angels;* for though above we divided the sentence into four parts, yet as the Rabbis do not interpret *shall be high* by itself, but declare that he will be high above something else, and similarly with each of the two following verbs, so the fourth part ('exceedingly') must belong really to the third, the idea expressed by which it serves to intensify.

---

[d] *B'reshith Rabbâ*, c. 24. [e] *Shemoth Rabbâ*, c. 12.

The whole, however, as I understand their method, 'goeth unto one place.' If now we return to the words of the text, we shall see that what God says to his only son Israel is this, that he will prosper in four different worlds. [14] From what source, however, does he merit all this? is it not because, *as many were astonished at thee* (i. e. at Israel) in the two desolations [of the Temple], so that every one that passed by 'was astonished and hissed' at the terrible disasters accompanying the two chastisements described in the Law, when even the stranger coming from a far land, when he saw the plagues of that land and the sicknesses laid upon it, was to hiss and ask in amazement, 'Wherefore hath the Lord done thus? what meaneth the heat of this great anger?' (Deut. xxix. 22–24.) According to the degree of their amazement, then, *so* was *his countenance marred from man*, in consequence of the magnitude of his sufferings: by this expression the prophet means to say that it *seemed* to be marred to those who gazed upon it; for man can never discern in a face the image of God, but only skin and flesh: the next phrase also, *and his form from the sons of men*, has a similar import, and does not at all imply that his form was marred in the eyes of God, who seeth that which is spiritual. Or the words may signify that *his countenance from man was marred*, i. e. what was derived in it from man, to the exclusion of that which was derived from the Almighty (viz. the image of God); and, again, that *his form from the sons of men* was disfigured, but not what came to him from above. [15] As the four high prerogatives assigned to him in ver. 13 became his in consequence of his sufferings, *so*, through the same instrumentality, *he will sprinkle many nations*, i. e. by these his deserts he will 'sprinkle the juice of them' (Is. lxiii. 3), that is, their blood, which will stream before him 'like a breach of waters.' And so brilliant will be his career before the eyes of the heathen, that *at him kings will shut their mouth*, thinking that none of his deeds can be adequately described; they will therefore close their lips and refrain from speaking. And all this will be caused by their having *seen what had never been told them;* for very many predictions which had been uttered by the prophets respecting events that would happen to them, had never reached them; for what the prophets spoke and wrote they did not usually communicate to a nation itself, they only heard of it in process of time: but now they see all clearly accomplished by the Messiah. Hence also *those who had not heard* of any of the deeds to be done by him began now to *attend;* for when the kings saw terrible deeds of which they had never heard done by the Messiah, they observed attentively, in order to discover whether the matter was really as it had appeared to be, or not: for their astonishment was so great that they were almost incredulous, and looked closely and carefully, doubting whether even their eyesight had not deceived them.

LIII. [1] The Almighty, however, says that there is no need for surprise at their attitude of incredulity in presence of these marvels; for *who believed our report*—the report, namely, which we made known to you from heaven, but which the kings had not heard of? so fearful was it, that in the eyes of every one who did hear it, it was too wondrous to be true; and *upon whom was the arm of the Lord revealed* as it was upon the King Messiah? The sum of the whole is that he obtained this honour for himself owing to his merits in enduring for Israel (as has been said) chastisements of love. [2] The contents of this and the following verses shew unmistakably that they are the words of the prophet, as it were instructing or guiding the people, and not the words of God: this is plain both from the phrase, *We saw him, but he had no beauty that we could desire him,* which would not be suitable for God to use with reference to himself, as also from the two expressions, *We esteemed him not,* in the next verse, and (verse 4), *Our sicknesses he carried.* From the fact of the Rabbis expounding the previous verses of the Messiah, it may be seen that these speak of the righteous who endures in the present world the chastisements of love; and therefore I maintain that up to this point we have had the words of God announcing the greatness of the Messiah in return for his sufferings, and designed to set forth the exalted dignity of him by whom those chastisements are borne. Here, however, the prophet seems to set before us the words of Israel endorsing the Divine declaration, and affirming in their own persons its entire truth: 'The "tried saying of the Lord,"' they exclaim, 'which he has made known to us concerning the King Messiah, has opened our ears and removed the blindness of our eyes; we beheld a man, just and perfect, bruised and degraded by suffering, despised in our eyes, and plundered verily before God and man, while all cried, "God hath forsaken him;" he must surely, therefore, we thought, be "despised" likewise in the eyes of the Almighty, and this is why he hath made him "an offscouring and refuse" (Lam. iii. 45). But now the Lord hath awakened our ear, and taught us that the chastisements of love are infinitely great; henceforward, then, will "his strength be magnified," when we see him just, and humble in spirit, stricken, and smitten: for then we shall all agree in concluding that what we had seen before meant nothing except that he was carrying our sicknesses; and that his sufferings were for the protection of his generation.' Such is the substance of what the prophet puts into the people's mouth. And first of all they say, *He came up as a sucker*, etc.; i. e. we see one who was as a sucker with water for it to suck up, and growing great and tall; he was like this, however, only *before him*, viz. before the Lord (named in verse 1); for though this just and perfect sufferer flourished and grew great before God in the upper world, yet in the earth which we see below, he was *as a root* coming forth *out of the dry earth*, and not a sucker (because there was no water for him to 'suck' up). Being lowly, therefore, in the sight of our eyes, he was without *form and comeliness* in the world: his form was 'darkened' by the blackness of his sufferings (cf. Lam. iv. 8), and 'his own leanness bare witness in his face;' neither had he any beauty that we could desire him on account of his righteousness, but, on the contrary, he was rejected in our eyes. (This is the reason why the ו in ונחמדהו is pointed with *Shwa'* and not with *Pathaḥ*, because the verb does not express an actual fact [f].) [3] Not only, however, was this just one despised in our eyes, but, as is now said, his sense of holiness caused him to be despised in his own eyes, not merely when he found himself amongst men of position, and in comparison with them held himself to be of slight reputation, but even when *forlorn of men*, i. e. when destitute of their society and having no companion but himself. Moreover, in spite of his holiness, he was *a man of pains and broken by sickness*: now there are two species of sickness, one when a man is in pain but is still able to move about, the other when he is attacked by some such disease as consumption or fever, when he is prostrated upon his bed, a 'couch of infirmity,' but is free from pain; in the latter case he is said to be 'broken' by sickness, because his complaint bows him down: cf. Jud. viii. 16. Or, perhaps, since instances happen in which men suffer from some disease and are then cured, and then from another and are cured of it likewise, and so with a third or a fourth, whereas, on the contrary, they sometimes have a complaint which, being constant, and more severe than any of the former kind, completely breaks them down, the expression ידוע חולי may refer to the latter, and mean that the person to whom it is applied is *known* through some one disease which, unlike the others that come and go, never leaves him. The prophet says that both these descriptions of sickness unite against the man here spoken of. But, besides this, *he was despised*, also, in his own eyes: it is not stated that he was humbled for his pride, since in reality men hid their faces from him, not for any fault of his own, but for the iniquity of his generation; though he himself (as the words of the text shew, *And 'twas as though the face-hiding came from himself*) looked upon the matter differently, imagining in his goodness and humility that he must be guilty,

[f] The words are not, 'he had no beauty, *and* we desired him,' but 'he had no beauty, *that* we should desire him.'

and was thus punished for his sins. Accordingly he was both *despised* in his own eyes, and we *esteemed him not.*
4 Yet in truth the cause of this 'face-hiding' lay not in him, but in the people; for, as we learn from the expression used in the preceding verses, *he* (הוא) *carried our sicknesses*, i. e. *he* was ready to carry them of his own accord, like R. Eleazar, the son of R. Simeon, who said, 'Come brethren, come friends[g]!' Again, as 'pain' was associated with 'sickness' in verse 3, so here it is stated that he bore the former as well, and was not like the man who exclaimed, 'Neither them, nor their reward[h]!' *We*, however, *thought* that he was not bearing them of his own accord, but that he was *stricken and smitten of God*, by a judgment of retaliation for his iniquities, and not out of love, as was the case with R. Eleazar. The prophet says *stricken*, with allusion to the expression ידוע חולי, and *smitten*, because he had at the same time called him איש מכאובות: we supposed him *stricken*, namely, with the strokes of men (i. e. through the powers of impurity) which fall upon a man as a consequence of one of those matters for which such strokes are appointed; *smitten of God* when afterwards God seemed to smite him, not from any desire to inflict upon him a chastisement of love, but in virtue of his attribute of justice, because he had not repented of his iniquity; and *afflicted*, when last of all (as is stated in verse 3) he was despised in his own eyes on account of the humiliation and affliction which had befallen him. Such is the signification of the three expressions, *stricken*, *smitten of God*, and *afflicted.*
5 It was not so in fact, however: it was because he was *wounded for our transgressions* that he was 'broken by sickness;' and because he was *bruised for our*

---

[g] I. e. invited his friends to see him, as though nothing were the matter: see Thalm. Bab., *Bâbha M'zi'ah*, 87[b].

[h] Alluding to a saying of R. Yoḥanan's (Thalmud of Babylon, *B'rakhoth*, fol. 5[b]), who when asked during an illness whether his sufferings were pleasant to bear in view of the reward they would bring after them, replied, that he found no pleasure either in the sufferings or in their reward.

iniquities that he became a 'man of pains' (for he was *stricken* for our 'transgressions,' and *smitten* for our 'iniquities'); and he was 'afflicted' with poverty, because—and this is the chief reason for which he was 'despised'—*the chastisement of our peace was upon him:* his being wounded and bruised for our iniquities had merely the negative effect of rescuing us from punishment; in order for us to enjoy positive peace and prosperity, further sufferings were needed, and these consisted in his being 'afflicted' with poverty. To express this, it is said that *the chastisement of our peace was upon him:* and it was well that this additional chastisement should rest upon him; for while the direct consequences of our sins had been averted by his sickness and stripes, something still was needed in order to confer peace upon us. Or the sense of the passage may be as follows: If he had 'carried our sicknesses,' it would have been sufficient to remove misfortune from us, but not to procure us prosperity: but we do possess prosperity; does it not follow then that he must already, at some time or other, have suffered sickness, being *made sick* (מחלל) *for our transgressions,* that pain must have lighted on him, being *bruised for our iniquities,* and that his calamities were prolonged, because *the chastisement of our peace was upon him,* and in order to benefit us positively?—for, so far as the mere removal of suffering was concerned, we were long ago *healed by his stripes.* 6 *All we like sheep had gone astray*—like sheep which all follow after their leader, so that if the leader strays, they all stray with him, because of the unity of the whole flock; as the Rabbis say, 'When the shepherd is angry with his flock, he makes their leader blind[i].' The prophet says, Would that only one had gone astray, and that only the unity of the rest had led them after him! for union, though it be with something evil, is a good, as it is written (Hos. iv. 17), 'Ephraim is joined unto idols; *let him alone;*' here, however, there is in two respects a difference for the worse: for

---

Thalm. Bab., *Bâbha Qâma*, 52ª.

in a flock only one goes astray, but in our case, as we learn from the expression '*All we* like sheep,' there were many straying; in a flock also the general error results from the unitedness of the whole body, but the phrase, '*Each* turned to his own way,' shews that with us this was not so, but that it resulted from the separate action of each individual. Had it indeed been otherwise, our guilt (as the passage from Hosea indicates) would not have been so great. But see now the mercy of God: after we had individually gone astray, he might have been expected to punish us individually likewise (for every man by his own separate iniquity creates an accuser to 'light' upon him for the purpose of punishing him); yet the Lord did not look to this, but counted us as one man, reckoning up *the iniquity of us all* together, and *causing it to light* upon this just one, who was accordingly sufficient to bear the whole of it, which would not have been the case had each one's iniquity been reckoned up against himself. 7 In the *B'reshith Rabbâ*[k], the Rabbis say, There is a 'drawing nigh' that is for prayer; as it is written (1 Kings xviii. 36), 'And Elijah *drew nigh:*' but although his prayer [for rain] was heard before his Creator, yet his piety prevented him from praying for a removal of his own calamity, or complaining of the bitterness of his sufferings, as he might have done had the saying, 'Neither them, nor their reward,' been his model. Elijah resembled rather Rabbah, who, although both he and R. Ḥisda were men of the greatest piety, prayed, and there came rain, and prayed again, and there came rain[l]; and yet in spite of this, when all his household were enduring the 'sixty pains' [felt by the tooth that hears its neighbour eating, and has nothing itself[m]], he did not pray for any alleviation of his sufferings. In like manner the prophet says here that the prayer of this just one was heard by God, that when he *drew near* (נגש) for the purpose of praying, *he was* at

---

[k] C. 93.

[l] Thalm. Bab., *Ta'anith,* 24[a].

[m] Thalm. Bab., *Bâbha Qâma,* 92[b].

once *answered*, even *without opening his mouth* (as in the promise, 'Before they cry I will answer them,' lxv. 24): still, however, in the endurance of injury done to his person he was *as a sheep led to the slaughter*, and in loss of his substance, *like a lamb which before her shearers is dumb*, insomuch that *he opened not his mouth* to entreat that even one of his troubles might be removed from him (for he rather rejoiced in them), or to exclaim, 'Neither them, nor their reward.' [8] While he was yet alive, he was our protector; and now that he is dead, *he was taken* מעצר וממשפט: i.e. *because of the shutting up*[n] of rain that was to ensue, and *because of judgment* to come, he was taken away. For, though he protected it before, yet inasmuch as his generation will not repent of its iniquity which had caused the judgment and the drought, their fate will be like that which we read of in the *Midrash Ne'lâm*, where R. Aḥa of Caphartarsha, when he would avert the plague, was told from heaven that he could avail nought, for sinfulness still lay upon the people, and he must therefore amend them by causing them to repent and devote themselves assiduously to the Law. In the same way, the prophet exclaims here, *As for his generation, would that some one would declare* to them *how it was cut off from the land of life* for the iniquity which the just one had before averted, because they did not repent. Hitherto, he means to say, this just one had been stricken for the people's transgression; but henceforward *the stroke* would be *upon themselves*, for there would be no one else to be smitten for them. It is possible, from his use of the singular '*transgression*,' that Isaiah means to allude to their sin in supposing that he had died for his own iniquity, and in not having been brought themselves by his death to repentance. [9-12] These verses also are all of them hard, and difficult to fix the sense of, though we shall not touch on everything which might be noticed. Our

---

[n] Compare the use of עצר in Deut. xi. 17, 1 Kings viii. 35.

Rabbis, I see, have in two places[o] expounded verse 12 of Moses our master, each 'Midrash' possessing its own particular features; and we may at least admit that the passage does allude to him, though any one adopting this opinion is bound to explain what connexion subsists between the verse relating to Moses and those which precede it. I think myself that properly these refer to him likewise: after having stated that the just one did good to his age, not only during his lifetime, by carrying their sicknesses, but also in his death, when *because of drought and judgment* he was *taken* out of the world in order to make atonement for them, the prophet now proceeds to ask, Will not the heart of man 'be embittered' when it reflects that for the sufferings endured in this present life, the just one ought at least not to miss enjoying elsewhere the reward for his obedience to the Law and the Commandment; whereas by dying for his generation he will be cut off from the Law and the Commandments, and so debarred from happiness both in this world and in that which is to come? He therefore says, *And he made his grave with the wicked*, i. e. I will shew you an instance of this in the chief of all the prophets, and the choicest of all creation, who, by still suffering after his death, endured a heavier penalty than others who had suffered for their generation: for he 'made his grave with the wicked,' i. e. Moses, who, as our Rabbis say[p], was buried away from the Promised Land, together with the wicked ones who died in the wilderness: for these were unworthy to enter into the world to come, had not Moses borne the disgrace of being buried by their side, in order that he might bring them into it with himself. And we cannot be wrong in interpreting the 'wicked' here of those who perished in the wilderness for the sin of the spies; for the Rabbis themselves explain *he was numbered with the transgressors* (verse 12) similarly. Moses was not, however, buried solely with these: in the wilderness rested also Qorah, who was '*rich*,' with all

---

[o] Above, pp. 8, 10.

[p] *Soṭah*, 14[a].

those who perished with him, when they complained that Moses and Aaron had killed the people of the Lord (Num. xvii. 6); with all these Moses made his grave, in order to bring them likewise into the future world. For it is well known that even Qorah and *his deaths*, i. e. those who died in his cause, will all rise up with him; since, as our Rabbis say[q], it follows certainly from the words of Hannah's prayer, 'The Lord bringeth down to the Underworld, and bringeth up' (1 Sam. ii. 6), that Qorah will return and come up from the Underworld, and *à fortiori*, those who perished with him, and in fact the whole generation of the wilderness. The prophet appeals thus to a known case: *he*, i. e. Moses, *made his grave with the wicked*, for he was buried in profane ground in order to bring them in with him [into the future world], and that, not only with the generation of the wilderness, but also *with the rich* [viz. Qorah] *in his deaths*—amongst those, that is, who perished with him—in order to bring them in likewise, *because he had done no violence*, like those who perished in the desert, which alone might have caused him to be left behind, *neither was there any guile in his mouth*, when he said, 'But if the Lord create a new thing,' etc. (Num. xvi. 30); in a word, he sinned neither with the disbelieving Israelites, nor in anything that he uttered in the matter of Qorah; on the contrary, he acquiesced for their advantage in the indignity of being buried away from the Promised Land. [10] But you will ask, Why should God do these two things, both *bruising* and *sickening* the just one during his life for the iniquity of his generation, and then cutting him off from the world on account of its sin? the Almighty can have no concern lest vexation should cause him to sin. To meet this, the prophet continues: You know, indeed, that the Lord was pleased to bruise and sicken him for the iniquity of his generation; yet afterwards *if his soul* is prepared to die, and thereby to *make* itself *a trespass-offering* on their behalf, he will no longer feel the trial, but

---

[q] *Sanhedrin*, 109[b].

rather rejoice; for God will comfort him with other words, saying, *He shall see seed, shall lengthen days:* he will even devote himself to the Law and the Commandments and *prosper* (which is what is meant by *the pleasure of the Lord shall prosper in his hand*), because there is no disannulling of the Law in the chastisements of love (which are what are sent to protect an age from punishment): he will thus be blessed both in this world and in that which is to come. 11 God now speaks, adding a further promise to the prophet's words, *For the travail of his soul*, etc. There is a saying of the Rabbis[r] on the verse, Prov. xxxi. 25, 'And she laugheth at the future,' that at the time when the just are taken out of the world they are shewn their reward, their soul is satisfied, and they themselves then fall asleep; and this is what is written in the same place that the soul of the just suffers hardship, because it can no longer in the present world pursue studiously the practice of the Law, and his body suffers hardship, because it must go and decay in the grave. Therefore the Almighty shews each man how his soul will reap satisfaction for all that he has done (and this is the meaning of 'their soul is satisfied'), and how his body, for what he has enjoyed, will be left as one asleep (and this is the meaning of 'they themselves will fall asleep'). And so it is said here: Let not the owner of this soul feel vexation at dying for the iniquity of his generation, alleging that it was his desire to live longer in order to satisfy himself with further acts of merit: will he not, *for the travail of his soul*, wherewith he laboured unto the day of his death, when he is taken away, *see* something which will *satisfy* him? *by his knowledge*—or will—I promise that the *just one*, i. e. *my servant, shall justify many, and* that he shall *bear their iniquities.* 12 For *I will divide him* a portion with the many, that he may receive a portion in the world to come with the many who by his means are meet to receive a reward for their sufferings: and because he after-

[r] *B'reshith Rabbâ*, c. 62.

wards died for the iniquities of his generation, therefore *with the mighty*, the patriarchs and those like them, *he will divide spoil, because he poured out his soul to die* for the sake of Israel, and also because he was *numbered with the transgressors;* for people said when they saw his sufferings that he was smitten of God for his sins, and classed him with the transgressors. This he knew, yet went on enduring, *and carried* this *sin of many*, not caring to be vexed with them, but, on the contrary, *interceding* with the Holy One *for*, i. e. on behalf of, *the transgressors*—those, namely, who spoke thus of him, not, like some, from ignorance, but from actual malice. Or the sense of the text may be that in his lifetime, in consequence of the sufferings he will experience, he will *see seed*, etc.: and therefore *by his knowledge*, i. e. in accordance with his will, *the just one*, i. e. *my servant, will justify many and bear* all *their iniquities* without solicitude, and without inquiring whether it is not a strange thing to endure distress for the sake of others after death. For if this be the case, why did Moses our master endure, for the sake of those who perished in the wilderness, to be buried with the wicked in a foreign land? But there is no real difficulty: 'on account of this very humiliation, I shall multiply,' says the Almighty, 'his reward; for *I shall divide him* a portion *with the many*, the whole of their merits will attach themselves to him, and I shall allot him an equal portion for all these, as well as for his own. Moreover, *with* all *the mighty*, i. e. with the chiefs and wise men of each generation who teach the law to every successive age, *he will divide spoil*, and share their reward with them.' And do not wonder, because this may seem excessive measure for him to receive: had it not been for him, they would never have entered into the world: did not Moses 'pour out his soul to die,' when he 'put his soul into his hand,' saying, 'But if not—blot me, I pray thee,' etc. (Ex. xxxii. 32), where he expresses his willingness to die in their stead? Moses also was on their account 'numbered with the transgressors;' for God said, 'How long refuse ye to keep my statutes and my ordinances?' (Ex. xvi. 28), classing him thereby with men who had profaned the Sabbath, as our Rabbis say[s], For the sake of one leaf, a whole branch is often injured; i. e. on account of the wicked, the righteous is reviled. Accordingly, it is said that 'he was numbered with them,' i. e. he felt no anxiety in having given his soul for them, and, besides this, that 'he carried the sin of many,' as God said to him, 'Go, get thee down' (Ex. xxxii. 7), as though to say, Descend from all thy greatness, because Israel has sinned; but still, in spite of this, 'he made intercession for the transgressors,' because in every place that Israel transgressed he interceded for them. And this is the prophet's meaning when he writes, *And he carried the sin of many, and made intercession for the transgressors.*

[s] Thalm. Bab., *Bâbha Qâma*, 92[a]. Compare Buxtorf, s. v. כרבא.

XXXVIII. R. SH'LOMOH LEVI.

Says Sh'lomoh, son of the honourable and exalted R. Yiẓḥaq, of the house of Levi (may the merciful God preserve and deliver him!): Throughout this prophecy, all the commentators exert their utmost upon its interpretation, and are at no small variance respecting the import of it. I myself also, 'with the latter ones,' have had a similar experience; I have laboured hard many years, and even now 'my witness is in heaven, and my record in the highest,' that the thirst of my desire has not been satisfied with what the net of my speculation has brought up for me out of the springs which extend themselves at the foundations of their writings. He who would have at his command the whole multitude of divergent opinions respecting it, must apply himself to the commentary of the blessed Don [Yiẓḥaq Abarbanel], and to the excellent words which he has uttered. To me, however, who am 'afflicted and of a broken spirit,' the object of the prophet seems to be to describe in general the varied forms of suffering to which the righteous are exposed, and, after having done this, to exhibit to us in particular how they all ultimately result in the greater perfection of the sufferer: he accordingly declares that the man who is perfect in theory (which is what he means by ישכיל) will also be perfect in practice, because he will be God's servant, i.e. will be one who performs his commandments. In other words, his meaning is this: *My servant* who obeys my commands, not as though they were merely human precepts to be learnt by rote (Is. xxix. 13), but with intelligence and reason, will assuredly *be high and exalted and lofty exceedingly.* By this he, perhaps, intends to say that he will be elevated above all the worlds. In reference to his elevation above the lower world, he says, *he will be high;* and this is possibly what the Rabbis meant when they said, 'He will be higher than Abraham,' for Abraham called himself 'dust and ashes' (Gen. xviii. 27). Alluding to the intermediate world, he says, *and exalted,* viz. above Moses; for, according to the Cabbalists, the attribute of Moses is called 'heaven,' and of him the words were spoken, 'Thou didst go up on high' (Ps. lxviii. 19); accordingly the Rabbis[a] tell of the numerous times that Moses went up into the mount. And, alluding to the world of angels, the prophet continues, *and lofty.* In addition to this, however, the Rabbis mean by their Midrash to express in what way such a man is perfected in the three essentials of the faith: he is *high* through the sufficiency of God declared to him by Abraham, *exalted* through the law from heaven delivered by Moses our master, and *lofty* through that providence which, as Maimonides[b] has remarked, may be shewn to exist by reason: these are they that 'sit first in the kingdom, and behold the king's face' (Esth. i. 14), being the constant objects of his providential care; indeed, some hold that, when Onqelos interprets פני ('my face,' Ex. xxxiii. 23) by *that which is before me,* he means to allude to the angels. Or *high* may allude to the perfect manner in which his private conduct is guided, *exalted* to his behaviour in public towards other men, and *lofty* to the theoretical principles which regulate both. Our Rabbis, in the Midrash *Tanḥuma,* have expounded the verse of the King Messiah, saying, 'He shall be higher than Abraham,' etc.: but although the righteous Don [Yiẓḥaq Abarbanel] has given a correct explanation of this Midrash, it appears to me that its meaning is rather this, that, in spite of all Abraham's nobility of character, the Messiah will be more noble still: for

[a] Thalm. Bab., *Sanhedrin,* 111[a].

[b] *Guide des Egarés,* iii. 130 ff. (ed. Munk).

although Abraham sware that he would not take 'from a thread even to a shoe latchet' (Gen. xiv. 23), yet the same verse indicates a deficiency in his nobility, since he should not have added, 'Lest thou say, I have made Abraham rich.' In the same way, the 'noble's daughter' (Cant. vii. 1) is said to be the daughter of Abraham; and the 'nobles of the people are gathered together, even the people of the God of Abraham' (Ps. xlvii. 10): accordingly the attribute of benevolence was granted to Abraham for a possession. The Messiah will also be more patient than Moses, who was 'exceeding meek, above all the men which were upon the face of the earth' (Num. xi. 3); but not more so than the Messiah, for, in spite of all his patience, he demanded, 'Have I conceived all this people?' etc., and, 'Wherefore hast thou dealt evilly with thy servant?' (Num. x. 12, 11.) From the words 'which are upon the face of the earth,' we learn that through enduring patiently he shewed that he was sprung from the earth: for the beasts, which have no intelligence to govern the material element of their nature, display no such patience: on the contrary, as knowledge and intelligence increases, so patience increases likewise. And when, lastly, they say, 'and loftier than the angels,' it must be understood that if we consider the verse (Ezek. i. 18) which they adduce in proof, the subject spoken of is אופנים, which, in the opinion of Maimonides, signifies the *elements*, but in that of all other commentators signifies the *spheres*: this, however, is no difficulty to the view of the Rabbis, for we know that he 'maketh the winds his messengers,' how much more then may not these existences be his messengers as well! The meaning thus is that he will have power to work signs and wonders by them, according as he may require; and hence the verse says that with all their loftiness there was coupled fear, because the righteous possesses the power to discomfit all their array. Thus three qualities are mentioned as belonging to him, each pre-eminently essential to a king: 1. nobility, 2. patience, 3. authority. The circumstance that Abraham alone is here named, and not Isaac and Jacob, they account for by supposing that the latter are alluded to in what follows, 'Who art thou, O great mountain?' which is immediately explained to mean that he will be greater than the patriarchs; for Isaac, they say, was great in the prerogative of might (which hence is named as his special attribute) when he laid his neck upon the altar (in accordance with the saying, Who is the man of might? The man that subdues his own natural impulse[c]): and Jacob was great in the prerogative of truth; as Scripture says, 'Thou gavest *truth* to Jacob' (Mic. vii. 20). [13] In the book *Zohar*, section וישב[d], the words *My servant shall have understanding* are referred to the attribute of royalty, which is *high*, because it receives its light from intelligence (בינה); and *exalted*, because it partakes of the attribute of mercy belonging to Abraham; *lofty*, because of Isaac; *exceedingly*, because of Jacob,—the meaning being that when the righteous man who is an inhabitant of this nether world is a true worshipper of God, all his acts are regulated by the Shekhinah that dwelleth here below, and by its commandments; and through such service of him he is made a servant of the Lord. [14] This verse, as well as the last, is supposed to be spoken by God himself, reminding the prophet *how many were astonished* at him, when he went 'naked and barefooted' (Is. xx. 2), like one despised and forlorn, and wondered whether he could still possibly be the 'servant' who is spoken of, at a time when *his countenance was marred beyond* any *man* (words describing his evil temperament) and *his form beyond the sons of men* (describing his defective constitution). The first of these expressions refers to his evil temperament, regarded as inherent in himself; the latter to his defective constitution, regarded also as derived from his parents: in saying *beyond man*, too, the prophet characterizes the imperfection of his nature in not possessing what ought properly to have belonged to him as a man, and in saying *beyond the sons of men* he characterizes his imperfections as a member of a species: the

---

[c] *Abhoth*, iv. 1.

[d] Compare above, p. 12.

distinction here drawn is noticed in the chapter *On temperaments* in the 'Canon[e],' *q. v.* [15]Although, however, he is thus circumstanced, and although it appears that the imperfection of his physical constitution would preclude him naturally from prophesying, or instructing others, nevertheless, as regards both quantity and quality *he will sprinkle*, i. e. preach and prophesy to *many nations:* not unsuccessfully because of him *kings will close their mouths*, so as not to speak (or, perhaps, *will leap* and hasten to tell wondrous accounts of him, because he will be perfecting them in knowledge): *for what had not* before *been told them* they will *see*, i. e. understand from him, and with quickened faculties of apprehension *perceive what they had not heard.* More precisely it should be said that the instruction to the 'many nations' will be concerning quantity, and that to the great 'kings' concerning quality; for after hearing his words they will shut their mouths, inasmuch as through his agency they will perceive by the sense of sight things which had never been told them, and apprehend by their intelligence what they had never heard in the company of other men.

LIII. [1]The prophet now adduces a proof in support of what God had said to him: At the beginning of our restoration, i. e. of the restoration of the people of Israel, who, at the time that we were making bricks in Egypt, resembled men in a condition of degradation, and sold in perpetuity as slaves, *who believed the rumour* or fame *of us* which went out into the world? *and for whose sake* (על מי) was *the* stretched out *arm* and mighty hand *of the Lord revealed* in Egypt? [2]Suddenly, *before* the Almighty, the people of Israel *came up out of the 'land of dryness* and the shadow of death,' i. e. out of Egypt, כיונק וכשרש, in other words, *as though* it had long been possessed of *root and branches* (or, perhaps, the sense may be that it rose so rapidly that the branches grew up first, and its root only extended itself afterwards, in consequence of being planted in a dry soil); yet

---

[e] Viz. of Avicenna: see I. ii. 1.

owing to its degraded state, we noticed that it had *no form* or perfection in the ordinary attributes of mankind; *nor comeliness* in graceful acquirements; and that, although in full possession of strength and might and all external blessings, it still had *no beauty that we might desire it.* Or the prophet may mean to say that it had no form or comeliness, *but* nevertheless *we gazed upon it;* and that it had no beauty, *but* still *we desired it.* Or, again, he may mean that it grew up *like one that sucked with his face* (for it is impossible to suck from a root which is planted in the dry soil)—according to the saying that a man is like an inverted tree, because all his nutriment is sucked in from above, and hence the countenance always looks upwards. The words *had no form*, etc., refer to the root—he had no *form*, viz., in the arrangement of his various limbs; no *beauty* in the union between his mental and his physical frame, or in the adaptation of the various parts of the body to one another; no *comeliness* in his disposition generally. [3] The prophet here applies his comparison explicitly, stating that the same will be the case with the man of understanding, i.e. the 'servant' of the Lord, who is despised on account of his defective constitution and frame,—a constitution which sums up the defects of a whole species, but does not exist in individuals, since it is not produced by differences of subject, or climate, or province, or country, etc.—according to the classification to be found in Avicenna[f]. He calls him a *man of pains*, for the blows and bruises visible in him; and because of his evil temperament he describes him as *known of sickness*, meaning to say that his condition was such as not to make it difficult to recognise him. And because we hid our faces from him, so as not to look upon his pain, he *was despised* by us, and we esteemed him not. Or the meaning may be that he had as it were hidden his face from him, i.e. from God; or that he, viz. God, had hidden his face from him, after his sufferings had left such marks upon him;

---

[f] See 'Canon,' *ibid.*

and that therefore *he was despised*, but we did not think of him even as despised—for he was so insignificant that the thought of him did not occur to us at all. 4 But he was not as we had imagined him: being perfect and without sin himself, he atoned for all besides—*our sicknesses*, i. e. our evil temperament, *he carried*, and *our pains*, i. e. the diseases common to us all, *he bare*. The expression *pains* is intended to include every description of pain, such as are enumerated in their proper place; and the prophet says *carried*, because it was his endeavour to take them really upon himself, adding afterwards *bare*, because all the time that they were upon him he never kicked against them. We, however, thought that he had been only justly *stricken and smitten* by such pains, *and afflicted* by an evil temperament: because 'evil are all the days of the afflicted' (Prov. xv. 15), i. e. of the man who has an evil temperament, or, as our Rabbis[g] say, who is weak. Or the meaning is, that we caused him to be so thought of; or that, as he was so sorely *stricken*, and, what is more, *afflicted* (the two being in no sense the same, as is plain from the words in Job xxxvi. 21, 'For this thou hast chosen rather than affliction[h]'), we thought him smitten in judgment, and not in love. 5 His evil temperament, however, was produced *by* the multitude of *our transgressions*, and the ordinary human sicknesses which befel him were in consequence of *our iniquities*: the double expression is an allusion to internal as well as to external complaints, and as 'transgressions' are more serious than 'iniquities[i],' so are internal complaints graver than those which are external. The prophet says that his troubles and sicknesses were for our *healing*: his sicknesses, namely, were for the purpose of securing and establishing our health, the *chastisement upon him* (by which is signified his evil temperament) as for *our peace*, and *by*

---

[g] See Thalm. Bab., *Bâbha Bathra*, 145[b].

[h] The bearing of the passage cited upon the distinction in question is obscure.

[i] Compare p. 25.

his stripes, i. e. by the common maladies of mankind, *we were healed* and cured of our sicknesses. [6] The prophet here explains his meaning, and says that we were suffering from two kinds of sickness, one common to, and shared by, our whole race, and implied in the comparison to a sheep—which suggests that we are all gone astray together; the other corresponding to the particular sins of the individual, and indicated by the words *we have turned each after his own way*. Now the sufferings of the righteous cannot atone for the special sins of the individual, but each man will have to pay his own particular penalty for them after death: *the iniquity of us all*, however, i. e. the iniquity common to our whole race, *the Lord laid upon him*, viz. upon the righteous who is punished for the iniquity of his own age. In the *Yalqut* there is quoted a Midrash from the Aggadah of Samuel:—Says R. Huna in the name of R. Aḥa: The chastisements are divided into three parts, one for David and the patriarchs, one for the generation of our present exile, and one for the King Messiah, as it is written, 'He was wounded for our iniquities,' and, 'But I have set my king[j],' etc. Now the plain sense of the first of these passages shews that it cannot include all three parts, but only the last; and hence, inasmuch as already, according to the opinion of the Rabbis, the verse speaks of the Messiah, it demonstrates also that he will suffer. The same conclusion is also arrived at from the words of Ps. ii. 6, one of the explanations of which, 'I have drawn him out of the chastisements,' clearly involves the fact of his suffering. To me, however, the saying seems to give an assurance that my view of the Parashah, that it relates, namely, altogether to the sufferings of the righteous, is sound and true. Of these sufferings there are three kinds: First, the chastisements of love, or trials such as those undergone by the patriarchs: with whom, on account of his dignity, is reckoned David also, for in reality David's sufferings were for the purpose of making to a certain extent

[j] Compare above, p. 10.

atonement for iniquity; the man, moreover, who reflects on the nature of extraordinary trials will see that he, too, came to atone for Israel's guilt by a species of trial, as I have myself described by the help of God. The sufferings of the second kind are those endured for the iniquity of a whole generation, which yet do not liberate it from its guilt; in such a case, possibly, the righteous only perishes, in order that his contemporaries may be the more implicated, as happened, in fact, with the generation at present suffering exile: those of the third kind, on the contrary, are such as do liberate a generation from its guilt, and effect atonement for it; and this is what will be the case with the generation of the Messiah. Perhaps, then, the expression *wounded for our transgressions* may allude to the first of these; *bruised for our iniquities*, to the second; *the chastisement of our peace was upon him, and by his stripes we are healed*, implying, as it does, that we are entirely free from all iniquity, to the third, or, in other words, to the generation of the Messiah. Thus, if your eyes perceive aright, you may see that the verses of the Parashah agree perfectly together, and indicate the three divisions that have been mentioned. As to the application of Ps. ii. 6 to the Messiah, the term נסכתי has been expounded (1) in the sense of *anointing*, so as to indicate his perfection in wisdom (for anointing with oil signifies plenitude of intelligence); (2) in the sense of *pouring out* (מסכה Ex. xxxii. 4), so as to indicate the completeness of his external blessings, such as riches; (3) in the sense of *fixing* (as in מסכת Judg. xvi. 13 f.), so as to indicate his irresistible strength; (4) in the sense of *making great* (as in the phrase נסיכי אדם Mic. v. 4), so as to indicate his glory; lastly, in the sense of *drawing out* from suffering, to indicate his perfection in all mental qualities, which are notoriously made perfect by suffering. The whole of this application you will find in the *Yalqut* on Ps. ii. 6, *q. v.* [7] The prophet now refers to the many righteous who suffer in the present exile, being slain or burnt for having *not done violence*. Each one of them, he says, was brought first of all to the court of judgment, where he was *oppressed and afflicted*, viz. with cruel blows, while being led before the judge; after this he was taken to prison, but *he opened not his mouth*. Next he was brought out thence to be condemned to death, and was as *a sheep led to the slaughter;* at the same time all his riches were confiscated, according to the words *like a lamb which before her shearers is dumb*, i. e. a lamb which if she were to cry out would only be shorn partially, but being silent, is shorn completely; like such a lamb the righteous was shorn of all his possessions, and like her also without opening his mouth. [8] In this seizure both the king and the judges made common cause, they all united to do injury to Israel; neither hindered the other, although it is a frequent occurrence both for the judicial power to rebuke the king, and for the king to rebuke the judicial power. This persecution, however, with the victim's subsequent death, affected those also who were still left alive; for *who* was there to *teach* and instruct his generation, that he had been *cut off from the land of the living*, i. e. from the righteous amongst them with whom he had been associating? [no one;] for, *for the transgression of* the rest of *my people*, i. e. of the wicked, *the stroke* fell upon them, viz. upon the righteous who were living, and were the friends of the murdered man. All these, as has been said, are the words of the prophet. [9] *He gave*, i. e. allowed, his burial and death to take place at the hands of the wicked; he also at his death gave up all his riches (for they had been confiscated to the wicked kingdom), *although he had done no violence* for his goods to be seized, and although there was *no deceitfulness in his mouth* for him to be murdered. Even 'while it is yet high day' are the righteous murdered in our present exile by men who devise against them schemes of wrong 'because they have done no violence, and there is no deceitfulness in their mouths.' The passage I have already quoted from the Aggadah of Samuel proves, as was said, the truth of this explanation: apply thyself to it, and see and understand; for our fathers have told us how these words, spoken as they are in truth, were fulfilled in their own cases in the provinces of Spain and all the districts of the Gentiles, where many of them were burnt or imprisoned for the Holiness of God and the Unity of his name. [10] The prophet here alludes to the particular kind of sufferings—such as those of the patriarchs or David—which come upon a man individually, whether as punishments for sin or as chastisements of love; though, indeed, in the opinion of the author of the *Moreh* [*N'bukhim*], there are no sufferings without sin; but, by the help of God, I have fully explained his view elsewhere, and it may be found in the treatise Leḥem Sh'lomoh, *q. v.* Isaiah says, *Him whom the Lord has pleasure in*—i.e. whom it is his good pleasure to make perfect (as it is written, Prov. iii. 12, 'Whom the Lord loveth—taketh pleasure in—he correcteth, as a father doth his son')—him *he bruiseth* with stripes, and *sickeneth* with many sicknesses, both external and internal together. Notwithstanding, however, that these are but the chastisements of love and not caused by sin, *if he regards* them as borne for the *trespass of his soul*, reflecting that, although in actual deed he may have done no wrong, he may still perhaps have sinned by the thought of some trangression, or there may be in his soul some fault, through its having failed to accomplish so much as it should have done, then it is certain that, besides its being *the pleasure* and purpose of the Almighty to perfect him by his counsel, or to perfect others with him, he may 'now know' and now declare that he will be as it were an ensign to all the nations, and *the pleasure of the Lord will prosper in his hand*, i.e. that his purpose will advance to completion—a result which will be sufficient for him by itself. He will, moreover, be rewarded by seeing seed, and lengthening days in the land, 'like the days of heaven upon the earth.' In *Berakhoth*, § 1[k], Rabba, son of R. Huna, says: Whom the Lord hath pleasure in, he bruiseth with chastenings, etc.; and the verse is then explained as I have stated, the words אם ישים אשם נפשו being taken to mean, 'If he applies his soul, or makes

[k] Compare above, p. 8.

it his pleasure, to receive his chastenings intelligently, and like a man presenting a trespass-offering, who performs the act in full knowledge of what he does and with the assent of his intellect.' The explanation there given of חפץ ה' בידו יצלח, viz. 'his doctrine shall be established in his hands,' is also compatible with my own, for it is God the instructor who teaches knowledge to man that is instructed; the man instructed is also the learner (disciple), and the doctrine taught, which is the 'Lord's pleasure or will,' is established in his hands. In saying *shall see seed*, etc., he denies that his seed will be like that of R. Yoḥanan, of whom it is said in the Gemara, that he had many sons, but they all died; and in declaring that his doctrine will be established in his hand, they affirm that his chastenings will not be such as to involve any interruption of the Law. In the book *Zohar*, section וישב, the verse is explained to signify that the Lord was pleased *to purify him;* and it is further stated that the subject of תשים (*shall make*) must be 'his soul,' as otherwise the prophet must have employed ישים (*masc.*), and also that the 'Lord's pleasure' is the Law, which is to prosper in his hand. [11] The last verse spoke of the chastenings that come as a correction for sin; the present verse speaks of those which come of love, for purposes of trial. *As he beholds*, it says, the travail of his soul, he *will be satisfied*, i. e. will delight and exult in the thought that he is righteous, and God's servant, 'my messenger whom I send' from this time onwards to make many righteous, to restore them by a complete conversion, and, in the manner before explained, to bear their iniquities. [12] God here makes his final declaration respecting the righteous one who is to atone for his generation, or who is tempted in order that by his trial the people may learn to know the Lord and to walk in his law, like Abraham when he was binding Isaac upon the altar: Behold, *I will divide him* in the world to come a portion *like* the portions of *the many* who returned through his means to the Lord; for there were many whom he justified, and the merits of them all shall attach themselves to him. Moreover, in the present world, he shall *divide spoil*, i. e. riches and honour and external goods *with the mighty*, i. e. with rulers; for, inasmuch as *he poured out his soul to die*, and in doing so *carried the sin of many*, I will allot him in the next world a portion as goodly as be those who were rendered fit to attain it through him; and since in this world *he was numbered with the transgressors* (either because they were appointed[l] to rule over him, or because he was thought to be one of them himself), *but* yet *entreated them* to amend their ways (or, *made intercession for* them), therefore *with the mighty shall he divide spoil*. It is further clear that it is because he sanctified my name among the many, that God promises to allot and grant him a portion in their midst, so that they will be unable to withhold it from him. And because his murderers and those who would seize his spoil are mighty and strong, therefore he will divide the spoil of his enemies in their very presence (את); and then distribute it to his own relatives and friends, in return for his having *poured out his soul to die*, and voluntarily choosing death rather than life; and although at the time of his murder he was ranked, in the sentence read out to him, with the generality of other transgressors, yet he took no count of it, knowing truly that he *carried the sin of many*, making it, as he did, his constant habit to *intercede for transgressors*, in order that atonement might be made for them. In *Soṭah*, § 1, R. Shimlai expounds this verse as follows: Why, he asks, did Moses long to enter into the Promised Land? etc.[m] This quotation shews the truth of my interpretation of the last verse; for the Rabbis explain it of Moses our master, concerning whom the saying goes[n], 'Moses was worthy himself, and made many others worthy as well; the merits of them all shall attach themselves to him.' They declare, too, that it would never have entered into his mind to be desirous of eating of the fruit, and of being satisfied with the good things

[l] A play upon נמנה and נתמנה.

[m] The entire Midrash will be found above, p. 8.

[n] Compare p. 273.

of the land of Israel, except that he might be enabled to testify to them how the Almighty had performed his promise that it should be perfect, not only in what was pleasant, but also in what was useful (these being what are signified by its 'fruit,' for milk is useful and honey pleasant), and also good (indicated by the expression 'good things,' descriptive of the abundance with which it is blessed), for without his testifying it, all this was before them, and it was perfectly well known to him to be so; but it was still his wish to fulfil there the commandments himself, and so to elevate them out of a condition of potentiality into one of action. God therefore said to him, 'Dost thou at all seek for anything except to secure a reward?'—i. e. to bring these commandments into action; for a 'reward' is given not for a mere capacity, but only for a completed act—'I will bring it to pass upon thee, as though thou hadst done them, for since thou art he who causeth Israel to do them, it is as though thou hadst done them thyself.' *Therefore I will divide him a portion with the many*—a portion the same as theirs, viz. of the Israelites who enter in, whether 'with the latter,' in which case, apart from the literal sense, there will be an allusion to the recompense of the world to come, or 'with the former,' which will refer to the recompense in the present world. Now the patriarchs were worthy of both these rewards, of the temporal no less than of the eternal; and Moses our master will, in addition, be held worthy in the resurrection, because he 'poured out his soul to die' for the sin of the golden calf (Ex. xxxii. 32); and therefore they apply to him the words *bare the sin of many*, etc., because he was numbered with those who perished in the wilderness, and also (according to one interpretation) the saying, With how many trials did the generation of the wilderness vex him! But further, he *interceded for the transgressors*, i. e. for the people in the wilderness, who, though continually vexing him, he still used to pray might be converted. There is besides quoted in the *Yalqut*, a Midrash from *Siphré*, which applies the verse to Moses our master in another way: for, inasmuch as all the perfections which were realised in Israel, were attained by his means, he will naturally receive as his reward a portion equal to that of all the rest; as it is written, 'And he came at the heads of the people,' because he had 'performed the righteousness of the Lord and his judgments with Israel' (Deut. xxxiii. 21), for Moses was continually in all their assemblies[o] executing justice. If now you are a man of sense, you will be able to understand how everything that is expounded of the 'righteous man, perfect in his generations'—how 'many and sore troubles' passed over him, and how again and again he was chastened with suffering—may be applied also to the nation at large: for all Israel are connected together like a single man [as in fact it is said even of the whole human race], 'And he called their name Man' (Gen. v. 2).

[o] Compare above, p. 10.

XXXIX. R. ABRAHAM OF CORDOVA.

§ 41. *An exposition of Isaiah* lii. 13–liii. 12.

The third opinion, appropriated by the wise men of Edom, is that the Parashah is descriptive of the Messiah, i. e. of Jesus, whose 'foundation,' in the writings of Isaiah, rests securely upon God, according to the words, *Who hath believed?* etc., the whole of which the Nazarenes assert that the prophet meant to apply to the Messiah, describing him, as he does, as 'without form or comeliness.' They then affirm and believe that the person in whom all this language was fulfilled was Jesus of Nazareth, who was stricken, smitten, despised, and killed through sickness of heart at the sins of the human race, and that this is what the prophet attests when he adds immediately afterwards, 'Surely he hath carried our sicknesses, and borne our pains,' etc. (verses 4, 5). I shall reply first of all by pointing out how it is a recognised custom of Scripture to speak habitually of the whole nation by the name of an individual—addressing it at one time by the name of Jacob, at another by that of Israel, and calling it on one occasion Zion, on another Jerusalem, and so forth. For instance, in accordance with this principle, Scripture says (Deut. vi. 4), 'Hear, O Israel, the Lord our God is one God.' The same practice seems to me to have been adopted by Isaiah, when he likens our nation in her 'desolation and mourning' to a man stricken and smitten of God: in fact, he opens his prophecy with the words, 'Israel doth not know, my people doth not consider' (i. 3), adding immediately afterwards, in the plural number (ver. 5), 'Where can ye be smitten more?' etc.; and again below, 'For the iniquity of his covetousness I was angry and smote him' (lvii. 17), speaking of the entire people in the wilderness as of a single man. Isaiah, moreover, adheres to the same practice when announcing the redemption of Israel under the name of Zion, in the words, lii. 7, 'That saith to Zion, Thy God is king,' etc.; and shortly before (ver. 1), 'Put on thy strength, O Zion: put on thy beautiful garments, O Jerusalem, for henceforth,' etc., assuring us that after the true Messiah has entered in, Jerusalem will no more fall into the hands of the uncircumcised, as she fell, without being able yet to rise again, shortly after the days when Jesus appeared. Indeed, this is an indication that Jesus was not the true Messiah, but a mortal. Isaiah, however, continues to employ the singular, saying, 'Shake thyself from the dust; arise, and sit down, O Jerusalem,' etc. (ver. 2), until, at the end of the chapter, he declares, *Behold my servant* (i. e. the whole of God's people, who are now spoken of as *Israel*) *shall prosper*, etc., to the end of ver. 15, using terms descriptive of our exile, wherein we who are here to-day have 'all like sheep gone astray' amongst the Gentiles. In the next chapter he alludes to the day of redemption, which will bring about a stupendous miracle in the midst of the Gentiles; for in it the Almighty will magnify Israel with signs terrible beyond what can be imagined, which their eyes will then behold, so that in their wonderment they will say one to another, Who would believe that which we now hear? and who hitherto hath ever been possessed of *the arm*, i. e. the might, *of the Lord*, so as in a moment to save his people Israel, and raise them to greatness? Did not WE esteem him *as a root* springing *out of the dry ground*, devoid of sap, and deprived of hope, without form or worth, and if we looked at it, displaying nothing which might excite our zeal on its behalf? He was *despised and forlorn of men*, etc., i.e. was incessantly persecuted by the Gentiles, in such a manner that we never ceased despising and cursing him, and cruelly heaping on him our sicknesses, pains, and blows, in the idea that this had been the Divine pleasure, and that he was really hated and loathed by the Almighty, being *stricken, smitten of God, and afflicted;* in a word, abandoned by him for ever. Now, however, that we have heard this, we see that the case is the reverse of what we thought: Israel was *wounded for our transgressions,* which we committed, at the time when we smote him mortally, in order to force him to listen to us, and to follow our counsels and the 'stubbornness of our heart.' This he never would do; but determined rather to endure our fierce anger, although contrary to justice and right, to support cruel plagues, 'sore sicknesses and of long continuance;' *like a sheep he was led to the slaughter, and like a lamb dumb before her shearers so he opened not his mouth* to scrutinize the decree of his Creator, but so accepted the sentence passed upon him by the Almighty that his sufferings became to us a source of iniquity. The meaning of the words, 'The chastisement of our Peace is upon him,' is this, that the Messiah will be called Jehovah-shalom [Jehovah is peace], like the name 'Prince of peace' (Is. ix. 5): it must be supposed that 'when the Lord doeth great things for us'—signs unsearchable and marvels without number—and when our Redeemer, the Lord our righteousness, is come, they will 'then say among the heathen,' as if speaking for themselves: *The chastisement* and penalty which should have been ours, for having invented the fiction of the advent of our Messiah, fell upon Israel instead during the long years of his bitter captivity, although he always steadily adhered to the truth, and would never acknowledge our errors; hence we never ceased to afflict him, imagining that *by his stripes* which were produced when, in zeal for our own lying belief, we visited him with the rod of our anger, we should secure for ourselves happiness and prosperity, and that by his pain we should *be healed.* But now we see that we had *all gone astray,* like sheep without a shepherd, each turning to his own way, one pursuing this path, and another that, none of us perceiving that by our hands which ought to have been helping him in his latter end, the Lord was *bruising* him, in order that he might be worthy of the great blessings which our eyes now see before us in his midst. The prophet, however, for the confusion of the Nazarenes, and to expose the nakedness of their faith, wishing to give to his words that true sense in which, to the absolute exclusion of any other, we have here explained them, enlarges on his theme, adding, 'For the transgression of my people was the stroke *upon them*'—as the word appears in the copy of our sacred and venerated books, written in our own ancient and truthful tongue, which no hand of the translator has ever touched for the purpose of transplanting it from the fields of truth and right—in order to shew with his very finger that the subject of the whole prophecy is not a particular individual of a generation, but the entire Israelitish nation; accordingly, in this one place, he intentionally substitutes the plural, *upon them*, for the singular, meaning that for their sin the stroke had fallen upon the Israelites,—as he says elsewhere, 'For the sin of her prophets, the iniquities of her priests,' etc. (Lam. iv. 13). And who is the man that will not open the eyes of his understanding to discern the craft and guile of the lying Hieronymus, who, in his version, so misused his inkpot as to trample on the word למו, contriving in his usual manner to misapply it to the Messiah (as, in fact, he distorted the sense of the whole prophecy) by the rendering, 'For the transgression of my people was there a stroke upon *him*,' meaning to imply that the Messiah was smitten for the sin of the people?—In conclusion, the prophet declares that Israel endured all these plagues and sufferings, *although he had done no violence, and there was no guile in his mouth:* and so, at the present day, when the truth is revealed, those who ravage and waste Israel admit that they hate him without cause, and injure him for nought, because even while in exile amongst the Gentiles he was content to fulfil the statutes and laws of the Lord. And this which he did in believing the Unity of God and the Advent of the Messiah, could *not* be imputed to him as *violence*, because all his words were truthful and just, neither was there guile in his mouth. As for myself, the author. I could not in this prophecy refrain from explaining each word one by one, when I saw how the Nazarenes construct with them nets and traps, and build up a great argument by extracting out of almost every word a demonstration that, after the time of Jesus, there can be no new future Messiah for Israel (on the ground that they have already 'devoured him with open mouth[a]') : they do this, I say, because they see that in reality the plain and unvarnished meaning of the prophecy, in all its parts, in all its words, and in all its syllables, is a cluster of 'bitter grapes' to them. Such, however, are their efforts to turn the platter upside down, by perverting the simple sense of the text, and fabricating falsehoods about them, that not only does the slightness of their foundation remain unexposed, but the pride of their heart is even confirmed; in their desire to seduce the wavering multitude, and to 'hunt the souls' of the poor and innocent, which are dragged along by the cords of their malicious devices, they are compelled to falsify the translation, so as to believe that the prophets spoke with reference to Jesus. So did Hieronymus, and was canonized for what he did, together with the 'company of his friends[b]' 'who went with him,' accepting his words and adopting his counsels, contending against the Lord and all his prophets: and every one who hears them or reads their translation steps in his simplicity into their impurities, like the blind man who defiles himself with blood in the street, and goes down alive into hell, sinking every moment deeper and deeper ; as for me, in the plain meaning of God's words will I rejoice; so may I not 'fall into the hands of man,' who is but ashes and blood.

---

[a] *Sanhedrin*, 99[a] : הלל אומר אין להם משיח לישראל שכבר אכלוהו בימי חזקיה.

[b] So the phrase (Gen. xxvi. 26) is understood by Onqelos and the Màsora.

XL. R. SH'MUEL LANYADO.

My servant, i. e. the King Messiah, *shall be high and exalted, and lofty exceedingly*—he shall be higher than Abraham, of whom it is written, 'I raise *high* my hand to the Lord' (Gen. xiv. 22); lifted up above Moses, of whom it is written, '*Lift* it *up* in thy bosom' (Num. xi. 12); and loftier than the ministering angels, of whom it is said, 'Their wheels were *lofty*' (Ezek. i. 18): and so again it is said, Thou art the 'great mountain' (Zech. iv. 7), which is greater than the patriarchs. R. Yiẓḥaq Abarbanel was unable to comprehend how the Messiah could be lifted up above Moses, of whom it is said that 'there arose no prophet in Israel like him' (Deut. xxxiv. 10); and still more how he was to be greater than the angels, who are spiritual beings, whereas the Messiah is born of a woman: it is, in fact, upon that expression that the idolaters [Christians] rest the chief article of their faith, the Divinity of the Messiah. Abarbanel rejects also the opinion of the learned En Bonet[a], who explains it of the doctors; 'for how,' he asks, 'could it enter into any one's mind to speak of the doctors as exalted above Abraham or Moses? besides, such a view has no support from the passages adduced in proof of it, for the verse from Ezekiel is admitted to refer to the host of heaven, how then can it be used to establish the application to the Rabbis?' The author of the '*Aqêdah*[b] writes as has been stated above in chap. xxviii, and carries En Bonet's view still further, supposing that the Messiah will be higher than

[a] See p. 154: compare also pp. 165–168.

[b] R. Yiẓḥaq Aramah.

Abraham in respect of his nobility, more exalted than Moses in lavishing all things needful upon Israel, loftier than the angels in the learning of the Law. Thus he himself applies the expression to the perfection procured by the agency of Messiah our righteousness. This he conceives to include, (1) the reality of faith, which was attained first by Abraham, when he 'believed in the Lord,' and made his people to believe likewise; it is said that in this respect the Messiah will be *higher than Abraham*, because through him the true faith will be promulgated even more than by Abraham, who 'raised his hand on *high* to the Possessor of heaven and earth :' and (2) acquaintance with the Law which was given by Moses for us to walk in ; the command, 'Lift it up in thy bosom, as a nurse,' etc., not referring to any bodily guidance, but being an injunction that he should teach and lead them to true knowledge and doctrine, like infants 'weaned from milk and removed from the breast,' which are carried by their nurse. This indeed was what Moses did, the Law which he set before the children of Israel being as a spread table; and therefore it is said that the Messiah will lead his people in the understanding of the Law, and *lift them up* even more than Moses. The expression does not allude to the power of prophecy, for the position of Moses was such that there 'arose no prophet in Israel like him.' Inasmuch, now, as the two high qualities just mentioned are intimately connected with tranquillity and rest for the righteous (when it is well with them, it is well also with the world!), the peace in the days of the Messiah will be multiplied exceedingly; and through the Divine providence constantly attending him, the angels who preside over the nations will become subject to him (for in God's providence he will 'visit the host of heaven in heaven, and the kings of earth upon earth,' Is. xxiv. 21); and this is what is signified by the phrase *loftier than the angels*—for the Almighty will 'give nations before him, and kings shall he subdue' (Is. xli. 2). R. Yizḥaq Abarbanel states that he has seen an interpretation that would regard the *Mem* before Abraham, etc., not as the *Mem* of superiority or comparison, but as the *Mem* of derivation or cause, supposing that in the Messiah there are to be three kinds of perfection; the first physical, and derived from Abraham; the second acquired, and derived from Moses, in whose Law he is to be trained; the third divine, in that an abundance of all things will be lavished upon him 'from the Lord out of heaven:' upon the last ground he is termed *higher than the angels.* The words of the text do not, however, accord with this explanation. Abarbanel himself, therefore, adheres to its literal meaning, supposing that the Messiah will be higher than Abraham, inasmuch as Abraham served the Lord for love, forsaking 'his land and his kindred and his father's house,' in order to follow after him, who received the seal of a holy covenant, and proceeded to bind his only son in order to fulfil the command of his God, and who after the victory over the kings was not penetrated by any feeling of pride, or a thirst for the glory achieved by their conquest, or any desire of their spoil, but said, 'I *raise high* my hands unto the Lord that I will not take,' etc.; because the glory which he loved was not carnal or material. The King Messiah, however, will be *high* in the fear of the Lord, and 'righteousness shall be the girdle of his loins,' etc. In the second place, in relation to the people, whom the Messiah, being 'mighty to save,' will redeem and rescue, it is said that he will be *lifted up above Moses;* for while the redemption of Moses only brought the nation out of Egypt into the land of Canaan, the Messiah will gather all Israel together from the four quarters of the world. In the third place, in relation to the Gentiles, that he will prevail and rule over them; for although their heavenly princes (Dan. x. 13) will pour down all blessings upon them, the Messiah will still bow them down and overcome them: what is meant by *higher than the angels,* then, is this, that the Almighty will 'visit the host of heaven,' so that their forces will be of no avail to the nations over which they preside, and that the Divine abundance will be shed down upon the Messiah directly, which is not the case with the angels, to whom it is only transmitted through a series of intermediate agencies. Thus far Abarbanel. A difficulty, however, at once arises on the first point; for, since the greatness of Abraham's service sprang out of love, the text which ought to have been appealed to was, 'The seed of Abraham who loveth me' (Is. xli. 8), in preference to the one before us, which by the expression 'shall be high' points rather to the passage in Genesis, 'I raise high my hand' (xiv. 22). In my own humble opinion it seems that in the first two parts En Bonet is right; for in point of nobility the Messiah will excel even Abraham, and therefore it is promised that he *shall be high;* for the noble man who (like Abraham, when he swore he would not take from a thread even to a shoe-latchet) despises gain, and even the wealth that is his own, will assuredly be exalted (for 'a man's gift maketh room for him, and bringeth him before the great'); and such, even to a greater degree than with Abraham, will be the case also with the Messiah our righteousness. And in the ability to guide Israel he will be superior to Moses; for Moses, when he was a shepherd, had compassion on the kid which escaped from him in order to drink, and brought it in his bosom: for for that purpose had the Almighty chosen him [c],—how much more then that he might guide and tend Israel? This then (as I have explained in the *Kh'li Hemdah*) is the meaning of Moses' words: 'Ask not of me things which are not in my power, as that I should give them flesh; for whence should I have flesh to give to all this people? Ask only that which is in my power, viz. that I should "*lift them up* and carry them in my bosom:" accordingly it is said, *Lifted up above Moses*.' And that he is to be far above both Abraham and Moses we learn from the word *exceedingly*, which stands at the end; for if this had not belonged to all the three preceding terms, but only to the last, we should have read not '*and* lofty,' but merely 'lofty:' the conjunction *and*, by coupling the three expressions together, indicates that

[c] *Sh'moth Rabbâ*, c. 2.

the adverb is intended to qualify them all. As regards En Bonet's explanation of 'loftier than the angels,' my judgment coincides with that of R. Yiẓḥaq Aramah and R. Yiẓḥaq Abarbanel, who reject it on two grounds: I think that the words should be understood in their natural sense, but believe also that they involve a mystery which no mouth can utter: it is, however, revealed in the book *Zohar*, in the section on Deut. xxii. 6 ('When a bird's nest chanceth before thee,' etc.); so that we need not wonder if, as is the fact, he is to be loftier than the angels. The text appears to me to refer simply to the fear and dread which he will inspire into all flesh even more than the angels, who yet are so awful that, as we know, when one appeared to Manoah and his wife, they exclaimed, 'We have seen God; we shall surely die' (Judg. xiii. 22). Accordingly the Messiah is said to be 'loftier than the angels,' in respect of the terror which their presence creates; since every one who beholds them, like Ezekiel, is 'afraid and trembles;' for in Ezek. i. 18, 'they had fear,' the meaning is not that the cherubim were filled with fear of the Almighty—a fact which there was no occasion to remark specially—but that they inspired fear into all who beheld them. And then, lastly, he is called 'the *great mountain*, which is greater than the patriarchs,' because each of the patriarchs helped in his turn to restore the world after it had been corrupted by the sin of our first parents [d]; and so it is stated in the book *Zohar* that Abraham did his part in this restoration, when he was thrown into the fire to fulfil the verse which says, 'The molten images of their gods ye shall burn with fire [e]' (Deut. vii. 25): thus Abraham, by tasting the torment of the flames, made atonement for man, and is hence called the 'great man.' Isaac, again, made atonement for bloodshed, inasmuch as, for the fear he felt (as it is written,

---

[d] Lit. 'the first Adam' or 'man:' cf. 1 Cor. xv. 45.

[e] Abraham, it was said, was treated in the same way that his descendants were to treat the heathen idols.

Gen. xxxi. 42, 'the *fear* of Isaac . . . .'), his own blood was as good as poured out upon the altar. And Jacob averted the consequences of a forbidden marriage by preserving peace between the two sisters, where any one else would have only been a cause of rivalry and discord; for it was just to obviate such that the prohibition was given not to take a woman as wife 'unto her sister to be her rival in her life' (Lev. xviii. 18).

The opinions of our wise men on the interpretation of this verse have now been discussed: but we do not gather clearly from their language whether they are speaking of Messiah son of Ephraim, or of Messiah son of David. The same doubt is suggested by Abarbanel, who thinks however that the former cannot be intended; for how, he asks, could it be said of him that he will 'be high and exalted, and lofty exceedingly?' If, on the contrary, we refer the prophecy to Messiah son of David, there is a difficulty in the expression *marred beyond man;* for Isaiah says, 'Behold my servant, whom I uphold; my chosen one in whom my soul delighteth; I have put my spirit upon him' (xlii. 1). And again, 'And a rod shall come forth out of the stem of Jesse' (xi. 1): how, too, can he say of him, *Stricken, smitten of God, and afflicted,* for Messiah son of David will be 'just and victorious' (Zech. ix. 9), and so far from being *despised and forlorn of men,* that 'unto him will the Gentiles seek' (Is. xi. 10)? Nor are the other verses more applicable to him, which declare how he will endure sufferings and death for Israel's sake. In a word, the explanation of the Rabbis and of the Targum of Yonathan cannot possibly be conceived as being truthful in the sense of being literal; it is allegorical and adventitious, consisting, as it does, in the adaptation of one of their traditions to the language of the text; and a proof of this lies in the fact that the Targum itself refers the subsequent verses to Israel, and not to the Messiah, and that one verse, the last, is referred by our Rabbis to Moses. Thus far Abarbanel[f]. A similar

[f] Above, p. 163.

difficulty was felt by 'Ibn 'Ezra, as I shall shew directly, when I transcribe his words later on. In my own humble opinion, who accept 'the words of the wise as goads' (Qoh. xii. 11), I believe that they mean to assert that the verse speaks solely of Messiah son of David, to whom all the gorgeous language in it will apply. The prophet next addresses the people of Messiah son of Ephraim, and encourages them not to be afraid of the myriads which were against them, assuring them that the degree of his future exaltation will be proportionate to the amazement with which they had previously contemplated him; that even though the son of Ephraim were slain, the Almighty would avenge him by the hand of Messiah son of David, who would *sprinkle* the blood of *many nations*. The words mean then, *As*, when thou, O Messiah son of Ephraim, wentest forth into the world, *many were astonished at thee*, wondering how it could possibly be that *his countenance* was so *marred beyond men*, and *his form beyond the sons of men*, whether also such was the usual appearance of a conqueror—*as* they thus mocked thee without measure, *so will* Messiah son of David *sprinkle* the blood of many nations: the fact is that the prophet here uses the third person, in order to shew that he means some one different from Messiah son of Ephraim, who had been mentioned just before, and one who will shed the blood of his enemies. Then kings too will put their hand upon their mouth (as he says, *At him kings shall shut their mouth*), since, so he adds, besides what was told them before the coming of Messiah son of David, *they* now *see* more terrible things still, even *that which had never been told them, and perceive that which they had never heard*: in other words, things which they were now for the first time perceiving, in virtue of the spirit of understanding, which enabled them to discern one thing hidden within another, were now increased manifold. After this, the Almighty, speaking for himself and the congregation of Israel (or for himself and the two Messiahs), enquires *Upon whom*, in days gone by, *was the arm of the Lord revealed* that they might be able to compare one thing with another? for although, as it is written, he 'laid it bare' against the Egyptians, and 'wrought with the arm of his might' (cf. Is. lii. 10), still he has not manifested it so openly now in the second Deliverance. The reply is, Upon Messiah son of Ephraim, who will *come up before him*, and in comparison with Messiah son of David (who will follow after him) be *as a sucker* or small branch, and *as a root out of the dry ground*, which is very small. He is to have *no form*, to be *despised, forsaken of men, and afflicted* with endless pains,—as our Rabbis relate of him, he will stand in the gate of Rome[g], binding up each wound separately by itself, lest the season of Deliverance arrive too suddenly; and his pains and sicknesses will make it seem *as though* the faces hidden from them were averted *because of himself* and his deeds, which had been the cause of our *esteeming him not. Yet* in truth it was otherwise: in all his sufferings he was guiltless: it was *our sicknesses* that *he bare*,—the sicknesses and pains which were in readiness to come for our iniquities upon us were carried by him instead, and we were in error in thinking him *stricken* and *smitten of God*, i. e. as Rashi explains, an object of his enmity. After his advent, to use again the words of Rashi, the son of Ephraim, who for a while had held sovereignty and executed *judgment* over Israel and the Gentiles, was *taken away*, because the Gentiles resolved to slay him; *and who* then *could tell of his generation* and the travail which befel him? *for he was cut off out of the land of the living*, and slain *for the transgression of my people*, the *stroke* intended *for them* being borne by him instead. In addition to this, he *made his grave with the wicked*, being buried amongst those who were slain at the time that the Gentiles assembled together against him, and was delivered into the hand of *the rich*, i. e. of the kingdom of wickedness, for death under all the forms which men could devise; he was not to be put to

---

[g] Above, p. 39.

death speedily, but tortured by every conceivable method of producing a severe and painful end; and hence it is that the prophet says not 'in his *death*' but 'in his *deaths*.' And all this happened because he had done no wrong in deed or word, but had kept the truth of God alone in his mouth; for it was *the Lord's pleasure to bruise and sicken him.* But *if thou*, O Israel, *puttest* before thy eyes *the trespass-offering* which would be incurred by his murder, and the preservation of his soul from death, and if thou lettest thyself be pained thereby, behold, this thy care for him will stir thee up unto repentance, and prevent him from being slain: thus he shall *see seed and have long days*, and *for the travail of his soul* which he endured he *shall be satisfied*, i. e. shall eat and be filled of the reward bestowed upon him for his sufferings; and although he will not hold the same rank and position as Messiah son of David, nevertheless, *by his knowledge he will justify many, and* by suffering himself *bear their iniquities*, until at last I *divide him a portion with the many*, etc.—Such is the sense of these verses, according to the opinion of those amongst our wise men who apply them to Messiah son of David, and to Messiah son of Joseph, who is of the tribe of Ephraim.

[Here follow the expositions of Rashi, 'Ibn 'Ezra, R. David Qamḥi, and Abarbanel (see above, pp. 37, 43, 49, 168). Upon Abarbanel, Lanyado passes the following criticisms: liii. 2, after the explanation of ונראהו (p. 174); His statement, however, raises some difficulty, for if the word relates to past time, the ו ought to have been pointed with *Pathach*: liii. 8 (p. 180), upon למו; This is not correct, for the plural must have been expressed by נגעים לו, 'there were *strokes* upon *him*:' liii. 9 (p. 181, l. 10), the custom alluded to is further illustrated; And similarly in the country of Ishmael, where, for the same reason, for the sake of distinction, the shrouds are dyed *yellow*: liii. 10 (p. 183); This objection, however, makes no difference; for even those who derive the word from חלה—which is the simplest way—have to account for the absence of the א; so that the third radical is still wanting: lii. 12 *end* (p. 188); A difficulty, however, still remains; for the prophecy cited relates certainly to Jerusalem itself, and not to the whole land: Josiah also was slain out of Jerusalem; but this being so, the words 'there shall no more enter into thee the uncircumcised and unclean' can have no reference to Josiah.]

LII. [13] In my own humble opinion, the Parashah must be supposed to describe the righteous worshipper of God. And the prophet says that being skilled as a servant in the understanding of the Law, he will deserve finally that the glory should come upon him, *he will be high and exalted*, etc.: he does not say, '*and* will be high,' but makes a break at the word 'my servant,' between 'will understand' and 'he will be high,' to shew that the former denotes the spiritual success constituted by the service of God, and that this will render him worthy of the analogous successes that are to follow; he will be *high*, namely, in the dignities of the present world, and *exalted* through the elation of soul occasioned by his successes, and *lofty exceedingly*, so that all who stand before him will be scorched by the brightness issuing 'from his chamber [h].' [14] Turning now to the Israelitish nation mentioned at the end of the previous Parashah, and speaking with them mouth to mouth, the prophet announces the reason why the servant of the Lord should be deemed worthy of such exaltation, saying, *As many*, O Israel, *were astonished at thee* when they saw thy calamities (for 'as they saw, so were they amazed')—in other words, in proportion to their astonishment that the order of creation was changed in him, *so* was the countenance of my servant *marred beyond man*, through pain for the misfortunes of the synagogue and of Israel, until a livid hue had destroyed all resemblance to human features, *and his form* or contour *beyond the sons of men*—for the miseries of Israel so bowed him down that, as he moved, his head was bent between his knees. [15] Being thus affected for Israel, however, it is *accordingly* (כֵּן) destined for him to

[h] An allusion to Ps. xix. 5.

sprinkle many nations, i. e. by his victories to diminish their numbers, and cause but a few to be left of them; as a man who, after dipping his finger into water, sprinkles a drop here and a drop there, so, when God's servant sprinkles, he will leave them 'very few indeed,' even as 'two or three berries on the top of a furthest bough' (Is. xvii. 6). *At him*, i. e. at his victory, *kings*, when they see the successes of Israel in the latter days, *will shut their mouth;* for *they will then see what had not been told them*—those splendid predictions having been announced not to themselves, or to their people, but to Israel, *and perceive what they had never* before *heard*—the promises of the prophets having been given only to Israel, and they themselves knowing nothing of them.

LIII. [1] Israel now asks, *Who believed* the glad tidings which they heard of our future exaltation? and *upon whom* were revealed the prophecies of the vengeance about to be executed by *the arm of the Lord* upon them that hate him? were they not revealed solely to us Israelites? and the Gentiles, when they heard that we were to attain security and prosperity, and even when the arm of the Lord displayed itself in vengeance, would not believe; so that, when they do perceive our successes, they will be seeing things which had never been told them. All this will happen on account of the one righteous who is here called 'my servant;' for 'the righteous is an everlasting foundation.' [2] Like a branch of the kind called suckers, because (Ps. lxxx. 12) they suck in [nourishment] from the rivers, so will the righteous, with his good deeds and understanding of the Law, *come up before him;* like a sucker constantly imbibing moisture, living in, and supported by, the divine fulness he will grow up before the Almighty. But before the sons of men he will appear simply *as a root* devoid of moisture rising *out of the dry earth*, without form or bodily beauty; nevertheless, *when we look* in hopes of beholding a comely aspect, although no brightness or beauty meets our gaze, we shall still desire him, for 'the Lord giveth grace and glory' (Ps. lxxxiv. 12). [3] He was *despised* and *forsaken of* wicked *men*, in consequence of being *a man of pains*, or one upon whom from time to time pains used to come, in addition to the chronic and permanent ailments expressed by the phrase *known of sickness:* and those who saw him thought wrongly that all these befel him because God had *hidden his face* from him on account of his iniquities: he was therefore so much the more *despised, and we esteemed him not*, regarding him simply as a sinner against God: in the words of Yonathan in the Targum [i], 'As though the presence of the Shekhinah had been withdrawn from us, they [the righteous] are despised, and esteemed not.' 4 But the facts were otherwise: *he himself* carried our sicknesses, and bare our pains, and by saying *he himself*, the prophet indicates that the righteous, of his own will, was pleased to carry them for Israel. The 'sicknesses,' denoting transient calamities which are curable like an ordinary ailment, are not so severe or distressing as the 'pains;' accordingly the prophet says with accuracy that he carried them himself: of the latter, however, which designate more painful misfortunes, it is not said 'he *himself* bare,' but simply 'he bare;' since, as immediately follows, it was in fact the Almighty who laid them upon him. 5 Here, again, with the lighter term 'wounded,' the pronoun is similarly made emphatic; not so however with 'bruised:' for although wounding is the penalty for 'transgressions,' and bruising for 'iniquities,' which are the less serious of the two [k], there is no difficulty upon this score, since, granted that transgressions are the severer, yet the iniquities which are most generally committed are those which produce 'bruising.' *We* however *thought him stricken of God* for his own sins, whereas in reality he was stricken for ours, being himself just and perfect. The view here taken obviates the surprise felt by Abarbanel, how, namely, one man could possibly suffer for another, if even 'the son shall not die for the iniquity of the father, nor the father

---

[i] Above, p. 5.

[k] Cf. *Yepheth ben Ali*, p. 25.

for the iniquity of the son' (Ezek. xviii. 20): for the righteous voluntarily and of his own accord bears the sicknesses of his generation, in order to merit the never-ending pleasure of making atonement for them. The meaning of the prophet may then perhaps be that we fancied the decree against him had gone forth from the Almighty, while in fact he was *stricken and smitten* of himself, not involuntarily, but by his own choice, and that he kept begging his brethren and friends to 'come and rejoice in his sufferings, for they would be the means of making atonement for the whole of Israel.' It is possible that the words, *He was wounded*, etc. (which are but a repetition of what was stated in verse 4, 'He himself carried our sicknesses,' etc.), denote minor forms of suffering which come upon the righteous in order that he may be able to make atonement for his generation, viz. (as with the trespass-offering offered in cases of uncertainty[l]) by holding the penalty over them in suspense, and in order that they may repent. The object of this suffering is that we, being punished, may make our peace with God; as the prophet indicates in the words *the chastisement of our peace* was thrown *upon him;* and in that which follows, *by his stripes it is healed to us*, not however so as to be cured entirely, for the text does not run 'we are healed,' but 'it'—i. e. part of the sickness—'is healed to us.' [6] I have heard that our learned, perfect, and most illustrious teacher, R. Mosheh El-Sheikh, understood the words, *All we like sheep went astray*, as denoting a fault in which we all shared alike; because, when a single sheep wanders astray, the rest in the flock follow after it: he adds a remark to the effect that he only wishes this were all; on the contrary, however, *we* also *each went after his own way*, all the ways being equally corrupt, and none better than the rest[m], etc. But, in my humble opinion, the expression *iniquity* (not *iniquities*) *of us all* is used,

[l] Lit. 'the suspended trespass-offering:' see *B'rêshith Rabbâ*, § 43.

[m] See p. 267.

because there are both general sins in which all people offend, and also particular sins of which only individuals are guilty: the former are the more serious, and hence our Rabbis say, There is no comparison between the few who fulfil the commandment and the many who fulfil the commandment; and in the same way the many who stumble and transgress are very different from the few who stumble and transgress. Accordingly, with reference to the general sins, the phrase is, *All we*—i. e. altogether, on a common track—*have gone astray like sheep;* and with reference to the particular, *We have turned each to his own way:* with regard to the latter, now, 'every man must be put to death for his own sin,' but with regard to the former, the prophet declares that the iniquity common to us all is *laid upon him.* Or the distinction may possibly be this: 'All we like sheep have gone astray' may denote *open* sins, such as are committed by all, and 'we have turned each to his own way' may denote *secret* sins committed by the individual which no one besides himself can see or be cognizant of: the open sins, now ('the iniquity *of us all*'), were laid upon the righteous, though they ought in strictness to have been visited upon us: the sins done in secret, however, did not affect him. In all these interpretations עון denotes simply iniquity, and not, as 'Ibn 'Ezra thought, the penalty of iniquity. 7 Abarbanel's view is not incorrect, viz. that *oppressed and afflicted and led to the slaughter* refer to his bodily sufferings, and *as a lamb dumb before her shearers*, etc., to the loss of his possessions; and that the words *he opened not his mouth* are repeated to indicate that he did not open it while undergoing either one or the other. It seems to me, however, that the repetition may possibly have a different significance: they may mean (1) that although oppressed and afflicted, he still never opened his lips to his tormentors, whether for purposes of imprecation or of entreaty, either while he was being led to slaughter, or while they were plundering his goods; and (2) that he did not open his mouth to murmur against the attributes of God, but admitted the justice of the sentence of heaven against himself. [8] I have heard it stated that the learned and illustrious Mosheh El-Sheikh explained this verse to signify that the righteous was rescued from the sufferings and judgment which were to be executed upon Israel; if so, then, he must have suffered with and for his generation till the time came when he was finally released and went to his eternal home: *who,* however, was there that *could* openly *acquaint his generation, when* the righteous that was amongst them *had been* thus *cut off out of the land of life,* that they must be warned to sin no more? for from that moment, *for the transgression of my people the stroke* was to fall *upon them,* i. e. upon my people, and not upon the righteous, as it had done before, while he was suffering for it: henceforward, therefore, by speaking thus the prophet, he conceives, bids the people be warned. But in my humble opinion, the verse signifies that *from the imprisonment and judgment* about to be the lot of his generation, *he was taken* in their stead; and who was there then to declare even in a whisper that he had made atonement for them, in that, by his being thus cut off from life, for the transgression of my people the stroke had fallen upon them (viz. upon the righteous)? There is, however, another possible method by which we may understand in what manner the death of the righteous effects atonement: we find it stated (lvii. 1) that 'the righteous is taken away because of evil (to come),' in order, viz. that vengeance may take its course: the difficulties arising in connexion with this subject I have examined in the *Kh'li Ḥemdah.* Or the meaning may be that, when his time has come, and he has completed his task or is taken away, he makes atonement for his generation, as it is written אשכל כפר (Cant. i. 14), i. e. 'a man in whom there is everything is a ransom,' or makes atonement: but the righteous who ought to have lived on and obtained perfection is cut off from the land of life, and so removed from impending vengeance. Accordingly, in view of the first point, it is said that while he was holding *sovereignty* and high office over Israel, and executing *judgment,* he was *taken away,* therein resembling the 'man in whom is everything, and who is a ransom' for his generation, as it is written (ib. vi. 2), 'My beloved went down into his garden, to the beds of spices,' etc.: hence it is added, *And who could tell his generation? for he was cut off* without having accomplished his destiny. Or the last words may mean that *he was cut off* not merely out of this present world, but also *from the land of life, on account of the transgression of my people*, for which *a stroke* would undoubtedly come *upon them*, from which the righteous was to be taken away: thus the verse will contain a double statement, (1) '*Who* could declare his generation?' i. e. the generation for which his death made atonement, and (2) 'For he was cut off from the land of life for the transgression of my people;' after which the 'stroke' is said to fall upon them for their wickedness in having thus caused his death. 9 During his lifetime the righteous in his humility acquired for himself the possession of a burial-place with the wicked; hence it is here said that *he* himself *made his grave with the wicked:* he also made it *with the rich in his death*, he was not poor, but in all his deaths could be counted with the rich—he was not 'hated' like the 'poor' (Prov. xix. 7): nevertheless, although his riches thus put it within his power to provide himself a grave with the righteous, and *although he had done no violence*, he yet chose one amongst the wicked. Or by the rich (עשיר) are denoted Esau [the Christians] (עשו), the meaning being that every form of death to which he was subjected was inflicted upon him by them, and that he accepted all contentedly *because he had done no violence;* for if he had committed violence as they had done, they would have buried him 'in the choice of their sepulchres,' and Esau would not have tortured him with such an exquisite variety of death ('deaths' in the plural). *Neither* was there any *guile in his mouth:* for it was not in a spirit of hypocrisy, but with perfect sincerity of heart, that he bade them bury him amongst the wicked. 10 *The Lord,* however, *was pleased to bruise* the righteous, *and to sicken him*—though only with a light ailment, in order that *if thou*, O Israel, *makest his soul*, i. e. the soul of the righteous, to be a *trespass-offering*—makest its affliction an occasion for the confession of thy sins—then assuredly this righteous one (who was bruised that he might be able to atone) shall be healed, and will *see seed and have long days, and the pleasure of the Lord*, which is that Israel may be purified, *shall prosper in his hand:* since his death will have had the same effect as all the usual trespass-offerings (such as those rendered for sacrificial mistakes, robbery [n], etc.) by which atonement is procured. Upon the interpretation here given, we remark that the change from the third person to the second is analogous to the one noticed above, lii. 14, where, after addressing Israel ('at *thee*'), the prophet turns to speak about the righteous in their midst ('*his* countenance,' '*his* form,' and in the previous verse '*shall* prosper'): so here 'if *thou* puttest' is addressed (as I have explained) to Israel, while 'to bruise *him*,' '*shall* see,' '*shall* have' refer to the righteous. [11] There are two descriptions of 'travail,' one the travail of the soul caused by the study of the Law, the other the travail of the body, or the toil undergone in the effort to amass riches, and to eat and drink: the perfect one who is the subject of this prophecy will reap no profit whatever in this world *from the travail of his soul:* it is all reserved for the world to come, where he may enjoy the brightness of the Shekhinah—as is indicated by the term *shall see*, here used metaphorically of attaining or comprehending: accordingly it is said, *On account of* (or *For* [o]) *the travail of his soul* he will attain the privilege of seeing spiritual prosperity and being satisfied therewith. It is possible that the words may allude to the opinion also held by the Rabbis that while the righteous is still alive in the present world, the Almighty shews him the reward reserved for

---

[n] Cf. Lev. v. 14–vi. 7.

[o] מן having the same force assigned to it as in ver. 8, *For* the transgression of my people.

him in the future, and that as he looks upon it his soul is satisfied: thus it is said in *B'rêshith Rabbâ*[p], in the Parashah *And Abraham died* [Gen. xxv. 8], 'Themselves sleep, and their soul is satisfied.' The *from* (מן) will in this case be partitive: *some of* the travail of his soul he will see in this world, but not the whole. *By his knowledge* the pure and innocent will guide other men in righteousness, and *justify the just.* Or the sense of these words may be that when two adversaries come before him, by his knowledge he will justify the righteous and condemn the guilty; and my servant will direct all his efforts towards *the many,* so as to render them worthy of happiness, bidding them 'do good,' in so far as he will *justify the just,* and 'turn from evil,' in that he will *bear their iniquities,* viz. by shewing himself ready to accept cheerfully the sufferings which ought to have fallen upon them. 12 *Therefore,* since he will thus justify many, the justice of the many will attach itself to him[q], and he will be rewarded for what he has done, as I have explained on the verse, 'He executed the justice of the Lord and his judgments with Israel' (Deut. xxxiii. 21); for all the righteous acts performed by Israel will be imputed to Moses, who made them worthy in the same way as if he had done them in company with Israel himself: upon the same principle also I explain 'I am a companion of all who fear thee' (Ps. cxix. 63), for since the Psalmist justified them, and was the cause of their fearing God, he had a common lot with them, and could call himself their companion. Similarly it is promised here, *I will allot him a portion with the many*—he will have a portion with the many whom he justified—and *he shall divide spoil with the mighty,* i. e. with those whom by his counsels he strengthened and confirmed in the way of righteousness, as our Rabbis explain on the verse, 'For mighty is he who doeth his word' (Joel ii. 11), i. e. God confers might upon the righteous that they may become doers of his word: with such then

---

[p] Cf. p. 272. [q] Cf. p. 287.

will he *divide spoil*, as though he were the chief and they the followers; for the deed is greater than the doer. The reason why all this happened is stated in the succeeding words: *Because he poured out his soul to die* in order to bear their iniquities, and so far deceived the judgment of the wicked as to be himself *numbered with the transgressors*, as though he were their companion in sin. So little, however, was this the case, that in fact he *carried the sin of many*, saying, 'Turn to me, let there be no iniquity, listen to my voice' (Job vi. 29); his words being listened to, because he was thought to be one of themselves; and so, too, whenever they were wishing to transgress, he would *appeal to them*, saying, 'Do not, my brethren, I pray you, do not this wrong' (Gen. xix. 6), entreating and begging them by every means in his power to desist from evil. Otherwise the first part of the verse may mean, Independently of his portion being a goodly one, I will further honour him by its being distributed to him in the midst of the whole assembly (as it is said, '*In* or *among many* will I divide to him')—for this he would feel to be a privilege and mark of esteem; and similarly *with the mighty he shall divide spoil*, i. e. in company with them, for his own chamber[r] will be in close proximity to theirs.

---

[r] Above, p. 304.

XLI[a].

XLII. R. ABRAHAM BEN Y'HUDAH ḤAZAN[b].

LII. [13] *Behold* in the latter days, *my servant* Jacob, i. e. the righteous who are in him, *will prosper*, etc.: in the Midrash, '*My servant shall prosper*, i. e. the Messiah; he shall be higher than Abraham, lifted up above Moses, and loftier than the angels.' [14] *As many* peoples were amazed at them when they saw their depression, and said one to another in the exile, See *how* their *countenance is marred*, i. e. dark and worn, *beyond* other *men*—for there are many nations who think that the features of the Jew are disfigured and unlike those of other men, and ask (as, for example, in the countries of Ishmael and Persia) whether a Jew has a mouth or an eye—[15] *so* now will his hand also be mighty, and Israel shall 'cast down the horns of the nations which have scattered him' (Zech. ii. 4). Qamḥi, however, explains יזה as meaning *will make to speak*, for people in their amazement at his greatness will be talking of him continually. יקפצו 'will *open*,' though others render 'will *close*,' as Deut. xv. 7: they may either *open* their mouth to tell of Israel's greatness, or *close* it by laying their hand upon it in astonishment at beholding it.

LIII. [1] Had we, they say to each other, had we heard from others what we are now beholding, *who would* ever *have believed it?*

---

[a] See Preface. [b] Compare Rashi throughout.

upon whom has the arm of the Lord ever yet *been revealed* in such splendour and greatness? [2] *Before* such greatness came upon it, this people was in deep depression, springing up out of itself *like a sucker*, and *like a root out of the dry earth*—the point of the comparison being that as it is a marvel if any root or plant be found growing in arid soil, so it was also a marvel when Israel *came up* out of captivity. He had *no form nor comeliness*, viz. while in exile; and *when we* first of all *beheld it, how were we to desire it?*—on the contrary, we rather felt a loathing towards it. [3] חדל אישים, i. e. the *most insignificant* of men; or, according to another explanation, *forlorn* of men, because they would not associate with him: *a man of pains*—alluding to the sufferings of exile, and *taught of sickness*, i. e. accustomed to have the yoke of exile pass over him. וכמסתר פנים ממנו, Rashi: For their depression they *hid their faces from us* that we might not see them, like a person stricken with leprosy who is afraid to look up. Qamḥi: We were *as* men *hiding their faces from him;* we could not look at him, because of the loathing we felt for him, and we accounted him for nought. [4] *But* now we see that this was not merely a consequence of their depression: Israel suffered in order that by his sufferings atonement might be made for all the wicked; yet *we thought* he had been hated of God, *stricken, smitten, and afflicted.* [5] מחלל *pierced*, as Num. xix. 16. מפשעינו *because of* our transgressions. מדכא *bruised.* מוסר וגו׳, he was punished, in order that the whole world might have peace: by חבורה are denoted the sufferings of exile. [6] It is now revealed how the seventy nations have erred: yet the Lord *let himself be entreated* by him and propitiated for the iniquity of us all, in that he refrained from destroying his world. [7] נגש *he was oppressed* in exile, and *afflicted* with stripes, yet *he opened not his mouth* to complain of what we did to him, but was *as a sheep led to the slaughter* and *opened not his mouth* to cry, or *as a lamb dumb before her shearers.* נגש denotes sufferings affecting his property, מענה those affecting his person. [8] מעצר from *sovereignty*, cf. 1 Sam. ix.

17; or, as others explain, from *confinement*, in which he had been kept by them. ממשפט, i. e. from the punishments he had hitherto endured. The meaning is, that the Gentiles will express themselves thus when, hereafter, they see Israel *taken* and released from bondage. *And his generation*, etc., *who* ever *said* or *suspected* that his generation would thus rise to fame? (or, *Who could declare* all the troubles which he underwent?) for *he was cut off from the land of life*, i. e. from the land of Israel. Others, however, think the verse to mean that while in exile he was really considered to have been cut off out of the land of the living; how then were we to expect that such greatness as this would ever be his? *For the transgression*, etc. Each nation will make this confession, saying that in consequence of their own transgression, and not Israel's, had the *stroke* fallen *upon them*. [9] He resigned himself to whatever form of burial might be decreed against him by the wicked who were ever condemning the Israelites to be murdered and then buried like asses in the bellies of dogs. He consented, then, to be slain according to the will of (את) the wicked, refusing to deny the God of Israel; and this is the meaning of *gave* . . . .; for if he had yielded, they would have released him; he would not do this, however, but preferred to meet death for the sake of the Unity of God. Nor was there any *guile in his mouth* so as to accept idolatry as the worship of God. [10] *But* the Lord was pleased *to bruise him*, and so to lead him back to prosperity; therefore *he put* him *to sickness*. The Almighty now says, *If his soul* is so devoted to my holiness as to *return* itself as *a trespass-offering* for all his rebelliousness, then I will pay him a goodly reward, he shall *see seed and have long days*. אשם is a fine or ransom, as in the account of the Philistines, 1 Sam. vi. 3. *Shall see seed*, as Ezekiel says, 'I will increase them with men like a flock' (xxxvi. 37). *Shall have long days*, as it is written, 'The days of my people shall be as the days of a tree' (Is. lxv. 22); and as Zechariah says (viii. 4), 'Each with a staff in his hand for very age.' *And the pleasure of the Lord*, etc.; for he will multiply him, and shew good to him exceedingly. [11] Up to this point the Gentiles have been speaking: now commence the words of God. *For the travail of his soul*, he says, which he bore in exile, *he shall see* good so as to *be satisfied* with it; and *my righteous servant*, i. e. Israel, *by his knowledge*—for all of them will know me, as it is written, Is. xi. 9, 'And the earth shall be filled with the knowledge of the Lord'—*will make many righteous*, as it is said, 'And many nations shall come and say, Come, and let us go up into the mountain of the Lord, and he will teach us of his ways' (Mic. iv. 2); *and their iniquities he will bear*, viz. by his righteousness, so that there will be peace and happiness throughout the whole world. [12] *Therefore*, because he does this, *I will divide him* a portion *with the great*, i. e. a *lot* and inheritance with the old patriarchs. Qamḥi explains, I will divide him the spoil of *many* nations, those, viz., who are to come with Gog to Jerusalem: but, according to the view which I have adopted, רבים signifies *great*. *Because he poured out his soul to die*, i. e. resigned himself to death in captivity, and *was numbered with the transgressors*, i. e. was punished as though he had been one of them himself, and *carried the sin of many*, the sin, namely, which they committed in heaping ill-usage upon him, and *interceded for the transgressors*, to call down blessings upon their land, notwithstanding the fact that they had transgressed against him.

XLIII. R. NAPHTHALI BEN ASHER ALTSCHULER.

Behold my servant. Since I see that unfortunately the Gentiles have built upon this Parashah a heap of vanity, I have undertaken the task of refuting their errors by a true and convincing method in accordance with the teaching of my relation, the great and illustrious Rabbi, Naḥman of Belsitz. 1. If the opinion [of the Christians] is correct, why is he [Jesus] called 'my servant?' is he not by their own arguments God? and if it be replied that he is called 'servant' in reference to the time during which he was still man, why does Isaiah say 'he will be high and exalted,' etc.? for even, by their own accounts, Jesus was never during his whole life in any position of authority: if again it be supposed that the expression relates to what will take place after the Resurrection, even then there is a difficulty; for even the Gentiles say that at that time he will be altogether God, how then could he be called a 'servant?' 2. The words 'so marred was his countenance beyond man' will not apply to this man, for [the Christians] themselves interpret of him the verse, 'Thou art fairer than the children of men,' etc. (Ps. xlv. 3): if then upon one occasion he is termed 'despised,' upon another 'fair,' their arguments refute themselves. 3. By whom are the words, 'As one that hid his face from him,' supposed to be spoken? if by Israel, they are untrue, for on the contrary (as they are well aware) they hardened their faces at him and contemned him ever so many times; if by the nations of the world, they are no less untrue, for the Gentiles were ultimately reconciled to his teaching. 4. The words in verse 4, 'He hath carried our sicknesses,' etc., are assigned, according to the Christian interpretation, to Israel as a confession that they would not acknowledge him as God, and thought that it was God who smote him, and that he had not come to make atonement for sin, as though (which God forbid!) they had been in error in thinking this: a difficulty however then arises, for if he makes no atonement for those who do not receive him as God, how can he 'carry their sicknesses?' 5. How can Israel declare that 'the Lord laid upon him the iniquity of us all,' if those who do not believe in his affliction derive, as the Nazarenes also admit, no advantage from it? If you urge that the words, 'He hath carried,' etc., are spoken by the Nazarenes, there is still a difficulty, for why, after thinking that he was smitten of God, and had not come for the purpose of making atonement by his suffering, did they proceed to accept him as God? and how, when they had followed after him themselves, could they say, 'All we like sheep have gone astray?'

LII. [13] I will now proceed to explain these verses of our own Messiah, who, God willing, will come speedily in our days! I am surprised that Rashi and R. David Qamḥi have not, with the Targum [a], applied them to the Messiah likewise. The prophet says he shall be 'high and exalted and lofty,' expressing the idea under various forms, in order to indicate that his exaltation will be something extraordinary. It is a proof that the Parashah refers to our Messiah, that, alluding to the future Deliverance, the prophet had said before, 'Break forth into joy, ye waste places of Jerusalem' (lii. 9), and 'How beautiful on the mountains,' etc. (ver. 7), and immediately afterwards continues, 'Behold my servant shall prosper,' etc. [14] *As many* nations *were astonished* when they saw Israel's depression, say-

---

[a] Above, p. 5.

ing to one another, How marred is the countenance of each one of them! See, how 'their form is black' (Lam. iv. 8) beyond other men! for the Gentiles think that the features of a Jew are disfigured and unlike those of other men, so that there are even amongst them those who ask whether a Jew has mouth or eye, as, for example, in the country of Persia ('Ibn 'Ezra [b]).
15 *So* will the King Messiah *scatter many nations; at this kings will shut their mouth*, in wonder at the glorious and God-sent successes which will attend him. *For that which was not told them* will *they have seen*,—it had never, namely, entered into their minds that our Messiah was still to come, for they believe that he has appeared already, but both their memory and their expectation will perish! The parallel, *and that which they had not heard*, is added for the sake of emphasis.

LIII. 1 *Who would have believed our report?* If we had heard, so they will say to one another, from others that which we now are beholding, we should never have believed it: *upon whom was the arm of the Lord* ever *revealed* in majesty and greatness, that it should now have been revealed upon a depressed people like this nation of Israel? The question is one expressive of contempt, as though to say, Who is this that it is thus revealed upon? 2 *Before* such greatness came to it, it was in depression, i. e. the name of the Messiah was not recognised in the world, but it *sprang up* out of itself like one of the suckers of a tree, and *like* the marvel of *a root* rising *out of the dry* ground, so Israel was brought up marvellously out of exile: at first it had no comeliness, beauty, or form, *and when we beheld it*, it had *no beauty*, so *how* can the Almighty *devise it* now? Or the meaning may be, that 'it had no beauty, *neither* did we desire it, but, on the contrary, loathed it.' 3 *He was despised* in our eyes, and *the most insignificant* of men (or, *forlorn* of men, because they would not associate with him); *a man of pains*, who passed all his days in anxious dread lest the

[b] Compare p. 44.

Gentiles should appear suddenly and attack them; *and taught of sickness,* being accustomed to have the yoke of exile pass over him. The prophet uses the singular, referring to the Messiah who is their king: thus the Messiah is termed 'despised' as representing Israel. Others think ידוע signifies *broken.* And he was *as though we hid* our *faces from him,* for we would not look at him because of the loathing which we felt for him; *and we accounted him,* i. e. Israel, for nought. [4] *But* now we see that this was not a consequence of his depression, but that he suffered in order that by his sufferings atonement might be made for the whole of Israel, as it is said of the prophet Micah, that the blood issuing from him made atonement for all Israel. The sickness which ought to have fallen upon us was borne by him: the prophet means to say, When Messiah son of Joseph shall die between the gates, and be a marvel in the eyes of creation, why must the penalty he bears be so severe? what is his sin, and what his transgression, except that he will bear the chastisements of Israel, according to the words *smitten of God?* Others consider that the passage speaks of the Messiah who is smitten *now* with the pains of the world to come (as it stands in the *Gemara*[c]), and endures so the sufferings of Israel. *And yet we*—it is Israel who are speaking—*thought* that he had been hated of God. [5] But it was not so: *he was wounded for our transgressions, bruised for our iniquities,* and *the chastisement* which was afterwards to secure *our peace* was *upon him.* [6] *Like sheep,* i. e. like sheep without a shepherd so long as the Messiah had not arrived, *we all went astray;* yet *the Lord let himself be entreated* by him and propitiated for the iniquity of us all, in that he refrained from destroying us. [7] *He was oppressed* under exactors and persecutors, *and answered* with words of treachery, yet he *opened not his mouth,* but endured in silence *like a sheep led to the slaughter, and like a lamb dumb before her shearers.* (The words ולא יפתח פיו refer to the 'sheep.')

[c] Above, p. 34.

[8] *From the confinement* in which he was kept by them, and *from* the *judgment* or sentence of punishment, *he was taken; and who said* or suspected that *his generation* would ever attain such greatness as it has attained now? *for* at first *it was cut off* and exiled *from the land of life*, i. e. the land of Israel; for *for the transgression of my people* had this *stroke* come upon the Messiah. [9] He resigned himself to be buried in whatever manner the wicked might decree, who were always condemning Israel to be murdered, and in accordance with (את) their judgment; and was ready for any form of death (מותים) according to the decision of *the rich*, i. e. of the [wealthy] magistrate. Why, however, should he have been thus punished *although he had done no violence*, etc., except that the Almighty was trying him? The words allude to Israel who are now in exile; though others hold that they allude to the Messiah. את will then signify *with*, the meaning being that when the wicked man dies, the Messiah will die likewise, as though his grave were *with him*: in the same way he will die *with the rich* who accumulates his wealth by robbery, although *he had* himself *done no violence*. [10] I will see, the Almighty now says, whether *his soul* is so devoted to my Holiness as to *return* itself as *a trespass-offering* for all his rebelliousness: if so, I will then pay him his reward; he shall *see seed* in this present world, and *prolong* his *days* in the world to come. אשם is the fine or satisfaction which a man gives to one against whom he has committed some offence. וחפץ ה׳ בידו, by transposing two of the words, *and the business in his hand the Lord shall prosper*. [11] *Of the labour of his own soul* he ate and was satisfied; he did not plunder other people. *By his knowledge he will justify the just;* the King Messiah will mete out right judgment to all who come to be tried before him; and *my servant* will become a prince *over many*—the word עבד being used as in the *Gemara*, 'When I make thee a prince, I make thee also a slave.' *And their iniquities he will bear*, as happens always with the righteous, as it is said (Num. xviii. 1), 'Thou and thy sons shall

carry the iniquity of the sanctuary.' 12 *Therefore I will divide him* a lot and an inheritance *with the great*, i. e. with the patriarchs in the garden of Eden; *and with the mighty*, i.e. with the patriarchs also, *he shall divide spoil*, viz. the spoil of the world to come—the word being used metaphorically—*because he poured out his soul to die*, resigned himself voluntarily to death, *and was numbered with the transgressors*, was punished as though he had been one himself, *and* for the sake of others *carried the sin of many*, and *made intercession for the transgressors*, inasmuch as through his sufferings prosperity came into the world. It may be remarked that Rashi explained this Parashah of the righteous who are in exile, and who endure there suffering and affliction.

XLIV. R. SH'LOMOH DE MARINI.

It might have been expected that, after describing the return of Israel to the Holy City, the prophet would at once have gone on to the prophecy, 'Shout, O barren one,' etc. (liv. 1): it seems, however, that he has interposed the present Parashah, because the words 'Depart ye, depart ye,' etc. (lii. 11) are addressed to the nations left in bondage after Israel's redemption, who as they 'bring meat-offerings unto the Lord' (lxvi. 20) and see the glory and exaltation of his people, will be filled with astonishment, amazed at the wondrous marvel done before their eyes, and eager to understand how this great thing could have happened in the world, for a nation to have been suddenly and in a moment changed from one extreme to another. An account is accordingly here given of the reflections which will occur to them, and of the considerations which their mode of thought will suggest to them on the two topics of Israel's depression and exaltation, and the confession of their own error, until at last they finally acknowledge the truth, justifying God's will in all that he does. The meaning of the reply made by God, after their own words are concluded, will be explained below: the prophet begins by premising in the first three verses an exact statement of the nature of the perfection and happiness which Israel is hereafter to attain, and at which *many will be astonished.* It should be remembered that this prophecy not only speaks at once both of the Israelitish nation and of the Messiah, but at the same time alludes also to any righteous one amongst them who may have been a 'sign and a portent' of what happened to the people at large: all three are styled 'my servant,' as, for instance, Moses (Josh. i. 1), Isaiah himself (xx. 3), and others besides; Israel (xliv. 21); and similarly the King Messiah (xlii. 1): since the text is intended to describe each of these separately, the singular number is used, in order to include every one bearing the same title. With the exception of those which have been specified, viz. the particular righteous individuals, the nation as a whole, and the King Messiah, the Lord's Anointed, who is to reign over them, no one is so designated; but in saying *upon them* (liii. 8), the prophet already lets fall a plural word to shew that he is alluding to the people. We may now proceed to the explanation of the text.

LII. [13] The words in this verse express all that either the mouth can utter or the heart conceive concerning Israel's future perfection and happiness. Our holy Rabbis have revealed to us their meaning in the saying, 'He shall be higher than Abraham, lifted up above Moses, and loftier than the ministering angels,' which shews that his true perfection will consist, first of all, in his perfecting himself as far as possible in the service, the fear, and the love of God, and afterwards in conferring the same perfection upon others as is done by the Almighty himself; by this he will find favour in the eyes of God and man, and will attain that consummate bliss which consists in cleaving to God as closely as possible, and enjoy the brightness of his Shekhinah, and be illumined in the light of his countenance. In this all happiness is embraced.

Now Abraham was the first who strove to perfect himself in the service of God, and to rise higher than any other man in fearing him and loving him, so as even not to withhold from him his only son. Moses, more than any one else (according to the saying, 'Moses was just, and justified many: the justice of many shall cleave unto him'), helped to make others perfect; for through him the Divine Law was given and became a source of instruction for Israel, and everything which we possess now, or which the wise of future generations will acquire, is derived from him. The angels are those who cleave to the Lord of all things, and stand before him in the fruition of the light of his Shekhinah more than any other creatures, in order that they may continue holy and separate from matter. But the king and nation here spoken of will one day ascend far above any of these in elevation and dignity (as it is said, *exceedingly*): for in Abraham's time the Law was not yet given, and what the patriarch did was done of his own righteous choice and upright character—for with the Highest Mind his own was in perfect harmony; but he who lives under the Law, and exerts himself through it to attain that dignity, is greater; and yet even Moses' teaching did not extend to other nations besides Israel. But at the time here spoken of all the nations 'will turn to know the Lord,' and happiness will become universal; and this, too, through Israel's agency, as it is written (lx. 3), 'And Gentiles shall come to thy light and kings to the brightness of thy rising.' And, lastly, the angels cleave to the Lord in virtue of a law of mercy from the Lord (for upon this condition were they created); but Israel will then attain their position through the merits of their own deeds, and while their body and soul are still united, as it is written, 'Thine eyes shall gaze upon the king in his beauty' (xxxiii. 17); and again, 'Eye to eye shall they look on when the Lord returneth to Zion' (lii. 8). [14] It is well known that all the early successes of Israel, and the other events of their history, since the time that they became a nation, did not happen in the natural course of the world; but the people grew victorious and mighty by the aid of signs and wonders; and similarly, when they were brought low as a punishment for their sins, they fell to the very lowest depths, and things happened to them which had never happened to any other nation in the earth. At such a strange history, every one beholding them *will be astonished* and amazed; or, as it is said in *'Ekhâ Rabbâthi*, 'There are three prophets who began their prophecies with *How*...!—Moses, Isaiah, and Jeremiah: Moses said, "How can I carry alone all this people?" (Deut. i. 12); Isaiah, "How hath the faithful city become an harlot!" (i. 21); Jeremiah, "How doth the city sit solitary!" (Lam. i. 1)—like a matron who had three bridesmen, of whom one saw her in her prosperity[a], etc.' In the same way Moses' exclamation was made when he beheld Israel in their prosperity and splendour, Isaiah's when he beheld them in their wantonness, Jeremiah's when he beheld them in their shame; for even the prophets themselves marvelled at Israel's history, wondering how these things could be: how much more then would the Gentiles be surprised! And so it is said, *As many had been astonished at thee*, on account, viz., of all the successes which had befallen thee in the past, *so was his countenance marred beyond man*, etc., for disgrace will fall upon this nation until the end, for in proportion as once their exaltation was great, so will their depression be great likewise when the Lord has hidden his face from them; and *so* also will there be cause for wonder when it reverts to its normal state, and ascends to an elevation higher than any which it had previously enjoyed. [15] *For that which they have not seen*, etc.: these words perhaps allude to the far off nations of the earth who had not heard the fame of them.

LIII. [1] Of the nations in Israel's own land who have seen the actual words of Scripture, the prophet, alluding to the manner in which, devising out of their own heart, they apply them to other events, announces that they will then ask, *Who* was there that *believed* in this distant rumour which we heard? *and the arm of the Lord* (which is said above to have been 'laid bare,' lii. 10), *upon whom has it been revealed?* for we ourselves did not conceive the matter so. (This sense follows from the connexion with the succeeding verses.) [2] The prophet declares how greatly the Gentiles will exert themselves to tell of the

---

[a] *'Ekhâ Rabbâthi*, c. 1: the quotation continues,—'the second in her wantonness, and the third in her shame.'

ignominy and humiliation of the nation, affirming that they could not find that he had either root or branch which would prosper, but that he was both needy and dejected, in want of every comfort. Was it credible that it would be reported that a people which 'the Lord had chosen for himself' would be spoiled and deprived of every worldly enjoyment, and, in addition, suffer exile and be tossed about in the lands of strangers, wandering about in search of bread amid reproaches and confusion of face, as in fact is actually the case? for, from the day that we were exiled from our land, our inheritance 'has been turned to strangers,' and 'we drink our waters for money,' although at the beginning the wells had been our own, and on Israel's account the showers had descended upon the ground out of heaven, and the plenty had extended even to other lands. But now all this is reversed: 'the handmaid is the heir of her mistress' (Prov. xxx. 23), and woe to the children who are exiled from their father's table to eat the bread of tears and drink the poisoned water. And this is the reason why they continually cast us in the teeth, saying, If the truth rests with you, and not with us, why are you left all these years in our hands for us to be rulers over you? Is the Lord's hand shortened that he cannot save or assist you, but has rejected you? for unless we had taken charge of you, and given you room to dwell in, ye would have had none remaining, but would have been all dead from famine and want. Such is the meaning of the expression *as a sucker before him*—Israel's growth was like that of a sucker standing apart, which has no root planted in the earth, but sucks in nourishment out of some other place, i. e. here, the land of the Gentiles. In addition to this, however, he was *as a root out of the dry earth*, sprung up, so to speak, from a poor and bitter root, a 'root bearing gall and wormwood'—an allusion to what seemed to them his destitution and insignificance. In the same strain they continue, *he had no form nor comeliness*—enjoyed no perfection whether of soul or body, no supereminent qualities of mind, no wisdom or riches or glory, no regal or

other dominion; but when *we looked at him*, we found in him nothing pleasant to our eyes, how then, seeing man judges only by the sight of his eyes, *could we* possibly *desire him?*
[3] We saw, moreover, that it was a people spoiled and depressed to such an extent, as to have lost all the vigour and courage necessary for prevailing over its oppressors; was not its heart, like the heart of a woman in travail, 'fearful and afraid' at everything, so that 'the noise of a driven leaf pursued them,' and of their enemies 'a single one would chase a thousand, and two would put ten thousand to flight?' each one of them, too, being *a man of pains and known to sickness*, a man upon whom time and destiny pressed hardly, and who was liable to every accident and every disease. And as we beheld in him all these imperfections, and saw besides that the Lord had *hidden his face from him*, and that signs and wonders were no longer wrought for him as in the days of old, we concluded that *he was despised*, and so we esteemed him not; for in the Babylonian captivity, although there Israel was an afflicted and needy people, still the kings of Babylon were compelled to award recognition to Israel on account of the signs wrought there for Hananiah, Misha'el, and 'Azariah, and for Daniel; and again in the Median captivity, the nations were forced to do the same by the aid of Mordekhai and Esther, and afterwards in the Grecian, by the Hasmonaeans; in this captivity, however, no such sign at all has ever been shewn. Possibly, however, the suffix in ממנו may point back to the Gentiles themselves ('from *us*'), asserting that the reason why they had so greatly erred was because the truth had been hidden from them, and the word of the Lord had never reached them, and they had never seen the light of the Law, but were as the blind groping in darkness. [4] '*But* the case was not as we thought: on the contrary, *he carried our sicknesses*, for it was we who were really sick, and the ultimate cause of his sufferings, and all the punishments spoken of, should have come rightly upon us, for they sinned merely by accident, whereas we have sinned in accordance with our inmost nature,

since they possessed a law of truth, to which we had no access.' This subject has been treated by the Rabbis in the Midrash on Cant. i. 6, 'Look not down on me, because I am black:'—'He carried the sickness, and bare the penalty of his iniquity'—as the text says (Amos iii. 2), 'Only you have I known of all the families of the earth; therefore will I visit upon you all your iniquities;' for Israel in the midst of the nations is compared to the heart in the midst of the body, for as the heart, being of a more equable constitution and purer than the other members, is the seat of the living soul, so Israel in its very root and substance is the seat of Divine truth. Accordingly, whatever happens to Israel as compared with the other nations, is analogous to what happens to the heart as compared with the other members of the body; so that, as from the purity of its blood, and abundance of breath, the heart has a clear and quick perception of any emotion which may strike it—whether it be anxiety, or sorrow, or fear, or resentment, or hatred, or love, or an alteration in climate or food, or change of position, or sleeping or waking, acting upon it—so it is more easily affected than the other members, as though it were something as light as a hair, and is consequently exposed to more diseases than they are, although at the same time far stronger and better able speedily to repel anything which may attack it (for in other parts of the body it is only possible to arrest a disease after the lapse of a considerable time), being for this purpose endowed with stronger health than the other organs. Similarly, Israel's position among the Gentiles is such that the Shekhinah is to them what the living soul is to the heart; and as the strength of the heart is necessary in order that by its aid the soul may reside in the body, so this nation must needs have perfect health, in order that through it the Shekhinah may reside in the world. Thus, on account of the purity and strength, which are characteristic of Israel, sickness and punishment will assail him, causing him to be continually in suffering and exile; and this is the reason why their iniquities will be 'visited upon them' without delay, in order, viz., that the sickness may not prevail over them until the measure of it which will produce complete destruction has been filled up. Such then is the sense of, 'You only have I known;' for in proportion to the degree of perfection in them are they 'known' of the Lord. This is the cause why, when they even sin but slightly, they are still punished: the Shekhinah will not take up its abode in them unless they are clear from every sin; they are therefore speedily sensible of their penalty. It also explains why Israel experiences such sicknesses, and why they are restored and purified so quickly, in order, viz., that the sin may not linger among them until it becomes confirmed, as it does among the Gentiles, of whom it is said (Gen. xv. 16), 'The iniquity of the Amorite is not yet full.' All this will in time be revealed to the nations, and they will then confess, saying, '*Surely he carried our sicknesses;*' it was we who were really sick, though we did not perceive it, whereas he, by his natural quickness, perceived it readily; thus the sickness speedily left him, and he was prepared to receive his cure. In addition, however, to the sore blow thus decreed against him for the purpose of blotting out transgression, we ourselves made our hand heavy upon him, and added to his pain, and this *our pain he bare*, or, in the words of the Psalmist's complaint, 'Him whom thou hast smitten they persecute, and tell of the pains of them that thou hast wounded' (Ps. lxix. 27), to which the Divine reply is, '*I* was wroth but a little, and *they* helped forward the affliction' (Zech. i. 15). The omission of the word הוא is noted by the Masora [b], in order to form an allusion to the passage, 'I am with him in affliction' (Ps. xci. 15), and, 'In all their affliction he was afflicted' (Is. lxiii. 9), meaning the congregation of Israel, as though God himself sympathised in the sufferings of his people. Yet we *thought him stricken*—thought that he would never be healed, while, in fact,

[b] Some MSS. insert הוא before מכאבנו: and in several editions (see De Rossi, or the *Minḥath Shai*) there occurs the marginal note הוא קְרי ולא כתיב.

his sickness was the very cause of his cure—*smitten of God and afflicted:* whereas we ourselves were all the time smiting him most cruelly with our own hands. Such are their reflections on the first statement about Israel's humiliation. [5] On the second statement (contained in the words 'despised and forlorn of men'), relating to his insignificance, they confess the truth in the words, *wounded for our transgressions*, admitting that all the sin and imperfection inherent in this people was owing to the wickedness of the nations amongst whom they were mixed, and who had become a snare to them; that from the time when they first became a nation in the land of Egypt, they had been defiled by the idols of the Egyptians, and after they had entered into Canaan, they had followed the ways of the Amorite, the heathen whom they preserved alive becoming 'pricks in their eyes, and thorns in their sides,' and seducing them to serve their idols; that afterwards, when they were in exile and mingled among the Gentiles, they had learnt their works; indeed, had they not swerved to the right hand or to the left of the words of the Law, they would not have had such power over them, as it is written (Deut. iv. 6), 'And ye shall keep and do them, for this is your wisdom and your understanding before the eyes of the nations,' etc. And this is what is alluded to in the words, 'Look not down upon me, because I am black, because the sun,' etc. (Cant. i. 6). And in *despising* him, for being devoid of all vigour and courage, they noticed that this was all decreed upon him, as it is written, 'I will bring faintness into their heart in the lands of their enemies,' etc. (Lev. xxvi. 36); and again, 'How could one chase a thousand, etc., except their Rock had sold them and the Lord had delivered them?' (Deut. xxxii. 30.) Thus Israel's depression caused such a change in their relative position that, as the one rose the other sank, as it is written, 'And it shall come to pass that, when thou shalt have the dominion, thou shalt break his yoke from off thy neck' (Gen. xxvii. 40). And all this may be understood from the language here, *The chastisement of our peace was upon him, and by his stripes we are healed.* 6 They will then, the prophet proceeds, be amazed that they had never perceived their error: if, indeed, all the other nations in the world had been observing one religion, and Israel another, and they had enjoyed prosperity while Israel had met with the reverse, then it might have been possible for them to suppose wrongly that the truth rested with them and that Israel was in error. On the contrary, however, the different nations and also their religions are divided amongst themselves, each repudiating the authority of their neighbour's, and, at the same time, they each enjoy dominion and power in the world, so that neither they themselves nor the kingdoms over which they hold sway can be any guarantee or sign of the truth of their religion; and the decline and fall of Israel's sovereignty can afford no argument that true religion is not to be found among them: the more so, inasmuch as, though they attempt to raise unfair charges against it, all nations practically admit the divine origin of their faith. And so they say here, *All we like sheep went astray*, alleging in proof of this that we *turned each to his own way*,—we did not all agree in one opinion or one faith, but repudiated each others' convictions; the reason, however, why we remained in prosperity, whereas Israel was in distress, was because *the Lord laid on him the iniquity of us all.* The explanation of these words is, that the cause of Israel's being exiled from their land was properly their own iniquities; but the cause which prolonged the withdrawal of the Divine blessing and the contumely of the world, was their idolatry; unquestionably, if all the Gentiles had now been calling upon the name of the Lord, to serve him with one accord, the world would have been regenerated; but his name being profaned amongst them is the occasion of pain and harm accruing to Israel while they are in exile. This condition of things is alluded to by our Rabbis in an Haggádah (*B'râkhoth*, § 1):—It is reported in the name of R. Me'ir, that at the hour of sunrise, when all the kings of the East and of the West place their crowns upon their heads, and bow down to the sun, forthwith the Almighty is provoked: it is asserted to be a sign of his provocation that at the same moment the red comb of the cock is changed to white. The meaning of this is explained by the commentator [Rashi] to be, that during the single moment of his provocation an eclipse takes place in the world below, and the greatest distress accrues from it upon all living; in its most poignant form, however, it rests upon Israel in particular, who, consequently, are the most deeply affected by it. [7] Besides this, however, in consequence of our error *he was oppressed* and spurned by us all (for there is no hatred like the hatred of religion), every one who bore the name of God's 'servant' being seized for us to punish him with sore chastisements, because he would not acknowledge our doctrines, and we even withheld from him permission to speak, so that he could *not open his mouth* at all for the purpose of explaining and demonstrating the principles of his faith: truth we cast down to the ground, and the false religion flourished and spread to such an extent that, *as a sheep led to the slaughter*, all those who came forward to oppose it, or to call in question its principles, were slain with indignity by hundreds and thousands, in order that its adherents might persevere unshaken. Moreover, we devised schemes of wickedness against them to plunder their goods, so that they became *as a lamb dumb before her shearers*, and *opened not* their *mouth*, for none can plead his case with effect against those stronger than himself. [8] We, moreover, attacked him with our arguments when we beheld this people *taken from sovereignty and from judgment;* for in the days of old it was called the people of the Lord, the Divine providence attended it continually, and so great was the love displayed for it, that God ordained that thrice in the year it should appear at Jerusalem in order that its members might submit themselves before him, as a son in excessive love before his father, and any one of the other nations who touched it was 'like a man touching the pupil of his eye.' At length, however, God removed his own from under his hand,

and Israel was smitten with great and sore judgments, and now we see it disgraced still more, for, instead of loving it, he has rejected it, and its enemies, or whoever else may desire to mock it, trample it under foot and devour it, none offering 'to plead his cause that he might be bound up' (Jer. xxx. 13), or to avenge him. And if that generation had prolonged its existence in the world, and not been wholly brought to an end, *who would declare it*, or think anything of it? for 'wherein was he accounted of in our eyes?' it seemed rather as if Israel no longer existed, for we thought he was *cut off from the land of the living*, ever saying, 'There is no salvation for him in God' (Ps. iii. 2); he is left however in the world in order not to become a proverb to us. And when he attempted to convince his fellow-citizens that he should not be so treated and punished, we all exclaimed, *For the transgression of my people there is a stroke upon them*—a saying which is the reverse of the text (Zeph. iii. 6 f.), 'I have cut off nations, their towers are destroyed: only fear thou me, only receive instruction!'
[9] It is possible that the subject of *gave* may be 'my people' in the last verse, the Gentiles here declaring that they had treated Israel ignominiously in two respects: for (1) Israel *made its grave with the wicked*, every man among them being buried with the burial of the wicked, 'his flesh' being 'pained upon him,' and his soul going to destruction; and (2) they esteemed him as *the rich in his death*, for the expression 'rich' is used generally as a term of reproach for one who trusts and glories in his riches, as it is written, 'And the rich man answereth roughly' (Prov. xviii. 23), 'The wealth of the rich is his strong city' (verse 11), and similarly elsewhere. The meaning thus is, that this nation, which is fired with the lust of gold, and of accumulating riches not by just means, but by robbery and fraud, will have to relinquish all their gains before they have finished half their days, and that their latter end will be so ignoble that they will be thought to have been wicked before both heaven and earth. *Because he did no violence*, etc., i. e.

because, in keeping the Law, he erred neither in intention nor in act, and his end justified his beginning, shewing that Israel had been the choicest of the human race, now the cause had appeared for which the Almighty had so long confined him in exile. 10 In truth so little had God rejected or abhorred Israel, that his *pleasure* and delight had always been in him: it was only in order to purify him that *he bruised him*, and in order to do good to him in the end that *he made him to be sick*. So our Rabbis teach in *B'râkhoth*: Said Rabbâ, Whomsoever the Lord hath pleasure in, he bruiseth him with chastisements; for is it not said that 'the Lord was pleased'—not to consume him utterly, but merely—'to bruise and sicken him,' in order that he might turn to him with all his heart? for those who are bruised with suffering are nearer to God than other men, as it is written, 'With him that is of a bruised and humble spirit I do dwell' (Is. lvii. 15); and, 'A heart broken and bruised, O God, thou wilt not despise' (Ps. li. 17). The sick person whose material strength is thus exhausted is strong in intellect, and he is protected by the Lord,—as the Rabbis say[c], 'The Sh'khinah is above the pillow of the sick;' and for the same reason the physical strength of this people was prostrated, in order that its heart might be bowed down, and that it might be able to cast off its unclean imagination, and be left pure and innocent (as it is written, i. 25, 'And I will purify as with lye thy dross, and remove all thy tin'). Thus, *if its soul makes a trespass-offering*, i. e. if it accepts its trial in a spirit of love, and feels that this is the reason for which it is sent into captivity, and 'rejoiceth not unto exultation' among the Gentiles, nor is mingled with them, and forgets not Jerusalem, but prays continually that it may still return to 'take its part in the Lord's inheritance,' and to serve him with an undivided heart, then *he will see seed, have long days, and the Lord's pleasure*

---

[c] Thalm. Bab., *N'darim*, 40[a].

will prosper in his hand. In these words are described three great consummations, for which we now are looking. The first of these is the complete redemption at the time of the Resurrection, when 'the heart of the fathers will be turned to the children, and the heart of the children to their fathers' who perished miserably, being martyred for the sacredness of God; all these will then behold one another and delight themselves together. The second is, the assurance that they will never again go into captivity, but will prolong their days, as it is written, 'The youth shall die an hundred years old' (lxv. 20); and again, 'He hath swallowed up death for ever' (xxv. 8): the same idea is expressed by the Rabbis when they say [d] that they will never return to their dust, but that after many years have passed over them, the substance of their bodies will be made as pure as heaven itself, and again become incorruptible—as is detailed at length by R. Abraham ha-Levi in his exposition of the Blessing at the new Moon. And the third is, that by the agency of Israel all other nations will become worthy to 'know the Lord, and to serve him with one accord,' and that in his light they will all see the light of the truth. [11] The text bears witness that so it was: in particular, of the just who were to be found at all periods in Israel, and who were put to death in the cause of truth, not one ever felt anxiety, or seemed to be sensible of all that he was suffering, but accepted it with gladness, in the anticipation of this exalted perfection. *Out of the travail of his soul he will see,* considering, viz. that all is for his advantage, *and be satisfied,* and find pleasure in the thought that, as Scripture says (Prov. xxxi. 25), 'Strength and honour are her clothing, and she laugheth at the future,' i. e. the soul of the righteous sings and rejoices even while still under the weight of affliction and misery, because it looks hopefully forward to the future, to the day when it will receive its full reward, and 'find its delight in the Lord:' and hence also its mind rests contented,

[d] Thalm. Bab., *Sanhedrin*, 92[a].

even while united with the body in this life. Similarly, Israel in the travail of its soul will *look and be satisfied*, watching for the day of Deliverance. *He will justify my righteous servant by means of many*, i.e. he will take an example from what happens to the righteous in his generation, who, although knowing well that he is perfectly upright, and a servant of God, still passes his days in pains and in the midst of many and sore calamities. Such, indeed, is the life of the majority of the just; but their mind is appeased by the recollection that all is to conduce to their ultimate happiness, and that the glorious promises cannot be realised except through suffering; for 'reproofs of correction are the way to life' (Prov. vi. 23). To the same purport Scripture says, 'Who is the man that will live, and not see death continually?' for even during life he is consumed away through the trouble of delivering his soul from the power of the grave. This is not possible otherwise, as it is said, 'If a man dies he will live, and if he lives he will die,' whence it follows that the fate of the righteous will befall Israel as well (as it is written, 'I am become a portent unto many'); and hence he knows that he will never attain this great consummation except by first bearing the yoke of a protracted exile. He will *bear their iniquities*, as the righteous bears those of his own generation. 12 Because, then, he hath done all this, *therefore I will allot him* this happiness *with many*, for the numbers of his children will be multiplied, and all the Gentiles in whose midst they are left will stand in awe of his righteousness: *with the mighty he shall divide spoil*, when he rises, namely, to a dignity superior to that of man—as our Rabbis say [e], 'Before the righteous the angels will sing songs,' for he who 'divides spoil' is in the enjoyment of something which did not before fall to his share. And this privilege will be is, *because he poured out his soul to die*, resigning himself to suffer martyr-

[e] Thalm. Bab., *Bâbha Bathra*, 75[a].

dom for the sanctity of the Name of Heaven, and so was awarded the right of acquiring a higher life than other men; and because he *carried the sin of many and interceded for the transgressors*, praying continually that the world might be restored through the establishment of the kingdom of the Almighty, and that all men might call upon the name of the Lord, to serve him with a whole heart. He was just and justified many: therefore the justice of the many shall cleave unto him, and he shall receive a reward equivalent to them all[f].

---

[f] Compare pp. 273, 287.

XLV. R. YIẒḤAQ LOPEZ.

The Nazarene:—Hast thou not magnified thy tongue above thy name in saying that in our hands are scales of deceit, and that they have deceived us, and prevented our understanding from comprehending mysteries? is it not rather you yourselves who are deaf and dumb, and who grope about like the blind? Behold here, now, is the conclusion of my words: 'We have sought it out; so is it:' every mouth amongst us confesses that all your words are 'dead flies which cause a stink,' whilst we possess the 'apothecary's ointment' which poureth forth concerning 'the word spoken by the king,' and that unto which 'his commandment reacheth,' so that even the shades below will be sensible of it, how much more 'they that dwell in houses of clay,' when their companions rise up against them, exclaiming, Surely we are not guilty; we are true men, seeing that we believe in Jesus our Messiah. I will now, therefore, bring thee proofs from the prophecy of Isaiah how he came and endured great sufferings, and afterwards died for the redemption of his creatures who were in Gehenna, and rescued them from the hand of Satan who was assailing them; if, therefore, thou art willing to acknowledge the truth, thou wilt find thyself unable to reply to all that I shall adduce. The prophecy is as follows.

LII. [13]*Behold my servant*, etc. Of whom are these words spoken except of Jesus? and the saying of your Rabbis upon this verse, 'He shall be higher than Abraham,' etc., although it is applied by them to the King Messiah, how is it possible to adapt its language to any child of man? for of Moses it is said that 'no prophet ever arose in Israel like him;' and there is no essence loftier than that of the angels except the Divine: you cannot, then, apply the verse to any but our Messiah, who is God and man. *As many*, etc., i. e. notwithstanding his exalted dignity, yet many were astonished at him, because *his countenance was so marred;* in other words, because his fleshly appearance was marred by his sufferings, and by the death which ensued upon his crucifixion. *So will he sprinkle*, etc., i. e. rule over *many nations*, and *kings will shut their mouths at him* when they see his miracles.

LIII. [1] *Who believed?* etc. to be understood in its usual sense. *Despised*, and *a man of pains*, viz. on account of the many sufferings and indignities which you heaped upon him. מוכה אלהים, as though to say that *God* was *smitten and afflicted* by bearing our distresses. *By his stripes we are healed*, i. e. by his death, for by it the iniquity common to all was atoned for, on account of which all mankind were liable to Gehenna. *All we like sheep*, etc., for, before he came, all the children of the world were in error on account of the iniquity that was in their hands; but when he came, *the Lord laid on him the iniquity of all* his creatures. *As a sheep*, etc., i. e. in his love and goodwill towards us, he endured death for the redemption of our souls. *He was cut off from the land of the living*, and *for the transgression of his people* death and suffering came *upon him*. *He made his grave with the wicked*, because, when they crucified him, two thieves were hung beside him, he being in their midst. *The Lord was pleased to bruise him*, etc., in order, namely, to cancel the spiritual penalty which had passed upon all for the sin of our first parent. Now, therefore, open thine eyes and see how, throughout the Parashah, the prophet speaks of Jesus our Messiah in a manner which thou wilt not be able to refute.

THE JEW:—Thou Rock of all the ages, wherefore wilt thou chasten us for ever, and punish us through such long years, that there is none left amongst us to stand up before the heathen? O reveal, now, thy glory upon us, that all the nations may know that thou art the God of gods, and that all those may be put to confusion who make their boast in idols, like thee [O Nazarene] and thy companions in error, when thou declarest that this Parashah refers to Jesus your Messiah: does not this opinion of thine contain flaws without number, which in the eyes of reason ruin it utterly? Since, however, it is from the verses of this Parashah more than from all the rest of Scripture that you gain strength for your arguments against us, do not lay it to my charge if I dwell upon it at some length, in order that you may understand how all your assertions are but words of vanity, and as a wind that passeth by bringing nothing with it, that the prophet's words will not, for countless reasons, bear the meaning which you would assign to them, and that they do not in the remotest degree allude to Jesus. Our Rabbis offer two explanations of this Parashah,—some referring it to Messiah our righteousness, as, for instance, Yonathan ben Uzziel, who is followed by many of our other doctors in the various Midrashim, and Naḥmanides; while others, as R. Joseph Qamḥi, and his son, R. David Qamḥi, and Rashi, apply it to Israel, who, they say, is here called by the Almighty his 'servant,' as often elsewhere in the same prophet. In support of the latter view it is pointed out further that the preceding and subsequent Parashahs are strongly in its favour: immediately before (lii. 12) Isaiah was predicting the gathering together of the exiles of Israel, and immediately afterwards the Parashah beginning, *Shout, O barren one* (liv. 1), is filled with glorious promises descriptive of the same events: it is urged, therefore, that the Parashah in the middle must of necessity be explained of Israel likewise. And this explanation is the right one; for even those who interpret it as a whole of the Messiah (as Yonathan ben Uzziel), nevertheless admit that some parts refer to Israel: such also was the opinion of the other doctors alluded to, there being indeed numerous obstacles in the way of explaining it in any other way. But in addition to this, you will find yourself, on many other grounds, unable to succeed in the attempt to explain it of Jesus. 1. The prophet says, *My servant* ישכיל, but how can this apply to God? if you suppose it to mean 'shall have understanding or knowledge,' then God, just because he is God, is knowledge itself, and knows all things from eternity and to eternity. How, then, could the prophet utter such a prediction of him, as though he were now deficient in understanding, and the time would one day come when he would acquire it? And if you suppose it to mean 'shall prosper' (as 1 Sam. xviii. 14), was his prosperity or success, then, carnal or spiritual? for 'successful' and 'not successful' cannot be predicated rightly [of God], besides which we know, from the history of his last moments, that Jesus did not 'have success.' 2. How can you suppose that God calls him his 'servant?' how could God call one who was of the self-same substance with himself his 'servant?' are not 'master' and 'servant' two distinct terms, each exclusive of the other? and if you say that there are three Persons, but one God in 'Substantia,' 'Potentia,' and 'Habitus,' yet how can you call the King of the highest potentates a 'servant?' Nor can you reply that this word is used relatively to his manhood, because the expressions 'shall understand,' 'shall be high and exalted, and lofty exceedingly,' are not applicable to his manhood, but only to what you consider to be his Godhead; accordingly, 'Ibn 'Ezra remarks that the expression *shall understand* does not suit the body, because the body, even whilst living, does not possess such an attribute: this being the case, then, it can only apply to his soul; in other words, to the Godhead. And if you urge that he is called a 'servant' with reference to the time during which he was in the form of man, and that he was made God and King only after his death, then is not the saying of Solomon fulfilled in him, 'Under three things doth the earth tremble . . . . *under a servant, when he becometh king?*' (Prov. xxx. 22.) And how can he have undergone the change and accident of death, when the prophet himself says,

'I the Lord change not?' (Mal. iii. 6.) Thus you refute yourself. 3. How can the words *shall be high*, etc., which relate evidently to future time, be made to adapt themselves to him? Tell me when this exaltation took place: was it while he occupied the position of a man, in things pertaining to the body, or while he was God? if you suppose the former, you then omit to mention that Jesus never was elevated or exalted at all; so that the words here were never fulfilled in him—on the contrary, he was condemned to death, exactly as might happen to any other unimportant person, and as in fact you contend is foretold by Isaiah himself—while, if you suppose the latter, then the announcement is an idle one, and why should the prophet have made it? for God, just because he is God, is for ever 'high and exalted, and inhabiteth eternity' (lvii. 15): how then can a period be predicted when he is to *become* high and exalted? And who, further, ever supposed that originally God was lowly and humble, and that he only afterwards would be exalted? is not such a supposition contrary to reason? 4. The prophet, speaking in the second person, says 'at *thee*' (lii. 14); but if he had been alluding to Jesus, he must have written 'at *him*:' for Isaiah is here addressing the persons to whom the prophecy was delivered. 5. He says, *So marred was his countenance*, etc.: now elsewhere you assert that the prophet calls him a 'flourishing olive tree, beautiful with well-favoured fruit' (Jer. xi. 16), and that David calls him 'fairer than the children of men' (Ps. xlv. 3), but now you maintain the reverse: at the same time the language here accords closely with the words below, *He had no form*, etc., and, *A man of pains*, etc.,—expressions which, one and all, teach that he was naturally troubled by melancholy, and was also of weak constitution and feeble frame. The facts, however, were otherwise; for I know well that it is not recorded anywhere, either in your own New Testament, or in the writings of your wise men, that Jesus was thus afflicted; he is always described as young and handsome, 'ruddy, and withal of a beautiful countenance' (1 Sam. xvi. 12).

Moreover, his constitution was so regular that he never had a pain—not even a headache—up to the day of his death: how then can you speak of him as 'a man of pains' and 'known of sickness,' phrases which would only be applicable to one who was constantly ailing? If you answer that these words have reference to his death, every one's countenance is altered when he is dead, so that he could not, on this account alone, be described as 'marred beyond men:' moreover, the expressions in question belong to one who is still living, since the sufferings which he endured in the hour of death would not be spoken of as a 'sickness,' but rather as a 'blow' (1 Kings ii. 25, 29) or mishap falling upon him. 6. It is said that he *carried our sicknesses and bare our pains*: expressions which you cannot explain of the sufferings borne by souls in Gehenna for the sin of their first parent, whence Jesus might have released them; because, forsooth, our first parent suffered for his sin a spiritual penalty, going down to Gehenna and remaining there: this, however, I cannot concede, for there is no mention to be found of it, either in the command given to Adam, or in the penalty or curse imposed upon him[a]. The words 'thou shalt surely die,' from which you derive the idea of a spiritual penalty, do not necessarily imply this: for we find the same phrase used upon other occasions where you cannot possibly so interpret it; does not Nathan say to David, in the affair of Bathsheba, 'The child that is born to thee *shall surely die*,' though it is certain that the child was never condemned to Gehenna? and Abimelech said, 'Whoso toucheth this man or his wife shall *surely be put to death*' (Gen. xxvi. 11), though it is evident that, not being God, he was not passing sentence of spiritual death. The same phenomenon occurs often; the word being doubled for the sake of emphasis. And even, though I were to allow that Adam suffered spiritual punishment for his sin, yet what did the men who came after him do to merit Gehenna? they did not sin

[a] Above, p. 156.

themselves, and 'the soul of the son shall not bear the iniquity of the father:' if, again, Adam's soul sinned, but Abraham's clave unto the Lord, and kept his commandments (as it is written, Gen. xxvi. 5), how could the Divine judgment condemn them both equally, and cause the 'righteous to be as the wicked?' And although, further, I were to allow that Adam's punishment was a spiritual one, and that its consequences affected his descendants, still, since the Almighty is pleased to accept atonement for iniquity, is his infinite hand 'shortened that it cannot save' for men to imagine he must clothe himself in flesh and endure sufferings? Is it not contrary to reason that justice should call for punishment upon him against whom others have sinned rather than upon the sinner? And if you contend that it was right that some one single individual of the human race should receive the penalty upon himself, and so atone for all mankind, it might have been expected that some prophet or wise man should have been the victim, rather than that God should slay his own Son: who ever heard of a king, who, when his servants had offended him, slew his own son to make atonement for their sin? In addition, however, to all the weak points which have been here enumerated, the supposition that the Almighty (who is infinite power) should take flesh, and so become finite, refutes itself. Other objections, stated by R. Ḥasdai [Crescas], I do not wish here to dwell upon. But how can you reconcile it with your creed that Jesus should be said to 'carry sickness and bear pain?' it is inconceivable that God should ever endure Gehenna, and if you think that the words may be applied to his death and the sufferings which were inflicted upon him, then there is still a difficulty in the term employed, for death is never spoken of as 'sickness.' The expression *smitten of God* is also difficult to explain; for it would seem to imply that God smote himself. And from the phrase, *The Lord laid upon him*, etc., it follows that he must be the patient and God the agent: it is clear, then, that the Almighty is the Master, and he the subordinate. The same conclusion follows from verse 10, *The Lord was pleased*, etc.: your contention, then, that he is God cannot be a just one. 7. The language in verse 8, *He was taken from sovereignty* (1 Sam. ix. 17) *and from judgment* is inapplicable to him; for Jesus (as I have shewn in § 15) was never at any time invested with authority or dominion: and what follows is no less unsuitable, viz. that he was *cut off from the land of life*—i. e. according to the most natural meaning, from the land of Israel, which is so designated—for it is well known that Jesus met his death in Jerusalem. And if you prefer to explain the expression of the *glory* in Paradise, from which he was cut off (inasmuch as that, too, is called the land of life), even this resource will not avail; because you yourselves believe that he rose again the third day, and ascended up to heaven, and sat down on the right hand of God, where he liveth for ever and ever: if, then, he is still in the 'land of the living,' he cannot be said to have been cut off from it. A difficulty also arises on account of the word למו ('to *them*'), which shews that Isaiah was referring to more than one, since otherwise he must have written לו ('to *him*'), as, in fact, is actually done by some of those who would falsely mislead you. If you answer that he used the plural number, in order to point to both the manhood and the Godhead at once, then you are corrupting your own faith, in which it is a fundamental article that Jesus did not endure suffering and death in respect of his Godhead, but only in respect of his manhood, or, as you term it, his *humanitas*. 8. The ninth verse is not applicable to him; for your theory that 'his grave' means his death, and that this took place amongst the wicked Israelites, has nothing to support it: had the prophet intended this, he must have said 'his death,' since it is not recorded in your books that he was in any sense maltreated at the time of his burial. Moreover, this prophecy would then contradict another prophecy of Isaiah's respecting the Messiah, in which he says that his 'resting-place shall be glorious' (xi. 10)—a passage which you have corrupted, your false guides rendering it, 'And his grave shall be glorious[b]:' the expression, *and the rich in his death*, is likewise unsuitable. 9. If Jesus was God, and consented to suffer for the purpose, as you maintain, of rescuing the souls of his creatures, it could not be said that *the Lord was pleased to bruise him*, as though it had been God's will to do this; for what is done without any assignable cause is attributed to 'pleasure,' and not what is done for some definite purpose. How, too, will the next words afford a congruous sense? if he was God, then his happiness could not depend upon a covenant or condition; how then can he suitably be supposed to receive a reward? are not all such expressions applicable to men rather than to God? And as to the promise that he should *see seed* and *lengthen days*, was it not his fate to die in the midst of his days, when thirty-three years old, and without any children? If you answer that his 'seed' means those who follow after his doctrine, the word used is inappropriate; for you will not find in the whole twenty-four books of the Old Testament that disciples are ever called 'seed:' they are only called 'children' or 'sons,' as Deut. xi. 19, 2 Kings ii. 3 al.: in this case, therefore, he should have written, 'he shall see *sons*,' for by 'seed' are denoted those who proceed literally out of a man's loins; and how could it be said of God that he had seed in this sense? And if you suppose that the 'length of days' mentioned by the prophet alludes to the Godhead, which lives for ever and ever, no need for Isaiah to have assured him of this: we know well that the Creator is the First and the Last, and that his years never come to an end, and that he, moreover, watches and observes both that which has been and that which is to be: there is nothing, therefore, either novel or appropriate in affirming long life except of flesh and blood. Besides, how could it be said that *the pleasure of the Lord* should prosper *in his hand*? Such a phrase as this could be used only of what a man performs through the agency of some one else, not of what he performs in his own person: the 'travail of his

[b] In the Vulgate, 'Et erit *sepulcrum* eius gloriosum.'

soul' is also an unsuitable expression, for you yourselves hold that his Divinity never endured travail or suffering, but only his manhood. 10. The words in verse 12 are likewise inapplicable to him; for even though you interpret *I will allot him a portion with the many* of the nations who accepted his doctrine and religion, what will you make of the clause which follows? you will not find it stated anywhere that Jesus carried on war or 'divided spoil;' and to refer the expression to his Divinity will only give rise to the unsuitable idea that the Creator should support himself by the division of spoil [c]. It is said, too, that he *interceded for the transgressors:* but, if he was God himself, with whom was he to intercede? Nor, lastly, can you reconcile with the facts what is here said, that he *poured out his soul to die*, which implies that he met death voluntarily, and without any compulsion: for I have already shewn in this very section that he died against his will. It is clear, now, from these ten considerations, that in accordance with the right interpretation and the true meaning of the prophecy, it is impossible to explain it, as you do, of Jesus your Messiah.

I will therefore proceed to put before you the correct explanation, as it has been given by R. David Qamḥi and Rashi and other expositors, which is to the effect that it alludes to Israel, and specially to the time when our exiles will be gathered together: the proof of this lies in what I have already stated, namely, that both before and after it the predictions delivered by the prophet relate to our redemption: he says, for example, 'Awake, awake, put on thy strength, O Zion,' etc. (li. 9, 17), 'How beautiful are the feet,' etc. (lii. 7), 'The Lord hath redeemed Jerusalem,' etc. (vers. 9–11), and then immediately breaks off into *Behold my servant*, etc. When the Parashah is ended, he again resumes the same strain, exclaiming, 'Shout, O barren one,' etc. (liv. 1), the sequel of which relates entirely to the period of our redemption. It will thus be clear to any one

---

[c] Cf. above, p. 124 *top*.

of intelligence that the Parashah before us must refer to the same occasion: it narrates, in fact, the comments made by the Gentiles on the nation in general, and on the righteous in particular, whose reproach and disgrace they had witnessed before, but whose exaltation they will then behold.

LII. [13] Accordingly the prophet begins, *Behold my servant*, i. e. Israel, who are so termed by him countless times besides, as xliv. 2, etc., *shall prosper*, emerging from the depression in which he had previously been. [14] *As many were astonished at thee*, when they saw thy depression, when your countenance and form was changed in consequence of the subjection in which you were held, *so will he scatter many nations*, i. e. rule over them with great power, his exaltation being such that *kings will open their mouths at him* in amazement when they behold his greatness, forthwith exclaiming (LIII. [1]) *Who believed our report* that this despised people would ever rise to such greatness? [3] *He was despised*, etc., viz. in consequence of the miseries which you ignominiously inflicted upon us: so great was the contempt in which we were held by you, that any one who wished to reproach or insult another called him a Jew: besides this, you also expel us from your lands. Many of you, too, *hide* your *faces* so as not to look at the countenance of a Jew: to do this is considered by you to be 'an iniquity for the judge.' And do not raise an objection at the expression, *a man of pains*, as though it referred only to an individual; because our nation is repeatedly spoken of as a man—for instance, 1 Sam. xvii. 2, Judg. xxi. 1, and often besides[d]: the prophet adds, lastly, that *he was* so *despised* that *we esteemed him not*. [4] You however will say, '*He carried our sicknesses and bare our pains:* previously, indeed, we imagined that sufferings had been sent upon Israel, as a punishment by the Almighty, and therefore *thought him stricken, smitten of God, and afflicted:* this was not so, however; they were endured by him on our account.' Or we

---

[d] See p. 175.

may take another line, and suppose that these are the words of Israel spoken by them with reference to the righteous—whose case they thoroughly suit: they will then express Israel's confession that the sufferings which they ought for our iniquities to have endured were borne by the righteous for their sake.
[5] Accordingly, Isaiah continues, *He was wounded for our transgressions*, etc., *and by his stripes we are healed*, i. e. by the stripes of the righteous we are forgiven. [6] Then the transgressors in Israel will say, *All we like sheep went astray*, we followed the stubbornness of our heart; *but the Lord laid upon them*, the righteous, *the iniquity of us all.* [7] These righteous, dwelling in the midst of the Gentiles, were *oppressed and afflicted:* their enemies murdered and persecuted them, and, but for the mercy of God, would have exterminated them altogether: [8] all day long they *oppressed* them with cruel judgments; and *who can tell* all the vexations and sufferings endured by each successive *generation* in exile for the holiness of God's name? *for he was cut off out of the land of life,*—alluding to the numbers of the righteous who were persecuted to death in the midst of their days; *for the transgression of my people was the stroke upon them*, i. e. the plagues which ought to have fallen on Israel for their transgressions came upon the righteous instead: accordingly, the prophet says למו, which is plural. [9] *He made his grave with the wicked,*—referring to the righteous who were slain like guilty persons condemned to death by the sentence of a court, and afterwards flung out unburied for the dogs; although he uses the word 'grave,' which might seem to imply that they were actually buried, yet we may suppose that their burial was like that of Jehoiakim, king of Judah, who was 'buried' by being 'drawn along and cast outside the walls of Jerusalem' (Jer. xxii. 19): thus the meaning will be, that as the wicked who are sentenced to execution are only buried on dunghills, the treatment received by Israel at the hands of the Gentiles was similar. *And with the rich in his death;* i. e. as the rich and wicked man who perishes without having done any good or righteous act in

his life is cursed at the hour of his death by all who know him, such is also the fate of the Israelites after they have been murdered; or perhaps the meaning may be, that the wicked Gentiles maltreat us not merely during our lifetime, but even after our death; for when we have buried our dead, they go 'in the pupil of the night and darkness' to their sepulchres and proceed to exhume the bodies in order to insult them and plunder their grave-clothes: especially if the dead person were sufficiently wealthy for them to imagine that his 'glory' and riches might 'descend after him' into his tomb. All this they did, *although he had done no violence and there was no deceit in his mouth.* [10] All the sicknesses and afflictions mentioned as falling upon the righteous only befel them by *the pleasure of the Lord*, for the purpose of cleansing them from the iniquity they had committed, and of making atonement for the transgressors in Israel; for 'the righteous maketh atonement for his generation,' as we learn from the case of Josiah, king of Judah, who, though perfectly upright himself, nevertheless was punished in the iniquity of his age. In the same way, king Solomon says, 'Whom the Lord loveth he chasteneth.' *If*, however, *his soul makes a trespass-offering*—i. e. if he accepts his sufferings of love, as though there had been some trespass in his soul, he will be worthy for his reward to *see seed* and *prolong his days*, etc. [11] *For the travail of his soul, he will see and be satisfied*, i. e. as a compensation for his travail, and because he bare their iniquities, all that has been mentioned will be granted to him. [12] *Therefore*, because of all this, *I will give him* a goodly portion of the spoil of *many*, and *with the mighty he shall divide* the *spoil* of all the nations who will advance against Jerusalem (as it is said, in the description of the battle with Gog and Magog, Ezek xxxix. 10, 'They shall spoil those that spoiled them, and rob those that robbed them, saith the Lord'), *because he poured out his soul to die*, viz. by undergoing martyrdom for the holiness of God, as our own eyes see is done now by those of our nation in Spain and Portugal, where numbers are being burnt alive for the sake of the truth. *And was numbered with the transgressors,* for sufferings and death were endured by these righteous as though they had been wicked and corrupt: in their death, therefore, they atoned for the sins of many, and in their lives sought for mercy on *the transgressors,* notwithstanding the oppression which they had endured at their hands.

You have now a clear proof that the whole Parashah relates to the future rewards and happiness which the Almighty will in due time bestow upon Israel in return for the misery and indignities which they underwent amongst the heathen in this present world: their exaltation and might will then be such that all people will be astonished (as it is written, Dan. xii. 3, 'They that *understand* shall shine as the brightness of the firmament'), and the transgressors in Israel will perceive that all the sufferings of the righteous were on their behalf, that through their death their own sins might be forgiven, and that by their merits the Redeemer might at length come and deliver us from this long captivity. With respect to the Haggadah (mentioned by you at the beginning), 'He shall be higher than Abraham, more exalted than Moses, and loftier than the ministering angels,' and the assertion that such exalted dignities could not be predicated of any one except of Jesus, who was both man and God, I have deferred replying to it until now, because, firstly, I have considered it important to answer you by appealing to the literal rather than to the allegorical interpretation of the text; and, secondly, because our Rabbis have laid down the principle not to reply to an Haggadah, and because I intend to treat all Haggadahs at full length in another place, 'whereunto thou mayest seek, and whither thou mayest come.' Nevertheless I will mention the explanation given of this Haggadah by one of our Rabbis, viz. R. Mosheh of Coucy, which is to the effect that the upright and perfect man is superior to the angels, because the angels are perfect through being devoid of an evil imagination, so that a being like man, who has the evil imagination, but maintains his integrity in spite of it, is morally their superior. And do not wonder how the perfection of a man can resemble that of an angel, for in Joshua it is said (v. 14), 'I am the captain of the Lord's host; now am I come,' which our Rabbis explain thus, '*Now I am come:* but Moses thy master had no pleasure in me, as it is written, If thy presence doth not go, take us not up hence,' which they further explain by saying that Moses himself took the place of the Metatron: since, then, the Messiah is more exalted than Moses, it is evident that he is also loftier than the angels [e].—Such, then, is the exposition which I have wished to give, in order to remove the hardness of thy heart.

---

[e] Above, p. 152.

XLVI. R. Y'HOSHU'A SEGRE.

You must know that the Nazarenes have yet another proof, which they imagine to be 'strong as a molten mirror,' and one which 'no craftsman or son of a craftsman can break up,' derived from the fifty-second and fifty-third chapters of Isaiah, two chapters upon which their learned men build their principal arguments, alleging that Jesus was the Messiah, and that he perished in the midst of many sicknesses in order to make atonement for guilt. Their interpretation is as follows:—'13 *My servant*, i. e. Jesus, who was God's servant, *shall* assuredly *prosper* in his divine essence; he shall be *high and lifted up, and lofty exceedingly* — the prophet distinguishing him by three terms, expressive of the highest exaltation, and corresponding to the threefold nature implanted in him, the Father, the Son, and the Spirit. 14 *As* in the days of thy life, when they knew not thy nature, *many were astonished at thee*, asking, as in fact they did ask, How can any son of man do such signs as this man doth?—so *bright*[a] *was his countenance beyond man, and his form beyond the sons of men*, for he had a fair face and comely eyes, and possessed a glass of such transcendent brightness[b], that his like could not be found amongst all mankind—15 *so will he sprinkle*, viz. with his own holy waters, the waters of

---

[a] Above, pp. 61, 67.

[b] A play, apparently, on the two meanings of the allied words מַרְאֶה and מַרְאָה. Compare *Wayyiqra Rabbâ*, § 1, where it is said, with reference to Num. xii. 8, ומראה ולא בחידת, that while all the other prophets saw through a soiled and darkened glass, Moses saw through one that was pellucidly clear. Compare also 2 Cor. iii. 18.

baptism, *many nations*—for these waters he hath appointed for every one that cometh into the world: *at him kings will shut their mouth;* they will run towards him to hear his wisdom and knowledge, as it is said, *Venerunt magi ab Oriente* (Matt. ii. 1), in allusion to the kings who, following his star, came from the East to behold his majesty and glory. *And that which had not been told them,* etc.: because they came to offer him worship and honour on account of the good fame which he had in all the earth.

'LIII. [1] The prophet, knowing that the Jews would not believe in Jesus, but would put him to death, now substantiates what he had said, asking, *Who believed our report,* the report which we gave, namely, that Jesus would come? [2] *He came up as a sucker,* which, when young and small, men do not regard at all: he will have at first *no form or comeliness; and we shall see him, but he will not shew* [c] (others), i. e. he will be a learner from other men, and not a teacher: being endued with a body and the capacities of a body, he will be forced to observe the ways of the body, and to be a recipient rather than a conferrer; and *we shall desire him,* for the Almighty hath desire towards his only son. [3] While among men, he will be *despised and forlorn of men;* for the Jews will deny his Divinity, declaring that he is a sorcerer and a deceiver of Israel, and therefore they will stone him and hang him on the cross: *a man of pains,* etc., for the Almighty will give him over into our hands and authorize us to put him to death, and be as though his face were hidden from him: he will be *despised,* and we shall *not esteem him.* [4] But the prophet bids them know that if the Almighty has thus hidden his face from him and abandoned him into their power, it is because he has *carried our sicknesses and borne our pains,* i. e. all the sicknesses and pains which ought to have fallen upon us for our sins: *we* however *thought him stricken and smitten of God* for his own wickedness, though in truth it was not so, and he was stricken and afflicted for our

---

[c] Taking מראה as a *partic. Hif'il.*

transgressions. [5] The whole is here summed up in the words, *Wounded for our transgressions*, etc., which state how all his sufferings were on account of our sins, for the purpose of making atonement for them and removing them from off us: *our peace is removed* utterly *because of him*, for through the stripes which he received when his hands and feet were pierced upon the cross, the sin which rested upon us *was healed*, and the guilt contracted by Adam's sin wiped out, so that the gates of Paradise, which had been closed then, were opened by the death of Jesus. [6] Of the Jews who were thus to treat him, Isaiah, seeing that they would rise up against him and crucify him, "through one that was wicked producing wickedness[d]," says, *All we like sheep went astray, we each*, after slaying him upon the hill, *turned to our own way: yet the Lord laid upon him the iniquity of us all*, for immediately after his death, the second Temple was laid waste, and Israel wandered in exile from their land "into the land of the children of Esau, who dwell in Seir." [7] The prophet adds: If ye are willing to acknowledge that Jesus, the Son, died by his own will and pleasure to atone for guilt, know also that in the hour of his death, he never lifted up his voice to cry, because he heard not, neither felt the sufferings which the Jews inflicted on him. [8] And what did his death achieve for the world? by being crucified *he was taken* out of the world in order to appoint and *preside over* (עצר) the second judgment in the presence of all that ever came into the world: *and his generation*, the inestimable benefits which he conferred in particular upon those of his own generation, *who can declare?* If he had not delivered himself up to die, the whole of that generation, as also all other generations, would have been *cut off from the land* of life, for until then the gates of Paradise had been closed; inasmuch as *for the transgression of my people a stroke* was *upon them*—they were unable to enter therein, because sin prevented them. [9] Nevertheless, he *made his grave with the wicked;*

---

[d] Cf. Thalm. Bab., *Shabbath*, 32[a].

[10] *and the Lord,* i. e. the Father, *was pleased to bruise him* with that sore sickness in order that in the future *the Lord's pleasure* might *prosper by his hand,* i. e. that men, by being obedient to his new law, might secure Paradise for themselves, and that [11] *for the travail of his soul,* the travail which each would undergo in the service of Jesus, he should *see and be satisfied. By his knowledge*—by that creed which in their language is styled a "confession"—he will *justify the just,* and ever afterwards *bear* all their *iniquity* if they believe in him and keep his commandments. [12] The Father here promises of the Son: *Therefore I will allot unto him,* and to his law, glory *among the many,* and *with mighty* nations *he shall divide* the *spoil* of his law, *because he poured out his soul to die, and was numbered with the transgressors,* being put to death between two thieves, who are called "ladroni," and *carried the sin of many,* and made atonement for it, *and interceded for transgressors,* always praying for them whenever they are willing to believe in him.'

The following are the doubts which tell with fatal effect against this most mendacious explanation, and force upon us the true one in its place:

1. How could the Almighty have called his only Son a 'servant'—a title appertaining to one who is passive, and in unconditional subjection to an active principle without? if the Nazarenes are right, he should rather have used the more dignified expression, and said, 'Behold, my *Son* shall prosper.' 2. The prophet says here, 'He will be high and exalted, and lofty exceedingly,' and below describes the subject of his prophecy as 'despised, and forlorn of men:' but how can attributes which mutually contradict one another, co-exist in a single individual? 3. He says that men were amazed at Jesus, because he had a form unlike the other children of men: but in what respect was it different? since if he means to allude to any halo of glory encircling him, this is untrue, for we do not find that people ever fled from him or were awed by his presence (as they fled from Moses), but that they seized him and put him to death.

And, moreover, not one of their writers has spoken of Jesus as being marked by such a halo. 4. They explain the words, 'So shall he sprinkle,' etc., of the holy water which he commanded to be poured upon the head of every man: but water was never thus poured upon his own head, nor did he ever with his own hands pour water upon the head of any one else; and the assertion that John the Baptist poured water upon him is altogether false, for that was not a case of pouring but only of immersion; nor did Jesus himself ever enjoin the pouring of water, which is a rite invented as time went on, like the rest of their practices, out of their own hearts. 5. How can it be said, firstly, that kings were to 'shut their mouth at him' (which they explain as relating to the three wise kings who were to come and worship him and hear his wisdom), and afterwards that he would be 'despised and forlorn of men?' 6. If, as must be admitted, he died 'for his own sin' (2 Kings xiv. 6), how could it be said of him that he was 'stricken, and smitten *of God?*' 7. As regards the explanation of the words, 'Wounded for our transgressions,' we may indeed remember what the Thalmud says, 'In Babylon they have the proverb, "Ṭobiah sinned, and Zagod was beaten;" and in Palestine, "Shechem had the pleasure, and Mabnai[e] was cut off:"' but can it be right that when other men have sinned, Jesus should then die for them? Is it in accordance with justice for the righteous to die for the purpose of rescuing the wicked? 8. What is the meaning of 'All we like sheep,' etc.? if it was the King's decree that Jesus should die in order to atone for sin and guilt, and if the Jews only executed his pleasure in putting him to death (for he must then have come into the world in order to suffer death upon the cross), how can it be said that they 'went astray' in so doing? did they not rather do what was right and fitting, if such was his pleasure? And the pleasure of any one is also his glory. 9. How

---

[e] Thalmud of Babylon, *Makkoth*, 11a. 'Mabnai' is explained to signify the inhabitants of Shechem.

can the words, 'He opened not his mouth,' be applied to Jesus? does not Luke certify in his Gospel that at the moment of his death he cried with a loud voice, saying, 'My God, my God, why hast thou forsaken me?' And did he not also cry out to God? if so, however, he was not himself God, for, as I shall explain in its place, men only cry out to one who is more powerful than themselves. 10. How do the expressions, 'He shall see seed, shall have long days,' apply to Jesus, seeing he died unmarried and childless when only thirty-three years old? In face of these objections all the arguments and interpretations of the Christians have come utterly to an end; for any explanation that labours under many grave doubts is a mere vapour and can have nothing in it.

It is indeed true that our forefathers have offered many explanations, new and old together, for this prophecy. Yonathan ben 'Uzziel indicates his own opinion respecting it, an opinion derived from tradition, in his Targum. Enough also, and more than enough, has been written about it by Rashi, by R. David, by R. Levi ben Gershon, by the great Don Yiẓḥaq Abarbanel, by R. Mosheh el-Sheikh, and by R. Sh'muel Lanyado (in the excellent treatise, the *Kh'li pâz*). All these, however, and in particular the illustrious Yaʿqob ben Ḥayim of Tunis (who printed the entire Bible), ended the fifty-second chapter with the words *what they had not heard have they perceived*, beginning the fifty-third with the exclamation, *Who believed our report?* for although this view was not the one entertained by Yonathan, his opinion has been disregarded by the side of the doctors of the Masôra: retain, then, their arrangement and explanation, which you will find in their several treatises. In my humble opinion, it would seem that a correct exposition of the prophecy must preserve the division, and that the reader should know that at the beginning of chapter l. the prophet was speaking of the Deliverance, and that he continues to treat of the same subject till the beginning of chapter liii, as we shall explain fully in the verses as they come, by the help of God.

LII. [13] After having detailed at length, in chapters l–lii, the great and marvellous events to happen in our midst, bringing us glory and renown, at the time of the true Messiah, the prophet says, in conclusion, *Behold my servant*, to whom I shall give the dominion, and whom I shall set over you as king in person, *will prosper* (ישכיל, as 1 Sam. xviii. 14); the land, in the days when the Messiah shall arrive, shall have rest from war, and Messiah himself shall be exalted before the eyes of the heathen, being perfect in every part of his mental nature, *high* in all relating to the soul, *exalted* in spirit, and *lofty exceedingly* in the breath (of life): he shall also be king over the whole earth, though at the same time my 'servant,' for his power and regal greatness will devolve upon him from me, and be in no way dependent upon his own ability or pleasure; for every being that possesses a body, or is created, is under the dominion of the Almighty, nor can anything be found in all the worlds which is not subject to him. [14] The prophet, addressing Israel, now says, *As many*, formerly, *were astonished at thee*, exclaiming, 'See, this is new; this people hath never been thus exalted in the ages which are past,' even those who had known thee in Egypt as a 'slave for ever' marvelling when they saw thee rise to greatness; *so destructive will his countenance be for men*—the brightness and beauty of his features will destroy all spiritual life from amongst men, and *his form* cause breath to cease *from the sons of men;* for they will be left in wonder and astonishment, gnashing their teeth. משחת is a noun formed from השחית by the addition of מ, like משכן from שכן, and refers to those who see the Messiah, and who will be awe-struck at his presence and be left appalled. [15] The prophet now narrates what the Messiah will do when he is come: he will *scatter the nations* and remove them from his presence, however *numerous* they may be, in return for their having made Israel's yoke heavy, while he was amongst them in exile, and for having treated him unbefittingly,—יזה is thus for יזרה, the ר being omitted for euphony. *Kings*, he adds, *will close their mouths at him*—the rulers of the Gentiles will answer no more, nor even know how to commence recounting his praises when they behold his wisdom and greatness; the end of the verse assigns the reason why their mouths are to be shut, because, namely, they have *seen what had never been told them, and observed* with their own eyes what they had never heard from the lips of their teachers or acquaintance.—Here ends the account of the Messiah, which had formed the subject of the prophet's discourse from the beginning of chapter l.

LIII. [1] The prophet now proceeds to depict the surprise which will be expressed by the nations in the future when they see the people of Israel elevated to greatness and honour such as they had never attained through the whole course of their previous history, representing them as exclaiming, *Who believed our report?* i. e. who is the man that believed the report which we spread concerning them, saying that their hope had perished, that the Lord had cast them off, and delivered them into the hand of fate? *and upon whom was the arm*, i. e. the prophecy, *of the Lord revealed* at the time when we thought that the future would bring misfortune to them? [2] Our anticipation we now see reversed. We imagined that Israel would never again rise from the ground; but now we perceive that they have sprung up *like a sucker* or *like a root, out of the dry earth* in which they were buried and lost. כיונק, Israel sprang up in all his greatness like one of those shoots upon a tree which are called 'suckers;' and לפניו refers back to the sucker at the beginning of its growth [*before itself*, i. e. before it has arrived at its full size]. And *like a root out of the dry earth*, which at first has *no form* and *no comeliness*, and, when we *look* upon it, displays *no beauty* to our gaze, but which, afterwards, mounts high above our heads, so that all who see it at once feel *desire* for it: such was Israel; but now he has risen to his full height, producing in our hearts an ever-growing desire to unite ourselves as closely as possible to him. [3] At this point the prophet makes it his aim to describe the wonder which the Gentiles will express in the future on the greatness of Israel, saying, What a people is this which was *despised and forlorn of men*—for all the days of our life we avoided holding converse with him, and none of our men were 'with them in the house'—and who was perpetually *a man of pains*—for one day we used to attack them with one form of craft or fraud, and another day with another—*and known by sickness!* and because he was thus known to us as ravaged by the sickness of penury, we therefore *hid* our *faces from him,* and because he was a people *despised, we esteemed him not,* and he was in our eyes 'as a broken sherd?' [4] *Yet* all the *sicknesses* and all the *pains* which we laid upon him *he bare,* although we made their weight so heavy on him with a yoke of iron upon his neck, that throughout his life he was never able to lift up his head, being *stricken, smitten of God, and afflicted,* and because his hope had perished. [5] But we have discovered that *he was panged* (מחולל, *Poʿlel* from חיל, Ps. xlviii. 7, as Qamḥi says in his commentary), and bare all these throes and pains *for our transgressions,* i. e. in order to increase our transgressions and be a cause of sin to us; and *bruised for our iniquities,* i. e. similarly, whenever he was left bruised, it added to our iniquities and only served to 'increase transgression to our sins.' This being the sense, then, מוסר must be, not a substantive, but a verb, and the clause will mean, *Our peace was removed* from us *because of him*—because, viz. of the evil treatment which we inflicted on him. *And from his stripes he was healed by us,* i. e. we were the cause of his being healed from them; ל signifying *because of.* The connexion is this: We had been the cause of his many and sore sicknesses, and now he was healed from the stripes which came upon him by reason of our sins, because of us—for we are humbled, and despised, and bruised, and afflicted, and in subjection to him. [6] Perceiving thus that, after having been long contemned and despised in their midst, Israel had at last risen to the highest consummation of honour and glory, and that all the penalties imposed by them upon him had been in opposition to justice, and that the misfortunes which they themselves were experiencing in the days of the Messiah were in accordance with truth and right, measure for measure, they confess, saying, *All we like sheep had gone astray* (תעה, as Gen. xxxvii. 15), *we turned each to his own way*—one going to meet another and look his companion in the face, as the manner is of those who are in bewilderment or surprise: *but the Lord*—God himself and his court of judgment—*hath* now laid upon us *the iniquity of us all through him*—*through him*, viz. because his iniquities mounted upwards in order to intercede against us, that the Almighty might not delay our punishment. [7] Seeing, then, the calamity impending, and themselves unable to escape from it, they proceed here to recount all the 'deeds which should not be done' which they had done towards Israel, and all the hard treatment which they had received at their hands, exclaiming, See, how this people, which now is in the height of fortune, was once *oppressed and afflicted*—so the word is to be rendered—and received all its sufferings without opening their mouth! they were unable to say a word before us, for the priests of the inquisition would prohibit them even to utter a whisper in any way opposed to their will, or to the ordinances of their kings and rulers: thus they were, moreover, in our eyes *as a lamb dumb before her shearers:* the thought is repeated in order to indicate two points about which the Gentiles will make statements concerning us: whether we slew them, they will exclaim, like a sheep led to the slaughter, or whether we seized their gold and silver and all the desire of their eyes, as though they were like a lamb dumb before her shearers,—in either instance alike they *opened not their mouth* for fear and trembling. [8] מעצר, i. e. from the confinement in which we held him: the root has here the same meaning as in Deut. xxxii. 36, where it is used of coercion or subjection under the heavy yoke of exile; the same explanation is given by Qamḥi in his commentary. From this *he was taken*, and so rose to greatness: *and* this *his generation*, now honoured and exalted, *who could declare it*, or make known that we never would believe in its redemption?

Yet now it is *cut off* from our hands, and gone forth from under our burdens, *because of the land of life*, i. e. in order that it may be brought in thither: and *for the transgression of my people* who laid *a stroke upon them* and severe sufferings, it was taken away from us and conducted into the position of honour in which it now is, although while amongst us the people were accounted only as so much cattle. [9] *And he made*, etc.; for we obliged Israel to 'buy their sepulchres at a full price' outside the city, like *the wicked* who are treated without any consideration: and even if one wealthier than the rest in the nation thought to expend much gold and so to purchase for himself a spot for his father's tomb, we never would give him permission to do so, but forced him to submit to burial *with his deaths*, i. e. in the same place with other men: so greatly was this nation oppressed and afflicted amongst us, although they had *done no violence, neither was guile in their mouth!* And treatment such as this is falling upon us continually in the course of our exile. [10] We now see, the nations proceed, that *the Lord was pleased to bruise* and punish *him*, and *to put him to sickness*, in order that afterwards, in the days of the Messiah, the penalty might fall upon us in the manner described, Ezek. xxv. 14, 'And I will lay my vengeance upon Edom by the hand of my people Israel;' for Nero Cæsar rose up to attack Israel and said, The Holy One desired to lay waste his house, and to wash his hands on the man who does it. He went, etc.[f] And *because* this people *putteth his soul* in his hand[g] to endure cheerfully all the repulses and other misfortunes which have befallen it, it shall *see seed* and *lengthen days*, for the Almighty will reward it with prosperity, and the wonders of celestial wisdom will be multiplied in it, one rich and perfect blessing bringing many others in its train; *and the Lord's pleasure shall prosper in his hand*, for 'God maketh a decree, and

---

[f] *Gittim*, fol. 56: the entire passage will be found above, p. 132.

[g] See Judg. xii. 3, 1 Sam. xix. 5.

the righteous annulleth it,' as our Rabbis say on the verse (2 Sam. xxiii. 3), 'A righteous man, ruling in the fear of God[h],' and also the book Zohar on Lev. v. 1. [11] Calamities will attack the nations, so that in spite of themselves they will reluctantly be telling the praises of Israel: how *for the toil* and misery which he endured, his *soul* should now *see* seed, and he should prolong his days with such increase of wisdom that at last *by his knowledge* this nation which once was but *my servant* should become ruler *over many*. [12] *Therefore I will allot to him* all the honour which his high position will demand; *and with the mighty* of his nation *he will divide* our *spoil;* and all this glory will be attained by him *because he poured out his soul to die, and was numbered with the transgressors*—for all held him to be an evil-doer—and received at their hands the sinful treatment denoted by the expression *the sin of many.* And now with the measure which we meted out to him he will mete to us again; for he will rise up as a lion beside the men who once transgressed against him, and smote him, and reviled him, and contemned him, and *attack* them, as David bade Benaiah attack Joab (1 Kings ii. 29). At this point, therefore, the prophet concludes, beginning the next chapter with the words, 'Shout, O barren one, burst forth into singing,' etc., by way of comfort to our nation, who are thereby represented beyond doubt as redeemed, and adorned with glory and honour.

---

[h] *Moʿed Qaṭon*, 16[b].

XLVII. R. DAVID ALTSCHULER.

A.

LII. [13] ישכיל, *shall prosper*, as 1 Sam. xviii. 14; for a man who prospers in anything is considered to have been guided in his actions by *discretion* (שכל). [14] שממו, *were astonished*, as Job xxi. 5. כן, *truly*, as Num. xxvii. 7. מראה, the fair and clear *complexion* of the face. תאר, the *form* of the person. [15] יזה, to *sprinkle*, as Is. lxiii. 3. יקפצו, to *close*, as Job v. 16. התבוננו, to *observe attentively*, as 1 Kings iii. 21.

LIII. [1] על מי, *for whose sake?* נגלתה, *revealed.* [2] יונק, a tender twig put forth by a tree, as Ezek. xvii. 22. ציה, barren and dry. הדר, *comeliness.* ונחמדהו, the ו stands in the place of ש: so Exod. xxv. 2, '*that* they take,' etc. [3] חדל, *forsaken.* אישים, for אנשים. [4] נשא, to *bear* as a burden. נגוע, *prostrated* and debilitated, as Josh. viii. 15. מענה, *afflicted.* [5] והוא, the ו is in place of או (*or*). מחלל, *panged*, from חיל (Ps. xlviii. 7). מדכא, *broken* and crushed. מוסר, *chastisement.* שלומינו, our *peace.* חבורה, *stripes*, as Is. i. 6. [6] תעינו, *went astray.* פנינו, from פנה (Hos. iii. 1). הפגיע, *caused to meet* on him for his injury, as 2 Sam. i. 15. [7] נגש, *was oppressed* by the seizure of his wealth; the word is used of the exaction of money, 2 Kings xxiii. 35. והוא, ו again in lieu of או (*or*). נענה, was *afflicted.* לטבח, *to slaughter.* יובל, as Is. xviii. 7. גוזזיה, the verb signifies *to cut off the wool.* [8] עוצר, the prison, or place of detention, in which he was confined; cf. Jer. xxxiii. 1. ישוחח, to *declare*, as Ps. cxliii. 5. נגזר, to be *cut off*, as Lam. iii. 54. נגע, *prostration* and weakness. למו = להם: inasmuch as the singular is used throughout to designate the whole nation, the prophet here intimates this by the plural *them*. [9] עשיר, *the ruler*, for a man who is wealthy is generally also in authority. במותיו, *in his deaths*. [10] דכאו, *bruised* or crushed. החלי, from חלה. אשם, *sin* or transgression. [11] עמל, *toil* or sorrow. [12] עצומים, the *mighty*. שלל, *spoil*. תחת, *in return for*. הערה, to *pour out*, as Ps. cxli. 8. נמנה, to be *counted*. נשא, to *bear*. יפגיע, to *intercede* or solicit, as Jer. vii. 16.

B.

LII. [13] *Then shall my servant* Israel *prosper:* the prophet speaks of them in the singular, as is constantly the custom in Scripture. *He will be high and exalted*, etc.: the idea is repeated under different words, in order to express the vastness of his dominion and greatness. [14] *In proportion to* the astonishment which *many* felt at their humiliation, saying, *Truly* (כן) *his countenance is marred beyond man, and his form* changed *beyond the sons of men*, meaning thereby to imply that he was deprived of all power, and devoid of courage, [15] *in exactly the same proportion* will he have dominion, and his hand will prevail, and his heart be strong, in order for him to *sprinkle* the blood of *many nations* devoted to idolatry. *At* news of *this*, the *kings* of those nations *will shut their mouths*, so as not to speak a word in the depth of their amazement: *because that which was not told them have they seen*—their own eyes have beheld greatness far transcending any report which might have reached them, and *that which they have not heard*—a repetition of the same idea—*they have perceived*, i.e. observed with the minutest attention what actually occurred.

LIII. [1] *Who*, the nations will then say, *believeth our report?* we have never hitherto seen it so with our eyes, and who amongst us all believes the report which we hear of the increase of greatness and power which has fallen to Israel's lot? *and the* strength of the *Lord's arm*, *for whose sake was it* ever *revealed* from the days of old, that we should believe it had now been revealed for the sake of Israel? [2] *Before this* greatness came to him *he sprang up like a sucker* which derives its nourishment not directly from the soil but from a tree, the prophet means to say that whatever affluence Israel had had, came to him through the intervention of the idolatrous nations amongst whom he dwelt. *And as a root out of the dry earth*, for the little which he derived from himself came speedily to an end like a root rising up out of the parched and arid soil which 'is quickly cut off and withered:' and just as such a root would have *no form or comeliness*, so the affluence enjoyed by Israel lacked all completeness and polish: *and when we looked at him*, we found in him *no aspect* of beauty which might lead us to *desire* him; in other words, we could detect in him no attractive feature—neither bodily prowess nor strength of heart; and hence we simply loathed him. [3] *He was despised* in the eyes of all, and *forlorn of men*, for none of the idolaters would associate with him on account of his humiliation; *a man of pains and known of sickness*, well known to all as a great sufferer, and, as though he had *hidden* his *face from us*, that we might not see him, we could never look him in the face: he was so afflicted and dejected by the exile and its attendant miseries, that we contracted an aversion to gaze upon him. *And so he was despised in our eyes, and we esteemed him not*, for we said, The hand of the Lord hath done this, because he hath rejected him. [4] But, in truth, the Lord had not so rejected him: every sickness and every pain which he endured was on our account, they were what we inflicted on him through our own evil will: yet *we thought* in error that he had been *stricken* and *smitten of God*, because he had rejected him, and that it was by his hand that he was thus *afflicted* with chastisements. [5] Or (ו) the truth might have been that these sufferings were sent by the Almighty, though not because he had rejected him for the evil of his doings: on the contrary, the measure of his *pangs* was filled up in order that the transgressions of all those who are devoted to false worships might be atoned for through them. *Bruised for our iniquities:* the same idea is repeated in different words. *The chastisement*, etc.: the sufferings which ought to have come upon us, in order, by blotting out our iniquity, to perpetuate *our peace*, fell *upon him: and by the stripes* which came on him the plagues of our iniquity *were healed*—they were atoned for, and so dispersed. The clause is parallel to the two which precede. [6] So great was our iniquity that *we all went astray* from the path of truth and right *like sheep*, for when one in a flock loses its way, the others following after it lose their way likewise: in other words, our fathers wandered from the way of truth, and therefore we also simply followed after them. *We have turned each to his own way;* i. e. would indeed that we had been only like such a flock, in which one lamb merely strays after another! it was, however, far otherwise: each one of us *turned to his own way*, and these ways were none better than the rest; they were all equally corrupt[a]: but, this being the case, what guilt is there resting on us! But *the Lord struck him with the iniquity of us all;* i. e. it was our iniquity which, by the decree of the Almighty, smote and punished him. [7] For this cause *he was oppressed* by the seizure of his wealth, *or afflicted* with punishment of the body, in case he were poor and had nothing to give: yet he *opened not his mouth* to murmur or complain, for he dreaded lest his persecutors might ill-use him the more, but was *as a sheep led to the slaughter, and as a lamb* standing before the man who shears off her wool; for the sheep *opens not its mouth*, and the lamb *is dumb* and emits no cry: in the same way, Israel under his exactors uttered no sound of complaint. [8] *From* the house of bondage in which he was confined, *and from* the place of *judgment* in which he had been condemned, *he was taken* off to this oppression or affliction: nothing would procure

[a] Compare above, pp. 267, 307.

his release: *and who could tell of* all the sufferings endured by him throughout the days of *his generation?* for the end of it all was, that he was *cut off from the land of life:* in a word, his sufferings accelerated his death. *For the transgression*, etc.: so every one will be saying, This *stroke* came not on them for their own iniquity, but for the transgression *of my people:* either, i. e. my people transgressed, when their evil purposes led them to afflict them, or they were plagued in order to atone for the transgressions of my people. [9] He resigned himself to be buried *with the wicked*—to be like them in the contempt and miserable treatment which is their lot; he would not disobey the Law in order to escape the same fate. *And with the rich in his deaths;* the sentence still depends upon ויתן: he resigned himself *in accordance with* (את) the will of the wealthy magistrate to all the forms of death to which he might sentence him, in order to abide firmly by his own faith. And yet, the prophet continues, such a sentence as this was passed quite gratuitously, and not because of the *violence* which he had done, or the *guile* which was in his mouth—he was guilty of neither the one nor the other—but simply from a spirit of malice. [10] Here the prophet, as it were, replies to the doubts supposed to be expressed by the idolaters, whether, namely, the calamities which came upon Israel were occasioned by the wickedness of their own hearts, and not by the decree of the Deity, or whether, again, they were sent from God in order that they might atone for the iniquity of the idolaters themselves. Neither of these suppositions, he tells them, is true: *the Lord was pleased to bruise him, he put him to sickness*, and by his decree all this took place: the object of Israel's calamities, however, was not that they might atone for the sins of other men, but rather to 'prove him and do good to him at his latter end:' God, as it were, said, I will see now *if his soul will make* itself *a trespass-offering*, not scrutinizing curiously into my dealings, but confessing that what came upon it had come justly, inasmuch as he had sinned and incurred guilt: if it does so, his reward shall be that all his life *he shall see* his *seed* with his own eyes, and *prolong* his *days*, and still none of them will die during his lifetime; *and the pleasure of the Lord* [will be this, that] *he shall prosper with his hands,* because he stood under trial, and did not question the divine justice. [11] *From the travail of his soul* which *he saw, he shall* receive profit and *be satisfied: by his knowledge my servant will* make it his aim to *justify the Just One,* acknowledging that what he had endured had been in order to blot out the guilt of sin, so that the reward for his good deeds might not be withheld. *My servant unto many:* the prophet means to say that Israel was not a servant *of the many* idolaters, as he would have been, had he hearkened to their voice in the matter of his religion, but that he was *my servant unto* or before them, not listening to their persuasions, but bowing his shoulder to bear whatever injustice they might exhibit towards him, as a punishment for his refusal to be persuaded by them. [12] Since, then, he thus endured the trial, *I will give him* a portion in the inheritance *of the many* nations, *and the mighty,* i. e. the idolaters who are strong, *he shall divide* to himself *as spoil,* in return for his having *poured out* and abandoned *his soul* to death, and for having been *numbered* by the heathen *with the* generality of *transgressors* and renegades, 'with full plenty of contempt and indignation' (Esther i. 18). *Yet he carried the sin of many,* i. e. bent his shoulder to endure all the sins perpetrated against him by the many nations which inflicted on him punishments and pains: *and unto* the idolaters, who were thus *the transgressors* against him, he *made supplication,* his eyes being ever fixed towards them 'as the eyes of servants unto the hand of their masters.' And hence divine justice has ordained that, in return for his past humiliation and subjection, he will, when the hour of redemption has arrived, assume the position of sovereign over them.

SHORT PASSAGES.

a. R. DAVID BEN ABRAHAM THE QARAITE.

אלם, Ps. lvi. 1. יונה here denotes the same people which are indicated, Cant. ii. 14, by the words, 'My dove in the clifts of the rock.' And they are styled *dumb*, on account of their silence even from the language of rightful complaint, comp. Ps. xxxix. 3, 10; and in the same way Isaiah, describing a portion of the remnant[a], says, 'He was oppressed, etc. . . , and as a lamb *dumb* before her shearers, so he opened not his mouth.'

b. R. YONAH IBN JANÂH.

חבר. The substantive חבורה denotes always a *wound*, or the mark of a wound, as Ex. xxi. 25, Ps. xxxviii. 6, Prov. xx. 30. From the same root comes, as I believe, חבורה, Is. liii. 5, which is not a substantive of the form גבורה, חלושה, Ex. xxxii. 18, בכורה, Deut. xxi. 17, but an infinitive, the relation which it bears to its suffix being the same as in קחם, Hos. xi. 3, which signifies *taking them*: in the same way the prophet means to say here, *in wounding him.* The sense is as follows:—After having described the excellence of this good man, so truly humble, yet so depressed in spirit through grief at the state of unbelief in which the people were sunk as regards the law, and despised by the men of his generation, as it is said,

---

[a] Compare p. 61.

'Despised and forlorn of men,' etc., the prophet continues, saying, We, when we beheld his sufferings and sickness, thought him put to sickness and pain by the Creator for his own deserts; but lo, his sickness was caused through his sorrow for our sins: *the chastisement of us all* and our wrongs reached him, and *by his wounds* and sickness *we were healed.* In thus wounding him, we all erred like beasts, and not one of us turned from his wicked way: God, however, 'brought upon him the iniquity of us all,' i. e. it was only for our iniquities that he thus tried him. שלומנו I explain to signify *the whole of us,* as in Jer. xiii. 19, where הגלת שלומים means 'they are *all* led into captivity.' מחלל, *made sick and wounded,* being the participle passive from the same verb of which מחוללת, Is. li. 9, is the active participle.

c. R. Mosheh ben Maimon.

What is to be the manner of Messiah's advent, and where will be the place of his first appearance? He will make his first appearance in the land of Israel, as it is written, 'The Lord, whom ye seek, will come suddenly to his temple' (Mal. iii. 1); but as to the manner of his appearance, until it has taken place, thou canst not know this so as for it to be said of him that he is 'the son of such a one, and is of such and such a family:' there shall rise up one of whom none have known before, and the signs and wonders which they shall see performed by him will be the proofs of his true origin; for the Almighty, where he declares to us his mind upon this matter, says, 'Behold a man whose name is the Branch, and he shall branch forth out of his place' (Zech. vi. 12). And Isaiah speaks similarly of the time when he will appear, without his father or mother or family being known, *He came up as a sucker before him, and as a root out of the dry earth,* etc. But the unique phenomenon attending his manifestation is, that all the kings of the earth will be thrown into terror at the fame of him—their kingdoms will be in consternation, and they themselves will be devising whether to oppose him with arms, or to adopt some different course, confessing, in fact, their inability to contend with him or ignore his presence, and so confounded at the wonders which they will see him work, that they will lay their hands upon their mouth; in the words of Isaiah, when describing the manner in which the kings will hearken to him, *At him kings will shut their mouth; for that which had not been told them have they seen, and that which they had not heard they have perceived.*

d. R. Meir ben Shim'on.

Behold my servant, etc. This Parashah is applied by the Nazarenes to Jesus; such an explanation, however, is untenable even on the ground of their own allegations. For example, they assert Jesus to be the son of God, and to be himself God, the whole being thus God, and at the same time one: but if so, how is he called *my servant?* Almighty God is not a servant; on the contrary, all are his servants. If to this it be replied that Jesus is termed *servant*, as being a servant of the Godhead, do not the Christians assert that he is God? how, then, can one who is the Creator of all and the Lord of all receive such a title? Again, how can it be said that he should *prosper?*—for this is the meaning of ישכיל, as in 1 Sam. xviii. 14: in what did his prosperity consist? were not his misfortunes and general ill-success patent to all, when the Pharisees and doctors and, in fact, the whole people condemned him to death (as is related in their own book), and he was slain with his disciples? And how can it be promised that he should be *high and exalted and lofty exceedingly?* Jesus in his lifetime was only thus exalted at the time of his crucifixion: do you not see how till then he was in fear and trepidation daily? If you reply that the phrase refers to his Godhead, not only is God called *a servant*, but, besides this, the Godhead is unchangeably 'high and exalted' through all eternity; how, then, could it be said that he '*will be* high' now? And if you suppose that he was 'high' through the multitude of miracles which he performed, he only did these in the manner suggested by the Pharisees and doctors, viz. by sorcery, which indeed he persevered in till at last they wreaked their will upon him in the way that they did. Again, it is said in the same Parashah, *He shall see seed*, etc.; but what 'seed' did Jesus see, and what 'length of days did he enjoy,' and what 'pleasure of the Lord prospered in his hand?' did not both he and his disciples perish after a short life? and did they not meet with ruin rather than prosperity in their undertakings? If you fall back on the supposition that this language refers to his Deity, the same objection will still hold which I mentioned above. Again, at the end of the Parashah, it is said, *Therefore I will divide*, etc.: but what 'spoil' was ever divided to Jesus 'among many,' and what happiness was ever his during life, when he was rather a 'wanderer and fugitive,' and in constant terror of death? If you suppose the words to relate to both his Godhead and his manhood (the latter of which you assert ascended up into heaven), the whole being God together, how does the prophet say, '*I* will divide him?' would not he rather be himself dividing to others? and, again, how does he say *amongst many*, when his ascension, by their own account, took place secretly, and not in the presence of any multitude? although, to be sure, a great miracle such as that ought to have been enacted (as I have said above) before as many witnesses as possible: in fact, neither in his days, nor since, have the events ever happened which I there indicated as bound to occur in the time of the true Messiah. Let every man of intelligence, therefore, understand, on the question of this Parashah, that it refers to the people of Israel, who are oppressed for the truth of the Creator and his Law, being daily plundered and despised, murdered and burnt, as Scripture says, 'For thy sake are we slain all the day long,' etc. (Ps. xliv. 23); and again, 'Thou hast laid thy back as the ground, and as the street, to them that went over' (Is. li. 23). It may however, at the same time, be explained haggadically of the Messiah and his followers—though the meaning is still practically unchanged—as expressing, namely, the assurance that, in the time of Deliverance, the Creator will *divide* amongst them the *spoil* of Gog and Magog and all his host, as it is written, 'And they shall spoil their spoilers, and plunder those that plunder them' (Ezek. xxxix. 10); and again, 'Instead of bronze I will bring gold,' etc. (Is. lx. 17)—an occasion to which numerous predictions relate. Isaiah says, *my servant* in the singular, as the manner is in prophecy; for example, Jer. xxx. 10, Is. xli. 8, and frequently besides. Although what we have stated here is sufficient for every one of intelligence, we shall nevertheless, by God's will, in § 3, offer an explanation of the entire Parashah, word by word, in accordance with its true import.

The Parashah before us is expounded in *Soṭah*, § 1, of the Messiah[b]: by the literal method it may, however, be explained of Israel, for there are several passages in which the prophets speak of the Israelitish nation in the singular number, as Is. xliv. 2, xlii. 1, and elsewhere, even before we arrive at the present Parashah. But the Nazarenes, in spite of this, apply it to the Messiah, whom they contend to have been that man [Jesus], who they affirm was the Messiah and also God, whose servants they are, and whom they accept as divine: it may be objected, however, that if he was God, both in body and spirit, he could not be termed 'servant:' whose servant, indeed, could he, under such circumstances, have been? Or, if it be thought that the expression relates to his body, how did the prophet say that he would be 'high and exalted?' we do not find that in his body he was ever 'exalted' except at his crucifixion: on the contrary, he fled, now into Egypt, now to other places: if, again, it be said to relate to his Godhead, how could the Godhead be

---

[b] Not to be found in our editions; but cf. the extract from *Yalqut*, p. 9.

termed a 'servant?' would he not then be the Creator, and all besides be his creatures and his servants? If, now, you reply that the allusion is to his flesh after the resurrection (for they say that he ascended on the third day to heaven[c]), who, pray, witnessed his ascension? if such a marvellous event took place, it should have been transacted in public before the whole people, just as his condemnation also had taken place in public: it is impossible to put faith in miracles which so easily admit of being controverted, that the Pharisees said, 'He did them openly that men might believe in him, in the name of devils.' But the miracles of his resurrection and ascension (which ought to have been achieved so as to be seen of all, in order that the people might not persevere in their rejection of him) were in fact transacted in secret; and the Law says (Deut. xxvii. 18), 'Cursed is he that maketh the blind to err in the way.' All this we have stated above, in another place. The *proof* that 'my servant' denotes Israel, is to be found in the passages already cited from the previous Parashahs, xliv. 2, xlii. 1; also xlii. 17, 'Who is blind as my servant?' after which the words, verse 22, 'But *this* is a people robbed and spoiled,' shew that the 'servant' is the nation plundered by their enemies in captivity—a conclusion which is further corroborated by verses 24, 25, 'Who gave *Jacob* for a spoil, and *Israel* to the robbers? did not the Lord, he against whom?' etc.

e. R. Mord'khai ben Y'hosafah.

This Parashah is said by the Nazarenes to refer throughout to their Messiah, who suffered for their salvation; and they affirm that this is indicated by Isaiah himself in the words, *But we thought him stricken, and smitten God, and afflicted,* which declare plainly that he who was thus stricken and smitten was

[c] R. Meir's acquaintance with the Gospels, it will be observed, is not distinguished for accuracy.

God. They omit however to take account of the expressions used in the text, or to consider that the prophet has been all along speaking of the captivity, as lii. 3, 'Ye were sold for nought, and not for money shall ye be redeemed,' and, 'Fear not Jacob, and my servant Israel' (xliv. 2, and often similarly besides); again, 'The God of Israel will be your rereward' (lii. 12) to gather in the outcasts of Israel, and that in continuation of the same idea he here begins, *Behold my servant shall prosper*, i. e. there will yet be a time in which my servant, already mentioned above, shall prosper and be exalted. And although while in exile his depression was so great that *his countenance was marred beyond man, and his form beyond the sons of men*, there still will come a time when men will be proportionately *astonished* at his exaltation; for then his salvation will sprout forth suddenly, and *come up before* the Almighty *like a sucker* shooting up before the tree that has been hewn down itself, whilst its stump revives. The nations now say, *Surely he hath carried our sicknesses*, etc.; for Israel bears during his exile all the pains and sufferings which they impose upon him: but *he*, i. e. either the servant Jacob, or the Messiah who will be king over the seed of Jacob, *was wounded or bruised* for the iniquity of the Gentiles, in order that he might receive the penalty on their behalf. *All we*, they continue, *like sheep went astray;* for Israel is to be *oppressed and afflicted*, yet *without opening his mouth*, for he will endure all for the glory of the Creator: *for coercion and judgment he was taken away,*—he was taken out of the world in consequence of the acts of oppression and injustice perpetrated upon him whilst in exile. But *who* at that time would believe, when *he was cut off from the land of life for the transgression of my people, a stroke to them*, that all that he had done to them was in consequence of their transgression, in order that the Creator might take vengeance on them? *And he made his grave with the wicked*, etc., for they spilt their blood and buried them with contumely in the sepulchres of the wicked, as it is written, 'Was Abner to die as a fool dieth?' (2 Sam. iii. 33): thus they resigned themselves to martyrdom, *the rich* even preparing himself to meet death under two forms ('in his *deaths*'), the actual dissolution of his person, and the destruction of his substance; for he loved the Lord not merely in 'all his soul,' but also in 'all his strength.' But the Almighty *was pleased* thus *to bruise him*, for the purpose of blotting out his iniquities. *If*, then, *his soul maketh a trespass-offering*, admitting its guilt and accepting its sufferings as sent upon it in love, then he will *see seed* and *have long life*, and *for the travail of his soul see and be satisfied*, i. e. 'see' the consolations of prosperity, and 'be satisfied' with delights. And for his sufferings in exile he will justify amongst many the Just One of the world, as the prophet says, *By his knowledge my servant will justify the Just One*—i. e. God—*unto many*, confessing him to be righteous; *and their iniquities*, i. e. those of the Gentiles, *he will bear* for their advantage. *Therefore*, because viz. he thus acknowledged the justice of the Divine judgment, the time will come when *I shall divide him amongst many*, or publicly, *the spoil of the nations*, and *the mighty he shall divide as spoil*, because he *poured out his soul to die* for the glory of God, and was *counted* in exile as a transgressor and sinner himself, and as a bearer of iniquity, although, nevertheless, like David, who said (Ps. xxxv. 13), 'But as for me, when they were sick, my clothing was sackcloth,' *he was* ever *making intercession* and supplication *on behalf of the transgressors* who smote him.

I have now explained for you the whole Parashah. There are many considerations which stand in the way of the Nazarene interpretation. 1. Heaven forbid the prophet to have used such an expression as *smitten God!* (verse 4.) The verse simply means that the Gentiles, during our captivity, imagined that it was of the Lord's hand that Israel was smitten, but that afterwards they will acknowledge that it was not so, and confess that he was 'wounded' for their 'own transgressions,' that the Almighty might take his vengeance upon them. 2. How could it be stated with any propriety of the Almighty that he was 'cut off out of the land of life?' 3. How could it be said of him that he would 'see seed, and have long life?' Does the Almighty need to be reassured by such promises as these? 4. It is said, 'The pleasure of the Lord (is that) he shall prosper with his hand:' and yet this Messiah of theirs is nowhere at all! 5. How could it be said, 'For the transgression of my people, the stroke was on *them?*' it should rather have been 'on him;' למו is plural, referring to Israel. 6. It is said, 'For the travail of his soul, he shall see and be satisfied:' but how is this applicable to him? In a word, the entire Parashah points to the very reverse of what they believe.

f. R. Mosheh of Salerno.

I will now, according to the best of my ability, explain in what way this Parashah refers to Israel. The prophet has already several times spoken of Israel and Jacob as 'my servant;' accordingly, when he begins here, *Behold my servant shall prosper*, it is plain that he alludes likewise to Israel who are now in exile, but who will in time be redeemed. Israel will then, he continues, *be high and exalted;* and *as many* were before *astonished at thee*, when they saw that *his countenance was marred* beyond any of the children of men—you know how many countries there are where people ask whether a Jew has a mouth, an eye, a nose, and so forth—*so he will make many nations to exclaim*—הזה has here the sense of *sprinkling words*, like הטף, Mic. ii. 6, which is from the same root as נטפי מים, '*drops* of water,' Job xxxvi. 27: *at him*, when they behold his greatness, *kings will open their mouth*, saying that *what had not been told them they had seen*—for, though something had been told them of Israel's greatness, yet this had in fact not been one-thousandth part of what they now beheld, and that *what they had not heard they* now *had perceived.* Israel themselves are next introduced as speaking: Who, they ask, was there amongst you that gave credence to the report of this greatness which we proclaimed in your ears? *upon whom*, except upon us, *has the arm of the Lord been revealed?* (Others suppose this verse to be spoken by the Gentiles declaring that they could not believe the matter upon report only, as they had not yet seen it.) He *came up*, wearing the appearance of a shoot out of a puny and blighted tree, without either *form or comeliness*, and when we looked at him there was *no beauty;* how then *could we desire him?* (The last clause an exclamation of surprise; or, perhaps, it may be rendered, *Yet we desire him*, viz. now.) For *he was despised* whilst in exile, *and forlorn of men, a man of pains and known to sickness*—a phrase which cannot be used except of one who has had ailments for a series of years, and hence strictly applicable to Israel, whereas the 'sickness' experienced by Jesus did not extend beyond the single day upon which he was put to death—and as he passed along the roads such was his humiliation and shame that men *hid* their *faces from him: he was despised and we esteemed him not.* Therefore the *sicknesses* and *pains* which ought to have fallen to our lot were *borne* and *carried* by him instead: yet *we thought him stricken, smitten of God, and afflicted.* But *he was wounded for our transgressions*—or, as Yonathan renders, *was profaned*, referring the words to the Sanctuary which is at present profaned for our transgressions: by his explanation of 'poured out his soul to die,' viz. resigned his soul to his murderers, Yonathan means, however, to refer to the Messiah, who for Israel's sake exposed himself to the perils of war, but never actually died: you will find a similar expression applied to Zebulun, Judg. v. 18, 'The people which despised their soul *unto dying*.' *The chastisement of the whole of us*, the sufferings which should have been ours, came *upon him*—שלום, from the root שָׁלֵם *to be whole*, is used as in Jer. xiii. 19, where it is equivalent to כל—*and by his stripes*—the stripes (Exod. xxi. 25) which he bore when 'stricken'—*we are healed. All we like sheep went astray*, were in error upon this point: *the Lord* had *laid on him the iniquity of us all,* whereas we thought him *stricken of God, and afflicted* [without any such cause]. *He was oppressed,* etc., *and opened not his mouth:* but how can this apply to Jesus? did not Jesus cry out, 'My God, my God, why hast thou forsaken me?' [It is true however of Israel; and Israel] also was in exile like *a sheep led to the slaughter. From* the *coercion* of captivity, *and from the judgments* to which he was there liable, *he was taken,* and released by God into 'an open space;' but who would have made such an announcement to that generation, while he was *cut off from the land of life,* i. e. from the land of Israel? *for the transgression of my people,* they will every one be saying, *the stroke was upon them,* viz. when, as the prophet said before, Israel was 'wounded for our transgressions.' *And he made his grave at the will of the wicked,* entrusted his death to the hand of the wicked and the wealthy who endeavoured to seduce him to false worships; he would never, however, comply, but preferred death, for *he did no violence, neither was there guile in his mouth.* (Or these words may mean that they slew him *without* violence or guile, i. e. although he had been guilty of neither one nor the other.) *He shall see seed,* etc. How can the heretics apply these words to Jesus? 'seed' is a term which never occurs except in its strict physical sense; but Jesus had no seed, nor long life.

The Parashah succeeding this, 'Shout, O barren, thou that hast not borne,' etc., 'For thy Maker is thy husband,' 'He hath called thee as a woman, forsaken and grieved in spirit, and a wife of youth, when thou wast refused' (liv. 1, 5, 6), is addressed to Israel (as the prophet had said before, l. 1, 'Where is the bill of your mother's divorcement?'): for who was 'grieved in spirit' but the congregation of Israel in exile? again (liv. 7), 'For a small moment have I forsaken thee; but with great mercies will I gather thee:' but who was there scattered that the Lord should 'gather' her, except Israel? again (verses 8, 9), 'In a little wrath I hid my face from thee, etc. . . . . . : I have sworn that I would not be wroth with thee, nor rebuke thee:'

but with whom was God 'wroth' so often as with Israel, whom he led captives to Egypt, to Assyria, to Babylon? . . . . . .

g. R. Yoseph Albo.

Sometimes, too, misfortunes light upon the righteous not as a punishment, but for the sake of a whole nation, that atonement may be made for it. This is because the Almighty takes pleasure in the preservation of the world, and knows that the righteous will bear his sufferings cheerfully, without quarrelling with any of his attributes: he therefore brings sufferings upon the just, as a satisfaction for the evil [otherwise] destined to afflict a whole people, in order that it may thus be averted: this is what our Rabbis mean by their saying[f], 'The death of the righteous worketh atonement.' We find the Law stated clearly in Scripture: God says to Ezekiel (iv. 4–6), 'Lie on thy left side; and I will place upon it the iniquity of the house of Israel, etc.[f], and thou shalt bear it: and when thou hast finished these things, then thou shalt lie again upon thy right side, and shalt bear the iniquity of the house of Judah.' In accordance with the same principle, the statements found in the Parashah, *Behold my servant shall prosper*, are all to be referred to Israel (who is here called 'my servant,' as Is. xliv. 2, xli. 8): when the prophet says, *Surely he carried our sicknesses, etc.; but we thought him stricken, smitten of God, and afflicted*, he means to say that when men see sufferings falling upon the righteous, they think they fall upon them on their own account, and are hence naturally surprised: it is not so in fact, however; they do not fall upon them for any sin they may have committed, but as an atonement whether for all the world, or for the entire people, or for some single city.

---

[f] *Mo'ed qaṭon*, 28[a].

h. R. Israel (Nagara ?).

[g] High and exalted and lofty exceedingly shall be my servant; yea, he shall prosper: | my servant, the 'branch,' shall cause redemption to branch forth; he shall gather the flock of my hand: | and upon him there shall rest the spirit of wisdom, and the splendour of my majesty! | The coming of Shiloh I will speed, that those who wait on me may not be ashamed: | my banner he shall set up, my feet he shall exalt, in order that every sorrowing heart may rejoice!

The gates of redemption he shall quickly open, so that none may shut: | the sick ones that wait for him, which are come into the prison, he shall redeem; | the sword that executeth the vengeance of the covenant he shall then gird on.

The breath of his lips shall slay the wicked, and hew in pieces the oppressor: | justice shall be the girdle of his loins, as he opens hidden places: | from the four corners of the world he shall gather unto himself the sheep which are cast far off.

As a prince he shall stand; yea, as an ensign of the peoples, whereunto the Gentiles may seek: | the place of his rest also shall be glorious; but the young lions shall lack, | and they which make their boast of false gods shall then be brought to confusion.

i. R. Eliyyah de Vidas.

It is said in the *Tana d'bê Eliyyahu*, during the thirteen years for which R. Shim'on ben Yoḥai was imprisoned in the cave, the depths of wisdom were revealed to him, and he attained knowledge of the future. In particular, he learnt how the man that has committed iniquities must suffer for them, and is not worthy to enter the celestial light (which is the oil of which David speaks when he says, Ps. xxiii. 5, 'Thou makest mine head fat with oil'), unless he first bruise and crush himself, as it is said

g The first letters of the several stanzas in the original form the acrostic *Israel*.

(Num. xxviii. 5), 'Mingled with *crushed* oil:' and this is that which is written, *But he was wounded for our transgressions, bruised for our iniquities*, the meaning of which is that since the Messiah bears our iniquities which produce the effect of his being bruised, it follows that whoso will not admit that the Messiah thus suffers for our iniquities, must endure and suffer for them himself.

It is related in *Wayyiqra Rabbâ*, on Lev. vii. 1, as follows: The Almighty said to Israel, My son, I am he who once declared to you that I had no pleasure except [h]in joyfulness and[h] in the man that was free from trespass: I have now changed; and I say that though a man commit countless trespasses, one upon another, yet if he repents, and humbles himself to the ground, and regards himself as only half pure—the other half of him having a trespass-offering hanging in suspense over it continually[i]—'lo, then I am with him in mercy,' and will accept his repentance, and will grant him sons who shall be diligent in the Law, and keep the words of my commandments in their mouth, as it is written, *The Lord was pleased to bruise him; if his soul makes a trespass-offering, he shall see seed, have long life, and that which the Lord hath pleasure in shall prosper in his hand.*

j. R. Hayyim Ibn Musa.

He states, moreover, that there are some of the Jews who declare that the Messiah will come into the world prostrate and bowed down because of our sins; and that this is clear from the verse, *But we thought him stricken, smitten of God, and afflicted.* Our answer is, that the words of Nicolaus, no less than those of the Jew whom he cites, justify no such inference; or, if it is a 'Midrash,' then there is no obligation to reply to it at all, for 'men do not reply to an allegorical exposition[k];' and

---

[h] In the extract, as cited p. 395, these words, which seem in this connexion to be superfluous, are absent.

[i] Above, p. 307.

[k] Cf. above, p. 124.

I myself also know of allegorical expositors among the Nazarenes whom many of their teachers utterly repudiate; for example, in this very kingdom the allegorizings of Frai Vincente Frère have been in many quarters repudiated, although he had an extraordinary reputation for learning and piety.

Nicolaus further asserts that his death is described by Isaiah, in the words, *As a sheep led to death.* Isaiah, however, in reality does not use such words; and granting that another has used them, still who can lay it down that they refer to Jesus? it must remain doubtful until he can give us demonstration of it. In truth, we believe that the verse refers to the people of Israel, or of Judah, who are spoken of as God's 'servant.'

Objection 9. From what Isaiah says of the Messiah (who is speedily to come in our own days!), *He shall see seed, shall have long days,* the Jews urge, he alleges, that, as Jesus had neither seed nor long life, he could not be the Messiah. They urge also, he continues, the same objection from the words of the eighty-ninth Psalm (verse 5), 'I will establish his seed for ever:' Jesus, they say, had no seed; and hence could not be the Messiah. In reply, Nicolaus points out that Jesus could not be expected to have material children, but only spiritual ones, for carnal union only brings with it folly; and maintains that he can derive the same inference from the verse, 'In Isaac shall thy seed be called,' which must mean that his seed is to consist of the Apostolate. But to this we rejoin, that the word used in Scripture with reference to God is not 'seed,' but 'sons;' if Jesus then, as they believe, was God, how could it be said that he would 'see seed?' And as to the other expression, 'have long days,' this was never fulfilled in Jesus, for he suffered at half the age usually allotted to man. Then the text, *If his soul shall make*, etc., since *If* expresses a condition, must imply that if he does *not* make his soul a trespass-offering, he will not either see seed or have long life: but language such as this would be blasphemy if spoken of God, though not if spoken only of the Messiah. And, thirdly, how can the expression,

'Make his soul a trespass-offering,' be in any sense applicable to God? And the passage adduced from Ps. lxxxix. is addressed by the Almighty to David as an assurance that carnal—not spiritual—kings will issue from his loins: this is the simple and entire truth.

k. Milḥamoth Adonai.

The Nazarene: We have now arrived at the Parashah, *Behold my servant shall prosper:* I have heard what you have once already told me in general terms, that henceforward all the predictions of joy and prosperity in this book refer to delivery either from the captivity of Babylon, or from that more protracted captivity of Edom in which you are now living, in accordance with the constant mention in them of Zion and Jerusalem. You also told me generally that I was a 'gleaner amongst the sheaves,' in maintaining that an individual verse need not of necessity be connected with what immediately precedes and follows it. But in fact, letter by letter, and word by word, this Parashah, from beginning to end, refers to him: for it relates how he fell into the hand of his enemies, and suffered himself for our iniquities, and was buried between the wicked; how, also, he was wounded for the transgression of the people, and we are healed by his stripes, and similarly many other incidents of his life: you have but to read it in order to see that it speaks plainly of him. I know also that your own great teachers unwittingly bear witness to the fact that the subject to whom it refers must be God, when they say, 'He shall be higher than Moses, and loftier than the angels:' who, indeed, is loftier than the angels, save God alone?

The Hebrew: This too I will wrest from your bosom: your opinion of the Parashah may in truth be refuted on ever so many grounds. 1. The prophet calls him *my servant:* though it is certain that the Godhead could not so address one who was no less God than himself; indeed, even the Father does not call his Son a 'servant;' for 'servant' as compared with 'master' implies a distinction of essence which does not subsist between 'father' and 'son'—the less so, as the very word 'son' itself (בן) is derived from בנה ('to build'), and so denotes one who is of the same structure with his father: hence the angels, and in like manner righteous men, are called 'sons' in virtue of their understanding. But the condition of a slave presupposes diversity of essence, though there may be an accidental connexion between him and his lord. When, however, the righteous are styled 'servants,' it is from a consideration of the commands—or prohibitions—imposed on them by the Almighty: and thus we may find the same person called a 'son' in respect of his understanding, and a 'servant' in respect of his subordination to God: thus, in the passage (Mal. i. 6), 'If I am a father, where is my honour? and if a lord, where is the fear of me?' the 'honour' is that which is owing peculiarly from a son, the 'fear' is that which is owing from a servant. 2. He is called a 'man of pains and *known* of sickness:' but such an expression is not used except of one who is habitually ailing; and such was not the case with Jesus. 3. He is said to be 'despised and forlorn of men, without form or comeliness:' but Jesus was handsome in person: was he not one of the seed royal, who assuredly were all 'goodly in form and well-favoured?' Nor can the description allude to the time of his death, for, since men *marvelled* at his elevation (lii. 13), the expressions must denote one who before had been constantly so circumstanced. 4. Isaiah says, 'For the transgression of my people was there a stroke upon *them*'—in the plural; but [had he meant to indicate Jesus] he ought to have said 'upon *him*:' we certainly find למו used occasionally as a singular, as Ps. xi. 7, but only as an anomaly. 5. He says, '*He* made his grave,' etc.; but he ought rather to have said, '*they* made,' since the allusion must be to Israel who buried him among the wicked. Or if you suppose that Jesus himself is the subject of the verb, did not the action in question take place after his death, when the body, we know, is devoid of all power of sensation? 6. He says of him that he shall 'see seed;' but you will nowhere find the term 'seed' used except of that which is born physically. 7. He says similarly, 'He shall lengthen days;' but this is a phrase which, according to its natural meaning, would denote some period which is terminable. For although our Rabbis[l] expound the words, 'Thou shalt have long days' (Deut. xxii. 7) as signifying infinite duration, this is an allegorical exposition, which however they are compelled to adopt, because the time mentioned has a beginning assigned to it; but time without either beginning or end cannot be denoted by the phrase 'length of days.' And if you reply that the words refer to his manhood, then this never had 'long days' at all. 7. The expression 'cut off from the land of life' is an unsuitable one to be employed of God.—Moreover, I can assure you generally that with respect to Messiah son of David, the Scriptures affirm consistently that he will be neither slain nor delivered into the hands of his haters: in fact, this is only said of Messiah son of Joseph, for reasons which we have already explained on the section *Ḥeleq*. You should also bear generally in mind that upon the man appointed to be the true Messiah signs and tokens will converge such as have never yet been manifested on any of those who have claimed to be the Messiah themselves: this was clearly shewn in the case of Bar Koziba, whom men quickly found to be no arbiter or judge[m] One of these signs characteristic of the Messiah is to be, as you know, the acquisition of vast dominions, as it is written, 'His dominion shall be from sea to sea' (Zech. ix. 10), and similarly, 'And to another people his kingdom shall not be left' (Dan. ii. 44): this, however, has never been fulfilled in him, or indeed in any one else, but least of all in Jesus, who never had any dominion whatever. And even the Romans, whose sway extended over the greater part of the world, when

---

[l] *Qiddushin*, 39[b].   [m] *Sanhedrin*, 93[b].

in course of time they embraced his faith, were reduced, and lost much of their power. Many other facts pointing in the same direction have been set forth in a previous part of this treatise: only remember that in truth the Parashah refers throughout to Israel and the Messiah, who will meet with extraordinary prosperity, so that all the nations who have before been only acquainted with our humiliation will be astonished both at him and at us. The entire explanation you will find stated with ampler details in our Commentary on Isaiah: as, in fact, we have shewn, the argument which you adduced from the saying of the Rabbis, 'loftier than the angels,' possesses no cogency whatever.

l.

ישכיל, i. e. will *prosper*. משחת, because his countenance and form were *marred* beyond those of other men. יקפצו, like the verse (Job xxix. 9), 'Princes withheld words, and laid their hand upon their mouth.' יונק, *a bough:* as though to say that Israel came up formerly before the Lord, and hence resembled a bough or root in arid soil, which does not grow large. ונחמדהו, R. H. . . . .[n]: 'he had no beauty *that* we might desire it.' כמסתר פנים, 'Ibn Janah: 'if he had but for a short time hidden his face from him, he would have been destroyed.' אכן—i. e. אם כן—*if* it was *so*, then, the sicknesses which we laid upon him he *carried*, and the pains which we occasioned to him he *bare*. *We thought him*, etc., i. e. as we plagued him, we imagined in our hearts that God had bidden us so to smite and afflict him. *He was wounded for our iniquities*, i. e. as we smote him, it seemed to us as though the Almighty had commanded us to do so; but now the same nations admit that 'he was wounded for our transgressions; in wreaking our vengeance upon him we were transgressing against him in his sickness, and in bruising him we were acting wickedly towards him.' 'Ibn Janah explains the

[n] The initial letter of this Rabbi's name (which is all that the Hebrew text offers) is not enough to enable him to be identified: similarly below, 'Z. A. B.'

words thus: We thought that God had smitten and corrected him; but it was not so: his sicknesses and pains were the effects of our transgressing against him. מוסר שלומנו, i. e. *the correction* or reproofs *of the whole of us* were *upon him*, and *by smiting him*[o] *we are healed*, i. e. he was smitten in our stead; שלום denotes here *the whole*, as in Jer. xiii. 19. R. Isaiah Mali, however[p], interprets the words to mean 'our peace was removed from off him'—we did not even allow him to have peace. ויי הפגיע בו, i. e. the Lord made him a 'stumbling-block and an offence before us.' מעצר וג׳, the meaning must be that when he was led to the slaughter, he was taken thither from prison and torture, i. e. he was first tortured, and then led off to execution (Z. A. B.) ואת דורו, *and his generation, who can declare* how it fared? (Z. A. B.) *For the transgression of my people*—or, as others prefer, of *his* people—which was actually—or, at least, was destined to be—*a blow to them* (Z. A. B.) *And he made his grave with the wicked*, i. e. according to 'Ibn Janaḥ, as cited by Qamḥi[q], he died before his time through their slaying him; and this, *although he had done no violence with his hands*[r], like the wicked who die before their time, or are put to death for their wickedness. מותיו, the plural of מות, for they were often put to death after being pierced through and through, or after having suffered cruel tortures (Z. A. B.) מעמל וג׳ (as the meaning seems to me to be), *for the travail* entailed by the troubles he endured, *he shall be satisfied;* notwithstanding this, however, *my servant* still *justified the just*, and did not, for what he had suffered, condemn him, but judged righteously in spite of all that he endured in bearing their iniquities, and so received the promise, *Therefore I will divide him a portion*, etc. (Z. A. B.)

---

o Comp. pp. 62, 373.

p P. 76.

q Perhaps Yoseph Qamḥi: this opinion of 'Ibn Janaḥ is not known from any other source.

r The author is thinking of the parallel passage, Job xvi. 17.

m.

LII. [14] *So* will he now prevail *and scatter many nations,* driving them from their land, like a man sprinkling water, when no one drop touches another (R. I[saiah Mali[8]]). Israel *came up like a sucker* which at first is scarcely perceived, but after a short time appears as a great tree: in the same way Israel were formerly depressed in their exile, but are now exalted over all: and *like a root* planted in *the dry earth* which men think to be hopelessly withered, but which at last shoots up, and produces a rich growth of foliage. Also Israel had at first *no form or comeliness, and when we looked at him, there was no beauty that we might desire it,* or exclaim, How beautiful the features of this Jew! (R. I[saiah Mali]). ידוע חולי, according to some, '*broken* of sickness,' as Judg. viii. 16. חדל אישים, since the prophet represents Israel as a single man, he speaks of him here as *ceasing from men,* i. e. as ceasing on account of his humiliation to be classed amongst other men (R. ʿImmanu'el). *But he carried* the *sicknesses* and *pains* which we occasioned to him: and for this reason he had no beauty: *yet we thought him stricken, smitten of God, and afflicted*—imagined that it had been God's will that we should afflict him. *But he was wounded for our transgressions,*—for when we wounded him, it was imputed to us as a great transgression by the Creator, and *bruised for our iniquities,* for similarly, when we bruised him, it was counted to us as an 'iniquity for the judge:' *our peace was removed* from *him,* for we did not allow him even to enjoy peace; *and by his stripes we were healed,* for as we inflicted upon him injury and wounds, we so rejoiced at his misfortunes that we seemed to be healed ourselves.

8 So the abbreviation must probably be interpreted; at any rate, both the explanations cited occur almost *verbatim* in the commentary of Isaiah Mali: see pp. 74, 75.

n. SEPHER ḤASIDIM.

Every one who is despised by the world, provided only it be not for deeds of wickedness, will be exalted in the future, as it is written, *Behold my servant shall prosper: he shall be high and exalted and lofty exceedingly.* Who is signified here? The same of whom it is written in the text below, 'He was the despised and forlorn of men.'

o. MIDRASH KONEN.

The fifth mansion in Paradise is built of onyx and jasper, and set stones, and silver and gold, and fine gold, surrounded by rivers of balsam: before the entrance flows the Gihon; a pavilion (?) is there of 'all trees of frankincense' (Cant. iv. 14), with sweet odours, and beds of gold and silver, and richly-variegated garments: there dwell Messiah son of David, and Elijah, and Messiah son of Ephraim; there also is the 'litter of the wood of Lebanon' (*ib.* iii. 9), like the tabernacle which Moses made in the wilderness; all the furniture thereof and 'the pillars thereof of silver, the bottom of gold, the seat of purple,' and within it, Messiah son of David who loveth Jerusalem. Elijah takes him by his head, lays him down in his bosom, holds him, and says, 'Bear thou the sufferings and wounds wherewith the Almighty doth chastise thee for Israel's sin;' and so it is written, *He was wounded for our transgressions, bruised for our iniquities,* until the time when the end should come.

p. 'ASÉRETH MÊMROTH.

The Messiah, in order to atone for them both [for Adam and David], will *make his soul a trespass-offering*, as it is written next to this, in the Parashah *Behold my servant:* אשם, i. e. cabbalistically[t], Menahem son of Ammiel. And what is written

[t] Lit. *by geometry*, thus: מנחם בן עמיאל = 40 + 50 + 8 + 40 + 2 + 50 + 70 + 40 + 10 + 1 + 30 = 341; אשם = 1 + 300 + 40 = 341.

after it? *He shall see seed, shall have long days, and the pleasure of the Lord shall prosper in his hand.*

q. Sepher ha-Gilgalim.

You must know also that the soul of celestial splendour no created being in the world has ever yet been worthy to obtain: the King Messiah, however, will receive it: it is accordingly said of him, *He shall be high and exalted*, etc., or, as our Rabbis say, 'He shall be higher than Abraham, exceedingly above Adam!'

r. Yalqut R'ubheni.

Said the old R. Ḥiyya: We have found no shepherd ready to sacrifice himself for his flock, except Moses, who said (Exod. xxxii. 32), 'And now, if thou wilt forgive their sin—and if not, blot me, I pray thee:' blot me out whence? from this world, and also from that which is to come, in order that the words might be fulfilled, *Because he poured out his soul to die.*

This is the law of the trespass-offering (Lev. vii. 1). The Holy One spake thus unto Israel: My sons, I said unto you, I have no pleasure save in the man in whom is no transgression; but my words I have changed: though a man commit a hundred transgressions one after another, yet, if he turn, and repent, and humble himself to the earth, and look upon one half of himself as guilty, and the other half as innocent, and consider the 'suspended trespass-offering' to be continually due from him, lo, 'I am with him in mercy,' and will accept his repentance, and grant him children of the Law—children diligent in the study and performance of it—and the words of the Law I will put for ever in his mouth, as it is written, *The Lord was pleased to bruise him* [u]. Says the Almighty to Israel, My son, think not of me as of this sand, which belongs neither to

---

[u] Above, p. 386.

the living nor to the dead; but let a man humble himself, and then, *if he puts his soul* in his hand, and (as it is said, Lev. vi. 6, 'brings a trespass-offering') offers atonement for himself, assuredly he shall *see seed* and *prolong his days*, i. e.—according to one explanation of the words—'see seed' in this world, and 'prolong his days' in the world to come.

Who is it that *carried our sicknesses and bare our pains?* Man himself, who first brought death into the world. Now learn what is secret from that which is revealed: Because he carried our sicknesses—for man himself by the rotation [of souls [v]] is Adam, David, and the Messiah—therefore he suffered in order to atone for the sin of our first parent who brought death into the world.

s. YALQUT HADASH [x].

The souls of the righteous wander to and fro in the world; and when they see amongst the sons of men those who are crushed by the sufferings undergone by them for the honour of God, and when they see also those wicked members of the generation who are the cause of the exile being prolonged, they come and announce it to the Messiah. Forthwith the Messiah proceeds into one of the palaces in Paradise called the Palace of the children of sickness; he enters thither and invites all the pains and sufferings of Israel to come and rest upon him. And did he not in this way lighten them off Israel, there would be no man in the whole world able to bear the penalties incurred for transgression of the Law; while Israel were in their own land they freed themselves from such sicknesses and other punishments by means of offerings, but now the Messiah frees them from them, as it is written, *He was wounded for our transgressions.*

---

[v] I.e. in accordance with the doctrine of transmigration.

[x] Comp. p. 14.

t.

The heretics explain this Parashah of Jesus. You may ask them, however, why he should be called a 'servant,' having no master? and if they reply that the Son is subject to the Father, then there are two distinct persons [in the Godhead], whereas they declare themselves that the whole is one. Or, if it be thought that he is called 'servant,' because he submitted himself to the will of his Godhead, why should men own the servant as lord and God? is it not better to serve God, the lord of all, than to serve the menial of a king? Again, the text says that he was *smitten and afflicted of God;* but he did not 'afflict him willingly' (Lam. iii. 33), for the Jews crucified him after the condemnation of Pilate. Again, it says, *The Lord was pleased to bruise him,* and yet they throw the guilt of his crucifixion upon us: but if God in his wisdom was pleased through him to accomplish the restoration of his world, why should men be punished for fulfilling his purpose? The text says also, *The Lord laid upon him the iniquity of us all;* but we Israelites are not saved by him at all, nor are even those who believe that he came to save men from Gehenna, and to repair the consequences of Adam's sin on Isaac, Jacob, and Moses our master (with whom God spake mouth to mouth, and of whom he took special charge at the time of his burial); the righteous and the foolish all die alike, and the just and the wicked are brought down to the Underworld together. This, however, reason can certainly not determine, nor intelligence endure; since, as it is said, 'Who is the man that feareth the Lord? .... his soul shall rest at ease,' etc. (Ps. xxv. 12 f.); and similarly in the assurance addressed by the Almighty to Moses, 'Behold thou shalt lie with thy fathers' (Deut. xxxi. 16): but what an assurance to give him, that he should rest with them in Gehenna! Men are sinful and disobedient now exactly as they were before he came: those who do evil go down into hell, and those who do good inherit Paradise (as, in fact, they assert themselves); yet if Jesus came for the purpose of repairing Adam's sin, then he ought to have repaired it entirely, and rescued men from all its consequences—destroying the enmity of the serpent, and the pain of childbearing, the toil necessary to 'eat bread,' the growth of 'thorns and thistles,' and all the murder and warfare which flow from the serpent's venom. But, in fact, everything attests that his coming has been a source of neither advantage nor detriment: how still does the curse pronounced when Cain slew his brother Abel ever grow in severity! And as to the words in ver. 10, which denote a condition that '*if* his soul makes a trespass-offering, he will see seed,' etc., where are the sons of Jesus? besides, if he be God, it is quite clear that such an expression as is here used cannot be applied to him.

By his stripes we were healed: yet how many of his disciples were prostrated by sickness! most of them, too, were crucified, or in other ways put to death, without the 'stripes' endured by Jesus making any manner of ransom for them. The truth is, that the Parashah relates throughout to any just man who is a 'servant of the Lord,' and who is ready for love of him to sacrifice his life by suffering martyrdom in his service.

u.

Flee, my beloved, until the end of the vision shall speak[y]; | hasten, and the shadows shall take their flight hence: | high and exalted and lofty shall be the despised one; | he shall be prudent in judgment, and shall sprinkle many! | Lay bare thine arm! cry out, and say: | 'The voice of my beloved; behold he cometh[z]!'

v. Buch der Verzeichnung.

The fifty-third chapter they call the golden chapter, and say that it refers to their Messiah; we, on the contrary, can prove

---

[y] *Or*, come speedily; see Hab. ii. 3. Comp. also Cant. viii. 14, ii. 17.

[z] Comp. Cant. ii. 8. The lines give the acrostic, בחיי חזק.

clearly that it refers to Israel; indeed, we see daily everything happening to them as is here described: besides, chapters fifty-two and fifty-four cannot relate to their Messiah. They say that their Messiah is God, whilst this Parashah begins 'My *servant* shall act prudently;' but a servant cannot be God: Moses, again, is called the 'servant of God,' and Scripture says that 'none arose like him.' They say, further, that he gave himself up willingly as a sacrifice for their sins, whereas in St. John's Gospel (viii. 59), when they threw stones at him, it is recorded that he went out of the way. At the end of the chapter it is written, *He shall see seed and prolong his days;* but how can God have 'seed,' and how long was his life? Much more might be adduced in order to shew that the Christians cannot go far with their arguments; but I prefer not to waste time by protracting the discussion further.

w.

We are shrunk up in our misery even until now! our rock hath not come nigh to us: Messiah, our righteousness, hath turned from us: we are in terror, and there is none to justify us! Our iniquities and the yoke of our transgressions he will bear, for *he was wounded for our transgressions:* he will carry our sins upon his shoulder, that we may find forgiveness for our iniquities, and *by his stripes we are healed.* O eternal One, the time is come to make a new creation: from the vault of heaven bring him up, out of Seir draw him forth, that he may make his voice heard to us in Lebanon, a second time by the hand of Yinnon [a]!

[a] One of the Rabbinical names of the Messiah, derived from Ps. lxxii. 17: comp. above, p. 7; Pusey, *Lectures on Daniel*, p. 481 (ed. 1864).

XLVIII. HERZ HOMBERG.

This prophecy is disconnected with what precedes it. According to the opinion of Rashi and 'Ibn 'Ezra, it relates to Israel at the end of their captivity; the term 'servant' and the use of the singular number referring to the individual members of the nation. But if so, what can be the meaning of the passage, 'He was wounded for our transgressions,' etc.? Who was 'wounded?' who are the 'transgressors?' Who 'carried' the sickness and 'bare' the pains? And where are the sick? are they not the same as those who are 'smitten' and who 'bear?' And if 'each turned to his own way,' upon whom did 'the Lord lay the iniquity of them all?' The Ga'on, R. Sa'adyah, explains the whole Parashah of Jeremiah: and there are indeed numerous parts of Scripture in which we can trace a great resemblance to what befel Jeremiah while persecuted by the false prophets. But the commencement of the prophecy, 'He shall be high and exalted and lofty exceedingly,' and similarly the words 'with the mighty he shall divide spoil,' will not admit of being applied to him. The fact is, that it refers to the King Messiah, who will come in the latter days, when it will be the Lord's good pleasure to redeem Israel from among the different nations of the earth. When he first manifests himself those who see him will marvel at him, asking, Who is this man without form or comeliness, that durst presume in his heart to bid all the kings of the earth set Israel free? In one country, people will revile and despise him, keeping in the distance and hiding their faces from him: in another, they will smite and buffet him till he is covered with bruises and stripes, and exhausted with pains; and if he betakes himself elsewhere, they will there attack him in order to slay him without justice or right, and to cast him forth into the grave of a criminal. And even the Israelites themselves will only regard him as 'one of the vain fellows,' believing none of the announcements which will be made by him in God's name, but being contumacious against him, and averring that all the reproaches and persecutions which fall to his lot are sent upon him from heaven, for that he is 'smitten of God' for his own sin. For they will not at first perceive that whatever he underwent was in consequence of their own transgression, the Lord having chosen him to be a trespass-offering, like the scape-goat which bore all the iniquities of the house of Israel. Being, however, himself well aware that through his pains and revilings the promised redemption will eventually come at the appointed time, he will endure all with a willing soul, neither complaining nor opening his mouth 'in the siege and distress wherewith the enemies of Israel will oppress him' (as is pointed out from the passage here in the Haggadah). And then, when the 'waters of indignation reach even to the neck,' the arm of the Lord will be revealed upon him to deliver him out of all his troubles; he will not give him over to die like a transgressor, but he will raise him on high, and exalt him exceedingly, and the Lord's pleasure shall prosper in his hand. And because he shewed himself ready to meet death for the sake of the many, or, in other words, for the general advantage, he will make him head over *the many*—i. e. over the children of Israel now in dispersion, and the kings of the earth will be astonished at him, because, though seeming to them at first to be despised and forlorn of men, he will then become as one of themselves, even 'dividing spoil with the mighty.' Perhaps upon this prophecy is based the opinion of Sh'mu'el[a],

---

[a] *Sanhedrin*, 99[b].

who said that the only difference between the present world and the days of the Messiah was in the submission of the kingdoms, which would then be consummated.

LII. [13] ישכיל, *shall prosper.* [14] שממו, *were astonished:* all the past tenses in this Parashah must be understood as futures; the prophet in his vision sees the events as though they were already accomplished. כן, *rightly*—a word serving to corroborate a statement. מִשחת, for מָשחת, *marred* or *spoilt.* [15] יזה, according to the Targum, *to scatter;* and so also Rashi, for in *sprinkling,* a man scatters the blood which has previously been massed together into innumerable drops. יקפצו, will *shut,* as Deut. xv. 7: in Qamḥi's words, 'Their astonishment will be such that they will lay their hand upon their mouth;' there is, however, no occasion to suppose this, for when a man is greatly amazed, his lips are shut and he is unable to speak.

LIII. [1] This verse is parenthetical, the prophet remarking that the kings will rightly be amazed; for who that heard our words could fail to believe them! *Upon whom* was it revealed, save upon him? [2] יונק, a small and weakly plant which clings to the earth, as a sucking child to its mother's breast. ונראהו, there will be nothing in his countenance to attract the eye of the beholder. [3] חדל, he will be *forlorn of men,* because all will hold themselves aloof from him. ידוע, chastened and *broken* by severe sicknesses, as in Judg. viii. 16. So R. D. . . . . כמסתר, i. e. he will be as one despised and rejected, from whom every one hides his face; comp. Deut. xxxi. 18. ולא חשבנוהו, for he seemed in our eyes to be worth nothing at all; comp. Is. ii. 22. [4] In accordance with the view which we have stated above, these are the words of Israel, recognising what was previously hidden from them, and exclaiming, Now we know that it was for our sins that he suffered. סבלם, the suffix is appended, although the substantive has preceded, for emphasis, as Exod. ii. 6 (R. D. . . . .) *But we* at that time erred in imagining that his sufferings were for his own sin. [5] מחולל, as חלל, Ps. cix. 22.

מפשעינו, *on account of* our transgressions,—מן as in מרבר, Josh. xxii. 24: so also מעונותינו. מוסר וג׳, i.e. whatever might *remove* or put an end to our peace he took upon himself. [6] *We went astray like sheep*, which go they know not whither. הפגיע: the root פגע, besides its usual and known significations, denotes also bodily or moral perception produced either by contact with a sensible object, or by a mental representation, or by some other influence affecting the subject: and so it said, A blockhead is not easily *touched*, i.e. has no feeling. עון, the *penalty* for iniquity, as Gen. iv. 13. [7] נענה, was *answered* with words of fraud (Rashi). [8] עצר: the ruler who is a protector of his people is called עוצר (a sovereign); comp. 1 Sam. ix. 17. משפט, i.e. the place in which the judges sit. לקח, *was seized*, as 1 Sam. iv. 11: and hence the spoil which soldiers take forcibly from their captives is termed מלקוח. The meaning is that they will seize him, and neither allow him to be brought before the sovereign for fear he should have compassion on him and rescue him from their hands, nor permit him to appear before the judges lest on trial he should be acquitted: thus he will be debarred *from* both *the sovereign and the judge*. ישוחח, to *declare*, as Ps. cxliii. 5: the clause, *And his generation*, etc., forms a parenthesis, in which the prophet asks, Who would even mention with his lips that cruel and wicked generation which would interdict him guiltless and uncondemned *from the land of the living?* The meaning of נגזר is not that they will actually kill him (else what can be the signification of 'he shall see seed, have long days,' and 'therefore I will divide him,' etc.?), but that they will devise to do so, and will *decree* that he is to have his grave with the wicked: God however will deliver him, and not leave him in their power: נגזר thus signifies *was decreed*, as Est. ii. 1. [9] ויתן: we have already shewn how they agreed together to condemn him as one accursed; so that if they succeeded in putting him to death, they would have buried him beside the wicked. עשיר, used as in Job xxvii. 19, 'The *rich* lieth down, and doth so no more,' where Job adds (verse 13),

'This is the portion of the wicked man:' the word appears, then, to be sometimes used especially of one who has enriched himself by robbery and violence, and is here, therefore, parallel to the 'wicked.' במותיו: the sense of the whole is, 'And he made in his deaths his grave with the wicked and the rich:' the plural *deaths* is used because piercing him, as cruel men do, through and through, they would, so to speak, be putting him to death again and again. [10] *But the Lord,* in his own deep purpose, *was pleased to bruise him,* as the prophet proceeds to describe: *if,* he says, addressing the Almighty, thou hast decreed to *make his soul a trespass-offering,* it is only in order that he may *see seed, and have long days,* the meaning being, that this had been done for the purpose of convincing the kings of the Gentiles that he was to be the messenger of God, sent to gather together the outcasts of Israel. [11] The travail of his soul he will see, i.e. feel, even to satiety; comp. Job vii. 4, 'I am *full* of tossings to and fro:' nevertheless, *in his knowledge* or reflection *he will justify* the judgment determined against him by the Almighty; for *my servant will be just for many,* i.e. there are some men who are perfectly righteous, and free from every taint of transgression, and who follow their Maker's will, but who at the same time are righteous only for themselves, and will not sacrifice their own lives for the sake of others: *my servant,* however, will be righteous *for many,* 'adventuring his soul freely' for the general good, and not sparing his own life if others might be benefited through his death, but enduring the burden of their sins in order to release them from punishment. [12] *Therefore,* because he thus sacrificed himself for the general advantage, the lot and good fortune of *the many* will be his portion, and the reward for his sufferings. שלל does not here signify the spoil of war, for nothing is said of any battle to be waged by him, but abundance and plenty of good things, as in Prov. xxxi. 11: the meaning being that like one of *the mighty* among the kings of the earth, he will live in affluence and plenty. הערה,

poured out his soul, emptying it from his body, as Gen. xxiv. 20. *He was counted with the transgressors*, because they appointed his grave by the side of the wicked. יפגיע, *he will intercede* for the transgressors, and for those who rise up against him.

XLIX. R. YAQOB YOSEPH MORD'KHAI HAYYIM PASSANI.

I am much surprised at those commentators who have applied themselves to investigate the meaning of this Parashah. One, for example, maintains that it was the intention of the prophet to allude to Moses; another, that he referred to the Israelitish people; a third applies it to king Josiah; a fourth dwells much upon the King Messiah, and so brings the Midrash into the text: for ourselves, however, we know with certainty that Scripture never bears any other than the simple and literal meaning; a different supposition will not enable us to 'reply to Epicurus [a].' Moreover, not one of the explanations mentioned is in complete accordance with the language of the text, or succeeds in satisfying us, still less does the opinion of the disbelievers who make these verses the foundation of their faith. Thus the words 'had no form or comeliness' cannot possibly be interpreted of Moses, for every one is well aware that Moses had a fine form and the strength of a lion. And if (as is indeed the case) the words, 'For the transgression of my people were they smitten,' allude to Israel, then the person described as suffering for the nation cannot be the nation itself. And Josiah, because the measure of the iniquities of his generation was then filled up, in spite of all the integrity of his heart, was still never vouchsafed such a signal favour as that

---

[a] See p. 114.

'kings should close their mouths at him,' etc.; nor could it be said of him that he would 'have long days,' for he perished prematurely in the prime of manhood. And as regards the explanation which refers it to the Messiah, we may say, Take heed, O wise men, in your words, even though the language be meant to be metaphorical and indirect. I have therefore been led to the conviction that the Parashah may after all be referred intelligibly and naturally to Hezekiah. For although, like all other prophecies, most of Isaiah's also point to the latter days, when the Messiah will have appeared, still there are particular ones which have reference to that just monarch, and to the fall of Sanherib, which took place in his days and through his merits [b].

LII. 13 *Behold my servant shall prosper*, as it is said, 2 Chron. xxxii. 30, 'And Hezekiah *prospered* in all his works:' he is rightly also called God's 'servant,' for he not only turned himself, but also brought back Judah, and a great part of Israel as well, to the service of God—an achievement which none of his ancestors, in spite of all their excellent intentions, ever contemplated. For he put away the high places, and 'sent letters into every tribe of Israel, saying, Turn ye to the Lord God of Abraham,' etc. (*ib.* xxx. 6), and restored the crown to its former state, entreating the favour of his princes and ministers, almost prostrating himself before them, while he said, 'Hear me, ye Levites, now sanctify yourselves, and sanctify the house of the Lord God of your fathers, and carry out the impurity from the holy place,' etc. (*ib.* xxix. 5 f.) *He shall be high and exalted, and lofty exceedingly;* for so it is said (xxxii. 23), 'And many brought gifts to the Lord, and presents unto Hezekiah king of Judah, and he was *exalted* in the eyes of all the nations.' 14 The dangerous illness which attacked him made 'the strength of his face to change;' and 'the fatness of his flesh grew lean,' as he drew near to the 'gates of death.' 15 Many kings and

[b] Compare Sa'adyah Ibn Danân, p. 204.

princes were amazed exceedingly at the miracle wrought for him, for not with sword or spear did the Lord save his anointed from the hand of Sanherib: but greater far was the miracle which displayed itself in the world when the orb of the sun turned backward before the eyes of all, and when Merodach-Baladan sent ambassadors to him to enquire about the portent which had occurred in the earth; this is what is meant by the words, *What had not been told them they have seen;* for they perceived clearly that so highly favoured was he in the eyes of the Lord, that the order of creation was altered for his benefit.

LIII. [1] *Who believeth our report?* so, feigning surprise, asks the prophet of his pious contemporaries; for good Hezekiah was a descendant of the wicked Ahaz, and upon him was *the arm of the Lord revealed* in the destruction of Sanherib. [2] At the period when all were immersed in idolatrous worships, Hezekiah *came up as a sucker or root, out of the dry* and weary *earth,* in which was no religion or fear of God. [3] As, from his birth upwards, Hezekiah rejected the deeds of his fathers, and the shameful customs of his age, the people abominated him, and held aloof from him, and hence he was *despised and forlorn of men,* his father in particular hating him even to the day of his death, for he 'made him pass through the fire to Moloch' (2 Kings xvi. 3, and *Sanhedrin,* fol. 69), though he was delivered miraculously by God[c]. Still, however, the few righteous who were to be found at that time felt a longing and desire for him, saying, O that the 'rod' were 'come out of the stump of Yishai, and the spirit of knowledge and of the fear of the Lord were resting upon him!' and this is the meaning of the words, *He had no beauty, yet we desired him.* [4] When, after his father's death, he ascended the throne, his servants were so much dissatisfied that, with Shebna at their head, they rebelled against him, and sought to submit themselves to the

---

[c] Compare above, p. 208.

wicked Peqaḥ, son of Remaliah, king of Israel, as Isaiah narrates (v. 6); and when they saw him afflicted with severe illness, their hatred carried itself still further, and they 'poured contempt' upon their 'prince,' judging maliciously that his sufferings were because he had despised their own wicked faith, and that the graven images of their gods had *hidden* their *faces from him.* [5,6] They did so still more when they saw that his affliction prevented him from maintaining the style and manners of a court (*Sanh.* fol. 94), for he would eat only a pound of flesh a day: since, then, he 'did what was right in the eyes of the Lord, with a whole heart, as David his father' (2 Chron. xxix. 2), and 'brought out the impurity from the house' (ver. 5) and restored all Israel to the true faith, the sufferings which he endured must have been for the sake of his generation; almost, indeed, had the Almighty determined to quench the coal that was left, and to give Jerusalem into the hand of Sanherib, and only in consequence of Hezekiah was the redemption of their soul achieved, and deliverance wrought for them by his transcendent merits, so far surpassing the sufferings which he bare. After this, however, all perceived that *he was wounded for* their *transgressions, and bruised for* their *iniquities,* in order to make atonement for them unto God; for the attribute of judgment, displaying itself before them, *laid upon him the iniquity of* them *all,* as the text says, *for the transgression of my people,* even *the stroke* which should have fallen *upon them.* [7] When his sickness was at its worst, he acknowledged the justice of God's judgment upon him, but 'like a dumb man which openeth not his mouth,' expected from hour to hour the moment of his death, as he declares himself in his writing (Is. xxxviii. 9), 'I said in the cutting off of my days, Let me go into the gates of the Underworld,' etc., and accepted his afflictions as sent upon him in love, without murmuring, or complaining of the shortness of his days. [8] When, however, he heard the prophet's command, 'Set thy house in order; for thou shalt die and not live' (ver. 1), he entreated God to grant him a longer life in order that he might be enabled to serve him; else he would have been *taken from sovereignty and judgment* in the prime of life and when his reign had but lately commenced: now, if his death had occurred immediately after the death of Ahaz, before he had had time to restore the faith of his people to its pristine integrity, *who would have told of his generation?* it would have been rather a generation 'departing in darkness' until it was all consumed without having seen the mighty acts of the Lord, wrought by him on behalf of this righteous king; [9] nor would he have left any memorial of himself after him, but would have been buried with his wicked father—as the text states, *And he made his grave with the wicked,* implying that it was so determined—in spite of the innocency of his hands, and the fact that *he had done no violence.* But it was the Lord's pleasure merely *to bruise him,* and to put the guilt of his generation on his soul; accordingly, after his prayer, when God had heard his supplication and seen his tears, the promise is given, *He shall see seed, shall prolong his days;* thus the Almighty added to his life fifteen years, and let him 'see seed,' for previously he had had no children. [12] *Therefore I will divide him a portion with many,* viz. the spoil of Sanherib, because he bare the iniquities of the age, and was counted as a transgressor, and above all interceded for the remnant that were still left (who were 'transgressors'), as it is said (2 Kings xix. 15), 'And Hezekiah prayed before the Lord,' etc.; and (2 Chron. xxxii. 20), 'And Hezekiah the king prayed,' etc.: this, then, is the meaning of *interceded for the transgressors,* in order, viz. that the city might not fall into the hands of the king of Assyria. And so, when all Judah and Jerusalem and the remnant of Israel returned to the service of the Lord, and the sanctuary was restored to its original purity, and the priests to their ministrations, and the Levites to their pulpits[d] (all which Ahaz had neglected), and when

---

[d] Whence they blessed the people.

they beheld the miracles, then all his servants began to love and honour him; and when he died, he did not 'make his grave with the wicked,' as had been determined, and as nearly took place, but he ended his life honourably and 'was buried in the ascent of the sepulchres of the sons of David' (2 Chron. xxxii. 33).

Such is the interpretation which I have been able to give of these verses. And if my view is not in accordance with the mind of the prophet, I pray the Almighty to grant me a reward for what I have done! May the Lord lighten mine eyes in his law! and may the purpose of mine heart be well-pleasing to him!

L. SH'MUEL DAVID LUZZATTO.

Behold my servant. From this point to the end of chapter liii. is a single prophecy, delineating the servant of the Lord, first as crushed beneath every description of suffering, and then as rising up in prosperity and great glory. We have already seen elsewhere in these prophecies how the 'servant of the Lord' is a designation for Israel: as, then, the prophet says there expressly 'Israel my servant,' and 'Jacob my servant' (xli. 8, 9, xliv. 1, 2, 21, xlv. 4), so here it is plain that he is referring likewise to Israel, and describing first their depression whilst in exile, and afterwards their greatness in the time of deliverance. In the same way the Parashah has been interpreted by Rashi, R. Abraham 'Ibn 'Ezra, R. Yoseph Qamḥi (in the *Sepher ha-gâluy*[a]), R. Mosheh ben Naḥman, R. David Qamḥi, Don Yiẓḥaq Abarbanel (in his first explanation); and amongst Christians, by Döderlein, and, following him, by Carl Georg Schuster, Eckermann, Eichhorn, Telge, and Rosenmüller. And that already in the days of the *Tanna'im*[b] this interpretation was adopted by the Jews, is attested by Origen[c]. The Christians, however, explain it in their usual manner; but they have been already answered by 'Ibn 'Ezra, Abarbanel, Rosenmüller, and Gesenius. Rosenmüller in his younger days, and after him Gesenius, referred the

---

a See above, p. 49; and compare also what is stated in the Preface.

b I.e. the doctors of the 'Mishna,' opposed to the אמוראי, or *Amoraim*, who lived *after* the redaction of the Mishna, and embodied the traditional teaching of the *Tanna'im* in the 'Gemara.'

c *Cels.* i. 55: the Jew with whom Origen once disputed maintained ταῦτα πεπροφητεῦσθαι ὡς περὶ ἑνὸς τοῦ ὅλου λαοῦ, καὶ γενομένου ἐν τῇ διασπορᾷ, καὶ πληγέντος, ἵνα πολλοὶ προσήλυτοι γένωνται, κ. τ. λ.

Parashah to the prophets (and very similarly Paulus, to the upright in Israel); but Rosenmüller himself abandoned this view on account of certain expressions which were inapplicable to them : I have pointed out before that the prophets did not form a company of themselves such as might be denoted by a collective term like 'my servant;' nor do we anywhere find that the word is so used explicitly of the prophets as a body, for the phrase employed above (xliv. 26), 'confirming the word of his *servant*,' does not refer to them as a collective aggregate, but to each and every individual prophet who has ever existed. 'Ibn 'Ezra at the end of the chapter gives it as his opinion that the prophet means to allude to himself; Yonathan and the *Korem* [d] apply the prophecy to the Messiah; Augusti to Uzziah king of Judah; Bahrdt and Kongnenburg to Hezekiah; Abarbanel (in his second part) to Josiah; Voltaire and Stäudlin to the prophet Isaiah. And R. 'Eli'ezer, the German, author of the 'Works of the Lord,' interprets it of Job. For my own part, I understand it of Israel in exile; though at the same time perceiving that the language used is applicable, not to the times of the Babylonian exile, but to the exile in which we are placed now. Accordingly, it appears to me that the prophecies following relate to the future redemption, and not to that from Babylon. And as, above, there came first (xxxix. 7) the prediction of the Babylonian captivity, which was then followed by a series of prophecies relating to the deliverance from Babylon, so here the picture of Israel in exile is succeeded by a number of prophecies describing the deliverance that is still to come.

LII. 13 *Behold my servant* Israel *shall prosper*, in compensation for his having been during exile in adversity, and his affairs uniformly unfortunate: nor will he only 'prosper;' he will moreover be *high and exalted, and lofty exceedingly.* 14 *As many were astonished at thee*, when they saw thy affliction in exile, so wilt thou then be high and lifted up, and shalt *scatter many*

---

[d] The title of Herz Homberg's Commentary above, No. XLVIII.

nations. *So marred* and altered *was his countenance beyond men*, etc., is parenthetical (Rosenmüller, Gesenius): the prophet, it may be observed, commences in the second person, but having in the parenthesis employed the third ('*his* countenance,' '*his* form'), he continues to make use of it, saying, 'So shall *he* startle,' etc. מִשְׁחַת: he should have written מָשְׁחָת, in which case it would have been the participle, as Mal. i. 14: the *Ḥireq* and *Pathaḥ* are, however, extremely difficult to account for. My pupil Rabbi M. Ehrenreich, the Levite, says that the punctuators pointed the word so for the reason which I have explained above (xlix. 7), to indicate, viz. that they did not connect the word with the meaning '*marred*,' but with that of *anointed*, as Lev. xxi. 12; and this view is correct. To Israel, however, in their present exile the expression is still eminently applicable; for their countenances are changed so as to be unlike other men's,—indeed, all who see them recognise them immediately, afflictions and subjection and 'terror on every side' being stamped visibly on our faces. But this could not be said of the prophets; for although at times the prophets had their enemies, yet they never stood in such awe of them as for their 'form' to be changed; if they had been faint-hearted, they would simply have ceased to prophesy altogether. [15] As formerly in his depression many were astonished at him, *so* now in his exaltation he will occasion in many nations the greatest wonder. יזה, from the root נזה, the fundamental meaning of which, in both Arabic and Hebrew, is *to leap*, as in lxiii. 3, Lev. vi. 20, 2 Kings ix. 33, all passages describing the 'leaping' or 'spurting' of blood from one place to another; accordingly, in Hif'il it signifies *to make to leap* or *spurt;* similarly, in German we have *springen*, to leap, and *sprengen*, to sprinkle. Here the meaning is that he will cause such great astonishment among the nations that in their amazement they will start from their place, as men do when they see something entirely unexpected. Since now he has thus alluded to the idea of 'leaping,' the prophet proceeds, *At him kings* יקפצו—a word which, in Cant. ii. 8, is parallel to מדלג, 'leaping,' though here, by the addition of פיהם, he gives it a different meaning, viz. that of *closing* the mouth as a sign of terror and confusion, as Mic. vii. 16, 'Nations shall see and be confounded at all their might, they shall lay their hand upon their mouth,' Job xxix. 9, v. 16, Ps. cvii. 42. Schröder, Rosenmüller, and Gesenius explain יזה as signifying 'fill with joy,' like *exsultare*, which is derived from *saltare:* this sense, however, does not suit well in this place, nor can it be appropriately connected with 'As many were astonished,' which precedes, or with 'At him kings shall close their mouth,' which immediately follows it. Jerome and others have interpreted '*will atone* for many nations,' from the notion of the sprinkling of blood; but this view has been already replied to by Schröder, who points out (1) that הזה is never used without mention of the object sprinkled, whether it be blood, or water, or oil: (2) that the phrase is not הזה איש, but הזה על איש or אל איש [not 'to sprinkle a man,' but 'to sprinkle *upon* a man'], for הזה signifies properly *to make to leap* or *spurt;* (3) that such a sense would be out of connexion with 'As many were astonished.' *For that which had not been told them they have seen*, viz. words the like of which had never been declared to them. The rendering 'shall startle many nations' agrees admirably with the supposition that Israel is here referred to: against the idea that the prophets are meant is the fact that their enemies and revilers were not the Gentiles, but Israel themselves, and that the prophets had no controversy with the Gentiles, but only with the children of their own people; if then the prophets are intended, what object could there have been in mentioning the Gentiles?

LIII. [1] After the words *For what was not told them*, etc., the prophet represents the nations as replying: If we had spread the news of this great event happening, *who would have believed our report?*—so strange and preternatural was the announcement: *And the arm of the Lord, for whom is it revealed?*—spoken contemptuously. 'Whom did the Lord choose, to manifest his power on his behalf? he ought, forsooth, to have revealed it to aid those who were in the possession of dignity and dominion; but he has done otherwise, he has chosen to himself "a people despised and spoiled," humbled and contemned: who could have believed this?' (Abarbanel.) לשמועתנו: many explain, 'the report which we received,' understanding the announcement of the prophet at the end of the chapter: but Isaiah rather conceives the nations as actually seeing what is described, not as merely hearing it from the mouth of the prophet. Gesenius supposes Isaiah to be speaking in behalf of himself and the prophets his companions, and asking who believed the announcements which they had made respecting Israel's future redemption. [2] The servant of the Lord *came up* and budded in exile *before him* and by his help, *like a sucker* or shoot issuing forth from a tree, or *like a root* notwithstanding that it was planted in the *dry earth:* exactly as no one can imagine a plant flourishing in a dry and uncultivated soil, so it was impossible to picture the servant of the Lord as springing up and growing high. The meaning of the whole verse is that 'he came up before him out of the dry earth like a sucker or root.' לא תאר לו ולא הדר ונראהו[e]: so these words must be joined, the sense being that his form had no beauty calculated to attract our gaze, nor did we care even to look upon it; nor, again, had he *any beauty that we might desire him* (R. Me'ir Obernik, Rosenmüller, Gesenius, and the Greek translator Symmachus). But the punctuators, as their custom is, devised a contrivance for the purpose of averting dishonour from Israel, and accentuated in such a manner that the meaning might be 'although he had no beauty, yet we looked at him and desired him.' The sense was also altered by Yonathan in the Targum: his rendering is, 'His form no profane form, and the terror of him not that of any ordinary man; his complexion a holy complexion, so that all that saw him gazed at him.' The words 'he had no form,' etc., refer to the servant of the Lord, not to the sucker or

---

[e] I.e. 'he had no form or comeliness that we might look upon him.'

the root; they contain, however, the reason why the people compared him to something emerging out of the dry earth, because, namely, his form was despised in their eyes. [3] *He was despised*, etc.: so is the servant of the Lord, i. e. Israel during the exile. חדל אישים, *frailest of men;* compare כסיל אדם, Prov. xv. 20, 'foolish of men,' i. e. the most foolish amongst men. חדל signifies 'ready to perish, frail,' as Ps. xxxix. 5 (Martini and Rosenmüller): not dissimilar is the first explanation given by Qamḥi, 'most insignificant of men.' Gesenius, however, and others have adopted Qamḥi's second explanation, 'forlorn of men,'—one from whom men *ceased*, and with whom they would not associate: but the root never bears the signification *forsake;* and Job xix. 14, the passage cited in proof of this, does not mean 'my neighbours *forsook* me,' but 'they *ceased* to be and appear as my neighbours.' ידוע חלי, '*acquainted* with sickness,' like מידע, Ps. lv. 14, a metaphorical expression, as though Israel were a friend and companion of every description of ailment; compare Prov. vii. 4, 'Say to wisdom, Thou art my sister, and call understanding thine acquaintance.' Rosenmüller and Gesenius explain, 'known on account of his sicknesses.' My pupil R. Ephraim Raphael Girondi takes the word in its ordinary sense, as signifying 'known to sickness,' as though the sicknesses were represented as returning to their lodging-place, and taking up their abode with one whom they recognised as ready to receive them; and this view is correct. וכמסתר וג׳: his appearance was such as almost to cause every one that saw him to hide their faces from him, in order not to look upon him. מסתֵּר is for מסתִּיר; compare וידבְּקו, 1 Sam. xiv. 22 (Qamḥi, Rosenmüller, Gesenius): it is accordingly Hif'il, and means '*making others hide* their faces.' נבזה וג׳, *he was despised*, and accounted in our eyes as nothing worth. [4] *But* the sicknesses which ought to have come upon us—as though to say, We, rather than he, deserved to be punished—it seemed as if *he bare* in our stead. *Stricken*, viz. by the hand of God: the 'God' mentioned immediately afterwards belongs to all three words ['stricken,' 'smitten,' 'afflicted']. מכה is beyond question in *stat. constr.*, and must be pointed with *ẓere* (as in the editions of Brescia and of 5278 A.M. = 1518 A.D.): in some copies, however, it is pointed with *segol*, but this is only an error: in the great Bible of the year 5285 A. M. (= 1525), it is with *ẓere*, and the Masôra on the word says distinctly, 'Twice with *qameẓ*, once written with *yod*, מכי חרב במלחמה,' i. e. מכה occurs on two occasions with *qameẓ qaṭon* (= *ẓere*), upon one of which (Jer. xviii. 21) it is spelt with *yod*. In the other great Bibles published at Venice, although the Masôra is printed at the side, it is nevertheless pointed with *segol*. 5 מחלל, *pierced*, as li. 9 ('Ibn ʿEzra, Rosenmüller, Gesenius), though there it is the active participle, while here it is the passive one. מפשעינו, '*on account of* our transgressions,' as Lam. iv. 13. מוסר וג׳, the sufferings bringing peace which ought to have been ours came *upon him*: possibly, however, the prophet intended שִׁלּוּמֵנוּ, 'our vengeance,' as xxxiv. 5, 'the year of vengeance,' Hos. ix. 7, Mic. vii. 3, for which the punctuators have substituted שְׁלוֹמֵנוּ, 'our peace.' ובחברתו: this ought to have been pointed ובחֲברתו; but the punctuators have again contrived otherwise, deriving the word from חברה, as was already done by Yonathan, who renders, 'And for that he was wholly devoted to his words our sins were forgiven us,'—the word נתנהי being formed from the root נהא, which denotes the *union* of hearts together for the purpose of repentance, as in 1 Sam. vii. 2, where the Targum has, 'And all the house of Israel *were gathered together* after the worship of the Lord;' and Jer. iii. 17, where נקוו is rendered similarly. In the clause in question, the prophet keeps up the metaphor by employing two correlative terms; in plain language, the meaning is that by what he endured we are in prosperity. Such a conception as this, however, is not really to be justified; as Qamḥi objects, one nation cannot suffer for the sins of another; it is only by a rhetorical figure that the prophet puts the words into the Gentiles' mouth, in order to indicate how completely they will recognise that

Israel are the innocent and they the guilty. It is further clear that all this cannot relate to the Babylonian exile; for at that time how many nations were in subjection to Babylon exactly as Israel was! and we do not find that the condition of Israel was worse than that of the rest. It is, however, eminently true of the present exile, during which from one generation to another Israel continues 'a people despised and spoiled,' a people treated as no other nation has ever been treated. [6] *All we went astray like sheep,* whose manner is to wander hither and thither; *we turned each to his own way,* we each followed after the stubbornness of his own heart—the allusion is to their corrupt deeds, not to their false beliefs—*but the Lord made to light upon him the penalty* owing by *us all.* Here I must mention another explanation of these three verses (4–6) which I found in a manuscript commentary on the book Cuzari, now in my possession; the writer cites it in the name of his master in his book, *A testimony for Israel,* likewise a commentary upon the Cuzari. According to this view, the prophet means to declare that our exile is in no way owing to our transgressions and folly, or to the absence of all knowledge of the Law: hence it is that he says at the beginning, 'Behold my servant shall prosper;' but in consequence of the sins and wickedness of that generation, viz. the generation in which Isaiah himself lived, as he expresses it afterwards, Israel was *wounded for our transgressions,* i. e. our condition was one of prosperity, and his one of suffering, and his stripes and strokes were our healing: for he bare what should have been borne by us, and so little was our happiness a result of our own integrity that 'we all went astray like sheep,' etc. And some support may be found for this view, if we consider that in point of fact it was solely the sin of Manasseh and of his age which was the first occasion of Israel's captivity. [7] נגש, perfect Nif'al, from נגש, *to oppress* or *exact,* Deut. xv. 2. נענה: the commentators explain, 'was afflicted;' but in this way a difficulty was felt from the word והוא, which at last led Martini (with whom Rosenmüller agreed) to correct, and read נגש הוא ונענה[f]. Gesenius understood the words to mean that 'they oppressed him *although* he was already afflicted.' But the right course is, with Cocceius, to take ענה in the sense of *humbling*, which it bears in Exod. x. 3: the prophet says that they oppressed him, yet he was not utterly cast down, but *endured humbly* and submissively, *and opened not his mouth*; so in the language of the Talmud נעניתי לך (*B'râkhoth*, fol. 28), i. e. 'I submit myself to thee,' and similarly *K'thubhoth*, 67ᵇ, *Yoma*, 22ᵇ—it is surprising that Rashi (on the passage in *B'râkhoth*) can explain, 'I have spoken more than was needed.' *And as a lamb*, etc.: the comparison to a lamb bears reference to the extortion of money (which is represented by the fleece): and נגש is used of exaction in 2 Kings xxiii. 35, Deut. xv. 2. The clause *and opened not his mouth* at the end of the verse belongs to the figure of the sheep, as though to say that his not opening his mouth was the conclusion of the whole. All this description tallies perfectly with the condition of Israel in exile; but, as 'Ibn 'Ezra observes, by no means with that of the prophets (as Gesenius thought), for if these had never opened their mouth with courage and might, they would not have been prophets at all, and if they had desisted from prophesying no one would have hated them. Gesenius alleges in corroboration of his opinion the words of Jeremiah (xi. 19), 'I am as a lamb led to the slaughter,' omitting to notice that Jeremiah compares himself to a lamb, not because of his patience, but because they laid wait for him without his knowledge, as in fact he immediately says, 'And I knew not that against me had they formed devices:' besides, how could it be thought that Jeremiah was patient like a sheep when in the very next verse he exclaims, 'Let me see thy vengeance of them?' [8] מעצר וג׳: Rashi, 'Ibn 'Ezra, and Qamhi explain these words to mean that he was rescued from his afflictions; but this will not agree with the context: Abarbanel, that he was

[f] Compare above, p. 76.

deprived of his authority; but in this case the prophet ought to have written, 'Sovereignty and judgment was taken from him:' Rosenmüller and Gesenius, that he perished under his sufferings; the sufferings of the righteous, however, could not be denoted by the term 'judgment.' It seems to me that, like many of the other words expressive of negation, מן here signifies *without*, as in Deut. xxxiii. 11, '*without* their rising again,' the meaning being that he was put to death *without* the authority of the *government, and without* the sentence of *a court of judgment:* any one that found him murdered him if he so chose; and such has at some periods been actually the condition of Israel. עצר, *government:* comp. 1 Sam. ix. 17, Judg. xviii. 7. ואת דורו וג׳: Rosenmüller and Gesenius render, 'And as to the men of his generation, who was there of them that considered that for the transgression, etc.?' but, in this case, Isaiah should have said ומדורו, 'and *of* his generation;' and שיח moreover means nothing except *to speak.* Rashi renders, 'Who could tell of all the sufferings which befel him?' but this is not denoted by the word 'generation.' In my opinion, את here signifies *with*, and the passage resembles Ps. cxxvii. 5, 'For they shall speak with their enemies in the gate:' '*who*,' Isaiah asks, '*was there* to be his advocate, and *to speak with* the men of *his generation* in order to reprove them for their treatment of him?' he uses the word ישוחח to indicate how none could be found to utter even the slightest sound on his behalf; and he says 'his generation,' for it was not one nation or even two that persecuted him, but the whole of his contemporaries *en masse.* עמי is here for עמים, as Ps. cxliv. 2: *for the transgression of the peoples* who were themselves liable to bear the stroke that was borne by him,—נגע למו, 'which was *a stroke to them*' (Martini and Hensler). Others render, 'The stroke came upon them' (he says *them*, because the servant of the Lord denotes all Israel); but it seems to me improbable that the prophet should employ expressions like נגע ל ['a stroke *to*' ...] and מכה ל for stating that a stroke came *upon* any one. In the Septuagint translation, the clause is rendered as though it read 'stricken unto death' (למות for למו), which has been adopted by Houbigant, Capellus, Michaelis, Kennicott, Lowth, Koppe; but how could it be said that he was 'stricken unto death' (which would imply that he was not dead before), when the prophet had both spoken of him already as 'cut off from the land of life,' and immediately proceeds, 'And he made his grave with the wicked?' [9] *And he made*, etc., i. e. he was buried like the wicked ingloriously. במותיו: since מָוֶת is incapable of a plural (except indeed in מותי ערלים תמות, Ezek. xxviii. 10, where, however, it is not really a plural from מות, for the prophet is addressing an individual, and how can a single individual die more than once?), it seems to me best, with 'Ibn 'Ezra and after him Lowth, Martini, Lockemacher, and Gesenius (in his second edition), to derive this from במה in the sense of an ornamental building constructed over a grave. As to עשיר, the majority of commentators treat it as equivalent to *wicked*, but there is no reason why the 'wicked' should here be designated as the *rich*, nor is there any undoubted instance of this signification in the rest of Scripture. The meaning, therefore, appears to me to be, that Israel was buried with the wicked, but being in fact righteous, he ought legitimately to have a mausoleum built over his tomb as a memorial of his goodness, like those erected for the wealthy: '*his* mounds' meaning 'the mounds which ought to have been his,' like '*our* sicknesses,' '*our* pains,' above. על לא חמס עשה, *not because of violence that he had done*—for he did none whatever: the construction in Job xvi. 17 is similar. [10] I agree with Gussetius in holding דכאו to mean *his bruised one*, one who had been bruised by him, and that it ought properly to be pointed דַּכָּאוֹ, but that the *shwa'* appears instead of the *qameẓ*, as in מקדשו, Num. xviii. 29, נדחו, 2 Sam. xiv. 13. דַּכָּא or דַּכָּה occurs as an adjective, Prov. xxvi. 22; and accordingly I explain here, *But the Lord was pleased* that *his bruised one whom he had put to sickness*, if his soul should make a trespass-offering, *should see seed*, etc., the whole being a continuation of the Gentiles' words in the future. החלי is the perfect Hif'il from חלה; it ought regularly to be החלה, but as we also see in תחלואים (Deut. xxix. 21, etc.), it is here conjugated after the analogy of ל״א verbs: the form is moreover an Aramaic one—אגלי being Aramaic for the Hebrew הגלה: העני, in the language of the Talmud, is similar. אם תשים וג׳, i. e. if his soul resigns itself to death, as though it were a trespass-offering: תשים signifies 'maketh *itself*,' as in Judg. ix. 23, where לשום is 'that it might *place itself* upon Abimelech,' etc.; and again, 1 Sam. xv. 2; the meaning being, that he would endure his afflictions as a means of atoning for his iniquities, and by so doing admit the justice of God's sentence against him. After this, though he was still in exile, the Lord was pleased that he should *see seed*, and *prolong his days*, not perishing in any way until at length *the pleasure of the Lord should prosper in his hand*—his pleasure being, that the nations should be converted to the knowledge of his unity and to his worship: for this will be the consequence of the signs and wonders which he will perform for Israel in their future redemption. Here end the words of the Gentiles, and their confession that Israel's sufferings whilst in exile were not in accordance with justice; that, in fact, it was they themselves who had rather been deserving of punishment, and that through Israel's merits in acquiescing in their afflictions as just, God had preserved them and perpetuated their existence until the time of their deliverance should arrive, which would be for the benefit of the whole world. Rosenmüller and the commentators explain דכאו as equivalent to לדכאו ('to bruise him'): it is singular, however, that God should be described as 'being pleased' in the affliction of his righteous servant: the prophet ought rather to have written, 'Yet the Lord *commanded* to bruise him,' for חפץ does not express merely 'will,' but is used of what a man wills with satisfaction or delight, as in Ezek. xviii. 23, 'Do I take pleasure in, or desire, the death of the wicked?' Moreover, the conjunction is absent before החלי, though, according to this opinion, the sense must be, 'was pleased to bruise him, *and* put him to sickness.' Gesenius took דכאו as a substantive, the *Dagesh* being euphonic, signifying 'his bruising,' rendering 'But the Lord desired and made grievous his bruising, or affliction,'—החלה, to make sick or grievous, as Mic. vi. 13, Jer. xiv. 17: the conjunction, however, is still wanting, and the statement that the Almighty has pleasure in the sufferings of the just still remains. Upon my explanation the relative is omitted after חפץ, as in Isaiah xlii. 21, 'It pleased the Lord *that* he should magnify the law;' it is likewise omitted after דכאו, 'his bruised one *whom* he put to sickness,' as in Is. li. 12, 'from man *that* dieth,' and frequently. The אשם ('trespass-offering') is understood by Rosenmüller and Gesenius (who appeal to verse 4) to allude to the atonement made by him for the nations: this however cannot be; for although they say there 'he carried our sicknesses,' because the calamities which ought to have come upon them came upon Israel, yet how could they say that Israel *gave himself* to make atonement for them? for the Israelites in suffering have surely no such intention as this, nor is it at all within their cognizance that their afflictions will be for the advantage of other nations. There is another reason also why this view must be false: we find the 'trespass-offering' spoken of as an atonement for the individual presenting it, never for other people: indeed, the fundamental idea denoted by the root is that of *repentance*, but how could Reuben 'repent' for the sins of Simeon? atonement for other persons is described as a 'ransom' or 'redemption,' but never as a 'trespass-offering.' *He shall see seed*, etc.; by Rosenmüller, Gesenius, and the commentators generally, this is referred to the period following the Deliverance: but it is unlikely that the Deliverance should be indicated by terms not one of which transcends the limits of ordinary physical phenomena. My explanation connects the words with the period of exile. The Septuagint and Yonathan, from the Aramaic sense of the root—טהר becomes דכי in the Targum—render דכאו, 'to purify him;' and it would seem that this was also the view of Rashi. But the root דכא or דכה never occurs with this meaning through the whole course of Scripture: in its stead we find the root זכה, which in Aramaic changes its ז into ד, like זכר, דכר [g]. R. Me'ir Obernik and R. J. S. Reggio take the first words of this verse as an exclamation: 'And that the Lord should be pleased to bruise him, and put him to sickness for ever! Nay; but after he has resigned himself as a trespass-offering, he shall see seed,' etc.: upon this explanation, however, it seems that חפץ should have been the future tense, and not the past, as Judg. xi. 23, Is. xxxvii. 11, 'And that thou shouldest be delivered!' Finally, from the expression used here, 'shall have long days,' after the language of verse 9, 'Made his grave with the wicked,' which implies that he was already dead, it is evident that the subject of the prophecy cannot be a single man, but must be the nation: to this some reply by rendering 'shall see seed, *which* will have long days,' although he himself will have perished; but it will be plain, from what I shall say on the next verse, the words do not mean this. [11] The Almighty begins here to speak. *Away from the travail of his soul:* so Gesenius, מן having much the same force as that which I assigned to it above on verse 8; on this meaning of the word, Gussetius remarks that similarly in Latin *absque*, 'without,' is derived from *a, ab*, 'from.' יראה ישבע, i. e. *he shall see* seed, *he shall have his fill* of days (so also, as I find now, Abarbanel): the Gentiles having just previously used similar language, the Almighty here confirms the promise definitely for the future, saying, If even hitherto he has been seeing seed and having long life in return for what he endured in exile, henceforth he shall be released from the travail of his soul, and shall yet again 'see' seed and 'be satisfied' with life. 'Ibn 'Ezra and Qamḥi explain: He shall see prosperity so as to be satisfied therewith; but this misses the principal point. Rosenmüller renders, He shall see, i. e. obtain, his needs so as to be satisfied therewith:

---

[g] The paraphrase of Rashi is להחזירו למוטב: cf. p. 39.

and Gesenius, He shall be satisfied with that which he shall see. *By his knowledge*, i. e. his 'wisdom and righteousness and fear of the Lord;' as in Mal. ii. 7, 'The lips of the priest keep *knowledge*,' Job xxxvi. 12, Prov. xxii. 12, 'The eyes of the Lord preserve *knowledge*,' i. e. they preserve the man of knowledge, the 'just man which feareth the Lord;' Hos. iv. 6, 'Because thou hast rejected *knowledge*,' etc.: in all these passages, by 'knowledge' is denoted a righteous and religious spirit, for knowledge is equivalent to wisdom, and wisdom is generally in Holy Writ synonymous with a cultivation of the ways of righteousness and the fear of God; for 'the beginning of wisdom is the fear of the Lord,' and 'the fear of the Lord is the beginning of knowledge.' With these words, *By his knowledge*, a new sentence commences: the preceding words, *Away from the travail*, etc., were merely the counterpart to what the Gentiles had spoken previously, *He shall see seed*, etc. Here, then, the prophet begins to recount the praises of Israel in the days of their exile, declaring how *my servant* Israel, by the divine knowledge that was then in him, *justified the Just One*, i. e. acknowledged the justice of God's sentence upon him, confessing 'the Lord is righteous, for I have rebelled against his commandment.' *My servant unto many* justified the Just One, for such was his wont, at the time when he was a servant unto many, being subjected to rulers and dignitaries; *and bare their iniquities*, i. e. bare all the acts of wickedness which they committed against him. The commentators refer the verse to the period subsequent to the Deliverance; but this cannot be on account of the phrase 'bare their iniquities,' which can only apply to the time of exile. Rosenmüller, Martini, Hensler, and others explain, 'He that bare their iniquities in his exile will justify many after his deliverance' (so likewise Abarbanel), in spite of the fact that they ill-used him and he endured their wickedness during the exile: indeed, this view is altogether very far-fetched. Gesenius supposed the words to mean, that even after the Deliverance he would bear their iniquities, viz. by restoring them to prosperity; but this is more improbable still. Rashi understands them to refer to the exile, supposing that he 'justified many' when he judged truthfully all who came to be tried before him. 'Ibn 'Ezra, Qamḥi, Abarbanel, Rosenmüller, and Gesenius render, 'The just one, my servant, will justify—or make righteous—many,' by bringing them, viz., to the service of God; but in this case there is a difficulty from the ל in לרבים, and also from the collocation צדיק עבדי. Lastly, R. Me'ir Obernik and the learned R. J. S. Reggio, while referring the clause to the time of exile, explain thus: My servant shall have his fill of travail and sorrow during exile; but by his knowledge he will justify himself in his heart, i.e. he will feel himself to be just, and on this account he will bear their iniquities: but in this exposition the language of the text is not expressed with sufficient accuracy. [12] *Therefore* I will do this to him after his redemption: *I will divide him* a portion *with the great,* I will make his portion equal to that enjoyed by the rulers and nobles to whom previously he was in subjection (De Wette and Gesenius); *and with* (Gesenius), i.e. like, *the mighty* (as above, '*with* i.e. like the wicked,' verse 9) *he shall divide spoil,* for he will be great and honourable in the eyes of the nations, and they will honour him with presents and tribute; and should any nation refuse to do so, and attempt to harm him, then he will fight against that nation and take its spoil. The prophet says both, 'I will divide' and 'he shall divide,' using the same word with a double meaning as an elegancy of style. 'Ibn 'Ezra, Qamḥi, Abarbanel, and Rosenmüller explain, 'I will divide him a portion of many nations, and mighty nations he shall divide as spoil;' but this does not express it clearly. R. Me'ir Obernik and R. J. S. Reggio render, 'I will divide him a portion amongst many,' i.e. I will give him his reward openly before the eyes of the whole world: though ברבים, however, might bear such a sense in the language of the Talmud, it could not in Biblical Hebrew: even the עצומים following is a proof that רבים must signify *great* or *mighty*. הערה, *laid bare* (as Lev.

xx. 18), according to an anonymous commentator cited by 'Ibn ʻEzra, the meaning being that he did not withhold his soul from death, did not seek to rescue his life at the cost of changing his religion. All other expositors interpret *poured out*, as Gen. xxiv. 20, Ps. cxli. 8 : this however seems to me improbable, for Israel never 'poured out' his soul. *And was numbered with the transgressors*, submitted to the indignity of being called one, because of his adherence to the faith of his fathers. This expression forms a strong argument against those who assert the 'servant of the Lord' to be either an individual prophet or the prophets collectively; for the prophets are never reckoned as transgressors; on the contrary, the transgressors hate them for the severity of their rebukes. *And made intercession for the transgressors*, הפגיע, as Jer. xxxvi. 25 : so 'Ibn ʻEzra, Qamḥi, Abarbanel, and Gesenius: this clause shews that the one following must signify that he *forgave* the sin of his oppressors—נשא having the same force as in Exod. xxxiv. 7, x. 17, Gen. l. 17, and elsewhere; if this be not admitted, the two clauses are entirely devoid of connexion. We now understand through what kind of merit Israel will be redeemed: it will be through their own merits in the endurance of sufferings and death, in forgiving their persecutors, and in praying for them, as though to shew that they loved the nations, and although they rewarded them evil, still bare no ill-will towards them.

LI. THE CLEAR FOUNTAIN.

Isaiah has also prophesied in the fifty-third chapter about the opinions of the Christians (Edom), the oppressors of Israel. They falsely apply the prophecy beginning *Who believed our report?* to the martyrdom of Jesus, but it really refers to Israel, stricken by all nations, past and present, viz. Babylonians, Persians, Greeks, and Romans, which latter became the Christians. This is to be seen clearly from the fifty-second chapter, which is connected with the following one. The error of the Christian doctors is the consequence of their taking the expressiom *my servant* (lii. 13) as a real singular, whereas it is a collective singular, referring to Jacob and Israel. God said by the mouth of his prophet Moses that he would bring the curses which Israel suffered in the land of their enemies and haters on the latter when Israel turns back from his wicked ways (Deut. xxx. 1–3). Isaiah prophesies the same (li. 22, 23), and promises redemption to the humiliated people, saying, *Behold my servant* Jacob and my people Israel, who laid down his body as a pavement for the passers by, *shall be prosperous, exalted, and extolled, and raised very high.* The prophet means to indicate by these three degrees of exaltation that the elevation of trodden Israel will be greater than its abasement was low in past and present days, for God shall have taken away from them the cup of the dregs and of his fury, and put it into the hands of his oppressors (li. 22, 23). [14] And the nations seeing such a wonderful redemption of a people so abased, the prophet says, *As many were astonished at thee*, etc. It may be seen how this designation *my servant* is a collective singular, because it says *what was not told them, them* in the plural number referring to Israel.

LIII. [1] Then, astonished, they will say, *Who hath believed our report?* which we have heard from men believing in our peace, viz. our Messiah, the messenger of God to the nations. Persuaded by the twelve men (the apostles), we Edomites made war against Israel and the law of Moses, but now *upon whom has the arm of the Lord been revealed?* [2] The Christian expositors apply the contents of this verse to Jesus, who was conceived without intercourse with man. This idea, however (as we shall prove by the help of God), is an astonishing blasphemy (Dan. xii. 10?). The prophet speaks here also of Israel abased, humiliated, avoided, martyred, and spoiled by all nations, growing up before the providence of God like a branch and a root out of a dry land in consequence of their sins (Jer. xvii. 5–8). Isaiah (xliv. 1, 2) uses[a] for the present exile the expression 'dryness,' and for the humiliated people 'roots in a dry land;' in the time when God shall pour out waters upon dryness and upon roots in a dry land and his blessing upon his children, then *that which was not told them they shall see, and what they have not heard they shall understand. Who has believed?* etc. Dispersed Israel is called a root in a dry land, as compared with other nations who have a king and possess a country. Micah also compares the providence of God to grass and drops falling upon it in time of drought (v. 7), by which providence Israel was preserved among all other nations more wondrously than in Egypt. Where are now the Assyrians, the Babylonians, and the Persians, with their different religions? They were mixed up in the time of drought with other nations, and disappeared. Jere-

---

[a] By the word 'womb' in the passage Israel is compared to a woman in labour hoping for the assistance of God.

miah (xxx. 11), as well as Hosea (ii. 3 and iii. 4), both allude to the above-mentioned period of drought. Isaiah continues: *He hath nó form,* for he grows in the present exile as a root in a dry land. [3] *Despised and rejected of men,* as was always the case with scattered Israel. *As hiding their faces from* the despised one. *And we esteemed him not,* the nations will say, Who would have believed that the arm of the Lord would reveal itself to a nation despised and rejected of men, which covered its face, from which everybody kept aloof, as from a wounded man, and which is *acquainted with sickness,* i. e. with being despised and humiliated by all nations, past and present. The fame of this wonderful redemption will even reach the inhabitants of Cush (xviii. 1–3). [4] The sufferings which we ought to have borne, as evildoers persuaded by our teachers (Obad. 1, 2), Israel bore, which is even the case in our days, when Israel suffers humiliation, death, and destruction for supporting the holy law, whilst the nations support blasphemies. *Yet we esteemed him stricken, smitten of God.* This the nations repeat even in our own days, saying that Israel is smitten of God because they put to death their God and Messiah and did not believe in him, but finally they will say, *Who hath believed?* etc. (p. 430). The same was the case in Egypt, when the magicians said (Exod. viii. 19), 'It is the finger of God,' whilst later they were obliged to confess that God was fighting for Israel ('finger' refers to a single nation, whilst of Christendom as a whole the word 'arm' is used). [5] We were mistaken in believing that God smote him for his sins, since in reality it was our sins which caused his humiliation. In fact, the cup of trembling and of fury which was destined for him, according to the words of God, was put into our hands (li. 22). *The chastisement* which we deserved for *our peace,* i. e. for the Messiah, who is called *Prince of peace* (ix. 6), and at whose coming universal peace ought to have been established, came upon Israel. *With his stripes we are healed,* i. e. Israel was healed for the sake of the stripes which he received from us. Thus the prophet says further on (ver. 10), *If thou shalt make his soul*, etc. If we take it in the sense of the Christian interpreters, *by his stripes we were healed*, then the nations confess in amazement that when Israel drinks the cup of trembling and of fury they are healed, for the rod and the staff with which God chastises his people are necessarily during the time of their chastising prosperous (x. 6, 7). In fact, Israel suffers oppression from the Christians who are healed by those sufferings. The prophet explains this fact in x. 12, where Assyria represents Israel's enemy; and to this allusion is made in Psalm xciv. 1 (where vengeance refers to the redemption), 12, 14. [6] *All we like sheep*, etc. At the beginning there were Arians and Catholics, now there are Calvinists and [Lutherans], so that everybody turns to his own way (Jer. xlix. 7?). Then the nations, amazed at such a great salvation, will exclaim, *The Lord hath laid on him the iniquity of us all.* Isaiah alludes to those sects, saying, 'Through the wrath of the Lord of hosts is the land darkened' (ix. 18), i. e. in consequence of those different sects and opinions which the prophet calls 'darkness.' For in darkness every one turns his own way, and the same is the case when people are blind in understanding. [7] *He was oppressed*, etc. This is the case now with the inquisition, when Israel is brought to the funeral pile, if they try to speak, a gag is put on their tongue. [8] *From prison and from judgment*, etc. עצר is employed by the prophets in a good and a bad sense. In a good sense of the last days of the Passover (Amos v. 22), and in a bad sense of mourning (Joel i. 13). Here we take it in the latter sense, i. e. the nations, amazed at the great redemption, will say, *Who hath believed our report?* etc., that Israel will be brought by us in chariots to the house of God, and taken away from their state of depression and the judgment which God had pronounced against them in the day of his wrath (Is. xviii. 7, Zech. viii. 22, Is. xlix. 7, and Jer. xvi. 19). Thus the prophet continues, *his generation*, etc. In the former redemptions Israel was counted by tribes and families, but in the present redemption God alone will be able to count and distinguish the families,

i. e. God will not choose his priests and Levites from the other nations, as pretended by those who bring Israel to the house of God, saying that Israel is mixed up with them, but he will distinguish and choose them from Israel alone. *He was cut off from the land of the living*, i. e. from the holy land (Ezek. xxxii. 23). *For the transgression of my people*, etc., i. e. for the transgression of the fathers the children suffer at the present time (Lam. v. 7). *To him* (למו) is a collective singular, referring to Israel, and not to the Messiah of the nations. [9] *He made his grave*, etc., i. e. the nations called Israel, who died for the law and the holy name of God, and who are *rich*, i. e. who possess many virtues, heretics and evildoers, and they make in consequence their grave amongst the wicked (Dan. xi. 32–34), which is indeed the case in this long exile. And all that, says the prophet, *because he had not acted falsely* in regard to the law of God, for which Israel always was and is now reprimanded, and *there was no deceit in their mouth.* They always considered Jesus as an enticer, and consequently subject to capital punishment, according to Deut. xiii. 10. The nations, on seeing the redemption of those whom they called heretics and evildoers, but who are rich in great virtues, etc., will exclaim, *Who hath believed our report?* etc. [10] If, persevering in the law of God, he accepts patiently the chastisement as a correction for his sins, *he will see seed*, etc. [11] *For the trouble of his soul*, etc., i. e. he will say to himself, Drink the cup of trembling, etc.; bow down that they may pass, etc. (li. 22, 23)[b]. *By his knowledge shall my righteous servant* Israel *justify many*, i. e. on seeing the great redemption the justified ones will confess, Surely he has borne the griefs which we deserved, etc. (Jer. xvi. 19, 20). These passages prove clearly that Israel will be justified by their confidence in God and by their martyrdom, but not by that of the pretended Messiah. [12] *Therefore I will divide*, etc. King David instituted a law (1 Sam. xxx. 24), according

[b] This passage is totally corrupt; see the text, p. 380.

to which the spoil was equally divided amongst those who were the victors and those who guarded the town. The prophet says accordingly that those who fight for the law of God and die for it, have the same part of reward as those whose souls fight against the body for the sake of the law. Therefore he will divide spoil with many and the strong who guarded the city, i. e. the law of God; for the martyred people poured out its soul unto death and was numbered with the transgressors.

The Christians apply all this to their Messiah, which is proved false by the following affirmative condition, which requires necessarily a negative one. The prophet says, *If he offer his soul as a trespass-offering he will see seed*, etc., consequently, if he does not offer his soul as a trespass-offering, he will not see seed, etc. How is it possible to apply this to a man whom the nations adore as God-man and the son of God, who consequently lives and rules with God? What an unintelligible story all that is! The prophet says he, Israel my servant, spoiled by many, bore in past time and endures now the chastisement which the nations, who are their rod, deserved on account of their blasphemies against God in falsely interpreting the words of the prophets. Israel does not dare answer, for they are brought *as a lamb to the slaughter*, etc. The prophet means to imply that Israel suffers also in the present exile for the sin of their fathers, with whom they will divide the spoil. Israel prays for the welfare of the nations under whose rule they live. This God commanded by his prophet Jeremiah (xxix. 7). The nations, amazed at this great redemption, will exclaim, *Who hath believed our report?* etc., that the abased and humiliated people will pray for us. Thus we have established the meaning of Isaiah's prophecy in this chapter, out of which the Christians make the greatest effort to prove that their Messiah suffered for the sins of all the nations. It would indeed be a false interpretation which does not apply this chapter to Israel humiliated and martyred by all nations, past and present. If any one objects, saying, How is it possible that the prophets should not have prophesied with regard to that Jew killed and martyred, adored for such a long time by all nations as God and Messiah, we have only to say that Isaiah, as well as Daniel, has clearly prophesied concerning him. This will be the subject of the following chapter of our book.

A. ABRAHAM GUER OF CORDOVA[a].

B. R. MANASSEH BEN ISRAEL.

Question XXIII.

Isaiah liii. 4. Verily he bare our sicknesses, and suffered our sufferings. 12. And he bare the sin of many.

Ezekiel xviii. 20. The soul that sinneth it shall die. The son shall not bear the iniquity of the father, neither shall the father bear the iniquity of the son, &c.

If this chapter is to be interpreted of the people of Israel, how comes Isaiah to say that it bare the sin of many, whereas every one (according to the testimony of Ezekiel) pays only for his own guilt?

Reconciliation.

The subject of this question demands long argument, and for our verses to be perfectly understood it will be necessary to explain the whole of the chapter, which we shall do with all possible brevity, without starting any objections which may be made against other expositions, as our intention is solely to shew what our own opinion is. Accordingly for greater clearness I shall set down the literal text with a paraphrase of my own, and then illustrate it by notes.

Isaiah prophesies—I. The extreme prosperity of Israel at the time of the Messiah. II. The wonder of all the nations at seeing them rise from such a low state to grandeur. III. How they will perceive their mistake, acknowledging themselves to

[a] See No. XXXIX, p. 290.

be the sinners and Israel to be innocent. IV. What they will think of their various sects. V. The patience of the people in suffering the troubles of the captivity; and the reward they will receive for their suffering.

Literal Translation.	*Paraphrase.*	
Behold, my servant shall prosper, he shall be exalted, and shall be extolled, and shall be raised very high.	Behold my servant Israel shall understand: he shall be exalted, extolled, and raised very high, at the coming of the Messiah.	lii. 13
As many were astonished at thee, his visage was so marred more than any man, and his form more than the sons of man:	As many of the nations were astonished at thee, O Israel, saying at the time of the captivity, Truly he is disfigured above all mankind in his countenance and form:	14
So he will cause many nations to speak; kings shall shut their mouths at him; what had not been told them they shall see; and what they had not heard they shall understand.	So at that time they shall speak of thy grandeur; even kings themselves shall shut their mouths in astonishment: for what they had never been told they shall see, and what they had not heard they shall understand.	15
Who will believe our report? and upon whom hath the arm of Adonai been manifested?	Who would have believed (the nations will say) what we see, had it been related to them? And look upon what a vile nation the arm of the Lord has manifested itself.	liii. 1
And he came up before him as a branch, and as a root out of a dry ground; he had no form nor comeliness; and we	He came up miraculously as a branch and a root out of a dry ground, for he had no form nor comeliness: we saw	2

	saw him, and there was no appearance that we should covet it.	him, but so hideous, that it did not seem to us an appearance, for which we should envy him.
3	He was despised and rejected of men, a man of sorrows, accustomed to sickness; and as they hid their faces from him, he was despised, and we esteemed him not.	He was despised and rejected from the society of men, a man of sorrows, accustomed to suffer troubles; we hid our faces from him, he was despised and unesteemed among us.
4	Surely he bare our sicknesses and endured our sufferings; and we esteemed him wounded, smitten by God, and afflicted.	But now we see that the sicknesses and troubles which we ought in reason to have suffered, he suffered and endured, and we thought that he was justly smitten by God and afflicted.
5	But he was pained by our transgressions, was crushed by our iniquities: the chastisement of our peace was upon him, and by his wounds we were healed.	Whereas he suffered the sicknesses and sufferings which we deserved for our sins: he bore the chastisement which our peace and felicity deserved; but his troubles appear to have been the cure of ourselves.
6	All we like sheep went astray, we turned every one to his own way; and Adonai (God) caused the sin of us all to meet upon him.	All we like sheep went astray: we followed every one his own sect, and so the Lord seems to have transferred on him the punishment of us all.
7	He was oppressed, and he was afflicted, and he opened not his mouth; he was carried as a lamb to the slaughter and was dumb as a sheep before	He was oppressed and afflicted: he was taken by us as a lamb to the slaughter and as a sheep before its shearers, depriving him of life and pro-

its shearers; and he opened not his mouth.

He was taken from imprisonment and judgment, and who shall declare his generation? for he was cut off from the land of the living: for the transgression of my people they were stricken.

And he made his grave with the wicked, and with the rich in his deaths, although he had not acted falsely and there was no deceit in his mouth.

And Adonai wished to crush him, made him sick: if he offer his soul as an expiation, he shall see seed, he shall prolong days, and the will of Adonai shall prosper in his hand.

From the trouble of his soul he shall see, shall be satisfied: by his wisdom my righteous servant shall justify many: and he shall bear their iniquities.

Therefore I will distribute to him with many, and with the strong he shall divide the

perty: and he was dumb and opened not his mouth.

From prison and these tor- 8
ments he is now delivered: and who would have thought of this his happy age when he was banished from the holy land? Through the wickedness of my people (each nation will say) this blow came upon them.

He was buried with male- 9
factors, and suffered various torments with the rich, without having committed crime or used deceit with his mouth.

But it was the Lord (the 10
Prophet says) who wished to make him sick and afflict him, in order to purify him: if he offer his soul as an expiation he shall see seed, he shall prolong his days, and the will and determination of the Lord shall prosper in his hand.

For the trouble which his 11
soul suffered in captivity, he shall see good, shall be satisfied with days: by his wisdom my righteous servant Israel shall justify the many, and he will bear their burdens.

Therefore I will give him 12
his share of spoil among the many and powerful of Gog

spoil: because he gave up his soul unto death, and was numbered with the transgressors, and he bare the sin of many: and he prayed for the transgressors.

and Magog, because he gave himself up unto death for the sanctification of my name; and was numbered with the transgressors; and he bare the offence of many, even praying for the very transgressors from whom he received injuries.

COMMENTARY.

LII. 13 'Servant' was one of many titles of honour with which the blessed God honoured Israel (Is. xli. 8, Jer. xxx. 10, Ezek. xxxvii. 25, Ps. cxxxvi. 22). And as the prophet in this chapter praises the fidelity with which Israel, as loyal servants, were ever constant in the service of the blessed Lord, suffering innumerable persecutions in this captivity, he therefore applies this title to them here. Whence it appears that the sole subject of this prophecy is the people of Israel; and that is the true meaning of it; and the certainty of this is further proved by its connexion with the preceding chapter, where the prophet says, 'Awake, awake; put on thy strength, O Zion,' etc. (lii. 1–12); and then he continues (verse 13), *Behold my servant shall prosper* or *understand*, etc.

It is seen how the prophet goes on with the same subject, and at the conclusion of this chapter he still enlarges on it in the following: 'Sing, O barren, thou that didst not bear' (liv. 1); and continuing this subject in the same lofty strain to the end of the book, he extols that happy period loaded with innumerable blessings.

This being taken for granted, it is to be observed that the prophet in this first verse expresses this supreme state by these four terms, ישכיל ירום נשא גבה, *shall prosper* or *understand, shall be exalted, shall be extolled, and shall be raised very high*, which attributes (as Don Isaac Abarbanel well argues) signify those four prerogatives and dignities which the people of

Israel enjoyed in their own country, lost subsequently in the captivity, and will again recover at the time of the Messiah.

The first was an exact knowledge and profound wisdom, as Moses says, 'Keep these precepts, for this is your wisdom and understanding in the sight of the nations, who will say, Only this nation is a wise and understanding people' (Deut. iv. 6); a truth confirmed by innumerable writers, who acknowledge that all the learning of the Greeks and Egyptians was derived from the Jews; thus Justin, Theodoret, and Clement of Alexandria assert that all the good the philosophers and poets knew was pilfered from Holy Scripture; for which reason they call Plato the Attic Moses, or Moses of Athens; Clearchus the Peripatetic writes of Aristotle, that he acquired most of his learning from a Jew with whom he had much intercourse; Ambrose says of Pythagoras, that he was by birth a Jew, and like a thief robbed them of innumerable things; and Alexander Polyhistor further says, that he was the disciple of an Assyrian Nazarite, namely, the prophet Ezekiel, and that from such a master came forth such a disciple. Lastly, it is certain (as I have shewn at length in an Apology in defence of the various readings of various books) that the knowledge of Orpheus, Plato, Anaxagoras, Pythagoras, Thales of Miletus, Homer, and also many other very wise men, was derived from the clear oceân of Moses, and from the professors and those who were learned in his most holy law; for to them, according to the Psalmist, God revealed his words, a favour which he did not shew to any other nation (Ps. cxlvii. 19, 20).

The second dignity was the kingdom of the house of David, the only empire which he established. For all other princes, as the Turks, the Romans, and many others more ancient, obtained the beginning of their greatness by tyranny and force of arms; but it was to David only that empire was given by the Sovereign Majesty, as the royal prophet says (Ps. lxxxix. 4, 5).

The third was the gift of prophecy, which prerogative he conceded to no other nation. Moses wished that he and the people of Israel should in this respect be different from all other nations, as he begged of the Lord, 'Let us be separated, I and thy people, from all the people that are upon the face of the earth' (Exod. xxxiii. 16), which petition was granted him; and so there was no other prophet equal to him, and no other nation possessed the gift of prophecy. And although Balaam, a Gentile, prophesied, this is well known to have been quite an accident, as is expressed in the narrative itself, ויקר, 'and the Lord happened to meet Balaam' (Num. xxiii. 4); and this was either for the greater glory of Israel, its being acknowledged by a Gentile, or for the condemnation of the nations, that they might not make it an excuse that they had no prophet to instruct them in the right way, since Balaam, a man of such great fame amongst them, predicted to them all the successes of Israel, and its wonderful and prosperous end at the advent of the Messiah.

Lastly, the fourth prerogative was their union with the Divinity and the special providence of God. For although the Lord left all other nations to the protection of the angels and the celestial powers, he took the people of Israel alone under his own charge and particular government (Gen. xvii. 7, Deut. iv. 19, Num. xxiii. 9, Deut. xxxii. 9, xxxiii. 29, Ps. cxliv. 15, Jer. x. 16).

Now, who is ignorant that the people of Israel in their captivity, being considered unworthy because of their ingratitude, have lost all these prerogatives which they enjoyed while in the favour of the Lord? since now that precise knowledge is lost, there are no longer prophets, they live deprived of king and prince, and the Lord has hidden his face from them; but when for his honour he shall return, when he shall restore Israel to its former state at the advent of the Messiah, the whole will again be recovered, as all the prophets with one voice testify. And Isaiah admirably sums this up in the four words before us. For ישכיל is derived from שכל, *understanding*, and signifies that then they will understand perfectly, with profound and sublime wisdom. ירום, *shall be exalted,* is applicable to the kingdom, as it is said in Numbers, 'And his king shall be exalted above Agag' (xxiv. 7). נשא, *shall be extolled,* is applicable to the gift of prophecy, as it is said, 'The prophecy (משא) of the word of Adonai;' and גבה, *shall be raised very high,* represents the union and connexion with the Divine Sovereign Majesty, whose title is גבוה, *Most High.*

14 The prophet addresses himself to the people, and shews that in the same manner as the nations of the world wondered at their low state and misfortunes, even going so far as to charge them with being disfigured, having a form unsuitable to man, and unlike other mortals, so at that period will they wonder at their prosperity and elevated state.

15 For seeing the sudden change in the fortune of Israel, rising from such extreme meanness to such extensive empire, all the kings of the earth will wonder and discourse on the subject. And he gives the reason of this, viz. because what had never been told them of any nation they see in the people of Israel, whose grandeur none ever equalled, and what they had never heard from their false preachers, they now understand. Or יקפצו signifies *they will shut* their mouth, speaking with great respect and modesty of that people which they had shortly before known as captives, subject to the will of their tyrannous power (Mic. vii. 15, 16).

LIII. 1 *Who will believe our report?* etc. explains the wonder of the nations. Who, they will say, would have thought of this new state of things which we see in the prosperity of Israel, and that the arm and favour of the Lord would manifest itself or act upon so vile and mean a nation?

2 This springing up has not been in the ordinary or natural way, but a prodigy; for as a branch from small beginnings springs up miraculously, and as a root out of a dry ground, where it soon withers, so we see him raised up and resuscitated from the death of the captivity. We thought he had no human form nor comeliness, and so we looked upon him; moreover we

considered his form to be such that we did not envy it, and made no account of him.

[3] His state was so mean that we deemed him wholly unworthy of our society, considering it disgraceful to hold communion with him (Is. xlix. 7, Ps. xliv. 13). *A man of sorrows, and accustomed to sickness*, that is, to suffer the troubles of the captivity, compared in Holy Writ to sicknesses (Is. xxx. 26, Jer. xxx. 12, Lam. ii. 13, Hos. vi. 1). *And as hiding their face* ממנו *from him* (or *from us*), *we saw him and we esteemed him not.* That is, we made as though we did not see him, to avoid the obligation of courtesy towards him, which arose from the light consideration we held him in. Or it may also mean, he himself, from mere timidity and mistrust, hid himself from us. And there is no difficulty in the nation of Israel being styled in this verse איש, *man* of sorrows, it being a very common usage in Holy Scripture to speak of Israel collectively under this individual term (Judg. xx. 17, 22, xxi. 1, 1 Sam. xvii. 2, etc.)

[4] We unbelievers more justly merited the troubles and calamities which this innocent people suffered in their captivity. But we were so blind that we considered him to be wounded, smitten, and afflicted by God, and not through ourselves, and that all this came on them for keeping themselves apart from the truth, and not joining with us in our religion.

[5] But it was quite the contrary, for our wickedness alone was the cause of his troubles; did they not arise from any hatred God bore them. *The punishment*, מוסר, or *discipline of our peace was upon him*, for, as grief always accompanies pleasure, the chastisement of this happiness appears to have fallen on him. Or it may also mean, when in the enjoyment of peace adversaries were wanting, we immediately turned our arms against this people, and what we established for the discipline and good government of our states, all redounded in measures against him, decrees of death, banishment, and confiscation of property, as experience daily shews. Or otherwise, the doctrine

[מוסר] taught by our preachers was that our tranquillity depended on our being irritated against him, and ultimately that we should find health in wounding him.

[6] But *all we like sheep went astray*, etc. That is, they will not only acknowledge the ill-treatment and bodily inflictions they had made Israel suffer, but at the same time their errors, attributing their wickedness thereto; for many will say, We all (Ishmaelites and Edumeans) like sheep went astray, each in his own way followed a new sect; just as the prophet Jeremiah says (xvi. 19). *And the Lord made to fall on him the wickedness of us all.* That is, we erred, they followed the truth; consequently they suffered the punishments which we deserved.

[7] We deprived them of their property as tribute, and afflicted their bodies with various kinds of torture, yet *he opened not his mouth*, etc. The experience of this is seen every day, particularly in the cruelties of the Inquisition, and the false testimony raised against them to take their wool and rob them of their property. And it is exactly this that the Psalmist says, 'Thou hast given us, O Lord, like sheep appointed for meat' (xliv. 12); and further on, 'For thy sake are we killed every day, we are counted as sheep for the slaughter' (xliv. 23), suffering daily with the greatest patience these acts of tyranny and fearful calamities.

[8] *He was taken from confinement and judgment.* These two words have each different meanings, for עוצר signifies *kingdom* and *confinement* or *prison*, which is the same thing. משפט denotes *judgment* and *punishment*, as is well known to those acquainted with the Hebrew language. Consequently according to the first sense it says, This nation so abased, so vile, and which we considered to be almost void of human form, was not originally of such low standing nor common nor of small renown; for it has been deprived of a wealthy kingdom, an admirable senate, and a tribunal of justice or Sanhedrin; *and his generation*, or the happiness of that former time which he enjoyed, *who will be able to declare*, when he is banished from the Holy Land? Or

it may also mean, Now he is already delivered from prison and punishment; and who would have thought or spoken of the happiness of this generation, this present time, when he was banished from the land of the living, that is, the promised land, which is called in Holy Scripture, the land of the living (Ezek. xxxii. 23–27, Ps. cxvi. 9). *For the transgression of my people were they smitten.* For our wickedness has been the sole cause of this expulsion from their country. It must here be observed that the word למו *lamo* has the same signification as להם, *to them,* as is well known to every one acquainted with Hebrew grammar. And thus it is evidently seen from this passage that although the prophet speaks in the singular, and of a single people, *all* the children of Israel are treated of.

9 The nations continue, We have frequently condemned this people to death, and buried them with malefactors, and with the rich, במותיו, *in their various deaths,* though it is certain that, in order to take away their property, we raised against them innumerable false testimonies, and martyred them, without their having committed any crime or our having any charge against them, except of having accumulated wealth, as he continues, *although he had committed no* חמס *robbery and there was no deceit in his mouth,* that is, allowing themselves to be robbed of the property they had not robbed, and to be killed for the sanctification of the Lord, and refusing to acknowledge with their mouth any other religion.

10 From this verse onward the prophet speaks in the name of the Lord, and relates the reason why these troubles were suffered, and the reward to be hoped from them. And firstly he says that the will and determination of the Lord has been to crush them and to make them sick by so many different calamities, that, being purified by these means, they may become worthy of such great felicity. *If he offer his soul as an expiation,* אשם, surrendering it for the sake of the Law; or, if he give himself up and acknowledge himself guilty, becoming repentant, as Joseph's brethren, who said, 'But we are guilty' (Gen. xlii. 21), *he shall*

see seed, that is, they shall multiply infinitely (Ezek. xxxvi. 37, Zech. x. 10, Deut. xxx. 5). *He shall prolong days.* The same prophet confirms this where he says, 'As the days of the tree,' that is, the tree of life, 'are the days of my people' (lxv. 22); and Zechariah, 'And every man with his staff in his hand from multitude of days' (viii. 4). Lastly, *and the will of the Lord,* which is to oppress him and make him sick with punishments for his greater glory, *shall prosper in his hand,* for the purpose and end to which they are directed will be attained. Or, the will of the Lord, which is that all should be saved and come to the holy knowledge of himself, will prosper through his hand and means and take effect.

11 At that happy period Israel will see the [fruit of the] trouble of his soul and be satisfied with it; different to that former time of which Moses says, 'And ye shall sow your seed in vain, and your enemies shall eat it' (Lev. xxvi. 16, Deut. xxviii. 30), because, by enjoying everlasting peace and universal empire, they will peaceably enjoy the produce of the Holy Land (Deut. xxx. 9, Is. lxii. 8, Amos ix. 14). Or it may mean, for the trouble of his soul which he suffered in the miseries and misfortunes of the captivity, he will see seed and be satisfied with days.

By his knowledge my righteous servant shall justify many. That is, Israel, who is termed 'a righteous people and holy nation,' justifies many by his knowledge and wisdom, bringing them with brotherly love over to the true religion, and separating them from their vain sects; and this at the very time that *he bears their iniquities,* patiently suffering the tyranny of their wickedness. Or it may otherwise mean, At that time my servant Israel will justify and make many nations meritorious (Mic. iv. 2, Zech. viii. 23).

And he shall bear their iniquities. For being a most religious and holy people, he will take charge of the spiritual administration of the observance of the Law, as Moses says to Aaron, 'Thou and thy sons with thee shall bear the iniquity of the sanctuary' (Num. xviii. 1).

[12] In this last verse he treats of the final conflict, the prelude to Israel's felicity, that is, of that war of Gog and Magog so extolled in the prophets, in which many nations will join (as is clear from Jer. xxx, Ezek. xxxvi, and Joel iii), and this too with immense riches (Zech. xiv. 1, 14, Is. lx. 5, lxi. 6). These, then, are the *many and mighty*, whose spoil the Lord promises that they shall divide.

Because he poured out his soul unto death, etc. The prophet here attributes four merits to them, for which they justly deserve the reward of that happiness; and again in the form of a compendium he recapitulates the contents of the chapter. 1. Because he delivered himself up to death, allowing himself to be killed for the sanctification of the Lord's name, and the observance of his most holy law. 2. Because he was reckoned among the wicked, patiently enduring to be called a heretic. 3. For having borne the sin of many, the wickedness and tyranny of others falling on his shoulders. 4. Lastly, in having observed the precept of Jeremiah, 'Seek the welfare of the city whither I have caused you to be carried captive' (xxix. 7); and this too so carefully that in all their prayers they pray for the health of the prince, and the peace of the kingdom or province wherein they reside; and what is more, it may be even for the welfare of those from whom they are receiving insult and wrong, which is highly meritorious, and a convincing proof of the constancy and patience with which they receive from the Lord's hand the yoke of captivity and the sufferings of its misfortunes.

Thus far extends the explanation of this chapter, in which brevity has been the chief object, in order to shew that the clearness of the subject does not require long arguments.

Returning now to the question with which we began, the solution of the difficulty is rendered easy; for as souls are from God, and do not proceed from the parents, the son cannot pay for the father, nor the father for the son; each pays for his own guilt, as Ezekiel plainly says, 'The souls are mine, as the soul of the father, so also the soul of the son; the soul that sinneth that shall die,' etc. (xviii. 4–19). These are infallible words by which the prophet shews that the wickedness of the father cannot prejudice the son, giving as a reason that the son receives existence from his father only so far as regards the body, receiving his soul as a direct creation from God, a truth likewise confirmed by Isaiah, who says, 'And souls I have made' (lvii. 16). So that every one pays for his own faults, and not for those of others which he has not committed, as that would be contrary to God's most strict justice, which is to reward every one according to his own actions, as the law expressly commands in Deuteronomy (xxiv. 16), that by earthly justice the father is not to die for the son, nor the son for the father, but that each is to die for his own guilt. Therefore neither body nor soul pays for more than its own actions. And Isaiah is not opposed to this, for in the first text he treats of what the nations will say, who, recognising that Israel professed the true religion and themselves the false, will admit that the troubles they justly merited were suffered by that innocent people. And the passage which says that he bare the sin of many signifies that he has always been the target that received the aim of their wickedness, as we have explained.

C. ISAAC OROBIO DE CASTRO.

CHAPTER XXIV.

Paraphrastic explanation of the fifty-third chapter of the prophet Isaiah.

Christianity has formed out of the fifty-third chapter of Isaiah its principal argument for proving the truth of the gospel history; for as this contains nothing more than the life, passion, and death of him whom they adore as very God and Messiah, and they find the same portrayed in this chapter in such vivid colours that its expositors call it *the passion chapter*, and Isaiah the evangelical prophet, they make use of it as a convenient proof that Isaiah predicted by divine inspiration all that is related in the gospel, and that the Messiah was to die and suffer for the sins of mankind; that in this the redemption God had promised the people of Israel so many ages before would consist; that this people will acknowledge this truth in the latter days, and being converted to the Christian faith will confess how unjustly it punished and put to death the Messiah innocent of all sin, and that Israel will wonder at the glorious end of him whom it had before executed on the charge of high treason against God. They pretend that all this is signified in this chapter in such express words that they appear incapable of admitting any other interpretation, notwithstanding the opposition the Jews have always made not to admit it. So the Christian doctors argue: but it is well worthy of consideration that, though they hold this chapter to be so clear and express in favour of their fundamental doctrine, yet Paul in the epistle he wrote to the Hebrews, in which he tries to convince them and shew that Christ is the true Messiah, in reference to whom he quotes out of the whole of Holy Scripture all the verses which he could directly or indirectly accommodate to his purpose, has made no mention in any way of this chapter of Isaiah, and has not quoted a single verse of it; but if he understood it to be so clear and evident, as the Christians afterwards pretended, who could acquit Paul of great negligence or ignorance in quoting for his argument such a number of verses of the Holy Scriptures that he can in no way apply to his purpose, and omitting those which formed the principal support of his object to persuade the Gentile and convince the Hebrew? whence we may gather that Paul in writing to the Hebrews did not understand this chapter of the Messiah, for he was well aware that they understanding the divine writings would not allow themselves to be deceived, and would not accept an application so strange, as we shall prove in the following discourses.

CHAPTER XXV.

The grounds Christianity had for believing that the Messiah was to die for mankind are proposed for consideration.

In order to be able to apply the fifty-third chapter of Isaiah to the King Messiah, as the Christian church pretends, it was obliged to suppose that the innocent had to die for the redemption of souls, on which supposition the whole Christian doctrine rests. But if that supposition be demolished and we prove it to be opposed to truth and natural reason, they have nothing left to claim out of the fifty-third chapter: since there will be no innocent being who dies to whom they can apply it, and they will be obliged to look for some one else as the subject of this prophecy.

They affirm that Adam's sin was infinitely wicked, because the offence was against an infinite God; that this sin, which they call original, was communicated to the whole human race, both Adam and all mankind becoming enemies of God, slaves of the devil, children of wrath, condemned to hell, and banished from glory. They say, moreover, that neither Adam nor any other man could atone for this or for any other sin, since, as the debt is infinite, so must the payment be, that is, the merits of the acts of man; but as man is in his nature finite, he could do no act which would possess an infinite value, particularly as since Adam's sin man's inclination is become corrupt; and, as the Protestants maintain, he is rendered incapable of doing any meritorious act; consequently mankind is lost, rejected by God, and condemned. They say, moreover, that God in his infinite power could easily pardon man's offence, because his mercy and power are infinite; but that it would be prejudicial to the divine justice, which demands a regular and complete satisfaction, without which it would fail in equity and righteousness, by forgiving an infinite debt for a satisfaction and payment of finite value, as all the acts of man are; accordingly, it was necessary that there should be a man whose works and merits should be of infinite value, in order that by his death he might pay the debt which the whole human race owed God, and that thus, by an innocent being dying that the innocence of one might pay for the wickedness of all, it might be delivered from eternal death, the debt which Adam incurred for himself and his descendants. No mere creature was able to effect this end, and, therefore, God pitying mankind sent his son into the world, who being also God in unity of essence and nature should take upon himself human flesh and be very man, in order that he might suffer and die for the sin of all men, taking upon himself not only the crimes but also the punishment for them, which he washed away by his death, because his works had infinite efficacy, he being God and man in one and the same person; accordingly he paid in total to divine justice all that mankind owed as remaining due for the sin of Adam, and for all those that men might commit afterwards, provided they believe in and avail themselves of the merits of the death of the Messiah, who is in this way the Redeemer of the world, and of Israel too, if they would believe him to be such. This is the faith, doctrine, and religion of Christianity; upon this groundwork all its theology rests.

Human intellect, particularly that of the Israelite, requires no great acumen to refute this fundamental argument; it is sufficient to have recourse to the Holy Scriptures, which are the rule of all that we ought to believe and observe; and since there are many dogmas that the Lord did not command us, it is sufficient to reject them and pay no regard to them : nevertheless, we shall discuss this matter briefly so far as may be sufficient to shew we are not ignorant of it.

In the first place, it is never said in the Holy Scriptures that the sin of Adam was infinitely wicked, that through it Adam and his posterity became enemies of God and slaves of the devil; it is not mentioned in the Law; the prophets never deplored it, nor made allusion to any such reprobation and banishment from God, as afterwards Paul deplored and bewailed it in all his writings, in order to introduce to the world by this innovation the necessity of the Messiah he preached: Adam sinned, the Lord condemned him, and executed the sentence on him, but there was not in that sentence a single clause about eternal enmity and condemnation to hell; now since God has not said this, it is useless to urge it on the belief of those who must believe only what God has said. Besides, the guilt of man could never be infinitely wicked, because from man, who is a limited principle, nothing good or bad can proceed that can be infinite; and if, as they affirm, the wickedness of the offence acquires its infinite nature by its being against God, whose excellence is infinite, then also good works will be of infinite perfection, since they are performed towards the same God, and in relation to his being, which is infinite; and indeed with greater reason, since man does not commit sin directly against God, for no one sins with the view of offending him, but in order to follow the sensuality of his own appetite; rather the sinner would wish that God should not know of it, and to conceal himself from his divine Majesty, if he could do so, as Cain did, denying his sin; hence it is certain that no one wishes to sin to offend God; and if he sins, he offends him indirectly, and, if it were possible, he would wish to sin without offending him. But good work, repentance and penance, is done directly for God, and in order to please him, and appease his anger by doing all that lies in him to return to the divine favour; hence it is more reasonable that the work done directly to please God should have perfection and infinite wisdom through the infinity on the side of God, towards whom it is directed, than that a sin committed without any intention of displeasing or offending God should be infinitely wicked or imperfect through the infinity of God, towards whom it is neither directed nor intended by the sinner. This is evident, and no Christian doctor will be able, with all his subtleties, to maintain the contrary, and for that reason the Lord did not say so, because infinite and supreme truth cannot say anything repugnant to itself.

But leaving aside this speculation, we suppose that man cannot pay God in proportion to his wickedness; it is unworthily concluded, however, that divine justice is injured by the Lord using his divine mercy towards his creatures in such a way that it is necessary to pay him the total or perish through the debt; this is contrary to his justice, contrary to his infinite mercy, his absolute power and liberty essentially independent of all. In the first place, they suppose that divine justice is after the manner of human, that God is obliged to act in such and such a way, and if he should act in any other way it would be contrary to justice, just as human judges, who judge according to certain laws to which they are subject, and which they must not transgress (and should they do so, they would act against justice), must not punish the innocent or pardon the crime of the guilty, but only observe the laws by which they are bound; who will be so blasphemous as to impose this manner of justice on the Creator himself? What are the laws which he has to observe? Not such is divine justice, for the Lord is absolute and independent in his action; we say he is just, because all that he does and can do is just, because he is justice itself; all that he does is supremely right and free from any kind of wickedness; when he punishes the sinner, he acts justly; when he pardons him and has mercy on him, he also acts justly; when he destroys the innocent in Canaan he is righteous, and when he pardons the repentant Ninevites he is just; he did not act less righteously and justly when he pardoned David than when he punished Saul, and had he been pleased to destroy David and pardon Saul, he would have acted with equal justice and righteousness. Whatever his divine Majesty wishes is true justice; the Lord obeys no laws, his infinite being is supremely good, and so his acts are infinitely good and right, whether he pardons or punishes; and his divine justice must be so understood that it can as well perform acts of benevolence by pardoning as of severity by punishing, although in our manner of understanding we call one justice and the other mercy: granted this truth, why could or would he not pardon the sin of repentant Adam as well as of his posterity, and use his just mercy and pitiful justice by taking from them what their poor nature can pay, namely, repentance for their crimes, particularly when the Lord has promised, in so many passages of Holy Scripture, that he will not despise the contrite sinner, that he does not wish the death of the sinner, but that he should be converted and live; that although his sins may be red as scarlet, he will cleanse them and make them white as snow, if the sinner will only humble himself and be converted? Thus says the Lord, thus he promises, because his divine wisdom does not demand impossibilities invented by the human mind. Who bound the Lord's hands that he should not use mercy? what laws oblige him not to be satisfied? who will demand an account from him for his having mercifully pardoned the poor penitent sinner? God never said such a thing, either through his law or by his prophets, nor could he have said it, for by such a suggestion he would necessarily have ceased to be God, and been deprived of his infinite liberty as regards all that righteousness which is so incomprehensible to us.

And granted (as the Christian will have it) that the sinner had to pay in full to divine justice all that he owes for his crime, there would never be place for mercy, because he who pays in full all he owes receives no grace or mercy from justice or his creditor; and this is not contradicted by one paying the debt of another, as the debt is no less paid off than if one paid for himself, since if the sinner is obliged to pay either by himself or through another all he owes God and his justice, there is no place left for mercy, which is contrary to the goodness of God, and is repugnant to all he has revealed in the Holy Scriptures, that his mercy is over all his works.

However this new dogma, destitute of any support in Holy Scripture, may be defended, namely, that in order to return to the grace of God it is necessary to satisfy in full his justice, Christianity will gain nothing by the death of the Messiah; for how could justice be well satisfied by the execution and death of a most holy and innocent man, who had never committed any crime nor inherited that of Adam? In truth, no greater injustice can be imagined than that of innocence suffering for the wickedness of the impious, the killing a righteous man that the wicked, the transgressors, may not die, when the Lord says that every one shall die for his own crime (Ezek. xviii. 20); distributive justice consists in giving each one what he deserves, although in the punishment divine mercy may interpose to moderate it with such righteousness that that very moderation is also divine. But justice would never be righteous if it punished the innocent for the crime of the impious; the Amalekite children did not die for the crimes of their fathers, but by the just judgment of God, that they might not be wicked like their fathers; and the same in the universal deluge of the world and similar instances in which the infinite wisdom foresaw great expediency in the death of those who had not yet sinned;

but he never destroyed any one to punish him for the sin of another, though it is well that the death of those who did not sin may also serve as punishment to the sinner who grieves over the death, as David grieved over the death of the child of the wife of Uriah; it was agreeable to the divine judgment that the child should die, but it did not die to pay with its life for the sin of David; although God punished David with the death of the child, it is impossible that one should commit the crime and another bear the punishment, so that the criminal may be acquitted of his sin and the innocent punished; that could never be agreeable or satisfactory to divine justice, which, as it cannot make the sin of one to be the act of another, can no more demand that the punishment be inflicted on any other than the actual one who committed the sin. And if the Messiah, whom they believe in, was most holy, innocent, just, incapable of sin, it could not be agreeable to divine justice that, being faultless, he should suffer, be executed, and die, and that he should bear the punishment for the crimes of others; never would divine justice be more offended than by so manifest an act of injustice; and if, as they confess, men killed him unjustly, it was the greatest injustice on the part of God to send him and prepare the express means that he should be destroyed. Nor is this doctrine contradicted by the case of the Gibeonites, for whose satisfaction David was by divine decree made to destroy the children and nephews of Saul, because these were accomplices in the pillage and murder of the Gibeonites, and therefore God demanded that they should pay for their sin, and his holy name should be glorified by punishing the violation of the ancient oath on Saul and his family, called in Scripture a house of blood, the Lord condemning not only Saul but his family, whom he justly wished to destroy by this means. But in accordance with right and natural reason his justice would be most satisfied and righteous by the guilty one paying on his part as much as he can, and by his forgiving him what he cannot pay, instead of exacting the whole of the debt from another, who is innocent and who owes nothing: this is tyranny, not righteousness nor justice, either human or divine. It might be objected to the doctrine which we have been expounding, that Adam's sin is experienced in the punishment that mankind now suffers from the curse that God passed on him and his posterity, while he and Eve alone were the perpetrators of that crime, from which it appears that God inflicted the punishment of their misdeed on those who did not commit it, and it is therefore called *original*, because the penalty for it came on the first parents.

This subject is very difficult, and this is not the place to treat it with any completeness. But we shall briefly state the true explanation: God punished Adam for his sin with no other punishment than that of leaving him in every respect conformable to his human nature, to which the Lord had granted great privileges for life, if he had kept righteous and obedient to his Creator; but as he transgressed the divine precept, God took them away from him and he was left deprived of them, and not only himself, but his wife and their descendants; they never merited them, because the Lord had bestowed them of his free mercy, and therefore he never deviated from justice towards their posterity in leaving man in all the perfection of human nature without any privilege; this is not God punishing mankind for the sin of Adam, but God not giving men what of his grace he had given Adam, and had afterwards in justice taken back; so it is true that the Lord never inflicted upon any one the punishment for a sin which another had committed, in order by that means to deliver the guilty from his own guilt.

And Christianity is not helped by the answer that the Messiah was willing to suffer and die for the sin of men; that it was his own voluntary act, and that hence God did him no injustice in letting him suffer and die; and that he could through his innocence merit pardon for all the guilty of mankind. This answer is contrary to reason, because, although a righteous man may be willing to give his life for the guilty, the righteousness of justice does not allow the judge to accept such an offer; and he who should accept it would be an unjust judge, much more so if he wished it and disposed the direct means to bring about that the innocent perish for the impious; but the Christian doctrine affirms that the eternal Father, who is the judge in this suit, sent his Son, and through the agency of the third Person, whom they call the *Holy Ghost*, made him man, only to the end that he might suffer that death from men; wherefore both the eternal Father and that other Person would be iniquitous judges, not only in accepting such an unjust death, but decreeing it and disposing the means to bring it about, bidding him suffer it patiently, which is clear from the gospel which relates that in his agony in the garden he prayed to his Father if it were possible to excuse his drinking that cup of bitterness, and if not, that his will might be done. And Paul says that he was obedient to death, even the death of the cross; consequently he suffered innocently by order of God, to atone for the sin which he had not committed, delivering the guilty, and himself bearing the penalty and curse, as Paul says, 'It is written, Accursed is he that hangeth on the tree;' but Christ wished to be accursed or be made a curse for our sake, to obey his Father who had sent him for that purpose, exacting satisfaction of his justice through the death of his innocent Son, in order in this way to pardon mankind, including even those who killed him. But by this divine justice was highly injured, and the righteousness of the Creator suffered the greatest insult in being pleased that innocence should suffer, and wickedness should escape punishment.

The whole of this Christian mode of reasoning results in nothing else than a denial of the infinite mercy of the blessed God towards his creatures; because, if we acknowledge his mercy, no reason is left why it should be necessary for God to come into the world to make himself man and die for men in atonement for their sins; and, if he did not come, the whole machinery of Christianity comes to nought; consequently they are forced to persist in maintaining that mercy could not find place nor sin be pardoned except by means of the death of God made man.

The Lord says the contrary in Holy Scripture, promising his creatures innumerable times absolute pardon of their sins, provided only they desire it and are disposed to receive that blessing, without his immortal Majesty or any innocent being or Messiah dying, but all living, turned away from their wicked ways towards the Lord their God, repentant and corrected of their transgressions. Thus he declares it to his people by Ezekiel (xviii. 30), saying, 'Therefore I will judge you, O house of Israel, every one according to his ways, saith Adonai God' (thus speaks the righteousness of justice); and then the equity of mercy follows, 'Repent and turn yourselves from your transgressions; so iniquity shall not be your ruin,' etc. This is what Adonai God says, but what the nations say is different and contrary to it.

The Christian says that neither Israel nor any of mankind can return to God; that let man do what he may he will always be stumbling in his sin, without any possibility of freeing himself from its snares; but the Lord says that your sin, if repented of, shall be no more a stumbling-block to you. They say that although man may in his contrition depart from sin, he must still die a spiritual death; but the Lord, supposing contrition, says, 'Why wilt thou die, O house of Israel?' God does not say that another shall pay the penalty for the guilt of man, but that man should depart from sin and be converted, 'Cast away from you all your sins, return to me and live:' he does not say that he will die for us that we may live, but that we should return to him and so we shall live: with that his justice, his righteousness, his mercy are consistent, and conformable to all the Holy Scripture, without there being in the whole of it a single word which directly or indirectly, in light or in shadow (as they say), signifies the contrary; there is nothing about Adam's debt, or infinite wickedness, or the impossibility of satisfying divine justice, or the death of the

God-man Messiah to pay, by dying innocent, what he did not owe.

Wherefore the foundation of Christianity is destroyed and disproved, and consequently it cannot apply the fifty-third chapter to the Messiah dying to expiate sin, since such a death never was nor could ever be accepted by God, and would not be of benefit to his creatures, as every one shall atone for his own sin, and neither God nor any one else will atone for them, as it is said, 'Therefore I will judge every one after his own ways, O house of Israel, saith Adonai God.'

CHAPTER XXVI.

IT IS PROVED THAT EVEN UNDERSTANDING THE FIFTY-THIRD CHAPTER AS THE [CHRISTIAN] DOCTORS WILL HAVE IT OF THE MESSIAH, THEY CAN IN NO WAY APPLY IT AS THEY CLAIM TO DO.

GRANTED the truth of the Holy Scriptures concerning the redemption of Israel, and how it is to be according to the divine promise, and the qualities and merits of the true Messiah, who will be an instrument of God and the chief of redeemed Israel, as all the prophets described him, in order that Israel might never be mistaken in recognising him, or admit before his advent others who might be proposed either by the wickedness of any of the people or by the ignorance of the Gentiles; and granted also the refutation of the Christian arguments by which they pretend to darken our truth, and the clearness and sincerity of the Holy Scriptures, by which we demonstrate that neither the Messiah nor any other innocent man was to die for the sins either of Israel or of the nations, it is well that we should come to the fifty-third chapter, from which they claim a full proof of all they affirm, and a refutation of ourselves; now although it is evidently shewn, by what has been said, that he whom they believe in was not the Messiah of Israel, since he accomplished neither the redemption nor any other of the effects predicted by the prophets, still it may be proper to examine if the contents of this chapter can be applied to him, so as to demonstrate that, even understanding it as they wish, it is not applicable to this subject.

Let us allow (although false and contrary to prophetic truth) that the Messiah was to die a violent death for the sins of man, and that this is expressed in this prophetical fifty-third chapter of Isaiah; and let us allow also (although very doubtful) that he whom they claim to be such said he was the Messiah, and that the Romans and the Jews punished him and hung him on the gallows, which was the cross on which they hung malefactors; would this perchance suffice to constitute him the true Messiah, if all the things contained in this chapter should not fit him? would his dying be sufficient, if he did by his death nothing else of what the prophet declares that the servant of God, whom he introduces there, was to do, and whose afflictions he relates? There will be no Christian who will say that it would be sufficient unless he did and fulfilled all that is prophesied of that servant of God. Let us see, then, how the principal verses of the prophecy are applicable to him.

LIII. [1] *Who believed our report, and upon whom was the arm of Adonai manifested?* Granting that the whole of the chapter speaks of the Messiah, upon whom they affirm the arm of Adonai was manifested, it may be easily gathered from these words that the Messiah is not Adonai but simply a man. Since it says that upon him Adonai manifested his arm, the arm is not Messiah's but that of Adonai, because, if he was man and God, his own arm would have been manifested upon him, and he would not have occasion to refer to another Adonai; since there can be but one, and that would be himself; by which it is clearly seen that he spoke of a creature favoured by its Creator, not of the Creator under the form of a creature; for, if he was the Creator, the prophet would have said that his own right hand and his holy arm had saved him. In the second and third verses he describes the abasement and mean state of the servant of God of whom he is speaking, who ought to be esteemed and venerated, and employs the fourth verse in describing the troubles and miseries he suffered, saying, *Surely he hath borne our sicknesses, and sustained our sufferings, but we esteemed him stricken and wounded by God, and afflicted;* and the fifth verse continues, *But he was wounded for our sins, crushed by our revolt, the chastisement of our peace was upon him, and by his wounds ours were healed.* These and other similar verses which follow are explained by Christianity of the sins of mankind which the Messiah took upon himself to atone for, or of the punishments which Israel and the nations deserved for their crimes and that original sin which they inherited from Adam: these the prophet calls sicknesses, sufferings, and his passion and death the cause of healing, which is the expiation and deliverance from sin and its effects.

It is necessary, according to the Christian doctrine, that the Messiah should bear our sufferings, and heal our sicknesses, that both things should be fulfilled in him whom they adore as God and Messiah; and to know if he did so, and if what the prophet says was actually fulfilled in him, we ask whether these sufferings and this healing are to be understood materially with regard to the temporal troubles and miseries of Israel, or spiritually in so far as it refers to the purity and expiation of the soul, so that they might enjoy the divine glory. If it were to be understood according to the former meaning, Israel could never say such a thing, nor can it be affirmed of that subject; as since his death Israel has remained scattered throughout the world as it was for 600 years before his advent; and much more so since the destruction of the holy city and the sacred temple, suffering extreme calamities, and the most cruel sufferings of captivity among the nations, which fact they acknowledge in continual aggravation of our misery: therefore he did not bear these sicknesses and sufferings, since they continue to this day; and with his wounds, passion, and death he was not the healing of Israel which remained oppressed by the same infirmity of its captivity; on the contrary, according to their belief, from his death originated our ruin, the persecutions, the extreme contempt, the mortal hatred, and the protracted wanderings from which we suffer. And if he was the true Messiah (admitting, for the sake of argument, that he was to die for the people), by his death he should have borne our sufferings, by his martyrdom he should have healed the tribulations and the great sicknesses of Israel among the nations: and so the people would confess it, if it could come to believe it; but it cannot say so at any time with truth, as after his death Israel not only was not healed of its tribulations, but experienced them even in a greater degree, and still suffers them at the hands of those who in the world believed in him.

But Christianity seeing that in this sense it could not verify the prophecy of this subject, has recourse, as it is wont to do, to the spiritual, and says that he bare our sufferings and sicknesses in the sense of our crimes and the punishments we deserved for them, that this is the spiritual healing, Israel and the nations being freed from the debt of original sin, as well as of that which we have created anew by our actual crimes. Let us examine if this is true, and if the world experiences this spiritual benefit through his death.

In the first place, as for the sin of Adam, Israel and the nations remain as they were before, without that stain and debt of mankind being washed away or expiated by his blood, for they themselves confess that all are born infected with original sin, enemies of God, slaves of the devil, whom God could not purify although he made himself man and died to make atonement; and they believe this to be so certain, that they hold as an article of faith that children who die unbaptized are deprived eternally of glory, being condemned to *limbo* for the sin of Adam. And in the opinion of the Protestants the children of parents who are not Christians are condemned to hell for ever for the original sin which they did not commit; so that they confess that human nature could not be healed of its spiritual sicknesses and sufferings by the death of that Messiah: accordingly it cannot be this man of whom the prophet speaks.

And the answer they make to escape from this argument is not a little amusing, namely, that he for his part healed all, but it is necessary that each one should believe that he was healed through his death, for if he does not understand it to be so, he will remain in a worse state than before; this healing therefore rests in the conception of the patient, and should he die in childhood or be born an idiot, he cannot be healed because he cannot conceive that he gets healed; the necessary consequence is, that the devil takes them and they remain everlastingly in hell, atoning for the apple which they did not eat, unless indeed it is not a sin that his father and mother or any other Christian should think or believe that the child was cured of his sin through Christ; because this belief, although not his own, may avail him, and if there is no one to take this trouble for him, he must go, as the Papist maintains, to limbo, or to hell as the Protestant says.

Since no spiritual cure is experienced of the actual sins which men voluntarily commit, for Israel and the nations, Mohammedans and Christians, as well as those that are called heathens, commit the same sins as before his death, they follow miserably the frailty of their appetite, the same inclination to vice, and the same aversion to rational uprightness, which are the sufferings and infirmities caused by Adam's sin; and they follow human malice, and, in short, as many are condemned to hell now as before his death and passion, nay, even many more, because Israel with the divine law of Moses, and the nations of the world with the law of nature could be saved by observing them, but since his death none can be saved (in their opinion) except by believing in him and his incredible mysteries. And the Papists deny salvation to all, although Christians with all their heart and soul, who are not in everything followers of the Roman Church, and of these only those who do not die in sin, and at least can obtain absolution from another man to be saved, which with respect to the world means almost none; and thus Bernard, a doctor of the church, understood it, who writes in one of his revelations that on that day so many millions of people had died in the universe, and only a good old woman and a monk of his order had been saved. And if all this coming of God, this death and passion, were for no other end but to save mankind, and the Messiah was to obtain all that, how did he obtain it according to what they preach? how did he bear our sufferings and our infirmities? how did he heal the world of their sins and the pains of hell which they deserve? Where is this redemption of souls? these sins which he took away? that health and medicine that we got because of him, through his passion and death? Where is the kingdom of God preached by the Gospel at every point, proclaiming that the kingdom of the devil is already ended? How can the devil reign more than by taking off to hell almost all mankind, as they confess?

When the Lord shall reign in his world, as he has promised, at the time of the redemption, and his Messiah shall be Adonai One, and his name One, and all creatures shall know him, and love him, and his own people more than all creatures, he will remove all idols from off the earth, and so war, falsehood, and discord, all will be peace, love of God, and observance of his divine decrees, the law of nature among the nations, the divine law in Israel, as a kingdom of Levites, a kingdom of God. Such medicine, made by the omnipotence of the living God himself, Israel and all the nations will receive, and if by the death of this person this had happened in the world, they would have a right to say that he bare our sufferings and our infirmities, and his wounds had been our healing; but it was not so, and could not be so, since it is only the Lord God who pardons, saves, redeems, and no one else: and if the Messiah was to be as they understand it in this chapter, this ought to have happened on his death; but since it has not happened, all that can be said of him is that he died, but not that he was Israel's Messiah promised by the prophets.

[9] The servant of God of whom the prophet speaks can of necessity do no evil act; no falsehood, deceit, or perverse doctrine can issue from his lips, or be the cause of others introducing it into the world; now this cannot be maintained, I mean, proved, of the person whom they proclaim: because, giving the Gospel credit as a witness on the same side, he did many things contrary to the law of Moses, by which he was bound as a Jew. He said other things which proved false. In the first place, he transgressed the divine law, he and his disciples breaking the Sabbath rest, permitting the plucking the ears of corn on pretext of necessity, to the scandal of the Israelites, though it was not necessary to satisfy hunger by that means, and they were in no danger of life in suffering it, and they might have gone to the village and asked for bread in God's name; then, on the Sabbath they were not allowed to go so far from the town; but he consented and even approved of plucking the ears, which is the same thing as cutting wood, for which crime the Lord commanded another man in the desert to be stoned. He absolved of her crime the woman convicted of adultery, whom the divine decree condemns to certain death, for no better reason than asking the witnesses if they were sinners, as if to prove a crime required the witnesses to be saints, so that there would never be witnesses against the guilty, for no man can affirm of himself that he is righteous and never sinned; but he said, 'He that is without sin among you, let him accuse her;' and as no one dared to say that he was a righteous man, he sent her away in peace, combatting by an unlawful sympathy the divine law. He said that what entered by the mouth did not defile the soul, though the Lord has said so many times about forbidden food: '*Do not defile your souls;*' and yet he and his followers, more particularly Paul, admit that the apple of Paradise defiled not only Adam, by whose mouth it entered, but also all mankind, simply because God had forbidden it; consequently it is false to say that what enters by the mouth does not defile the soul.

He said, moreover, that power had been given him in heaven and on earth, though the Lord has said that he will not give his glory to another. He said things which proved to be false. Being asked by the apostles how it was that, being the Messiah, he did not unite the twelve tribes of Israel, a question surely very necessary and agreeable to the Holy Scriptures, he answered that they had no concern in knowing the day and the hour, but he assured them that that generation in which they lived would not pass without his returning in the clouds of heaven for that purpose, wherefore the church in those first hundred years expected with very certain faith that he would come as he had promised; on strength of which in the time of Tertullian great rogations and processions were made throughout the countries of Christendom, but he never returned, nor was what he had said fulfilled or verified. Afterwards his followers formed in his name many dogmas repugnant to truth,—they invented a plurality of persons, contrary to the very simple unity of their Creator, who being infinitely One, can in no sense be many; although this falsehood was published many years later. And what falsehood can be greater than that of confining him, whom heaven and earth cannot contain, within the trammels of humanity, within the narrow limits of a womb, the small compass of a wafer, affirming on his word that that is and there dwells the mighty God as he is present in heaven, converted into a crumb of bread and a drop of wine. The Gentile adoration of Bacchus as the god of wine was a great deceit, but a still greater deceit is that of adoring a little wine as the God of all. How then can the verse be verified which says, *There was no deceit in his mouth?*

10 *If he offer his soul in atonement he shall see seed,* etc. Cipriano de Valera renders it, *he shall see lineage,* which is the same as seed, descendants, or posterity. Let us see then if this verse can be applied to their alleged Messiah. The prophet promises three things of the subject or servant of God whom he there introduces, and all under a condition. The condition is,

if he offer his soul in atonement for sin; if, at the risk of his life, he will correct himself of his transgressions, loving the Lord his God more than his own soul or life, he will obtain the three following blessings: he will see his offspring, generation, and fortunate progeny, which is the same blessing which the Lord gave to the patriarchs, and they to their children. The second blessing is, that he will live a long time on the face of the earth, a blessing which the Lord gave his chosen and the observers of his divine precepts; the shortening of life, on the contrary, being the punishment with which he threatens transgressors; and thus to the subject of this prophecy, as a reward for his tribulations and sufferings, is promised that continuing with contempt for his own life in such a holy endurance, he will extend the days of his life, will be preserved alive in this world: so reads Valera, who translates it thus, He will live long days; and in the same manner the learned Arias Montanus also. The third blessing is, that the will of the Lord will prosper in his hand, that what the Lord wishes, what is agreeable to him in his world, will be effected through his servant,—for although the will of the Lord must always be carried into effect, he says that this will be by means of his servant,—using him as an efficacious and sufficient instrument for that end. This being granted, let us examine if these three things can be affirmed of that man who they say offered his soul for sin. The first, which is, *he will see his seed*, cannot fit him, for he died, as they affirm, without offspring or descendants; but to this they answer that he had a spiritual seed by generating the Christian church, and this, not natural children, must be understood by *seed*. This answer is contrary to the sacred text, and is the only means of escaping from the difficulty, because in Holy Scripture the word *semen* never signifies spiritual children, but those after the flesh. *Son* signifies many times spiritual son, but *seed* never anything but natural propagation. Cipriano de Valera translates *semen* by 'lineage,' which is the proper natural descendants, and nobody says that there is a spiritual lineage, accordingly it is necessary that this person should have a natural posterity to succeed him, which that man had not, and therefore this circumstance of the verse does not apply to him. Then the second, which is, *he will prolong his days*, or as Valera says, 'he will live long days,' is still less fulfilled in their Messiah, because if he died, as they say, at thirty-three years of age, it cannot well be affirmed that he shall live a long life, dying in the best period of his youth: this is called dying cut down by the hand of God: how then can lengthening of life, enjoying the blessing of a long life, be made to agree with being cut down in the best of his days? and if they should say that in another world he prolongs his days by living eternally, that is no particular prerogative, but the universal lot of all souls, even of those condemned, who will never die, but live eternally, either in pain or in glory; accordingly, 'he will prolong his days' is in no way fulfilled in him. The third is, that *the will of Adonai will prosper in his hand*, or through his hands, which still less can be applied to their purpose, for as we see in all the places we quote about the Messiah, it is the will of the Lord that he should congregate Israel from all parts of the world; that all nations should be converted to his divine worship and adoration, without false sects or idolatries; that sins should end, and that all human creatures should enjoy a perpetual peace, love, and spiritual and temporal tranquillity; this was and is the will of the Lord, and that which the prophet says will prosper through the hand of that servant of whom he speaks. Even the Gospel says so, where it states that the angel declared it to Joseph when he fled jealous of the premature pregnancy of his wife Mary, saying to him that she would give birth to a son, who should be called Jesus, and that he would take away the sins of his people (Matt. i. 21). And John in his Gospel says, speaking of the same, 'Behold the Lamb of God, behold him who takes away the sins of the world' (i. 29). They cannot then deny even from their Gospel that such was the will of God, and that it had to prosper and have its effect by the hand of his Messiah. But how will they apply this to him whom they introduce and adore, with whose advent all the contrary has happened, and up to this day nothing of what is the will of God has been performed or has prospered? Now if he was promised and sent to Israel, it was the will of God either that Israel should kill him and be lost for the sake of the Messiah, or that it should receive him and enjoy the blessings and benefits of his advent; the former is absurd and contrary to divine goodness and truthfulness, and the Holy Scriptures; and as for the latter, the will of the Lord did not prosper by the hand of that man and was not fulfilled; since Israel by denying him and killing him increased its sins and negotiated, as they say, its own utter perdition and ruin; consequently he did not remove the sins of his people, as the angel in the Gospel says to Joseph; nor is he the Lamb of God who removed the sins of the world, as John says. Admitting that on account of this child, this lamb, the perdition of his people followed, how do his followers preach him, if it be not the same thing God wishing to save it and condemn it by the same person? And if God wished to save it by means of the Messiah, and this salvation did not happen, but the contrary, the prophet should rather have said, 'And the will of God will *not* prosper in his hand;' since in the rest of the world outside Israel, of which John says, 'This is the Lamb of God which taketh away the sins of the world,' the will of Adonai prospered still less; since the world that God wished to redeem, and extricate from the snares of sin and the power of the devil, has remained, as we have said above and is manifestly seen, full of the same abominations, prevarications, and sins; consequently, this Lamb of God did not take away the sins of the world, nor did the will of the Lord prosper in his hand, as it has to, according to the prophet, by the servant of God of whom he speaks.

11 *By his wisdom my righteous servant shall justify many.* No wisdom did that man teach many, there was nothing he himself said, or which the Evangelists wrote in his name that was just and holy, that the Lord had not already said before in

his divine law and the prophets, without their being able to add to the divine law anything good for the spiritual life of man; wherefore the doctrine or wisdom to justify the soul did not spring from the Messiah or his disciples, but from that which the Lord revealed to Moses in the divine law which he gave his people; and what they added is nothing else than an affectation of holiness contrary to the natural reason itself, and prejudicial to human government. Among many things which we omit, let the case serve as an example in which he did not permit a son's last act of piety towards his own dead father, to whom, when he wished to go and give him burial, he said, 'Leave the dead to bury their dead, but come thou and follow me' (Matt. viii. 21, 22); an action surely, let them comment on it as they please, most impious and scandalous. He bids another youth, who was seeking for the way to perfection, sell all he possessed and give it to the poor (Matt. xix. 21); a doctrine contrary to reason, since the temporal goods which the Lord grants must be gratefully received, we should return thanks for them to the divine goodness that has been thus pleased to allot us a part of its bounties, should use them with sobriety, and relieve with alms the necessities of our neighbour by sharing them with him, but not so as to impoverish ourselves. And thus the Lord says by the prophet, 'Share thy bread with the poor' (Is. lviii. 7), but he does not say give him all the bread, for that would be a foolish and irrational charity. Still less tolerable was what the apostles afterwards commanded, that all converts to Christianity should sell all they possessed and entrust the money to themselves, as it is said in the Acts of the Apostles, 'And they sold all that they possessed, and placed the price at the apostles' feet' (iv. 34, 35). This was a doctrine repugnant to the government of mankind, for without some difference in temporal goods no one would be willing to work to acquire them, and if all were equal no one would discharge those servile offices which human society requires for its preservation, and it would amount to nothing else than opening the gate to idleness, the mother of all vices. And they not only by this means introduced idleness, but also by teaching that no one should take thought for the morrow, but should live joyfully without providing clothes to dress in, or food to live by; that the lilies without asking for it grow up better adorned than Solomon on his throne; that the birds of heaven are fed and grow fat without gathering in the wheat or providing for the future; that God, who takes care of these creatures, knows what men need, and will give it them. This wisdom is contrary to human providence, and is tempting Providence to sustain mankind miraculously without man using his reason, which the Lord has given him for his government, both temporal and spiritual, thus preferring to institute a rabble of mendicants instead of an honest and providently-managed government. The evangelical wisdom affected humility: it bids one, if offended with a slap on the face, offer the other cheek to receive another blow; an unreasonable piece of advice and out of character with all perfection, for to suffer blow and insult with patience, to bear no hatred and not to seek revenge on the offender, fulfils in man all the perfection of the spiritual life, and what the Lord commanded in his divine law, 'Do not bear hatred nor seek revenge.' But to wish purposely to be more offended, is not consistent with human intellect, or that for the sake of practising humility one should offer one's neighbour the opportunity, if in a moment of irritation he sins by giving a blow, of committing sin again by repeating it, and this time a greater sin; for the more the offended party shews himself humble, the more the guilt of the offender is increased, which would be avoided by his suffering humbly and retiring, careful that his enemy may not sin by continuing to give way to the effects of his wrath. The wisdom of the Gospel teaches that it is not sufficient, not to hate one's enemy, but that one must love him and all those who have done us harm; whereas the divine wisdom is contented with our not bearing hatred or not seeking for revenge on our enemies; it did not bid us love them, because such a command would be neither just nor possible;

one can love only what is good, and no one can conceive it good to be offended and to love it; it suffices not to hate it as bad: and if we are not obliged to love those with whom we have never spoken or communicated, for there is no reason which leads us to love them, how shall we love our enemies? It is true that we must be charitable to them, feel for their misfortunes, and help them if in need of us; this, however, is not to love our enemies because they do us harm, but not to hate them, and avenge ourselves by not wishing to do them good; but, on the contrary, to attend to their necessities by the general precept of charity towards all, without mentioning or recollecting their enmity. This is the wisdom of the Law, the other is that of men who affected more piety than the Law itself; but Christianity now acknowledges all this, and practises as we have said, since there is no one who does not seek the means of his own maintenance, no one who sells all that he possesses and gives it to the poor, no one who offers his face for a second blow, no one, however pious, who loves his enemies. Its doctors now say that they are advice, and not precepts, but still it remains doubtful whether they are good advice; although the Protestants would have them to be precepts, yet up to this day no one observes them or justifies himself by this wisdom, except a few bare-footed friars and Capuchins, who have given up everything to observe this evangelical wisdom, and raise themselves to higher stations by means of Christianity, living, as they say, an evangelical life: but not so, however, the head of the church and his hierarchies, whose riches, majesty, sovereignty, rivalry, revengefulness, ambition, and every quality opposed to the wisdom of the Gospel are not considered to be against this wisdom, which, like that of the Messiah which it preaches, never justified nor will justify anybody. The principal point in which this Christian wisdom has always consisted is in depreciating and running down the greatness of the divine law which the Lord promulgated on Sinai, because that which they invented was not compatible with it. Paul says that it was deadly, that it gave no holiness nor justification, nor eternal life to Israel; that it operated on men no better than a curse; that sin entered the world through the Law; that all were under a curse through it; and other similar blasphemies, of which his whole theology is composed. This is the wisdom which emanated from that Messiah and is so much extolled by his followers; he who best knows how to defend these dogmas is the wisest; he who writes with the greatest acumen to destroy the observance of the divine law, and who is most ostentatious in depreciating by his own wisdom the greatness of that which the Lord taught his people on Sinai is the most righteous; but the Lord himself declares its quality, saying at the time of its promulgation, 'This is your wisdom, this is your understanding;' by this wisdom the righteous servant of the Lord will make many righteous, not by that wisdom which flooded the world after the advent of that man, filling it with various religions repugnant to his unity and the immensity of his infinite and impassible divine existence; consequently he did not fulfil the verse which says that that servant of God would make many righteous by his wisdom.

It may be gathered from all that has been said that the fifty-third chapter, even if understood of the Messiah, as Christianity alleges, still cannot be applied to him in whom they believe, since what we said before about the redemption of Israel and the offices of the true Messiah, and what Isaiah wrote in this chapter about the servant of God of whom he speaks, were not fulfilled in him whom they introduce as such; so that in whatever way they explain it, this chapter in no way serves their purpose. Nevertheless, more to satisfy the curiosity of some people, than to meet the wants of their conscience, we shall state how this chapter must be understood, and who it is of whom the prophet speaks in it.

Explanation of the Fifty-third Chapter of the Prophet Isaiah.

For the more exact understanding of this chapter we must remark that the prophetical books are not divided into chapters, but form one continuous piece of writing from the beginning to the end of the prophecy; only for the sake of greater clearness and facility in quoting verses they were divided into chapters either by Jerome or by somebody else before him; and therefore when a chapter ends it must not be inferred from that that the prophet ends there with the discourse or subject on which he is engaged, and that he treats of a different matter in the following; but, on the contrary, that the same subject is continued, and that the prophecy was subsequently divided into chapters. Whenever, therefore, we wish to understand a chapter, we should examine what the preceding and following chapters contain, what subject is treated in them, and the purport of it, so as to see if the same subject is treated in what follows.

The prophet had spoken at great length and with perfect clearness of the redemption of Israel in the fifty-first chapter, and continues the same subject in the fifty-second, addressing the people of Israel and the holy city of Jerusalem, calling on them to awake from their sleep, to return to their ancient vigour, to lay aside their mourning apparel and put on garments of gladness, to shake off the dust of their ruins, as they will not only be restored to their ancient splendour, but their city will be for ever holy for its inhabitants, and will never more be profaned by the uncircumcised Gentiles, because the captivity of Israel is now ended, and being redeemed it will enjoy liberty again. The prophet continues addressing the same people, not the Gentiles, who would honour themselves with that name, but that people whom he led out of Egypt, and scattered among the nations for its sins, as is shewn by verses 3–6, 9, 10; and he proceeds to predict the wonderful effects of the redemption, that there will be no more impurity in Israel, or in the sacred vessels of the temple, that the Israelites will no longer go about with haste or by flight, but in safety and confidence, guided by God himself, who will gather and congregate them into their holy country; all this the Lord says by his prophet in words so clear that one has only to read them to understand them. And the Christian cannot deny that this happiness and redemption are promised to the true Israel whom he sent to sojourn in Egypt and afterwards brought out with a powerful hand, and not to the Gentile nations who never dwelled in or went out of Egypt, and who are called in this very place impure and uncircumcised; nor can they explain it of the return from Babylon, by what we have already proved, and because not one of the circumstances to which reference is here made can apply to it, either the holiness and purity or the perpetuity he promises when the impure and the uncircumcised shall no more enter Jerusalem, for, on the contrary, that redemption was very different to the one here promised by the prophet as glorious and wonderful in the eyes of all creatures, bringing the utmost greatness to the holy city as well as the redeemed people. After depicting the redemption of Israel as the Lord has decreed it, the prophet continues the same subject, describing the state in which the people will be in that happy time, both with regard to itself and the nations, saying in the thirteenth verse, '*Behold my servant shall be prosperous, shall be exalted and extolled, and raised very high.*' The Lord says, My people whom I formerly enslaved in Egypt and afterwards amongst all the nations, being now freed from its yoke, shall be no longer their servant but mine; my servant, over whom all the nations were prosperous before, shall now be prosperous himself, and as they formerly trampled him down, humiliated him, laid him down like dust to walk on, so now my servant shall be exalted. Therefore he said before: 'Awake, awake, Jerusalem, shake thyself from the dust,' that thou and thy people may be exalted; and if in captivity he suffered contempt, if the world conspired to dishonour him with reproaches, with vile and false evidence, with the imputation of abominations, now my servant shall be exalted, all the nations who blasphemed him with their abuse shall celebrate his happiness with praises, singing a new song to Adonai who hath performed truth and fulfilled his word to the house of Israel; and so his people will be exalted among the nations of the whole universe, and thus Israel will be a kingdom of priests, the chief of the whole world, and will become a subject of fame and praise in all the lands of his captivity, as the Lord promises by the prophet Zephaniah (iii. 19, 20); and so Isaiah says in this verse, repeating the idea in lxiii. 9, and before in xlix. 21. Israel is called 'servant,' a name by which the Lord frequently honours those whom he loves, as well individuals, like the patriarchs and Moses, as the whole congregation of Israel: so he calls it by the same Isaiah in many passages (xli. 8, 9, xliv. 1, 2, 21, xlix. 3).

It is unnecessary to multiply further proofs, for it must be considered established, that throughout Holy Scripture Israel is styled servant of God, and that Isaiah retained this designation throughout his prophecy, and preserves it in the first verse of our exposition; announcing the redemption and the very happy state that will follow from it, he says that Israel his servant will be prosperous; and so he promised before by the same Isaiah (xlviii. 15).

14 Israel being miraculously raised to such greatness, and declared God's servant in the presence of the nations, the prophet contemplates the wonder and fear that will fall upon them, after having known it for so many centuries as an abased, miserable people, in their opinion, forsaken by God, so much so that they themselves wondered how, after having been a loved and chosen people, his punishment reached such extreme severity; which wonder compelled the nations to enquire what sin Israel could have committed so grave that should compel divine justice to such lasting indignation, the most astute, the Christians, believing that his crime could have been nothing less than the murder of the incarnate God himself; so much

did the nations wonder at Israel in its long and painful captivity: and therefore the prophet says, *As many wondered at thee;* so the Lord had foretold in Leviticus xxvi. 32, and in the same manner Ezekiel v. 15. He gives next the reason why the nations wondered at the sufferings and miseries of the people, because they saw *its form marred beyond that of man,* and his appearance unworthy of the children of man, so disfigured that they did not appear to be a people or nation, nor to participate in human nature, nor as individuals to be reputed men; nor did they shew any manly vigour, but a submission so humble towards all nations that they never raised their hand in their own defence, and thus did not seem to be of the same species. It is therefore said that its aspect was marred more than that of man, and its form more than that of the sons of man; no quality shone in them to indicate their being either sons of man, or of the same nature as other men, but they seemed inferior to brute animals, for those defend themselves against their persecutor; but persecuted Israel was never moved to its own defence, and therefore the same prophet called it worm in chapter xli. 14, 'Fear not, thou worm of Jacob,' who art no man nor like a man among the nations, but like a worm which, by reason of its littleness, is not able to resist or to strive and defend itself against its oppressor. But when it is redeemed, then it will no longer be a worm, but valiant and manly; so the Lord promises in the chapter and verse quoted, depicting to the eyes of the nations both states, that of humiliation and that of its highest grandeur: 'Fear not, worm of Jacob, men of Israel;' the former meaning, in captivity like a worm, the latter in the redemption like men. When the nations shall see the people of Israel in this state, they will remember his miserable condition among them for so many centuries, when he was without the form of children of men, and his appearance so marred that it retained not even the shadow of man, but rather was that of the humblest worm of the earth; no action was seen in him to indicate that nobility which naturally belongs to human nature, he was always so patient and defenceless against injury, reproach, and persecution; therefore many nations wondered at him, his appearance being marred more than any man. And in this state Isaiah portrayed him in the first chapter, saying, 'From the sole of the foot even to the head there is no soundness in it,' etc., which is the same as his appearance being marred more than any man. If the nations wondered at Israel's change from being the people of God, to being a scattered and captive people, without form or resemblance of its ancient splendour, much more will they wonder at the brilliant change from this meanness, from the reproach of captivity to the more noble state which neither the wise men of the Gentiles could have comprehended, nor Israel itself imagined, had not God foretold it of its future happiness. The nations will wonder at this felicity, on seeing him elevated, exalted, and raised very high, the most contemptible littleness being changed into the most extraordinary grandeur, which must be understood of the people who persevered in the divine worship and observance of the divine law, for those who abandoned it and preferred for their own worldly ends to mix themselves with the nations, not having truly and evidently suffered in the midst of them the opprobrium and the degradation of captivity, will not be elevated or exalted, being treated as rebels against the law, and strangers to the people of God.

15 The prophet continues to describe the wonder of the nations when they see the wonderful and unexpected redemption of Israel; he describes the effects of this wonder such as naturally follow a great change, an extraordinary event; some talk over the event magnifying it, others are speechless, amazed and stupefied at the portent; he says that the kings will close their mouths, because it chiefly concerned the princes and kings of the world to oppose the happiness of Israel, they being the most powerful in obstructing it, and the most interested in preventing it, as Pharaoh in Egypt; then they count Israel as a large number of subjects, and those who were slaves

before become rulers, kings having to bend their neck to the new kingdom which the Lord will raise up on the earth, a kingdom which will have no end, as he said by Daniel. God says they will then close their mouths, as they will not reply or be able to gainsay the divine power, as he said before at the redemption from Egypt, 'And no dog sharpened its tongue' (Exod. xi. 7); the kings will remain confused, ashamed of their own vanities, and of the iniquity of the laws with which they afflicted Israel for so many years; their power will not suffice to injure him, nor their interest to hasten his ruin; nay, they and their princes will prostrate themselves humbly before Israel, as he promised in xlix. 7, and so in lx. 3; and at the tenth verse of this chapter, the Lord, speaking of Israel, says all that we have already explained so formally as to admit of no doubt or difference of opinion. The prophet, speaking in the name of the Lord, says to the people, Because I struck thee in my wrath, in the anger and severity of my divine justice, because I put thee in a state in which thou hadst no longer the look or appearance of a man or a son of man, and reduced thee to the lowest degradation, and thou didst suffer with patience and constancy the effects of my indignation; for that reason I will now in my benevolence have pity on thee, I will use my mercifulness with thee; I will bring about that thou shalt be elevated, exalted, and raised high, and the nations shall submit themselves to thee and rebuild thy ruins, and their kings shall serve thee humbly, themselves rising up in thy presence from their royal thrones on which they used to preside, and their princes falling on their knees before thee; kings will see and will stand up, they will start to their feet on seeing thee exalted and raised so high, and the lords will humble themselves, because they will know that the Holy One of Israel has chosen thee. And at verse 12 he says, 'That the nation and kingdom that will not serve thee shall perish, and the nations shall be utterly destroyed,' because at the sight of thy wonderful redemption no one will be able to ignore thy glories, and thou wilt make many nations speak of them, and kings will close their mouths, as Micah repeats in chapter vii. of his prophecy, at verse 16. *For what was not told them they saw, and that which they had not heard they understood.* The prophet gives the reason of the kings being dumb struck in amazement, and of the nations talking, excited at the marvellous change in Israel, saying, *Because they saw what they had not been told of.* The nations were not ignorant that Israel persevered in its hope, but they regarded that hope as vanity and superstition; not one of their wise men told of it as a credible reality, but as a contemptible fable worthy of ridicule; wherefore it was the same as not to have told it and to ignore it: *and what they had not heard they understood,* and they came to a practical understanding of that which they never wished to hear and could not understand; but when Israel is exalted and lifted up, they will see as an infallible truth that which no one had ever told them, and they will be compelled to understand what they had always wished to ignore, and will hear that which they had never wished to hear and understand; and this sight of what they had never thought of, this understanding of what they had never heard of, this practical experience of what they had never understood before, will be the cause why many nations talk of Israel, and the kings humiliated and prostrate close their mouths, *since what was not told them they saw, what they had not heard they understood.*

These are the last words of what they divided into the fifty-second chapter; but any one who fairly considers them will see in them an imperfect sentence, which still leaves the mind of the reader in suspense, for it says, *thus he will cause many nations to talk,* and does not say in continuation in what way or what the nations will say; wherefore either the sentence must be imperfect, or the word or expression *thus,* which is equivalent to *in this manner,* must be superfluous, a supposition we cannot admit in the case of the sacred text, and therefore the discourse must necessarily follow, saying in what way and what he will make the many nations say; and what they have to say could not possibly be said except by continuing it in what they have divided into the fifty-third chapter, their express words continuing the meaning in this manner: thus he will cause the kings to shut their mouths, thus he will cause many nations to talk, who believed our report? and on whom has the arm of the Lord been manifested? the nations continuing throughout the chapter to describe with the highest admiration the sufferings of Israel and its wonderful change. The Christian interpreters have tried hard to obscure the connexion of these last words of the fifty-second chapter with the fifty-third, because they do not wish the nations but the Jewish people to be speaking in this chapter, otherwise they cannot apply the chapter to their Messiah. For this reason, with cunning foresight, they translate the Hebrew word for *he will cause to talk* by *he will sprinkle*, availing themselves of the proper meaning of the word, which signifies *to sprinkle*; and in this way they introduce into the fifty-third chapter Israel talking of the Messiah, in order to exclude the nations talking of Israel; but this cunning in no way serves their purpose; on the contrary, they shew they defend a bad cause, for although it is true that the Hebrew word signifies *to sprinkle*, this meaning does not suit the verse, and the comparison which the prophet makes is out of place and meaningless if we translate *sprinkle* instead of *make to talk;* the comparison is in this form, *As many wondered at thee, his visage was so marred more than any man, so will he sprinkle many nations.* The wondering at him of many people has no relation with his sprinkling many nations; but if he says *will cause to talk,* the comparison is appropriate and quite rhetorical, *as they wondered at thee,* poor and abased, so thou wilt cause the nations to talk and burst forth into exclamations of wonder on seeing thy change. Besides, the expression *kings will close their mouths* clearly shews that the contrary is said of the nations who will talk, wondering at the unexpected happiness of the people, and there is no point in saying he will sprinkle many nations, and kings will close their mouths; but it is a highly rhetorical figure, which is called antithesis, to place together two contrary things, as the prophet does here; he will cause the kings to be silent and the nations to talk, . . . what follows in the fifty-third chapter; and if it were not so, this chapter would in no way fit in by introducing Israel saying what it contains; and this the most enthusiastic Christian can notice, as the fifty-second chapter ends with these words, *He will cause many nations to talk, and kings will close their mouths, because they saw what had not been told them, and understood what they had not heard. Who believed our report, and upon whom was the arm of Adonai manifested?* etc. It is impossible that this beginning of the fifty-third can have any connexion with that end of the fifty-second, unless it is the nations who talk and say, *Who believed our report?* and it would be necessary, in order to understand Israel to be speaking the contents of the chapter, that at the end of the preceding chapter or at the beginning of the fifty-third he should say: And then Israel will say thus, *Who believed our report?* but since there is no such expression, without occasion and against the connexion the Jewish people is brought in to speak what is said in the fifty-third chapter; consequently it must be the nations who talk, and not Israel, as they vainly pretend. And as to the Hebrew word which we render *talk*, it is true that it signifies to sprinkle, but the same word, to sprinkle or drip, occurs very frequently in Holy Scripture in the sense of to talk: and for the Christians the authority of Pagninus is sufficient, who says on this very verse of the fifty-second of Isaiah, *he will sprinkle*, that is, he will make to talk; and since Pagninus understánds it so in his Hebrew Dictionary, giving as an example this very verse, no further proof is required; and it is certain that when a word has two significations, it must be understood according to the sense of the subject-matter, and in the present case it is clearly seen that of *sprinkling* does not apply.

LIII. 1 Then the nations, wondering at the redemption of Israel, say, *Who believed our report?* Who ever imagined, or held it certain, that what we now see was to happen? He said before that *they understood what they had not heard*, and returns to the same words, saying, Before we neither heard nor understood, but now we both hear and understand that Israel is redeemed, and before none believed what we now hear of the glory and restoration of Israel to the grace of the Lord his God, and the possession of the holy land; he had said that the nations and kings will wonder, because they had not been told, nor had heard or understood it; and the same he says in chapter xliii. 9, 'Who among them can declare this, and shew us former things?' as if to say, None of the nations announced or related it as true, or foretold it so that we might believe it and hear it, which is the same as what he said above, *that which was not told them they saw, and what they had not heard they understood.* But the Lord answers them in the eleventh verse of the same chapter, that he announced it and told it, and will cause them to hear and understand what they never heard or believed; if there was no one among the nations to announce it, I Adonai have announced it by my prophets, I myself have fulfilled my word in saving Israel as I promised; I have saved because there is none else who can save; no man, no creature, is able to save Israel, but I alone: and by redeeming it now before the eyes of the nations, I will cause them to hear what had not been told them, and I will cause them to know what they did not before understand, and they will then in wonder say, *Who believed our report?* or who ever gave credit to what we do now hear about redeemed Israel?

And upon whom was the arm of Adonai manifested? This sentence has two meanings, both literal; one interrogatively negative, thus: to whom was revealed or manifested the strength of Adonai, his infinite power, the effects of which we now hear of in the exaltation of Israel? both portions of the verse making a whole in their meaning: who ever believed what we now hear, and to whom did Adonai reveal that he would use his divine power to redeem this people, for that was never considered in the world to be probable or possible? But with still greater propriety it can be understood in a positive sense, making it a question of surprise: who is this *upon whom the arm of the Lord was manifested* and the greatest proofs of his love and omnipotence? They might well excuse this question of the nations, as it could be no other than the people of Israel upon whom the Lord many times said he had manifested and would manifest the strong arm of his divine power. Thus he announced it by the same Isaiah in the preceding chapter (verse 10), 'Adonai hath manifested the arm of his holiness in the eyes of all the nations.' Then if the Lord says that he manifested his holy arm upon Israel, and that all the nations will see this, they had no reason to doubt it, and there is no occasion for the question, *and upon whom was the arm of Adonai manifested?* But this is more an exclamation of surprise than a question, for when such an extraordinary thing occurs as that of Adonai consoling his people and redeeming Jerusalem in the sight of the ends of the earth and under the eyes of all the nations, they justly burst forth into shouts of wonder, saying, *Who believed our report, and upon whom was the arm of Adonai manifested,* except upon God's afflicted and despised people, of whom we never heard or believed such happiness? The prophet said the same in chapter xl. 11, describing the redemption of Israel in these words, 'Like a shepherd he will feed his flock, he will gather the lambs with his arm.'

2 The prophet compares Israel in his mean captive state to a branch whose roots are in a barren ground, because there is no water to give it life, whence necessarily all its verdure fades, its leaves fall, and it remains shorn of the ornament which nature gave it, a branch whose dry roots it seems impossible can be green again and bear fruit. In this condition the Lord said by the same Isaiah (i. 30) that he would place Israel for its transgressions, 'Ye shall be as an oak whose leaves are falling off, and like a garden that hath no water;' so he placed him in its captivity, and from that state he will rescue it at the time of the

redemption : *and Israel will rise like a shoot before him, and like a root out of the arid earth.* The prophet says as a root out of a dry ground, but does not say as a dry root out of the ground, and the difference is well worth consideration; for it points to nothing less than the hope of Israel, for a dry root has lost the plant's vitality, and there is no hope of its becoming green again; but that which is in a dry ground, although withered and apparently dead, by the beneficial help of water returns to its former state; and as Israel, although in its captivity it was deprived of its ancient splendour through want of that special and miraculous providence which, like living waters, made it live and fructify, was nevertheless to revive and flourish at the time of its redemption, the prophet did not call it a dry root, but a root in a dry ground, of which hope never failed that it might be green again, and therefore it will come up like a branch, and like a root out of a dry ground, when the Lord pours upon it the waters of his mercy, as he promised by Isaiah (xliv. 3, 4). As long as the Lord does not shew this mercy to Israel, and keeps it in its captivity, in the barren desert of the nations, it remains as a root in a dry ground; but when his divine power redeems it in love, when it receives the watering of his pity, it will come up like a green willow, as a branch out of the dry ground, in which for so many centuries it struck its roots; and so the Lord promised by the same prophet, at xxvii. 6, 'In the coming days Jacob shall take root, Israel shall sprout and blossom;' and then, coming up like a branch which springs again out of the ground, Israel will experience what the prophet says in lxvi. 14, 'Your bones shall flourish like a shoot.'

He hath no form nor comeliness. As the branches and root in a dry ground have no form or resemblance of what they ought to be or what they were, and there is no sort of beauty in them, so the house of Israel in captivity shews nothing of what it was, and does not exhibit a shadow of what it is to be; it stands like a root in a dry ground, without splendour and without form or figure to be admired; it stands divested of the beauty imparted to it by those wondrous rays of light which the Lord shed on it on Sinai. With this disfigurement, with this decay of beauty, the Lord had threatened it through Isaiah (v. 14); hence the nations say of Israel in its captivity and meanness, *He hath no form nor comeliness.* This loss of its former beauty, through which all the nations refused to recognise it, was predicted by Isaiah (xxviii. 1), 'Woe to the crown of pride of Ephraim! its desirable beauty shall fall like a sprig: its desirable beauty shall be a fading flower.' Thus Jeremiah in his Lamentations bemoaned it (ii. 1), 'How hath the Lord cast down from heaven to earth the beauty of Israel!' Therefore the nations will say, seeing Israel in this state, *He hath no form nor comeliness. And we saw him, and there was no appearance in him that we should desire him,* for Israel being so disfigured as to retain not even the figure of man, his deformed and uncomely appearance resembling a root in a dry ground, the nations had nothing to covet in him, none of the nations wished to be or even to look like an Israelite; the race of the Jewish people being offensive to all, all held it as the scum of mankind. And even converted to their sects, the Jew lacks the esteem that native converts gain, or which the Turks and the Moors have for the Christians; any barbarian who may choose to follow their Koran is esteemed and raised to the highest honours, but the Jew who embraces their sect remains always oppressed and despised, for they desire nothing from this people, they see nothing in it worthy to be desired, *for it has no form nor comeliness,* nay, it seems to them wholly detestable, contemptible, and odious, an example of meanness, old ruins of a desolated edifice, a deceitful superstition. So the Lord said it would be with him in his captivity, that such would be the consideration in which he would be held by the nations among whom he would be scattered (Deut. xxviii. 37). How then in such a state would the nations wish for him? who ever coveted desolation or a desolated thing? who ever took notice of a pattern of misery? and who ever coveted what he held as falsehood and a laughingstock? Therefore the nations, as if to exculpate themselves of their error in the recognition of Israel, will say that God had placed him in such a state that when they saw him his appearance was not worthy of being desired: *We saw him, and there was no appearance in him that we should desire him.*

3 The nations say that Israel was despised, and this the nations of the universe will not now deny, and there is no need of greater proof than their own confession of it; since they say that nothing is so contemptible as a Jew, thus fulfilling not only what the Lord predicted in Deuteronomy, but also what the same Isaiah prophesies in xlix. 7, and so David before in Ps. xliv. 14, 15. Thus the Lord wished that Israel should be, and thus the nations performed, as Isaiah predicted (xlv. 17 and 20). Therefore the verse continues, *rejected of men:* a regular consequence in human society; when a man is unfortunate all forsake him; as Israel fell into contempt in the eyes of the nations, so all abandoned him, considering him unworthy of all dealings and communication, because they saw *his appearance marred more than any man, and his form more than the sons of man;* they saw him despised, and held communication with him to be dishonouring, admitting him only when their own interests advised it; but in the absence of that motive there are no men who will not avoid Israel, and prohibit or forbid his friendship; for oppression and persecution he will be sought after by the men of the nations, but for good or true friendship he will be forbidden, or rejected by men, who will look upon him with loathing and disgust as a foul and despicable object, as Jeremiah lamented (iii. 4, 5); Isaiah saying the same thing here, *shunned by the great. A man of sufferings and accustomed to sicknesses.* He calls the people of Israel 'a man of sufferings,' continuing to use the metaphor of an afflicted individual for the whole collective people, a style frequently employed in Holy Scripture (Judges xx. 17, 22, xxi. 1, 1 Sam. xvii. 2). In this same signification and style Isaiah calls Israel in our verse *a man of sufferings,* speaking of the whole people

in the singular as of a single individual. Jeremiah followed the same style (Lam. iii. 1), calling Israel 'a man in his afflictions.' He means by *sufferings* those which in his wanderings the nations caused him to suffer, both in body and in mind with unutterable pains and afflictions, fulfilling what the Lord foretold in Deuteronomy (xxviii. 60, 65); Isaiah depicting it in the same way in i. 5. *And accustomed to sicknesses*, used and habituated to these sufferings and sicknesses of reproach, miserable slavery, and depression; and it is said *accustomed*, used to, because these evils were not to be short or for a limited time, as the captivities under the Judges and the Babylonian, for they were to be evils and sicknesses lasting through long centuries, so as to be to all appearance incurable. Thus the Lord predicted in Deuteronomy (xxviii. 59), 'Great plagues, and of long continuance, and sore sicknesses, and of long continuance,' as Israel has had to suffer more than two thousand years amongst the nations, and therefore it is now accustomed to troubles; accordingly they will very appropriately say that it was a people accustomed to sickness. The prophet Micah (vi. 13) uses this phrase in speaking of the people, 'And also I made thee sick in smiting thee, and in making thee desolate because of thy sins.' *And he was as one who hid his face.* That is, Israel in its captivity does not dare to shine or ever shew himself, but fearful that the more he is seen the more he is noticed, and the less the people attend to him the more his life and peace are ensured, he conceals and hides his face, for he would rather they should not remember him, because the nations never mention him for his good, but for his oppression, to invent new ways to increase his troubles and drive him to new wanderings throughout the world without being able to find rest amongst any of the nations. Therefore the prophet said, *As one who hides his face*, like a man who in his timidity does not dare to be seen, but covers his face so as not to be recognised, and in his confusion withdraws from one place to another to escape the harshness of the powerful one who endeavours to injure him. The Lord said in Deuteronomy (xxviii. 65) that so it would be with Israel amongst the nations, that in his faintheartedness he would hide himself, wandering from one country into another. Therefore Israel hides his face, dares not appear before the nations, because his heart is always in fear, either because they do persecute him, or because he fears they will, even though they forget him, as it is foretold in Leviticus (xxvi. 17), 'And ye shall flee when none pursueth you.' This is what the prophet says in this verse, *and as one hiding his face*, always fleeing, always fearful; he predicted the same at iii. 8, 9, 'Because their tongue and their doings were against Adonai, the shew of their countenance witnessed against them;' that is, the sins of Israel frightened him so that he dares not shew his face, which is what Ezekiel predicted at vi. 9, 'And they shall be cut in their faces for the wickednesses they committed;' and at vii. 18, 'And shame shall be upon all their faces;' all which Isaiah said here in one word, *and as one who covers his face*. He says moreover, *He was despised and we esteemed him not;* it would seem to be one and the same thing, because 'despised' and 'not esteemed' are synonymous, and there is no difference between despising and not esteeming; but this is not so: the prophet expresses very different things by those two terms. He means to say that no nation felt esteem for Israel, because he was seen to be always despised by all, the contempt which he suffered from all being the reason for his not being esteemed by any, which is not the lot of slaves or any kind of captives, for these, though in another nation they suffer subjection and slavery, in their own hold power, government, and lordship, and there they are not despised; and as such they are considered even when in subjection and captivity, because they belong to a free nation and can become free again, as the Turks, the Moors, and other nations; but Israel is despised throughout the world, because it has no dominion, power, or government in any part of it, and thus he seems to every nation unworthy of the least esteem, every nation esteeming him of no account, because they see him despised by all; thus the nations will say, *He was despised and we did not esteem him;* for since all the nations despised him, there was no reason why any one should esteem him.

[4] The nations confess a truth evident and well known to all: they say the people of Israel bore their sicknesses, and suffered their sufferings; the sicknesses, troubles, and sufferings which they caused him in his captivity by their continued persecutions which they suffered and endured with the utmost patience and such wonderful forbearance for so many centuries; the nations call them *their* sufferings, *their* sicknesses, as the effects of their harshness and hatred, in the same way as we say in common conversation, 'he suffered patiently his master's blows,' 'the pious man bears God's trials, pains, and punishments with patience.' One clearly sees that the punishment is called God's, he being the acting cause, for it can be God's in no other sense, and the blows cannot be the master's except in the sense that they are the effect of which he is the cause. Grammarians teach this rule in all languages; and in Latin they give as an example Achilles' wound, which may mean either that which Achilles inflicted or that which he received from another; so in this verse the nations say, *he suffered our pains,* Israel bore with patience and endured the sufferings and sicknesses which we harshly inflicted on him, and which the Lord had already many times announced to him in the sacred law as Deut. xxviii. 60, 'And he will bring upon thee all the sufferings of Egypt.' The Lord says the sufferings of Egypt, not those which Egypt suffered, for Israel never suffered those in his captivities, but those which Egypt brought upon the people in their captivity, styling them 'of Egypt,' as effects of that cause. Thus the nations say *our sufferings,* those which the other nations caused them in their present captivity, just as above those which Egypt caused the Hebrews, and they are theirs because they are their own actions springing from their own power and wickedness. These sicknesses and sufferings which the nations would cause scattered and captive Israel are spoken of in the last clause of the verse just quoted from

Deuteronomy: the divine justice threatening that Israel would suffer not only the sufferings and troubles that Egypt inflicted on him, but others very different and of an extraordinary nature, that were not mentioned in the book of the law, when he should be cast out to suffer amongst the nations; and these are the sicknesses and sufferings which the nations will say that Israel suffered and endured with such wonderful constancy. This manner of speaking is an ordinary style in the sacred text, e. g. Ezek. xxxvi. 15, 'Neither will I cause thee to hear the shame of the nations, neither shalt thou bear the reproach of the people.' But it is clear that the nations did not bear the shame and the reproach, but that they caused them to Israel, and therefore he calls them 'of the nations.' Thus spake Zeph. ii. 8, 'I heard the reproach of Moab, and the revilings of the children of Ammon, who reproached my people;' and in the same sense the nations will say, 'he bare our sufferings,' as if they would say, he suffered our reproach, our shame; for the style and phraseology is all the same, which is seen also in many Psalms of David, for example, xl. 16, 'The nations shall be desolate in reward for their ill-usage;' it is clearly seen that it does not mean for the ill-usage or reproach which they suffered, but that which they caused Israel, nevertheless he calls it theirs because they are the cause of it, as of the sufferings and sicknesses of Israel which the nations called theirs in the same sense, as being the effect of their wickedness. Although this verse is thus clearly explained without varying a letter's point, yet, since our opponents make much out of it, it seems proper to explain it somewhat further, so as to leave no doubt or scruple about its meaning; and this interpretation will be accommodated to the doctors of Christianity themselves as far as possible, not to Nicolas de Lira in his epistles, and to the Bishop of Burgos in his additions, and many others who understand the verse not of the sins of men, as others understand, which the Messiah was to take upon himself, but of the bodily pains and sufferings, of hunger, thirst, and other human passions, which they affirm he had to suffer like other people, and explain 'he suffered our sufferings, our sicknesses,' that is, he had sufferings or sicknesses, hunger and thirst like ourselves, and in this respect he wished to be the equal of other men, though he was able, if he wished, to escape them. But these doctors do not properly explain that word *our*, and it is not agreeable to reason and good logic to say that, because a person suffers troubles similar to those endured by another, one bears the sufferings of another, as each one suffers what he feels in himself, or what he is caused to suffer, although the pains and passions may be alike and of the same kind; wherefore this explanation is neither plausible nor consistent. Other doctors explain this verse by saying that the Messiah suffered the sicknesses and the sufferings of Israel, and this people on repentance will say *he endured our sicknesses and sufferings;* this opinion is worthy of examination, because the Messiah had to suffer either the pains which the Jewish people deserved for their sins, or those which the same people made him suffer, for he could not bear or suffer the same pains and sicknesses which the people had in themselves, because it is impossible for one individual to suffer pain and another to suffer and bear the very same; it would be necessary then, if he had to suffer the pains of the people, that they should be either those which the people deserved for their crimes, he taking them upon himself to suffer them, or those which the people inflicted on his own body, and in either case it would be verified that he bare the pains of the people. And in truth no other manner of understanding it is left, and this interpretation is refuted by their own form of argument, we applying it to Israel in relation to the nations who afflicted him, as they do to the Messiah in relation to the people who was injured; and as they explain it that the Messiah suffered the pains which the people deserved or those which they caused and inflicted on his person, and therefore the Jews will say *our sufferings*, so we by the same form of argument explain it to our purpose, saying that the people of Israel suffered and endured the sufferings which the nations deserved for their sins, or those which they caused them by their harsh treatment; and they called them *our* because they were the cause of them, which is the same meaning as that of the Christian theologians, changing only the subjects, *they* say that the people would say *our sufferings* of those which the Messiah would suffer, and *we* say that the nations will say *our sufferings* for those which the people suffers in captivity; consequently, they can in no way oppose our interpretation without first refuting their own, for this is an *argumentum ad hominem*, which is refuting the opponent by his own reasoning. We observe that Nicolas de Lira and other interpreters utter loud exclamations, thinking we say that Israel bears the sins and sufferings of the nations, wishing to suffer for them, enduring the penalty which they deserved, and accepting it as an atonement for their own guilt, wherefore they make fine ridicule of our doctrine; but they are mistaken, because Israel never imagined nor believes such a thing, or that one can atone for the sin of another. We only say that the nations, acknowledging the errors in which they lived, and the truth which Israel always professed in its wanderings, will say with humility and submission, that they deserved for their errors the troubles and punishments which Israel endured and was made to suffer, though innocent of all the falsehoods which they charged them with in their divine worship; and accused by their own conscience they will own: *surely he bare our sufferings and endured our sicknesses*, both those which we deserved, and those we caused him by the continued severity of our persecutions; *and we esteemed him stricken, smitten of God, and afflicted.* The nations say that Israel seemed to them to be punished by God, because they saw him sick, burdened with sufferings and troubles; and in truth the nations were not mistaken, for so it is, and Israel confesses throughout the world that the Lord made him a captive, and scattered him among the nations to opprobrium, contempt, and afflictions, causing him to appear on the stage of the world in the part of a *man of sufferings*. But the prophet says that the nations will understand the contrary, and will retract their former opinion that 'he suffered our sufferings' had no wider signification; 'but we esteemed him as wounded and smitten by God;' that is to say, we were mistaken, believing that he was punished by God, when he bare our sufferings, our afflictions and wounds, which is contrary to the truth; since Israel was wounded, smitten, and punished by God, as the nations believed, which opinion they had no occasion to retract; but if we weigh the meaning of the words, they signify something else quite clear and proved throughout the world, which neither the nations will deny, nor we ourselves ignore it that the Lord punished Israel for his rebellion, wounded and cast him out throughout the nations, afflicted him for his guilt, as a father punishes his son, that being corrected of his vices he may follow the path of virtue, and attain the perfection that the most loving Father desires him to possess. But the nations did not consider Israel to be punished as the first-born Son of God for his future happiness, but wounded with a mortal incurable blow, abandoned of God, stricken with the leprosy of infidelity towards his Creator, and forsaken for ever as lost and reprobated; so all their authors write; so they preach in their churches; this is what they throw in the face of the children of Israel, from the most accomplished to the most vulgar of them, from the wisest to the most ignorant, mocking at our hope of recovery, and holding our wounds to be mortal. The Lord gives the lie to the nations, and prepares for them disappointment and punishment by the prophet Jeremiah (xxx. 11–14), concluding by contradicting the wickedness of the nations and their false judgment: 'For I will restore health unto thee, and I will heal thee of thy wounds, saith Adonai, because they called thee outcast, Sion' (verse 17). Thus the Lord promises to heal Israel of the wounds with which he wounded him by the nations; he will not leave him perpetually wounded and cast off as impure and leprous for having murdered his Messiah; but, on the contrary, he will heal and cure him, and Israel will at the same time serve Adonai his God, and his King Messiah, as he promises in verse 8. The nations will not understand this, because even God does not wish them to understand it; and they believe that Israel is wounded and smitten by God, because he will not forsake the divine law and admit their creeds. All agree that he is rejected by God, that it is a virtue to persecute him and torment him, by making him bear their unjust inflictions, by promulgating laws to ruin him, and efface his name from the earth. And thus of the very sufferings which they inflict on him they say continually that it is a punishment from God; that it is the effect of his reprobation, because they understand and teach that God wishes them to act thus, but when, at the wondrous redemption, they see him exalted and lifted up, they will give up the false conception they had formed of Israel during his troubles, and they will confess their error, saying, *And we esteemed him to be wounded, smitten of God, and afflicted,* thinking that this wounding was his reprobation for his eternal ruin, not a loving means to bring about his highest glory; and they will acknowledge that the Lord wounded his people to heal them afterwards, as he said by Isaiah (lvii. 17, v. 25). This wounding had been determined by the Lord in the wilderness (Lev. xxvi. 17).

5 This verse does not differ in substance from the preceding one; on the contrary, it follows the same reasoning and style, the nations confessing their wickedness and rebellion against God our Lord in impiously using their power against an innocent people, which never offended them, or gave occasion for their tyrannical laws in order to afflict and oppress them with every kind of calamity; therefore they confess that Israel was afflicted by their harshness, wickedness, and revolt against the humility of the afflicted people, and against God, whom they offended by persecuting and murdering the innocent, and seeking after cunning false witnesses to affirm horrible things of them, to accuse and incriminate them. Therefore they will

say, Israel is afflicted through our revolt, crushed through our iniquities; our hatred and malice were the cause of Israel's miseries, of his going ill-used and crushed throughout the world. Thus the Lord reproves the nations through the same Isaiah (iii. 15), 'What mean ye that ye beat my people to pieces, and grind the faces of the poor?' Then in penitence the nations will say, *He was afflicted through our revolt, crushed by our iniquities*, and the malicious hatred which we bore to him, without respecting the faces of the poor or the aged, for although Israel is submissive and humble, his humility does not help him to escape being persecuted and bruised by the nations. And even more clearly David said so in Psalm xciv. 5, 'They break in pieces thy people, Adonai, and afflict thine heritage;' and that through the malice of nations, as he said in the preceding verse; and then he continues, 'They break in pieces,' etc., which is the same as what Isaiah says, *afflicted by our revolt, crushed by our iniquities.* And for the better understanding of this verse we must remark that the rebellion and guilt which afflicted and crushed Israel must not be understood as a final cause, as if it were said, He who orders the rebellion and guilt of the nations was afflicted, in order to remove or expiate them by his wounds, or by his afflictions and troubles, but as an efficient cause, that the guilt and rebellion of the nations afflicted, wounded, and crushed Israel, and in this sense it is said, *crushed by our revolt*, which is the same as to say, by our iniquities and wickedness we crushed him; an ordinary way of speaking in all languages, as if any one should complain and say, By the wickedness and iniquity of the witnesses I find myself imprisoned, wounded, and afflicted; no one will understand it to be to atone for the iniquity of the witnesses, but that they are the efficient cause of his troubles; so the nations say that because of their wickedness and guilt Israel was crushed, tormented, and persecuted. This form of expression is very common in Holy Writ: Numbers xvi. 26 will suffice as an example, in which passage it is very clear that they had not to die for the sins of those criminals, as a final cause to atone for them, but as the cause or occasion of their death. Isaiah says the same in the name of the nations: through our sins and malice the people of Israel suffered their calamities; and thus Arias Montanus understood it in his interlinear Latin translation, where he expresses the revolts and iniquities as the agent after the passive voice, just as when we say the world was created by God, God is the acting cause; so he says, using the same grammatical form, *was crushed by our iniquities*, wherefore the iniquities are the efficient cause; and the Latin he uses can admit of no other sense than that the nations will acknowledge that their rebellion and iniquities were the occasion and the cause why Israel should suffer such oppressions, miseries, and troubles. *The punishment of our peace was upon him.* Arias Montanus translates it, 'The punishment of our pacifications was upon him,' because the Hebrew word is in the plural number; and he interprets it very well in this way, particularly because this word not only means peace as opposed to war, but every kind of good, quiet, security, mental enjoyment, and general prosperity. David, in speaking of the end of the righteous man, says in Psalm xxxvii. 37, 'Mark the perfect man, and behold the upright, for the end of each is peace;' so Isaiah calls repose and quiet *peace*, promising it to his people in xxxii. 17. Among other things which the nations will confess, seeing how unjustly they persecuted Israel, they will say, *The punishment of our peace was upon him;* our peace, our prosperity, was always a punishment for Israel, the effects, the fruits of our greatness and sovereignty, and the prosperity of our monarchies were for that people only punishments and persecutions, and as Montanus reads, 'our pacifications' or the happinesses which we enjoyed brought upon Israel punishments, afflictions, and the greatest misfortunes; indeed this clause admits of no other interpretation, because it says the *punishment of our peace;* and there is no punishment for peace, because it is not a vice or crime that deserves punishment; on the contrary, it is in every sense a blessing which God grants to men; punishment for war if it were unjust might be said appropriately, but punishment for peace would be very improper; it is therefore necessary to understand it in reference to another individual who is injured, for the peace of one side causes misfortune to the other, as if we said, the punishment of the peace of England was upon France, because the consequence of that peace was losses to the other kingdom; thus the nations say *the punishment of our peace*, of our prosperity, was upon that people; all our pacifications and states of happiness resulted in captivity, banishment, and severe punishments for Israel. That the nations will say this with all reason and truth, and that it was always just as they confess is well known to all those who are not ignorant of divine and human history. Thus when Sennacherib, the king of Media, prospered, extending the limits of his kingdom through Persia as far as Syria, his peace and greatness were a punishment to the ten tribes which Shalmanezer carried away captive; when the Chaldean monarchy prospered, Nebuchadnezzar took Judah captive, transferred the people to Babylon, and converted Jerusalem and its sacred temple into ashes; in the prosperity of the Persian monarchy, although the rebuilding of the temple and of the holy city was begun by order of Cyrus, the work was sadly stopped, being hindered by his son Cambyses at the request of the neighbouring nations; and as long as this empire lasted the Holy Land suffered unspeakable oppressions and miseries; while the Greek empire prospered, its peace was a punishment to Israel, his troubles being multiplied until the impious Antiochus, who blasphemously tried to put an end to the observance of the divine law, profaned the sacred temple and led into captivity a great number of Israelites; and no king of that time enjoyed peace, tranquillity, and prosperous circumstances who did not turn his scourge against the people of God to afflict them; and lastly, the Roman empire, which began with gentleness, protesting friendship to the Jewish people while it was in the beginning of its greatness, and had not yet attained the highest degree of prosperity, or the peaceable possession of the universal empire to which it aspired, when (as Justin, a Roman author, says) it sought the friendship of different Eastern nations to hold them in its devotion, whenever it might wish to invade their neighbours for conquest, then it flattered the Jewish people and honoured them with bronze plates inscribed with the title of friends and companions; but when it reached the highest greatness, and enjoyed the peaceable possession of the greatest wealth, then the punishment on Israel began; the people began to feel the punishment of the peace of Rome first by cruel governors who afflicted them, conspiring against their lives, property, and what is still more against the observance of the sacred laws (as Josephus narrates), until at last the total punishment of the peace and prosperity of Rome fell upon Israel, the holy city and temple being set fire to, and the people taken captive and scattered throughout all countries of the world up to this day. In the kingdom of France, as long as it was kept under by the English who possessed a part of it, the rest being divided among different princes, the Jews were received and for the needs of the kingdom well esteemed; the English departed, many provinces were united under one crown, France flourished, became prosperous, enjoying peaceably the universal sway of the Gallias, and the punishment of this tranquillity, this peace, fell upon Israel, the clergy, who were themselves the lords of France and its people, rising against them and butchering numbers of Jews throughout the kingdom, until the streets and squares ran with the innocent blood, and those who could escape travelled in their flight into Poland, Germany, Hungary, and Bohemia. When Spain was a wretched corner in the mountains of Oviedo, Leon, and Old Castile, and all the rest of the country possessed by numerous Moorish kings, with whom it waged continual war, the people was received and esteemed, because they were necessary to help with their money the military expeditions; but the Moors being expelled, the provinces of the kingdom being conquered, including last of all even the kingdom of Granada, all Spain being thus left under one monarch, who was Ferdinand the Catholic, at that very same instant when he conquered Granada, he made the decree on the field of battle by which the Jews, who had helped him with their wealth for that and his other conquests, were to depart at a short notice as exiles from the kingdom, some of them abandoning the divine law through want of means or courage to go abroad, others departing for troubles, death, and dishonour throughout the world; Spain was prosperous, became great, enjoyed the peaceable possession of all her kingdoms, and the punishment of her peace was upon Israel. Twenty thousand families passed over into Portugal, and were received by king Don Juan III on payment of a large sum of money of which he stood in need for his foreign conquests. Don Manuel was his heir, conquered many kingdoms in the Indies, increased his kingdom by the marriages and peaces with Castile, and with the riches of the East enjoyed peaceably the greatest tranquillity; but the punishment of his peace fell upon Israel, whom, as soon as he was prosperous, he inhumanly banished from his kingdoms, practising the notorious tyrannies which are narrated in his Life and Deeds by Osorio, bishop of Silves in Algarve, taking from them with barbarous cruelty their own innocent children, forcing those who had no time to embark to become Christians, and in default impiously declaring them slaves, as if he had conquered them in legitimate war. Yet war was not the cause of the miseries of the people, but the peace which the Lord in his just judgment granted him in his kingdoms was a punishment upon Israel. In short, the nations never flourished in prosperity and peace without that peace proving a punishment for the people of God; and this is what Isaiah means in this verse, that the undeceived nations will say *the punishment of our peace was upon him*, because our happiness, our peace, always proved to be miserable punishment upon Israel; when the Lord delivered him, for his sins, into our hands, we impiously treated him as a slave, using our prosperity to his damage; about which the same Isaiah reproves them (xlvii. 5), 'Thou didst shew them no mercy, upon the aged thou didst heavily lay thy yoke.'

And by his wounds we were healed. Certainly the divine prophet used a very subtle figure of rhetoric in this verse, which consists in turning the proposition by another contrary; the preceding clause said, that the nations will say, our prosperity, our peace, was a punishment to Israel; and then he converts it: and the wounds or punishment of Israel will be for us peace, welfare, and happiness; our peace caused him punishment, sickness, and wounds; and his wounds will cause us comfort and health; he was wounded for our peace, and we are healed through his wounds; and thus he says, *The punishment of our peace was upon him, and through his wounds we were healed.* The prophet says that from the troubles of Israel health resulted to the nations, and so they themselves will confess: he does not mean to say that Israel by his captivity will make expiation for the sins of the nations, as the Christian doctors say and impute to us, for our captivity is for our own sins, not for those of the Gentiles; but we also understand that Israel bearing patiently this painful captivity, and remaining firm in the divine faith and law of God, prepares himself for and makes himself worthy of the universal redemption for which he hopes, to which the infinite mercy of the Lord will contribute much more than our own merits; and we know, from the teaching of Holy Writ, that from these troubles and sufferings good will result not only for Israel, but also for many nations, who will participate in the happiness of God's people at that happy time, when they will be cured of their defiling sickness of idolatry, as Isaiah has said (ii. 17, 18, xlv. 23): the nations will be cured of their envy, their hatred, and their vain covetousness, enjoying perpetual tranquillity and perpetual peace, being united in one cheerful worship of God and mutual love. This health the Lord promises the nations at the time of the redemption of Israel by the same prophet (ii. 4). Such is the health the nations will obtain when they turn humbly to their Creator, and recover from their Gentile rebellion, with which for so many centuries they persecuted Israel, obliging him to transgress the divine laws, and to profane the days which the divine Majesty wished should be consecrated to his honour; recovering from this restlessness, they will pass into the happy extreme of health, as Isaiah prophesied in his last chapter (verse 23), and as the Lord promises by Zechariah (xiv. 16). This is the health that the nations will enjoy at the redemption of Israel; this is the fruit that the pious of them will gather from the troubles and wounds which he suffered in his captivity, from the patience with which he endured his sufferings and sicknesses for so long a time; and then they will say, Our tranquillity, our peace, was for his punishment, and his wounds were in order that at the time of his redemption we might be jointly purified of our uncleanness. And this the nations will confess, saying, *The punishment of our peace was upon him, and through his wounds we were healed.*

6 The nations continue their confession, and say that they all went astray like sheep, and followed their own ways like strayed sheep which, being lost, follow different paths, getting far away from their flock and from the true track which they ought to have followed to go to their shepherd; thus the nations confess that they went far astray from the path of truth, deviating through different tracks, divided into various sects, and following forms of idolatry and superstition not commanded by their Creator; the nations do not say that they sinned, but that they went astray, because they intended to refer to the vanity of the false worships which they followed; and so, although on repenting they confess their weakness, if they do not exculpate themselves, at least they endeavour to defend themselves on the plea of ignorance; they say that they erred, believing that they were right; and indeed the pious among the nations would not have followed the evil path had they been well informed of the right one, and even some of the impious would not have persisted in their errors had they been sure they were in error. Thus

the prophet calls them errors in distinction from the other sins which belong to human frailty; he does not speak of those sins inherent in all mankind ever since Adam, and there is no man who would justify these before the Lord, but he speaks only of the false rites and vain sects into which the Gentile nations are subdivided, and still persevere in, till Israel with his redemption shall be the cause of their true enlightenment, and the retractation of their errors, when they will say our fathers taught us falsehood. Now our opponents cannot understand this confession to be made by Israel, for although, as they pretend, he may have erred in his divine worship, which is impossible, it could not be affirmed of him, that each one went on in his own way, for Israel always followed one and the same way, the sacred law of Moses, without dividing into different sects; on the contrary, the whole of Israel always was and still is agreed in one and the same faith, and one and the same observance throughout the world; therefore it could never be said of the Israelites that every one followed his own way; and as this clause has no reference to personal or ordinary sins, it remains evident that it is fulfilled only in the Gentile nations, who follow so many different sects and ways in their worship, as is well known. *And Adonai caused the sins of us all to fall upon him.* This is the same as was said before, that the sins of the nations crushed the people, wounded and afflicted them; only now he expresses it by another more elegant phrase, that the Lord wished in his just judgment that the iniquity of the nations should be exerted against Israel, as a target against which the arrows of their cruelty and hatred were to be shot. This is signified by the word *to fall upon* or *against him,* for in the sacred language it is the same as to attack, to meet another, to kill or hurt him. The same expression is met with in 2 Sam. i. 15, 1 Kings ii. 31, 34, 1 Sam. ii. 17, which passages prove that the Hebrew word which we render *to fall upon* is the same as to encounter or attack anybody; and so the Christian doctors teach, more especially those most learned Hebrew scholars

Buxtorf and Cocceius in their dictionaries. If this is granted, the nations say that the Lord desired that their iniquity and malevolence should fall upon Israel to destroy him, and afterwards afflict him in his captivity; in this same sense the Septuagint renders it, 'And delivered them up to the wickedness of us all,' which is equivalent to saying that he exposed him to the attack of our wickedness, to suffer its cruelty; and so it is fulfilled in that people, on whom the malignity and mortal hatred of all the nations fall and make their attack, causing him exile, death, and every kind of misery. Therefore the meaning of the whole verse is as follows: *All we went astray*, each nation following paths far distant from God's way, being divided into various sects, from which resulted detestation and abomination of Israel, because he persevered in the divine law which his forefathers professed; but notwithstanding this, that we were in error and he was right in the true worship, still, in his divine judgment, he permitted the iniquity and malevolence of our errors to be employed against Israel, falling upon and attacking him with all possible means to ruin him, and caused the sin of us all to fall upon or attack Israel. But it might be objected to this interpretation of this verse, that it seems inconsistent that the wickedness of the nations should fall upon Israel to injure him, and that they should confess it to be so, and say at the same time that the Lord desired it to be so, and that he caused their sins and wickedness to fall upon Israel. But this is no inconsistency, but a part of the divine economy which the majesty of God has always followed in the government of his creatures, making the sins of the one to be instruments for the punishment of the other; yet he who is God's instrument is not therefore acquitted of sin. Pharaoh and his people were an instrument with which God afflicted Israel; God ordered that Joseph should be sold by his brethren, as he himself told him after Jacob's death, that for their good the Lord sent him thither; but the brethren were not acquitted of their sin. God punished David, using Absalom as his instrument to afflict him, but Absalom sinned grievously in persecuting David. Nebuchadnezzar was God's instrument for the destruction of Jerusalem and her people; but God says that he would severely punish Nebuchadnezzar for having executed this punishment. God avails himself of the wickedness of one man to punish the sins of another, and the man uses his free-will in being wicked, and wilfully incurs the sin of injuring another; for God obliges no one to be wicked, nor takes away from him his liberty to be good; only God, knowing that one man will spontaneously be wicked and cruel against another, permits it to be so, and makes use of the spontaneous wickedness of that man for the necessary punishment of him who deserves it. This is what the nations will say, that the Lord wished to make use of their sins and wickedness, setting them against Israel, as an instrument to punish and afflict him, as he made use of the iniquity of Pharaoh and Nebuchadnezzar to punish the crimes of his people, and so he threatened by the same Isaiah (ix. 10), 'And Adonai will strengthen the adversaries of Rezin against him, and join his enemies together, Aram on the east, and the Philistines on the west, and they shall swallow Israel with open mouth;' which means that the Lord would make use of all these hostile nations to vent their hatred and iniquity upon Israel and worry and destroy him, as they did in the past and present captivity, at the end of which the nations will acknowledge and confess this, saying, 'And Adonai made our iniquity to fall upon him; he was oppressed and afflicted and did not open his mouth; he was carried like a lamb to the slaughter-house, and like a sheep before the shearer he was dumb and did not open his mouth.' After having related this confession, the nations owning the injustice with which they treated Israel, the prophet goes on to describe the sufferings and immense patience of the people in their captivity, and foretel their future happiness; and beginning with this verse, he says, He was oppressed and afflicted, but for all this he did not open his mouth; although continually persecuted, afflicted, exiled, and treated worse than the vilest slaves,

Israel never attempted his own defence, or took courage to resist his injuries, conscious that his own transgressions and sins held his hands tied up, and that the nations would never have been able to injure him if the Lord in his divine justice had not ceased to protect him against them as he did before, and holding before his mind's eyes God's predictions in his law foretelling the oppressions of this captivity (Deut. xxxi. 17, xxxii. 30). This being known to Israel, he suffered without seeking means of defence, and never opened his mouth ; on the contrary, he was humble like a lamb at the slaughter, and like a sheep before its shearer, suffering death with ignominy and amid the imprecations of the populace, losing liberty, property, and even his own children at the hands of tyranny. So Isaiah expresses it in this verse, and before him David had said it in the same words (Psalm xliv. 12, 23).

8 *From restraint and judgment he was taken*, etc. Arias Montanus translates, *He was taken away from confinement*, understanding it of incarceration; the version of the LXX says *from opposition*, that is, from oppression, distress; but other Christian doctors well versed in the holy language, as Cocceius in his Hebrew Dictionary, translate with full propriety *from power*, because the Hebrew word which we render *restraint* properly signifies *power, reign, domination*, as Buxtorf explains it: and this is clearly seen from the sacred text. In 1 Sam. ix. 17, speaking of Saul, the Lord makes use of the same word, 'This same shall reign over my people ;' and in Judg. xviii. 7, 'He who should possess power or command,' the same word is used as here employed by the prophet, which can be also rendered *restraint*, as the king restrains his subjects within the limits of the laws. And so we shall translate not only in agreement with the truth and propriety, but also supported by the interpretation followed by the Christian doctors : *He was removed from the kingdom and judgment ;* that is to say, they took from him the power and kingdom of Israel, and the judicial power or government which he administered for himself,

which the Lord had instituted for him in the desert, since it is the same thing to say they removed him from the kingdom and government as to affirm that the one and the other were removed from him. And this is what happened to Israel, whom the nations deprived and dispossessed of the rule over his own lands, and of his own ancient government and jurisdiction which he freely exercised on his own subjects in accordance with the sacred laws, carrying off his kings and his populations into a miserable captivity, desolating his towns and fortresses, without leaving any form of state or government, and fulfilling what the Lord had predicted in Deuteronomy (xxviii. 36, 49, 50, 52). For the fulfilment of this divine decree the Lord employed the instrumentality of the nations, who deprived Israel of his king and judges, stripped him of his dominion, of his many strong towns and provinces, of his government and judicature, both civil and ecclesiastical, both of which were instituted by the divine law which he promulgated on Sinai; and the prophet says in our verse, that this will become well known to all the world, that among the greatest troubles of Israel, the most lamentable was the taking away his kingdom, and the depriving him of his judicature; and therefore it is said, *from restraint* or kingdom *and from judgment he was taken away. And who will declare his generation?* etc. He means, when once expelled from his holy country and deprived of his jurisdiction and government, who will celebrate his wonderful generation? who will esteem or make account of his miraculous beginnings? when deprived of dominion, state, tribunal of justice, and native land, and scattered and despised, who will talk of, or set any value on his glorious generation and origin? who will proclaim that from the very beginning of the formation of the world God chose him as a rule for all the other nations of the earth, creating and arranging the world in proportion to the children of Israel? So it is expressed in Deuteronomy xxxii. 8: 'When the Most High divided to the nations their inheritance, when he separated the children of man, he set the bounds of the people according to the number of the children of Israel.' This is what the prophet says, that Israel outside the land of the living, which is the land of Israel, dispossessed of his kingdom and jurisdiction or government, scattered like a vile slave among the nations, must necessarily fail to gain that celebrity and estimation which his illustrious generation or origin deserves; no one will speak of it to honour it; on the contrary, they will seek in it what they can find to despise, and say, that the natural race of Israel was never held in estimation by the Lord his God, nor deserves to be held so by men; that another spiritual Israel, composed of the nations themselves, is the beloved of God, and the one worthy to have his generation celebrated and proclaimed, not that of the Israel they call carnal, as being the true and real successor of Jacob, for this generation has been for many centuries condemned and rejected by God. This forms the complaint of the prophet, that Israel in his dispersion and slavery will have no one to celebrate his generation, but only to reproach and despise it: *And who will declare his generation?* as if to say, None of the nations, since none of them will hold it in estimation. That by the land of the living the land of Israel is meant, is clear from Holy Scripture, e.g. Psalm xxvii. 13, lii. 7, cxvi. 9, cxlii. 6; and still more clearly Ezekiel xxvi. 20, where, the Lord speaking against Tyre, who grew proud against Jerusalem, the prophet threatens Tyre with destruction and ruin from the king of Babylon, but that Jerusalem would return in future time to her former splendour, calling her 'the land of the living.' And in xxxii. 23 he prophesies against Pharaoh, the king of Egypt, and all his people, that they will be killed and destroyed for the injuries which they inflicted on Jerusalem, 'Because they caused terror in the land of the living;' and he repeats the same phrase in many of the following verses; so Isaiah says here, *For he was cut off from the land of the living*, Israel was driven out of Jerusalem and every part of the Holy Land which is styled *the land of the living*, because Israel lived in it a spiritual life through the special assistance of the Lord, who breathed his divine Spirit upon that people through the sacrifices, and on departing from it he finds himself deprived of that influence, that special connexion with his Creator, and consequently of that spiritual life which he then enjoyed, and to which he now aspires by observing the divine law, although with greater difficulty and more imperfectly, through lacking that life or influence which he enjoyed in the land of the living, in his own holy country.

For the transgression of my people was he wounded. We might well translate, following the true meaning of the Hebrew word, *they were wounded* [literally *wound to them*], and not *he*, for it is really in the plural and not in the singular, as the Christians translate it, in order to apply this and the whole chapter to a single individual, the Messiah. But those of them who understand the sacred language will know themselves that it is plural and must be read *they were wounded*, which would leave no doubt that the whole of the chapter refers to Israel; but as on doctrinal grounds they cannot understand it so, but only as the Gospel requires, they are obliged to take it singular, although the word really requires the plural number *they;* and seeking for some example in Holy Scripture to defend that interpretation, they avail themselves of the verse of the prophet which says, *They made idol and bowed down to it* (Is. xliv. 15). There the word *to it* is the same as the word *to them* in our chapter, and therewith they think they have proved their object, that is, that although it always has a plural import, it can sometimes be translated singular, as in the text adduced, where it cannot be rendered *to them,* since it says *idol* in the singular, and it would not be good grammar to say, 'he made an idol and bowed down *to them,*' but *to it,* in accordance with the number. But they cannot escape in this way, for even in the quoted passage they must render, 'they made idol and bowed down to them,' want of numerical concord being a very frequent style in Holy Scripture, just as it is many times said, 'and all Israel assembled *themselves,*' instead of saying *himself,* 'and all the people *they* said,' 'thy people *they* all saints,' while in strict grammar ought to say *he* 'all saint.' This takes place when the noun does not imply a singular object, but a collection or multitude of objects, even when in the singular form, as *people, Israel,* and similar words, which, though singular, imply a multitude; so in our verse it is said, 'they made idol;' although it is true that *idol* is in the singular, yet it still denotes a multitude, every kind of idol, just as when God says, 'thou shalt make no idol for thyself,' we must not understand merely one in the singular, but the whole collection and every kind of idol;' and in the verse which they allege it is not said that they made any particular idol, but that 'they made idol,' that is, that they fell into the sin of idol-making, not one only but many, 'and they bowed down to them.' Accordingly it is always true that the Hebrew word (*lamo*) is plural, and means *to them,* and therefore the verse we are explaining will say *they were wounded;* for although it had before spoken of the people in the singular, now it says in the plural *they,* which happens at every turn in Holy Scripture; and by translating it so, it becomes quite clear that the nations speak of Israel and not of any particular individual. But it does not the least affect the interpretation of the verse whether it says *they were* or *he was wounded;* and we shall continue to render it *he was wounded,* that it may not appear to offer any difficulty to the sense in which we explain the chapter, in which the nations say all that we have stated and explained in the preceding verses from the first, *Who believed our report?* to the sixth, which concludes, *and Adonai caused the sin or iniquity of us all to fall upon him.* Up to this point the nations make their confession, but in the remainder of the chapter they are no longer introduced, and the prophet alone speaks, pitying the miseries of the people, and saying things which the nations could never have said or meant at the time of the redemption, some being matters which they never heard of or understood, others absolutely prophetical, as the last verses (10, 11, and 12).

The prophet, after predicting the future ruin and dispersion of the people, saying how it would be afflicted, would not open its mouth, and would be taken away as a lamb, would suffer its troubles with the highest patience, and as a sheep before the shearer, and would be banished from its holy land and kingdom, deprived of power and jurisdiction over its own people, concludes by telling the cause of so great a punishment, and justifying the justice of God in expelling from the land he had miraculously given to their forefathers, his people he had chosen, loved, and favoured with such wonders, and in delivering it into the hands of its enemies to suffer the cruel wounds of its prolonged captivity; and he says that this was for no other cause than Israel's rebellion against the Lord its God, from whom it had received so many and such wonderful favours, a crime of high treason, from the punishment for which not even the first-born son can escape; he mentions the crime in a single word which comprehends the highest wickedness: *For the rebellion of my people was he wounded;* my people was wounded, says the prophet, for his rebellion, because he rebelled against his Creator, transgressing the divine law by idolatry, murder, incest, hatred, and every kind of crime, reaching at the time of the second temple such an enormous pitch of corruption, that Josephus says it was impossible for God to forbear from executing his anger upon a people which continued to perpetrate such atrocities, without respect for God, the holy temple, or the sacred things it contained—rivalry, ambition, and tyranny alone prevailing. In short, Israel rebelled against the Lord his God, and he poured upon him the curses he had foretold in the divine law; and therefore the prophet says, justifying God's severity and justice, *For the rebellion of my people was he wounded;* Israel was wounded for his crimes, was stricken and left without comeliness, and disfigured for his sins and rebellions against his Benefactor, being ungrateful for such supernatural favours, as Moses predicted in his song (verse 6). But Israel ungraciously rebelled, and the Lord promises to expose him wounded before the eyes of the nations, as he said by Isaiah (i. 4), 'They have forsaken Adonai, they have provoked the Holy One of Israel unto anger, they are gone away backward. Why should ye be stricken? will ye revolt more and more? The whole head is sick, and the whole heart faint. From the sole of the foot even unto the head there is no soundness in it, but wounds, and bruises, and putrifying sores; they have not been healed.' Such is the condition to which Isaiah says the Lord would reduce his people for its rebellion, and so he is represented by the nations in this chapter and in the same words; therefore no doubt is left that Israel is the subject of whom they speak; and the prophet repeats the same thing speaking of the same people, and recapitulates in the fifty-third chapter what he had said in the first, when he says, *And for the rebellion of my people he was wounded*, or they were wounded, which is the same; *he*, speaking of Israel collectively, *they*, distributively, the individuals forming the people. The prophet calls him *my*, either in the name of the Lord, who never ceased to call Israel *my people*, even when least obedient, and when his divine Majesty was most irritated by his excesses; or the prophet speaking in his own name, who in his love and sympathy for his brethren even considers it an honour to call them his people, just as the Lord, on the occasion of the sin of the golden calf, speaking to Moses, said, 'Thy people hath sinned,' thus inculcating that, although Israel may sin, no one should think himself dishonoured by acknowledging him as his own people, since God himself does not despise him, but, on the contrary, tenderly caresses him, saying, 'O my people, what have I done unto thee? and wherein have I afflicted thee? answer me.' Isaiah was well acquainted with this teaching, and therefore says, *For the rebellion of my people*, for although sinful and rebellious, he is still my people, and there is none other under heaven with whom I can be honoured.

9 The prophet says that Israel received three punishments at the hands of the nations, the deprivation of his power or

kingdom, of the jurisdiction and government which God had instituted for him while in the desert, and exile from the holy land among the nations; he says that he departed from the land of the living, and then follows the state in which Israel will remain among the nations. He was necessarily dead amongst them, since he had been cast out of the land of the living, being deprived of that spiritual life which he enjoyed through the divine influence, as we have stated above. And as death is followed by burial, so Israel dying among the nations is buried among them. Therefore the prophet says, that being exiled from the land of the living, he gave or made his grave amongst the wicked, he was deprived of that spiritual life and buried amongst the nations. And the Lord has said by the prophet Ezekiel (xxxvii. 11–14), that the house of Israel outside the holy country is to be considered dead and buried; in this passage the Lord very clearly says, that Israel being uprooted from the holy land is dead and buried among the nations, that it has lost its life because it has gone forth from the land of the living, that he will bring them out of the graves which he made amongst the wicked of the nations, and will restore him to the holy land, to live again not only the natural but also the spiritual life by means of his divine inspiration which he communicates in the land of the living; therefore he concludes, 'And I will put my Spirit in you and ye shall live;' I will breathe on you that gracious influence which vivified your parents, that ye may live. Accordingly Isaiah in this verse says nothing different from what the Lord says by Ezekiel, but the same thing in almost the same words, *Because he was uprooted from the land of the living, he made with the wicked* (that is, with the nations) *his grave*, which the Lord promises to open and restore him to the land of Israel that he may live.

And with the rich in his deaths. Well might Israel, had not his sins been so enormous, be buried among the nations, being deprived of that spiritual life which he before possessed in his country, without suffering other bodily torments which continually harass him in his exile; but he provoked the wrath of his Creator, and so he determined not only to deprive him of that spiritual life, but also to give him up to corporal torments and miseries, which he was to suffer at the hands of the powerful among the nations; and therefore he says not only that as dead he made his grave with the wicked, but also with the powerful in his deaths, that is, his troubles and calamities, not only the *deaths* which that people has suffered through the cruelty and tyranny of those who rule over him throughout the world, but also other innumerable evils sometimes more painful than death itself. He says *the rich*, which in the holy language is the same as powerful: and so the Christian doctors interpret it, and put the word in the singular, the rich one instead of the rich *ones*, adopting this idiom of the holy language, the use of one number for the other. The literal meaning of the whole verse then is, that Israel being deprived of his kingdom, of his government, of his home, in the holy land, would be deprived of the spiritual life that there was communicated to him, and as dead would make his grave among the wicked, who are the nations of the earth, suffering at the same time the deaths, vexations, and tyrannies of the powerful of this age, until the time of his redemption arrives; and so he says, *He made his grave with the wicked, and with the rich in his deaths; although he dealt not falsely and there was no deceit in his mouth.* The prophet said in the preceding verse that Israel suffered the cruel wound of captivity for his iniquity and rebellion, and now he says in this verse that he did not act falsely, and there was no deceit in his mouth, which appears contradictory, as at the same time he condemns and acquits him, declares his innocence and accuses him of crime: but it is not so; the divine Spirit affirms both without any shadow of inconsistency; he first considered Israel with respect to God, whom he offended by his ingratitude for his mercies and wonderful acts of kindness, and Israel deserved the cruel wound of the nations for that crime of ingratitude and rebellion; therefore he said, *And for the rebellion of my people was he wounded.* He next considers Israel with respect to the nations, suffering at their hands the horrible calamities and sufferings which they made him undergo when under their power, and with respect to them he says that Israel suffered undeservedly, for he never deserved their contempt, their hatred, and the continued persecutions with which they all and every one afflicted him, since Israel never dealt falsely or violently towards them, and there was never deceit in his mouth; but they always had the worst opinion of him as if he were unworthy of all confidence, always enclosing him in a special district, separating and confining him, branding the Israelites in their attire with differences from that of the natives and of all other nations, and all that through mistrust and a hateful supposition that, if not separated and marked out for recognition, they would perpetrate atrocious crimes, a stupid apprehension of powerful communities about a weak, helpless worm, with no other means of living among men but his continuous invocations of the mercy of the Lord his God, and a humble submission to all the nations of the earth. They always abhorred him because he remained constant to the divine law, and bore him mortal hatred for his obstinacy in the faith which he inherited from his forefathers, to whom God commanded it; they judged him, condemned him, and often murdered him in different kingdoms for diabolical superstitions which their malevolent designs attributed to him. Such was the opinion the nations formed of him, and from it followed all the torments and miseries endured by Israel in his captivity. The prophet contradicts this false opinion, affirming that although the Lord punished Israel, and wounded him for the sins which he committed against his divine laws and sacred precepts, wickedness and malice were the sole motives of the nations in executing this punishment, Israel being with regard to them quite innocent of all the motives and pretexts they invented in order to persecute him; whereas he never gave them any occasion for being justly provoked to inflict punishment, and so the prophet says, that Israel being buried amongst the nations by divine judgment, suffered the vexations, injuries, and oppressions of the mighty, and they heaped upon his head charges and crimes which he never imagined, with the object of destroying him, and this *although he did not deal falsely, and there was no deceit in his mouth.* Hence the solution is obtained to the difficulty proposed, namely, in considering Israel guilty with regard to the divine justice, but innocent with regard to the wickedness of the men who unjustly persecuted him.

The nations lay great stress upon this verse, endeavouring to prove that this chapter must not and cannot be understood of the people of God, but of some person who is sinless; as it cannot be truly affirmed of Israel in his captivity or before it, that he never acted falsely, and there was no deceit in his mouth, since he sinned from his very origin, and at all times committed every kind of sin which attends human frailty; and so far from Israel being able to deny this truth, he clearly confesses it, imploring God's mercy for his crimes, which cast him forth into captivity, and still keeps him in it; but if the wise men of the nations would consult the Holy Scriptures, they would find a very clear answer to their argument without any difficulty being left; and they ought to find no difficulty in our own explanation, since long before David said the same thing and with the same form of words as Isaiah uses here, David speaking distinctly of Israel scattered and captive among the nations in Psalm xliv, where, after celebrating the mercy which in former times the Lord shewed to his people, he describes the miseries to which he abandoned him for his sins, and in the sixteenth and following verses he clearly affirms that the people, being punished by God through the instrumentality of the nations, vindicates itself, saying, that it had not dealt falsely in the divine covenant, it had not deviated from the paths of righteousness, nor had its heart declined from the divine worship. Then, if David speaks so, cannot the same truth issue from the mouth of David as from the pen of Isaiah? If David says that

Israel did not deal falsely or deceitfully in the covenant, will not Isaiah be right in saying that there was no falseness in Israel nor deceit in his mouth? And the wise men of the nations do not dissent from this truth when they explain this Psalm xliv. of the present captivity of Israel by the Romans, as Nicolas de Lira explains it in his commentary. Still it is necessary to know in what sense David and Isaiah justify the people of Israel; since he is a sinner and punished by God for his transgressions, no one excuses him for the sins that usually follow our frailty, and the inclination of our material appetites; indeed these sins never led the nations to punish and persecute Israel; they do not despise and abominate him as robber, traitor, homicide, or for any other similar crime, but for his constant observance of the divine law, which in their hatred they style Jewish obstinacy, because he always scorned their divinities, and because he holds as profane what they venerate as divine. So Pliny says (xxiii. 5), 'The Jews are a perverse nation, and remarkable for their contempt of the gods;' and Tacitus says, 'All that other nations hold divine, they count profane.' It is for this reason that all the nations raise their scourge against Israel, the Moors, Turks, Persians, Arabs, and other nations, and all because he does not cease to observe, as far as time and place in his captivity allow it, the divine Law which he received on Sinai: all concur in saying that Israel is sacrilegious, that he falsifies it, that it is not perpetual, that it is now abrogated as useless, obsolete, and deadly: but Israel scorns persuasions, dangers, death, and contempt, for the sake of obeying and observing it, because it is perpetual and indestructible in spite of all human violence. The nations abominate this truth, and for it they abhor and persecute Israel. So David says in his Psalm, and of this he complains to God in the name of the people, that the nations destroy, scorn, and even murder him, for his having remained constant in the knowledge and true worship of his Creator, without declining to the paths of the Gentiles, or following their intricate windings; that therefore he was slaughtered like a lamb; he does not deny having committed other sins, but says that he has been insulted by all the nations simply for following the divine truth; this is exactly what Isaiah says in this verse, that the people was persecuted by the nations, because *he dealt not falsely, and there was no deceit in his mouth:* all the deceits and falsehoods that the nations imputed to him against the sacred religion which he professes by the eternal command, were pretexts of the malevolence of the Gentiles to ruin him and blot out his memory; because all that he said, all that he affirmed, in support of the observance of his religion, was holy, true, pure, and derived from that same spring from which he drank in Sinai; and guided by its light *he dealt not falsely, and there was no deceit in his mouth*, as the prophet says in this verse.

10 *But Adonai was pleased to bruise him*, etc. The prophet answers an implied question which the preceding verse might suggest to the mind; then, if Israel is innocent, if there was no deceit in his mouth, why did the nations seek such pretexts to depreciate and destroy him? How can it be consistent to say in the preceding verse that Israel suffered his wounds for his rebellion, and then immediately after to say that he did not deal falsely, and there was no deceit in his mouth, but that the will of God was pleased to punish him, whereas the righteousness of divine justice, which is God's goodness itself, does not permit that there shall be punishment without fault, or that innocence should suffer? And if in his righteous judgments he permits it for some good end, which we cannot fathom, is not permitting it the same as desiring it? But the prophet says that Adonai was pleased to bruise him, and that he should suffer punishment from the nations, notwithstanding that he did not deal falsely, and there was no deceit in his mouth. But, if the words of the prophet are properly considered, he says a very different thing: we stated before that Israel is innocent with respect to the nations, because he never acted violently to them, for the Hebrew word which we translate *falsely* means that,

and so the Christian doctors interpret it; the people never injured them and always suffered meekly their injuries, nor did he teach them any deceitful doctrine, which was what they imputed to him, but the infallible truth of the true God and his divine law, and therefore they were unjust in afflicting him with their continual vexations; but with respect to God, Israel was rebellious and guilty. The prophet says, then, that although Israel gave no occasion to the nations for persecuting him, the divine Majesty being offended was pleased to punish him and make use of the wickedness of the nations as the instrument of this punishment; they oppressed him unjustly, and the Lord in conformity with his justice and righteousness was pleased that they should oppress him. David says the same in Psalm xliv, already quoted; after having said that Israel did not fail in the divine covenant, that his heart turned not back, and that his footsteps declined not from the ways of the Lord (which is what Isaiah says, *He dealt not falsely, and there was no deceit in his mouth*), he continues, 'Why didst thou bruise us in the place of serpents, and cover us with darkness?' and this is the same as Isaiah says, *And Adonai was pleased to bruise him, made him sick.* There can be no more evident proof that David and Isaiah speak of the same subject, namely, Israel, both using the same form, not only of reasoning but even of expression, and saying that Adonai wished to bruise him, although he was innocent of what the nations imputed to him. *If he offer his soul in atonement*, etc. The prophet has already stated the reason why God wounded Israel, namely, for his rebellion and wickedness; and then he gave the reason why, being innocent with respect to the calumnies of the nations, he delivered him into their hands, namely, to wound and persecute him, because in his righteous judgment he was pleased that it should be so, for otherwise they could not have done it; now he states the final cause of his permitting this, of this apparent abandonment and forgetfulness of his chosen people, that it was not to destroy and make an end of him, as the nations believe, but that being corrected of his faults he might return into the grace of the Lord his God, and secure the wonderful favours which are promised in this verse and those which follow as far as the end of the chapter; therefore he says, *If he offer his soul in atonement he shall see seed, shall prolong his days, and the will of Adonai shall prosper in his hand;* that is, if he expose his life to dangers in atonement for his sins, he shall see seed, etc. God commands Israel in his divine law to love him with all his heart and with all his soul and with all his substance, which is to love the Lord more than one's own soul, and what is more than living in such a way, that out of love to him man should not hesitate to sacrifice his soul, his life, should it be required, for the glory and honour of his holy name. In this man's highest perfection consists,—in loving his Creator more than his own existence, his own life. On this love obedience to the divine law and its precepts depends, for if man bears God all the love he owes him, he will rather die than disobey him.

The prophet then says, that God having punished Israel for his disobedience, and bruised and weakened him among the nations, if he will offer his soul in atonement for his sins, if he will return to love him with all his heart and with all his soul, despising his own soul, which is his own life, to love and obey him, despising for his glory and honour all the dangers and injuries from the nations, he will be favoured of God, he will return into the divine favour as before, and God will fulfil to him the promise which he gave in Deuteronomy (chap. xxx), And thou shalt return and obey the voice of Adonai, and do all his commandments which I command thee this day; for Adonai will again rejoice over thee for good, as he rejoiced over thy fathers,' which is the same as what the prophet says, *If he give his soul in atonement he shall see seed.* He says, *If he give in atonement*, which would seem to be spoken conditionally and with doubtfulness,—if Israel will do so, or do the contrary, and that he promises him the consequent favours only on a condition. But this is no condition which leaves the consequence uncertain, but a style of Holy Scripture, even in matters that are infallibly to be, and this too in the case of acts depending on man's free will. For although our Lord in his absolute wisdom knows what man will do of his free accord, and how his own will will incline him, still he does not oblige or force him, nor is God's knowledge the cause of what man chooses, although he cannot fail to choose what the Lord already knows, because his wisdom cannot err. Therefore, although he knows what man will do, still he says, *if* thou do so and so; but he cannot fail or omit to do so. This is clearly shewn in Deuteronomy (xxx. 8), where it is said absolutely that Israel will turn from his iniquity, 'And thou shalt return and hear the voice of Adonai;' and at verse 11 he speaks conditionally, '*If* thou turn unto Adonai thy God with all thine heart, with all thy soul;' but this condition does not oppose the absolute promise which he had already made, it only shews that Israel using his free will will return to Adonai his God; for unless it were so, there would be no merit in returning. Just in the same way the prophet says here, that if Israel will offer his life for his sins or as an atonement for them, which means, Israel, by offering his life for his guilt, despising the dangers he met among the nations, and remaining constant to the divine law, will obtain the following rewards,—*he will see seed,* the Lord will fulfil the blessing which he promised in Deuteronomy (xxx. 5), 'I will multiply thee above thy fathers;' this multiplication Isaiah expresses by *will see seed,* that is, offspring and large posterity. He says the same thing in lxi. 9, 'And their seed shall be known among the nations, and their offspring among the peoples; all that see them shall acknowledge them, that they are the seed which Adonai hath blessed.' In this excellent way he says that Israel, if he offers his soul in atonement, will see the blessing which God gave to Abraham (Gen. xiii. 16), and to Hagar, the angel blessing Ishmael (Gen. xvi. 10). He makes the same promise through Ezekiel (xxxvi. 37), saying, 'I will increase them with men like a flock.' Isaiah says the people will obtain this blessing as promised in the divine law, that he will be a numerous people, that he will multiply and his descendants will be innumerable, that he will see seed and prolong his days. He adds another promise—that he will prolong the days of his life, that his happiness will be permanent, that he will experience no more ruin, diminution, or captivity, nor will his progeny, as in past redemptions, be such as to require a repetition of similar sufferings among the nations, nor will it commit sins compelling the anger of the Lord to inflict punishments. This duration and perpetuity of life in the land of their fathers is a reward which God offered in the Law for its observance, as here in Isaiah for his repentance and return to the divine mercy: therefore he says, *He will see seed, and prolong his days.* Isaiah repeats the same blessing at lxv. 20, 22; and at lxvi. 22 he extols the eternal duration of Israel, saying, 'As the new heavens and the new earth which I will make shall remain before me, saith Adonai, so shall your seed and your name remain.' Isaiah keeps this thought in the fifty-third chapter, and makes use of the same phrase, promising as a blessing to redeemed Israel that he will lengthen his days. *And the will of Adonai will prosper in his hand.* The prophet concludes the verse by saying that when the people have suffered the troubles of the captivity, and borne them, keeping constant to the divine law, and return in repentance to the divine grace, as of old, the will of Adonai will be in every respect accomplished, which always was that Israel should turn from his sins, that he should offer his soul in atonement, in order to welcome him and preserve him as his first-born son, to exalt him among all the nations, to communicate in his love his favours in the land which he gave to his forefathers as a perpetual inheritance, all which Israel had prevented by his sins, rendering himself ignorant of that will of God, being unmindful of his favours, as it was declared in Deuteronomy (xxxii. 28, 29), in the wonderful song of Moses. Such was and is the will of God, and this will be realised, and will prosper in Israel; for as the power of losing himself was in his own hand, so will be that of afterwards returning, which is the will of God, therefore it is said, *And the will of Adonai shall prosper in his hand;* and so it was promised through the same Isaiah (lv. 11), 'It shall accomplish that which I please, and it shall prosper in the thing whereto I sent it.'

[11] The prophet continues describing the rewards Israel will receive after the troubles of his captivity, and besides his multiplication and the perpetual happiness of his spiritual and temporal condition, he says in this verse that through the affliction of his soul he will see signs and fruits of the redemption of Israel, in accordance with the whole of Holy Scripture, that is, that he will see what for so many centuries he had wished to see; he will see his wonderful redemption, his kingdom re-established and exalted above all the other kingdoms, he will see his King, a son of David, on his throne, full of grace and divine spirit, his holy temple rebuilt, his priests and Levites purely performing the sacrifices; and in addition to this, he will see that in which the grandeur of his redemption principally consists, the affluence of grace and holiness, which, like full rivers, will be poured over all the children of the people, they circumcising the hearts of themselves, of their offspring, and uniformly loving the Lord their God with all their heart and with all their soul; he will see in all the nations of the universe a humble submission to their Creator, and will see them coming from all parts to Jerusalem in the name of Adonai, and the house of Jacob and Judah from the north to the land, the inheritance of their fathers; he will also see the divine secrets, enjoying as before the prophetic inspiration, for so many years denied to Israel, and this is properly called *seeing* in Holy Scripture (Joel iii. 1); the Lord had punished them by depriving them of the prophetic vision, and promises to restore it at the restoration. All this is expressed by the prophet in a single word, since it had all been said by the Lord in the Law and in the prophets in many parts and with perfect clearness, depicting the future redemption; and unless it happens so, it

is useless to try to persuade Israel that he is already redeemed, neither ought he to believe it, and the nations have no ground to prove that it is so; and the fact that Israel does not see what the Lord says he shall see in the happy time of his restoration is a sufficient answer to all the arguments and subtleties of our opponents. *And he will be satisfied;* that is, he will have abundance of all spiritual and temporal wealth, and he will use them so conformably with right reason and the divine precepts, that they will not cause in him pride or jealousy, or envy or avarice, vices which belong to those who, however much they possess, are always longing for more, being never satisfied, finding no end to their insatiable desires; but Israel will be satisfied, and will have nothing to desire, and will be free from that vice which accompanies the possession of material wealth; for if Israel in former times waxed fat and kicked through the possession of these good things, now he will use them with such moderation and temperance that material luxury will not divert him from holiness and justice; he will not proudly rebel, but he will eat and be satisfied, and will bless Adonai his God; this is what Isaiah says, *He shall see and be satisfied. With his wisdom my righteous servant shall justify many.* The Lord again gives Israel the title of his servant, as he did in the beginning; for if in all this chapter he represented him as the servant of all the nations, amongst which he suffered the troubles and miseries alluded to, now being freed from all he deserves to be the servant of the Lord his God alone, who redeemed him from such cruel chains, for there will be no one to rule over him, nor will he acknowledge any other authority than that of the Lord, whose power could now draw him out of the clutches of the Gentiles, as it did formerly out of Egypt The prophet says that the servant of the Lord, that is, Israel now justified, will with his wisdom justify many, all of the Gentiles who wish to avail themselves of his wisdom and teaching, and make themselves capable of receiving it; for as God is in his very nature supremely good, he communicates his goodness to his creatures, when they are capable of receiving it; there is no work of his that is not full of goodness; the redemption of Israel is the work of God alone, and thus it is necessarily good and communicable to all to whom it is possible to communicate his goodness. Many impious Gentiles will perish at that time in the blindness of their false sects, as all the prophets write, and particularly Ezekiel and Zechariah, and many will enjoy the fruits of the redemption with Israel, aroused by the miracles and wonders which they will see performed in favour of this redeemed people; these will join him humbly, and will surrender not only their persons in obedience as subjects, but also their souls, their wills to the true doctrine, faithfully asking them from those whom they will now acknowledge as taught by God, as his first-born son, whose wisdom will give to the pious of the nations the true and pure tidings of their Creator, and the worship with which they ought to serve him, forgetting the false ones which wickedness had invented, and ignorance preserved. Redeemed Israel will with his wisdom remove this ignorance, that the nations may be justified, and being sanctified and united with Israel all nations may praise the Lord and all may come to drink of this wisdom, as Isaiah said before at ii. 3, 'And many people shall go and say, Come ye, and let us go up to the mountain of the Lord,' etc.; and through Jeremiah (xvi. 19) he says that all the nations will come to Israel, confessing the ignorance in which they lived, and asking for the light of his true wisdom for their salvation; and similarly by Zechariah (viii. 23), 'And ten men shall take hold of the skirt of him that is a Jew, saying, We will go with you, for we have heard that God is with you.' Finally, Israel will be God's instrument in bringing back the nations to the knowledge of him through the wisdom of the divine law, which will abound in all the people, of which Moses said, 'This is your wisdom, this is your understanding;' and thus Isaiah confirms him by saying, *And my righteous servant will justify many with his wisdom. And he will bear their iniquity;* Israel will bear patiently the iniquity of the nations. But it would seem that Israel being already in this happy condition described by the prophet has nothing more to suffer, the iniquity of the nations can no longer hurt him, as they are supposed to be now vanquished and Israel to be redeemed, exalted, and raised very high; nevertheless, having said so so many times in this chapter, he now repeats it, but with a different purpose; before the nations were accused of the crimes which they committed against captive Israel, but now the prophet celebrates the benevolence of Israel after his liberation; for he was obliged to suffer the troubles of his captivity, having to persevere in the sacred laws; but that Israel, now that he is glorious, favoured by God and liberated, should repay the greatest injuries with the greatest kindness is a thing worthy of being celebrated by the prophet. It is for this reason that he calls him *righteous servant*, for it was only through being righteous that he could act so righteously as not only not to seek revenge for his injuries, but to solicit the salvation of those who oppressed him; they erred in seeking his ruin, and he with his teaching and wisdom will seek to remove their errors; they made him wander through painful paths, and he with his wisdom will guide them along the path of truth to the grace of their Creator, which will be the greatest benefit which the nations ever experienced; Israel will not be intolerant, or cherish the remembrance of the crimes they perpetrated on him; on the contrary, with the greatest forgiveness he will seek a remedy for them, by bearing them till they obtain the divine mercy; and as the priest bore the sins of the people to obtain pardon for them, so Israel will bear the guilt of the nations, fulfilling what the Lord says, 'And ye shall be named the priests of Adonai' (Is. lxi. 6), 'And ye shall be unto me a kingdom of priests' (Exod. xix. 6); and thus Isaiah says in this verse, *And he will bear their guilt.*

12 The prophet concludes this discourse by recapitulating all that he has said in the preceding verses; he considers the end of this battle which Israel in his captivity had to fight with the nations, resisting with invincible patience the powerful attacks

they made both against his spiritual nature (endeavouring to convert him to their various sects) and against his body by their cruel punishments, severity, and butchery, all which Israel, keeping true, courageously resisted, entrenched behind the fortifications of the divine law, which alone constituted his defence and gave him the glorious victory over all the nations of the universe; then the prophet says, The triumph of this victory I will make him share with many, I will give or apportion him the possession of many nations as spoils gained in the war; the Lord will fulfil what he said through Isaiah, he will possess those who possessed him, and will make subject those who had made him subject, he will employ as slaves the surrendered nations, and the nation that shall withstand him shall be destroyed, as the same Isaiah (lx. 12) says, 'For the nation that will not serve thee shall perish, and the nations shall be utterly wasted,' etc. The Lord will apportion to him the riches of the nations as spoils; as before by divine decree he spoiled Egypt of its riches, so he will do to all the nations, and so the Lord promised him through Isaiah (lxi. 6), in order that the servant of God may thus be elevated, exalted, and raised high above all the nations, not only in spiritual wealth, in which the perfection of the soul consists, but also in the temporal wealth which satisfies the wants of the body within the limits which reason, directed by the divine precepts, permits. *And he shall divide the spoil with the strong.* He says that he will divide these spoils, which the Lord will give to Israel, among the strong and valiant children of the people who bravely fought in their afflictions, and faithful to the Lord their God persevered till they gained the victory, without being vanquished either by fear or a kind of vanity (conversion) of the false Israelites, imposed upon the nations, which however they never believed and in no way esteemed; and with those who were brave he will divide the spoils; and he gives the reason why these are to enjoy the fruit, the spoils of this wonderful victory, *because he gave his soul up to death, and was reckoned among the rebels,* which means, because he exposed his life to dangers for the sake of the divine law, and made no account of the opinion of the nations, or of being held by them as a vile, obstinate, and pertinacious Jew, the reproach which all the nations throw in the face of Israel, by whom he is considered a criminal, and as such reckoned among the most sacrilegious criminals, being charged with high treason against God. But those who bore this opprobrium, these insults, with a brave spirit, with strength of mind, despising life, if required, and the honours of the Gentiles, which are of no value, if they did not conceal themselves, timid and wretched, in order not to be known and reckoned among the transgressors of Israel; if they felt greater esteem for the divine law, suffering contempt, than for the hostile opinion of the Gentiles, then *because he offered his soul to death and was reckoned with the transgressors*, because he bare the sins of many who exerted themselves to injure him, resisting only with patience their malevolence and tyranny, he will enter into the share of many, and with the powerful of Israel will divide the spoils of the nations who persecuted him. *And for the rebellious he will intercede.* Finally, when the servant of God is exalted, Israel elevated and raised very high, victorious over all the nations, dividing them under his own sway, and enjoying the spoils of victory, this greatness in temporal wealth will be no obstacle to the perfection of his spiritual life, in which the most valuable greatness consists, the summit of all happiness before reaching the celestial glory of the next world; for their hearts being circumcised, those of stone removed and those of flesh put in their place, Israel will preserve a perpetual union with his Creator; he will be his God, and Israel his people, and as such always worthy to share in his divine favours, which he will liberally and lovingly bestow on him; one of which will be that Israel will no sooner pray than he will be heard and his prayer accepted, as it is promised by the same prophet (lxv. 24), 'And it shall come to pass that before they call I will answer, and while they are yet speaking I will hear;' for Israel to call will be the same as to be answered by God; he will be praying, and at the same time he will experience the fulfilment of his prayer; his intercession will avail that the divine justice may pitifully pardon the nations their abominable sins, even those they committed against Israel, while innocent of all the falseness and deceit they charged him with, since he did not act falsely to them and there was no deceit in his mouth; for Israel, full of the love of God and his divine Spirit, will pray for the rebellious, will be the mediator of peace between the Lord and the nations, praying for them, not with an ineffectual prayer, but one so effectual that his entreaties will always have a happy result in mankind being benefited; and then the nations will make this spontaneous confession of their mistake and the injustice with which they treated Israel, which Isaiah narrates in this chapter, and what the Lord had said in the song of Moses will be fulfilled, 'Sing, ye nations, of his people, for he will avenge the blood of his servants, and will render vengeance to his adversaries, and will pardon the earth for his people' (Deut. xxxii. 43).

D. JACOB IBN AMRAM.

Non obstat tertio principaliter Isai. cap. liii. vers. 4, ibi: *Langores nostros ipse tulit, etc.*, vers. 7, secundum versionem Latinam, ibi: *Oblatus est, quia ipse voluit,* et vers. 8, secundum eandem Latinam, ibi: *Propter scelus populi mei percussi eum, etc.*, quae omnia videntur verificari in Jesu Messia et Deo Christianorum a Judaeis facto occidi, et non in alio.

Caeterum immerito. Imprimis, quia verba illa *quia ipse voluit* sunt temere supposita: quamvis vero sensui, quem ad praeoppositum caput liii. praestamus, non officiant. Eisdemque supposititiis verbis refragatur Matth. cap. xxvi. vers. 39, Marc. cap. xiv. vers. 36, Luc. cap. xxii. vers. 42.

Deinde, illa *percussi eum* sunt etiam iniquissime traducta. Nam veritas Hebr. habet *plaga eis,* seu *percussi eos,* ex verbo *lamo* in plurali. Unde constat, non loqui de uno, et multo minus de Jesu.

Praeterea, pro Christianis nullatenus facit. Primo, quia de tempore occisionis nihil ibidem dicitur, ut debeat praecise intelligi de Jesu Christianorum occiso; si quando illum, qui Judaeis promissus est Messias Davidicus occidi oporteret; quod falsum est, ut patebit inferius. Item et percussio de multis aliis intelligi potest, qui se Messiam simulabant.

Rursus, si pro Christianis loqueretur, dicere debebat *propter scelus populi mei ipse populus* Judaicus *percussit eum.* Ast secundum quamlibet literam, Deus sibi tribuit actum percutiendi; solamque causam applicat populo Judaico. Item et percussus non est unus, sed plures, ut patet ibi: *Propter scelus populi mei percussi* ego Deus *eos, etc.*

Denique convincuntur ex vers. 1, ibi: *Si posuerit pro peccato animam suam, videbit semen, prolongabit dies, etc.* Tum quia Deus aperte ibidem loquitur de puro homine, et humanis ac temporalibus praemiis eidem conferendis: Christiani vero intelligunt omnia spiritualiter (ut est ipsorum solitum effugium) et de praemiis non ipsi Messiae (quia Deum esse putant) dandis, sed hominibus, inquiunt, ab eo salvatis. Tum quia, dum conditionaliter loquitur ibi: *Si posuerit, etc.*, clare ostendit, se loqui de puro homine, cujus libero arbitrio Deus relinquit opera meritoria.

Quapropter dicendum est, Isaiam intelligi de populo Israel in novissimo dierum, ut nunc est, et jam antea fuit in omni genere afflictionum. Loquitur enim de uno, qui plurium vicem gerit, ut est populus Israel ex Deut. cap. iv. a princip., et cap. v. a princip., et cap. vi. vers. 4, et passim; de quo etiam promiscue pluraliter loquitur. Et idcirco dicit: *Propter scelus populi mei* Judaici, qui multifariam illuc usque peccaverat, *percussi eos,* id est, eundem populum Judaicum successive venientem; quia nempe, novissimo praesertim tempore, erit captivus, dispersus, afflictus, angustiatus, exactus, et percussus. Quod etiam clare deprehendetur ex praecedenti cap. lii. et cap. liv. sequenti ejusdem Isaiae.

Nec oberit dicere, quod videtur inconveniens, ut idem populus propter scelus ejusdem populi a Deo percussus dicatur: cum immo in proposito a prophetis dici soleat, 'Patres nostri comederunt uvam acerbam, et dentes nostri obstupuerunt,' vel 'Patres nostri peccaverunt, et non sunt, et nos pro eis patimur,' Jerem. cap. xxxi. vers. 26, et in Lament. cap. ult., Ezechiel cap. xviii. a princip., quia sumitur idem populus pro diverso tempore. Haec sufficiebant, ut Christiani destituerentur inani fundamento ex praeopposito cap. liii. Isaiae.

Verum, quia textus iste singularis est, et plusquam obscurus, utpote propheticus super omnibus angustiis, et miseriis, quas ubique locorum Israel passus est, patitur, et perpessurus est, in hoc longo exilio et dispersione inter gentes; quarum etiam tyrannidem versus Israel praedicit, et tandem ejusdem Israel venturam felicitatem: operae pretium duximus in eo tantisper immorari, eo potissimum, ut evidentius convincatur error gentium, quae ad instar solertis piscatoris solent in turbidum flumen rete jacere, ut aliquid videantur expiscari. Quae ut methodice expediantur, nota istud cap. liii. connecti praecedenti (ut statim patefiet) in quo propheta praedicit futuram gloriam Sion et Jerusalem, ut patet in princip. ibi: 'Quia non adiiciet ultra, ut pertransiat per te incircumcisus et immundus.' Quod adhuc impletum non est, ut evidens fit ex frequenti incircumcisorum et immundorum adventu et sede. Assentit propheta Nahum cap. i. in fin., Joel cap. ult. vers. 17: 'Excutere de pulvere, consurge, sede Jerusalem, solve vincula colli tui captiva filia Sion: quia haec dicit Dominus, gratis venundati estis, et sine argento redimemini, etc.' Praedicit quoque redemptionem et reversionem Israel a vers. 9 et vers. 12, ibi: 'Et congregabit vos Deus Israel, etc.;' et tandem subnectitur vers. 13 quem sequitur dictum cap. liii, in quibus sunt innumera vitia versionis Latinae Jeronymi; partim forsan ex ignorantia sacri idiomatis, partim ex malitia ut videbitis.

Eapropter praemittemus seriem verborum prophetae juxta veritatem Heb. (ex quo obiter error aut falsitas Latinae versionis colligetur) postea interpretamenta adhibebimus, quae verosimiliora videbuntur ad mentem Isaiae.

Inquit itaque in praecedenti cap. lii. a vers. 13: *Ecce intelliget servus meus, exaltabitur, et elevabitur, et sublimis erit valde. Sicut obstupuere super te multi, sic corruptus de viro aspectus ejus, et forma ejus de filiis hominum: sic*—non *iste,* ut in Latina—*asperget gentes multas,* vel faciet loqui gentes multas: *super eum continebunt Reges os suum; quia quod non fuit narratum illis viderunt, et quod non audierunt intellexerunt.*—Succedit praeoppositum cap. liii: *Quis credidit auditui nostro? et brachium Domini super quo*—non *cui,* ut in Latina—*revelatum est? Ascendet sicut virgultum coram eo, et radix de terra sicca: non forma ei, neque decor; et vidimus, et non aspectus, et desiderabimus*—non *desideravimus,* ut in Latina—*eum, despectum, et deminutum hominum*—non *novissimum*—*virum dolorum, et scientem infirmitatem, et abscondentem*—non *absconditus*—*vultum a nobis,* vel etiam a se, *despectum, et non reputavimus eum. Vero langores nostros ipse tulit, et dolores nostros portavit: et nos aestimavimus eum plagatum, percussum a Domino, et afflictum. Et ipse dolorosus propter iniquitates nostras, attritus propter scelera nostra: disciplina pacis nostrae super eum, et livore ejus sanati sumus. Omnes nos sicut oves erravimus; unusquisque in viam suam declinavimus, et Dominus fecit occurri in eo*—non *posuit in eo*—*iniquitatem omnium nostrum. Exactus*—non *oblatus,* ut alias et ipsa Latina traducit in Deut. cap. xv. post princip., ibi: Exiges—*et ille afflictus*—quod deest in Latina, a qua tum falso supponitur, Quia ipse voluit, o impia corruptela!—*et non aperiet os suum: sicut agnus ad occisionem ductus est, et sicut ovis coram tondentibus se obmutuit, et non aperiebat os suum. De detentione*—non *de angustia:* radix autem Judaica (id est, aethymologica) denotat regnum sive dominium; lib. Samuelis sive Regum I, cap. ix. vers. 17, ubi Latina etiam vertit *dominabitur:* detinet enim, sive cogit, qui imperat—*et de judicio sublatus est. Generationem ejus quis enarrabit? quia abscissus fuit de terra vitae, propter scelus populi mei plaga eis*—non *percussi eum*, in singulari. *Et dedit impiis sepulturam ejus*—non vero *dabit impios pro sepultura*, ut in Latina—*et divitem in morte ejus, super quod non fecerit falsitatem, nec dolus in ore ejus. Et Dominus voluit conterere eum, et fecit infirmari. Si posuerit pro emendatione*—poenitentia, non peccato—*animam suam, videbit semen, prolongabit dies, et voluntas Domini in manu ejus prosperabitur. Pro labore animae suae videbit, saturabitur: cum sapientia sua justificabit justus servus multos, et iniquitates eorum ipse portabit. Ideo dispertiam ei cum plurimis,* sive *magnis, et fortitus,* sive *fortium, dividet spolium; pro eo quod tradidit animam suam morti, et sceleratis,* seu *transgressoribus, annumeratus est: et ipse peccata multorum tulit, et pro sceleratis rogabit.*—Haec est vera traductio ex Hebraico in Latinum, et conformiter menti prophetae. Jam vides, pie ac sapiens lector, quam vitiosa sit Latina versio, et difformis veritati Hebr., in iis praesertim quae pro stabilienda fide sua ab eisdem Christianis perpenduntur: adeo, ut ad illum, illosque propulsandos ab umbra hujus sacri eloquii, sufficiat rectitudo, et restitutio versionis, de qua supra.

Qua supposita (quod attinet ad Judaeos) non parva est

difficultas in adhibendo sensum verbis obscurissimis Isaiae in praesenti; indigent plane spiritu prophetico. Unde antiquiores magistri nostri et reconditiores in varia abierunt interpretamenta; utrique tamen longe remoti a Christianorum expositione. Nos eorum sumus secuti expositionem, qui diffiniunt, Isaiam hic loqui de populo Israel: cum idem propheta in praecedenti cap. lii. ante finem (cui in themate succedit praeoppositum cap. liii) de eodem populo redimendo aperte loquatur. Quapropter inde trahenda est interpretatio, sicut et Isaiae mens.

Incipit itaque in dicto cap. lii. a vers. 13: *Ecce intelliget* lii. 13
servus meus, exaltabitur, elevabitur, et sublimis erit valde. In hoc prophetiae principio quatuor praeeminentias, quas Israel habuerat, et exilio et dispersione inter gentes perdiderat, recuperandas propheta praedicit: nempe intellectum, sive sapientiam; regnum; prophetiam; et providentiam Dei particuliter assistentis. Quae ex praescriptis verbis (quae alias in Latina versione videbantur synonima, et ideo otiosa, videlicet exaltabitur, elevabitur, et sublimis erit) juxta aethymon Hebraicum eleganter extrahit, et docte percurrit D. Isaac Abarbanel ibidem, quasi propheta dicat: Ecce populus meus (Judaicus) iterum plane intelliget, ad obsequendum Domino: regnabit super omnes gentes: prophetabit, id est, plene noscet voluntatem Domini, ut infra nota[t]: et a Domino protegetur particulari providentia, sicut a principio, et uberius. Non faciat vobis dubium, quod nomine servi intelligatur populus Judaicus. Nam Israel servus Domini vocatur, ut per eundem Isai. cap. xli. vers. 8, Jerem. cap. xxx. vers. 10, Psal. cxxxv. Confitemini: vers. 22 et passim. Plerumque in his locis loquitur Isaias in singulari, quamvis intelligat de populo Israel, ne quis putet, se intelli-

gere de aliquibus ex dicto populo, qui patiuntur pro peccatis patrum; sed potius de toto unite populo, quippe totus nunc patitur pro patribus, et eodem antiquo populo, qui
14 graviter, et saepissime peccavit. *Sicut obstupuere super te multi, sic corruptus de viro aspectus ejus, et forma ejus de filiis hominum;* id est, quemadmodum admirati super te multi, quia (ita expone illud *sic*) corruptior aspectus ejus (Israel), quam ut viro competat, et forma ejus, quam ut hominibus assimiletur. *Sic asperget gentes multas* vel *faciet loqui gentes multas; super eum continebunt reges os suum, quia quod non fuit narratum illis, viderunt; et quod non audierunt intellexerunt;* id est, sic (hic respondet admirationi gentium) vincet ac propellet huc illuc gentes multas, vel faciet loqui gentes multas, videntes populum Judaicum, antea abjectum, et omnino despectum utpote servilem, tunc exaltatum nimis valde; et propterea super eum reges orbis cum moderamine et pondere aperient [os] suum, quia vident et intelligunt, quod nec illis narratum erat, nec antea audierant: immo totum contrarium, scilicet populum Judaicum a Deo omnino expositum fuisse, ut gentibus serviret, subque ipsarum dominio viverent dispersi. Quae verba alias praepostere intelligit Paulus in epist. ad Romanos cap. xv. vers. 21. Quid autem loquentur reges mundi, cum continentia et pondere prosequitur Isaias in sequenti et nobis opposito cap. liii, nempe:

liii. 1 *Quis credidit auditui nostro, et brachium Domini super quo revelatum est?* Duo hic inculcat propheta cum admiratione gentium: Primum, stuporem ipsarum gentium super suo lapsu; quod scilicet a Judaeis victae, vel prae timore eorum, loquuntur de eisdem cum continentia et pondere, ob incogitatam felicitatem, et exaltationem Judaeorum, quasi

ita exclamat: Quis unquam tale audiri de nobis putasset, aut
quis credidisset, quod nos audivimus? Secundum, siquando
in mentem regum orbis venisset vicissitudo populorum aut
regnorum, quis eam applicasset populo Israel? aut dixisset,
super Israel brachium Domini, id est, ejus favorem ac
potestatem, iterum manifestandum? Unde praeposita verba
perperam intelligit Johannes in Evangelio, cap. xii. vers. 38,
ubi etiam pro *auditui* reponit *dicto* contra veritatem; et
Paul[us] absone exponit ad Roman. cap. x. vers. 16.—*Et* 2
ascendit sicut virgultum coram eo; et sicut radix de terra
sicca. Hic reddit rationem stuporis Regum orbis; quia
nempe a parvis initiis profectum, sicut virgultum, viderunt
in altum ascendere populum Israel, paulo antea abjectum,
et sicut radicem (quae vivida non speratur) de terra sicca (in
qua alias omnia arescunt, et moriuntur) coram Deo iterum
favente Judaeis. *Non forma ei, neque decor, et vidimus,*
et non aspectus, et desiderabimus eum. Dictae rationis
rationem reddit, et auget; quia populo Israel (Judaeis) in
captivitate et dispersione nulla forma est, nullus oris
splendor; et attente considerabimus eum, nec adhuc ei
aspectus (humanus) nobis visus erat. Et quis imputabit
nobis quod non desideraremus eum? id est, non speraremus
illius vicissitudinem, sive mutationem in gloriam? cum ante
de eo tale quid non imaginaremur: praecedit namque desi-
derium, sive spem, imaginatio; quod etiam confirmat in
seqq. *Despectum, et deminutum hominum, virum dolorum,* 3
et scientem infirmitatem; id est, si exulem Israel contem-
plabamur, ab omnibus spretum videbamus, caeteris homini-
bus inferiorem, vel ab hominum consortio ablegatum (quia
scilicet omnes gentes Judaeos a se propulsant, aut saltem
cogitant vel desiderant exterminare), dominum dolorum,

quia non nisi doloribus abundat, et assuetum infirmitatibus propter continuum in Exilio pavorem, et inde subcrescentem maerorem. *Et sicut abscondentem vultum a nobis*—vel *a se—despectum, et non reputavimus eum;* id est, adeo despectus erat, ut ipse affectaret abscondere vultum a nobis gentilibus: vel ita simulabat se, ne forte a se ipso agnosceretur Judaeus, ut passim evenit. Et si quando cognitus esset, spretus erat ab omnibus, et contumeliis affectus: et ideo non reputavimus eum in numero hominum, de quibus
4 posset vicissitudo iniquae sortis sperari. *Vero langores nostros ipse tulit, et dolores nostros portavit;* id est, langores, et dolores, quibus nos (Reges et nationes orbis) dedimus causam (et propterea *nostros* dicimus, *n.* 633) ipse perpessus est. Nam ex continua oppressione, tyrannide gentium, et servitute ac timore Judaeorum, incidunt ipsi Judaei in dolores, et langores. Loquitur itaque propheta de langoribus, et doloribus propriis, et ab ipso populo Judaico personaliter perpessis, ex causa tamen aliena, ut patet ex vers. seq.: unde etiam colligitur absona expositio Matthaei, cap. viii. vers. 17. *Et nos aestimavimus eum plagatum, percussum a Domino, et afflictum;* id est, cum sit quod propter malitiam nostram (gentium) Israel incidebat in langores, et dolores; nos putabamus, illum esse plagatum, percussum, et afflictum a Domino; non vero a
5 nobis, nec causa nostra. *Et ipse dolorosus propter iniquitates nostras, et attritus propter scelera nostra;* id est, non quidem Israel in hoc exilio propter peccata sua plagatus principaliter a Domino erat, ac percussus; sed ei potius adveniebant langores et dolores propter nostras iniquitates et scelera: inique enim, ac scelerate agebamus cum eo. *Disciplina pacis nostrae super eum, et livore eius sanati*

sumus; id est, cum nos (Reges et nationes orbis) eramus in pace, quidquid statuebamus pro disciplina et regimine Reipublicae nostrae, totum vergebat in perniciem Judaeorum, ut videlicet vel ejicerentur e finibus nostris, vel aliter punirentur, morte, sive (quod durius et iniquius est) coacta conversione ad religionem nostram; et tandem non quiescebamus, nec sanabamur, a cura persequendi Israel, nisi percusso eo et livore ejus.—Vel etiam expone, quod stante pace inter gentes (nam bellum inter illas mentem distrahit a Judaeis, et illorum religione) si forsan aliquid sinistri succedebat, *v. c.* mortalitas, vel morbus epidimialis, statim in plateis, in triviis, in suggestis, fiebant sermones, praedicationes, et exclamationes ab eorum magistris et sanctonibus (qui alias solent gentem suam corrigere, et castigare, ut ad ipsorum Deum, vel Deos, convertantur), et haec tota doctrina et castigatio (in statu pacis eorum) vertebatur super Israel, ut nempe Judaei publicentur causa illius mali occurrentis, et ita vel occidantur, vel ablegentur; et plane occidebantur, vel ablegabantur, cessabatque communis mortalitas, sic permittente Deo. Et hinc livore eorum gentes (ut putabatur) sanabantur.—Vel denique intellige, quod disciplina pacis sumatur omnino pro pace corporali, id est, sanitate, et valetudine corporis: ita ut valetudo generalis gentium sit super Israel, ut quando supervenit aliquis communis morbus, pro illius curatione agatur de castigandis Judaeis, velut causa morbi; in eoque versatur tota disciplina, sive doctrina pacis corporalis gentium, ut ita de plano procedat, quod propheta subjungit *et livore ejus sanati sumus.* Triplex ista, et quaelibet expositio impleta jam saepissime est in hoc longo Judaeorum exilio, nunc in hoc, nunc in illo regno, et aliquando in omnibus simul. Unde perperam praedicta

verba alias adducit Petrus in Epist. i. cap. 2, ante fin.
6 *Omnes nos, sicut oves erravimus, unusquisque in viam suam declinavimus, et Dominus fecit occurri in eo iniquitatem omnium nostrum*; id est, cum nos omnes sicut oves erravimus, Edom in viam suam, Ismael in viam suam, et caeteri similiter: attamen unusquisque nostrum unanimiter et indifferenter contra Israel statuebat ex propria diversaque religione, et indifferenter a quolibet nostrum patiebatur Israel. Et quod notabilius est, Deus ita dirigebat iniquitatem nostram, ut Judaeos offenderet: singuli enim putabamus Judaeos castigari debere quia religionem nostram non amplectebantur: et consequenter Judaei ipsi portabant, seu supportabant, iniquitatem nostram sive errorem, poenam indebite patientes, nempe ex diversa sive contraria causa,
7 respectu Christianorum, Maurorum, etc. *Exactus, et ille afflictus, et non aperiet os suum: sicut agnus ad occisionem ductus est; et sicut ovis coram tondentibus se obmutuit*; id est, ab illo severe exigebamus pecuniam, ut ultra corporis afflictionem, in bonis etiam pateretur, et non aperiet os suum; sicut agnus ducebatur ad occisionem, ut comederetur a nobis, et sicut ovis muta coram tondentibus se ita Israel coram nobis praedantibus eum, ut in inquisitione Hispaniae. De patientia Israel loquitur propheta, de praeterito, et de futuro; quia non unus sed plures actus successivo tempore denotantur. Huc usque loquuntur (ut praedicit Isai.) Reges et nationes orbis, stupefacti ob lapsum et ruinam imperii ipsorum, sublevato Israel, quem jam non reputabant populum denuo exaltandum, percurrentes ejusdem variam et infelicem fortunam ob iniquitatem ipsarum gentium. Incipit
8 modo loqui propheta de eodem Israel. *De detentione et judicio sublatus est; generationem ejus quis enarrabit?* id

est, iste populus Israel, quem Reges et gentes terrae reputabant non populum, non virum, sine forma et decore, despectum ac deminutum, plenum doloribus et assuefactum infirmitatibus, non fuit ita a principio; penes illum namque erat dominium sive regnum (quod *detentione* significatur, ut superius ostendimus), et sublime illud justitiae tribunal, sive judicium Sanhedrin: quis celsitudinem illius generationis, id est temporis illius (nam verbum דור *dor*, quo propheta utitur, et *generationem* Latinamus, tempus denotat: Exodi cap. iii. vers. 5, et patet ex omnibus concordantiis sacrae paginae) enarrare poterit? in quo florebat regali dominio excelsoque judicio, et tamen regno ac judicio privatus est a Domino, cui peccaverunt patres nostri. Loquitur propheta de privatione regni et judicii in terra sancta. Vel, quis tempus illud (nempe, miseriam et calamitatem ejus) enarrabit? in quo privatus fuit regno, et judicio; partim occiso Israel, partim expulso a terra sancta. Quem sensum probat vers. seq.: quid autem somnient Acta Apostolorum, cap. viii. vers. 33, penitus ignoratur, dum contra veritatem Hebraicam et Latinam etiam traducunt ibi: 'In humilitate judicium ejus sublatum est, et suam generationem (pro *genitura*) quis enarrabit?'—*Quia abscissus fuit de terra vitae, propter scelus populi mei plaga eis.* Hic rationem reddit aerumnarum Judaeorum, quod regno et tribunali justitia privati sint, et refert principalem, quod nempe a terra sancta ipsorum patria abstracti sint; quod durius erat occisione eorum. Et quae fuit causa ob quam occisi et expulsi sint a terra vitae? (sancta terra vitae solet appellari, Ezechiel cap. xxxii. a vers. 24; notat ex Christianis Adricomius Delphus, in Chronico mundi anno 3374.) Illud certum est, quod propter scelus populi mei (patrum varie peccantium) *plaga,* afflictio, exactio, ablegatio, et dolor successit *eis,* id est, filiis, sive populo Israel successivis temporibus in timore Domini, et legis custodia persistenti. In hoc etiam versu somniant Acta Apost. cap. viii. vers. 33, dum contra veritatem et Latinam etiam versionem ita invertunt ibi: 'quia tolletur de terra vita ejus:' Deus autem ob culpam patrum percutiebat Judaeos descendentes, interventu Regum et gentium orbis, ut supra. *Et dedit impiis sepulturam ejus, et divitem in morte ejus;* id est, propter scelus populi mei non solum perdidit Israel regnum et judicium, sed etiam cum exterminio a terra sancta sepulturam quam mortuus sortiretur in eadem terra Deus iratus dedit impiis immerentibus qui in eadem terra sancta sepeliuntur. Item, loco Regis Judaei dedit, sive posuit, divitem, id est, dominum (non Regem) ex gentibus in eadem terra sancta, ut regeret; quod experientia comprobatur. Quam terram sanctam, quia jam destituta est populo suo Israel (eo vel expulso vel subjecto) non vocat vitae sed mortis ejus. Nam respectu Judaeorum expulsorum, aut in eadem occisorum, merito dicenda est terra mortis; non enim vivunt in ea, vel serviliter vivunt; tum quia possessam ab alienis non decet appellari terram vitae, sed mortis. In versione hujus vers. crassissime hallucinatur Latina Jeronimi traductio, ut supra notavimus in correctione literae. *Super quod non fecerit falsitatem, nec dolus in ore ejus;* id est respectu gentium imperantium sibi falsitatem non fecit Israel, nec in ore ejus inventus est dolus contra tales nationes ac Reges eorum (quicquid a gentibus contrarium asseratur), Sophonias, cap. ult. vers. 13, ibi: 'Reliquiae Israel non facient iniquitatem, nec loquentur mendacium, et non invenietur in ore eorum lingua dolosa,' etc., Daniel, cap. xii.

vers. 7, ibi: 'Et cum completa fuerit dispersio populi sancti,' etc., ubi dispersum Israel, ut modo est, vocat populum sanctum. Similiter Isai. cap. lxiii. vers. 18, ibi: 'Quasi nihilum possiderunt (ut nunc possident) populum sanctum tuum,' etc. Peccaverunt tamen patres contra Dominum Deum suum; ea propter meriti sunt exilium et dispersionem, et in eadem permanent filii eorum, custodientes legem Dei. *Et Dominus voluit conterere eum, et fecit infirmari;* id est, quamvis in Israel non inveniatur falsitas aut dolus adversus gentes imperantes sibi, Dominus voluit affligere, et debilitare eum (putantibus gentibus Israel esse falsarium et dolosum, et idcirco castigantibus eum), tum ob purgandam patrum culpam, juxta Jerem. cap. xxxi. vers. 29, et in Lamentat. cap. ult., cum similibus: tum etiam ob propriam contra Dominum; non tamen ut extingueret eum, aut abjiceret, sed ut poeniteret ac reverteretur, juxta Levit. cap. xxvi. vers. 44, Deuter. cap. xxx. a princ., Jerem. cap. xlvi. vers. ult. *Si posuerit pro emendatione* (poenitentia) *animam suam, videbit semen, prolongabit dies, et voluntas Domini in manu ejus prosperabitur;* id est, cum Dominus non in perditionem populum suum ablegaverit et disperserit, si eum iniquitatum suarum ac patrum contra Deum poenituerit, reducetur ad feliciorem aetatem, quam fuerit prima, ut praedicit Deuter. cap. iv. vers. 30, et cap. xxx. vers. 1, et passim; generabit beatam prolem, quam vivam videbit; satiabitur diebus, quos prolongabit; et erit semper gratus Domino, et obtemperans. Hic etiam innuit propheta de iis qui constanter exponunt sive ponunt animam suam pro legis (quam violaverant ipsi vel patres ipsorum) tutela, et vel cremantur, vel aliter necantur ex judicio gentium. Jesus non prolongavit dies, quia anno 33 aetatis periit in cruce:

nec vidit semen, id est, legitimum ex foemore suo, ut semper
11 intelligitur in sacra pagina, ut late *n. 667. Pro labore animae suae videbit, saturabitur;* id est, post redemptionem et reductionem Israel ad terram sanctam, videbit satietatem (pro qua laboravit colens terram), et ipse satiabitur; aliud erat antea, ex Levit. cap. xxvi. vers. 16, et Deuter. cap. xxviii. vers. 30, et vers. 33, quasi dicat, in novissimo dierum, cum Israel redemptus et reductus fuerit ad terram sanctam suam et viderit ubertatem ejus, ipse non alienus fruetur ea, Deuter. cap. xxx. vers. 9, Isai. cap. xxxii. vers. 8, et cap. lxv. à vers. 21, Amos cap. ult. vers. 14, cum similibus; tum etiam pro labore animae quam pro Deo exposuit supplicio gentium. *Cum sapientia sua justificabit justus servus meus multos, et iniquitates eorum ipse portabit;* id est, tempore quo Israel in praedictis angustiis positus justus erit, justificabit multos ex gentibus, quos docebit, vel aliter trahet ad Dei vexilla. *Cum sapientia sua;* id est, sapienter; quia nonnisi sapienter, argute, ac subtiliter (ob metum gentium) ostendit ipsis errorem ipsarum: atque ita illos sapienter convertit ad Dominum (rari namque ex gentibus sponte quaerunt, et audiunt de absoluta Dei voluntate, et justitia legis Moysaicae) et propterea dicuntur justificati cum sapientia Israel. Et horum iniquitates (antea contractas, ob quas non merebuntur justificari; vel a quibus alias purgari debebunt) Israel ipse portabit, ut proprias. Sive propter dictam conversionem multorum gentilium ad Deum, ab Israel causatam, quam gentes alias iniquitatem putant, ipse Israel convertens tormenta patietur: et consequenter reputatam iniquitatem conversorum (ad Deum Judaeorum) portabit, seu supportabit Israel convertens, seu justificans. Nam apud Christianos praesertim, convertens

ad legem Moysaicam gravissime punitur, ut est notum. *Ideo dispertiam ei cum multis* (vel *magnis*) *et fortibus* (sive 12
fortium) *dividet spolium;* id est, propter meritum populi mei praenotatum, dabo ei partem cum multis justis, ut inter eos appareat quantum meritus est. Vel, dabo ei partem cum magnis, illis nempe primis parentibus, Abraham, Isaac, et Jacob. Nam idem verbum *rabim* pariter multos, ac insignes quoque et excelsos viros significat. Itidem fortibus, eis scilicet qui pro veritate, nempe Deo, et ejus sacra lege animose steterunt, Israel dividet spolium gentium peccatricum. Vel, fortium dividet spolium, id est, victoriam reportabit (tum enim spolia dividuntur) electarum gentium, quae convenerint contra Jerusalem in notissimo tempore, ac bello, ut per Ezechiel, cap. xxxviii. et seq., ubi loquitur de fortibus gentium qui cadent victi in montibus sanctis, notabiliter Joel, cap. iii. Zacharias (ubi etiam meminit spoliorum gentium), cap. xiv. et tandem generaliter Jeremias, cap. xxv. vers. 30. *Pro eo quod tradidit morti animam suam, et sceleratis annumeratus est; et ipse peccata multorum tulit; et pro transgressoribus rogabit;* id est, praemiorum (quae superius retulimus Deum in novissimo dierum daturum populo Israel) causae hic per Epilogum proponuntur; et imprimis, quia animam posuit pro Deo et sancta lege ejus inter gentes quarum ritus noluit amplecti et idcirco varie passus est. Nam si vellet a lege Domini deficere, reciperetur equidem a gentibus cum praemiis. Deinde, quia maluit sceleratis annumerari (quatenus, licet injuste, ei opponitur quod interfecerit vel non receperit Jesum, aut aliorum sectas, ut clamant Edom, et Ismael, etc.) quam legem Domini Dei sui deserere, quidquid eadem verba perperam exponat Marcus in Evangelio, cap. xv.

vers. 28, et diversimode Lucas, cap. xxii. vers. 37. Praeterea, quia peccata patrum tulit qui comederant uvam acerbam (peccaverant), propter quod dentes filiorum obstupuerunt, vel filii passi sunt; quae proverbialis ratio usque ad postrema tempora erit in ore Judaeorum, ut per Jerem. et Ezechiel. praecitatos. Vel quia gentium ab ipsis conversarum iniquitates perpessus est, ut praediximus. Denique, quia (quod supremum justitiae est) pro sceleratis filiis Israel transgressoribus legis (ut nunc sunt et fuerunt plurimi, proh dolor!) rogabit dominium, et quotidie deprecatur. Ob has itaque causas optimam partem in futuro saeculo sortietur, et omnibus erit celsior Regibus et nationibus, eisdemque imperabit Israel. Haec abunde dicta sunt ad saepe nobis oppositum Isai.; quod jam ut paremia est lippis et tonsoribus gentium.

---

(840)

Adducitur secundo principaliter Isai. cap. liii. vers. 4, ibi: מוכה אלהים juxta expositionem Bellarmini *De verbo*, lib. ii. cap. 2, vers. argumentum quartum, dum inquit, Relata Isaiae verba Latine verti possunt, *percussum Deum*, ut ita deitatem crucifixo tribuat, de quo totum illud cap. liii. Christiani intelligunt.

Caeterum, cum hi fallantur in hoc, ita et Bellarminus decipitur in sua versione. Nam caput illud loquitur de uno plurium vicem gerente, id est, populo Israel; ut jam supra ex puritate text. Hebraici late sumus interpretati a *n.* 613.

Praeterea, versio Bellarmini aperte repugnat elementis grammaticae Hebraicae, ut est notissimum quibusque illius professoribus: verbum enim מוכה *muge* est *Samuh*, et ponit sequens substantivum (*elohim*) in genitivo, idque est, *percussum Dei.* Jeronimus vertit, *percussus a Deo:* nec versionem Bellarmini Jeronimus praetermitteret, aut ignoraret (cum longe Bellarminum excelleret in sacro idiomate) si rationabilis aut tolerabilis esset, cum alias remotissima et alienissima quaeque ad Christianorum mentem trahat, ut saepe vidistis.

LII. Y'HUDAH BEN BAL'AM.

LII. [14] מֻשחת, participle of Hof'al. The regular form would be מָשְׁחַת like מֻשְׁלָךְ (2 Sam. xx. 21). ותארו with Holem like פעלו (Jer. xxii. 13), the regular forms of both being with Qamez Hatef, as פעלו (Job xxxvi. 24). I am surprised at one who, while adhering to the usual explanation of the word in Jeremiah, maintained, in his *Letters of Friendship* [a], that in Job it was an active participle signifying *worker* or *labourer*. In that case שכרו must be understood after לא יתן לו. When I was explaining the verse in question, I saw that in fact פעל meant *wages*, and that the phrase referred back to the preceding passage ברעהו יעבד חנם, describing the man who employs his neighbour's services, but does not pay him the wages he earns. [15] יזה: he will judge them by sending calamities upon them, amongst which will be the *sprinkling* of their blood (Is. lxiii. 3).

LIII. [2] מסתר, infinitive. [5] מחולל, passive participle of Piel. The meaning is that he was prostrated by our sins, and stricken by our offences, just as though he were punished for us. This eminent saint, while bearing the chastisements which came upon him as a trial (since he had committed no sin), attracted to himself, as it were, all the chastisements due to us, and gave us *peace* for them; thus they came upon him, and *by his stripes*

---

[a] A series of letters by R. Samuel the Nagid (i. e. the Prince), containing criticisms against R. Yonah (Abu-l-Walid) ibn Janâḥ. See Derenbourg's preface to his edition of R. Yonah's *Opuscula*.

we were healed. חבורתו, a substantive. We have already explained the possibility of God's acting in such a way, in virtue of a substitution decreed by him. [7] נענה, participle Nif'al in the sense of *afflicted* (Exod. iii. 7), and, in the feminine, נענה (Is. lviii. 10), except that there the ה is the mark of the feminine, whilst the radical ה is dropped. [8] *He was removed from affliction and trial*, and no one can *tell of him*, for his fame was *cut off from the land of life*, and *through the sin of my people he was tempted.* למו for לו, i. e. his suffering was only for the sake of the nation's sin, and not because he deserved it at all himself; as it is said, *although he did no violence*, etc. [10] החלי from חלא like החטיא (1 Kings xvi. 26). The sense of the verse is that the Lord willed his sickness in order that his soul might see guilt as guilt, i. e. that he might avoid it, in opposition to the man who does not see sin as a sin, but perseveres in his disobedience. There is a similar saying in Arabic, where one of the preachers says, By the Lord, shew me error as an error in order that I may abstain from it, rectitude as rectitude in order that I may follow it. [12] הערה, *he laid bare his soul to death*, i. e. he exposed it to terrible dangers. *And was numbered with the transgressors*, was as if he were reckoned amongst them in consequence of the afflictions resting on him. Any one not knowing his mind, would think there was some evil in him, for which he was being punished, whereas in fact he was carrying the sin of others, as it is said, *But he bare the sin of many*, etc. יפגיע, *interceded* and prayed for them, as Jer. vii. 16.

It has been asserted that the person alluded to in this prophecy is Jeremiah; and the description given in it is quite consistent with such an interpretation. Ibn Jiqatilia[b] applies the Parashah to the king Hezekiah: but I do not know at what time Hezekiah was *stricken, smitten of God, and afflicted*, or *oppressed, and opened not his mouth.* Indeed, it is surprising

---

[b] R. Mosheh hak-Kohen, who lived about 1200 A.D. See Mr. Nutt's preface to his edition of Ḥayyuj's treatises (London, 1869).

how this commentator can have entertained such a view; he must have overlooked the words, *Came up as a sucker before him, and as a root out of the dry land*, etc., applied by the prophet to the saint here described. And I am not aware of any of Hezekiah's ancestors since Solomon who possessed greater personal beauty or majesty than Hezekiah himself.

LIII. R. THANḤUM OF JERUSALEM.

LII. [13] ישכיל, *will prosper*, as 1 Sam. xvii. 14, Josh. i. 8. [14] עליך, 'at thee,' is equivalent to עליו, 'at him,' referring to 'my servant,' as מראהו and תארו, in both of which the suffix is that of the third person. משחת, equivalent to נשחת, and denoting his changed and marred appearance; he was at first in their eyes marred in figure and abhorred, the object of neither reverence nor esteem, but vile and unclean, despised and poor, exactly as the prophet represents him above (xlix. 7), 'Despised in soul, abhorred of the nation, slave of rulers.' In consequence of this his miserable condition, men dreaded and abhorred the sight of him, and shunned his presence, until his appearance again altered and he became such as is indicated by the words immediately following the passage cited, 'Kings shall see and shall stand up, princes, and shall do homage.' [15] The prophet continues in a similar strain, *So will he sprinkle many nations*, etc., for they were exceedingly astonished at his condition, wondering how any person or nation could pass thus strangely and suddenly from one state to another, without any visible cause, but by the command and secret counsel of God. And there was indeed reason for this astonishment. יזה (as lxiii. 3), *will sprinkle* their blood and pour it abroad, slaying them either with an open sword in field of battle, or else with a secret sword, as happened to Sanherib and his people. Or יזה may be understood to mean that he will *scatter* them and disperse their company as though it were some fluid which, when sprinkled, becomes so parted and broken up that it is impossible to gather it together again, as it is said (2 Sam. xiv. 14), 'We are as water spilt on the ground, which cannot be gathered up again.' The expression will then be metaphorical. *At him kings will close their mouth*, for reverence and awe, or in astonishment at his condition: compare Ps. cvii. 42, Job v. 16.

LIII. [2] ויעל, as xxxiv. 13; he *grew up* like a small shoot. יונק, as Ps. lxxx. 12: a similar metaphor is employed in chap. xi. 1. *He had no form*, etc.: at the beginning he had no cheerful countenance such as might inspire a desire to gaze at him. [3] *He was despised* (as it is said above, xlix. 7), *and the frailest of men* as regarded his body, although stronger than other men in so far as his soul was concerned. וכמסתר וגו׳, when he hid himself from us, and was concealed from our sight, in consequence of his ignoble and despised condition, no one *thought of him*,—no one cared whether he were absent or present, or indeed bestowed a thought upon him at all. [4] *But* he was regarded by us as a sinner enduring punishment: in other words, we thought that his pains and sickness were a punishment sent upon him from God, and merited by him for his sins and crimes: accordingly we ever viewed him with an eye of scorn and contempt. But now we know of a surety that his separation from us and his isolation resulted only in our punishment: for in his sicknesses and sufferings he was wholly concerned with what would conduce to our welfare and advantage: these were consequently, in fact, our sickness and punishment. [5] Notwithstanding this he was pained continually at our failure to secure deliverance and prosperity; and in spite of his own prostration, was concerned further with sympathy for us. *The chastisement of the whole of us* came upon him,—שלומנו, as in Jer. xiii. 19, where הגלת שלומים means that the entire mass of Judah was taken captive. מחולל וג׳, i.e. he was pained and grieved at seeing our sins and our being far from righteousness. מחולל as מחוללת (chap. li. 9), i.e. broken, destroyed, and bereft of strength. The meaning is: His severe pain and sufferings of heart and soul resulted purely from his distress for our sins and for what he saw of our failings. בחבורתו, *by his union* and connexion *with us* healing at last reached us, and our sickness and punishment came to an end. [6] *We all were going astray* like sheep, every one went, as he chose, after his own devices, for want of a leader or shepherd to guide us, i. e. our actions were like those of beasts which just follow the path pointed out by nature, without thought or reflection, and without distinguishing what is hurtful from what is beneficial. Seeing this state of things, he was so pained by it, that at last God caused the sins of us all to attach themselves as a punishment to him; in the words of the prophet, *But the Lord caused the iniquity of us all to light upon him.* Others explain *let him intercede,* from the sense borne by the root in Jer. vii. 16; God, that is, accepted his intercession for them, liberated them from their sins, and gave them his aid. [7] Unceasingly he was *oppressed*, tormented, *afflicted*, and pained in heart; נגש with the same idea of oppression and distress as Exod. v. 13, Deut. xv. 2; and נענה in the sense of broken and humiliated, as Exod. iii. 7, x. 3, Is. lviii. 10. [8] *He was taken from imprisonment* and restraint, for judgment was pronounced against him, i.e. he was one of the generation which suffered unjust judgments in exile, and there was no one who would declare about him: עצר, as 2 Kings xvii. 4. According to others מעצר means *from sovereignty*, compare יעצור, 1 Sam. ix. 17; the former explanation is however sounder, and gives a better sense. ואת דורו וגו׳, there was not one among his contemporaries who would describe his perfection or declare his excellences. שוחח, as Ps. cxliii. 5, formed by doubling the last radical from שיח, Ps. cv. 2. *For he was cut off from the land of the living*, i. e. his merits were not known, nor his perfections and excellences described, until after his death, and his departure from the world of the living, i. e. the present world of sense, as in Job xxviii. 13 (where the words 'neither is she found in the land of the living' mean that wisdom is not found or known in the living world). And the same has been the fate of all the prophets and of all pious and learned men. They are not known or described as their merits and excellences really deserve; no one thinks to obtain a blessing through them or visits them to gain their intercession, until they are removed from this world; as long as they are alive no one pays them any attention. למו for לו, or למו itself must be taken in the sense of *every one of them*. The meaning is that all his afflictions, all the punishment and sufferings of captivity which fell upon him, were for their sins and transgressions, in virtue of the justly merited judgment of God. It is thus that when they have paid the debt which God has adjudged to be due from them, he then sends them a person who will guide them and deliver them. The person here described is such a guide or deliverer, who rescues them from captivity and from their enemies generally. 9 This is the description of his former condition: he was necessarily associated closely with the wicked, obliged to frequent their company and share their fortunes, for the purpose of giving them counsel and direction, and bringing them out of darkness into light, and from death into life; and also for another reason, viz. because in his day he could find none with whom to associate at all, except such as those. But he behaved amongst them as though he were as dead as they were themselves; he did not imitate them in their deeds of wickedness, he only had to do with them so far as was necessary for their guidance to the right way, discarding all complicity with their works, for the sake of his own happiness. The version of the translator[a] is :—'And he made him a grave with the evildoers, desiring to die, and with the rich in his death, as though wicked himself[b], although he had done no violence, neither was there any guile in his mouth.' In spite of all this, the will of God will ultimately be accomplished by his hands, and through him his pleasure will prosper and be established. 10 Only, as God desired to prove him, he broke him by sickness, and distracted him with pain, in order that the perfection of his character and his resignation might be visible to the world,

---

[a] R. Saʿadyah, the Ga'on: see p. 18.

[b] Sense doubtful.

as also his unalterable devotion to his Maker, in enduring patiently his judgments without wavering or perturbation of mind. The א of החליא is in place of the radical ה in חלה, the word being formed as החטיא from חטא; the regular form would be החלה, like הקרה, Gen. xxvii. 20. [12] *Because he laid bare his soul to death,* hazarding his life in the presence of his enemies in the accomplishment of God's purpose; and for this end exposed his soul to terrible dangers. לכן וגו׳, *therefore will I give him a portion with the noble,* i. e. with the great ones of that time, *and with the mighty,* i. e. with illustrious potentates, *he will divide the spoil,* the general sense being like that of the verse 1 Chron. xvii. 8: amongst all kings and nobles he will be specially protected, and every one who attempts to oppose him he will spoil, and drive back discomfited. And all this after he had been *numbered amongst* sinful *transgressors,* since men judged only from his external appearance and did not penetrate to his hidden nature, the mystery connected with him not being revealed to them. They imagined, therefore, that all this was a punishment on him for the enormity of his sins, whereas in fact he had committed no sin worthy of such punishment at all, but was even *interceding for transgressors,* that so their sins might be forgiven. Such is the meaning of the prophet's words, *But he bare the sin of many;* compare Ps. lxxxv. 3, Exod. xxxii. 32: in spite of that he made intercession for those wicked ones who thought evil of him: in his humility he did not hate them for their behaviour towards him, or forsake them and withdraw himself from them, but *interceded* for them (יפגיע, like תפגע, Jer. vii. 16). By פושעים are denoted those specially guilty sinners who make defection in the fundamental doctrines of religion and deny them, according to the use of the word פשע in Scripture of repudiation or denial (Exod. xxii. 8).

The exposition here concluded has followed throughout the plain and open sense of the words of the text, and their orderly progression one after the other (as you have seen), in accordance with the principle that there is nothing allegorical in the terms employed, a principle established by the general custom not only of the prophet in all the rest of his writings, but also of the other prophets in most of theirs. As we have explained, the method of the prophets is to represent figuratively to the multitude such truths as they can comprehend by words and phrases with which they are familiar, and in this way to imprint in their mind useful doctrines concerning matters of this world, so far as the majority are able to grasp them; for the masses have not the mental power to understand things such as these in their true nature, as they are understood by the prophets, and by wise or learned men. And the further principle has also been kept in view that in no part of these verses is there anything hyperbolical beyond what is elsewhere permitted (as has been frequently explained), or indeed any other departure from the usual custom of the prophets in their discourses, such as we have several times remarked on in previous parts of our commentary. We repeat that we have adhered throughout to the clear and palpable sense borne by the words of the text.

LIV. THE KHOZARI AND ITS COMMENTATORS.

A. Y'HUDAH HAL-LEVI.

We [i. e. the Israelites] are not in the condition of those who are dead, but in that of a person emaciated by sickness, of whose recovery the physicians despair, but who still desires eagerly to be cured by some miracle or interruption of the ordinary course of nature: as it is said, 'Can these bones live?' (Ezek. xxxvii. 3.) Similarly in the description given of the subject of the Parashah *Behold my servant*, 'He had no form nor comeliness, and we hid, as it were, our faces from him' (Is. liii. 3), i. e. his disfigured and loathsome appearance caused him to be treated like some filthy object, the sight of which fills people with disgust, and impels them to turn their faces from it: *Despised and forlorn of men, a man of pains and known to sickness.*

Says the Khazar: How can that be an allusion to Israel, when the prophet continues, *Surely he hath borne our sicknesses?* whatever has fallen upon Israel has fallen upon them for sins of their own.

Says the Ḥaber: But Israel is amongst the nations what the heart is amongst the members of the body[a]: it suffers most of all, and is in health most of all.

B. R. SH'LOMOH BEN M'NAHEM[b].

LII. [13] The prophet having foretold the exile and the advent of the Redeemer, describes now the prosperity of our nation

---

[a] Cf. pp. 228, 246.

[b] Introduction in O: The commentator says, Perceiving the diversity of opinion on the interpretation of the Parashah *Behold my servant*, insomuch that some of our Rabbis apply it to the King Messiah, while others (amongst

under the two figures that follow (ver. 13). First of all, he assures us that, in spite of our being in captivity, we shall never revert to a condition of imbecility or other mental incapacity; but, on the contrary, that the more we suffer, the more we *shall be wise*, and the greater our knowledge will become; and afterwards, when the Redeemer is come, he announces that we shall be *high and exalted.* [14] In this verse he describes the pains and the sufferings which will befal Israel in exile, declaring how, by Israel's single-hearted devotion to the contemplation of wisdom, he forsook all carnal desires, and freed himself from the yoke of the material world: *As many were astonished at thee,* etc., i. e. so completely did he give his reason the control of his desires, that many were amazed at him, at the sight of his marred and altered form. [15] The kings of the nations and their nobles will *shut their mouth* at this marvel, and not utter a word: for the news of it did not reach them merely by hearsay, but they beheld it eye to eye.

LIII. [1] The kings of the nations are next represented as asking, *Who would have believed* such a thing, had it reached him by hearsay or tradition? Or it may be that Isaiah means here to allude to the 'servant' mentioned above, asking, with reference to him, *Who could believe* this *great marvel? And the arm of the Lord,* i. e. his greatness and the rich profusion known to be in him, *upon whom has it been revealed?* [2] This rich profusion is like a young plant having its root in a dry and

---

them the Ḥaber) think that it relates to our captivity, I have thought it well to give the explanation of my master, as contained in his *Testimony to Israel* [a commentary on the Khozari], in which he follows generally the opinion of the author of the Khozari.

Introduction in M: The words of the Ḥaber in explanation of this Parashah are few. In order to convey his meaning somewhat more fully, I shall give here the exposition of my master in his work, the name of which is known in Israel as the *Testimony to Israel.* In this exposition he follows closely the author of the Khozari, but expresses his views at considerably greater length.

desolated soil, and lacking its proper moisture; it cannot, therefore, but be something superhuman [c] and spiritual. *He hath no form nor comeliness*,—the profusion which has come upon him from God is entirely intellectual and not material, and *we see it* with the eye of the intellect, although *it has no form*, but is entirely abstract, therefore *we desire it.* [3] And this also is a great marvel, how such an intellect, clothed in a form transcending all others, could be with that 'wise' servant, while he was *despised and frailest of men:* in what follows the prophet declares how this pain and sickness was incurred by him designedly, because he *hid his face* from his body, being cruel towards his material frame, through commiseration for his soul. It was of his own will that he was thus frail in body, and *despised;* but we did not understand this at the beginning, for we thought that such sufferings were natural to him. [4] His calamities are not the consequence of his own deeds, but on account of the multitude of our sins and iniquities, yet *we esteemed him stricken and smitten of God* for his own sins. [5] The general sense expressed by the prophet in these verses is, that our exile is not the result of our own transgressions, our follies, and want of knowledge (and hence he begins, 'Behold my servant shall deal *wisely*'), but has been caused by the sin and wickedness of the evil generation of his own time [d]. Accordingly he continues here, *But he was wounded for our transgressions, bruised for our iniquities*, etc., i. e. we are enjoying prosperity and peace, whilst he remains under chastisements; thus *his stripes* are healing for us, because he bears what ought to have been borne by us. [6] Our prosperity is certainly not in consequence of the integrity of our way, for *all we like sheep have gone astray.* [7] *He was oppressed*, etc., *yet he opened not his mouth*, for he bare the punishment of his own will. [8] *From sovereignty*, from absolute power and the unlimited control of his bodily desires, *he was taken; and* the history of *his generation*, or the many afflictions

---

[c] *Lit.* glorious. [d] Comp. p. 419.

which will befal him in his days, *who can declare* or describe? *For*, besides all this, *he was cut off from the land of life*, i.e. from the chosen land. [9] *He made his grave with the wicked* in an unclean land, *and* his death *with the rich* or with 'princes that had gold,' that 'fed delicately,' but who will remain for ever in the ruin of their intelligence. [10] *Yet it pleased the Lord to bruise him;* the prophet represents him in exile as a broken-down invalid, despaired of by physicians, who can only recover by means of a miracle. The prophet next uses, with reference to him, a phrase implying the highest praise, *If his soul shall make a trespass, he will see seed*, etc., as though to say that his exile was not forced upon him, but was incurred voluntarily, for if he had taken it upon his soul to accept the creed of his enemies, he would have *seen seed* and *prolonged his days* in 'quietness and rest' (to use the Ḥaber's own phrase [e]); indeed, a single word, which could have been spoken by him without the slightest trouble, would have made him the equal of his oppressor. And therefore *the pleasure of the Lord shall prosper in his hand*, viz. (as explained by Abraham ibn 'Ezra) 'by cleaving to him' (Deut. xi. 22), both at the beginning and at the end [i. e. continually]. Or the verse may be understood to mean that the Lord was pleased to bruise him in order to see *if his soul* would *take* the *guilt* upon itself, saying, 'My sins have caused this' (Jer. v. 25); and therefore that in the end he should *see seed*, should *prolong his days* in his kingdom, *and the pleasure of the Lord* should *prosper in his hand.* [11] God's servant, Israel, will, however, do still more in exile: he will tell every one how *for the mischief*, i. e. the falseness and wickedness, *of his soul he will see* calamities, and *have his fill* of chastisements. But Israel will also accomplish something further: *by his knowledge*, i. e. by his intelligence and perfect wisdom, *he will* cleanse and *justify* the many former generations from trespass and sin, declaring that they were righteous and

[e] See p. 559.

had not sinned; while with himself the case would be the contrary, for *their iniquities he should bear.* [12] The prophet now foretells to him the deliverance, the general gathering of exiles and their return to the chosen land with abundance of worldly possessions. *Because he bare the sin of many*, etc., i. e. because he bare in captivity the guilt of former generations; but in spite of this he will judge them with leniency, and *intercede* with the Almighty that he would bring them forth out of exile for their own merit. Such, briefly, is the view, presenting some novelties of interpretation, which I have to offer of the general sense of this Parashah.

LV. R. GERSHOM BEN NATHAN.

LII. [13] *Behold* in the latter days *my servant*, i. e. the righteous ones, shall *prosper*. *Shall be high*, etc., i.e. shall be exalted exceedingly. [14] *As many were astonished* and amazed at your humiliation, saying of you, '*So marred*,' etc., i. e. 'so disfigured are their countenances that they no longer bear any resemblance to other men,' *so* will Israel now *cut off*, and scatter the 'horns [a]' or reputation of the nations, so that they will be amazed at him, and *kings will shut their mouth* at the greatness then to be discerned in Israel,—greatness so extraordinary that (as it is written, Ps. lxv. 1, 'Unto thee silence is praise') none will be able to tell it,—and will be observing diligently that which is done for them.

LIII. [1] *Who would have believed?* etc.: If, the nations will exclaim, if we had merely heard the like of this, and had not seen it, we should not have believed it; nor should we have credited that *the arm* and might *of the Lord* had been *revealed*, as it has now been revealed, upon Israel: for previously all greatness had belonged to the nations. [2] *He came up* like a young plant: whereas before they had been in a condition of extreme lowliness, they have now started up rapidly to great dignity. And *like a root* which, emerging at first out of the dry and arid soil, and devoid of comeliness, becomes in time a beautiful tree. And *when we looked at them* at the beginning, they had no beauty such that we might desire them; rather were they

[a] Comp. Zech. ii. 4; and see p. 37.

humiliated and *despised;* but now all this is reversed. [3]*Despised and forlornest of men,* viz. in former times: the prophet speaks of Israel collectively as an individual, as repeatedly elsewhere. *A man of pains,* i. e. of afflictions; *and broken of sickness,* i. e. the sufferings of sickness: such also was their abasement that, like men stricken [with leprosy], they hid their faces and were ashamed. And this was the estimation in which we held them universally. [4]*But* now we see that the sickness and pains which properly were ours were borne by them on our account; for by the sufferings of Israel atonement will be made for all nations. Yet we imagined that they were *smitten of God* for guilt of their own: this however was not so; they were *stricken and smitten* for our sakes. מחלל, *pierced* or *wounded,* as חלל, Jer. xiv. 18 etc.: מדכא, *bruised,* as דך, Ps. lxxiv. 21. [5]מוסר שלומנו עליו, an inversion (as it appears to me) for שלומנו מוסר עליו, as though to say that the *peace* which we enjoyed was not owing to our own righteousness, but because Israel for their iniquity had received upon themselves the punishment which ought to have come upon us. ובחברתו נרפא לנו, i. e. in consequence of the *stripes* (Exod. xxi. 25) which fell upon him, *we were healed.* [6]*We have* now *gone astray,*—it is here declared how all the nations have erred in their belief. *We have turned each to his own way,* i. e. up to the present time each of us has been following his own evil course. הפגיע, the Almighty, unwilling to destroy his world, is represented by the prophet as punishing Israel; for Israel suffered in our stead. [7]*He was oppressed,* bowed down, *and* sorely *afflicted* under the hands of the Gentiles, yet he *opened not his mouth* in spite of all the abuse and violence to which he was exposed continually. יובל, *was brought. Before her shearers,* i. e. before such as are desirous to shear her. *Dumb,* viz. from terror. *And openeth not his mouth,* referring to the sheep led to the slaughter, because 'sheep' is masculine, whereas 'lamb' is feminine. [8]*From* the *confinement* in which he was kept amongst us in exile, *and from* the *judgment* of sufferings and afflictions in the midst of which he lived, Israel now is taken. All this is supposed to be spoken by the Gentiles in the future. *And his generation*—i. e. all the punishments which befel them one generation after another—*who* is able to *describe? for* from the beginning, they have been *cut off* and expelled from the land of Israel, here termed the *land of life. For the transgression of his people* this *stroke*—i. e. the distress which they suffered—came *to them.* The prophet means to refer to Israel. למו, i. e. came *to him.* 9 *He made his grave at the will of the wicked,* i. e. resigned himself to be buried in the manner determined by those wicked heathen who decreed death against him. *And at the will of the rich in his deaths,* for before the rich magistrate Israel was forced to submit himself to all the varied forms of death to which he was sentenced. And why was Israel thus treated? The prophet gives the answer: because he would not consent to do wrong—e. g. to rob or commit violence—like the nations, and because there was *no deceit in his mouth,*—his mouth was like his heart, and would in no way acknowledge their false worship. 10 But the Almighty *was pleased to bruise* Israel, and so to lead him back to prosperity[b]: he therefore afflicted them with sore sicknesses. אם תשים וג׳: the Almighty says, *If his soul* is so devoted to me in holiness as to *return* itself to me as *a trespass-offering*—which makes atonement for iniquity—then he shall *see seed,* etc., i. e. shall see his descendants walking before him in his life-time, and shall *prolong* his *days,* and *desire from the Lord shall prosper in his hand,* i. e. what he desires to obtain from him, God will send into his hand and cause it to prosper. 11 *From the travail of his soul he shall see and be satisfied*—he will be worthy to see the labour of his hands in his own possession, and to reap the full enjoyment of it, being neither dependent upon the assistance of others, nor reduced to the necessity of stealing. *By his knowledge he will justify the just,* i. e. establish his innocence, and not pervert justice. *My servant to many,* i. e. my servant will award

---

[b] Comp. p. 39.

justice, will mete out judgment faithfully, *to many. And their iniquities*—i. e. the iniquities of the many—*he will bear,* as happens generally with the righteous, one interceding for others in order that they may escape unpunished. [12] *Therefore,* i. e. on account of this, *I will divide thee* a lot and an inheritance *with the many,* i. e. thou shalt appear to the multitude, and be reckoned by those who see thee, to be as the old patriarchs. And similarly *with the mighty,* i. e. with those distinguished for valour, *he shall divide* spoil. *Because he poured out his soul to die,* i. e. resigned his life for the sanctity of heaven, *and was numbered with the transgressors,* endured much suffering as though he had been a sinner and transgressor himself. Yet in this he *bare the sin* of others, *and made intercession for the transgressors,* i. e. for the transgressors who were suffering, the prophet interceded with the Almighty, and the Almighty through his means gave prosperity to the world.

x. Levi ben Gershom.

It follows necessarily from this verse (Deut. xxxiv. 10) that no prophet whose office was restricted to Israel alone could ever arise again like Moses; but it is still quite possible that a prophet like Moses might arise among the Gentile nations. In fact the Messiah is such a prophet, as it is stated in the Midrash on the verse, *Behold my servant shall prosper*, etc., that he will be 'greater than Moses,' which is explained to mean that his miracles will be more wonderful than those of Moses; Moses, by the miracles which he wrought, drew but a single nation to the worship of God, but the Messiah will draw all nations to the worship of God, as it is written (Zeph. iii. 9), 'Then will I turn to the people a pure language, that they may all call upon the name of the Lord,' etc.[a] And this will be effected by means of a marvellous sign, to be seen by all nations even to the ends of the earth, viz. the resurrection of the dead.

y. R. Liwa of Prague.

The Messiah, who is the perfection of the world, will be *high and lofty and exalted*: now, inasmuch as he is the perfection, he is also the consummation, and the consummation is above all things, for all tends thereto: and this is why it is said of this Messiah that he will be *high and exalted and lofty*.

'A star shall proceed out of Ja'qob, and there shall arise a sceptre in Israel:' the King Messiah is here spoken of as a *star*, for (as we have explained above) his position and dignity will be of the highest, since it is said of him, *He will be high and exalted and lofty exceedingly*. He is here, therefore, compared to a star, because a star is elevated over all things.

---

[a] Comp. p. 79.

Alterations and Additions to page 40.

[14] *As many were astonished at thee*, saying, *His countenance is marred beyond man:* how is it possible that, in the manner that we see, the countenance of this people should be marred beyond man, and *his form* beyond the other sons of men? [15] . . . . *For what had not*, etc. Not merely all the consolations foretold by the prophets, but even the good things of which the nations had never been told, they will see then fulfilled in Israel.

LIII. [2] . . . . had formerly; for a countenance vexed with grief and distress is widely different from one smiling with happiness. *And we desire him:* for now they are all 'pleasant to the eyes.' [4] . . . . for our iniquity in following after idolatrous worships. . . . [5] . . . . since they kept righteous ordinances, and the law of truth was in their mouth. . . . [6] . . . . of falsehood. *We went each after his own way*,—each in the name of his god; but all were vanity and 'a work of deceits.' Now, however, we know that in all the earth there is no God except in Israel. *And the Lord laid upon him*, upon Israel, *the iniquity of us all.* [7] *He*—i. e. Israel—*was oppressed*—such is the meaning of נגש, as in 1 Sam. xiii. 6, where it is parallel to צר. נענה, i. e. *was humbled, humiliated*, as the Targum renders the word in Exod. x. 3. *And opened not his mouth:* when any one of them was led forth to execution, he opened not his mouth before the magistrate who condemned him, but like a sheep dumb before the slaughterer, or a lamb before her shearers, so the Israelite was silent before his executioner. [8] *From coercion and judgment*—from the punishments which he endured in exile—*he is* now *removed; and in his generation*, at the time when he was bearing the yoke of exile, and cut off from the land of life, from all those of his generation who were still alive, *who could tell* that they would ever rise to such greatness? who ever believed this of them in the days *when* they were dropping off from the land of life? *For the transgression*, etc.: the men of every nation will say that during the whole course of their affliction in exile no stroke ever fell upon them which had not been caused by the transgression of their own people: it will be impossible to assert that they were smitten with desolation for any fault of their own, because since we see their gods confirming now their deeds, we learn that they must have kept the law of truth. This being so, it is impossible to ascribe the calamities which befel them to guilt of their own: they fell upon them *for the transgression of my people*—for the sins of the nation observing such statutes as I do myself. [9] Every nation which condemned an Israelite condemned him to the punishment of the wicked, as, for instance, of murderers or those guilty of incest; and whatever form of death was thus selected for Israel, Israel received it. *And the rich in his deaths:* he endured the death to which any powerful and wealthy nation might sentence him. And since there was *no violence in their hands* they were murdered upon any arbitrary pretext; for the nations of the world tyrannized over them and consigned them to cruel deaths, because (as the next verse says) the Almighty desired to justify them in the day of judgment. [10] As Solomon says (Prov. iii. 12), Whom the Lord delights in, he bruises him with chastisements; and happy the man who thus suffers, and admits the justice of God's judgments, as the prophet proceeds to declare, *If his soul makes a trespass-offering, he shall see seed*, etc. [11] As a reward for his deeds, *he will be satisfied*,—for having, viz., justified the Just One by bearing cheerfully and heartily the yoke of exile in order to make the many righteous, as the prophet says, *My servant, the just one*—i. e. Israel the 'righteous nation'—*will justify the many by his knowledge*, by acquiescing intelligently and willingly in his exile, *and their iniquities he will bear.* [12] It is only fair that the nation which justified the many should have also a portion allotted to it *among the many;* he will, moreover, *divide spoil with the mighty, because he poured out his soul to die*—Israel resigned themselves to martyrdom for the unity of God—*and was numbered with the transgressors*—for there was no nation in the world which did not deem Israel to consist of transgressors.

Addition to page 89, *end.*

The disciples of Jesus vainly object that this Parashah refers to him. But if this were so, how could the Almighty call him his 'servant,' and say, 'He shall see seed, shall have long days?' if he is God, how can he see seed? And again, how could he promise that he would 'divide him spoil with the great?' [a] only if they admit that he was [not more than] a prophet is such an application within the range of human possibility [a].

Correction.

Page 387, line 4, *for* Frère *read* Ferrer; and see Grätz, viii. pp. 116–118.

---

[a] From a more modern MS.

INDEX.